JOURNAL FOR THE STUDY OF THE PSEUDEPIGRAPHA
SUPPLEMENT SERIES
30

Sheffield Academic Press

The Herodian Dynasty

Origins, Role in Society and Eclipse

DS
122
.K65
seab

Nikos Kokkinos

Journal for the Study of the Pseudepigrapha
Supplement Series 30

Published by Sheffield Academic Press Ltd
Mansion House
19 Kingfield Road
Sheffield S11 9AS
England

Printed on acid-free paper in Great Britain
by Bookcraft Ltd
Midsomer Norton, Bath

British Library Cataloguing in Publication Data

A catalogue record for this book is available
from the British Library

ISBN 1-85075-690-2

TO THE YOUNGER MEMBERS OF THE KOKKINOS FAMILY:
MY SON THEODOSIOS AND MY DAUGHTERS SARAH AND RACHEL

Aristobulus

The palace is in tears, the king is in tears,
King Herod laments inconsolably,
the entire city is in tears for Aristobulus
who was so unjustly drowned, by accident,
while playing with his friends in the water.

And when they learn of it in other places too,
when the news is spread up in Syria,
even among the Greeks many will be saddened;
many poets and sculptors will mourn,
for they had heard of Aristobulus,
and never before had their vision of a young man
compared with such beauty as this boy had;
what statue of a god had Antioch deserved
as fine as this child of Israel?

The First Princess, his mother, the most eminent
Hebrew lady, laments and weeps.
Alexandra laments and weeps over the calamity.—
But when she finds herself alone her sorrow alters.
She groans; she rails; she reviles and utters curses.
How they have deceived her! How they had duped her!
How their purpose has finally been realised!
They have ruined the house of the Asamonaeans.
How the criminal king has achieved his end;
the crafty, the villainous, the wicked.
How he has achieved his end. What an infernal plot
that even Mariamme should detect nothing.
Had Mariamme detected, had she suspected,
she would have found a way to save her brother;
she is queen after all, she could have done something.
How they will triumph now and secretly gloat,
those wicked women, Cyprus and Salome;
those vulgar women, Cyprus and Salome.—
And that she should be powerless, and obliged
to pretend that she believes their lies;
not to be able to go before the people,
to go out and shout it to the Hebrews,
to tell, how the murder was done.

K.P. Kavafes, Alexandria 1916/8
(trans. Dalven 1961: 89-90)

CONTENTS

Part I
IDUMAEA AND THE ORIGINS OF THE HERODS

Chapter 1
FROM EDOM TO IDUMAEA

Chapter 2
EARLY HELLENISTIC IDUMAEA

Chapter 3
LATE HELLENISTIC IDUMAEA

Part II
THE HERODIAN FAMILY AND SOCIAL STRUCTURE

LIST OF MAPS, FAMILY TREES AND CHARTS

List of Maps

List of Family Trees

List of Charts

PREFACE

This book is a revised and expanded version of my doctoral thesis written between 1987 and 1991–92, although preliminary research (also involving some publications) goes back a decade earlier. The original version was approved by the University of Oxford in 1993, at a time when I was fighting for my life after serious illness. My existence is owed totally to the expert hand of Mr Stuart Saunders, Consultant at St George's Hospital, Tooting, who showed interest in my work and did his best to fulfil my desire to publish.

The revisions were made in 1995–96, from the position of Honorary Research Fellow of the Greek and Roman Department at the Institute of Archaeology, University College London, where two people must be thanked in particular for nominating me, Professor John Wilkes and the now retired Mr Peter Parr. An attempt was made to update the bibliography, though it was impossible to do so thoroughly across many fields covered in some 1,100 notes and 10 appendixes. But perhaps no apology is necessary, since the volume of new publications has increased dramatically in recent years.

Breaking from the tradition of devoting many pages to various acknowledgments, I shall restrict myself to a few, main credits. Financial support for my programme I had from the British Academy, the Craven Committee (Oxford), St. Hugh's College (Oxford), and the Graduate School (UCL). Significant help was also received from two family members: my sister Kalliope and my brother Ioannes—the former being a particularly sweet and dear person. Moral support came from my colleague Peter James (who also read through an early version of my conclusion), but of course by far the most crucial encouragement was that of my wife Rikki. For my work's sake she has suffered continously for days, months and years.

In terms of academic support I shall be bold to thank one and *only* one person: Professor Fergus Millar. No one dealing with the Graeco-Roman Near East could have wished for a better supervisor. I am extremely lucky to have worked in the most important modern centre for the ancient world, the Ashmolean Library, under the direction of Fergus. Without his help this study would never have been completed. Not only has he spent dozens of hours in talking and drinking black coffees with me, but also corresponded, edited, and corrected extensively. His precious feedback was always given generously, and under difficult circumstances whether due to the pressure of Oxford administration and teaching, or due to his many scholarly endeavours. He is a master in avoiding personal conflicts of opinion, by offering subtle but expert comments, always cautious but open-minded, always strict but not without allowing breathing space. I do not recall him to have crushed outright any of my new ideas, either out of superiority or inertia, while his criticisms were consistently qualitative. Fergus was an amazing supervisor to me, frequently going beyond the call of duty, not only by repeatedly offering me books and photocopies, but even paying for the binding of my thesis when life was tough! I just hope that my hypothesis here, whether it be generally accepted or not, can live up to half of his standards.

N.K.
London, June 1996

ABBREVIATIONS

AAS	*Les Annales Archéologiques de Syrie*
AASOR	Annual of the American Schools of Oriental Research
ABSA	*Annual of the British School at Athens*
AD	Ἀρχαιολογικὸν Δελτίον
ADAJ	*Annual of the Department of Antiquities of Jordan*
AE	*L'Année Epigraphique*
AEM	*Archäologisch-Epigraphische Mittheilungen aus Österreich-Ungarn*
AEph	Ἀρχαιολογικὴ Ἐφημερίς
AHB	*The Ancient History Bulletin*
AION	*Annali dell'istituto orientale di napoli*
AJA	*American Journal of Archaeology*
AJBA	*Australian Journal of Biblical Archaeology*
AJC	Y. Meshorer, *Ancient Jewish Coinage* (New York: Amphora Books, 1982), vols. 1–2
AJP	*American Journal of Philology*
AJSR	*Association for Jewish Studies Review*
ALUOS	*The Annual of Leeds University Oriental Society*
AN	*Annuaire de Numismatique*
AnBib	Analecta biblica
AnBoll	*Analecta Bollandiana*
ANET	James B. Pritchard (ed.), *Ancient Near Eastern Texts Relating to the Old Testament* (Princeton: Princeton University Press, 1950)
ANRW	Hildegard Temporini and Wolfgang Haase (eds.), *Aufstieg und Niedergang der römischen Welt: Geschichte und Kultur Roms im Spiegel der neueren Forschung* (Berlin: W. de Gruyter, 1972–)
ANSMN	*The American Numismatic Society Museum Notes*
ARSP	*Atti della Reale Scuola Normale Superiore di Pisa*—Lettere, Storia e Filosofia
AS	*Ancient Society*
ASTI	*Annual of the Swedish Theological Institute*
AUSS	*Andrews University Seminary Studies*
AW	*The Ancient World*
BA	*Biblical Archaeologist*

BAIAS	*Bulletin of the Anglo-Israel Archaeological Society*
BAR	*British Archaeological Reports*
BARev	*Biblical Archaeology Review*
BASOR	*Bulletin of the American Schools of Oriental Research*
BASORSup	*Bulletin of the American Schools of Oriental Research,* Supplement Series
BASP	*Bulletin of the American Society of Papyrologists*
BCH	*Bulletin de Correspondance Hellénique*
BE	*Bulletin Epigraphique* (in *Revue des Etudes Grecques*)
BGU	*Aegyptische Urkunden aus den Königlichen Museen zu Berlin: Griechische Urkunden* (Berlin, 1895; repr. Cisalpino-La Goliardica, Milan), vol. 1
BHLS	E. Vogel (ed.), *Bibliography of Holy Land Sites* (parts 1-3, *HUCA* 42 [1971], 1-97; 52 [1981], 1-92; 58 [1987], 1-63)
BIA	*Bulletin of the Institute of Archaeology of the University of London*
Bib	*Biblica*
BICS	*Bulletin of the Institute of Classical Studies*
BJRL	*Bulletin of the John Rylands University Library of Manchester*
BJS	Brown Judaic Studies
BLE	*Bulletin de littérature ecclésiastique*
BMB	*Bulletin du Musée de Beyrouth*
BMC	(various eds.), *Catalogue of the Greek Coins in the British Museum* (London: B.M. Publications, 1873–1927), vols. 1-29
BMCRE	H. Mattingly and R.A.G. Carson (eds.), *Coins of the Roman Empire in the British Museum* (London: B.M. Publications), vols. 1–16
BMCRR	H.A. Grueber (ed.), *Coins of the Roman Republic in the British Museum* (London: B.M. Publications, 1970), vols. 1–3
BR	*Bible Review*
BSac	*Bibliotheca Sacra*
BTB	*Biblical Theology Bulletin*
BTS	*Bible et terre sainte*
BZ	*Biblische Zeitschrift*
CA	*Classical Antiquity*
CAH	*Cambridge Ancient History*
CAJ	*Cambridge Archaeological Journal*
CBQ	*Catholic Biblical Quarterly*
CD	*Cairo Damascus Document*
CHI	E. Yarshater (ed.), *Cambridge History of Iran.* 3.1. *(The Seleucid, Parthian, and Sasanian Periods)* (Cambridge: Cambridge University Press, 1983)

CHJ	W.D. Davies and L. Finkelstein (eds.), *Cambridge History of Judaism*. 2. *(Hellenistic Age)* (Cambridge: Cambridge University Press, 1989)
CIG	*Corpus inscriptionum graecarum*
CII	*Corpus inscriptionum iudaicarum*
CIL	*Corpus inscriptionum latinarum*
CIS	*Corpus inscriptionum semiticarum*
CO	*Les Cahiers de l'Oronte*
CP	*Classical Philology*
CPJ	V.A. Tcherikover, A. Fuks and M. Stern (eds.), *Corpus papyrorum judaicarum* (Cambridge, MA: Harvard University Press, 1957–64), vols. 1–3
ClQ	*Classical Quarterly*
CQR	*Catholic Quarterly Review*
CR	*Classical Review*
CRE	H. Mattingly (ed.), *Coins of the Roman Empire in the British Museum* (London: B.M. Publications, 1976), vol. 1
CREAM	C.H.V. Sutherland and C.M. Kraay (eds.), *Catalogue of Coins of the Roman Empire in the Ashmolean Museum*. 1. *Augustus* (Oxford: Clarendon Press, 1975)
CRINT	Compendia rerum iudaicarum ad Novum Testamentum. 1.1-2 S. Safrai and M. Stern (eds.), *The Jewish People in the First Century* (Assen: Van Gorcum, 1974–76); 2.2 M.E. Stone (ed.), *Jewish Writings of the Second Temple Period* (Assen: Van Gorcum, 1984)
CSSH	*Comparative Studies in Society and History*
CW	*Classical Weekly*
DaM	*Damaszener Mitteilungen*
DBSup	*Dictionnaire de la Bible, Supplément*
DHA	*Dossiers Histoire et Archéologie*
DJD	Discoveries in the Judaean Desert
EAEHL	M. Avi-Yonah (ed.), *Encyclopedia of Archaeological Excavations in the Holy Land* (Jerusalem: Massada Press, 1975–78), vols. 1–4
EI	*Eretz Israel*
EncJud	*Encyclopaedia Judaica*
EMC	*Echos du Monde Classique*
ESI	*Explorations and Surveys in Israel*
FGrH	F. Jacoby (ed.), *Die Fragmente der griechischen Historiker* (17 vols.; Berlin: Weidmann; Leiden: Brill, 1923–58)
FHJA	C.R. Holladay (ed.), *Fragments from Hellenistic Jewish Authors* (Chico, CA: Scholars Press, 1983–89), vols. 1–2
GLAJJ	M. Stern (ed.), *Greek and Latin Authors on Jews and Judaism* (Jerusalem: Israel Academy of Sciences and Humanities, 1976–84), vols. 1–3

GRBS	*Greek, Roman, and Byzantine Studies*
GSAI	*Giornale della Società Asiatica Italiana*
HSCP	*Harvard Studies in Classical Philology*
HSM	Harvard Semitic Monographs
HTR	*Harvard Theological Review*
HUCA	*Hebrew Union College Annual*
I.It.	*Inscriptiones italiae*
IBM	*Ancient Greek Inscriptions in the British Museum*
ID	*Inscriptions de Délos*
IEJ	*Israel Exploration Journal*
IG	*Inscriptiones graecae*
IGLS	*Inscriptions grecques et latines de la Syrie*
IGRR	*Inscriptiones graecae ad res romanas pertinentes*
IGUR	*Inscriptiones graecae urbis romae*
IK	*Inschriften Griechischer Städte aus Kleinasien*
ILS	*Inscriptiones latinae selectae*
IMJ	*The Israel Museum Journal*
INB	*Israel Numismatic Bulletin*
INJ	*Israel Numismatic Journal*
IPL	*Israel—People and Land* (Eretz Israel Museum Yearbook)
JANES	*Journal of the Ancient Near Eastern Society*
JAOS	*Journal of the American Oriental Society*
JARCE	*Journal of the American Research Center in Egypt*
JAC	*Jahrbuch für Antike und Christentum*
JBL	*Journal of Biblical Literature*
JC	L.I. Levine (ed.), *The Jerusalem Cathedra* (Detroit, MI: Wayne State University Press, 1981–83), vols. 1–3
JDAI	*Jahrbuch des Deutschen Archäologischen Instituts*
JEOL	*Jaarbericht. . . ex Oriente Lux*
JH	*Jewish History*
JHS	*Journal of Hellenic Studies*
JIWE	D. Noy (ed.), *Jewish Inscriptions of Western Europe. 2. The City of Rome* (Cambridge: Cambridge University Press, 1995)
JJS	*Journal of Jewish Studies*
JNES	*Journal of Near Eastern Studies*
JOAI	*Jahreshefte des Österreichischen Archäologischen Institutes in Wien*
JP	*Journal of Philology*
JPOS	*Journal of the Palestine Oriental Society*
JQR	*Jewish Quarterly Review*
JRA	*Journal of Roman Archaeology*
JRAS	*Journal of the Royal Asiatic Society*
JRASC	*Journal of the Royal Astronomical Society of Canada*
JRASup	*Journal of Roman Archaeology*, Supplement Series
JRS	*Journal of Roman Studies*

JSJ	*Journal for the Study of Judaism in the Persian, Hellenistic and Roman Period*
JSNT	*Journal for the Study of the New Testament*
JSNTSup	*Journal for the Study of the New Testament*, Supplement Series
JSOT	*Journal for the Study of the Old Testament*
JSOTSup	*Journal for the Study of the Old Testament*, Supplement Series
JSS	*Journal of Semitic Studies*
JTS	*Journal of Theological Studies*
KAI	H. Donner and W. Röllig, *Kanaanäische und aramäische Inschriften* (3 vols.; Wiesbaden: Harassowitz, 1962–64)
KBS	*Kölner Beiträge zur Sportwissenschaft*
LA	*Liber Annuus*
LGPN	P.M. Fraser and E. Matthews (eds.), *A Lexicon of Greek Personal Names. 1. The Aegean Islands, Cyprus, Cyrenaica* (Oxford: Clarendon Press, 1987)
MDAI(A)	*Mitteilungen des Deutschen Archäologischen Instituts* (Athen. Abt.)
MFR	M.-Th. Couilloud (ed.), *Les Monuments Funéraires de Rhénée* (Paris: de Boccard, 1974)
MGWJ	*Monatsschrift für Geschichte und Wissenschaft des Judentums*
MH	*Medical History*
MHR	*Mediterranean Historical Review*
MM	*Mercure Musical* (Sociéte Internationale de Musique)
MNRAS	*Monthly Notes of the Royal Astronomical Society*
MUSJ	*Mélanges de l'université Saint-Joseph*
NB	F. Preisigke (ed.), *Namenbuch* (Heidelberg: Gelbverlag, 1922)
NC	*Numismatic Chronicle*
NCir	*Numismatic Circular*
ND	G.H.R. Horsley (ed.), *New Documents Illustrating Early Christianity* (North Ryde: Macquarie University, 1981–89), vols. 1–5
NEAEHL	E. Stern (ed.), *New Encyclopedia of Archaeological Excavations in the Holy Land* (Jerusalem: I.E.S., 1993), vols. 1–4
NovT	*Novum Testamentum*
NovTSup	*Novum Testamentum* Supplements
NTS	*New Testament Studies*
O. Petr.	'Ostraca in Prof. W.M. Flinters Petrie's Collection at University College, London', in J.G. Tait (ed.), *Greek Ostraca in the Bodleian Library at Oxford and Various Other Collections* (London: Egypt Exploration Society, 1930), I, pp. 82-152
OGIS	W. Dittenberger (ed.), *Orientis graeci inscriptiones selectae* (Leipzig: S. Hirzel, 1903–1905), vols. 1–2

OJA	*Oxford Journal of Archaeology*
OLP	*Orientalia lovaniensia periodica*
OTP	James Charlesworth (ed.), *The Old Testament Pseudepigrapha* (Garden City, NY: Doubleday, 1983–85), vols. 1–2
P. Cairo	B.P. Grenfell and A.S. Hunt (eds.), *Greek Papyri: Catalogue Général des Antiquitées Egyptiennes du Musée du Caire* (Oxford: 1903; repr. A.M. Hakekrt, Las Palmas de Gran Canaria), vol. 1
P. C. Zen.	W.L. Westermann and E.S. Hasenoehrl (eds.), *Columbia Papyri 3: Zenon Papyri 1* (New York, 1934; repr. Cisalpino-La Goliardica, Milan)
P. Hamb.	P.M. Meyer (ed.), *Griechische Papyrusurkunden der Hamburger Staats- und Universitätsbibliothek* (Leipzig and Berlin, 1911; repr. Cisalpino-La Goliardica, Milan), I
P. L. Bat.	P.W. Pestman (ed.), *Papyrologica Lugduno-Batava* (Leiden: Brill, 1980–81), vols. 20–21
P. Lond.	T.C. Skeat (ed.), *Greek Papyri in the British Museum. 7. The Zenon Archive* (London: B.M. Publications, 1974)
P. Mich.	C.C. Edgar (ed.), *Michigan Papyri* (Ann Arbor, MI: University of Michigan, 1931), I
P. Ness.	C.J. Kraemer, Jr (ed.), *Excavations at Nessana* (Princeton, NJ: Princeton University Press, 1958), III
P. Paris	J.A. Letronne *et al.*, *Notices et textes des papyrus grecs du Musée du Louvre et de Bibliothèque Impériale* (Paris, 1865; repr. Cisalpino-La Goliardica, Milan)
P. Ryl.	J. de M. Johnson *et al.* (eds.), *Catalogue of the Greek Papyri in the John Rylands Library, Manchester: Documents of the Ptolemaic and Roman Periods* (Manchester: Manchester University Press, 1915), II
P. Vin. T.	P.J. Sijpesteijn and K.A. Worp (eds.), *Fünfunddreissig Wiener Papyri* (Zutphen: Terra, 1976)
P. Yadin	N. Lewis (ed.), *Y. Yadin, The Documents from the Bar Kokhba Period in the Cave of Letters: Greek Papyri* (Jerusalem: Israel Exploration Society, 1989)
P. Zen.	C.C. Edgar (ed.), *Zenon Papyri* (Cairo, 1925–40; repr. Hildesheim: G. Olms Verlag), vols. 1–5
PBA	*Proceedings of the British Academy*
PCPS	*Proceedings of the Cambridge Philological Society*
PdP	*La Parola del Passato*
PEFQS	*Palestine Exploration Fund, Quarterly Statement*
PEQ	*Palestine Exploration Quarterly*
PIASH	*Proceedings of the Israel Academy of Sciences and Humanities*
PIR²	E. Groag *et al.*, *Prosopographia imperii romani: saec. I, II, III* (Berlin: W. de Gruyter, 2nd edn, 1933–)
PJ	*Palästina-Jahrbuch*

PLRE	J.R. Martindale (ed.), *Prosopography of the Later Roman Empire*. II. AD *395–527* (Cambridge: Cambridge University Press, 1980)
PP	W. Peremans *et al.* (eds.), *Prosopographia Ptolemaica* (Louvain: Bibliotheca Universitatis, 1950–68), vols. 1–6
PS	*Population Studies*
PSAS	*Proceedings of the Seminar for Arabian Studies*
PSI	G. Vitelli (ed.), *Papiri greci e latini* (Società Italiana) (Florence: Casa Editrice Felice Le Monnier, 1917–25), vols. 4–7
QDAP	*Quarterly of the Department of Antiquities of* Palestine
RA	*Revue Archéologique*
RAC	*Reallexikon für Antike und Christentum*
RAO	*Recueil d'Archéologie Orientale*
RB	*Revue Biblique*
RBPH	*Revue Belge de Philologie et d'Histoire*
RDAC	*Report of the Department of Antiquities, Cyprus*
RE	A. Pauly *et al.* (eds.), *Realencyclopädie der classischen Altertumswissenchaft* (Stuttgart: J.B. Metzler, 1893–)
REA	*Revue des études anciennes*
REJ	*Revue des études juives*
RES	*Répertoire d'épigraphie sémitique*
RevQ	*Revue de Qumran*
RG	*Revue Germanique*
RHD	*Revue d'histoire du droit Français et étranger*
RivB	*Rivista biblica*
RIC	M. Rosenberger (ed.), *The Rosenberger Israel Collection* (Jerusalem: Yail, 1972–78), vols. 1–4
RIDA	*Revue Internationale des Droits de l'Antiquité*
RMP	*Reinisches Museum für Philologie*
RN	*Revue Numismatique*
RP	*Revue de Philologie*
RPC	A. Burnett, M. Amandry and P. Pau Ripollès (eds.), *Roman Provincial Coinage* .1.1-2. *(From the Death of Caesar to the Death of Vitellius, 44 BC–AD 69)* (London: B.M. Press; Paris: Bibliothèque Nationale, 1992)
RSF	*Rivista di studi fenici*
RSO	*Rivista degli studi orientali*
SB	(various eds.), *Sammelbuch Griechischer Urkunden aus Aegypten* (Wiesbaden: O. Harrassowitz [later volumes], 1915–), vols. 1–16
SCI	*Scripta classica israelica*
SCO	*Studi classici e orientali*
SEG	*Supplementum Epigraphicum Graecum*
Sem	*Semitica*
SH	*Scripta Hierosolymitana*

S K	*Sovetskiî Kollektsioner*
SM	*Schweizer Münzblätter: Gazette Numismatique Suisse*
SNG(ANS)	Y. Meshorer (ed.), *Sylloge Nummorum Graecorum: The Collection of the American Numismatic Society*. pt. 6. *(Palestine-South Arabia)* (New York: A.N.S., 1981)
SP	*Studia patristica*
SPA	*The Studia Philonica Annual*
SPB	Studia postbiblica
SPh	*Studies in Philology*
S R	*Studies in Religion/Sciences religieuses*
STS	*Studia Theologica cura ordinum Theologorum Scandinavicorum edita*
SVM	E. Schürer (rev. and ed. G. Vermes, F. Millar *et al.*), *The History of the Jewish People in the Age of Jesus Christ* (Edinburgh: T. & T. Clark, 1973–87), vols. 1–3.2
TA	*Tel Aviv*
TAPA	*Transactions of the American Philological Association*
TIRIP	Y. Tsafrir, L. Di Segni and J. Green (eds.), *Tabula Imperii Romani: Iudaea Palestina* (Jerusalem: Israel Academy of Sciences and Humanities, 1994)
TSAJ	Texte und Studien zum Antiken Judentum
TU	Texte und Untersuchungen
TynBul	*Tyndale Bulletin*
VT	*Vetus Testamentum*
Wadd.	H. Waddington (ed.), *Inscriptions grecques et latines de la Syrie* (Paris: Didot, 1870)
WGEN	W. Pape (ed.), *Wörterbuch der griechischen Eigennamen* (Braunschweig: Vieweg, 1911), vols. 1–2
WHJP	M. Avi-Yonah and Z. Baras (eds.), *The World History of the Jewish People*. VII. *The Herodian Period* (London: W.H. Allen, 1975)
WUNT	Wissenschaftliche Untersuchungen zum Neuen Testament
YCS	*Yale Classical Studies*
ZAW	*Zeitschrift für die alttestamentliche Wissenschaft*
ZDPV	*Zeitschrift des deutschen Palästina-Vereins*
ZPE	*Zeitschrift für Papyrologie und Epigraphik*

The issue of the Gutenberg Bible in 1456, the first book of the Western world to be printed from movable type, only three years after the spectacular fall of Constantinople, meant that the spreading of the new spirit of the Renaissance was now guaranteed, followed by the inception of modern scholarship.

Up to this time Herod the Great, the famous king of the Jews, had been a common character in both the dramatic and the non-dramatic literature of the Middle Ages, his portrait always being based on that of the New Testament, the Apocrypha or the Church Fathers. For example, he features in an eleventh-century fragment of a 'liturgical' play *Magi* from Compiègne, as well as in a celebrated twelfth-century Latin play *Herodes* (see Parker [R.E.] 1933: 61-63). In the pre-Elizabethan Early English drama, Herod appears in many plays of the 'miracle' cycles, with central role in the *Pageant of the Shearmen and Taylors* of the Coventry Cycle. Scene 4 (outside Herod's palace) has the king boasting:

> I am the mightiest conqueror that ever walked on ground,
> For I am even he that made both heaven and hell,
> And with my mighty power I hold up the world around.
> Magog and Madroc both did I confound,
> And with this bright sword their bones I cut asunder,
> That all the wide world at those blows did wonder.
> I am the cause of this great light and thunder;
> It is through my fury that they such noise do make;
> My fearful countenance the clouds so encumber,
> That oftentimes for dread thereof the earth doth quake.
> Look! When I with malice this bright sword do shake,
> All the whole world, from the North to the South,
> I may them destroy with one word of my mouth.
> To recount unto you my innumerable substance,
> That were too much for any tongue to tell;
> For all the whole Orient is under mine obedience,
> And prince I am of Purgatory and chief captain of Hell;

> And those tyrannous traitors by force may I compel,
> My enemies to vanquish and even to dust them drive,
> And with a wink of mine eye not one to leave alive...
> (modernized version by J. Gassner)

No doubt it was such a Herod that William Shakespeare had in mind later when he made Hamlet say that an actor who was over-performing a murderous king was 'out-heroding Herod' (3.2.14). The same image of Herod is also encountered in the non-dramatic Middle English writings, such as the fourteenth-century poems *Cursor Mundi* and *Piers Plowman*, or Geoffrey Chaucer's *The Canterbury Tales* (cf. Hussey 1964: 256-58).

With the appearance in print of the Latin text of the Jewish historian Josephus from 1470, and particularly of the Greek *editio princeps* in 1544, a radical change was possible in the portrait of Herod in drama. Indeed, Hans Sachs's five-act play of 1552 was the first to dramatize the Josephan king as distinct from the religious king of previous times. It is remarkable that from Sachs to Stephen Phillips in 1900, over 25 full-length plays were devoted to Herod in the Western world (Fletcher 1922: 293), while by the Second World War a more thorough search could review not less than 37 (Valency 1940). But something more important and totally uncontemplated before was now also possible: Herod could be taken out of the theatre and become the object of rational, historical enquiry.

Thus partly due to the invaluable work of Josephus, and partly because of immense Christian interest, the history of the Herodian dynasty has attracted attention for almost five hundred years. While preliminary work began in the sixteenth century, the *Rabbini et Herodes* of Nicolaus Serarius was written in 1607, *The Unfortunate Politique* of Nicolas Caussin was already translated into English in 1638, and the epoch-making *Historia Idumaea, seu de vita et gestis Herodum diatribe* of Christianus Noldius appeared in 1660. Of course, at that time research was concentrated on Herod the Great, and it naturally involved an elementary approach to the basic historical evidence.

It was in the second half of the nineteenth century that the first extensive treatments of the dynasty appeared in the great Jewish and New Testament Times *Histories*, mainly of German scholars, such as Graetz, Schneckenburger, Ewald, Hitzig and Hausrath, as well as in separate studies such as those of van der Chijs, *Dissertatio Chronologico-*

historica inauguralis de Herode Magno (1855); von Schuller, *Herodes* (1859); Willett, *The Life and Times of Herod the Great* (1860) and *Herod Antipas* (1866), Derenbourg, *Essai sur l'Histoire et la Géographie de la Palestine* (vol. 1, 1867); de Saulcy, *Histoire d'Hérode, roi des juifs* (1867), and Brann, 'Biographie Agrippa's II' (*MGWJ* 1870–71), 'Die Söhne des Herodes' (*MGWJ* 1873) and *De Herodis, qui dicitur, magni...* (1873). But the clear example for a critical investigation was set in 1874 by the giant Emil Schürer, who considered all sources (literary and non-literary) available to him— though archaeology had yet to shed any light.

Between the time of the original work of Schürer and the beginning of its latest revision and English translation in 1973 (*SVM*), a stream of general and specific accounts were published, the most substantial of which were: Schegg, *Das Todesjahr des Königs Herodes* (1882); Stilgebauer, *Herodes* (1891); Wahl, *De Regina Berenice* (1893); Farrar, *The Herods* (1898); Vickers, *The History of Herod* (2nd edn, 1901); Caraccio, *Erode I. Re degli Ebrei* (1903); Reimarus, *Geschichte der Salome* (1906–1909); Daffner, *Salome* (1912); Caldecott, *Herod's Temple* (1913); Otto, *Herodes* (1913); Willrich, *Das Haus des Herodes* (1929); Momigliano, 'Herod of Judaea' (1934); Hollis, *The Archaeology of Herod's Temple* (1934); Kastein, *Herodes* (1936); Charlesworth, *Five Men* (1936); A.H.M. Jones, *The Herods of Judaea* (1938); Blinzler, *Herodes Antipas und Jesus Christus* (1947); Klausner, *History of the Second Temple* (1950, in Hebrew); Mireaux, *La Reine Bérénice* (1951); Abel, *Histoire de la Palestine* (1952); Minkin, *Herod King of the Jews* (2nd edn, 1956); Busch, *The Five Herods* (1956); Perowne, *The Life and Times of Herod the Great* (1956) and *The Later Herods* (1958); Frankfort 'Le royaume d'Agrippa II' (1962); Krawczuk, *Herod Krol Judei* (1965, in Polish); Bruce, 'Herod Antipas' (*ALUOS* 1966); Sandmel, *Herod: Profile of a Tyrant* (1967); Wirgin, *Herod Agrippa 1. King of the Jews* (1968); Schalit, *König Herodes: der Mann und sein Werk* (1969); Grant, *Herod the Great* (1971); Hoehner, *Herod Antipas* (1972); and M. Stern, 'The Kingdom of Agrippa I' (*Amorai Volume* 1973, in Hebrew).

The 'new' Schürer was soon to be followed by further useful works: M. Stern, 'The Reign of Herod' (1974) and 'Agrippa II' (1975); Jordan, *Berenice* (1974); Smallwood, *The Jews under Roman Rule* (1976); Prause, *Herodes der Grosse* (1977); Sullivan, 'The Dynasty of Judaea' (1978); Busink, *Der Tempel von Jerusalem, von Salomo bis*

Herodes (vol. 2, 1980); Baumann, *Rom und die Juden* (1983); Moliterni, *Hérode le Grand roi des Juifs* (1986); Harari, *Hérode le Grand* (1986); Kasher, *Jews, Idumaeans and Ancient Arabs* (1988); Holum *et al.*, *King Herod's Dream* (1988); D. Schwartz, *Agrippa I: The Last King of Judaea* (1990); S. Schwartz, *Josephus and Judaean Politics* (1990); Shatzman, *The Armies of the Hasmonaeans and Herod* (1991); Horbury, 'Herod's Temple and "Herod's Days"' (1991); M. Stern, *The Kingdom of Herod* (1992, in Hebrew); and Millar, *The Roman Near East* (1993).

Despite a plethora of examinations, it is extraordinary that previous studies have had no *real* depth in terms of social and family history. Only important individuals have been looked at, usually from a prosopographical point of view, with attention directed to the literary evidence, and very little more. Secondary members of the family, and their contribution to society, have simply been left out. With few exceptions, the same is also true for the dynasty's economic, military and administrative mechanisms. In short, the Herodian dynasty has been thoroughly examined only *externally*.

Fundamental questions such as the origins of the family, the social and political conditions in Idumaea in the second century BCE, the strongly Hellenized ideology of Herod the Great, the complexity of his genealogy, the status of the members of his family in Roman Judaea after the fall of Archelaus, their role during the time of the Jewish Revolt, their remarkable centrality in the workings of the Eastern Roman Empire, the gradual eclipse of Agrippa II, and the transfer of Herodian power from Palestine to the wider Greek world in the second century CE, have never been considered together.

Unless the dynasty is treated from beginning to end as an entity in its own right—being the most important dynasty of the Greek world in the Roman period which is known to us in such detail—and in particular treated *internally*, our understanding of it will never be complete. One needs to step inside the Herodian court's door for an entirely new viewpoint to appear. Regrettably, by mainly focusing on the literary evidence, research has seldom taken into account documentary material. New sources provided by the expanding archaeological work have yet to be fully assessed. What has been conspicuously lacking is a picture using all types of evidence. It is true that Josephus will always predominate. But without him being checked against, supplemented with, and corrected by contemporary documents and archaeology, no conclusion can claim to have been soundly based on facts.

It might be objected that other 'client'-kingdoms have come to seem less important, just because they did not happen to have a Josephus behind them. But for all we know of such kingdoms, and we do possess a respectable amount of evidence, no comparison can be made with that of Judaea, which is firmly a class apart. More than any other dynasty, the Herodian fully deserved the Josephus it got—and thus the considerable interest in it of several disciplines, beginning with ancient history, archaeology and theology.

It is certainly undeniable that the first volume of the 'new' Schürer has marked the end of an era and the beginning of another—yet one which is already almost a generation old! Also the framework of this monumental handbook has been criticized in the past, notably by Bowersock (1975), who thought that the arduous scholarship of Millar and Vermes might have better been devoted to a completely new work. Regarding the Herodian period, the 'new' Schürer appeared to Bowersock 'disproportionately weighted in favour of the literary sources' (compare now a directional U-turn in Millar 1993b). The present study has made efforts (within limited space) to tackle the historical evidence in combination with all materials at our disposal, at least those which actually *can* contribute to the writing of history.

Another observation of Bowersock (1975) goes straight to the heart of the matter: 'From antiquity to the present the obloquy of Christians and Jews alike (for different reasons) has blocked the way to a balanced view of Herod'. This book hopes to put this problem on a new footing, and to present us with an alternative understanding of this major client-kingdom of Rome—one that opens new historical perspectives on life in Hellenistic and Roman Palestine, and on Judaism and early Christianity. It is an attempt by a Graeco-Roman historian and archaeologist, with Graeco-Semitic early education (which he acquired as a member of a highly mixed ethnic society once flourishing in Egypt), who appreciates a remark recently made to him by an American professor, that 'it is very important that the classical historians 'recapture' Herod from the biblical [i.e. Christian] scholars'. But a psychological barrier has to be crossed by Jewish scholars too, some of whom may feel that my research seems to rob a significant character from their history. Herod may have been hated by the Jews in antiquity, but his achievements are useful in some current Jewish interpretations of the past. Having said that, of course, there would also be many, particularly among those working in earlier Jewish periods, who will find no reason to feel uncomfortable with my conclusions. For example, when I mentioned to one renowned for her Early Iron Age excavations that I have been working on Herod the Great, her reply was spontaneous: 'that bloody Philistine?'

As realistic as this reaction may be, it is as simplistic as the superficial understanding of a mainly geographical tag attached to Herod by Josephus: 'Idumaean'. This book illustrates the social complexity in Palestine of the Second Temple period, to the extent, for example, that an individual could legitimately be characterized as *Phoenician* by descent, *Hellenized* by culture, *Idumaean* by place of birth, *Jewish* by official religion, *Jerusalemite* by place of residence, and *Roman* by citizenship—with more than one definition possible in some cases. These diverse, but by no means incompatible, identities could coexist, although the degree of ascription to each would vary from person to person. Naturally, individuals who could be so characterized would lay stress to one or the other identity according to circumstances, always to their advantage. Paul the Apostle, who made varying claims while moving freely between the Hebrew, the Greek and the Roman worlds, is just a vivid, if somewhat restricted, example.

Ethnicity or cultural identity is a notoriously plagued question for both the ancient and the modern world (see in context only recently Goudriaan 1988; Friedman 1990; Østergård 1992). What is clear is that ethnicity cannot equal nationality in so far as the word 'nation', as an independent 'state', is a modern development. But to avoid tedious anthropological, sociological and political arguments, is to remember some bare essentials. Hellas may not have been a 'nation' in the sense that this word has had since the French Revolution, but it was as close as it could have been. The concept of a Greek nation may have remained an abstract idea, for which the fragmentation into sovereign polities was responsible, but a series of strong perceptions always provided an unbreakable bond between Greeks everywhere: common *blood*, common *language*, common *religion*, and common *way of life* (with all its customs and artistic expressions). The much-quoted words which Herodotus (8.144.2) put in the mouth of the Athenians preclude any misunderstanding (cf. Walbank 1972; and now Cartledge 1995):

... there is not enough gold in the world anywhere, nor territory beautiful
and fertile enough, that we should take it in return for turning to the Persian interest and enslaving Greece. There are many great things that stand
in our way of so doing even if we wanted to; there are, first and greatest,
the shrines of the gods and their images... then there is our common
Greekness (ἑλληνικόν): we are one in blood and one in language; those
shrines of the gods belong to us all in common, and the sacrifices in
common, and there are our habits, bred of a common upbringing.

The primary element in this Greek identity, namely the biological
descent, could not be emulated by a non-Greek (even if it could be
falsely claimed). Other elements, however, were there to be adopted—
either voluntarily or from a conscious or unconscious imposition since
the age of Alexander the Great; thus the phenomenon of Hellenization,
which is discussed in Chapter 2.

The impact of Hellenization on native cultures, and the creation of
'double' ethnicities (and later 'triple' in view of the rise of Judaisation), is a headache for the historian of the Near East—very much so,
due to the frequent movements of populations in the general area.
Geographic mobility by definition affected ethnicity, creating cultural
affiliations, which resulted in the introduction of new, isolated habits,
or even in broader linguistic and religious metamorphoses. The
research is still in its infancy, but at the crudest level, nevertheless, it
is possible to estimate the relative strength of this impact on different
ethnic communities. For example, the Hellenization of the native
Arabs or Jews (even at élite level) *before* CE 70 was considerably
inferior to that of the coastal Phoenicians by any judgment. Whether
this was due to geography, politics, or a prehistoric racial relationship
(via Mycenaean or Archaic connections) does not matter. It would
thus be a paradox to observe that individuals displaying Hellenization
of the order seen among the Herods are in general terms far closer to
the ethnic concessions made by the Phoenicians (whether of the coast
or of those who moved inland) than by the Arabs or Jews (namely of
local stock and not of the diaspora). No other family known to us
breeding among the Jewish community *in* Judaea ever reached such a
level of Hellenization as that of the Herods, as summed up in the conclusion. The native Jewish community of the Second Temple period
adhered to a strict Judaism, normally in conflict with paganism, which
must *not* be confused with the openness towards pagan ideas observed
in some areas of pre-exilic Hebraism or later Mishnaic rabbinism
(compare Chapter 2 n. 130). An investigation of the 'biological' and

cultural origins of the Herods is therefore imperative. A pragmatic Herodian background may help to conceive what was mentioned above as the remarkable centrality of the dynasty in the workings of the Eastern Roman Empire, and the readiness with which its members were chosen to serve as 'client'-kings and later Roman senators.

My conclusion could only be presented as a hypothesis (since inevitably its value remains to be seen), but one which I believe to be strong. Many questions answered in the conclusion are those raised in seminars and by my two examiners. Whether or not they seem the most relevant, they could not be excised. I am sure that dozens of new questions will be raised, perhaps more pertinent, or from people who know (or think they know) better, and in due course they will be answered too.

Apart from Josephus and the primary documentary sources (epigraphic, papyrological, numismatic and archaeological), I have utilized the New Testament, at least in the notes (see the discussion in Chapter 3 n. 75). My aim was purely historical. The points I selected are those that I believe to be valid as evidence—thus the usually approving nature of my New Testament citations (compare Chapter 10 at n. 21). I have concerned myself comparatively little with the opinion of theologians regarding such points, because my historical and archaeological background provided a safer basis upon which to judge. So my treatment of the Christian testimony has nothing to do with any conscious pro-Christian stance. Whoever has read my Greek book on Jesus (1980), for which I was nearly excommunicated by the Orthodox Church (following the novelist Nikos Kazantzakis who was, and the Marxist historian Yiannes Kordatos who nearly was), must know how critical I have been of organized religion, even if this book was the fruit of research far too early in my life and thus quite immature (much was preliminarily published in 1977 when I was 22). But no degree of criticism or scepticism must impede a historian from giving credit where credit is rightly due. To all intents and purposes, 'the world of the Gospels *is* that of Josephus', as my supervisor clearly stated (Millar 1990b: 357).

Since the time of Bowersock's observation concerning the unbalanced approach to Herod (mentioned above), the development of a general attitude towards our literary sources has come further to hinder progress in scholarship: 'hypercritism'. It is currently a trend, often presented as a virtue, to be hypercritical of ancient historical writing. Together with Greek and Roman records, the Old and New Testaments have come to suffer in particular. But wholesale rejection, without careful weighing in the scale of reasonableness, using controls now afforded by a variety of external sources, is simply too glib. Natural scepticism and good old criticism must continue to be enough in satisfying our scientific minds—surely. Unless we are prepared to face the danger of creating a situation in which systematic dismissal can leave us with no sources at all for writing any history (compare Kokkinos 1996). I cannot help but remember an international conference on early Christianity in which an American professor was delivering a lengthy eulogy on Luke's Acts, when a voice in the background complained: 'Don't you think you make a lot out of Luke?'. The professor's answer, which was followed by unstoppable laughter, was clinical: 'it is better to make a lot out of Luke than a lot out of nothing'!

My use of Luke in this book may surprise some modernists, but the decision was not taken naively. I believe that what are sometimes seen as Luke's 'errors' in relation to the Herodians, are not in fact errors if we pay attention to the details of the history of the Herodian dynasty—for example, the lack of Berenice II's title of 'Queen' in Luke (for which see Chapter 10 n. 194), or the use of the popular title 'Herod' for Agrippa I (for which see Chapter 8 n. 78; compare Chapter 10 n. 60), not to mention the notorious, though quite different, problem of the birth of Jesus under 'Herod' (for which see Chapter 8 n. 78 end). Of course there are unrelated mistakes in Luke, like numerous similar mistakes in Josephus (for example see Chapter 10 n. 9; Chapter 8 n. 20, etc.) or indeed in the highly praised Tacitus, Suetonius and Dio, to mention a few broadly contemporary historians of the Roman period. What does this mean? In our context it means absolutely nothing! There is no such thing as infallibility in historical writing whether ancient or modern. I agree that theology in the New Testament should be left to theologians, but its historical and archaeological wealth can only be put under the direct control of Graeco-Roman historians, and the sooner the better. Luke's work is too important to be treated lightly, not to say insultingly. In spite of kerygmatic shortcomings, it is an invaluable source of information for the Eastern world of the first century CE, filling a significant gap between Philo and Josephus (for example see Chapter 7 n. 82).

Turning to the rabbinical sources, it must be recognized that they are late compositions, too late to throw primary light on the history of Palestine before CE 70 (compare Chapter 10 n. 222). Nevertheless, occasionally they too contain relevant material, which should not be dismissed simply on the basis of date. I have selected some points which in my opinion must be genuine recollections or traditions of the first century CE (for example see Chapter 3 n. 41; Chapter 10 n. 67, etc.). But rabbinical evidence is above all useful for passive judgments in a variety of questions from geography to religion—for example, it provides later parallels to the early products of the land (for which see Chapter 2), or to the economy of manual labour (for which see Chapter 10 n. 244).

The last category of pertinent sources is the standard Greek and Roman literature, which has been used extensively in my reconstruction of the wider political world in which the Herodian dynasty functioned since its birth in the Hellenistic period. However, for the specific question of the origins and personal culture of the Herods, and how important, clear or valid is the way they were described by Greek and Roman authors, this literature is found to be basically useless. Nineteen surviving pagan writers briefly refer or allude to members of the dynasty, but not a single passage throws any indisputable historical light on our question. My exclusion of these writers is not arbitrary, and the reasons are given in the conclusion. Hopefully my arguments will be carefully considered, rather than hesitantly being taken as special pleading, though I doubt whether many experts will disagree with me—my supervisor certainly did not! An odd satirical or poetical remark, sometimes of a late writer, full of ambiguity and imprecision, intended or unintended, is no evidence that can be taken *a priori*. Any critical analysis has to reject such distant bits of information, and in any case we should not expect such writers to either know or be willing to testify on something so complex as the definition of an ethnic identity existing in a part of the world which they never understood or visited. The strongest view must remain that extracted from local writers, whether Greek, Jewish or Christian.

For the important subject of chronology I have made a special effort and devoted much space. It is clear that almost every major event of the Herodian period is liable to a chronological readjustment. I have decided to expose many cases, and not for fun—as much as I enjoy going back to basics and forcing conventional wisdom to be laid bare (for example see my contributions on proto-history in James *et al.* 1991)! The corrections suggested here are usually minor in magnitude, and the exercise might have been thought as trivial. Yet, there is nothing to supplement precision, if this is achievable. Such precision throws beams of light on political history otherwise totally lost to us (see further comments in Chapter 4 end).

Perhaps it is worth mentioning that although no university thesis on the dynasty as a whole has ever been undertaken, restricted dissertations have sporadically been submitted, of which the following remain unpublished: Harlan, 'Evidence of the Hellenistic Influence of the Herods upon New Testament History' (1943); D'Ancona Porte, 'The Art and Architecture of Palestine under Herod the Great' (1966); Vardaman, 'Corpus Inscriptionum Herodian[ar]um I' (1974); Fry, 'The Warning Inscriptions from the Herodian Temple' (1974); and Small, 'Herod at Masada and Herodeion: An Attempt to Identify and Characterize Herod's Domestic Architecture' (1984). There is also a thesis in progress by Jacobson, 'The Place of Herod's Temple in the Architecture of the Augustan Age'.

Finally, it is also worth mentioning that the greatest Roman historian of our time, Sir Ronald Syme, in his *Anatolica* (published posthumously in 1995), a collection of Strabonian studies which he left unfinished in the 1940s, planned to include a chapter entitled 'Strabo on the House of Herod'. Anthony Birley, the editor of this publication, notes in the introduction that 'an apparently complete draft on the House of Herod lacked notes' and that for other reasons too it seemed preferable to omit it (Syme 1995: xvii). It would have been interesting to know Syme's position (even if out of date) on such an important subject, and although I was invited to examine this paper by Fergus Millar, the literary executor of the Syme Archive at Wolfson College, I regret that I did not find the time to do so. Hopefully, my assessment of the ancient geographer in various notes of the present volume, together with the essential commentary of Menahem Stern (*GLAJJ* 1, 261-315), will adequately cover this matter in lieu of a published, specialized discussion.

Part I

IDUMAEA AND THE ORIGINS OF THE HERODS

Chapter 1

FROM EDOM TO IDUMAEA

After the death of Isaac his sons divided the territory between them, not retaining that which they had inherited. Esau, for his part, left the city of Hebron to his brother and taking up his abode in Saeira[1] ruled over Idumaea, calling the country thus after himself: for he bore the surname of Adom[2] which he had obtained under the following circumstances. One day, while yet a lad, he was returning from the chase, fatigued with his hunting and famished, when, meeting his brother who had just prepared for his midday meal a dish of lentils of a rich tawny hue, which still further whetted his appetite, he asked him to give him to eat. Jacob, thereupon, taking advantage of his famished state, required his brother to sell to him in exchange for the food his rights as firstborn son; and he, instigated by hunger, surrendered to him his rights under an oath. Hence by reason of the ruddy colour of the pottage, he was jestingly nicknamed by his youthful comrades Adom—*adoma* being the Hebrews' word for 'red'[3]—and that was how he called the country: the more dignified name of Idumaea it owes to the Greeks.

This traditional story as related by Josephus based on the biblical account is all we know of the first steps toward the creation of Edom, the ancient kingdom east of the Arabah.[4] The chief mountain range of Seir[5] extended almost the entire length of the Edomite homeland from Wadi el-Ḥesa in the north to Wadi el-Ḥismeh in the south. The early history of Edom does not concern us here—its government seems to

1. Gen. 14.6 שעיר בהררם—LXX ἐν τοῖς ὄρεσιν Σηείρ; cf. Num. 24.18.
2. Gen. 25.30 אדם—LXX Ἐδώμ.
3. Heb. אדום; cf. Gen. 36.1.
4. Josephus, *Ant.* 2.1-3; for the history of Edom, see the works of Bartlett 1969; 1972; 1973; 1977; 1979; 1982; 1983; 1989; where bibliographies; and now Vikander Edelman (ed.) 1995.
5. שעיר, modern Jebel esh-Shera. A second tradition in Gen. 25.25 explains Esau's nickname by the redness and hairiness of his skin. The word 'Seir' does mean hairy, shaggy, covered with brush or forests.

have collapsed soon after the middle of the sixth century BCE beyond recovery.[6] Formal Edomitic rule was never extended west of the Arabah,[7] and even if the Persians established a province over Edom, despite the repeated statements of Herodotus to the contrary,[8] there is no evidence that the Greeks called this province by that name. In the early Hellenistic period the region (or at least the northern part of it) was probably known as 'Gabalitis', whereas under the Hasmonaeans it was referred to as 'Arabia' or 'Nabataean Arabia'.[9]

Thus the use of 'Idumaea' in the passage of Josephus has strictly speaking been applied to the wrong area.[10] It will be seen later that the Greeks named Idumaea the place which is metaphorically called 'Western Edom'. At any rate, Josephus's context would support by implication the view that people of Edomite stock had once moved into South Judah and that they were gradually established there as 'Idumaeans'. The land around the region of Hebron would be naturally attractive to any group claiming to be the descendants of Esau, who must have felt that they should be the rightful owners of it, since traditionally their patriarch lost it to his brother Jacob by deception. The recognition of such a continuous tradition bound to the area is

6.   The latest mention of a king of Edom dates to the beginning of the sixth century BCE (Jer. 27.3). Ostracon 6043 from Tell el-Kheleifeh testifies that the Edomitic government was still active around the middle of the sixth century BCE (Albright 1941; Naveh 1966: 28-30; Glueck 1971: 226-29; cf. Cross 1975a; Cross 1986). Edom perhaps submitted to the Neo-Babylonian king Nabonidus in 553 BCE (Lindsay [J.] 1976: 23-39). If Lindsay is right in reading [A]dummu (in fact [U]- du-um-mu as in Grayson 1975: 282b ad 105, I.17) in the Nabonidus Chronicle, this would be the only reference to Edom in all surviving Neo-Babylonian and Persian records (by contrast Edom is found earlier in the records of Assyria).

7.   It used to be accepted that Glueck's surveys (1936: 152; 1967a: 436) showed that there was no pre-exilic expansion of Edomites west of the Arabah. The recent discovery of Edomite pottery in a score of sites in the Negev, believed to date from the seventh century BCE, has now altered the view (Bartlett 1982: 15-16; Bartlett 1989: 141-43)—but see below n. 27.

8.   Herodotus 3.88, 97, 107; see de Geus 1979–80: 54; Bartlett 1989: 164.

9.   For Gabalitis see Josephus, *Ant.* 2.6; cf. Jones [A.H.M.] 1971: 450 n. 19; for Arabia or Nabataean Arabia, see 2 Macc. 5.8; 1 Macc. 5.25; 9.35, etc.; cf. Diodorus 2.48.6.

10.   The same type of application and anachronism can be observed in the LXX when mentioning Edom, e.g. 1 Kgs 11.14-15; also cf. 1 Kgs 9.26 against 2 Chron. 8.17, etc.

alluded to in the book of Job.[11] The book of *Jubilees* also adds that Esau was buried in Adoraim a town close to Hebron,[12] while 1 Maccabees admits that 'the children of Esau' were to be found at Hebron.[13] The question then is: when and why would Edomites have migrated to the west and northwest of their original territory?

Relevant information is obtainable again from the biblical and apocryphal record. When Nebuchadrezzar II besieged and captured Jerusalem in 597 and 587 BCE, the Edomites joined his forces and exulted at the destruction of their ancient enemies.[14] Although it may be true that all the vindictiveness against Edom displayed in the prophecies of Ezekiel, Joel, Amos, Obadiah and Malachi cannot be connected exclusively with the events of 597 and 587 BCE,[15] much of this hostility must have derived from precisely these disastrous occasions.[16] It is reasonable to assume that the Edomites had profited from the resulting

11. Job 15.18, dated not later than the Persian period (Soggin 1989: 453-54); cf. Pfeiffer 1926.

12. *Jub*. 38.8. A conflicting tradition in the *Test. XII Patr.* (*T. Jud.* 9) places the burial of Esau on Mount Seir, but its location is sometimes confused in the Pseudepigrapha, taken as being near Hebron, as in *Liv. Proph.*, 10.9, mentioning the cave of Kenaz the first Judge and leader of an important Edomite tribe (cf. Pseudo-Philo, *frag.* 25.3; Josephus, *Ant.* 5.182; and Judg. 3.9 referring to Othniel son of Kenaz). Both *Jubilees* and *Testaments* are thought to date to the second century BCE (Wintermute 1985: 43-45; Kee 1983: 777-78; Doran 1989; cf. Mendels 1992: 44-45, 97-98). For an unconvincing hypothesis of calling 'Seir' a mountain area west of the Arabah, see Davies [G. I.] 1979.

13. 1 Macc. 5.65; cf. Millar 1993a: 35.

14. Ps. 137.7, referring to the Edomites who in the day of the destruction of Jerusalem were shouting 'Raze it, raze it! Down to its foundations!'; cf. Lam. 4.21-22; Ezek. 35.15; Obad. 10-16; also the direct accusation in the apocryphal 1 Esd. 4.45 '...build up the temple, which the Edomites burned when Judaea was made desolate by the Chaldees'.

15. Ackroyd 1968: 224; cf. Dicou 1984; Glazier-McDonald 1995. This hatred goes back a long way. Peaks of animosity can be observed in the Bible, including in Esau's story, the refusal of the Edomites to let the Israelites pass through their territory after the exodus, and the battles over the control of the 'King's Highway'. Haggadic literature dealing with Jacob and Esau extended the conflict to their descendants. Beyond the confrontation of Gen. 32–33, some traditions have Jacob slay Esau (*Jub.* 37.1–38.14; *Test. XII Patr.* (*T. Jud.* 9); and as late as the *Chronicle of Jerahmeel* 37.1-14). For the hatred of Esau in the New Testament, see Rom. 9.10-13, and for the continuation of the conflict in medieval times, see Cohen [G.D.] 1967.

16. Contra Morgenstern (1956: 101) and Bartlett (1982: 23).

deportation to Babylon of a part of the Judaean population and from the flight generated by the assassination of Gedaliah.[17] Many of them would have settled in the southern part of Judah with Hebron as their centre.[18] This is in agreement with at least one apocryphal statement, apparently of the Early Hellenistic period, also known to Josephus, referring to the Early Persian period when Darius I (521–486 BCE) decreed that Edomites should evacuate Judaean villages.[19]

How does this picture compare to the archaeology of the area? Interestingly, recent work has succeeded in distinguishing between 'Midianite' and 'Edomite' pottery, thus opening an avenue for understanding the precise distribution of these wares.[20] But first we should be reminded of the positive attitude towards pottery, as expressed by Parr:

> The connection between potsherds and people is always being made, of course, and even if there has been a reaction in recent years... it is still an important—perhaps the single most important—assumption in

17. Jer. 40–44; 2 Kgs 25.22-26; cf. Bright 1981: 330-31. In Ezek. 35.12 there is clear confirmation: 'the mountains of Israel... are laid desolate, they are given to us (Edomites) to devour'. According to Soggin (1984: 252-57; cf. Smith [M.] 1971: 64) the literary evidence suggests that outside Jerusalem only a small proportion of the population (mainly the nobility and some craftsmen) was actually removed (cf. Barstad 1988; Mitchell [T.C.] 1991). At all events, the texts do give the impression of the creation of a vacuum in the area, enough to be taken advantage of by the Edomites (cf. Torrey 1898).

18. It is possible that the book of Judith (1.9) preserved the Edomitic name of the original centre at Hebron: 'Betanei' (cf. 'Kiriath-Arba' in Josh. 14.15; Judg. 1.10, etc.); for later 'Idumaean' Hebron, see Chapter 2 n. 69. That Lachish served as the capital in the area is only based on the theory of 'Western Edom' as a Persian province, and on the existence of a palatial 'residency' (Avi-Yonah 1977a: 25-26; Tufnell 1977: 746; Rainey 1983: 18), the date of which is disputed (Aharoni 1982: 269; Ussishkin 1977: 39; cf. Ussishkin 1993: 910-11).

19. 1 Esd. 4.50; Josephus, *Ant.* 11.61; for the late history of Edom, cf. Myers 1971: 377-92; McCarter 1976: 87-92; and generally Bartlett (above n. 4).

20. For 'Edomite' pottery, see Oakeshott 1983; for 'Midianite', see Rothenberg and Glass 1983. It should be noted that the Midianite pottery is dated by Rothenberg and Glass (1983: 76) not later than the twelfth century BCE (contra Bimson 1981), thus postulating a settlement at Tell el-Kheleifeh dating back to the thirteenth–twelfth centuries BCE (contra Glueck 1965). But in view of the fact that Midianite sherds were found at Tell el-Kheleifeh Period IV (seventh–sixth century BCE), an acute chronological problem remains (see Glueck 1967b: 10-15; cf. James *et al.* 1987: 66-67; James *et al.* 1991: 201-203).

archaeological methodology that the movements and activities of specific groups of people can be distinguished in the archaeological record most readily and certainly from a study of ceramic typology.[21]

Edomite painted pottery has now been found in a score of sites west of the Arabah.[22] Concentrations of this constitute a tiny proportion of the total pottery assemblage in these sites, and they could be taken simply as evidence of trade.[23] The Edomites had economic interests in the Mediterranean port of Gaza, particularly after the gulf of Aqaba in the Red Sea came under their control, and Gaza was reached only by crossing the Negev.[24] It is also possible that the sudden appearance of Edomite pottery west of the Arabah coincided with the history of the North Arabian tribes, the strength of which was increased during the waning years of the Assyrian power:[25] Arabs could have brought Edomite pottery to the Negev through expansion and commerce. However, some of the sites have produced qualitative evidence which clearly suggests Edomite settlement in the area. Some 30 per cent of the pottery from Tel Malhata was Edomite, an ostracon from Horvat 'Uza was actually written in Edomitic, while Horvat Qitmit functioned as an Edomite cultic centre.[26]

Archaeology thus seems to verify our historical evidence,[27] and the

21. Parr 1978: 203; cf. Meyers 1993.

22. At Kadesh-Barnea in the Negev; at Aroer, Horvat Qitmit, Tel Malhata, Tel Masos and Tel 'Ira in the Beersheba region; at Tell esh-Shariah and Tel Haror on the banks of Nahal Gerar; and apparently at Tell Jemmeh in the extreme west (see Mazar [E.] 1985: 264; Beit-Arieh 1988: 35; Beit-Arieh 1989: 125; and now Beit-Arieh 1995a with additional sites); plus Edomite evidence on ostraca from elsewhere (see below n. 26).

23. The overall evidence certainly cannot support Noth's theory (1956: 311) of the existence of a 'Greater Edom' in the early Neo-Babylonian period. For an example of trade, cf. the Nabataean coins and pottery discovered in non-Nabataean sites west of the Arabah, including at Jerusalem (Wenning 1987: esp. 134-37).

24. Cf. 2 Kgs 16.6; 2 Chron. 28.17; cf. further Glueck 1967a: 441; there was a trade in slaves between Gaza and Edom in the eighth century BCE (Amos 1.6).

25. Eph'al 1982.

26. Kochavi 1977: 774 (Tel Malhata); Beit-Arieh and Cresson 1985 (Horvat 'Uza); Beit-Arieh and Beck 1987; Beit-Arieh 1988; and now Beit-Arieh 1995b (Horvat Qitmit); also note a seal (Biran and Cohen 1976: 139; Biran 1983: 34) and a fragmentary ostracon (Biran 1982: 162; Naveh 1985b: 120-21, no. 13) from Aroer; and possibly unpublished ostraca from Tel Malhata (Kochavi 1977: 774), and Tell esh-Shariah (Oren 1982: 160).

27. A remaining problem is surely chonology. The Edomite pottery in question is

discoveries at Arad have taught us a significant lesson. An Israelite fortress on the site (Stratum VI) was destroyed by Edomites (in 595 or 587 BCE according to the excavators—but probably later), as implied by a Hebrew ostracon, associated with the destruction of Stratum VI on palaeographical grounds:

> To Eliashib... From Arad 50 (men) and from Kin[ah 100 men]. And you shall send them to Ramat-Negeb by the hand of Malkiyahu the son of Qerab'ur and he shall hand them over to Elisha' the son of Yirmiyahu in Ramat-Negeb, lest anything should happen to the city. And the word of the king is incumbent upon you for your very life! Behold, I have sent to warn you today: [Get] the men to Elisha'—Lest Edom should come there.[28]

Other excavations east of Beersheba present a similar situation, according to which Judahite sites were destroyed during the sixth (and probably fifth) century BCE.[29] Further, the nomenclature of the Aramaic ostraca from Beersheba, dated from the mid-fourth century BCE, is overwhelmingly Edomitic and Arabic, testifying to the settlement of such people in the area. A mingling between the two races may even be indicated by that time. In fact, the inhabitants of at least the northern part of the Negev in the fourth century BCE have been recently termed 'Edomite Arabs'.[30]

By similar reasoning one can assume that during the late Neo-Babylonian period the Nabataeans (another Arabian tribe) would have

dated from the seventh century BCE, but it should be from the sixth, if a substantial number of Edomites had moved into southern Judah after 587 BCE. The accepted ceramic dating is thus forcing many to contemplate an Edomite westward expansion in the First Temple period (Stern [E.] 1982: 279 n. 49; Beit-Arieh 1989: 129-31; Bartlett 1989: 143; Beit-Arieh 1995a), which is not what our historical sources tell us. The solution to this conundrum may be found in the revision proposed by James *et al*. 1987, 1991, 1992. For a recent chronological debate, see Finkelstein 1992a; Finkelstein 1992b; Bienkowski 1992a; Bienkowski 1992b.

28. Aharoni (ed.) 1981: 46-49, no. 24 (unstratified); cf. Aharoni 1982: 279; also see nos. 12, 40 (Aharoni [ed.] 1981: 26, 71).

29. E.g. Tel Masos (Kempinski 1977: 818; Fritz 1983: 30; cf. Kempinski 1993), Tel 'Ira (Beit-Arieh 1981; cf. Beit-Arieh 1993a), Tel Malḥata (Kochavi 1977: 774; cf. Kochavi 1993), Aroer (Biran and Cohen 1976; cf. Biran 1993), Ḥorvat 'Uza (Beit-Arieh and Cresson 1982; cf. Beit-Arieh 1993b). Note that under current stratigraphical chronology very few sites east of Beersheba show any sign of reoccupation in the Persian period, e.g. Arad (mostly due to ostraca) and Ḥorvat Rithma—Stern [E.] 1982: 251.

30. Naveh 1979: 195.

profited from the migration to the west of a number of Edomites and would have begun gradually pressing into Edom from the southeast (and perhaps the east).[31] Although written information about the southern Transjordan for the period between Nebuchadrezzar II's war against Ammon and Moab in 582 BCE and the beginning of the Hellenistic era is not available, one finds Nabataeans by the end of the fourth century BCE firmly established in the former Edomite territory, and soon with Petra as their capital.[32] In the process, Nabataean assimilation with local people can safely be inferred.[33] A later record

31. By the fifth century BCE Edom had been completely taken over according to Malachi (1.3-5), one assumes by the Nabataeans. On a southeastern origin of these people, see Parr 1968–69. Bartlett (1979: 65) has argued for an eastern origin based on the theory that the 'Na-ba-a-a-ti' (Assyrian), '*nbyt*' (Teimanite) and 'Nebaioth' (Hebrew) are Nabataeans (cf. Broome 1973)—but see Eph'al 1982: 221-23.

32. Diodorus 2.48.1-7; 49.1; 19.94.1-10; 95.1-2; 97.1-2; cf. Negev 1976a. Hieronymus of Cardia (*apud* Diodorus 19.94) portrays the Nabataeans in 312 BCE as breeders of cattle, camels and sheep—but not as farmers (Hammond 1973: 13; Hammond 1991: 37). Archaeology at Petra has shown that sedentary life began in the mid-third century BCE (Parr 1965: 528-30; Parr 1970: 369), while monumental architecture dates from the beginning of the first century BCE (McKenzie 1990; cf. Kokkinos 1992b). Strabo (16.4.26) noted costly Nabataean stone houses and moulded works.

33. De Geus (1979–80: 70) is misled in saying that the Nabataeans are lately identified less and less as Arabs—on the contrary they are identified more and more as such (Eph'al 1982: 206, 221-23; Shahîd 1984: 5, 9-10; Negev 1986a: 60; Healey 1989; and now Macdonald 1993: 377-82). It is the increased Arabization of the later Edomites, both those who moved west of the Arabah (Naveh 1979: 194-45) and those who stayed in Edom, together with the fact that the Nabataeans were using Aramaic, the *lingua franca* (Starcky 1960: 924-26), that have confused de Geus. Our classical sources are clear: Diodorus 2.48.1 Ἄραβες οὓς ὀνομάζουσι Ναβαταίους; Josephus, *Ant.* 13.10 Ναβαταῖοι Ἄραβες; cf. *Ant.* 1.220-21 (Millar 1993a: 31); and the Nabataean-Arabic bilingual inscription from Oboda confirms this fact (Negev 1986b: 150). Moreover, de Geus cannot be justified in denying any migration from Edom on the basis of a certain continuity between the Edomite and Nabataeans cultures (as advocated by Bartlett 1979). Even if such continuity could be argued, by the hypothesis of a return to nomadism which would account for the lack of archaeological evidence (a break in occupation, suggested by Glueck, is confirmed by excavations [Bennett [C.M.] 1966; 1977; 1984] and surveys [Hart and Falkner 1985: 268]), nothing dictates against a partial migration of the original inhabitants of Edom. In fact evidence examined here demands it. That many Edomites were left behind can be illustrated by the ostracon from Heshbon (Cross 1973), dated to the end of the sixth century BCE and more than 50 years after the beginning of the assumed

preserved in Strabo, in spite of being misleading in its details (see Chapter 3, contra Kasher), does generally give the right impression for both movements, that is of the Edomites and the Nabataeans, as described above:

> The Idumaeans are Nabataeans, but owing to a sedition they were banished from there, joined the Judaeans, and shared in the same customs with them.[34]

Of course, a better understanding has been formulated today: the Idumaeans or, initially, Edomites were not Nabataean tribes[35] and their conversion to Judaism, as we shall see, was not a voluntary act but one to which they were compelled to submit by force.

What exactly happened in the early stage of the history of 'Western Edom' is difficult to determine at present. Several questions come to mind: were the Edomites given a certain autonomy over a province in South Judah by the Neo-Babylonian rulers after their settlement there? If so, how far south into the Negev, north toward Jerusalem and west toward the coast were their boundaries drawn? What effect would the subsequent Persian invasion have on such a new land division in the area? Would this division be adopted as a subdivision (like Judah and Samaria) of עבר נהרה (the fifth Persian satrapy which included all the country from Northern Syria to the borders of Egypt),[36] or would it

movement west of the Arabah, which mentions the 'men of Gubla', one of the Edomite tribes (Ps. 83.8); also by the only cuneiform tablet of the Persian period from Tawilan (Dalley 1984), attesting an Edomite here in 521 BCE, the first year of Darius I (though it could also be Darius II, 423 BCE, or Darius III, 335 BCE); and by the worshippers of Qos living in Nabataea down to the Roman period (Bartlett 1989: 200-201, 206; cf. Hammond 1991: 38).

34. Strabo, 16.2.34; he only means that they came from Nabataea, as when he calls the Jews 'Egyptians', since they arrived from Egypt following the exodus.

35. As we saw, the biblical record associates Esau (the son of the Hebrew patriarch) with the Edomites. It is thought that Edomitic language was a Canaanite dialect akin to Hebrew, Moabite and Ammonite, not only in the first half of the first millennium BCE, but as late as the Persian period (Cross 1969: 23; Naveh 1971a: 28; see now Vanderhooft 1995). The Edomites adopted the Hebrew script under the influence of Judah, which later became increasingly Aramaized due to the Assyrian expansion (Naveh 1982: 100-12). A degree of Arabization upon the Edomites (both in Edom and in the Negev) is understandable, and it should not be taken to signify that the Edomites were originally Arab tribes (contra Shahîd 1984: 5, 13). Stephanus (s.v. *Edoumaioi*), shows that even in the sixth century CE there was speculation as to whether Idumaeans (or Edomites?) were of Arab or Hebrew stock (s.v. *Idoumaioi*).

36. Herodotus, 3.91; *Ebir nâri* (Aram. עבר נהרה see Ezra 4.10; Heb. עבר הנהר

be united with Judah proper to form a larger province?

One thing is certain: the Edomites were not the only inhabitants of southern Palestine during this period. It is evident from Nehemiah that surviving Jewish communities were still living in South and West Judah.[37] In his memoirs mention is also made of unfriendly Arabs, evidently in the south, with Geshem of the late post-exilic or early restoration period as their leader.[38] The Jewish reformer is apparently

see Ezra 8.36) meaning 'beyond the river' is the Assyrian administrative term known from the time of Esarhaddon and perhaps even earlier (1 Kgs 5.4)—cf. Schalit 1954: 68; Avi-Yonah 1977a: 12; Rainey 1969: 51.

37. Neh. 11.25-30. Although Nehemiah's list has been criticized as reflecting earlier periods (Aharoni 1966: 355-56; cf. Stern [E.] 1981: 17), one cannot see how this can be proved (Williamson 1987: 28). The fact that he does not mention the Edomites in South Judah shows: (a) that by his time 'Western Edom' had yet to be established as a province (it will be suggested here that it may have formed a part of Judah, which in turn, but only very early under Persian rule, may have been a part of Samaria—Alt 1953: 316-37; cf. McEvenue 1981; but see Williamson 1988; Eph'al 1988); (b) that by now prejudice was too great to allow a mention of Edom possessing former Israelite land; and (c) that the Edomites seem to have evacuated a considerable part of Judah at the beginning of the Persian period.

38. Neh. 4.1; cf. 2.19; 6.1, 6. The identification of Geshem the Arab with Gashmu the father of Qainu, King of Qedar (Dumbrell 1971), and with Gashmu the son of Shahru, Governor of Dedan (Winnett and Reed 1970: 115-17), as well as the presence of a Qedarite king, Iyas son of Mahlai, at Lachish (Lemaire 1974; cf. Lemaire 1990: 47-50), cannot be proved (Bartlett 1979: 59-62; Eph'al 1982: 214). However, based on the finds from Tell el-Maskhûta, the first identification is reasonable. Although only one silver bowl mentions 'Qedar', we are dealing with a considerable votive cache (Rabinowitz 1956; 1959), belonging to a shrine of the Arab goddess han-'Ilât ('Αλίλατ of Herodotus, 3.8; אלת in Nabataean and Palmyraean inscriptions, e.g. Cooke 1903, nos. 80.4; 99.1; 117.6; *'ll't* in the Qur'ân, Sûra 53.19; often equated with the sky-goddess Urania—Irvine 1973: 293). The connection of a king of Qedar with an Arab shrine in the Eastern Delta at the time when Nehemiah and the Greek sources (see below n. 39) refer to Arabs in southern Palestine is indicative (cf. de Geus 1979–80: 60-61). Certainly by the fifth century BCE Arab nomads dwelt here with the consent of the Persian authorities—apparently serving as a garrison for this important border of Egypt (Rabinowitz 1956: 9); cf. the Nabataean inscriptions from Tell esh-Shuqafiya (Strugnell 1959; Jones [B.W.] *et al.* 1988; Fiema and Jones 1990). Arab shepherds or guards in the Fayûm are proved later by the Zenon papyri (Tscherikower 1937: 27). Qedarites may well have been transferred here from their eastern homeland. Their king would have had no alternative but to serve the Persians as a client-king wherever he was placed. Tiglath-pileser III the Assyrian had already put such a programme into action, when he entrusted the tribe I-di-ba-'-il-a-a with a similar task in this area (Na'aman 1979: 68-90; cf. Eph'al

in agreement with Greek writers such as Herodotus, Diodorus, Polybius and Arrian, who testify to an Arab presence both here and in the
Transjordan during the fifth and fourth centuries BCE.[39] Additionally
in the western part, the Shephelah region, remnants of Philistine communities[40] together (or intermingled with) some Phoenician groups

1982: 215-16). But there is no reason to believe that the Qedarites enjoyed excessive
powers by which they seized the whole of Edom, as well as 'Western Edom', and
ruled over the entire south (Myers 1971: 386). Nehemiah's reference to Geshem the
Arab can only be understood by Arab presence to the extreme south, i.e. south of
'Western Edom' (contra Cross 1955a: 46-47; cf. Rainey 1969: 65). This accords
with the position of the Arab territory in Herodotus (3.5) and apparently in the book
of Judith (1.9). The nomenclature of the Aramaic ostraca from Beersheba testify to
Arab influence in the southern border (Naveh 1973; Naveh 1979: 182-95). We
should remember that Nabataean settlement in the Negev detectable by archaeological
means begins only in the third century BCE with the founding of Eboda and Elusa
(Negev 1986a: 29-30). The earliest Nabataean inscription from anywhere in Palestine
dated to the beginning of the second century BCE is from Elusa (Cross 1961: 161;
Naveh 1982: 154; Negev 1986a: 17); cf. comment by Graf (1992: 455) about an
unedited text in the Damascus Museum of the third century BCE.

39. Herodotus, 3.91; cf. 3.5; also cf. Arabs on racing camels who took part even
in Xerxes' campaign to Greece in 480 BCE (7.86-87, 184); Diodorus, 13.46.6;
15.2.4 for Arab participation in coastal and overseas operations in 410 and 386 BCE;
cf. Arabs in Gaza when Antigonus was on his way to Egypt (20.73.3); Polybius,
16.40; Arrian, 2.25.4 relates that Arabian soldiers defended Gaza against Alexander;
see Eph'al 1982: 197.

40. For the Philistines see Macalister 1913; Mazar [B.] 1964; Tadmor 1966;
Kitchen 1973; Dothan [T.] 1982; Sandars 1985; Mazar [A.] 1985; Brug 1985;
Dothan and Dothan 1992; Bierling 1992. From an early period Philistines and
Edomites were allies against Judah (e.g. 1 Sam. 14.47; 1 Chron. 18.1-13; 2 Chron.
28.17-18; Isa. 11.14; Ezek. 16.57; 25.12-17; Obad. 19; cf. also later reflections in
Sir. 50.26 and *Jub.* 37.10) to the wars of Judas Maccabaeus against both (1 Macc.
5.65-68) and the Dead Sea Scrolls where Edomites and Philistines are enemies of the
'sons of light' (1QM 1.1-2 and implied in 11.6-7, cf. Num. 24.17-19). A convo-
cation of the two is mentioned in a Nimrud letter (XVI—*ANET* 287), dated to the
time of Sargon II's campaign in 712 BCE. The last Philistine kings mentioned in
cuneiform documents are those of Gaza and Ashdod, found together with the
Phoenician kings of Tyre and Sidon, in a list (*ANET* 308) of high court officials at
the palace of Nebuchadrezzar II (first half of sixth century BCE). King A-ga-' of
Ascalon, mentioned in 592 BCE, must have been in the same company (Weidner
1939: 928). Also from about 600 BCE is the famous Aramaic letter of King Adon,
apparently of Ekron (Porten 1981). The last mention of Philistines in the Bible
belongs to the mid-fifth century BCE. In spite of the submission to Sennacherib
(*ANET* 287-88), the 29-year siege by Psammetichus (Herodotus, 2.157) and the

that had slowly crept down the coast,[41] as well as with various people of Greek origin,[42] seem to have formed a part of the population. In

deportations of Nebuchadrezzar II (Jer. 25.20; 47.2-7; Zech. 9.5-6), the ancient language of Ashdod was still alive at the time of Nehemiah (13.23-24). It will be seen later that a Philistine *ethnos* (perhaps now reinforced by Phoenician and Greek blood) still existed in the Hellenistic period (1 Macc. 5.68; 10.83-84; 11.4) and probably later (Strabo, 16.2.2).

41. For the Phoenicians see Baramki 1961; Harden 1963; Jidejian 1968; Moscati 1968; Jidejian 1969; Brown [P.J.] 1969; Jidejian 1971; Katzenstein 1973; Ap-Thomas 1973; Niemeyer (ed.) 1982; Moscati (ed.) 1988; Bikai 1990; Culican 1991; Lipinski (ed.) 1991; Aubet 1993. According to Josephus (*Ant.* 7.74) the Philistines were assisted by Phoenicians in their war against David, and Ps. 83.7-9 lists among the enemies of Judah all three: Edomites, Philistines and Phoenicians. It is written in *Jub.* 24.28: 'Cursed be the Philistines... May the Lord make them as scorn and a curse and (the object of) wrath and anger... in the hands of the Kittim', perhaps alluding to the gradual takeover of their land by various Phoenician and Greek groups (for Phoenicians as 'Kittim' see Ezek. 27.6; cf. Eustathius, *Comm. in Homeri Iliad.* 1.349). Phoenician influence and trade to the south is detectable from the eighth and especially from the fifth centuries BCE, with inscriptions from Akko to Ascalon and down to Arabia and Egypt (see Cross 1964; Cross 1968; Cross 1979; Glueck 1971: 229-31; Delavault and Lemaire 1979; Naveh 1987; Lemaire 1988; Lemaire 1989: 92-93; cf. Amos 1.6-7 for the slave trade between Tyre and Edom). Unquestionable Phoenician settlements on the coast of Palestine begin under Persian rule (Elayi 1982: 102-103; Lemaire 1990); for archaeological evidence in Ashdod (Jamnia, Tell eṣ-Ṣafi, Tel Ṣippor, Tell el-'Areini) and Idumaea (at least Lachish), see Stern [E.] 1982. The inscription of 'Eshmun'azor, King of Sidon, shows that he received from the Persians (for the date see Peckham 1968: 78-87; cf. Kelly 1987) some Philistine territory which included the cities of Dor and Joppa (*ANET* 505). The *Periplus* of Pseudo-Scylax, dated to the fourth century BCE (cf. *GLAJJ* 3, 8-12), adds invaluable evidence by presenting several coastal cities as belonging either to Sidonians (e.g. Dor) or to Tyrians (e.g. Ascalon). Straton's Tower (*CPJ* 1, 121-22, no. 2a; Josephus, *War* 1.408), later Herodian Caesarea-on-the-coast (Levine 1975: 5-6; cf. Foerster 1975; Roller 1983; Roller 1992), seems to have been founded by king 'Abd'Ashtart I of Sidon, of the time of Artaxerxes II (*RE* 7, 273, s.v. *Stratōn*; cf. Levine 1973; see coins in Betlyon 1982: 11-14; but cf. Arav 1989b; Stieglitz 1993). Nehemiah (13.16) refers to a Tyrian community in Jerusalem (cf. the place [χωρίον] called 'Straton's Tower' in Josephus, *War* 1.80, probably reflecting a living quarter of Phoenicians from the coastal city), while Herodotus (2.112) refers to another at Memphis in Egypt, and a third is assumed from ostraca at Elephantine (Lidzbarski 1912: 4-19). For Hellenistic evidence pertaining to Phoenician settlements in Palestine and beyond, see Chapter 2 n. 49. In connection with the Shephelah suffice it here to mention the Sidonian colony at Marisa (*OGIS* 593).

42. Greek pottery (from Geometric to Classical) is scattered across the Eastern

fact such a conspicuous socio-ethnic instability in this area will continue to be apparent in the succeeding eras, which are the main concern of the work at hand. With the addition later of the Hellenistic element this instability will reach a maximum degree.

The inadequacy of the available evidence renders difficult any attempt to answer with certainty the questions posed above. Nevertheless it seems most unlikely that the Neo-Babylonians would have had

Mediterranean, from Al Mina to Tell Jemmeh (see Boardman 1980: 35-102; Wenning 1981; Wenning 1991; cf. Coldstream and Bikai 1988; Boardman 1990; Waldbaum 1994). Trade with Greece and the arrival of mercenaries may not explain the total of this impact. At Ashdod, Assyrian records tell of a 'Ia-ma-ni' (Assyrian spelling for *yawan* which denotes a Greek or Ionian) who was put up as king by rebels. His uprising was crushed by Sargon II in 712 BCE (*ANET* 286). This was the time of the prophet Isaiah, and in Isa. 9.12 of LXX, the name of the Philistines (פלשתים) is given as ῞Ελληνες, instead of the usual ἀλλόφυλοι. This may be explained as a Hellenistic updating (Seeligmann 1948: 81, 87), but the Greeks were termed ἀλλόγλωσσοι from much earlier (Herodotus, 2.154.4; cf. Abu Simbel text in Meiggs and Lewis 1969, no. 7; also cf. the 'non-Hebrew' language of Ashdod—Neh. 13.23-24). In the early sixth century BCE Ezekiel (27.13) addressing Tyre pronounced: 'Ionians... were thy merchants', and it was then that Alcaeus's brother served the Babylonians in the battle of Ascalon (Quinn 1961; *GLAJJ* 3, 1-4). A Greek inscription from the beginning of the fifth century BCE from Tell el-Ḥesi mentions a person with a Greek- Phoenician name (Chapter 2 n. 105). Greek mercenaries at Akko are attested in the fourth century BCE by Isaeus (*Orat.* 4.7) and Demosthenes (*Orat.* 10.52—*in Callipum*, 20); for a Cretan inscription from Gaza, possibly of the mid-fourth century BCE, and the כתים and קרסי in the ostraca from Arad, see Chapter 2, nn. 104, 113-14; for Greek ligatures impressed on handles of amphorae from Shiqmona and Jaffa, see Stern [E.] 1982: 198; cf. now the significant evidence from Dor (Stern [E.] 1988: 6); for reflection beyond the coast and the Shephelah, see the Greek pottery north of Jerusalem at Tell en-Nasbeh (McCown 1947: 62), and the coins from Beth-Zur, Tell Zakariyah and Hebron (Stern [E.] 1982: 198, 218), as well as the Samaritan coins with Greek letters (Meshorer and Qedar 1991: 13-17). Pre-Alexandrian influence has always been realized (Iliffe 1933: 26; Sellers 1933: 41; Cross 1963: 114-15; Auscher 1967; Weinberg 1969; Smith [M.] 1971: 46; Stern [E.] 1989; cf. Colledge 1987: 134-38). The fact that Philistia and its vicinity attracted Greeks of the Archaic and Classical periods (as well as Hellenized Phoenicians later) may not be coincidental. There is a characteristic continuity here which must not be overlooked (cf. Naveh 1985a: 14, 21). The question certainly is that of the origins of the Philistines—see Amos. 9.7 from 'Caphtor' (כפתר). Past theories, although not in agreement, have pointed toward the Aegean, Crete, Cyprus or Anatolia. Yet, from the point of view of the material culture, as stated by Mazar ([A.] 1985: 105): 'The Mycenaean cultural heritage of the Philistines is demonstrated by their pottery and by cultic clay figurines such as the so-called "Ashdoda" and "mourning women" types.'

any motive for giving to Edomites, apart from permission for settlement in the southern part of Judah—a fair exchange for the help provided in the war against the Judahites—real measures of autonomy.[43] Also, the Edomite influx probably occurred in several waves and, therefore, 'Western Edom' would initially be an area in constant progress of occupation; thus too unconsolidated for regular assessments of produce and taxation. In other words not an ideal area for transforming into another administrative division, but perhaps merely a 'district' belonging to a larger province.

The same can be said for the Persians who would not have granted Judahite land to Edomites,[44] the collaborators of the Babylonians, especially after allowing the Jews to return to their country and looking favourably upon Jewish affairs.[45] Darius's decree, mentioned above, ordering Edomites to evacuate Judaean villages fits well at this juncture. A further allusion, stated in more dramatic terms, may be discerned in a later Apocryphon, the *Testament of Job*:

> Then the devil, when he had come to know my heart, laid a plot against me. Disguising himself as the king of the Persians, he stood in my city gathering together all the rogues in it. And with a boast he spoke to them saying: 'This man Jobab is the one who destroyed... the temple of the great god... Therefore, I also shall repay him... Come along then and

43. Contra Alt (above n. 37) who maintained that at the beginning of Neo-Babylonian rule the area of Idumaea was separated from Judah.

44. Contra Avi-Yonah 1977a: 25-26 and Aharoni 1966: 361, who took it *a priori* that from the very beginning of their rule the Persians established a province called Idumaea. Recent studies modified this to the first half of the fourth century BCE (de Geus 1979–80: 61; cf. Lemaire 1990: 51-54). Yet this view also fails to show that a different name was carried by the presumed individual land complex. In spite of the poor state of evidence, 'Judah' and 'Samaria' are known as provinces, but there is no mention of 'Idumaea'. Moreover, it is not clear as to whether some administrative or military functions asserted from the Aramaic ostraca of Arad (Naveh 1981) and Beersheba (Naveh 1973; Naveh 1979), imply an independent province (de Geus 1979–80: 62-63; cf. Stern [E.] 1982: 240). The Persian period continues to be obscure, especially in southern Palestine, and much depends on the precise dating of Iron Age IIC local material (James *et al.* 1991: esp. 171-75).

45. See generally Stern [E.] 1984; cf. Tadmor 1994. With the exception perhaps of the time when the revolts that marked the end of Persian rule spread into the entire Fifth Satrapy and had to be crushed by the Persian armies (Barag 1966; Smith [M.] 1971: 60, 185; Cross 1975b: 5; Widengren 1977: 501). Note that when the Persians arrived in Egypt (525 BCE) they destroyed many local temples but not the Jewish temple at Elephantine (*ANET* 492).

gather spoils for yourselves of all his animals and whatever he has left on the earth... Most of his possessions I have already destroyed by fire. The others I confiscated. And as for his children, I shall slay them.'[46]

It is conceivable, of course, that the Edomites were not totally exterminated or expelled from the entire land, but perhaps the majority was confined to the south, with no special privileges and, as far as one can assume, under some kind of supervision by the Judaean governor. The famous list of Nehemiah, also mentioned above, clearly includes 'Western Edom' in the Persian province of Judah: 'they encamped from Beersheba to the valley of Hinnom'.[47] This further fits with the reference to the Arab territory which thus had to be situated south of Beersheba, as already discussed.

By contrast the subsequent Hellenistic regime had every reason to care for the rights of foreign populations (particularly those with some Greek background such as that of the Shephelah) and by implication the Edomites, and would have readily proclaimed the autonomy of Idumaea, against Jewish feeling. Besides, the vigorousness of the Hellenistic administration, taken together with the maturity now reached by the Edomite occupation in South Judah, might seem to have provided enough economic and political instigation for the establishment of a separate province.[48]

It must be noted that more is known of Samaria and Judah under the Persians. In terms of epigraphic material from this period (and with due respect to the important recent finds of ostraca), extraordinary

---

46. *T. Job* 17.1-6; cf. Job 1.17; Mal. 1.4; Aristeas, *Concerning the Jews* (*apud* Eusebius, *Praep. Evang.* 9.25.1-4); also cf. Hecataeus (*apud* Josephus, *Apion* 1.193) referring to the fact that when pagan temples and altars were erected in Judaea, the Jews 'razed them all to the ground, paying in some cases, a fine to the satraps and, in others, obtaining pardon'.

47. Neh. 11.30. For a different understanding of this list, see above n. 37. Avi-Yonah (1977a: 14) is also against it, but only because it does not fit his theory of a limited Persian province of Judah (for a greater Judah, as suggested here, see Abel 1938: 120). Stern ([E.] 1982: 249) refers to an agreement among scholars that villages mentioned in this list are outside Judah's territory, but he offers no evidence behind this agreement.

48. Cf. Jones [A.H.M.] 1971: 239-40; Hengel 1974: 21; Kasher 1988: 6. Stern ([E.] 1982: 249-50) does not seem to commit himself—he may be allowing for the possibility that 'Idumaea' was a Hellenistic creation (cf. Stern ([E.] 1981: 11-12); see Kindler 1974: 74-75.

discoveries such as the 'Wadi Daliyeh papyri' and coins of Samaria,[49] or the 'post-exilic seals and bullae' of Judah[50] and, indeed, the 'YHD coins'[51] and the 'Elephantine papyri'[52] are lacking from Idumaea.

Yet, concerning the numismatic evidence many problems remain and the last word is still to be said. Although it is unanimously accepted that the יהד (and evidently יחזקיה הפחה, יוחנן הכוהן and ידוע') coins represent the Persian province of Judah, it has so far been proved impossible to demonstrate that they were struck in Jerusalem. While a few come from Jerusalem, most of these specimens have curiously either been, or reported as, found at locations in the south.[53] Since such a consistent distribution cannot simply be explained by the process of diffusion, this may shed some light on the relationship between Judah and its southern territory. For one thing if the YHD coins, as formal Judaean currency, were struck and circulated in the south, it would seem logical that Judah either included, or claimed to administer, the land of 'Western Edom'. In this case, the latter could scarcely have become an independent province named 'Idumaea' before the Hellenistic era, as concluded here.

49. See preliminary publications by Cross 1963, 1966, 1971, 1975b, 1985, 1988; and Lapp and Lapp 1974; for the coins see Meshorer and Qedar 1991.

50. Avigad 1976.

51. Mildenberg 1979; Rappaport 1981a; *AJC* 1; Barag 1985; Betlyon 1986; Barag 1986–87; Meshorer 1990–91; Mildenberg 1994 and his bibliography for other contributions.

52. Cowley 1923; Kraeling 1953; Driver 1957; Porten 1968.

53. Jerusalem (Ariel 1982: 277 n. 13); Bethzur (Sellers 1933: 73-74 n. 9); the Bethlehem-Hebron area (Spaer 1977: 203); Tell Jemmeh (Rahmani 1971) and 'near Gaza' (*BMC* Palest. 181, no. 29); see Rappaport's important comments (1981a: 4-5, 8 n. 39); cf. the existence of the southern mints of Gaza, Ashdod, Ascalon and the so-called Philisto-Arabian coins (Mildenberg 1994: 67-70); cf. Chapter 2 n. 32.

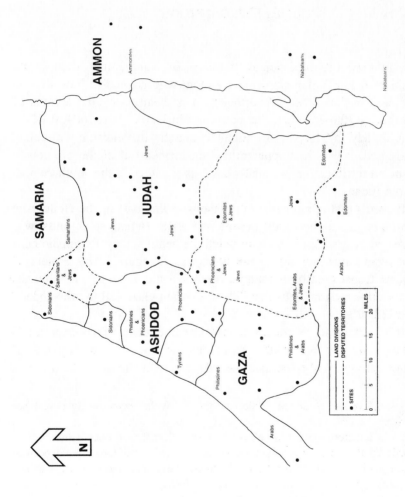

Southern Palestine in the Persian Period, c. 538–332 BCE: Ethnic Distribution

Chapter 2

EARLY HELLENISTIC IDUMAEA

The first definite reference to 'Idumaea' by name is that found in the archive of the Ptolemaic official Zenon, who arrived in Palestine on business in 259 BCE.[1] Nevertheless it is clear from Hieronymus of Cardia (c. 300–250 BCE), as preserved in Diodorus (c. 60–30 BCE), that already in 312 BCE a Ptolemaic eparchy in Palestine was called Ἰδουμαία.[2] This had apparently been formed out of the previously disputed territory (or 'no man's land' as it were), in the southern area of old Judah.

It seems that administrative divisions in this part of the Hellenistic world began to be made before 301 BCE (when Antigonus was defeated at Ipsus), the date in which the century-long Ptolemaic control over Palestine and Coele Syria was inaugurated by Ptolemy I Soter.[3] Consequently one may assume that the institution of Idumaea occurred sometime between 332 BCE (when Gaza fell to Alexander)[4] and 312 BCE.

It is difficult to be precise. Our historical evidence for this period is unfortunately scanty. Under Alexander we barely know the names of a few satraps. But given that one, Bessus, a Persian, held the office at

1. See esp. *P. Zen.* 1.59006 and 59015; for the second century BCE, see 2 Macc. 12.32.

2. Diodorus once calls it an ἐπαρχία (19.95.2) and once a σατραπεία (19.98.1). This may give the impression that the division of Greek provinces was based on the previous Persian system, but in reference to Idumaea the term can only be seen as metaphorical. The Vienna papyrus of Ptolemy II Philadelphus's tax edict shows that the official name of a district in Syria was in fact ὑπαρχεία (Liebesny 1936: 266; *SB* 8008; cf. Austin 1981: no. 275).

3. Abel 1935; Heinen 1984; Hengel 1989a; cf. Schalit 1954; Schwartz [S.] 1994; see conveniently Hengel 1980: 21-32.

4. Arrian 2.25.4-27.7; Rufus 4.6.7-30; Diodorus 17.48; Plutarch, *Alex.* 25; Hegesias (*apud* Dionysius of Halicarnassus, *De comp. verb.* 18).

Damascus from 329 to 325 BCE,[5] it seems that until then very little change had been made in the former, main administrative division: the Persian satrapy of עבר נהרה. Under the Diadochoi, the first attempt of Ptolemy I to annex Palestine took place in 320 BCE (when he attacked the satrap Laomedon).[6] Although his victory was short-lived and in the years that followed (until 301 BCE) the area changed hands several times, this may have been the starting point for the territory's organisation. It is also possible that it was then that Jerusalem was subdued, as Agatharchides informs us.[7] The *Letter of Aristeas* (if it too belongs here) says of Ptolemy:

> He invaded the whole of Coele-Syria and Phoenicia... some of the people he moved from their settlement to other places (μετώκισεν) and others took prisoners (ἠχμαλώτισεν), bringing everything into subjection by fear... he removed from the land of the Jews into Egypt up to one hundred thousand people...[8]

5.   Arrian 4.7.2 and discussion of Hengel 1989a: 43; for the few satraps, e.g. Andromachus and Menon (Curtius Rufus 4.5.9; 4.8.11), see Bosworth 1974. Josephus's story of Alexander and the Jews (*Ant.* 11.326-39) is mistrusted by many (see Momigliano 1979; Cohen [S.J.D.] 1982–83; but cf. Golan 1982). The Bible is silent, exept from a few allusions in Zech. 9–14 (Delcor 1951).

6.   Diodorus 18.43; Appian, *Syr.* 43.

7.   *Apud* Josephus, *Ant.* 12.6; *Apion* 1.210; cf. Appian, *Syr.* 50.252; for the 320 BCE date, see also Droysen 1878: 167-68; but given as 312 BCE by Abel (1952: 31), and even 302/301 BCE by Tcherikover (1959: 56-57), followed by Hengel (1980: 19); cf. *GLAJJ* 1, 108. Old dies of Aramaic YHD (יהד) coins were reused in Early Hellenistic Judaea, replacing the title with the Hebrew YHDH (יהדה). If the early chronology proposed by Betlyon (1986: 642) for these coins is correct (beginning at c. 330 BCE), formal Hellenistic rule here already under Alexander may have been indicated by numismatics. But Alexander had consistently promoted his universal coinage of *Alexandreis*, which made it difficult for local autonomous issues to survive (though there were a few—cf. Rappaport 1981a: 11). Furthermore, such YHDH coins were reminted later bearing the likenesses of Ptolemy I Soter and Berenice I (Jeselsohn 1974: 60; Spaer 1977: 200-203; cf. Mildenberg 1979: nos. 26-28; Mildenberg 1994: 65-66). The earliest known currency struck outside Egypt depicting Ptolemy I and his queen is that from Cyrenaica dated to 305–285 BCE (Svoronos 1904: nos. 314-21). One could therefore suggest that the entire series, in which the reused YHD coins are followed by those carrying the head of the king and queen of Egypt, was initiated by Ptolemaic control after 320 BCE (i.e. the earliest possible Ptolemaic date), rather than under Alexander. Autonomous coins in Cyrenaica were produced as early as 323–313 BCE while the area was subject to Ptolemy I (Svoronos 1904: nos. 59-60).

8.   Aristeas, *To Philocrates* 12; Fraser (1972: 2.970-73) dated this work to the

Admittedly, however, more effective Ptolemaic control would have been imposed on areas in the interior of Palestine only after the Battle of Gaza in 312 BCE, in which Ptolemy inflicted a devastating blow upon Demetrius Poliorcetes.[9] Such an understanding may be inferred from Hecataeus who mentions that Ptolemy now became 'master of Syria', and 'many of the inhabitants…desired to accompany him to Egypt and to associate themselves with his realm', chief among whom was one 'Ezekias, high priest of the Jews'.[10]

This being the case many questions can be raised, some of which will be treated briefly here, as a general background, before proceeding to the Maccabaean period and the birth of the Herodian dynasty: (1) Why was it that Idumaea came into being? (2) What was approximately its geographical extent and internal divisions in the Early Hellenistic period? (3) Were new cities founded within its area, or old ones refounded? (4) How was it governed? (5) How large was its population? (6) What was its ethnic composition? (7) Did 'Hellenization' affect it?

1. *Creation and Economy*

In the previous chapter several possible reasons were given for the creation of Idumaea as an eparchy. Apart from the crucial strategic position it held for the Ptolemies in their confrontation with the Seleucids, this area reflected broader political issues, such as the

end of the third century BCE; Bickermann (1976: 109-36; cf. Murray 1987) opted for the end of the second; Shutt (1985: 9) settles for a date around 170 BCE.

9.   Hecataeus *apud* Josephus, *Apion* 1.185; Diodorus 19.80; Justinus 15.1.6-9; Plutarch, *Demetr.* 6.

10.   *Apud* Josephus, *Apion* 1.186-87. Another story is recorded later, under Antiochus IV Epiphanes (175–164 BCE), in which a high priest, Onias, together with his followers migrated to Egypt (see Kasher 1985: 7-9; Parente 1994). The similarity of the two need not compel us to doubt either. Ezekias has been presented as a 'chief' rather than 'high' priest (*GLAJJ* 1, 40-41), but this does little to differentiate the stories. The fact that Hebrew coins of Judaea (of the mid-fourth century BCE) refer to one יחזקיה הפחה (Ezekias the governor) makes Hecataeus's story plausible and, indeed, the identification of the two Ezekias's tempting. The question whether a high priest could have also been the governor may be answered by the coin (Barag 1986–87) bearing the inscription יוחנן הכוהן (Yohanan the priest), and by the fact that other priestly dynasties in charge of city states are known to have struck coins at this period (Seyrig 1971).

complicated relationship of its mixed local population.[11] The Hellenistic policy of caring for the rights of foreigners in any particular area (to ensure their loyalty), went hand in hand with the fact that Edomite occupation at least had now become established in this disputed territory. Besides, there were great economic forces at work here making the establishment of a separate province necessary.

As will be seen later, although the inhabitants of Idumaea could not have remained unaffected by the influence of Hellenism, no Ptolemaic attempt as such was made to Hellenize the place; for one thing the Ptolemies—in contrast to the Seleucids—did not carry out a vigorous urbanizing policy. It seems that the decisive factor which shaped urban life in southern Palestine was almost exclusively the economic competition between the two superpowers, and the exaction of taxation. In order to retain a complete monopoly over maritime commerce, the Ptolemies kept tight control of the inland caravan trade routes.[12] This they achieved by promoting the establishment of fortresses and garrison posts in strategic points, which turned Idumaea into a main artery of Palestinian commerce by sea, land and desert. Huge profits were made not only from the transit trade of the highly valued incense from Arabia (for the regulation of which a special official was appointed at Gaza—ὁ ἐπὶ τῆς λιβανωτικῆς) and the popular wine from Rhodes,[13] but also from a rich local production.

From the archive of Zenon only the principal trade in slaves (testifying to the existence of private estates) is directly connected with Idumaea,[14] yet some of the main exports recorded generally for Syria-Palestine—wheat, oil, wine, dates, honey, caviar, meat, figs, and purple dye[15]—would have been Idumaean. Other products also bought by Zenon—dried fruit, cheese, pickled goods, salted fish-meat, sea-fish,

11. Cf. Tscherikower 1937: 49-51.
12. See Bowersock 1971; cf. Seyrig 1968; Smith [R.H.] 1990: 124.
13. For the Arabian spice trade at Gaza, see Glucker 1987: 86-93; for the official, see *P. Zen.* 1.59009; *PSI* 6.628; for the frankincense, see Groom 1981; for the Petra-Gaza road, see Cohen [R.] 1982; for the imported Rhodian wine, see conveniently Broshi 1984: 28-29.
14. *P. Zen.* 1.59015 verso; cf. the trade in slaves (probably mostly Idumaean) by Ascalonites on Delos (Leiwo 1989: 577).
15. E.g. *P. Lond.* 7.2141; *P. Zen.* 1.59069; *P. Lond.* 7.1930; cf. Palestinian diet conveniently in Broshi 1986; for modes of production in general, see Safrai 1994: 104ff.

pomegranate seeds and mushrooms—were probably Syro-Palestinian in origin.[16]

From later sources of the Roman period (especially the rabbinical literature) we can gather a few references to the products of Idumaea, which in this case do not seem to be out of place here. Vine trees were found as far south as Kefar 'Aziz, and while Jamnia was a centre of the wheat trade, barley was cultivated in the drier southern parts.[17] Weaving industries, oil production and the raising of doves in the lower hills (see below), as well as the valuable purple-dyeing indus- tries on the coast, thrived. The latter might possibly be connected with the wool brought from the mountainous Hebron, the sheep of which was particularly appreciated.[18] Moreover, purple-dyeing extended to the south where whole townlets at one time were engaged in this trade, 'so that everybody's hands bore the marks of it'.[19]

The fishing industry was naturally important on the coast, exploited from the Persian period by Phoenician settlers, and as late as the Byzantine Empire when Jewish fishermen are attested at Jamnia Par- alus.[20] Over the other side of the eparchy, on the shores of the Dead Sea, from En-Gedi to Livias beyond Idumaea in the north, the pro- duction of balsam, a wood resin used for making perfumes and medi- cines, continued down to the fourth century CE.[21] The processing of

16.   E.g. *P. Zen.* 1.59013-14; *P. Lond.* 7.1930; *P. Zen.* 1.59006; see Tscheri- kower 1937: 24.

17.   *m. Kil.* 6.4 (vine trees); also Ascalon was renowned for its date groves, onions and wines (Avi-Yonah 1977a: 195; Mayerson 1993); for the wine of Gaza, see Marcus Diaconus, *Life of Porph.* 58; Broshi 1984: 25; Glucker 1987: 93-94; Mayerson 1992; cf. an Aramaic ostracon of the fourth century BCE from Ashdod referring to the 'vineyard of Zebadiah' (Naveh 1971b; Dothan [M.] 1975: 117); *Gen. R.* 76 (wheat); *m. Ket.* 5.8 (barley); both wheat and barley are attested in the Aramaic ostraca of the Persian period from Beersheba (Naveh 1973; Naveh 1979), and in the Greek papyri of the pre-Islamic era from Nessana, which also add grapes, olives, figs and dates (*P. Ness.* nos. 60-67).

18.   *b. Men.* 87b.

19.   *Tanḥ. Nissah* 8.

20.   Neh. 13.16; Peter the Iberian 126 (edn Raabe); cf. the 'ship of Jacob' in Jamnia Paralus in the *Test. XII Patr.* (*T. Naph.* 6), and the 'boat' and 'fishing' of the Zebulon tribe further north (*T. Zeb.* 6).

21.   Diodorus 19.98 (cf. Theophrastus, *Hist. Plant.* 9.6.1; Strabo 16.2.41; Pompeius Trogus, *apud* Justinus 36.3.3-4; Pliny, *Hist. Natur.* 12.111-13; Tacitus, *Hist.* 5.6); and *b. Šab.* 26a; a document from the time of Bar Kokhba points to the importance of En-Gedi as a spice-growing centre (Yadin 1962: 255-56 no. 46);

leather at En-Gedi is mentioned in two Aramaic ostraca from the Persian period, and the place was known to the *Wisdom of Ben Sirach* and to Pliny for its palm trees and dates.[22] Here also was the region described by Diodorus as the place in the Dead Sea from where asphalt was extracted and then sold at a considerable price to Egypt for embalmings.[23]

In the lowland, Shephelah, were situated wealthy estates, which must have prospered under the 'scientific management' of the Hellenistic era.[24] They belonged mostly to Hellenized Phoenicians and Edomites, though the population elsewhere was multiracial, mainly a mixture of Philistines, Edomites, Jews and Arabs (see below §6). The form of the Phoenician/Edomite organization was essentially urban, while the Arabs lived in a tribal framework. However, in some areas Arabs seem to have been leading a semi-sedentary life, since a number of them occupied the city of Gaza.[25] The Nabataeans provide the first

note the Herodian pharmaceutical *officina* at 'En Boqeq (Gichon 1976: 365-69; Gichon 1993).

22.   Stern [E.] 1982: 39 (ostraca); *Sir.* 24.14; Pliny, *Hist. Natur.* 5.73 (cf. Josephus, *Ant.* 9.7; Solinus, *Collect.* 35.12; cf. Diodorus 19.98); given these references to the groves of palm at En-Gedi, one may disagree with Stern (*GLAJJ* 1, 316) who thinks that Virgil (*Georg.* 3.12-5), Lucanus (*Pharsal.* 3.216), Valerius Flaccus (*Argon.* 1.12), Silius Italicus (*Punica* 3.600), Statius (*Silvae* 1.6.13; 3.2.138; 5.2.139), Martial (*Epigr.* 10.50) and Juvenal (*Sat.* 8.160), must *all* mean 'Judaean' when they refer to 'Idumaean' palm trees, fertile slopes, fruitful orchards and perfumes. Only in Martial, and perhaps Valerius Flaccus, there seems to be a clear confusion between the two; for the products of En-Gedi, see further Song 1.3; 7.12-16; cf. Josephus, *War* 4.496-70; Galen 14.25; Eusebius, *Onom.* (edn Klostermann 86); *Beresh. R.* 14.7, etc.

23.   Diodorus 19.99.1; cf. Strabo, 16.2.42; Josephus, *War* 4.480; Tacitus, *Hist.* 5.6.3; Solinus, *Collect.* 1.56; 35.2; Hammond (1959) attributed the exploitation of asphalt to Nabataeans.

24.   Rostovtzeff 1941: 351, 1403 n. 149; cf. Herz 1928; Mittwoch 1955; Gil 1970. Cendebeus's army fled to 'the towers in the fields of Azotus' (1 Macc. 16.10); these towers must have been agrarian; they were attached to cultivated fields of villas, as watchtowers, used for storage but inhabited in times of danger (e.g. in Samaria—Applebaum *et al.* 1978: 96). Rural estates existed from the monarchical period (e.g. למלך stamps—Rainey 1982), but their special promotion in the Hellenistic era is suggested by different evidence including the Zenon papyri, the Hefziba inscription, etc. (Applebaum 1979–80: 164; Rappaport *et al.* 1994: 75-76; cf. Gibson [S.] 1982).

25.   E.g. Herodotus, 3.5; Aramaic ostracon of בר עבדמראן from Raphia (Naveh 1985b: 118-19, no. 9); Arabs were still called νομάδες under the Seleucids, but their

clear example (third to first centuries BCE) of an Arab tribe of this region changing its lifestyle from nomadic to sedentary (Chapter 1 n. 32).

The predominantly agricultural character of the economy is evident from many sources. From the time of the monarchy King Azariah (c. 772–747 BCE) had invested in the cultivation of the land in the lower hills, the plains and even the desert.[26] In the Persian period Nehemiah makes clear that property, at least among the Jews, consisted of vineyards, olive yards and houses; taxes were collected in corn, oil, wine, cattle, sheep and poultry.[27] The *Letter of Aristeas* (regardless of precise date of composition and the presence in it of some innacuracies) has preserved the most remarkable description of Early Hellenistic Palestine (including Idumaea), which must be quoted here *in extenso*:

> The terrain (of the country) was ample and beautiful; parts were flat, such as the area around Samaria and the neighbourhood of Idumaea; other parts were hilly, such as the neighbourhood of Judaea. Continuous attention to husbandry and the care of the land is necessary, to ensure good yield as a result for the inhabitants. When this attention is paid, all farming is accompanied by abundant yield on all the aforesaid land. In such of the cities as achieve large size and its accompanying prosperity, the result is abundance of population and neglect of the land, because everyone is bent on cultural delights, and the whole population in its philosophy is inclined to pleasure... The zeal of the farmers is indeed remarkable. In fact their land is thickly covered with large numbers of olive trees and corn crops and pulse, and moreover with vines and abundant honey. As for the fruit trees and date palms which they have, no number can be given. They have many flocks and herds of various kinds, with ample pasture for them. So they perceived clearly that the areas needed to be well populated, and designed the city and the villages accordingly. A large quantity of spices and precious stones and gold is brought to the area by means of the

appearance in great numbers in northwestern Idumaea should only be explained by their arrival there to fight (2 Macc. 12.11).

26. 2 Chron. 26.10; for his dates, see Hughes 1990: 275.

27. Neh. 5.11, 15, 18; cf. the sacrificial allowance of animals, wine, oil, frankincense, flour, wheat and salt given to the Jews by Antiochus III (Josephus, *Ant.* 12.140); see Eccl. 2.4-9 (cf. Song 4.13), satirizing the wealth of Jerusalem in Late Persian or Early Hellenistic times, which would not have been inferior to that of Shephelah; cf. Hecataeus's brief description of the Jewish land as 'most excellent and fertile... productive of every variety of fruits' (*apud* Josephus, *Apion* 1.195); Strabo (16.2.2) calls the inhabitants of Palestine γεωργικοί; cf. Broshi 1987: 32.

Arabs. The land is agricultural and well fitted also for commerce; the city is the home of many crafts, and there is no lack of goods imported from overseas, because of its convenient harbours which supply them, such as Ascalon, Joppa, and Gaza, and also Ptolemais... The district is well watered everywhere, has everything in abundance, and is very secure. The river Jordan flows around it and never dries up... Other torrents, as they are called, also flow down, covering the parts toward Gaza and the district of Azotus. The countryside is surrounded with natural defenses, being difficult to invade and not negotiable for large numbers because of the narrow approaches, with overhanging precipices and deep ravines, and the whole mountainous surroundings of the entire area being very rugged. It used to be said that copper and iron mines were formerly sunk in the neighbouring hills of Arabia, but in the time of the Persian supremacy they were abandoned...[28]

2. *Geography, Divisions and Centres*

The geographical extent of Idumaea in the Ptolemaic period (301–200 BCE) can be delineated, though its precise borders may only be assumed in a tentative way. In the south, a series of linked-up wadis— Ghazzeh-Shallaleh-Beersheba-Malhata—which run almost the whole distance from the Mediterranean coast (south of Gaza) to the southern edge of the Dead Sea, and which have determined the area's geo-politics from remote antiquity, served as a natural division. These major wadis separated the arable land from the vast desolate Negev which opened to the south.[29] Throughout history Beersheba was reckoned to be the end point of the Land of Israel.[30] This southern boundary is confirmed by archaeology, in the discovery of Hellenistic fortresses and garrison posts along its course (see below).

In the west, the Dead Sea itself provides another natural boundary; Diodorus's statement that the lake is situated 'in the middle of Idumaea' must only be taken as referring to its approximate geographical position in relation to the northern and southern limits of the province.[31]

28. Aristeas, *To Philocrates* 107-20; cf. *1 En.* 26-31; Josephus (*War* 4.534-37) briefly describes the landscape of Idumaea (noting towns, villages and vegetation), in the course of the First Jewish Revolt.

29. Aharoni 1958; Aharoni 1966: 23-24, 28-29; cf. with reservations Gichon (1967), and see Shatzman (1994: 132) on Isaac's work.

30. Judg. 20.1; 2 Sam. 17.11; 24.2; 1 Kgs 4.25; Neh. 11.26.

31. Diodorus, 19.95.2; cf. 98.1; 99.1 for people on both sides hostile to each other; Avi-Yonah 1977a: 37.

In the north, the Azekah-Keilah-Bethzur-Tekoa line, which had marked the southern border of Persian Judah 'proper',[32] was adopted by the Early Hellenistic administration. Diodorus (above) described Idumaea as stretching between Judah and Beersheba. That Bethzur continued to function as the dividing point between the two provinces is clear in the preparations of the Maccabees on the eve of their revolt: 'and fortified Bethsura to preserve it: that the people might have a defence against Idumaea'.[33] Furthermore, during the Maccabaean period the city of Hebron is implicitly mentioned as lying in the northern part of Idumaea, and the same may be said for Adora and Marisa.[34]

The western limits of the province seem to have included the entire region of lower hills,[35] and part of the plain down to the coastal strip of Gaza and Ascalon. However, its northwestern extent is not easily identifiable. Given the thorough restructuring of the Persian province of Ashdod in the Hellenistic period, of which even the capital was transferred from Azotus to Jamnia,[36] it will be reasonable to suggest that the Ashdodite territory was united with Idumaea. Thus the latter would have gained an important access, as it were, to the Mediterranean, even though both ports of Ascalon and Gaza had close relationships with Idumaea at that time (as known from Zenon).

At any rate, the frontier guard (χωροφύλαξ) mentioned in the Zenon papyri, which was stationed at Pegae (future Herodian Antipatris), clearly indicates the existence of a division there between two major land units.[37] Could these be Idumaea (represented by the Ashdodite territory) and Samaria? Judging from the fact that after his defeat by Judas Maccabaeus, Gorgias the governor of Idumaea retreated

32.   Called 'proper' here to exclude the then 'disputed territory' in the south, which was presumably under Judahite influence (Chapter 1, end). The distribution of the YHD seal impressions shows that the province of Judah was never officially expanded south of Bethzur (Stern [E.] 1981: 19; Stern [E.] 1982: 246-47). The fact that these stamps date from the Late Persian to the Early Hellenistic periods shows that the borderline remained unchanged. On the problem of En-Gedi, see below n. 41.

33.   1 Macc. 4.61.

34.   1 Macc. 5.65; cf. Josephus, *Ant.* 3.257; *War* 1.63.

35.   For a definition of the Shephelah in the biblical period, see Rainey 1980; Rainey 1983.

36.   Avi-Yonah 1977a: 37-38; for Ashdod (Azotus) see *SVM* 2, 108-109; Dothan [M.] *et al.* 1971; Dothan [M.] 1975; Dothan [M.] 1993: 101-102; for Jamnia see below n. 67.

37.   *PSI* 4.406; cf. *P. Zen.* 1.59006.

to his lands in 'Idumaea and Azotus and Jamnia', it seems that this may well have been the case.[38] It is true that the information about Gorgias dates to the beginning of the Maccabaean period, but there is no reason to assume that the unification of the two provinces was necessarily carried out by the Seleucids, even though the latter are known to have united certain administrative districts;[39] the Idumaean/Ashdodite arrangement could have been initiated earlier by the Ptolemies.

The internal division of the province into three main units can thus be assumed. These would officially be called τοπαρχίαι, and they would in turn consist of groups of κῶμαι or villages.[40] The invaluable papyri of Zenon strongly imply that Western Idumaea with its capital at Marisa became the first toparchy, while Eastern Idumaea with its capital at Adora was the second one.[41] The Ashdodite territory with Jamnia as its new centre may be thought to have functioned as a third toparchy.[42]

38.   2 Macc. 12.32; 1 Macc. 4.15; cf. Josephus, *Ant.* 12.308; also *Ant.* 12.351 where he is called στρατηγὸς of Jamnia; see further Bar-Kochva's comments (1989: 270). This may also be supported by Diodorus 19.95.2, where Idumaea seems to extend to the coast of the Ashdodite territory.

39.   Avi-Yonah 1977a: 48; de Geus 1979–80: 64.

40.   τοπαρχία being the Egyptian term for the subdivision of a νομός (cf. 1 Macc. 10.30, 38; 11.28, 34); the latter was equivalent to the ὑπαρχία in Syria-Palestine; see Bagnall 1976: 14.

41.   By Josephus's time the capital of Eastern Idumaea was En-Gedi, while that of Western Idumaea (since Marisa was destroyed in 40 BCE) was possibly Beth Govrin (cf. de Geus 1979–80: 65; Kloner 1993a: 195-97); though under Herod probably Ascalon (see Chapter 3 n. 102). Both Idumaeas became toparchies of Judaea (Josephus, *War* 3.55; cf. Ptolemy, *Geogr.* 5.16.8). The transfer of En-Gedi to Judaea would have taken place under the Maccabees (Josephus, *Ant.* 13.257; see Tel Goren II's tower erected in the time of Alexander Jannaeus—Mazar [B.] *et al.* 1966: 46), i.e. if Pliny's source (which has En-Gedi and Idumaea independent from Judaea—*Hist. Natur.* 5.70) dates to Herod's reign, when Idumaea was indeed separate from Judaea (Josephus, *Ant.* 15.254; cf. *GLAJJ* 1, 475-76), or better to the time of Gabinius's partitions (Kanael 1957: 105, fig. 1), or else to the Early Hellenistic period. Stern ([E.] 1982: 245-49) places En-Gedi in Judah already under the Persians on the basis of YHD seal impressions. But the examples from En-Gedi are few and late in type (Seleucid?). Further, the discovery of a statuette in Persian En-Gedi runs counter to Stern's opinion; such objects are generally unknown from Judaean sites (see below §7). It would seem preferable to place Ptolemaic En-Gedi within Idumaea (see Map 2; cf. the case of Gezer—Chapter 3 n. 7).

42.   See in context *P. Zen.* 1.59006.

Marisa, mentioned in three papyri,[43] must also have served as the administrative centre of the whole of Idumaea. An ancient Hebrew town, refounded and fortified by Hellenized Sidonian colonists (apparently under the aegis of the Ptolemies), Marisa, old Mareshah, became one of the most important crossroads for trade in the south.[44] On travelling from Egypt to Syria through Palestine in 259 BCE (like another Wenamun, the official from Thebes, eight centuries earlier),[45] Zenon bought from Marisa three young slaves, who managed to escape and returned to their former masters. This act initiated a long correspondence on the part of Zenon, which, as we shall see later, is helpful in any consideration of ethnic composition.

The excavation of Marisa in 1900 revealed the most striking and well-preserved city of its time in Palestine.[46] Its square plan, surrounded by walls and rectangular towers, its temple, agora, rich tombs, significant oil industry (16 oil presses have so far been identified) and dove-raising industry (as inferred from columbaria in around two hundred caves) furnish us with an amazing corpus of material for the study of this period. Taken together with the plentiful epigraphic evidence (from tell, tombs and caves alike—including some 50 limestone tablets with invocation oaths), Marisa is undoubtedly unique. The plan of the city is Eastern Hellenistic, that is a blend of Greek elements with Oriental overtones.[47] Such a plan would not

43.   *P. Zen.* 1.59006; 59015Vᵒ; *P. Zen.* 4.59537.

44.   Josh. 15.44; 2 Chron. 11.8 etc.; *OGIS* 593; evidence for Marisa in the Persian period is lacking, but Phoenician presence at that time is attested at Lachish, only four miles away (Stern [E.] 1982: esp. 158-59, 180, 185, 194).

45.   See Lichtheim 1976: 224-30.

46.   Bliss 1902; Peters and Thiersch 1905; Ben-Arieh 1962; Oren 1965; Avi-Yonah 1977b; *SVM* 2, 4-5 n. 8; Oren and Rappaport 1984; Kloner and Hess 1985; Kloner 1985; Kloner 1987–88; Kuhnen 1990: 69-81; Kloner 1991; Kloner 1993b.

47.   Cf. Horowitz 1980. His re-examination of Marisa was superficial. Horowitz was right that Hellenistic culture was brought here by the Phoenicians, but he was wrong in other conclusions. The street pattern, fortifications, agora, public buildings and private houses show a small (natural) continuity and a large discontinuity from Palestinian architecture. Horowitz did not discuss the tombs or their material evidence, nor the stratigraphy of the site. Under the first Hippodamian city was detected a 'Jewish' one (see למלך stamps) of unknown plan, but probably different from the Hellenistic (as Israelite cities were). Above it rested a 'Maccabaean' city with a distorted plan, which prompted Avi-Yonah (1977b: 783) to observe that: 'The inhabitants were apparently no longer prepared to accept the urban plan imposed on them from above'. Whether this is true or false, the Greek elements do deteriorate

have been unknown to Greek-Phoenicians—for example it existed in the Persian-Hellenic Al Mina III (430–375 BCE) on the Syrian coast.[48]

Other Sidonian colonies of the Hellenistic period are known in Palestine: in Shechem and Jamnia Paralus.[49] No contemporary description of Marisa has survived, but we do possess a brief account of Shechem which might be appropriate to compare with Marisa here. Written at the end of the second century BCE by Theodotus, a Hellenized inhabitant of Samaria (conceivably of Phoenician origins and probably a convert to Judaism),[50] it throws light on the type of environment the Phoenicians were looking for when settling inland:

in the uppermost city (see changes in the onomasticon). Marisa's plan cannot be claimed to be typically oriental. Hippodamian plans during the fifth to second century BCE are found in areas sunk in Hellenic or Hellenistic influences, as shown by their culture (Segal [A.] 1978; Barghouti 1982; Peters 1983). The earliest planned towns in Palestine (dated to the Late Persian period) are Tel Megadim, Shiqmona and perhaps Tell Abu-Hawam II, all with Greek influences (Broshi 1977; Stern [E.] 1982: 48-49; cf. Arav 1989a; Kuhnen 1990). The Late Iron Age examples cited by Horowitz, mainly Megiddo III, are fraught with dating problems (Wightman 1985; cf. James *et al.* 1991).

48.   Wooley 1953: 175, 180.

49.   For Shechem see Josephus, *Ant.* 11.344; 12.259, 262; Delcor 1962; Hengel 1974: 2.195 n. 233; cf. below n. 80; for Jamnia Paralus see new text of 163 BCE (Isaac 1991); see also the well-established Hellenized Phoenician settlement at Tel Anafa in Upper Galilee (Herbert 1993; Herbert 1994); to these must be added the Sidonian and Tyrian colonies of the Persian period (Chapter 1 n. 41); in Hellenistic times Phoenician traders ventured to all directions, south to Petra (Parr 1970: 369) and Arabia (Bron 1988), and north to the Aegean: Rhodes (Morelli 1956: 170; Fraser 1970), Cos (Herondas, 2; see Mandelaras 1986: 69-81), Delos/Rheneia (Moutèrde 1964: 156-61; *MFR*, 325), Piraeus (Sidonian colony—*KAI* 60), Athens (Pope 1947: 144-45), Oropos (*IG* 7.4262) and Demetrias (Arvanitopoulos 1952–53b); see generally Masson 1969; Baslez 1986; and now Grainger 1991: 187-219; for the west see Whittaker 1974; for earlier background, see Gjerstad 1979; Coldstream 1982; Negbi 1992; Strabo (16.2.34) refers to Phoenicians in Galilee, Samaria, Jericho and Amman; for later influence see Chapter 3 n. 105.

50.   Theodotus is thought to have been a Hellenized Samaritan or Jew (*GLAJJ* 1, 129; *SVM* 2, 561-63; Collins 1980; Pummer 1982; Fallon 1985; Mendels 1987: 110-16; *FHJA* 2, 68), mainly because when writing about Shechem he evidently justified the Hasmonaean aggression there. But the inhabitants of Samaria, as with Idumaea, were a highly mixed population, the most Hellenized section of which was Phoenician (see Chapter 8 §5), like the Sidonians of Shechem. It is not beyond reason that our Theodotus is identical to the Greek-Phoenician writer of that name in Josephus, *Apion* 1.216, and Tatian, *Orat. ad Graec.* 37.

Thus the land was good and grazed upon by goats and well watered. There was neither a long path for those entering the city from the field nor even leafy woods for the weary. Instead, very close by the city appear two steep mountains (i.e. Ebal and Gerizim), filled with grass and woods. Between the two of them a narrow path is cut. On the side the bustling Shechem appears, a sacred town, built under (i.e. the mountain) as a base; there was a smooth wall around the town; and the wall for defence up above ran under the foot of the mountain.[51]

3. *Urban Communities and Military Settlement*

Under the Ptolemies there is no evidence for any *new* city foundation within Greater Idumaea, nor even in the surrounding areas.[52] By 'foundation' here is meant the creation of a new city on a site formerly empty or occupied only by a village (for example Alexandria). One exception would be Anthedon on the coast (northwest of Gaza), perhaps settled by people from Boeotia, but the earliest reference to it is from the Maccabaean period, and it could have been founded by the Seleucids after 200 BCE.[53] Another possible exception is Arethusa, but its location is unfortunately unknown (though close to Jamnia—perhaps Tel Ya'oz?), and again it may have been a Seleucid foundation.[54]

It is of interest that the Nabataeans at this time began creating permanent settlements. Apart from their capital Petra itself, where the earliest houses were constructed in the mid-third century BCE,[55] the

51.   Theodotus, *apud* Alex. Polyhistor, *apud* Eusebius, *Praep. Evang.* 9.22.1; cf. the coins of Neapolis/Shechem depicting the temple on Mt Gerizim under Hadrian (Meshorer 1985: 46-52).

52.   Millar 1987: 114-16; cf. Tcherikover 1959: 90-116. As a comparison, see the foundation of Arsinoe in Cilicia under Ptolemy II Philadelphus (283–246 BCE) mentioned in a new text (Jones and Habicht 1989).

53.   Josephus, *Ant.* 13.357; *War* 1.87; cf. *Ant.* 13.395; see Tcherikover 1959: 95; Jones [A.H.M.] 1971: 449 n. 16; *SVM* 2, 104; it is commonly identified with Khirbet Teda (Avi-Yonah 1977a: 100), but the site has not been excavated.

54.   Josephus, *Ant.* 14.75; *War* 1.156; also mentioned in a text from Delos (*MFR*, no. 185); the remains of Tell Ghazza (Tel Ya'oz), 4 km northeast of Jamnia Paralus, surveyed in the early 1950s (Dothan [M.] 1952: 112), indicate a substantial Hellenistic settlement (see now Isaac 1991: 140 n. 31).

55.   Some roughly built houses, 2–3 m beneath the Colonnaded Street, were dated by coins 'of a type minted in Aradus in the mid-third century B.C.' (Parr 1970: 369). A problem presented by the ceramics, similar types of which are dated in Samaria IX to 500–300 BCE (Parr 1965: 528), may be solved by the chronological revision in James *et al.* 1991: 187.

establishment of Eboda (from c. 300 BCE) was the first in a series of Nabataean towns which grew up west of the Arabah in the Negev, namely Elusa (c. 250 BCE), Nessana (c. 200–150 BCE), Kurnub/ Mampsis (first century BCE) and Subeita (first century BCE).[56] No doubt the same economic forces (principally the spice trade) governed both these towns and the south Idumaean fortresses (see below). Foundations like these became vital stepping stones in the caravan route from Arabia to Gaza through the desolate Negev. Their role was to protect the trade, as well as to provide stations for resting and importantly for praying.[57]

While there is no evidence that the Ptolemies ever issued a royal charter making a place a *polis*, or that any old city within Greater Idumaea was formally refounded, it might be reasonable to assume that the principal town of Marisa underwent some kind of governmental reform. By this is meant no more than a legal and financial transaction: the king would receive a considerable price, while the city would be granted the right to revise its constitution along Greek lines, and be governed by its own representatives—for example the case of Jerusalem.[58] The change would have provided the city with a number of benefits, but it was certainly not a question of 'freedom': the royal civic governor would have been removed, but the royal military governor with his garrison and some officials would have remained *in situ* for supervision.[59]

If Theodotos the ἄρχων, and Apollophanes the ἄρχων and ἀγορανόμος of Sidon, are necessarily accepted as Hellenistic civic officeholders,[60] then the Apollophanes who held the same position in

56.   See generally Negev 1986a; Wenning 1987: 137-82; but cf. Negev 1988: 35: 'the presence of Nabataeans in the central Negev during the fourth to first centuries BCE still needs substantiation'.

57.   See the temple of Zeus Obodas and the shrine of Aphrodite in Eboda, under which apparently once stood a Nabataean sanctuary (Negev 1976b: 345; Negev 1981: nos. 3, 7; Negev 1986b; Negev 1991a); cf. the pagan temple at Beersheba (below n. 139); and from an earlier period the Edomite cult centre at Ḥorvat Qiṭmiṭ (see Chapter 1 n. 26; cf. Beck 1993), and even earlier the religious station at Kuntillet 'Ajrud (Meshel and Meyers 1976; Meshel 1978).

58.   2 Macc. 4.9; see basically Tcherikover 1964; Jones [A.H.M.] 1971: 250-51; Hengel 1974: 277-83; cf. Millar 1983: 61.

59.   Tscherikower 1937: 44.

60.   *P. Mich.* 3; Haussoullier and Ingholt 1924: no. 4; Robert 1925; on Theodotos see Bagnall 1976: 23; these texts are not in Millar 1983: 62, and thus a degree

Marisa (ἄρξας τῶν ἐν Μαρίσηι Σιδονίων) would indicate that this old town, and new Sidonian colony, was granted certain rights of a *polis* by the Ptolemies.[61] This would be harmonious with the fact that Marisa possessed an extensive officialdom. Among other positions we can infer those of τεταγμένος ἐπὶ τῆς πόλεως for Pesistratus, ἐπιστάτης τῶν φυλακιτῶν for Pasicles, and φυλακίτης for Epicrates.[62] We are also aware of an ἀγορανόμος, whose name, Agathocles, is inscribed on two lead weights found at Marisa,[63] and perhaps a military ἱππάρχης, Libanius, from a tomb painting.[64] Further agreement may be found in the archaeology of the site as described above. Nevertheless in contrast to its successor, Beth Govrin, a little to the north, founded fully as a city (Eleutheropolis) by Septimius Severus in CE 200, Marisa never issued any coins.[65]

The extremely scanty information concerning Adora, the other principal town, does not permit us to comment on its status,[66] nor

of Greek constitution in Sidon may have to be accepted.

61.   *OGIS* 593; cf. Tcherikover 1959: 104-105; the same civic position may also be found in Samaria under the Seleucids: a fragmentary inscription of one Philochares son of Philochares (Reisner *et al.* 1924: 1.197, fig. 121; 2: pl. 59b) could be restored as [ἄρχ]ων of the city, and could date to Year 161 (τὸ ἕν (one) ξρ (160) ἔτος) in the Seleucid era (151/150 BCE); however, *SEG* 8.97 takes the era to be that of Sebaste (which began in 27/26 BCE), thus dating the text to CE 134/35—the restored office would then be [στρατηγεύ]ων; but the space needed for this word does not seem to be available, and the palaeography may not conform.

62.   Tscherikower 1937: 40-42; cf. Hengel 1974: 24.

63.   Bliss 1902: 61, fig. 28, an undated copy; Oren 1965: 222, a dated copy (108–107 BCE); cf. Lifshitz 1976: 180-81, no. 32, with the name wrongly given as 'Agathon' and the date as 107/106 BCE; not in Qedar 1986–87: 34-35; a similar Macedonian shield, with which these weights are decorated, interestingly appears on a coin of Herod the Great (*AJC* 2, pl. 1.2-2b; Meshorer 1990–91: pl. 25.2c); under the Seleucids, Jerusalem also had an ἀγορανόμος (2 Macc. 3.4); for other *agoranomoi*, see below n. 70 (Gaza) and n. 72 (Joppa).

64.   Rostovtzeff 1941: 520—but I read: ἵππος Λιβανίου ἱππ[άρ]χου; cf. *SEG* 7.326 from Khoraïbé (Qana) of one Δορυμένης Αἰτωλὸς ἱππάρχης.

65.   Spijkerman 1972; Meshorer 1985: 64—Eleutheropolis is the only inland Palestinian city, south of Jerusalem, ever to have issued coins.

66.   Adora is mentioned in Josephus's list of Greek cities as one freed by Pompey (*Ant.* 14.75; *War* 1.155), and later restored by Gabinius (*Ant.* 14.88; *War* 1.66); for Adoraim, the stronghold in the period of the monarchy, see 2 Chron. 11.9 (cf. Josephus, *Ant.* 8.246); Adora was visited by Zenon (*P. Zen.* 1. 59006); Edomites seem to have been the majority here (cf. *Jub.* 38.8-9) and they may have built an important temple to Qos/Apollo, if this is inferred from the story of Mnaseas (*apud*

does that of Jamnia,[67] though the establishment of a military κατοικία here may be conjectured (for which see below). A conspicuous silence surrounds Hebron, presumably a major post-exilic centre of the Edomites (Chapter 1). Zenon's archive has nothing to say about it. 1 Maccabees describes it simply as fortified with round towers, burned to the ground by Judas Maccabaeus in 154 BCE.[68] Even archaeology, though admittedly restricted in this area, has failed to uncover any substantial Hellenistic remains.[69]

On the coast, north and south, close to Idumaea, some major old cities may have been refounded. For example, Gaza, which had been destroyed by Alexander the Great and was rebuilt anew;[70] also perhaps Ascalon, although it was only in the second century BCE at the

Josephus, *Apion* 2.112-14); Adora is mentioned in 1 Macc. 13.20 (cf. Josephus, *Ant.* 13.207, 209); it was subsequently captured by John Hyrcanus (Josephus, *Ant.* 13.257; *War* 1.63; cf. further *Ant.* 13.396; 14.88); it is thought to be located in the modern village of Dura, southwest of Hebron (Abel 1938: 239).

67.   For Jabneel or Jabneh in the Bible, see Josh. 15.11; 2 Chron. 26.6; cf. Josephus, *Ant.* 5.87; 9.217; Jamnia was the place where Gorgias retreated after his defeat by Judas Maccabaeus (1 Macc. 4.15; cf. Josephus, *Ant.* 12.308), and from there he attacked Joseph and Azariah (1 Macc. 5.58; cf. Josephus, *Ant.* 12.351); Apollonius the governor of Seleucid Coele Syria came to Jamnia with a great force in his preparation for war against Jonathan (Josephus, *Ant.* 13.88); for later references, see *SVM* 2, 109-10; Yavneh has not been excavated, but it has been surveyed (Dothan [M.] 1952: 44-45; Mazar [B.] 1960); Philo (*Legat.* 200) speaks of Jamnia as 'one of the most populous cities', inhabited by a mixture of Jews with alien races (ἀλλόφυλοι), 'intruders for mischief from the dwellers in adjacent countries... (who) made themselves a pest and a nuisance... by subverting some part of the institutions of the Jews'; cf. Chapter 3 n. 5.

68.   1 Macc. 5.65; Josephus, *Ant.* 12.353.

69.   Campbell 1965: 32; for the excavation of Tell Rumeideh and the Hellenistic finds of Area I.7, see Hammond 1968: 256-57; cf. Ofer 1986: 93; Ofer 1993; for early historical references, see Chapter 1 n. 18; for a valuable description of Hebron at the time of Josephus, see *War* 4.529-33.

70.   Arrian 2.27.7; cf. Josephus, *Ant.* 17.320; *War* 2.97 (Ἑλληνίς); *Ant.* 13.364 (βουλή); Gaza's importance under the Ptolemies is highlighted by numerous mentions in the Zenon papyri (*P. L. Bat.* 21, index); it was certainly a *polis* under the Seleucids—see coins ΔΗΜΟΣ ΣΕΛ[ΕΥΚΑΙΩΝ] and ΓΑΖΑΙΩΝ ΔΗΜΟΥ (*BMC Palest.*, lxix, 143-44), and the lead weight of Apollonius the ἀγορανόμος dated to 122/121 BCE (Lifshitz 1976: 173-74, no. 11); for later weights see Chapter 3 n. 153; on the history of Gaza, see Rappaport 1970; *SVM* 2, 98-103; Kasher 1982; Glucker 1987; Katzenstein 1989; Mildenberg 1990; Katzenstein 1994.

expense of Gaza that it reached its peak,[71] and Joppa, which began minting coinage under the Ptolemies.[72]

Apart from placing garrisons in the principal towns of Syria,[73] the Ptolemies seem to have been responsible for the rebuilding of many old Hebrew forts. The importance of Idumaea's ὀχυρώματα continued down to the time of the Maccabees, the Herods and Vespasian.[74] To the early part of the Hellenistic period may be attributed the excavated fortresses of En-Gedi (Tel Goren III), Ḥorvat 'Uza, Arad IV, Tel 'Ira, Beersheba I and perhaps Tell Jemmeh—also possibly the slight evidence from Aroer and Tell el-Far'ah (south)—along the southern border of the eparchy.[75] These strongholds, extending on an approximate line from the Arabah to the Mediterranean, could not have been intended to protect the country from the Seleucids, who were situated a great distance to the north, but they would probably have been established to regulate the passing of trade.[76]

Lastly, it would seem to be logical to suppose that a few settlements of veteran soldiers (κληροῦχοι) were planted in the rich countryside of Greater Idumaea. To be sure direct evidence is missing, but it is possible that the offices referred to in Jamnia were connected with a

71.   Avi-Yonah 1977a: 39; cf. *P. Zen.* 1.59010; see Rappaport 1970; *SVM* 2, 105-108; Meshorer 1989a; note the coin of 168 BCE with ᾿ΑΣΚΑΛΩΝΙΤΩΝ ΔΗΜΟΥ (Chapter 3 n. 160); on Ascalon see Chapter 3 §4.

72.   *BMC* Palest., xxiv; Kindler 1985–86; cf. *P. Zen.* 1.59011, 59093, *P. Lond.* 7.2086, *PSI* 4.406; *SVM* 2, 110-14; Meshorer 1985: 24; note the inscribed handle of an ἀγορανόμος with the Seleucid date ΓΠΡ (130/129 BCE)—*SEG* 18.627; for other cities further away, such as Akko/Ptolemais, Philoteria, and Rabbat-Ammon/ Philadelphia, see Tcherikover 1959: 90-105; Kashtan 1988.

73.   Bagnall 1976: 14; cf. Diodorus 18.43.2; 19.59.2; 20.113.2; Josephus, *Ant.* 12.138; *PSI* 5.495; see also Bikerman 1938: 53-54.

74.   2 Macc. 10.16; Josephus, *War* 4.447, 552.

75.   Tel Goren III (Mazar [B.] *et al.* 1966: 46; Barag 1976: 376); Ḥorvat 'Uza (Beit-Arieh and Cresson 1982; Beit-Arieh and Cresson 1983); Arad IV (Herzog *et al.* 1984: 29); Tel 'Ira (Biran and Cohen 1979); Beersheba I (Aharoni 1975a: 167; Aharoni 1975b: 163-65); Tell Jemmeh (Amiran and van Beek 1976: 548; cf. van Beek 1993: 672-74); Aroer (Biran 1983: 34 n.); Tell el-Far'ah (south) (Cowley 1929: 111-12; but see Naveh 1985b: 116, no. 2).

76.   Settlements grew around such forts (e.g. Beersheba I), depending on the road, on sheep and goats, and on cultivation of the arable land of the wadi bottoms; for this type of agriculture, using run-off water, see Evenari *et al.* 1958; cf. Stager 1976: 157; for the questionable Herodian *limes* later, see references above n. 29 end.

military κληρουχία—positions such as those of ἀκροφύλαξ, φυλα-
κάρχης, δικαστής, γραμματεὺς and ἀρχυπηρέτης, reflect military
functions.[77] From *P. Zen.* 1.59006, Rostovtzeff inferred that another
such colony was established near Gaza.[78] This may be supported by
the existence of a Cretan-Aetolian family of mercenaries in the area,
attested in an epigram to be discussed later. Looking wider, we are
certainly aware of a κληρουχία in the land of the Tobiads in Ammanitis, where a Greek force stationed there included soldiers of other
nationalities, under the command of the local prince Tobias who was
serving Ptolemaic Alexandria.[79] Another example is Samaria, for
which Eusebius reports that it was settled by Macedonians, and he is
supported by overwhelming archaeological evidence from the site.[80]
Furthermore, one should note Sidon in the north which may also have
possessed a Ptolemaic military colony—if this is how the 22 names of

77.   *P. Zen.* 1.59006; see Bagnall 1976: 16; cf. the veterans settled in Idumaea
by Herod the Great (Josephus, *War* 2.55).
78.   Rostovtzeff 1941: 348; but cf. Tscherikower 1937: 60; see also Avi-Yonah
1978: 106-12.
79.   *P. Zen.* 1.59003; cf. 59005; 59075; 59076; *P. Lond.* 7.1930; for the Tobiads see Mazar [B.] 1957; cf. McCown 1957; for Joseph son of Tobias (Josephus,
Ant. 12.154ff.), see Goldstein 1975; Gera 1990. This important Hellenistic Transjordanian centre is located at 'Araq el-Emir, and although its main buildings (Qasr el-
'Abd, Square Building and Village IV) are currently dated from c. 200 BCE, a few
coins, sherds, and two Aramaic graffiti mentioning טוב ביה, are of the third century
BCE (see generally Lapp [N.L.] [ed.] 1983; Lapp and Lapp 1993). Qasr el-'Abd, the
monumental building complex, has been identified as a palatial *paradeisos* (Dentzer *et
al.* 1983: 147), i.e. the residence of the governor, and not a temple as previously
thought (Lapp [P.W.] 1976: 530-31; Campbell 1979: 163). However, a *paradeisos*
has no parallel in the Persian world, whereas Greek styles are evident here (cf. Arav
1989a: 109, 162; Kuhnen 1990: 54-58).
80.   Eusebius, *Chron.* [edn Schoene 2: 114]; cf. Curtius Rufus, 4.8.9; see
Jones [A.H.M.] 1931a: 79; for Samaria see *SVM* 2, 160-64; for the archaeology see
conveniently Avigad 1978: 1046-47, 1049; cf. the recently discovered fortified town
on Mt Gerizim (Magen 1986; 1990; 1993a); note how strikingly similar is the palaeography of Hegesandrus's inscription from Samaria (Crowfoot *et al.* 1957: 37, no.
13, pl. V.1) to that of Hegesidicus's wife from Philippi in Macedonia (Koukoule-
Chrysanthake 1979: 331, pl. 144d); cf. the fact that Herod the Great assigned
Samaria's land to veteran pagan soldiers (Josephus, *Ant.* 15.296); further cf. Applebaum 1979–80: 163 n. 26: 'As definite Macedonian colonies we may identify
Samaria, Gadara, Abila, Pella, Philoteria, Gerasa, Hippos and Dium...'; also note
Stern ([E.] 1989: 116-21) on Dor.

Greek soldiers preserved on painted stelae found there are to be dated and interpreted.[81]

Cohabitation of Greek soldiers (and even of some private individuals) with Palestinian women need not be doubted;[82] in fact the phenomenon would not have been uncommon since at one time it required legislation in defence of local females who were unjustly enslaved. The fundamentally important tax edict of Ptolemy II Philadelphus, dated to 260 BCE, states:

> As for people serving the military and the others who are settled (κατοικούντων) in Syria and Phoenicia, those who are living with (συνοικοῦσιν) native wives (γυναιξὶ λαϊκαῖς) need not declare them (i.e. as slaves)...[83]

Moreover, Hecataeus hinted at the fact that other foreigners and Greeks settled among the Jews:

> ...when they (the Jews) became subject to foreign rule, as a result of their mingling with men of other nations—both under Persian rule and under that of the Macedonians who overthrew the Persians—many of their traditional practices were disturbed.[84]

It would therefore seem reasonable to accept that there was a degree of Greek military, as well as private (as new evidence from Khirbet Za'aquqa now proves—see below n. 107), migration into Palestine, though how significant this was is difficult to assess from the sparse evidence at our disposal. On balance one may tentatively agree with Millar who noted that

> there is no positive evidence to suggest that there was private immigration (the statement would extend to the military) on a scale which would by

81.   Jalabert (1904: 15) and Jidejian (1971: 71) refer to them as Seleucid, but most probably they were Ptolemaic (Bar-Kochva 1989: 574; cf. Bagnall 1976: 17 n. 30); cf. the case of the Ptolemaic mercenaries further north at Ras ibn Hani (Rey-Coquais 1978).

82.   See generally Launey 1949–50: 642-75, 690-700; cf. the story of Diophantus, a Macedonian, who married a local woman and settled at Abae in Arabia (Diodorus 32.10.2); also the Macedonians in Marisa (Peters and Thiersch 1905: nos. 21, 31-32 from Tomb 1); cf. the כסמים at Arad (below n. 104).

83.   Liebesny 1936: 258-59, recto ll. 12-15; cf. above n. 2.

84.   Hecataeus, *apud* Diodorus 40.3, *apud* Photius 244; cf. Philo's quotation above n. 67; and Ezra's (9.1-2) and Nehemiah's (13.25) objections to mixed marriages.

itself have brought profound changes in culture, social relations or the economy.[85]

But the Hellenized Phoenician settlement (particularly in Greater Idumaea and Samaria) was on a large scale (as literary, epigraphic and especially archaeological material shows) and it would deserve further attention. The subject is intimately related to the wider problem of 'Hellenization' and it will be touched upon briefly later.

4. *Administration*

The question of how Idumaea was administered by the Ptolemies is another one for which no final answer can be given. Because no general governorship is attested in the available documents, it is thought that the entire province of Syria-Phoenicia lacked a supreme office, supervised directly from Alexandria.[86] Polybius mentions Theodotus, a τεταγμένος ἐπὶ Κοίλης Συρίας in 221 BCE, Nicolaus, a στρατηγὸς in 219 BCE, and Andromachus, another στρατηγὸς after 217 BCE, but these were specially appointed military commanders from Egypt, rather than locally established civil administrators.[87] Yet, since in the financial realm there was a διοικητὴς for the whole province, it is possible that a civil or perhaps military governor (of whom we have no record at the moment) also existed.[88] By analogy, the Seleucids later maintained this high office in the region, as στρατηγὸς καὶ ἀρχιερεύς.[89]

At the level of the hyparchies within Syria-Phoenicia, individual ὕπαρχοι are thought to have been appointed, but again the case of the best candidate, Keraias, who defected to the Seleucid Antiochus III, has often been disputed.[90] However, as with the διοικητὴς of the province, each hyparchy (including Idumaea) certainly possessed a

85. Millar 1987: 116; contra Fuks [A.] 1974: 57; but cf. now Lund 1993.
86. Tscherikower 1937: 39; Avi-Yonah 1977a: 33.
87. Polybius 5.40.1, 46.3; 5.61.8; 5.87.6.
88. The financial administrator is referred to in Ptolemy II's edict as διοικοῦντος τὰς κατὰ Συρίαν καὶ Φοινίκην προσόδους (Liebesny 1936: 258-59, recto ll. 18-19; cf. above n. 2). In fact, we may now have a record of a military governor based in Tyre under Ptolemy IV Philopator (221–203 BCE), mentioned as στρατηγὸς Συρίας καὶ Φοινίκης (Rey-Coquais 1989: 614-17).
89. *OGIS* 230; Landau 1966; Bertrand 1982; cf. 2 Macc. 3.5; 4.4.
90. Polybius 5.70.10, 71.11; see Welles 1934: 371; Bagnall 1976: 14-15; cf. Theodotas (*PP* 15044).

financial official termed οἰκονόμος.[91] It should be emphasized again that in both cases it is economy that matters. At the level of the toparchies within separate hyparchies, we do not have specific information about individual τοπάρχαι (unless Pesistratus of Marisa functioned as one rather than τεταγμένος ἐπὶ τῆς πόλεως—see above), though some subordinates in the officialdom of towns and military κατοικίαι have already been discussed. At village level there were the κωμομισθωταὶ (those buying the tax contracts for the villages) and the κωμάρχαι,[92] one of whom may have been Ieddous, almost certainly of Idumaea (not Judaea), who owed a sum of money to Zenon.[93] In lower positions we encounter several agents and minor officials, including the τελῶναι (tax-farmers), as well as the wealthy estate owners, like the Marisan brothers Zaidelus and Kollochutus, from whom Zenon bought slaves.[94]

5. *Population*

A mere impression from the Zenon papyri concerning the population of Greater Idumaea (in respect of the three major cities of Marisa, Adora and Jamnia) is that it was considerable, not to mention prosperous. The same is true of what is recorded in the *Letter of Aristeas*.[95] Strabo knew that Jamnia of the past was so thickly inhabited that its territory could provide 40,000 fighting men. This would indicate a

---

91.   Liebesny 1936: 257 (l. 1), 258 (l. 37); cf. above n. 2; in the case of Judaea, and since the local governors of the Late Persian period disappear (see also Schwartz [S.] 1994: 162), it is not impossible that the high priests functioned as economic agents to the Ptolemies (*viz*. Josephus, *Ant*. 12.161); cf. the case of the Tobiads in the Transjordan, above n. 79.

92.   Liebesny 1936: 259 ll. 18-19.

93.   *P. Zen.* 1.59018 = *CPJ* 1, 129-30, no. 6. It is unlikely that he was living in Judaea; the circumstances of Straton's journey on behalf of Zenon (*P. Zen.* 1.59015) suggest that Ieddous (Ἰεδδοῦς) was a Jewish κωμάρχης in Idumaea. A Yaddua (ידוע), a Jewish official of Arad, is mentioned in 16 (out of 45) Aramaic ostraca of the Late Persian period in accepted chronology (Naveh 1981: nos. 1-3, 5-9, 13, 15, 17, 19, 22, 28, 34, 36), and a Yaddua (ידוע) appears on a YHD coin (Spaer 1986–87; cf. Meshorer 1990–91: 115, no. 6). Iaddous (Ἰαδδοῦς) was also the name of the high priest (Josephus, *Ant*. 11.302) in the story of Alexander's alleged visit to Jerusalem—see above n. 5.

94.   *P. Zen.* 1.59804; *P. Zen.* 1.59015.

95.   Aristeas, *To Philocrates* 107-108, 113.

population of at least c. 200,000, but the figure seems an exaggeration by the geographer or his source.[96]

At the time of Herod the Great it is said that an army of 3,000 Idumaeans were transferred to Trachonitis, while the Zealots later invoked the aid of 20,000 Idumaeans, and Simon Bar Giora had 5,000 attached to his army.[97] Unfortunately, although these numbers may be interpreted as populations of c. 15,000, c. 100,000 and c. 25,000 respectively, they are general numbers, not connected with a single village or town. Yet Vespasian is said to have attacked two Idumaean villages, Betabris (Beth Govrin?) and Caphartoba (Kefar Tov?), killing over 10,000 and taking 1,000 prisoners.[98] If the future emperor managed to exterminate as many as one third of those living there, each village at that time might have had around 15,000 people.

We have no historical means of arriving at exact figures for the province as a whole. Based on Josephus it has been estimated (but not without criticism) that the whole of Palestine in the first century CE had a population of about 2,500,000.[99] Naturally the Roman period cannot be compared with the Hellenistic in numbers, but if we assume that from c. 250 BCE to c. CE 50 the population tripled, and if Greater Idumaea possessed roughly a quarter of it (counting mainly Galilee,

96.   Strabo 16.759; data on the recruitment capacity of a population in the Classical world are as follows: Athens recruited 15 per cent of the free population (Gomme 1933: 5-6, 47); Republican Rome around 10 per cent (Brunt 1971: 54, 419); a notional maximum of 20 per cent is here adopted for calculations.

97.   Josephus, *Ant.* 16.285; *War* 4.235; 5.249.

98.   Josephus, *War* 4.447-48.

99.   Byatt 1973: 56; cf. Avi-Yonah 1977a: 219-21; *GLAJJ* 2, 62-63. Broshi (1980) estimates only one million, based on the quantity of grain that the country could provide for its inhabitants, but it may be safer to adopt the population's recruitment potential—thus Bar-Kochva (1989: 56-57) calculated 400,000 people in Hellenistic Judaea alone. It may be useful to note more about the Jews. The returnees from the exile after c. 538 BCE numbered 42,360, without counting 7,337 slaves and 200 singers (Ezra 2.64-65). But not all returned or were deported in the first place (Chapter 1 n. 17), and many continued to occupy parts of the area which later became Idumaea (e.g. Neh. 11.25-30 and Arad ostraca). At the end of the fourth century BCE the number of Jews was thought to be 'vast' (Hecataeus *apud* Josephus, *Apion* 1.194). Ptolemy I is said to have taken 100,000 Jewish prisoners to Egypt (Aristeas, *To Philocrates* 12), and similar figures of recruited men are given in 1 Macc. 5.20; 12.41 etc. Philo (*Flacc.* 6) in the first century CE testifies that there were 1,000,000 Jews in Egypt, while Bar Hebraeus [edn Pocock: 73] refers to 6,944,000 under Claudius in the whole Empire.

Samaria, Judaea and Idumaea), then a mere guess would be that under
the Ptolemies this hyparchy had as many as 200,000 people.

An archaeological survey of Idumaea, with the view of assessing its
settlement density in the Hellenistic period, could improve our understanding (despite many limitations). In the mainland 15 excavated sites
have produced Hellenistic material: Arad, Beersheba, En-Gedi, Tell
el-Far'ah (south), Tel Ḥalif, Tell el-Ḥesi, Tel 'Ira, Tell Jemmeh,
Lachish, Marisa, Masada, Tel Nagila, Khirbet el-Qôm, Tell esh-
Shariah, Ḥorvat 'Uza. In the Ashdodite territory, suggested here to
have formed a part of Idumaea (thus 'Greater Idumaea'—see Map 2),
another seven excavated sites have shown signs of Hellenistic occupation: Tell el-'Areini, Azotus, Azotus Paralus, Gezer, Tell Judeideh,
Tell eṣ-Ṣafi (Gitta or Geth?) and Tel Ṣippor.[100]

To these 22 sites must be added Adora, Jamnia and Jamnia Paralus
(incl. Tell Ghazza) which are known from historical sources and a
field survey, while the little work carried out at Hebron remains
unpublished.[101] As regards strictly the Early Hellenistic (c. 332–167
BCE), this is attested in most of the mentioned places, but not in
Masada, Tel Nagila, Tell esh-Shariah and possibly Tell Judeideh.
Furthermore, the scanty information (basically one ostracon) from
Tell el-Far'ah (south) is debatable.

The material evidence from some of these sites is in the nature of
pottery and/or coins (Tell eṣ-Ṣafi, Tel Ṣippor, Jamnia Paralus),
ostraca (Tell el-Far'ah [south], Tel 'Ira) or inscription (Jamnia Paralus), barely confirming the existence of a settlement. Nevertheless, a
few clear strata of occupation are to be found (Tell el-'Areini, Gezer,
Tel Ḥalif), including building remains (Tell Ghazza). Moreover, one
should point to the granaries of Tell Jemmeh, the plastered storage
pits of Tell el-Ḥesi (the contents of which testify to a large spinning
and weaving industry), and the complex of pools at Azotus Paralus (an
extensive purple dye industry). Of particular interest are the temples
excavated at Lachish and Beersheba, the square plan and agora of
Azotus, the reused city-gate of Gezer, the massive tower of Arad, the
fortifications and tower at En-Gedi, the fortress of Ḥorvat 'Uza, and
the houses butted on the defence wall system of the town of Khirbet

100. To avoid a long bibliography here, seven main sources will provide the relevant references: *EAEHL* (*NEAEHL*); *BHLS*; Stern [E.] 1982; Arav 1989a; Kuhnen
1990; *TIRIP*.

101. See above nn. 54, 66-67, 69.

el-Qôm. Archaeologically, beyond question, the most important Hellenistic site is Marisa, as already discussed.

From the point of view of the number of settlements, another hypothetical estimate of population may be worked out. If each of the (about) 20 known Early Hellenistic Idumaean sites had at the most 10,000 people (towns had many more, but fortresses many less),[102] then a population of 200,000 would be calculated, which seems to agree with the initial guess above.

6. *Ethnic Composition*

The name of 'Idumaea' itself must indicate that in the Early Hellenistic period a considerable section of the population was 'Edomite'—the people who had settled primarily in the south and the east of the eparchy from the time of the Babylonians (Chapter 1).

Utilizing testimonies predating his own time, regarding the *ethnē* living in Syria-Palestine, Strabo stated:

> Some writers divide the whole Syria into (the tribes of) Coele-Syrians (= Ituraeans), Syrians (= Aramaeans) and Phoenicians, and say that four other tribes are mixed up with these, namely Judaeans (= Jews), Idumaeans (= Edomites), Gazaeans (= Arabs) and Azotians (= Philistines)...[103]

This list of native tribes hardly differs from that concerning the people residing in Idumaea from the sixth to the third century BCE, which can be built up from various other sources. Only the foreign Greek element, at least for the later part of this period, needs to be added here (Strabo's source listed 'native' tribes), but as we have gathered it could not have been great.

In terms of Greek epigraphical evidence, the whole of Palestine can be briefly surveyed here. Yadin's claim that an ostracon belonging to Arad IX (currently dated to the eighth century BCE) is written in

---

102. Josephus (*War* 3.43) says that the smallest village of Galilee had over 15,000 people, but this must have been true only of the largest village. His claim (*Life* 235) that there were 204 villages and towns in Galilee, which would give a population of over 3,000,000 for that province, is grossly exaggerated (Hoehner 1972: 52, 291). It seems unlikely that the largest village in Idumaea of the Hellenistic period could have had more than about 10,000 people.

103. Strabo 16.2.2.

Greek cannot be substantiated,[104] and the earliest Greek inscription is
that found at Tell el-Ḥesi in Idumaea, which seems to date to the fifth
century BCE;[105] the person named (Arēebal) is evidently of Greek-
Phoenician origin. To the mid-fourth century BCE (excluding letters
on amphora-handles[106]) may be assigned a Cretan epigram found
south of Gaza (but presently reckoned to be of a later date—see
below), to the end of the century a new group of funerary graffiti
from Khirbet Zaʻaquqa, while texts of the third century BCE include a
Greek and a bilingual (Greek and Aramaic) ostraca from Khirbet el-
Qôm, a bilingual inscription from Tel Dan, three texts from Marisa
(tell), two from Samaria, and one each from Joppa and Hefziba.[107]
The second century BCE (again excluding writings on imported
amphorae[108]) is represented by a respectable corpus of texts from
Marisa (tombs, caves and tell), three inscriptions from Samaria, two
from Akko/Ptolemais, one each from Jamnia Paralus, Gezer and Jerusalem, an inscribed handle from Joppa, and perhaps by two ostraca
from Arad III.[109] Moreover the second century BCE has produced

104.   Yadin 1974: 30-32: only a redating of the site's stratigraphy (lowering Arad
IX to the seventh century BCE—cf. James *et al.* 1991: 171-75), together with the fact
that probably Greek mercenaries (כתים) are mentioned in the Hebrew ostraca
(Aharoni [ed.] 1981: nos. 1-2, 4-5, 7-8, 10-11, 14) from Arad VI (to be lowered to
the fifth), could make Yadin's claim plausible; for the conventional chronology, see
Herzog *et al.* 1984. An inscribed Greek sherd from Al Mina on the Syrian coast presumably dates from the seventh century BCE (Boardman 1982).
105.   Bliss 1894: 104-105; cf. Stern [E.] 1982: 244; this inscription, scratched
across the base of a small limestone stand, is not mentioned by Sevenster (1968),
Fitzmyer (1970) or Hengel (1974). A text in the Greek language but written in
Cypro-syllabic of c. 400 BCE (on a Phoenician votive scapula conventionally of
c. 600 BCE) was excavated at Tel Dor (Stern [E.] 1994).
106.   From Shiqmona see Elgavish 1978: 1104-105; cf. Stern [E.] 1982: 198;
Broshi 1984: 29.
107.   Khirbet Zaʻaquqa (Kloner *et al.* 1992); Khirbet el-Qôm (Geraty 1975;
Geraty 1981; Geraty 1983; cf. Skaist 1978); Tel Dan (*ND* 1.105: no. 67; cf. Millar
1987: 132-33); Marisa (Avi-Yonah 1977b: 784); Samaria (Crowfoot *et al.* 1957: 37,
no. 13 = *SEG* 8.95; cf. Fitzmyer 1970: 509 n. 26; *SEG* 8.102); Joppa (Lifshitz
1962a: 82-84, no. 6; cf. Sevenster 1968: 100-101); Hefziba (Landau 1966).
108.   E.g. recently from Dor (Ariel *et al.* 1985) and Jerusalem (Ariel [ed.] 1990:
13-98).
109.   Marisa (Wünsch 1902; Peters and Thiersch 1905; Moulton 1915; McCown
1921–22; Abel 1925; Oren and Rappaport 1984; Kloner 1985; cf. *SEG* 8.245-61);
Samaria (Reisner *et al.* 1924: 1.250, no. 1; Reisner *et al.* 1924: 1.197, fig. 121;

official lead weights, for example from the cities of Gaza and Marisa, and possibly to the end of the century (if not the beginning of the first) should be dated the inscription from the Tomb of Jason in Jerusalem.[110]

Among the Aramaic ostraca from southern Palestine—the main source of Semitic epigraphy in the area from c. 500 to c. 200 BCE (on conventional terms)—there are many dated to the Hellenistic period (and more should be).[111] These have been found in the following locations: Raphia, Tell Jemmeh (twelve), Tell el-Far'ah (south), Tel 'Ira, Horvat 'Uza, Arad, Khirbet el-Qôm (six), Marisa (an Edomitic marriage contract of 176 BCE), Tell el-Hesi, Jerusalem, Tell el-Fûl ('Early Jewish' of the late second century BCE), and Qumran (several of second–first centuries BCE).[112]

Since the main concern of this chapter (apart from politics and economy) is the ethnic composition of Idumaea, the above material, particularly the ostraca that include proper names, are of great value. It is important to stress that the same names were often adopted by different groups of people, but it is true that by and large Hebrews

Tushingham 1972; cf. *SEG* 8.96-97); Akko/Ptolemais (Avi-Yonah 1959 = *SEG* 18.622; Landau 1961 = *SEG* 19.904; cf. Schwartz [J.] 1962 = *SEG* 20.413); Jamnia Paralus (Isaac 1991); Gezer (*CII* 1184; Gabba 1958: 31-32, no. 9); Jerusalem (Applebaum *et al.* 1981–82: 108, no. 18); Joppa (*SEG* 18.627); Arad III (Lifshitz 1981).

110.   For the lead weights, see Lifshitz 1976: 187; cf. Manns 1984; Qedar 1986–87: 33-35; for the inscription on the theme 'enjoy life' from the Tomb of Jason, see Puech 1983: 491-94.

111.   For the period c. 500–200 BCE, the only other sources are a few Phoenician inscriptions (for references see Chapter 1 n. 41), the YHD coins and stamps (Chapter 1 n. 51), and probably a couple of MSS from Qumran (Naveh 1982: 113; cf. Cross 1955b). For the tension in palaeographic chronology (due to insecure pottery dating—Chapter 1 n. 27), see the Aramaic ostraca from Tell Jemmeh, dated between c. 250 and 200 BCE by the excavator, but in the fourth century by Naveh (1992a: 52).

112.   Raphia (Naveh 1985b: 118-19 n. 9); Tell Jemmeh (Naveh 1992a; Naveh 1992b: 53; cf. two South Arabic inscriptions—van Beek 1972: 246); Tell el-Far'ah (south) (Cowley 1929: 111-12; but see Naveh 1985b: 116 n. 2); Tel 'Ira (Biran and Cohen 1979; cf. Naveh 1985b: 118 n. 8); Horvat 'Uza (Beit-Arieh 1984; Beit-Arieh 1993a: 1497; cf. Misgav 1990); Arad (Naveh 1981: 170 n. 44); Khirbet el-Qôm (Geraty 1983); Marisa (Eshel and Kloner 1994); Tell el-Hesi (Rose and Toombs 1976: 47); Jerusalem (Cross 1981); Tell el-Fûl (Rast 1981); and Qumran (de Vaux 1973: 103).

used Hebrew names, Arabs Arab, Edomites Edomite, and Greeks Greek—hence the bilingual ostracon from Khirbet el-Qôm (above) of Nikēratos and Qos-yadaʿ; the latter also named in Greek as 'Kosidēs'. At all events when ambiguity is involved, broader archaeological evidence can assist in determining the question. For example, the Hellenistic pagan temples of Lachish and Beersheba (above) provide a reasonable criterion for distinction: worshippers there could have hardly been Jewish, and certainly not by faith.

The Greek epigram from Gaza suggests the existence of a Cretan colony in this area, possibly as early as the mid-fourth and certainly by the end of the third century BCE.[113] Interestingly, Cretan influence here is reflected in both earlier and later records: the Old Testament, a Hebrew ostracon from Arad, Tacitus, Roman coins and Christian literature.[114] We thus know the names of six members of a mercenary family in Gaza: Charmadas the son of Tascomenes, his son of the same name and daughter Archagatha, her husband Machaeus the Aetolian and their daughter Cleodoxa.

We already saw how the onomasticon of the Aramaic ostraca from Beersheba, dated from the mid-fourth century BCE, attests to a predominance of Edomites and Arabs in the south.[115] By contrast the Aramaic ostraca from Arad in the east persist with Jewish names—such as Eliashib, Shallum and Yaddua—but not without the introduction

113. First published by Iliffe (1931; cf. *SEG* 8.269) as a third century CE epigram, but then redated to the Hellenistic period by Tod (1933) and by Roussel (1933)—more recently referred to by Fitzmyer (1970: 509 n. 26) and Hengel (1974: 26 n. 77); I intend to suggest elsewhere a mid-fourth century BCE date for this text, which seems to fit better the political circumstances of that period both in Crete and Egypt.

114. Cf. the Philistines (Chapter 1 n. 41); for the 'Cherethites' (כרתי[ם]) see 2 Sam. 8.18; 15.18; 20.7; 20.23; 1 Kgs 1.38-44 (cf. Albright 1920–21; Delcor 1978); for the 'Qerosites' or sons of 'Qeros' (קרם—Ezra 2.44) and the קרם of an Arad ostracon (Aharoni [ed.] 1981: no. 18), see Garfinkel 1988; for a confused but instructive legend about the Jews and Crete, see Tacitus, *Hist.* 5.2.1-3 (cf. now van der Horst, 1988); for the Roman coins with the Gazaean Marnas (e.g. *BMC* Palest. 146 no. 17), his epithet 'Cretogenes' (Marcus Diaconus) and the equation of Gaza and Minoa (Stephanus), see Hill 1913; and now Mussies 1990; cf. Aramaic ostracon from Raphia (above n. 25).

115. See Chapter 1 n. 30; for the Arabs cf. Polybius 5.79.8; 1 Macc. 12.10-12; Pliny (*Hist. Natur.* 6.156-57) refers to Lihyan and Thamûd Arabs south of the Nabataean realm (cf. Qur'ân, Sûra 8.71-7; 11.64-71 etc.); Agatharchides (*apud* Photius, *Bibl.* 92) also acknowledges the Thamoudians (see Diodorus 3.44.2-6).

of some Edomitic ones: קוסינקם, קוסבה, [ד]קוספ.[116] The onomasticon of Marisa in the west is overwhelmingly Greek and Hellenized Phoenician, with the occasional appearance of Edomitic, Egyptian, Jewish and other Semitic names. In some cases the ethnic origin is given directly: Ortas the Macedonian, Eikonia the Sidonian, Philōtia the Sidonian.[117] Other times it is implied: the 'priest' Balsalō (Baal hath prospered?), the worshippers of the goddesses Aphroditē and Korē, the theophorically named Audokōs (אבדקוס), or Athēnaios.[118]

But generally the highly mixed population of southern Palestine in the Hellenistic period is best illustrated by a list of 'locals' employed by Zenon in his travelling party of 259 BCE. Here we have the perfect assortment of Greek, Phoenician, Edomite and Jewish people working side by side together: 'Hippostratos, Auaēlos, Panabēlos, Zabalnos, Philōn, Menōn, Zēnōn, Hosaios, Annaios, Sannaios, Kousnatanos, Nikōn...'[119]

7. Hellenization

Plutarch presents us with the standard Hellenic view of Alexander the Great, as the universal conqueror, an educator with philosophical training, a 'reconciler of the world', who 'civilized barbarian kings', 'founded Greek cities among the wild peoples', and 'taught laws and peace to lawless and uneducated tribes'.[120] It is interesting to contrast the Semitic view of Alexander as given in the *Sibylline Oracles*: 'a

116. Naveh 1981: nos. 20, 32, 43; for the Edomitic theophoric name of 'Qos', see Bartlett 1989: 200-207; cf. Israel 1979; for its Hellenistic equation to 'Apollo' note the list in *SB* 681; cf. Qos-nathan = Apollo-dotos (*P. L. Bat.* 20: no. 18); for the Idumaeans in Egypt, see Chapter 3 n. 12.

117. Peters and Thiersch 1905: no. 31 (Tomb 1); no. 42 (Tomb 2); Moulton 1915: no. 10 = *SEG* 8.258 (cf. Abel 1925: no. 12).

118. Peters and Thiersch 1905: no. 43 (Tomb 2); no. 33 (Tomb 1); Wünsch 1902: 168, no. 26; Oren and Rappaport 1984: no. 14 (Tomb E.8); no. 22 (Tomb N.9). For further diagnostic examples from the West, see the Greek sisters Rodion (or Rodia?) and Athēnion (or Athēnia?) from the large family buried at Khirbet Za'aquqa (Kloner *et al.* 1992: 40*, no. 5b and 42*, no. 9a = *SEG* 42, 1443b and 1447a), the Phoenician Ba'alpaday (בעלפדי) from Tell Jemmeh (Naveh 1992a: 49, no. 1), and the Edomite Qosram son of Qosyad (קוסרם בר קוסיד) from the Marisan marriage contract of 176 BCE (Eshel and Kloner 1994).

119. *CPJ* 1, 124-25, no. 3.

120. Plutarch, *De fort. aut virt. Alex. Magni* 1.6 (329C); 1.4 (328B).

faithless man clad with a purple cloak on his shoulders, savage,
stranger to justice, fiery', who 'wished to destroy' races foreign to his,
and before whom 'all Asia bore an evil yoke'.[121]

Nevertheless, the Hellenization of the Eastern world had started
long before Alexander (Chapter 1 n. 42), and it was a gradual process—in fact a complicated cultural phenomenon to which in many
cases individuals subscribed of their own accord. We only need to be
reminded of the story in Herodotus about Scyles the king of the
Scythians, who was 'given to Greek ways', took on 'Greek clothes',
'made offerings to the gods in the Greek fashion', built himself a
house in a Hellenic environment with 'sphinxes and griffins made of
white stone' standing all about it, 'married a wife' from the same area,
was 'initiated in the rites of the Bacchic Dionysus', and at the end lost
his life to his angry compatriots who were guarding their own
Scythian customs.[122] In agreement with elements from this story, the
criteria of Hellenization have been seen to include, in the words of
Sherwin-White and Kuhrt, 'not merely the adoption of Greek coinage,
names, institutions and Greek words, but also Greek political practices, lifestyle, and literary, artistic and architectural ideas...'[123]

It will be of benefit to quote the current expert opinions on the
vexed question of the Hellenization of Syria-Palestine. A maximalist is
Smith, who concluded that

> the cultural history of Palestine from the beginning of the Persian period is
> one of constant subjection to Greek influence, and...already in the
> Ptolemaic period every sector of the country must have been shaped by
> that influence more or less.[124]

A less extreme view is the now apparently revised theory of Hengel:

> A more thorough (Hellenization), which also included the lower classes,
> only became a complete reality in Syria and Palestine under the protection
> of Rome...[125]

Towards a minimalist position is that of Millar, who concludes that:

> the positive impact of hellenistic rule was relatively slight.[126]

121. *Sib. Or.* 3.388-400; cf. 11.215-18; Collins 1983: 359, 439.
122. Herodotus 4.78-80.
123. Sherwin-White and Kuhrt 1993: 145.
124. Smith [M.] 1971: 54.
125. Hengel 1980: 53.
126. Millar 1987: 129; cf. now Wasserstein 1995.

An extreme minimalist view is that of Feldman:

> even after the Maccabees (i.e. in the Roman/Herodian period) the degree
> of Hellenization was hardly profound...[127]

These fundamental (and formidable) studies provide most of the evidence that can be put together from literary and epigraphic sources alike, for the analysis of the phenomenon of Hellenization—though archaeological results have yet to be fully analysed; only a brief overview will be possible here.

There is no particular reason to restate the general argument, or redefine our terms. The extreme opinions of Smith and Feldman can safely be put aside, and it is really between Hengel and Millar that a balance may be found. From the Roman/Herodian period onwards the impact of Hellenism was fundamental—even in the extreme national-istic environment of the Bar Kokhba revolt in the 130s CE, a docu-ment from the Cave of Letters frankly states why it was written in Greek: 'because reasons were not found to be written in Hebrew' (διὰ τὸ [ἀφο]ρμὰς μὴ εὑρηθ[ῆ]ναι Ἑβραεστὶ γ[ρά]ψασθαι)![128] As late as the end of the Byzantine period, deep into the Negev, the papyri of Nessana still display an incredible degree of Hellenization.[129] If we exclude the significant, but perhaps not profound, impact of Aegean cultures on coastal Palestine since the Late Bronze (Mycenaean) and the Iron Ages (Philistines and Greek mercenaries), it is with the Late Persian period that the main process begins. But what is important is that the carriers of Hellenism at that time were more often than not Phoenicians. In the Hellenistic period this process—be it the use of Greek language, ideas, style or building—accelerated, to reach a peak by the end of the Herodian rule.

Meaningful material evidence, such as the YHD coins and seals, *loculi* tombs, early *unguentaria*, figurines and altars from *favissae* and temples, can clearly betray Greek, Ptolemaic and Hellenized Phoeni-cian origin. Any study of the first coins minted in Judah and Judaea

127. Feldman 1988: 85; cf. now Feldman 1993.

128. Lifshitz 1962b: 247; Fitzmyer 1970: 514; corrected by Obbink 1991: 54 (however, διὰ τὸ [ἀφο]ρμὰς sounds awkward); cf. Rajak 1990: 264, who refers to the 'sealed-off environment' of Qumran; see further the Hellenization of the Hauran (Chapter 10 n. 228), and Millar's observation (1993b: 504) about this area: 'the lan-guage of communal life, as expressed in written form, down to village level, was Greek'.

129. See Kraemer's comments in *P. Ness.* (p. 18).

will conclude that they variously date from the end of the Persian to the beginning of the Hellenistic period (Chapter 1 n. 51). Greek influence is undeniable. The series can simply be described as pagan, or at least syncretistic.[130] Were these coins to date from a later time, when an organized attempt to Hellenize the Jews was made under the Seleucids (instigating the Maccabaean revolt), their meaning would have been evident. Yet this is not the case. The numismatic evidence suggests that in the late Persian period Jewish society was exposed to Hellenic pressure, while in the early Ptolemaic this turned into Hellenistic. Surely it would be logical to assume that at least a circle of Jews (no matter how small and probably amongst the élite) must have approved this type of influence at that time.[131]

The case of the *unguentaria* (descendants of the Greek *lēkythoi*), often used in burials, is also diagnostic. Kahane suggested that they were introduced into Palestine being 'a Hellenistic heritage, most probably of eastern (Alexandrian?) provenience'.[132] Conceivably their initial users would have been Gentiles, and since Ptolemaic Egypt is one of the areas where such *unguentaria* were manufactured, their first appearance in Palestine may be sought in the third century BCE. The earliest known type of *unguentarium*, the fusiform (heavy ware), is found in a score of sites in Idumaea and Judaea: Tell en-Nasbeh, Jericho, Jerusalem, Gezer, Azekah, Bethzur, Marisa, Lachish and Tell Jemmeh. This was dated by Lapp to c. 200–150 BCE, but, as Stern

130.   Unlike pre-exilic Hebraism and later Mishnaic Rabbinism, the rigid ritualistic conceptions of Judaism in the Second Temple period would not have tolerated Greek religious symbols in the form of human and animal representations produced locally (Josephus, *Apion* 2.75; see Urbach 1959; Guttmann 1961; cf. Sanders 1992: 242-47). The owl, the male divinity with Dionysiac emblems, the heads of Pallas Athena, Ptolemy and his wife Berenice I, some unbearded young males, the eagles and the mask, pose a real problem of interpretation. The ornamental design of the ירשלם sealing (350–250 BCE?) displays a five-pointed star ('shield of Solomon'), rarely met within Jewish art but connected with magical beliefs of Pythagorean origin (Garbini 1962: 63); see Tomb 1 at Marisa (Peters and Thiersch 1905: 19, and next to inscription no. 33); but cf. Cook 1930: 213-14; also cf. assumed Pythagoreanism among the Essenes (Josephus, *Ant.* 13.371; Hengel 1974: 1.245; cf. *SVM* 2, 589), with the LXX fragments among the Dead Sea Scrolls (Ulrich 1984).

131.   See Rappaport 1981a: 15.

132.   Kahane 1952: 139; for the history of *unguentaria* after Kahane, see especially Lapp [P.W.] 1961: 21, 197-99; Hellström 1965: 23-27; Drougou and Touratsoglou 1980: 123-29 (with references to Macedonian finds); Khairy 1980; Anderson-Stojanovic 1987.

observed, a small ointment bottle of Late Persian times is 'indistinguishable from the Hellenistic unguentaria', which thus must have existed from 'the third to first centuries B.C.'. The Late Persian bottle is represented by examples from Gil'am, Tell en-Nasbeh and Lachish. According to Stern it originated in the west: 'in Cyprus, Rhodes or Greece'.[133]

Soon after their introduction *unguentaria* began to be produced locally, and gradually they were adopted by the native cultures—even the Maccabees later do not seem to have wished to reject them.[134] By analogy, Ptolemaic Alexandria is also reckoned to be the place from where the *loculi* or *kokhim* tombs with their characteristic art and architecture (best displayed in the necropolis of Marisa) were introduced into Palestine in the Early Hellenistic period, although such cemeteries are also known in 'Asia Minor, Cyprus and Phoenicia'.[135] In fact, this type of burial, which was taken up by the Jews and continued in use as late as the first century CE, is thought to have been 'a convenient solution, for contemporary Jewish laws required the careful separation of individual interments in the tomb'.[136] Naturally fusiform *unguentaria* were found inside the Hellenized Phoenician *loculi* tombs of Marisa.[137]

The two commonest types of cult objects from the Late Persian and Early Hellenistic periods are figurines and incense altars. Figurines are often found in *favissae* ('sacred' refuse pits), either being or supposed to be associated with temples. In the south of the country *favissae* have been recorded at Tell eṣ-Ṣafi, Marisa, Lachish, Tell el-'Areine, Tel Ṣippor, Jamnia, Ascalon, Gaza, and Beersheba. Individual figurines have been found also stratified at Tell Jemmeh and En-Gedi. Altars are known from Azotus, Lachish, Tell esh-Shariah, Beersheba,

133.   Lapp [P.W.] 1961: 197; Stern [E.] 1982: 125, A.3.

134.   Cf. Lapp ([P.W.] 1961: 228): 'the fact that the form of the containers in which the Jews obtained the ungents required for their burials was not Palestinian in origin... should not be understood as any kind of compromise with Hellenism'.

135.   Oren and Rappaport 1984: 150; cf. Goodenough 1953: 65-78; cf. McKenzie (1990; Chapter 1 n. 32) on the architectural origins of the monuments at Petra.

136.   Oren and Rappaport 1984: 150; this type of tomb almost became the canonical form of Jewish family grave (Finegan 1992: 297).

137.   E.g. Oren and Rappaport 1984: 119 (Tomb 1, grave goods no. 8); cf. Bliss and Macalister 1902: pl. 60.6-11.

Tell el-Far'ah (south) and Tell Jemmeh.[138] Existing stone temples have been excavated at Lachish and Beersheba, while historical sources postulate the existence of others, including at Gezer, Azotus, Ascalon and Gaza.[139]

The examination of the figurines and altars throws light on popular cults, allowing us to identify contemporary trends.[140] These cults have many Helleno-Semitic affinities and their distribution seems to be confined to the largely non-Jewish areas. Obviously the followers of Judaism in their rites could not have utilized objects directly opposing their religious precepts. In the majority of cases the cult has been linked to the Phoenicians and Arabs.[141] On the evidence of these types of cult objects, a peripheral Hellenization, arriving in southern Palestine primarily through Phoenicia, has to be accepted for both the pre-Ptolemaic and Ptolemaic periods.

138. Stern [E.] 1982: 158-95; for background references cf. the discussion on altars by Forte 1967.

139. For the temple at Lachish, see Aharoni (ed.) 1975, but with wrong interpretation (cf. Stern [E.] 1982: 63; Kuhnen 1990: 58-60); for the temple at Beersheba, see Aharoni 1975b: 163-65; Derfler 1981; Derfler 1993; for the historically attested holy places, see Chapter 3 §1; for a possible Hellenistic temple at Adora, see above n. 66; the Marisan temple would also have been Hellenistic (contra Avi-Yonah 1977b: 788).

140. Due to the strains in post-exilic archaeological chronology, only a broad date is given to the various *favissae* of figurines and altars: Persian to Early Hellenistic. Most of the figurines are made of terracotta, and the commonest representations in Eastern dress are a male god (Ba'al type), a fertility goddess (Astarte type), a pregnant female (Tanit Pane Ba'al) and 'rider deities'. In Western dress appear Apollo, Heracles, Hermes, the 'temple boys' and Dionysiac reclining figures, as well as a standing female goddess (Aphrodite type) and seated goddesses (Demeter/Korē type). The features are Phoenician, Cypriot and Greek, in agreement with the clay used for the largest assemblage from Tel Ṣippor (Negbi 1964). The incense altars are made of limestone and some were found together with figurines, providing the best evidence that they belong to the same cult. As Stern ([E.] 1982: 194) has shown their background is almost certainly Phoenician.

141. Stern [E.] 1982: 158.

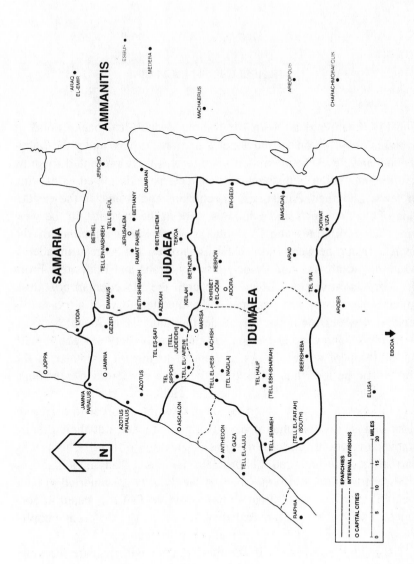

Southern Palestine in the Early Hellenistic Period, c. 332–165 BCE

SAMARIA

AMMANITIS

JUDAEA

IDUMAEA

JOPPA

LYDDA

EMMAUS

GEZER

JAMNIA

AZOTUS

JAMNIA
PARALUS

AZOTUS
PARALUS

ASCALON

ANTHEDON

GAZA

TELL EL-AJJUL

RAPHIA

TEL
SIPPOR

[TELL
JUDEIDEH]

[TELL EL-'AREINI]

TEL ES-SAFI

[TELL EL-HESI]

[TEL NAGILA]

LACHISH

MARISA

TEL HALIF

[TELL ESH-SHARIAH]

[TELL EL-FAR'AH]
(SOUTH)

TELL JEMMEH

BEERSHEBA

ELUSA

EBODA

AROER

TEL 'IRA

ARAD

HORVAT
'UZA

[MASADA]

KHIRBET
EL-QOM

HEBRON

ADORA

BETHZUR

KEILAH

AZEKAH

BETH SHEMESH

TEKOA

BETHLEHEM

RAMAT RAHEL

JERUSALEM

BETHANY

QUMRAN

TELL EL-FÛL

TELL EN-NASHBEH

BETHEL

JERICHO

EN-GEDI

ARAQ
EL-EMIR

ESBUS

MEDEBA

MACHAERUS

AREOPOLIS

CHARACHMOBA/CLIS

N

MILES

0   5   10   15   20

——————— EPARCHIES
- - - - - - INTERNAL DIVISIONS
O CAPITAL CITIES

Chapter 3

LATE HELLENISTIC IDUMAEA

The first chapter dealt with the remote geopolitical background of Idumaea, focusing on the movements of ethnic groups under the Babylonians and the Achaemenids. Evidence was there presented to show that the population in this area was characteristically mixed, consisting of Jews, Edomites, Philistines, Phoenicians and Arabs. In the eastern side of the area Jews and Edomites were in the majority, in the west prevailed Philistines and Phoenicians (both likely remnants of the ancient fusion between old coastal Canaanites and Aegean invaders), while the south was mainly occupied by Arabs and Edomites. From the administrative point of view, up until the Macedonian conquest, Idumaea seems to have remained a disputed territory (or a 'no-man's land' as it were), but apparently under the influence of Judah.

As the second chapter has shown, the same variety of people, with the addition of some Greeks, continued to inhabit Idumaea in the Hellenistic period, thus making the question of Herodian genealogy (the beginnings of which fall into Late Hellenistic times) a complex one to answer, though by no means impossible. To call the Herods 'Idumaeans' (as Josephus does) is simple—to find out their precise ethnic connections in such a multiracial society is difficult. This is why past studies have ignored this problem. Ultimately, any attachment to cities or towns that early members of the dynasty are reported to have had, will prove to be of great value—provided that it is taken in conjunction with the geographical distribution of the different peoples living in Idumaea before the arrival of the Romans (see Map 1).

The evidence presented in the third chapter will indicate (contrary to previous beliefs) that the origins of the Herodian dynasty are to be sought in the western part of Idumaea; and since this was largely occupied by Hellenized Phoenicians, the whole subject now takes a new and unexpected direction.

1. *Idumaea and Maccabaean Judaism*

The troubled Seleucid domination of southern Palestine did not last long (200–165 BCE, and then in marked decline until 143 and even 129 BCE),[1] although it left a most remarkable scar on the history of this period, that is the attempt to Hellenize Jerusalem and the Temple (168–165 BCE). A serious reaction to this attempt was the Maccabaean revolt (167–143 BCE), carried out by Mattathias of Modein and his five sons: John, Simon, Eleazar, Judas and Jonathan.[2]

Seleucid Idumaea was first invaded by Judas Maccabaeus (165–161 BCE) after the reinstatement of the Jewish cult. During his invasion he not only strengthened Jewish positions but also carried out a series of acts of retribution against Hellenized neighbours who had apparently either assisted the Greeks in their desecration of the temple, or had at least welcomed the result.[3] Although the attack on Jamnia, undertaken by Joseph and Azariah against Judas's explicit commands, ended in disaster for the Jews,[4] Judas came back to fight the Idumaeans successfully in, among other places, Hebron, Marisa and Azotus, where 'he pulled down their altars and burned their carved images with fire'.[5]

1.   Bouché-Leclerq 1913–14; *SVM* 1, 125-215; for a basic bibliography see Soggin 1984: 286-308; note Tcherikover 1959; Bickermann 1962; Smith [M.] 1971: 286-308; Efron 1987; *CHJ* 2.

2.   *SVM ibid.*; Bickermann 1937; Mørkholm 1966; Hengel 1974; Millar 1978; Rajak 1990; Kasher 1990: 55-191; Sievers 1990; Rajak 1994; Feldman 1994; for the dating of the occupation of the Temple by the Greeks, see Grabbe 1991.

3.   For Judas see Bar-Kochva 1989. Among those punished by Judas were Edomites who had settled in the region of Acraba or Acrabeta (1 Macc. 5.3; cf. Josephus, *Ant.* 12.328), probably on the eastern boundary of Judaea and Samaria (Avi-Yonah 1977a: 65, 112, 153; cf. Josephus, *War* 2.235). Edomite presence here is known from the Wadi Daliyeh material (Chapter 1 n. 49; cf. Judt. 7.18). One is reminded of the destruction of the Temple by the Babylonians with Edomite help. The old enmity between Jews and Edomites continued in the Hellenistic period as illustrated by the story of Mnaseas of Patara (*apud* Josephus *Apion* 2.112-14; *GLAJJ* 1, 99-101 n. 28); cf. *Sir.* 50.26, detesting 'those that dwell among the Philistines'. Of other locals who paid for their pro-Greek attitude, the Scythopolitans are said to have been 'a thorn in the side of Israel in the days of the Greeks' (*Scholion* to *Meg. Ta'an.*, under 15 and 16 Sivan; cf. below n. 27).

4.   1 Macc. 5.56-61; cf. Josephus, *Ant.* 12.350-52.

5.   1 Macc. 5.65-68; cf. Josephus, *Ant.* 12.353 (for Josephus's apologetics, see Feldman 1994: 65-66); cf. Judt. 8.18 referring to the fact that 'idol worship had disappeared in our generation' (cf. Hecataeus in Chapter 1 n. 46); Jamnia itself was

Azotus and its renowned temple of Dagon later became the object of another attack by Jonathan (161–143 BCE), this time apparently acting on behalf of Alexander Balas, the usurper of the Seleucid throne, in his conflict with Apollonius the governor of Coele-Syria. For his victory Jonathan was even awarded the Idumaean (ex-Ashdodite, ex-Philistine) territory of Akkaron (Ekron).[6]

Gazara (Gezer), a Gentile city in the post-monarchical period and probably part of Ashdod/Idumaea in Hellenistic times,[7] was captured by Simon (143–135 BCE) in his effort to consolidate his independent Jewish state. Before he occupied Gazara, where he built a palace for himself, Simon took care to clean 'the houses wherein the idols were'.[8] Similar procedures could have taken place again at Jamnia, if the city was briefly conquered by this Maccabaean leader, as Josephus believed.[9]

However, the drastic subjugation of Idumaea became a reality only around 127 BCE as part of the expansionist policy and religious

so heavily burned by Judas that the fire could been seen from Jerusalem (2 Macc. 12.9); for Jamnia see Chapter 2 n. 67.

6.   1 Macc. 10.78-89; cf. Josephus, *Ant.* 13.99-102; see *SVM* 1, 181; for the excavations at Tell Miqne (Ekron), see Dothan and Gitin 1982; 1993.

7.   On the basis of YHD seal impressions, Stern ([E.] 1981: 19) argued that in the Persian period Gezer belonged to Judah (but cf. En-Gedi—Chapter 2 n. 41). If this were so, the city would have changed hands in the Hellenistic period, for Simon later to reclaim it. The subsequent history of Gezer is problematic. On circumstantial evidence it is thought that under Hasmonaean rule Emmaus replaced Gezer in importance (cf. *Ant.* 14.275; *War* 1.222), but this does not mean that Gezer became part of Emmaus's toparchy (contra Schwartz [J.] 1990: 54). Only in the Late Roman period it is possible (though again not certain) that Gezer fell within the sphere of Emmaus/Nicopolis (Eusebius, *Onom.* [edn Klostermann 68]); note that Ekron, to the south, was then inclined towards Azotus (Avi-Yonah 1977a: 149-50). In fact Josephus may imply that Gezer belonged to the Jamnian territory. In his list of toparchies (*War* 3.54-5; cf. *Ant.* 18.31; *War* 2.167) he does not mention Gezer, but singles out Jamnia (*War* 3.56) as a city with 'jurisdiction over the surrounding localities' (*War* 3.56); see Chapter 7 n. 58; for the excavations at Gezer, see Dever 1976, 442-43; Dever 1993: 506; Γαδάροις or Γαδώροις under Gabinius (Josephus, *War* 1.170; *Ant.* 14.91) cannot be Gezer, and since it is unlikely to be Gadara (contra Smallwood 1967a), it needs to be read as Ἀδώροις, i.e. the Idumaean Adora (Kanael 1957: 103).

8.   1 Macc. 13.43-48; cf. Josephus, *War* 1.50; Strabo 16.759; note the Gezer inscription (Chapter 2 n. 109), which is supposed to refer to a Pampras who wished to see Simon's palace on fire, but this reading is hardly confirmed by the original photograph (*PEFQS* 1905, 100).

9.   Josephus, *Ant.* 13.215.

purification carried out by John Hyrcanus (135–104 BCE).
1 Maccabees, our primary source for Palestine under the Seleucids,
stops at the beginning of John's rule, but announces a *History of Hyrcanus* which evidently brought the narrative down to the end of the
second century BCE.[10] Although this book must have been lost at an
early age, it is not impossible that stories from it were available to
Josephus.[11] Besides, other written sources known to him (such as, for
example, historians of the Late Hellenistic/Early Roman era who
covered Jewish affairs and are known to us only from fragments)
would have referred to the actions of John, particularly the conversion to Judaism which he forced upon the Idumaeans (see below).[12]
Likely candidates are Posidonius of Apamea,[13] Apollonius Molon,[14]
Timagenes of Alexandria (who is reported to have given an account
of the forced conversion of the Ituraeans by Judas Aristobulus I in
104 BCE),[15] Alexander Polyhistor (who based his work on various
Hellenistic Jewish authors),[16] Teucer of Cyzicus,[17] Hypsicrates (who

10.   1 Macc. 16.24.

11.   According to *SVM* (1, 20; 3.1, 185-86) Josephus did not know the *History
of Hyrcanus* which had already been lost in his time. However, the possibility that he
was acquainted with stories from it cannot be excluded (cf. Thoma 1994: 131). It
seems that such stories were utilized by the author of the historical work *Megillath
Ta'anith*, composed in Aramaic more or less when Josephus wrote (Zeitlin 1919–20:
256-58).

12.   This event would have been remembered especially in Egypt, where many
Idumaeans (Greek-Phoenicians and Edomites) seem to have fled to avoid the
Maccabaean oppression. There is clear evidence for their presence here in the second
century BCE (Launey 1949–50: 556-59; Rappaport 1969; Thompson [D.J.] 1984;
Thompson [D.J.] 1988: 99-105); cf. Theodoros from Marisa in Athens (*IG*
2^2.9285), and the 'Gate of the Idumaeans' in Rome (Juvenal, *Sat.* 8.158-62; *GLAJJ*
2, 102).

13.   *GLAJJ* 1, 141-47; cf. *SVM* 1, 20-22.

14.   *GLAJJ* 1, 148-56; cf. *SVM* 3.1, 598-600.

15.   *Apud* Strabo *apud* Josephus, *Ant.* 13.319 (contra Kasher 1988: 79-85); see
GLAJJ 1, 222-26; cf. *SVM* 1, 22-23.

16.   *GLAJJ* 1, 157-64; *GLAJJ* 3, 16-22; cf. Strugnell 1985; *SVM* 3.1, 510-12;
Alexander's 'Jewish' sources included Demetrius, Eupolemus (possibly of Phoenician origins), Artapanus, Cleodemus-Malchus (possibly of Punic origins), Aristeas
the Exegete, Philo the Epic Poet and Ezekiel the Tragedian, but these seem to have
given accounts of earlier biblical periods (see *FHJA*; *SVM* 3.1, 513-28, 559-61,
563-66; *OTP* 2, 781-84, 803-19, 843-72, 883-903).

17.   *GLAJJ* 1, 165-66; cf. *SVM* 1, 40.

mentioned the expedition of Antipater, Herod's father, to Egypt),[18] Pompeius Trogus (whom we know referred to John Hyrcanus),[19] Strabo of Amaseia in his *Historika Hypomnēmata* (with references to Jewish affairs as known from Josephus), and Nicolaus of Damascus (also referring to Hyrcanus).[20]

Josephus describes the events in the land of Idumaea at the last quarter of the second century BCE, which are our main concern here:

> Hyrcanus also captured the Idumaean cities of Adora and Marisa, and after subduing all the Idumaeans, permitted them to remain in their country so long as they had themselves circumcised and were willing to observe the laws of the Jews. And so, out of attachment to the land of their fathers, they submitted to circumcision and to making their manner of life conform in all other respects to that of the Jews. And from that time on they have continued to be Jews.[21]

A version of the same story was already known to one Ptolemy, most probably the grammarian of Ascalon who seems to have lived at the end of the first century BCE, and who wrote a biography of Herod the Great:

> Jews and Idumaeans differ... Jews are those who are so by origin and nature. The Idumaeans, on the other hand, were not originally Jews, but Phoenicians and Syrians; having been subjugated by the Jews and having

18.   *Apud* Strabo *apud* Josephus, *Ant.* 14.139; see *GLAJJ* 1, 220-21; cf. *SVM* 1, 24. Hypsicrates may have been of Hellenized Phoenician origins, as perhaps his predecessors Theodotus (see Chapter 2 n. 50) and Mochus (see Hengel 1974: 2.58 n. 219). All three are mentioned by Tatian (*Orat. ad Graec.* 37; cf. Clement, *Strom.* 1.21.114; Eusebius, *Praep. Evang.* 10.11.10;), as having been translated by Laitus, who thus should post-date them (cf. *GLAJJ* 1, 128-30; Geiger 1990, 149). Another Hellenized Phoenician writer may have been Theophilus (*GLAJJ* 1, 126-27; cf. *SVM* 3.1, 556-57), but he probably wrote earlier than 125 BCE; also earlier would have been writers of Phoenician histories such as Menander of Ephesus, Dius, Philostratus, Hieronymus the Egyptian and Hestiaeus (*GLAJJ* 1, 119-25; Josephus, *Ant.* 1.94, 107; *Apion* 1.144).

19.   Pompeius Trogus, *Hist. Philip.*, Prol. 36; cf. Diodorus, 34–35.1; Plutarch, *Reg. et Imp. Apoph.* 184F; see *GLAJJ* 1, 332-43; cf. *SVM* 1, 68.

20.   Nicolaus, *apud* Josephus, *Ant.* 13.251; see *GLAJJ* 1, 227-60; cf. *SVM* 1, 28-32; Toher 1987. For writers such as Conon, Zopyrion, Hermogenes and a few others (Josephus, *Apion* 1.216) nothing is known, and we cannot speculate whether their works had included events in late second century BCE southern Palestine (*GLAJJ* 1, 350-51, 450-54; cf. Wacholder 1962, appendix).

21.   Josephus, *Ant.* 13.257; cf. Josephus, *War* 1.63; *Ant.* 14.88; 15.254-55; also cf. Josippon 10.71; 29.9-11; 59. 2-3; for the date see Smith [M.] 1978: 5-6.

been forced to undergo circumcision, so as to be counted among the Jewish nation and keep the same customs, they were called Jews.[22]

The testimonies of Ptolemy and Josephus have not been fully comprehended, and recently were even discounted *a priori* by Kasher.[23] One of the problems with Kasher is that he takes the 'Idumaeans' mentioned as having been 'Edomites', and thus finds it hard to believe that the latter were uncircumcised. But the reference is to the inhabitants of Hellenistic Idumaea, who, as we saw, were a highly mixed population. In fact in the wealthy western part (where Hyrcanus's attacks were largely concentrated) Edomites were in the minority, and it makes sense therefore that Hellenized Phoenicians (the main population here—note Ptolemy's 'Phoenicians and Syrians') who decided to stay, were compelled to be circumcised. That the Phoenicians under Greek influence had abandoned the habit of circumcision is already made clear by Herodotus.[24]

Kasher's resort to post-Talmudic information in his effort to show that forced conversion was in conflict with Jewish law cannot be taken seriously—apart from the fact that the evidence in question is very late (earlier sources are conspicuously silent about it), the circumstances in the Maccabaean period were surely exceptional.[25] Smith

22.   Ptolemy, *apud De Adfinium Vocabulorum Differentia* (s.v. *Ioudaioi*); this work, attributed to Ammonius (or to Herennius Philo of Byblus), is dated to the end of the first century CE (*SVM* 1, 27-8). Stern (*GLAJJ* 1, 355-56) accepts that Ptolemy would have discussed the difference between Jews and Idumaeans in connection with Herod's origin, but he doubts whether Josephus knew him. Yet, the characterization of Herod as ἡμιιουδαῖος by Josephus, accords well with what Ptolemy says and, even though this may have been common knowledge, it could not have been found in the writings of Nicolaus of Damascus who favoured Herod (see below Section 3). Further, our Ptolemy could not have been the brother of Nicolaus, because he evidently gave an unprejudiced account of Herod's descent. The abusive language of Antigonus from the walls of Jerusalem perfectly parallels the historical reactions of people in moments of an extended siege—for example, Athens in 87/86 BCE, Perusia in 41 BCE, etc. (see Kajava 1990: 59-60); cf. below n. 41.

23.   Kasher 1988: 44-78.

24.   Herodotus, 2.104; cf. Josephus, *Ant.* 8.262; *Apion* 1.171.

25.   Kasher 1988: 50, citing *Masekhet Gerim* 7; Kasher thinks that Josephus in *Life* 112-13 gives the impression that Jewish society deplored any forced conversions. On the contrary, in this episode the historian relates how he needed to argue against such an act until he 'brought over the people to my (his) way of thinking'. Besides, at the time he wrote in Rome (after the fall of Jerusalem), the last thing he would have wanted to stress was that he agreed with compulsory conversions

claimed that Hyrcanus's policy was an imitation of the Roman success
in forcibly extending citizenship,[26] but there is no evidence of such
forcible imposition on individuals by the Romans—Hyrcanus's policy
was simply a reaction to the conversion to Greek religion (and
abolition of circumcision) which his fathers had suffered at the hands
of Antiochus IV Epiphanes a few decades earlier. Kasher's denial of
Maccabaean campaigns involving compulsory conversions is totally
unrealistic. To build a case on a superficial statement of Strabo (see
explanation in Chapter 1 n. 34) and concurrently ignore Ptolemy and
Josephus is unacceptable. Archaeology, too, would support our
sources, since the pagan temples so far excavated (that is at Lachish,
Beersheba, and perhaps Marisa) were violently destroyed at about this
time.[27]

Of course submitting by force to Judaism was one thing, accepting
it wholeheartedly was another. It would have taken several generations for Idumaea to be fully assimilated, and if this ever happened it
would not have been before the mid-first century CE. Idumaeans (with
the circumcised Edomite element in the front line) felt themselves to

(cf. Smith [J.Z.] 1980). But the fact that he could not reject them as having occurred
in the past (for example, under Hyrcanus), demonstrates their historical significance
(cf. Rosenbloom 1978: 94-96; Cohen [S.J.D.] 1990: 211-16). It is no wonder the
History of Hyrcanus did not survive!

26.   Smith [M.] 1978: 5-6; cf. Goodman 1992: 64.

27.   See Chapter 2 n. 139; cf. Hyrcanus's destructions at Shechem and Mount
Gerizim (Josephus, *Ant.* 13.255-6; *War* 1.63; cf. *Meg. Ta'an.* under 21 Kislev; see
Schwartz [S.] 1993), as well as Samaria (Josephus, *Ant.* 13.281; *War* 1.64; cf.
Meg. Ta'an. under 25 Heshvan) and Scythopolis (Josephus, *Ant.* 13.280; *War.*
1.66; cf. *Meg. Ta'an.* under 15 and 16 Sivan); cf. further the destruction of sacred
places in Idumaea by Judas and Simon, and later the forced circumcision of the Ituraeans by Judas Aristobulus I (above n. 15), and of the children found uncircumcised
in Judaea (1 Macc. 2.46); and finally, Theodotus's poem in which he chose to
include the biblical story of the compulsory circumcision of Shechemites in Jacob's
time, betraying the date of its composition to be around the time of John Hyrcanus
(see Chapter 2 n. 50); cf. above n. 5. Schwartz's question ([S.] 1991: 18-19) of
whether the Hasmonaeans had an adequate military force to conquer such extended
territory should not have arisen. With armies, it has always been a matter of discip-
line, mobility and speed—not numbers. We only need to remember that the nucleus
of the army of Alexander the Great, which conquered the entire Near East, numbered
15,000 Macedonians, and appropriately the Bible gives us a feasible picture of the
tactics required by a relatively small Israelite force of invaders to capture well-
defended Canaanite cities (Malamat 1982).

be Jews (and they were probably seen as such) only at the end of the Second Temple period.[28] While their loyalty at that time may not be questioned,[29] this was not the case earlier. Josephus, referring to their past record (but obviously irritated by current events, since the Idumaeans sided with the Zealots during the revolt he describes), says of them:

> ...they were turbulent and disorderly people, ever on the alert for commotion and delighting in revolutionary changes, and only needed a little flattery from their suitors to seize their arms and rush into battle as to a feast.[30]

The first real defection that comes to our attention is the one which took place around c. 38 BCE at the end of the rule of Antigonus, the last of the Hasmonaeans.[31] Under Herod the Great a major revolt with the view of returning to the old Hellenistic order (with the help of Cleopatra VII of Egypt), was attempted by Costobarus, who openly opposed Judaism.[32] As his name betrays, and as is noted by Josephus, the Idumaean cult of Qos was never forgotten.[33] Even after the death of Herod in 4 (or 5) BCE we hear of an uprising of his veterans settled in Idumaea, which spread among the local population, apparently in

28.   Josephus, *War* 4.243, 265, 273, 275-76, 278-79, 281, 311; at least up to the end of the Maccabaean period they could still be termed ἡμιιουδαῖοι, or 'half-Jews' (Josephus, *Ant.* 14.403); cf. above n. 22.

29.   E.g. Josephus, *War* 2.43; 4.234; 7.267; cf. Mk 3.8, the only reference to Idumaea in the New Testament.

30.   Josephus, *War* 4.231; the Idumaeans were known as fighters—Herod the Great settled 3,000 in Trachonitis to restrain brigandage there (see Chapter 10 n. 224).

31.   *War* 1.326 (cf. *Ant.* 14.450 with a wrong reading). It seems that this uprising at the time of the Roman officer Machaeras was directed against Herod (cf. *War* 1.303), but not necessarily in order to embrace Antigonus's cause (certainly not by the majority of Idumaeans). As later uprisings show, Idumaea had always hoped for independence.

32.   Josephus, *Ant.* 15.253-58; see Chapter 7 §1.

33.   Cf. above n. 12, and the worshippers of Qos living in Nabataea until the Roman period (Chapter 1 n. 33 end; Flusser 1976: 1074-75); for a reassessment of the cult of Qos, see now Dearman 1995: 123-27. A small altar with 'Qos' on its base (reference in Ronen 1988: 215 n. 6) was discovered at Ramat el-Khalil (Mamre), north of Hebron, where the paganized (largely Edomite/Phoenician) Terebinthus stood (Sozomen, *Hist. Eccl.* 2.4), which at one stage was enclosed by a massive wall of Herodian workmanship (cf. Applebaum 1977: 777; Magen 1993b; and now Taylor [J.E.] 1993: 86-95).

the hope of breaking from Jewish rule. It should not be surprising to learn that the instigators of the trouble, whom Augustus punished, were in fact of 'royal blood'—lesser members of the Herodian family either positioned in or having great influence upon Idumaea (see Chapter 5 nn. 20-21).

2. Herodian Beginnings

Although Josephus does not say so, we may logically assume that when faced with Hyrcanus's ultimatum many Hellenized Phoenicians (and other non-Jews) living in Western Idumaea took the decision to flee the country. An exodus of natives shortly after 127 BCE, and mainly toward Egypt, may be expected (see above n. 12). Nevertheless, out of necessity and in fear of losing their belongings, the majority of the population (particularly the wealthy) had to conform to the new *status quo* imposed by Jerusalem. Long established families, besides those of mixed marriages (e.g. Phoenician/Edomite or Arab/Phoenician), accepted Judaism if this was the price for being allowed to continue their business locally.

Under Alexander Jannaeus (103–76 BCE) the Maccabaean kingdom reached its peak. Among his conquests in neighbouring districts, the capture of the important city of Gaza needs to be pointed out, for it was an act which would have affected relations with tribal Arabs and especially the Nabataeans.[34] Nevertheless, apart from expansion Alexander's policy was the strengthening of occupied territories. His rule over Idumaea, now converted to Judaism, achieved consolidation in this period,[35] not only by the building of fortresses,[36] but also by the appointment of an appropriate *stratēgos*. To reduce the danger of insurrection Alexander entrusted the province to an Idumaean of Hellenized stock (as his name implies), Antipas. This is the earliest member of the Herodian family referred to by Josephus:

34.   Josephus, *Ant.* 13.358-64; cf. *War* 1.87; see *SVM* 2, 101; Kasher 1982: 70-73; Glucker 1987: 4.

35.   Josephus, *Ant.* 13.395-96; Stern [M.] 1981; Meshorer's initial suggestion (1981) that Jannaeus was the first Maccabaean ruler to strike coins, has now been abandoned by him (1990–91: 106); cf. Sievers 1990: 152-54.

36.   E.g. En-Gedi (Tel Goren II)—Mazar [B.] *et al.* 1966: 46; and probably Masada (many coins of Jannaeus)—Yadin 1966: 205; see Meshorer 1989b: 86-87 nn. 19-102.

... King Alexander and his wife appointed (him) governor of the whole of
Idumaea (i.e. of all its divisions), and they say that he made friends of the
neighbouring Arabs and Gazaeans and Ascalonites, and completely won
them over by many gifts.[37]

Apparently as a result of his masterly diplomacy, cultural background
and wealth (see below), Antipas was able to handle the multiracial
society of southern Palestine better than any Jew could, notably the
rough soldier Jannaeus, who lacked all adroitness in his conduct.[38] No
doubt Antipas's centre will have been established in the capital city
Marisa (see Chapter 2 §2), and it will have been here that his sons
Antipater, Phallion and Joseph I were raised.

Near the end of Alexander's rule, when a relative degree of peace
(in which Antipas must have played a significant role, certainly along
the Jewish-Arab-Phoenician frontiers) was effectuated, the governor
of Idumaea arranged the marriage of his, apparently first, son Antipater with a most 'noble' Arabian lady, Cyprus.[39] This was the best
alliance possible to contrive at that time, since a new king (c. 84 BCE)
had ascended the throne of Nabataea. Aretas III, to whose family
Cyprus may have been connected, was a philo-Hellenic figure (as
shown by his coins) and thus their agreement would have been easier
to reach.[40]

37. Josephus, *Ant.* 14.10.
38. E.g. Josephus, *Ant.* 13.372-73; *War* 1.88-89; cf. *m. Suk.* 4.9.
39. Cyprus had a Greek name (Ilan 1989: 194 n. 30). For Aretas to count
seriously on this 'matrimonial alliance' (Josephus, *War* 1.181), and later to take the
young woman with her children into his care (*Ant.* 14.122), may suggest that her
'distinguished Arab family' (*Ant.* 14.121) was no other than the royal Nabataean—
though Josephus is not explicit (cf. later the marriage of Herod's son Antipas to a
daughter of Aretas IV—Chapter 8 §2). The date of Cyprus's marriage (c. 80 BCE?) is
deduced from the fact that her first son, Phasael, was born not later than 77 BCE (see
Chapter 6 §1). We do not know whether she was the first (or only) wife of
Antipater.
40. For his coins from Damascus, which call him ΦΙΛΕΛΛΗΝ, see Meshorer
1975: 12-16; and cf. Schmitt-Korte 1990: 107, 125, who makes Aretas III the first
Nabataean king to mint coins. Aretas III reigned from c. 84 to 60 BCE, even if he is
attested for the last time in Josephus in 62 BCE (cf. *BMCRR* 1, 483-84). The date on
the Nabataean inscription from Tell esh-Shuqafiya was initially wrongly read as
'Year 14' of Cleopatra (39/38 BCE), which was also wrongly thought to equal 37/36
BCE (Jones *et al.* 1988). The new reading, 'Year 18' (Fiema and Jones 1990), translates into 35/34 BCE, which means that Malichus I's reign (his 26th year, also
referred to in this text) began in 60/59. Malichus must have succeeded Aretas III.

During the reign of Alexandra (76–67 BCE) Antipater seems to have succeeded his father in the position of Idumaean *stratēgos* at Marisa.[41] By that time his wife Cyprus had given birth to at least three of his sons: Phasael, Herod and Joseph II. Thus Marisa would need to be regarded as Herod the Great's 'home town' (see below).[42] Like his

That an 'Obodas II' existed between these two kings (*SVM* 1, 580; Meshorer 1975: 16-20; and cf. Wenning 1994: 33; Schmitt-Korte and Price 1994: 96-97, 117!) is highly unlikely.

41.   The time of his appointment is deduced from the fact that his father Antipas is referred to under Jannaeus and Alexandra, but not later, in conjunction with the remark that Antipater was already 'an *old* and bitterly hated foe' of Aristobulus II in c. 65 BCE (Josephus, *War* 1.123). He is variously described in Josephus as 'an Idumaean' who had 'a large fortune' and 'by nature a man of action and a trouble-maker' (*Ant.* 14.8); 'an Idumaean by race, his ancestry, wealth and other advantages put him in the front rank of his nation' (Josephus, *War* 1.123; cf. *b. B. Qam.* 82b 'an old man who had some knowledge in Grecian Wisdom'; cf. Wasserstein 1995, 120-21; contra Wiesenberg 1956, 230-31); 'held in the greatest esteem by the Idumaeans' (*Ant.* 14.121); 'a man of good sense' (*Ant.* 14.101); 'a man of great energy in the conduct of affairs' (*War* 1.226); 'from a house of common people and from a private family' (*Ant.* 14.491; cf. *Ant.* 14.78, 489; *b. B. Bat.* 4a 'you are neither a רכה (= *rex*) nor the son of a רכה). Moreover, Antipater is assessed by Josephus as 'a man distinguished for piety, justice and devotion to his country' (*Ant.* 14.283); a man with 'valour', in the words of Nicolaus (*Ant.* 16.52); but in the words of the last Hasmonaean king, Antigonus, also as 'governing the people by violence', acting 'lawlessly' (*Ant.* 14.140), and in his 'insolence, repeatedly do[ing] outrage to the nation' (*War* 1.196; cf. Herod's character in *War* 2.84-85; *Ant.* 17.191, 304-305; 19.329). Herod, Antipater's son, was seen as a 'low-born upstart' (*War* 1.313; cf. *Pss. Sol.* 17.7 'a man alien to our race'; see Laperrousaz 1989; also cf. *T. Mos.* 6.2 'a wanton king, who will not be of a priestly family'), and so too his sister Salome and her daughters (*War* 1.477-78; cf. below n. 64 on Agrippa I), and further as 'reigning over a kingdom in which he was an alien' (*War* 1.521), and 'a commoner and an Idumaean, that is a half-Jew' (*Ant.* 14.403). The last remark may not be totally justified, because despite the fact that Herod practised Judaism only in diplomacy, he was a 'third generation' convert to Judaism, and thus (halakhically speaking) potentially a full-Jew (Deut. 23.9), though we cannot be sure given that his mother was Nabataean (cf. Baumgarten [J.M.] 1983; Kasher 1988: 126-27). On allusions to Antipater in the *Pss. Sol.* 4, 11 and 13, see Aberbach (1950–51); on his Roman citizenship, see Gilboa 1972; note Kanael (1952), who thought that Antipater's monogram (A) appears on coins of Hyrcanus II (cf. Meshorer 1974; Meshorer 1981), but these coins are now attributed to Hyrcanus I (Barag and Qedar 1980; Meshorer 1990–91: 106), and the (A) may indicate the minting place, i.e. Ascalon (see below §5).

42.   Cf. Schalit 1962: 109-10; Schalit 1969: 257 n. 382; Oren 1968: 59; Hengel

father, Antipater cultivated wide friendships with princes of the neighbouring lands, including rulers in Syria and even the Jews guarding the entrances to Egypt.[43] But his greatest influence was upon the Nabataean Aretas III, as demonstrated by his persuasion of the latter to join the Idumaean forces and march against Aristobulus II, as well as by his being persuaded to agree to Scaurus's terms.[44] On the Roman authorities later, Antipater had considerable effect: Pompey, Scaurus, Gabinius, Cassius, Antony, and above all Julius Caesar, held him in high regard.[45]

Antipater befriended Alexandra's older son Hyrcanus II (then the high priest), and strongly disapproved of the actions of her younger son Aristobulus II. The new governor soon became instrumental in leading the royal brothers to war (c. 65 BCE), when the younger took over the throne by force after the death of Alexandra.[46] While the war was raging Antipater's wife and children were protected in the Nabataean court at Petra.[47] It was only in 63 BCE, after the conquest by Pompey, and after his brother Phallion had fallen in battle,[48] that Antipater moved to Jerusalem and established there the first Herodian 'court'. He further instituted his own special forces, referred to in Josephus as ἐπίλεκτοι or ἑταιρικόν.[49] From this point his power rose steadily to surpass later even that of Hyrcanus: he 'was courted by the nation as if he were king and universally honoured as lord of the

1974: 1.62; 2.45 n. 34; also cf. later discussion on Costobarus and the sons of Baba and Marisa (Chapter 7 §1).

43. Josephus, *Ant.* 14.121; *War* 1.181; for the Arab and Syrian rulers, see *Ant.* 14.128-29; cf. *War* 1.187; for the Jews above Pelusium, see *Ant.* 14.131; cf. *War* 1.175; *Ant.* 14.99; further cf. *Apion* 2.64 referring to the Jews as river guards.

44. Josephus, *Ant.* 14.14-16 and *War* 1.124-25; *Ant.* 14.32-33 and *War* 1.127; Josephus says that this was done because Aretas felt Antipater to be a very good φίλος (*Ant.* 14.17; cf. *War* 1. 124-25), or ὄντα συνήθη (*War* 1.159), or due to the ὑπάρχουσα ξενία (*Ant.* 14.81).

45. Josephus, *Ant.* 14.81 and *War* 1.159; *Ant.* 14.103; *Ant.* 14.120 and *War* 1.180; *Ant.* 14.326, 381, 383 and *War* 1.244, 282; *Ant.* 14. 143 and *War* 1.199; *Ant.* 14.137, 16.53 and *War* 1.194; cf. below n. 50.

46. Josephus, *Ant.* 14.19-21; *War* 1.126; on the identity of Alexandra, see Ilan 1993; on Hyrcanus II, see Schwartz [D.R.] 1994.

47. Josephus, *Ant.* 14.122—Herod being seven years old; for the Nabataean court in general, see Parker [S.T.] 1986 (chapter 5); cf. Appendix 4.

48. Josephus, *War* 1.130; for Phallion see Chapter 5 §1.

49. Josephus, *Ant.* 14.84; *War* 1.162.

realm'.[50] The fears on the part of Aristobulus, that he would snatch the throne from under the feet of the weak Hyrcanus, almost came true. Antipater's royal manner of dress, with purple robes, metal ornaments and other finery (which in the past had greatly irritated Aristobulus) could at least now be rendered more acceptable.[51]

Under Malichus I (60/59–30 BCE) relationships changed drastically, apparently because of the Nabataean's hostile response to Hellenic ideas, in conjunction with Antipater's growing philo-Roman attitude. The latter did not prevent Gabinius from marching against Malichus in c. 56/55 BCE (at a time when he was *epimelētēs* in Jerusalem and capable of influencing the Roman governor).[52] None the less it seems that he still managed to persuade the king of Petra to send troops in aid of Caesar to Egypt in 48 BCE, as he did with other Arab and Syrian rulers.[53] For his extraordinary performance and bravery, apart from being made *epitropos* of Judaea by Caesar in 47 BCE, Antipater achieved a grant of the Roman citizenship, exemption from taxation and other honours and marks of friendship. He clearly became 'an enviable man'.[54] All these privileges were evidently also

50.   Josephus, *War* 1.207. Kanael (1957) argued that it was only in 55 BCE that Antipater became an important political figure. If so, he would not have established his 'court' at Jerusalem before the mid-50s, and presumably he would have remained in Idumaea. But Josephus (*Ant.* 14.80) strongly implies that Herod's father was already based in Judaea, since it was from there that he supplied Scaurus with grain in 62 BCE. Also Strabo (16.2.46) has Pompey appointing him (even though Strabo is confused in calling him Herod).

51.   Josephus, *Ant.* 14.44-45; cf. Samaias's irritation at Herod's manner of dress (*Ant.* 14.173); when older Herod also dyed his hair (*War* 1.490); further cf. later Agrippa I's extravagant appearance (*Ant.* 19.344), as well as that of Agrippa II and Berenice II (Acts 25.23).

52.   Antipater was left in Jerusalem 'to do what he pleases' (Josephus, *Ant.* 14.103; cf. *War* 1.178). His position now was that of a 'financial' procurator (*Ant.* 14.127; cf. 139) as opposed to the 'political' governor he became later (*Ant.* 14.143; *War* 1.199).

53.   *Bellum Alexandrinum* 1; cf. Josephus, *Ant.* 14.28; *War* 1.187; the enmity later of Malichus towards Herod can thus be understood (*Ant.* 14.370-72; *War* 1.269).

54.   Josephus, *War* 1.194; *Ant.* 14.137; 16.53-54; for the citizenship see above n. 41 end. The nature of many privileges granted to Antipater and his children may be inferred from the various awards received by Hyrcanus and his sons, as known from the Roman decrees reproduced in Josephus (*Ant.* 14.190ff.). In one case this can be confirmed. The Senate was obliged to give an answer 'within ten days at the

3. *Late Hellenistic Idumaea*

extended to Herod and strongly shaped the destiny of his remarkable dynasty.

What exactly happened to Idumaea in the war between the Hasmonaean brothers is not clear. The large cities (Marisa, Adora, Jamnia, Azotus and the mysterious Arethusa—see Chapter 2 §2-3) seem to have been destroyed in the retaliations launched by Aristobulus, if Gabinius had to rebuild them (c. 55 BCE) after Pompey had them returned to their original inhabitants.[55] Josephus says that these cities were incorporated by Pompey in the province of Syria, but if so then Idumaea would have been restored to Herodian control either by Gabinius during his reforms of Palestine, or by Cassius in 52 BCE, or later by Caesar in 47 BCE.[56] One question remains: why do we not hear Antipater appointing one of his sons to the post of *stratēgos* there? By contrast he is known to have named Phasael governor of Jerusalem and its district, and Herod of Galilee.[57] The answer to this may be that the Idumaean position was already occupied by a member of his family, such as his brother Joseph I (see Chapter 5 §2 and below n. 59), and thus not a current appointment for Josephus to

latest' to any request by a member of Hyrcanus's (read Antipater's) family (*Ant.* 14.210). Indeed when Herod made his request in 40 BCE, he was given an answer within 'only seven days' (*Ant.* 14.387). For Herod's Roman citizenship, see now Jacobson 1993–94.

55. Josephus, *Ant.* 14.88 has Gabinius rebuilding these cities, 'which had long been desolate'—as if from the time before Pompey. The fortress of Masada (cf. above n. 36) is said to have been destroyed in the war between Gabinius and Aristobulus (*War* 7.171), presumably in c. 63 BCE (*War* 1.140; cf. *Ant.* 14.37), though it may equally be the second defeat of Aristobulus in c. 56 BCE (*Ant.* 14.92-97; *War* 1.171-74). The latter placement would be more in accordance with the decision of Gabinius around this time to demolish some key desert fortresses, including Machaerus, Hyrcania and Alexandreion (*War* 1.168); for the fortresses, see Tsafrir 1982; Netzer 1993.

56. On Gabinius's reforms see Kanael 1957; cf. Smallwood 1967a; on Cassius see *War* 1.180; *Ant.* 14.120-21; on Caesar see *Ant.* 14.205, 207. In 39 BCE, a year after Herod became king of Judaea, M. Antonius presented him with additional territories, including Idumaea (Appian, *Bell. Civ.* 5.75; cf. Chapter 10 n. 151), which Herod thus must have reclaimed; note that since for these areas Herod had to pay taxes according to Appian, it is unlikely that Judaea went tax-free (*GLAJJ* 2, 189-90; contra Momigliano 1934a: 349), though later (perhaps after 30 BCE), these taxes would have been dropped (*SVM* 1, 413-20; Gabba 1990: 164; Kokkinos forthcoming 2).

57. Josephus, *War* 1.203; *Ant.* 14.158.

record, had he known about it. Anyway Antipater's third son, Joseph II, was conceivably too young for a command (see Chapter 6 §2).

During this clouded period between Pompey's and Herod the Great's conquests of Jerusalem, real contact with Idumaean affairs is lost to us. Nevertheless, something may be pieced together by following the adventures of Herod before he became a king. After the murder of Antipater in 43 BCE and the return of Antigonus with the help of the Parthians in 41/40 BCE, Herod was forced to flee from Judaea. He terminated all of the family's business there, tranferred the most valuable possessions to a secret location in the south,[58] and, since he was not welcomed in Petra, moved the entire Herodian court (relatives, functionaries and slaves) to Masada.[59] When the Parthians invaded Jerusalem and found no treasures, all enquiries seem to have led them to one place in Idumaea: *Marisa*. The city was immediately and entirely devastated, another indication of its having being connected to Herod.[60] But Herod was clever enough to avoid the old Herodian centre (possibly the then headquarters of Joseph I), and the Parthians left empty-handed without accomplishing their goal. When Herod later returned as king from Rome, the Idumaeans were united in following in his final assault against the Hasmonaean Antigonus in 37 BCE.[61]

3. *The Question of Origins*

Where did Antipas, the father of Antipater and grandfather of Herod, come from? Is there any way of looking further back into history to

---

58. Josephus, *War* 1.268; *Ant.* 14.364; it is unlikely that Herod would have hidden his valuables in the obvious Marisa or in Masada, or even the small Idumaean fortress called Rhēsa (see Chapter 6 n. 37), the only places mentioned by Josephus in his account of Herod's flight; it would have made more sense to transfer them further away to Ascalon, the progenitor Herodian base (see below §3), which lay in a Greek environment and had strong walls to protect it; subsequently this city may have served as the administrative centre for Idumaea, since Marisa was never rebuilt after its destruction in 40 BCE (Chapter 2 n. 41; see below n. 102).

59. Josephus, *War* 1.264; *Ant.* 14.358; Herod's brother, Joseph II, plays a crucial role in Idumaea at this juncture (see Chapter 6 §2), and one wonders whether there is confusion in Josephus here between this young man and Herod's uncle Joseph I, who might at that time have been the local *stratēgos* as conjectured above.

60. Josephus, *War* 1.269; *Ant.* 14.364.

61. Josephus, *War* 1.293-94; *Ant.* 14.398, 411.

determine the real origins of this family? Apart from the comparatively vague account of Josephus pointing to 'Idumaea', there were
two other conflicting accounts available in antiquity, which will now
be investigated. The first evidently emanated from Nicolaus of Damascus, the court historian of Herod, but from the beginning it was
rejected by Josephus himself:

> Nicolaus of Damascus, to be sure, says that his (Antipater's) family
> belonged to the leading Jews who came to Judaea from Babylon. But he
> says this in order to please Antipater's son Herod, who became king of
> the Jews by a certain turn of fortune... [62]

Elsewhere Josephus made a special effort to explain the main purpose
of Nicolaus's work:

> ...he wrote...to be of service to him (Herod), dwelling only on those
> things that redounded to his glory, and transforming his obviously unjust
> acts into the opposite or concealing them with the greatest care... through-
> out his work he has been consistent in excessively praising the king for
> his just acts, and zealously apologizing for his unlawful ones. But, as I
> said, one may fully forgive him since what he produced was not a history
> for others but a work meant to help the king.[63]

62.   *Ant.* 14.9; cf. Yosippon 37 [edn Hominer 129]; contra Wacholder's (1989:
164) partial defense of Nicolaus. The case of Nicolaus is naive to discuss. It is
obvious that Jewish ancestors had to be sought far away from Judaea, precisely
because it was impossible for Herod to claim local Jewish roots. For the same
reason, and very unlike the Hasmonaeans, Herod never dared to claim the priesthood. In the conflict between the Jews and the Hellenized Phoenicians (called Σύροι
in *Ant.* 20.173 and Ἕλληνες in *War* 2.267) of Caesarea-on-the-coast ('in Phoenicia'
according to *Ant.* 15.333) in the late 50s CE, the first are said to have claimed
precedence because Herod, the founder of the city, γεγονέναι τὸ γένος Ἰουδαῖος.
However, this can only mean that they were pointing to the fact that he had been a
converted Jew (contra Zeitlin 1963: 7; cf. Cohen [S.J.D.] 1994). If there was a side
that could claim a 'racial' connection with the founder of the city, it would surely
have been the Hellenized Phoenician; cf. later the case of Agrippa I in Alexandria
(Chapter 10 n. 96); for the Greek and Roman sources referring to the Herods, see
Conclusion.
63.   Josephus, *Ant.* 16.184-86. Wacholder (1962: 79) believes that in some
cases Josephus himself is no less apologetic of Herod than Nicolaus, and equally
biased when he dealt with events of his own day such as his treatment of Vespasian
and Titus. This is almost a balanced assessment. It should be remembered that the
central position of Nicolaus in the court at Jerusalem cannot be compared with that of
Josephus in Rome, not to mention the different aims of the works of the two
historians. From the surviving fragments of Nicolaus one gets the clear impression

The 'non-Jewish' background of the Herodian family had evidently been a handicap,[64] which Nicolaus sought to conceal by proclaiming that the family's origins went back to Jewish returnees from the Babylonian exile. Although Herod would have had general political interests in keeping good contacts with the Jews beyond the Euphrates, Nicolaus's story may have influenced him to tighten links with the Jewish communities there—thus boosting the invention and making it sound deceptively real.[65] Many families, in one case under special state concessions, were encouraged at that time to re-emigrate to Palestine, including the famous house of Hillel.[66]

The invention of Nicolaus was not without precedent in this part of the world: one need only to think of the notorious family of the Tobiads in the post-exilic period. The major opponent of Nehemiah, Tobiah the governor of Ammanitis, was in high favour with the leading men of Jerusalem who were bound to him by marriage relationships. He maintained a special room in the temple, from which

that his protection of the Herodian interests was far greater than Josephus's of the Roman (cf. Goodman 1994: 336-37). Wacholder praises Nicolaus for at least being consistent in his exposition of Herod, whereas Josephus lacked coherence. However, for the purpose of historical enquiry one would have wished that Nicolaus had been less consistent, since Josephus's hesitation often provides the opportunity to form our own opinion.

64.   See above n. 41. The non-Jewish origins of the dynasty were still a problem at the time of Agrippa I, who is said to have shed tears when he came to read Deut. 17.15, where it is written that only Israelites may be appointed king, and the people had to assure him that he was their 'brother', i.e. a full Jew (*m. Soṭ.* 7.8; *Sifre Deut.* 157; *Midr. Tan.*, 104; Allon 1961, 70 n. 53; Neusner 1970, 64; for refs see Chapter 10 n. 67; cf. Philo, *Spec. Leg.* 4.157; see Cohen [N.G.] 1990). In the episode of Simon, a pietist, Agrippa I was accused of being ineligible to enter the Temple because of his alien ancestry (Josephus, *Ant.* 19.332-34: the right word for the natives is ἐγγενεῖς)—the question is whether proselytes were excluded from the Temple, and until what generation (Baumgarten [J.M.] 1983; cf. Segal [P.] 1989; Schwartz [D.R.] 1990: 124-30); cf. Agrippa I's bringing of the first-fruits as far as the altar (*m. Bikk.* 3.4), etc.

65.   Contra Neusner 1976: 50-52.

66.   On the house of Hillel, see Derenbourg 1867: 176-92; Neusner 1971: 1.185-340; *SVM* 2, 363-67; Neusner and Avery-Peck 1982; on the house of Ananel, see Josephus, *Ant.* 15.22, 34, 39-40, 51; on the house of Zamaris, see Chapter 10 n. 102; on returnees under Herod, see Stern [M.] 1976: 570-71; cf. the enigmatic Aramaic inscription (written in Palaeo-Hebrew) discovered in a tomb of the Herodian period at Giv'at Hamivtar, referring to the return from Babylonia of the remains of a Mattathiah son of Judah (Naveh 1976; Ilan 1987: 12-13).

Nehemiah ejected him.[67] Apparently Tobiah (Hebrew 'Yahweh is good') had claimed to be of Jewish descent from the pre-exilic monarchy, since members of his family sought to be registered among those enrolled in the native genealogies. But such a thing could not be proved, as categorically implied by Ezra and Nehemiah.[68]

In the case of Herod the question that arises is whether he would have needed to distort or even destroy official genealogies kept in the Temple, in order to allow for Nicolaus's invention? An answer to this will emerge as our discussion proceeds. For the moment it is important to remember that, being a priest, Josephus must have had good knowledge about the state of genealogical archives in the pre-70 CE Jerusalem (see below n. 79), and good reasons to reject what Nicolaus had claimed.

The second account of the Herodian origins (without counting Josephus's own) was preserved by the early Christian church (its main advocate being Africanus); note that already the evangelists (particularly Luke) show a remarkable familiarity with the Herods, independent of Josephus. That the Jewish historian was unaware of this version, which we may call 'Ascalonite', points to the fact that it was circulated shortly after he wrote—unless it had appeared earlier (for example in the lost *History of Herod* by Ptolemy of Ascalon, mentioned above) and Josephus chose to ignore it. It is also possible that this version had a long oral tradition before it was written down, perhaps soon after the death of Agrippa II. In this case a relevant, lost work that immediately comes to mind is that of Justus of Tiberias, which happened to be a vital source of Africanus.[69] Schürer's assessment is interesting:

> Josephus and Julius Africanus are basically in agreement in regard to the Idumaean descent, the only difference being that according to Josephus, Antipater's background was distinguished, and according to Africanus lowly (he particularly emphasizes the poverty). In addition, Josephus gives the father of Antipater as Antipater, whereas for Africanus it is Herod. Certain connexions of King Herod with this town speak in favour of an Ascalonite descent... But for the rest, the story of Julius Africanus

67. Neh. 6.17-19; 13.4-9.
68. Ezra 2.60; Neh. 7.62; for the Ammonite background of the Tobiads, see references in Chapter 2 n. 79.
69. Gelzer 1880: 246-65; Schürer 1890: 68-69; *FHJA* 1, 372; Bowman 1987: 365-66. Africanus is explicit about the corroboration of his story by Greek sources: ταῦτα μὲν δὴ κοινὰ καὶ ταῖς Ἑλλήνων ἱστορίαις (below n. 80).

reveals so much spite and malice that it is impossible to avoid the sus-
picion that it is a Jewish or Christian fabrication... See also W. Otto...
correctly rejecting the Ascalon tradition...[70]

Let us for a moment analyse this position. Although Schürer finds a
'basic agreement' between Josephus and Africanus, and although certain connections of Herod 'speak in favour of an Ascalonite descent',
the 'spite and malice' revealed in the story of Africanus makes him
reject the Ascalon tradition. But this surely does not do total justice.
Would one reject the Ascalon tradition as a whole on the basis of
the 'spite and malice' added to it by the Christian hand? Should not
Schürer rather have said that the spite and malice in the story are
evidently a Christian fabrication, though the core of the Ascalon tradition itself (being in agreement with Josephus and 'certain connections
of Herod'), cannot be excluded *a priori* and could have been based on
authentic information?

The earliest writer known to us to mention the tradition connecting
Herod with the city of Ascalon is the Christian apologist Justin, the so-
called Martyr,[71] in his work *Dialogue with Trypho the Jew*:

> And it was prophesied by Jacob the patriarch[72] that there would be two
> advents of Christ, and that in the first he would suffer, and that after he
> came there would be neither (Jewish) prophet nor king in your
> tribe... and that the nations who believed in the suffering Christ would
> look for his future (second) appearance... that in your tribe there never
> failed either (Jewish) prophet or ruler, from the time when they began
> until the time when this Jesus Christ appeared and suffered, you will not

70.   *SVM* 1, 234 n. 3; the new Schürer seems to have been influenced by Otto
(1913: 1-2, 17-19) and Schalit (1962; 1969). The latter's conclusion on this subject
has remained unchallenged for far too long (Hoehner 1972: 5-6 n. 2; Rajak 1973:
367; Smallwood 1976: 19-20 n. 50; *GLAJJ* 1, 242; Kasher 1988: 130; Horbury
1991: 119-20). Earlier scholars, such as Stark, Gelzer, de Saulcy and Phythian-
Adams were readily prepared to accept the Ascalon tradition.

71.   See *Acts of Justin and Companions*, but cf. Eusebius, *Hist. Eccl.* 4.16.7-8.

72.   *Viz.* Gen. 49.10; cf. *Test. XII Patr.* (Jud. 22); *4QpGen*[a] (4Q252), col. 5.
This is not the place to discuss the interpretation of this prophecy as messianic by,
among others, the New Testament and early Christian writers. Although it seems
unlikely, it is certainly not impossible that Herod also might have tried to capitalize
from such a prophecy, making a claim for himself (as argued by Schalit and criticized
by Stern [M.] 1960: 55-57); were this to be true, a dimension would be added to the
question of his followers, the so-called 'Herodians' (Rowley 1940; Daniel 1970;
Hoehner 1972: 331-42; Yadin 1985: 81-83; Bickermann 1986: 22-33; Braun 1989),
as first noted by Ps.-Tertullian (*Adv. Haer.*, 1.1).

venture shamelessly to assert, nor can you prove it. For though you
affirm that Herod, after whose (reign) he suffered, was an Ascalonite,
nevertheless you admit that there was a high priest in your tribe, so that
you then had one who presented offerings according to the law of
Moses... also you had prophets in succession until John (the Baptist)...
But after the manifestation and death of our Jesus Christ, in your tribe
there was and is nowhere any prophet: nay, further, you ceased to exist
under your own king, your land was laid waste, and forsaken like a lodge
in a vineyard...[73]

Since Herod was caught up, as it were, in the process of this
prophecy's fulfilment, from the Christian point of view it was imperative that his non-Jewish origins were clearly demonstrable. This reference to Ascalon was made public at Rome around the middle of the
second century CE, where Justin was active. Nevertheless, the apologist would have known about it from much earlier, certainly before
CE 135, when he engaged in his disputation with Trypho at Ephesus.
There is no reason to suspect fabrication specifically involving Ascalon: why was this city chosen and not another Greek, or non-Jewish,
city of the area?

It is important to note that Justin's parents were pagan and that he
was born in c. CE 100 at Flavia Neapolis, the ancient Shechem of
Samaria.[74] As we saw (Chapter 2 §2), Shechem was a Sidonian colony
and the existence of Phoenician remnants here up to the time when the
place achieved the status of a Roman city need not be doubted (cf.
below n. 105). Since Ascalon had also been a Phoenician colony, one
may suggest that there is a conceivable likelihood as to how Justin
knew of Herod's past—the families of both would have had essentially
the same ethnic background. Besides, Justin may have studied the
work of another Hellenized Phoenician writer (if this is what he was),
Ptolemy of Ascalon, the biographer of Herod, or he may have read
Justus of Tiberias, if either one had recorded the Herodian origins
(see above). Moreover, oral tradition preserved (for reasons still
eluding research) within early Christian circles in Palestine (and later
perhaps at Ephesus, an important centre of the Early Church) may
have been a supplementary source for Justin. The existence of such an
oral source[75] is made clear by Julius Africanus, the next Christian

73.   Justin, *Dial.* 52.3.
74.   Justin, *Apol.* 1.1; see Barnard 1967.
75.   Oral traditions concerning the Herodian family were transmitted by the early
Christians. Luke's writings (ignoring red herrings) are the most informed in the New

writer to mention this tradition, and in fact in its fullest version.

Sextus Julius Africanus was born pagan in c. CE 160 probably in Jerusalem (that is Aelia Capitolina);[76] he was educated in Alexandria and later settled in the Judaean Emmaus (Nicopolis). His most famous work was a 'Chronography of the World' in five books, while he was believed to be one of the most eminent scholars of his day, handling information from 'every department of literature and science'.[77] In his letter *To Aristides*, an ingenious but unconvincing attempt to reconcile the contradictory genealogies of Matthew and Luke, Africanus claimed to have had access to records handed down by the *desposynoi*, the human relatives of Jesus Christ.[78] These records apparently sought to support the Davidic descent of the founder of Christianity (as advocated by Paul and the Evangelists, who may have utilized information from the same circles), by giving reasons why the family could only provide a tentative genealogy. It had been made up partly from memory and partly from what appears to be a book of 'Chronicles' (βίβλος τῶν ἡμερῶν), because the original document was lost, one presumes under *familiar* circumstances.

According to the *desposynoi*, it was Herod the Great who burned the records of the noble Jewish families kept in the Temple, in his

Testament on this subject followed by Mark (see Chapters 7 §2 and 10 §1), and without dependence on Josephus (Hunkin 1919; cf. Feldman 1984: 717-23; contra Schwartz [D.R.] 1990: 215-16 n. 12). The obvious oral source available to Luke (other than that of the δεσπόσυνοι to be discussed next), was Paul the Apostle (see Hengel 1992). A Jew of the Greek-speaking diaspora (Acts 21.37) and a Roman citizen (Acts 22.28), he was educated at Jerusalem in the school of Gamaliel (Acts 22.3), becoming employed there in CE 36–37 (in what seems to have been a police force, possibly of Herodian origin—cf. the persecution of Jesus' followers, Acts 8.3). His sister was apparently a wealthy lady (van Unnik 1962), whose young son could enter the building (Herodian palace?) where Paul was held (Acts 23.16-19). Later at Caesarea Paul was presented to Agrippa II and Berenice II (Chapter 10 n. 194). He refers to a 'Herodion', conceivably from the house of 'Aristobulus', as his συγγενής (Chapter 10 nn. 21, 169). Although it cannot be proved, it is not impossible that Paul's sister had been married to a royal courtier or even to a lesser member of the Herodian family (cf. Chapter 7 n. 107). Such a connection would solve a number of problems in Paul's life.

76.   The Suda [edn Bekker, s.v. *Afrikanos*] wrongly asserts that Julius was born in Libya (see Gelzer 1880; Thee 1984; and Habas 1994).

77.   Socrates, *Hist. Eccl.* 2.35.

78.   *Apud* Eusebius, *Hist. Eccl.* 1.7.2-16; cf. Africanus, *Chron., apud* Syncellus [edn Dindorf 1: 561]; on the *desposynoi* see Bauckham 1990: 354-64.

effort to alienate their surviving descendants and to cover up his own inferior background.[79] The victims' families were unable to reconstruct with accuracy their destroyed genealogies, but being aware of their own ancestry they made it a priority to remember at least their enemy's 'low' origins:

> When Idumaean brigands attacked the city of Ascalon in Palestine among their other spoils they took away captive from the temple of Apollo, which was built on the walls, Antipater the child of a certain Herod, a hierodoulos, and since the priest was unable to pay ransom for his son, Antipater was brought up in the customs of the Idumaeans and later was befriended by Hyrcanus the high priest of Judaea. When sent on a mission to Pompey on behalf of Hyrcanus he won for him the freedom of the kingdom which had been taken away by his brother Aristobulus, and so was himself fortunate enough to gain the title of overseer of Palestine. Antipater was assassinated from envy of his great good fortune, and succeeded by a son Herod (the Great), who later was appointed by Antony and by decree of the august Senate to be king of the Jews. His children

79.   Although Josephus does not refer to this event (since it would not have been mentioned by Nicolaus had it been historical), he does reveal (*Apion* 1.34) that the genealogical archives sustained damage, at least when Jerusalem was invaded by Antiochus IV Epiphanes, by Pompey and by P. Quinctilius Varus (Urbach 1966: 7-8; Urbach 1977: 87). The Syriac *The Cave of Treasures* [edn Budge: 195], mentions Herod's destruction, but this fourth century CE work will have depended on Africanus. At all events, such an act was not incompatible with his character and it is in line with Nicolaus's invention. We know that Herod killed the members of the Sanhedrin (*Ant.* 14.175), and consistently tried to dispose of all opposition, whether Hasmonaean or presumably Davidic (Jeremias 1969, 275ff.; see significant new evidence in Flusser 1986). According to *b. B. Bat.* 3b Herod killed the sages who expounded Deut. 17.15 'from the midst of thy brethren shalt thou set up a king' (cf. above n. 64). Schalit (1967–68) theorized that Herod created for himself a Davidic genealogy, via the family of Hillel, who might have claimed such a descent (*y. Ta'an.* 4.68a = *Gen. R.* 98; *y. Kil.* 9.32b = *Gen. R.* 33; *b. Sanh.* 5a, *b. Ket.* 62b, *b. Šab.* 56a). Josephus's information on the public archives is important (*Apion* 1.31; cf. *War* 2.427; 6.354), as is the survival of his own genealogy (*Life* 1-6; see below n. 83); cf. the 'sacred books [and]... (lacuna)', which Josephus gained from Titus when Jerusalem fell, thus saving them from oblivion (*Life* 418). Furthermore, note the tomb inscription of the priestly family buried in the so-called 'Tomb of James' (*CII* 1394), dated to the first half of the first century CE, which mentions members going back four generations, who claim to be the 'sons of Hezir' (בני הזיר). The priestly house of Hezir is mentioned in 1 Chron. 24.15, and a Hezir was associated with Nehemiah (Neh. 10.20).

were Herod (Antipas) and the other tetrarchs. *So much is shared with the histories of the Greeks also.*[80]

Epiphanius later, who was born actually in the area of Marisa (Beth Govrin/Eleutheropolis), is also aware of the Ascalon tradition, and curiously not via Africanus, as his version indicates:

> ...Herod was the son of Antipater of Ascalon, a *hierodoulos* of the idol of Apollo. This Antipater's father was named Herod, and he was the son of Antipas. Antipater was taken prisoner by Idumaeans and fathered Herod during his stay in Idumaea. Since his father was poor and could not ransom his son—I mean Antipater—he remained there for a long time as a slave. But later, with his young son, Herod, he was ransomed by public subscription and returned home. This is why some call him an Idumaean, though others know him as Ascalonite. Afterwards he made friends with Demetrius, was appointed governor of Idumaea, and became acquainted with the Emperor Augustus. Because of his governorship he became a proselyte, being circumcised himself and circumcised his son Herod. The kingship of the Jews fell to Herod, but he was king in Judaea as a tributary ruler, under the Emperor Augustus.[81]

It would be pointless to defend this story in all its details, since it is partly confused and probably exaggerated. Yet, again, there is no compelling reason to reject the core of the tradition. In fact the Herodian ancestry presented here—with one extra generation—could make better sense, though one may still trust Josephus (even if he himself was unsure)[82] as regards the name of Herod's grandfather (that is Antipas instead of Herod). Perhaps as a compromise one may expect in the genealogical sequence the great-grandfather to be called Herod. The following tabulation of the three authorities indicates the suggested restoration in Josephus:

80.   *Apud* Eusebius, *Hist. Eccl.* 1.7.11-12 (my italics); cf. the accusation of low origins (ταπεινότης) Herod had to face (Josephus, *War* 1.313; *Ant.* 14.430; cf. *War* 1.478); see references above n. 41.

81.   Epiphanius, *Panar.* 1.20.1.3-5. In the fifth century CE Sozomen from Bethelia, near Gaza, mentions Herod as Idumaean from his father's side and Arab from his mother's (*Hist. Eccl.* 1). Theodoret of Cyrrhus, the most original writer to stem from Syria in that century, calls Herod ἀλλόφυλος, stating that his father was an Ascalonite and his mother Idumaean (*Eranist.* 1.63). Among other sources to be noted are Eusebius (references in *Chron.*, *Quest. ad Steph.*, *Ad Luke*, *Dem. Evang.*, *Proph. Eclog.*, and fragments of Procopius); Ephraem Syrus; Sulpicius Severus; *Chronicon Paschale*; George Hamartolos; Bar Hebraeus; etc.

82.   Josephus, *Ant.* 14.10: τοίνυν.

Africanus	Epiphanius	Josephus
	Antipas of Ascalon	[Herod of Ascalon?]
	|	|
Herod of Ascalon	Herod	Antipas
|	|	|
Antipater	Antipater	Antipater
|	|	|
Herod the Great	Herod the Great	Herod the Great

Assuming that Antipater was about 70 years old when he was poisoned in 43 BCE, he would have been born in c. 113 BCE. If Antipas was about 35 when he became the father of Antipater, he would in turn have been born in c. 148 BCE.[83] The family tree below follows this chronology through to the generation of Herod the Great:

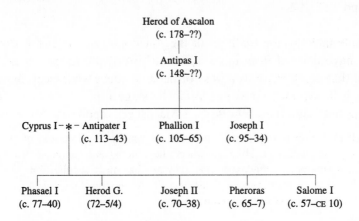

The question remains of how much it is necessary to deviate from the Christian versions of the story to allow for error and distortion.

83.   For Antipater's death, see Josephus, *War* 1.226; *Ant.* 14.283; we know he was an old man (*War* 1.123; *b. B. Qam.* 82b; see above n. 41), and his son Herod also died at a similar age (Chapter 6 n. 2); the fact that Antipater would have become father to Herod when he was 40 is not a problem, for it is perfectly within range of Herodian patterns of fatherhood (see Chapter 4). Josephus's own genealogy may not necessarily be doubted (see Rajak 1983: 15-17; Fuks [G.] 1990): he was born in CE 37, his father Matthias in CE 6, his grandfather Joseph in c. 68 BCE, and his great-grandfather Matthias Curtus in c. 135 BCE (*Life* 4–5). Had his purpose been simply a deceitful extension back to the Maccabees, why did he not add a generation or two? Josephus himself had his last son Simonides/Agrippa when he was 40 (*Life* 427)!

Two possible alternatives will be explored. The first will accept almost verbatim (with some control from Josephus) the essentials found in Africanus/Epiphanius, while the second will put forward a hypothetical reconstruction paying attention to evidence from 1 Maccabees:

a) A band of brigands from Idumaea attacked the temple of Apollo at Ascalon in c. 140 BCE, robbing it of all its treasures. In the process the son of Herod, the temple's priest (who was from a locally established family of high standing and wealth),[84] was abducted for ransom. However, perhaps because the total loss had been too great, the blackmail was not met, and the child Antipas (about eight years old) remained a hostage in Idumaea. The boy was destined to grow up and become *stratēgos* under Alexander Jannaeus (103–76 BCE) over the people of the land which kept him in bondage—but not before he was converted to Judaism in the situation created by John Hyrcanus around 127 BCE.

b) Alternatively, the tradition of the Ascalonite origin of the Herods may have derived from quite different historical circumstances. The point that might serve as a link for understanding what went on (even though it cannot be proved), is the 'hostageship' of the boy. At an appropriate time (in c. 144 BCE), 1 Maccabees reports the following:

> Then Jonathan went forth... and when he came to Ascalon, they of the city met him honourably. From whence he went to Gaza, but they of Gaza shut him out... Afterward, when they of Gaza made supplication unto Jonathan, he made peace with them, and took the sons of their chief men for hostages, and sent them to Jerusalem...[85]

---

84.   The family's wealth is made clear by Josephus (see above n. 41); for the Apollo connection see below §4. The priestly background is of interest: in a confused passage Strabo (16.2.46) says: 'Now Pompey... appointed Herod (*sic*) to the priesthood; but later a certain Herod, a descendant of his... received the title of king...' By the first Herod, Strabo must mean Antipater (contra *GLAJJ* 1, 310), and of course we know that Pompey appointed not Antipater but Hyrcanus as the High Priest. The confusion over a 'priestly' Herod, who was an ancestor of Herod the Great, may thus be instructive.

85.   1 Macc. 11.60-62; cf. *b. B. Bat.* 3b-4a; *b. Qid.* 70b 'slave of the Hasmonaeans'; see Josephus *Ant.* 14.491 'from a private family that was subject to the kings'; cf. Maccabaean officials with the name Antipater (1 Macc. 12.1-4, 16; Josephus *Ant.* 13.163-70 [advisor and envoy of Jonathan]; *Ant.* 14.248 [father of Aeneas, envoy to Rome]).

True, in this passage only Gaza is directly said to have submitted young hostages. But since this was done as a gesture of supplication (in view of the ravaging of the Gazaean suburbs by the Jewish forces), and Ascalon had also made an agreement with Jonathan on the occasion (as also testified by Josephus),[86] it may be legitimate to assume that Ascalon too had offered some young hostages.

Antipas the son of Herod, a leading man of Ascalon and priest of the temple of Apollo, may have been taken to Jerusalem and grew up there. His Hellenized background would have been useful to the royal Hasmonaean court, from which he would slowly have emerged with a high reputation and perhaps even with an appointment in Idumaea. There he would have had to be converted to Judaism by Hyrcanus in c. 127 BCE. Under Jannaeus (103–76 BCE) Antipas succeeded in becoming *stratēgos* of this place—he knew how to handle the converted Hellenized Phoenicians. We saw how Josephus particularly stressed Antipas's special influence over Ascalon, Gaza and the Arabs.

There are no adequate means of determining which one of the proposed models is likely to be historically accurate; but the fact is that the Ascalon tradition can no longer be ignored. The wider historical context shows complex relations between Judaea, the inland cities of Idumaea (such as Marisa) and the coastal ones (such as Ascalon), as well as the important fact that forcible conversion affected the general area. In fact a Hellenized Phoenician (Tyrian/Sidonian) origin for the Herodian family, with an initial establishment at Ascalon

---

86.   Josephus, *Ant*. 13.148-49. The Ascalonites had learnt their lesson from Joseph the Tobiad (a generation or two earlier according to Josephus, though several according to Goldstein 1975), who extracted from them taxes by force, after putting to death 20 of their leading men (*Ant*. 12.181). Further, as explained in 1 Macc. 10.86; 11.60, Ascalon welcomed Jonathan first because of antagonism with Gaza, and second because the city was under the influence of Ptolemy Philometor who was friendly with Jonathan (1 Macc. 11.5-7; cf. Stern [M.] 1981: 26 n. 23). Ascalon subsequently maintained good terms with the Maccabees, and it was only by the mid-first century CE that hatred for the Jews was stressed by Philo (*Legat*. 205) and later by Josephus (*War* 3.10). Under Alexander Jannaeus the friendship reached a climax, apparently due to Herodian Antipas, who kept firm ties; note also the era of Ascalon beginning in 103 BCE when Jannaeus rose to power (below n. 169); and tentatively *m. Sanh*. 6.4, mentioning the hanging of witches in Ascalon by Shimon ben Shetaḥ, presumably under Jannaeus (*SVM* 1, 231 n. 7; Stern [M.] 1981: 27 n. 24; Efron 1987: 218 n. 352; Efron 1990; but cf. Hengel 1984).

and later development in Idumaea, may be supported by a parallel examination of this important coastal city. To do so will be to look at the Herods for the first time against their own cultural background. There seems to exist circumstantial as well as hard evidence hitherto overlooked.

4. *The Culture of Ascalon and the Herods*

Some relationship of the Herodian family to the city of Ascalon was familiar to Josephus, who refers to it, even if cursorily. We saw the example of Antipas's dealings with the Ascalonites. The same is implied in the case of Antipater and his orchestration of Caesar's attack on Egypt, precisely from Ascalon.[87] When Caesar later issued his decrees favourable to Hyrcanus and the Jews (clearly as a result of Antipater's performance), he ordered copies to be deposited in the temples of Sidon, Tyre and Ascalon.[88] Surely this was not only because these three Phoenician cities were the most important on the Levantine coast.

Josephus is explicit about Herod's extensive building programme in this city: 'baths, sumptuous fountains and colonnades, admirable alike for their architecture and their proportions'.[89] It is true that Herod was an extraordinary benefactor to well over 20 cities outside his kingdom, with architectural projects in at least 13 of them,[90] but it is also

87.   Josephus, *War* 1.187; *Ant.* 14.128; cf. Hypsicrates, *apud* Josephus, *Ant.* 14.139; and the *stēlē* raised by Caesar in Alexandria (Josephus, *Apion* 2.37).
88.   Josephus, *Ant.* 14.197.
89.   Josephus, *War* 1.422.
90.   Pagan cities outside Herod's kingdom benefitting from his building projects included: Ascalon (baths, fountains, colonnades and a palace—*War* 1.422, 2.98; *Ant.* 17.321); Ptolemais (gymnasium—*War* 1.422); Tyre (temples and market places—*War* 1.422); Sidon (theatre—*War* 1.422); Damascus (gymnasium and theatre—*War* 1.422); Berytus (halls and porticoes—*War* 1.422); Byblus (wall—*War* 1.422); Tripolis (gymnasium—*War* 1.422); Laodicea (aqueduct—*War* 1.422); Antioch (pavement and colonnade for broad street—*War* 1.425; *Ant.* 16.148); Rhodes (restoration of buildings and temple of Apollo—*Ant.* 14.378; *War* 1.424); Chios (reconstruction of portico—*Ant.* 16.18-9); Nicopolis (greater part of their public buildings—*Ant.* 16.147). In many other cities (including Phaselis, Balanea, Pergamon, Ilium, Cos, Samos, Athens, Olympia, Sparta) and whole regions (in Cilicia, Cappadocia, Ionia, Lycia, Paphlagonia, Phrygia) Herod showed his liberality in the following ways: grants of land (*War* 1.422-23); revenues to maintain gymnasiarchies (*War* 1.423); payments for shipbuilding (*War* 1.424); grants of corn (*War*

true that he possessed no royal palace in any Hellenized city other than Ascalon. Augustus made this a present to Salome I (Herod's sister), after the death of the king.[91]

Concerning this building there seems to have existed an ancient palace complex, which Herod would have had to refurbish.[92] No doubt Salome would have made it her main residence until she died in c. CE 10.[93] In fact she may already have been staying there periodically, following the careers of her three husbands, all of whom seem to have been appointed *stratēgoi* of Idumaea (see Chapter 7 §1). As has already been suggested (above n. 58), it is possible that after the destruction of Marisa, Ascalon served as the administrative centre for the southern part of Herod's kingdom, even though strictly speaking it may have lain outside its borders (but see below n. 102). This will

1.424); payments to meet general needs (*War* 1.425; cf. *Ant*. 19.329); unspecified offerings and donations (*War* 1.425); revenues to maintain games (*War* 1.427); enumeration of debts (*War* 1.428); discharge of taxes (*War* 1.428); general gifts (*Ant*. 15.327); reconciliations (*Ant*. 16.26); support for rights (*Ant*. 16.27-61; cf. 12.125-27); revenues to maintain civic functions (*Ant*. 16.146); unspecified benefactions (*Ant*. 16.146); payments for sacrifices and ceremonies (*Ant*. 16.149). On Herod and the Greek world, see Kokkinos forthcoming 1; cf. Merkel 1988: 820-22). For the building projects of Herod within his kingdom, see Netzer 1981; cf. Netzer 1987a; Small 1987; Segal [A.] 1989: 147-50.

91.   Josephus, *War* 2.98; *Ant*. 17.321.

92.   The palace of the last Philistine king of Ascalon (Weidner 1939: 928), must have been destroyed in the Babylonian attack of 604 BCE (Stager 1996), but it would have been rebuilt to accommodate a governor in the area. Indeed the βασίλεια were known to Ps.-Scylax in the Persian period, when Ascalon was under Tyrian control (*GLAJJ* 3, 10, no. 558). In the Hellenistic period this building may have been passed on to Herodian hands, if members of the family held office there (see below §5). Herod the Great would have modernized it—note Josephus's mention of it as τὸ βασίλειον and τὰ βασίλεια (above n. 91).

93.   Josephus, *Ant*. 18.31; cf. *War* 2.167. *Ant*. 17.322 reads αὐτῆς ὁ οἶκος ἦν ἐν τῇ Ἀρχελάου ἀρχῇ, translated in the Loeb as 'her residence was in the territory ruled by Archelaus', which may sound as if her 'house' after 4 BCE was situated in Judaea. But this is a bad translation. The passage really means that the area in which the estates given to her by Augustus were situated (i.e. Jamnia, Azotus and Phasaelis), was controlled by Archelaus. This can be shown by the reading of *War* 2.98, τὸν δὲ οἶκον αὐτῆς ὑπὸ τὴν Ἀρχελάου τοπαρχίαν ἔταξεν, which the Loeb translates as 'her estates, however, were placed under the jurisdiction (toparchy) of Archelaus' (cf. Avi-Yonah 1977a: 102).

explain why Augustus decided to give the palace to Salome, the person most familiar with it.

Although previously unnoticed, in the closing stages of the Hasmonaean history Josephus further hints at the Herodian-Ascalonite relationship. After the final fall of Aristobulus II and his second imprisonment in Rome, his wife and children were apparently given residence at the Herodian palace of Ascalon.[94] His elder son Alexander was later executed (48 BCE), but Antigonus II and his two sisters, probably due to a plan contrived by Antipater,[95] were claimed by Philippion the Ituraean[96] and were taken away from their mother who was held at Ascalon.[97] With her there probably remained Alexandra II, the wife of the deceased Alexander, and her children.[98] During this period Herod must have spent some time with his father in Ascalon,

94.   Aristobulus II's wife had made a deal with Gabinius in c. 57 BCE, to surrender the desert fortresses held by the Jews while being permitted to retain her children (Josephus, *War* 1.174; *Ant.* 14.97). The seclusion of the family at Ascalon (below n. 97) would have served the purpose of safeguarding its members in the Herodian environment of a Greek city—cut off from their main Jewish contacts. It is of interest that in the superior *Ant.* the MSS reading is Ἰδουμαία, not Ἰουδαία, for the place where the children returned after they were granted their freedom, but the text is emended as a scribal error!

95.   Josephus, *War* 1.196; cf. *Ant.* 14.140. As time went on the Herods must have felt that it was not safe to keep the Hasmonaean family even at Ascalon, especially since the children (including two boys) were getting older. In fact one of them was soon risen up in rebellion.

96.   Philippion was the son of Ptolemy, king of Chalcis, who had once been attacked by Aristobulus II (Josephus, *Ant.* 13.418; cf. *War* 1.115; for the Ituraean coins see Kindler 1987–89). Philippion married Alexandra III, one of the Hasmonaean girls, but he was soon slain by his father who took her as his wife (*War* 1.186; *Ant.* 14.126). The history of Chalcis is dark after this point (cf. Chapter 10 n. 151), but any possible offspring from this union (e.g. Soaemus—*Ant.* 15.185, 204-207, 216, 227-29), would be of interest for the last phase of the Hasmonaean history and the later acquisition of the area by the Herods.

97.   Josephus, *War* 1.185-86; *Ant.* 14.123-26; her name is not known—she was the daughter of Absalom the brother of Alexander Jannaeus (*Ant.* 14.71; cf. *War* 1.154).

98.   The marriage of Alexandra II and Alexander, which would have taken place in Ascalon in c. 55 BCE, produced the following children: Mariamme I (born c. 53 BCE), Aristobulus III/Jonathan (born c. 52/51 BCE) and an unnamed female (c. 50/49 BCE), who became the wife of Pheroras, brother of Herod (Josephus, *War* 1.483)—it will be useful to append a family tree:

and this is where the first arrangement to marry the daughter of Alexandra, Mariamme I,[99] would have been made.

The wife of Aristobulus II seems to have died at Ascalon, possibly a few years after 48 BCE when she is last attested in our sources. Her daughter-in-law (Alexandra II) and granddaughter (Mariamme I) apparently followed Herod to Jerusalem (upon the latter's betrothal in 42 BCE), because when the Parthians attacked the city in 41/40 BCE they were among the members of the Herodian court which Herod led to Masada for safety.[100] A small pro-Hasmonaean circle which would have been created in Ascalon may have existed for a long time, since Alexander (the son of Herod and Mariamme I) had 'friends' in this city, who were allegedly prepared to supply him with a poison to kill the king.[101]

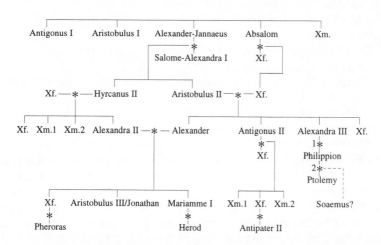

99.   Mariamme I was then only a little girl. Herod was betrothed to her in 42 BCE when she would have been about 12 (Josephus, *War* 1.241; *Ant.* 14.300), and he married her in 37 BCE at about 17 (*War* 1.344; *Ant.* 14.467).

100.   Josephus, *Ant.* 14.352-58; *War* 1.264.

101.   Josephus, *Ant.* 16.253; cf. a pro-Hasmonaean circle at Marisa (Chapter 7 §1). Alexandra had good connections with Cleopatra VII of Egypt (Chapter 7 n. 17), and Ascalon was an ideal place for such a development. The city was directly influenced by Cleopatra—she appears on its coins from 49 to 38 BCE (Brett 1937: 455-56). According to *SVM* (1, 298) in 37/36 BCE (but probably late in 36—Chapter 7 n. 14) Antony presented to Cleopatra the entire Philistine/Phoenician coast (except Tyre and Sidon), i.e. including Ascalon. Although Josephus (*War* 1.361; *Ant.* 15.95) does not explicitly say so, this may have been the case. However, Herod at this point

Therefore, as is claimed by the early Christian sources, Ascalon
seems to have had an important link with the Herods. Although from
103 BCE onwards the city was autonomous and no direct literary
evidence of *formal* incorporation into Herod the Great's territory has
reached us,[102] the King did retain a strong influence (and probably a
legal tie) that could conveniently explain his ancestral connections with
it. It will be necessary to examine briefly the culture of Ascalon,[103]
illustrating the various ways in which the Herodian dynasty fits in.

We have already said that when the Babylonians conquered the city
they evidently drove away, as was customary, a part of its population
(the royal family itself is recorded in exile). Under the Persians
Ascalon was not restored to Philistine control (in contrast to the re-
establishment of the Jewish state); instead it was handed over to the
Phoenician Tyrians. In the Hellenistic period, and at the expense of

could have leased Ascalon from Cleopatra (as he did with Jericho—*War* 1.362; *Ant.*
15.96; cf. 132), otherwise it is inconceivable why the Egyptian queen disappears
from the city's coins (see next note).

102.   It is thought that Ascalon continued to be independent, because it is not
referred to among the cities given to Herod in Josephus's lists, and while Pliny
(*Hist. Natur.* 5.13) calls it an *oppidum liberum*, its era (beginning in 103 BCE)
persisted until the Late Roman period. But Josephus's lists are not complete—for
example, Azotus and Jamnia are missing (*Ant.* 15.217; *War* 1.396; see *SVM* 2, 92
n. 22). Pliny may refer to the status of the city before Herod's time—his source was
probably Gabinian in date (Chapter 2 n. 41; cf. Jones [A.H.M.] 1971: 260-63). As
for the era of Ascalon, although it continues uninterrupted, no known coins advertize
'autonomy' after 38 BCE (see below n. 171). It is possible then that the city belonged
to Herod (he owned the palace there), and if not unconditionally, he may have held it
on lease (see above n. 101), or perhaps only been assigned with its supervision. We
should remember that even cities of the Decapolis, like Hippos and Gadara, had been
placed under Herod's jurisdiction from 30 BCE (*Ant.* 15.217, 320; *War* 1.396;
2.97), and that from time to time Herod was given broad powers over the region—
for example, according to Josephus (*War* 1.399) Augustus granted him the procuratorship of all Syria. Herod also held some unusual powers over autonomous
cities, such as 'no sovereign had been empowered by Caesar', since he could
'reclaim a fugitive subject even from a state outside his jurisdiction' (*War* 1.474)!

103.   For the history of Ascalon, see Phythian-Adams 1921; Rappaport 1970;
SVM 2, 105-108; note the tradition of Xanthus (*apud* Nicolaus *apud* Stephanus, s.v.
Askalōn), concerning the Lydian general Ascalus who invaded Syria and founded the
city; another version had Mopsus, the son of Lydus, instead (*apud* Mnaseas *apud*
Athenaeus, 8.346e-f; see Astrour 1967: 53-67); cf. Mopsus, a Greek hero from Troy
(Callinus *apud* Strabo, 14.4.3); for excavation see Garstang 1924; Avi-Yonah and
Eph'al 1975: 127-29; and now Stager 1991a; 1991b; 1991c; 1991d; 1996.

Tyre, the city of Sidon emerged as the leading Phoenician force, while making obvious concessions to the Greek way of life.[104]

Most of the Canaanite coast, as well as various inland locations (notably Marisa, the suggested birthplace of Herod the Great), came increasingly under its sway. Sidonian trade and commerce extended in all conceivable directions: south to Egypt and Arabia, north to the Aegean, west to the limits of the Mediterranean—an explosion in many ways similar to the good old days (ninth to seventh centuries BCE) of Tyrian colonization.[105] Accompanying that expansion were many aspects of Phoenician civilization.

Ascalon developed into an important Hellenized centre, with its own local characteristics, at least if one is to speak of its religious cults and its famous people. Although the entire Phoenician pantheon (to a large extent common Canaanite-Philistine-Phoenician), known to us basically from the Ugaritic texts and Philo of Byblus (that is El, Baal, Astarte, Anath, Melkart, Dagon, Eshmun, Reseph, Hauron, etc.),[106] will have been worshipped in coastal Palestine, at Ascalon it was Astarte/Aphrodite Urania ('the heavenly one') who held the highest status. Herodotus says that her temple was among the oldest of its kind and that it was from there that her cult was introduced to Cyprus and Cythera.[107]

104. See Chapter 1 n. 41 and Chapter 2 n. 49; cf. the Greek named [Dio]timos, a hitherto unknown son of Abdalonym the king of Sidon (Kantzia 1980; Sznycer 1980); the onomasticon of the next few centuries presents the best evidence (Austin 1981: no. 121; Jidejian 1971: 71-72).

105. The Phoenician achievement was still underlined in the first century CE by Pomponius Mela (*De Chron.* 1.12). Coastal cities were still described as Phoenician by Josephus, for example Caesarea-on-the-coast (*Ant.* 15.333) and Dora (*Life* 31; cf. *Ant.* 16.285), and in the second century by Dionysius, for example Joppa (*Perieg.* 904-12; cf. Eustathius, *Com.* 910). Pausanias (7.23.6) met a Sidonian in Achaea who would argue for the priority of his mother-city's religion over that of the Greeks. The Phoenician script (e.g. legends such as בדמלקרת) persisted on coins until the time of Gordian III in the mid-third century CE (Hamburger [H.] 1954: nos. 137-39); cf. at that time the Φοινικάρχαι (*OGIS* 596; Welles 1938: no. 188), and the ἔθνος Φοινίκων (Ewing 1895: no. 112; cf. Wadd. 2432). There is no escape from the impression that the Phoenician culture did not break up before the triumph of Christianity in the fourth century CE (Albright 1955: 2; Millar 1983: 57-58).

106. See Rawlinson 1881: 150-80; Albright 1953; Dahood 1958; Baumgarten [A.I.] 1981; Ribichini 1988: 104-25.

107. Herodotus, 1.105; cf. also Delos (*ID* 2266) and Athens (Pausanias, 1.14.6); already Jeremiah (7.18; 44.25) may condemn a worship of Aphrodite

Diodorus knew of Derceto or Δερκετοῦν (probably from the Ugaritic *drkt*, meaning 'dominion'), who is identified with Atargatis, but also with Astarte/Aphrodite.[108] It seems that in the Hellenistic period the cult of the Aramaean/Syrian goddess Atargatis began to spread down the Levantine coast, being gradually at various places assimilated with that of Astarte/Aphrodite Urania.[109] At Ascalon, Derceto/

('Queen of Heaven') in Jerusalem; for Phoenicians in Jerusalem, see Chapter 1 n. 41; cf. later Roman temples in Aelia Capitolina (Sozomen, *Hist. Eccl.* 2.1), Eboda (Chapter 2 n. 57), and Gaza (Marcus Diaconus, *Life of Porph.* 59, 64). Other gods worshipped at Ascalon were Heracles-Belos (*SB* 8452) and Poseidon (*ID* 1720, 1721; cf. Bruneau 1970: 474; Teixidor 1977: 96); from Roman coins Hill (1912: 10-13) identified Astarte, Osiris, Isis, Dioscuri (cf. Hill 1911: 62) and Heracles; see also *SVM* 2, 31-32.

108.　For the identification of Derceto with Atargatis, see Hill 1912: 9; Cook 1930: 171; with Aphrodite see Teixidor 1977: 96. Tempting as it might seem to identify all three goddesses, Lucian (*De Syria Dea*) distinguishes between Derketo of Ascalon and Atargatis of Hierapolis (cf. Oden 1976), while two goddesses are implied in the myth of Derketo's daughter Semiramis, who was brought up by doves (Diodorus, 2.4.20). Dedications at Delos (*ID* 1719, 2305) may also imply two goddesses: Astarte Palaestine and Aphrodite Urania. Cook (1930: 173) believed, perhaps based on Dussaud (1904: 242), that since Urania was a sky goddess she was of the Anath-type (cf. the Gazan temple of the thirteenth century BCE—Albright 1955: 1-2) and should not be identified with Astarte or Atargatis. The latter would have replaced Urania in Ascalon at a later date. Yet, besides fluidity between Astarte and Anath, according to Philo of Byblus (*FGrH* 790, F2) Astarte was the daughter of Uranos. Further, Albright (1953: 74) argued that the name Atargatis is a combination of Astarte and Anath, and this seems to be supported by the presence of an Atargateion at Ashteroth Karnaim in the Bashan (2 Macc. 12.26; cf. 1 Macc. 5.43-44); see also the Astarte temple at Beth-Shean in the time of Saul (1 Sam. 31.10).

109.　This process is illustrated by the discovery at Akko/Ptolemais of a second century BCE dedication to Hadad and Atargatis by a Hellenized Phoenician family (Avi-Yonah 1959). The Mishna ('*Abod. Zar.* 3.4) mentions a bath of 'Aphrodite' at Akko. A bronze statuette with a female head and the body of a fish, identified with Atargatis, was found at Azekah (on the Judaean/Idumaean border)—Cook 1930, 172, pl. 35.1). At Memphis in Egypt there was a sacred pool in the temple of Aphrodite and Proteus the fish-god (Herodotus 2.112). By the first century BCE Atargatis appears among the Nabataeans in the reliefs of Khirbet et-Tannur, where she is also seen as the dolphin goddess (Glueck 1937; see Patrich 1990: 109-11; cf. Glueck 1993). Tradition would seem to point to an earlier period for the transformation of Astarte/Aphrodite into Atargatis at Ascalon: while Herodotus (1.105) mentions the plundering of the temple of Aphrodite Urania by invading (or retreating) Scythians in c. 620 BCE, Xanthus (*apud* Mnaseas, *apud* Athenaeus, 8.346e-f) had Mopsus the Lydian (above n. 103) drowning Atargatis and her son Ichthys in the

Aphrodite possessed a sacred temenos close to the city, with a large pool full of fish.[110] Thus fish were sacred to her. But, above all, it was her doves that became a strict local 'taboo', persisting for centuries, as shown by the coins.[111] Philo of Alexandria, in his *De Providentia*, gave us a brief but interesting description of these doves:

> In Syria by the sea is a city named Ascalon. When I arrived there—at that time I was sent to the paternal temple (in Jerusalem) to fulfil a vow and offer sacrifices—I saw an impossible number of doves at the crossways and about every house. When I asked the reason, they said it was not permissible to catch them; for the inhabitants, from a remote period, had been forbidden to enjoy them. So tame is the creature through security that it always lives not only under the same roof with man but at the same table, and abuses its immunity.[112]

It cannot be coincidental that at Marisa there was discovered a group of about 200 caves, known as *columbaria* caves (due to the thousands of small niches cut in long rows on their walls), which served for raising doves. It is clear from the size of the niches and from the presence of a few conical pillars (which remind us of Phoenician ritual), that they could not have served for placing burial urns (as in the famous *columbaria* of the city of Rome), but rather for

nearby lake, where she was devoured by fish. Embroiled myths said that the goddess was actually 'saved' by a fish ([Eratosthenes], *Catast.* 38), or that she was 'changed' into a fish (Diodorus 2.4.2-6; 2. 20.1-2) and her daughter Semiramis into a dove (Ovid, *Met.* 4.44-8). But the goddess of Ascalon still appears as fully human (not half-fish like Atargatis) in the Hellenistic period, for example at Athens (on a herm from the Agora—Papachatzes 1974: 282, fig. 160).

110. A circular depression called by the Arabs the 'Well of Ibrahim' (cf. Abraham's wells in Gen. 26.18), was identified by Garstang (1922: 113) with this sacred pool. In c. CE 180 Origen (Contra *Celsum* 4.44) refers to wells at Ascalon, of 'strange and extraordinary style of construction', and in c. CE 570 Antoninus Placentinus (*Itiner.* 33) mentions the *puteus pacis*, 'made like a theatre, in which one goes down to the water by steps'. However, the current excavator takes the depression to be an actual theatre of the first or second century CE, which had a *parados* with water channels, and which by the fourth century was in ruins (Stager 1991c: 38-39). That a theatre existed at Ascalon in the Roman/Byzantine period is certain (Segal [A.] 1989: 164; cf. the theater ticket of 'Phamoles' found at Ascalon— Stager 1991c: 38), but Stager's identification does not necessarily coincide with that of Origen and Antoninus.

111. See Meshorer 1985: 26-28; and below coin discussion.

112. *Apud* Eusebius, *Praep. Evang.* 8.14.64; for this work of Philo, see *SVM* 3.2, 864-65.

sacred doves of the Astarte/Aphrodite cult.[113] Also Herod, as Josephus testifies, built a great number of special 'cots for tame pigeons' in his palace at Jerusalem, as well as at Masada, as revealed by the excavations there.[114] Moreover, the rabbinical literature was aware of the domesticated type of doves called *yonei Hardissaot*, the Herodian doves.[115] Last, but not least, of particular importance is a dedication to Atargatis in her temple at Qalaat Fakra in the Lebanon, for the 'safety' of Agrippa II and Berenice II, the great-grandchildren of Herod (see Chapter 10 n. 214).

As we saw, the Ascalonite temple of Apollo is referred to in Christian sources. Excavations in the early 1920s, at the eastern portico of what was then called the 'Bouleuterion' with 'Herod's Peristyle', revealed what was interpreted as being a shrine dedicated to Apollo (on the basis of a fragmentary statue of this god found therein).[116] Although it is now known that the building complex is a basilica of Severan date, the function of the shrine seems still to be accepted, and there does not seem to be reason to exclude the possibility that Herod's project (that is colonnades, etc.—see above n. 89) was previously located here.[117] If Africanus's source is to be trusted, the original temple of Apollo may have stood close to the walls of the city, which in the Hellenistic period could have encircled the vicinity.

The head of Apollo has been identified on coins of Ascalon, and as a god he was in many ways identical to the Phoenician Resheph and the Mesopotamian Nergal.[118] Teixidor, perhaps following Cook, saw Apollo as represented by Phanebalos, a local deity also depicted on

113. For the caves see Ben-Arieh 1962; for the sacred doves and the pillars of Astarte, see Oren 1968; analysis of debris from the niches of a subterranean *columbarium* complex, exclude the possibility that they were used for the ashes of human cremations (Kloner and Hess 1985: 124).

114. Josephus, *War* 5.181; cf. the περιστερεών on the Mount of Olives (*War* 5.505); for Masada see Yadin 1966: 134-39.

115. For the יוני הרדיסאות see *m. Šab.* 24.3; *m. Ḥul.* 12.1; *b. Ḥul.* 139b; doves, sacred in Ascalon, were regularly sacrificed in Jerusalem (Mk 11.15; Mt. 2.12; Jn 2.14, 16; Jeremias 1969: 48; cf. Sanders 1992: 103-104); some may have been used by Herod for communication between Jerusalem and his desert fortresses.

116. Garstang 1924: 28-29, pls. 1-2, building S.

117. Avi-Yonah and Eph'al 1975: 126 (no. 4 in plan), 127-29; Stager 1991c: 39-41; Stager 1991d: 43-45; Stager 1993, 110-111.

118. Reseph 'the burner' was the exact opposite of Eshmun 'the healer' (Dahood 1958: 54; cf. Albright 1953: 79).

coins.[119] However, Pane-Baal or 'the face of Baal' was an epithet of the goddess Tanith, despite the fact that the figure at Ascalon wears helmet and cuirass, and carries a *harpē*, a round shield and a palm-branch. The sex is certainly not clear and an androgynous deity cannot be excluded.[120]

The cult of Apollo was widespread in southern Palestine. A temple of his is also documented in nearby Gaza.[121] The Idumaeans identified their principal god Qos with Apollo. This is proved by various items of evidence: the Greek translation of their theophoric onomasticon; the story of Mnaseas concerning Apollo at Adora and reflecting the Jewish-Idumaean struggle before the conversion to Judaism; and the decree of the Idumaeans inscribed in the temple of Apollo at Memphis.[122] The husband of Herod's sister, who bore the theophoric name Costobarus, had been a worshiper of Qos/Apollo, and he was the one, as we saw, who opposed Judaism. The temple at Marisa was probably dedicated to Apollo, if we judge from the frequent use of his theophoric equivalent in the area.[123] Archaeology confirms the extent

119. Teixidor 1977: 97; cf. Cook 1930: 179; coin e.g. *RPC* 1, 4884; 4889; 4893.

120. Hill 1912: 11; Phythian-Adams (1921: 82) thought that Phanebalos might represent Heracles-Belos, a combination of Baal, Sarapis and Eshmun, who is known to have been worshipped at Ascalon in the third century CE (*SB* 8452; and coin under Macrinus according to Hill, 1912: 13), and that he might be the figure riding on a lion ('Asclepios the lion-carrier') which appears on later coins. Hill (1912: 9) thought that Phanebalos might be identified with Eshmun assimilated to Melqart/Heracles, with the lion skin. Since Sidon's two main deities were Eshmun and Astarte, while Tyre's were Melkart and Astarte, and since Astarte/Aphrodite is present at Ascalon, Eshmun or Melqart are wanted. Thus the combination of the two makes sense.

121. Marcus Diaconus, *Life of Porph.* 64.

122. For the onomasticon, see Chapter 2 n. 116; the significant concentration of Qos/Apollo names in *SB* 681 should be stressed here: Qosadoros, Qosramos, Qosmalachos, Appolophanes, Apollonios and Apollodoros (see Thompson [D.J.] 1984: 1072; cf. Thompson [D.J.] 1988: 100); for Mnaseas see Chapter 2 n. 66; for the Apolloneion at Memphis, see *OGIS* 737.

123. E.g. Peters and Thiersch 1905: nos. 9, 12-13, 24, 44; Oren and Rappaport 1984: nos. 10, 13-14, etc.; cf. Cook 1930: 203; the three compartments do not presuppose a temple of an Idumaean trinity, and there is no evidence that it was erected by Gabinius (Avi-Yonah 1977b: 788). The only deities named in the Marisan texts are Aphrodite and Korē (see Chapter 2 n. 118), the latter also introduced to Samaria (Flusser 1975). Herod was familiar with Korē (Kokkinos 1985), and after

of the cult of Apollo in Idumaea, by the discovery of figurines at sites such as Lachish, Tell el-'Areini and Tel Ṣippor (also Tell Megadim in the north).[124]

Herod's coins, which are full of pagan symbols (such as the caduceus, the cornucopiae and the eagle) directly connected to Hellenistic deities,[125] also depict the 'tripod with lebes' of the Apollo cult. It is known from Josephus that Herod honoured Apollo (also the god of his patron Augustus) by building a temple to him at Rhodes.[126] Alexander, Herod's son, cultivated a close friendship with Euaratus a prominent Coan, identified with Caius Julius Euaratus the priest of Apollo at Halasarna.[127] Antipas's inscription from Delos (the mythical birthplace of the god) was dedicated to Apollo and placed in front of his holy temple on the island.[128] Finally an inscription from al-Mushannaf in the Hauran, set up for the safety of Agrippa I, seems to refer to Apollo as 'the ancestral god' (πάτριος)—possibly of both the dedicator and the Herodian family.[129]

None of the ingredients of Hellenized Phoenician culture were absent from the city of Ascalon, above all the development of Greek *paideia* and literature. Among its famous people the city boasted

Augustus's initiation into her cult, he appears to have built a temple (νεώς) to her at Sebaste (Josephus, *Ant.* 15.296 in Niese's text; for the probable site, see Sukenik 1942; Wright 1959: 72)—not to be confused with the Augusteum (Netzer 1987b; Barag 1993).

124. See generally Stern [E.] 1982: 179, tab. B.

125. Jacobson 1986: 159-65; contra Meyshan 1959. According to Meshorer (*AJC* 2, 7-9; cf. Meshorer 1984) after 19 BCE the Tyrian shekels—depicting the head of Heracles—were minted by Herod in Jerusalem (but see Appendix 9 end). Herod's religious persuasion has never been explored (cf. above n. 41); see Herod's 'piety' in Jacobson 1988: 391-93, and contrast the weak understanding of Richardson 1986.

126. Josephus, *War* 1.424; *Ant.* 16.147; no doubt at Athens and Nicopolis, and perhaps Sparta and Cyprus, the shrines of Apollo were also benefitted by Herod (Kokkinos forthcoming 1); cf. the statue of Apollo or Aphrodite from Caesarea-on-the-coast (Gersht 1983–84).

127. Josephus, *War* 1.532; *Ant.* 16.312; *IGRR* 4.1101; cf. Sherwin-White 1976: 185; 1978: 249-50.

128. *OGIS* 417; *ID* 1586; cf. Gabba 1958: 45-46, no. 15; inscriptions of other Ascalonites from Delos clearly show the respect of these Hellenized Phoenician people for the cult of Apollo (*ID* 1717, 1718, 1722, 1724, 1934).

129. *OGIS* 418 (see Chapter 10 n. 92)—the word is πάτριος (or perhaps πατρι[κ]ὸς as corrected by Dittenberger) not πατρῷος which may have meant the epithet of Apollo, as known, for example, from his temple in the Athenian Agora.

Antiochus the Stoic (or eclectic) philosopher, and his brother and successor Aristus, who lived in the first century BCE.[130] Another native of Ascalon was Ptolemy the grammarian, who, as we saw, was probably the biographer of Herod the Great. Also three other Stoic philosophers (Sosus, Antibius and Eubius), another grammarian (Dorotheus), probably an epigrammatist (Euenus), as well as two historians (Apollonius and Artemidorus) are on record.[131] Ascalonites excelled in trade and business overseas: Aphrodisius the son of Zenodorus held the prestigious position of πρόξενος on the island of Delos, where also Philostratus the son of Philostratus became a renowned banker.[132]

Herod's education followed Hellenized Phoenician standards, at least judging from his intellectual pursuits as related in a fragment of

130. Antiochus was born a little before Strabo, as the geographer himself testifies (16.2.29).

131. Stephanus, s.v. *Askalōn*; see Hengel 1974: 1.86-87; Geiger 1990: 147; Geiger 1991–92: 117; among famous people from later periods, the family of Julian the architect is discussed by Geiger (1992).

132. Aphrodisius is known from three inscriptions (Roussel 1987: 12 n. 3), while Philostratus from eighteen (Mancinetti-Santamaria 1982; Leiwo 1989). Merchants and others from Ascalon are known to have been active, or died, in a number of places: on Rhodes (*IG* 12.118; Maiuri 1925: nos. 161-62, 175; cf. Morelli 1956: 148) two men (Alexander son of Sosus and Apollonius) and two women (Eirena and Plousia wife of Antaius the Laodicean); on Rheneia (*MFR* nos. 21, 87, 228-29, 241, 284, 436bis, 468) five men (Dionysius son of Prytanes, Nikandrus and Diopeithes sons of Dionysius, Diophantus son of Diopeithes, and Hippo [crates?]) and three women (Artemisia daughter of Phile, Armonia daughter of Akesandrus and Aline); on Delos (*ID* 1723, 2033, 2305, 2593, 2599) five men (Diodotus son of Antipater, Damon son of Demetrius, Apollophanes, Antipater, and another whose name has not been preserved), but without counting a son (Theophilus—*ID* 1934) and a friend (Zenon—*ID* 2253) of Philostratus the banker; in Athens (*IG* 2².8388-90) two men (Antipater son of Aphrodisius, and Zenon son of Zenon) and one woman (Megiste daughter of Asclepiades and wife of Demetrius the Antiochean), while a young Ascalonite (Zenon son of Moschus) is also mentioned in a list of *ephēboi* (*IG* 2².1028.148); at Demetrias (Arvanitopoulos 1909: nos. 80, 151; Arvanitopoulos 1949: no. 257; Arvanitopoulos 1952–53a: nos. 322, 347, 349; cf. Sznycer 1979) six men (Sillis son of Zoilus, Diocles son of Phil[on?], Jason son of Antipater, Dorotheus son of Apollo[phanes?], Zenon son of Antipater and Mettounmikim son of Abdeleb); at Puteoli (*CIL* 10.1746) one man (Herod son of Aphrodisius); in Rome an actor (Apelles) worked for the court of Caligula (Philo, *Legat.* 203-206), while a soldier (Yamur son of Asam) served in the eighth praetorian cohort (*IG* 14.1661 = *IGUR* 590); and, of course, from near Alexandria (*IBM* 4.1072).

124 *The Herodian Dynasty*

Nicolaus's autobiography (and absent from Josephus):

> Herod again having given up his enthusiasm for philosophy, as it commonly happens with people in authority because of the abundance of goods that distract them, was eager again for rhetoric and pressed Nicolaus to practice rhetoric with him... Again, he was seized by love of history... and becoming eager to study this subject, also influenced Nicolaus to busy himself with history... Then Herod, when sailing to Rome to meet Caesar, took Nicolaus with him on the same ship, and they discussed philosophy together.[133]

It was only natural that Herod would eventually be led to compose his own work—no doubt his *Hypomnēmata* were written in Greek.[134] Although of his early years we know very little, Herod would have been taught Greek at Marisa or Ascalon.[135]

Under Herod the Great Greek learning became more widely available, even at Jerusalem itself, in such institutions as apparently the school of Hillel, and the synagogues of Theodotus and the Libertines.[136] Perhaps this is in line with the staunch programme undertaken by the King, in building and promoting *gymnasia* in Phoenician, Syrian and Aegean cities (at least in Ptolemais, Tripolis, Damascus and Cos).[137] The tutition Herod provided for his children was strongly

133. Nicolaus, *apud* Constantinus Porphyrogenitus (*FGrH* 90, F135; *GLAJJ* 1, 248-50 no. 96).

134. Josephus, *Ant.* 15.174; in composing his memoirs Herod may have followed the example of Augustus and Marcus Agrippa, but of course Hellenistic royalty have had scholarly interests (Préaux 1978: 1.212-20), and other client kings of Rome became well-known writers, such as Archelaus of Cappadocia and Juba of Mauretania.

135. Hengel (1989: 35-36) maintains that Herod was taught Greek in Jerusalem under Hyrcanus II, which is rather easy to say. First, the Herodian court in Jerusalem was established in 63 BCE (cf. above n. 50), at which time Herod was nine or ten (see Chapter 6 n. 2), and his schooling must have begun before Hyrcanus. Second, it is not clear whether appropriate Greek education became available in Jerusalem immediately after 63. The *gymnasium* established there in 175 BCE (1 Macc. 1.14) was a peculiar case, which would not have survived. The only mention in Josephus (*Ant.* 15.373) of young Herod attending lectures of a teacher (διδάσκαλος), does not make clear where or when.

136. For Hillel's school, see *b. B. Qam.* 83a, but note Neusner above n. 66; cf. generally Momigliano 1981: 328-30; for Theodotus's synagogue, see *CII* 1404; Gabba 1958: 79-82, no. 23; for the synagogue of the Libertines, see Acts 6.9; Hengel 1992: 32, 42-43.

137. Josephus, *War* 1.422-23; see above n. 90.

Graeco-Roman,[138] though certainly with a Semitic basis.[139] Members of the Herodian family to the time of Agrippa II and beyond, safeguarded their Hellenized Phoenician tradition—Josephus says that they were 'persons thoroughly conversant with Greek *paideia*'.[140]

As we know, proper Greek education focused not only on the training of the mind, but also on the skills of the body. Accordingly the physical prowess of Herod the Great became almost proverbial:

> Always foremost in the chase, in which he distinguished himself above all by his skill in horsemanship... As a fighter he was irresistible; and at practice spectators were often struck with astonishment at the precision with which he threw the javelin, the unerring aim with which he bent the bow.[141]

Herod's general culture is self-evident, as was to be shown by his massive contributions to the pagan world, his Hellenized royal court and building of theatres and hippodromes in his own kingdom.[142] Faithful to the Hellenized Phoenician passion for sport, Herod did not hesitate to introduce athletic games in Jewish territory. Many texts clearly indicate that Phoenicians took an active part in the Greek games.[143] Herod himself became patron of the Olympic Games; the position with which he was honoured (διηνεκὴς ἀγωνοθέτης) was

138. E.g. Josephus, *Ant.* 16.203, 242; 17.95; cf. Otto 1913: 90.

139. This may be gathered from Herod's own speeches to the people of Jerusalem (regardless of whether they have been embellished by Nicolaus or Josephus—e.g. Josephus, *War* 1.457-65; *Ant.* 15.382-87), which must have been in Hebrew, and later by Agrippa I's understanding of Marsyas's Hebrew message (*Ant.* 18.228), and his reading of the Torah in the Temple (Chapter 10 n. 94), as well as the speech of Agrippa II at the time of the Jewish Revolt (see discussion in Chapter 10 n. 206).

140. Josephus, *Life* 359; cf. the Greek learning of Julius Archelaus (Chapter 7 n. 87), and the total Hellenization of the descendants of Alexander II (Chapter 9 n. 37).

141. Josephus, *War* 1.429.

142. For Herod's contributions to Greece, see above n. 90; for his Hellenized court, see Chapter 4; for building of sports facilities at Caesarea, Sebaste, Jerusalem and Jericho, see *SVM* 1, 305-306 n. 56; *SVM* 2, 55 n. 155; Netzer 1987a: 440 map.

143. Herod introduced games at Caesarea (Josephus, *War* 1.415; *Ant.* 16.136-41) and Jerusalem (*Ant.* 15.267-76); see Harris [H.A.] 1976; cf. Ascalon's festival games (*IGRR* 3.1012); for Sidonians in the Theseian, Nemean and other games, see *IG* 22.960; Wadd. 1866a; *SEG* 1.466; cf. Jidejian 1971: 70-77.

totally unprecedented.[144] No wonder, therefore, that the king admitted that he felt 'much closer to the Greeks than to the Jews', according to Josephus.[145]

Hence it needs to be stressed that Herod's Hellenizing policies should not be understood simply as a political design (common among client-kings) to show loyalty to Rome, or only as 'euergetism', or megalomania for building and honours,[146] but primarily as a deep-rooted attitude reflecting personal circumstances, that is the origins of his family from a Hellenized Phoenician environment. The Roman world happened to be ideal for the display of his inner thoughts and beliefs, although he had no alternative but to avoid enforcing them on the Jews in Palestine.[147]

The Greek names of Antipater and Herod are well-attested among people from Ascalon, Gaza and the Phoenician coast. Antipater (Ἀντίπατρος) was the name of famous individuals, like the epigrammatist of Sidon (second century BCE) and the philosopher of Tyre (first century BCE). Antipater was also the father of Nicolaus of Damascus, the principal counsellor of the Herodian palace. There had been many Antipaters in respectable positions during the Hellenistic period, for example an ἐπιμελητὴς and a τριήραρχος in Egypt.[148] The island of Delos and the city of Demetrias have each produced at least two inscriptions referring to Antipaters who came from Ascalon: on Delos—the father of a Diodotus, and probably another individual;

144. Josephus, *War* 1.426-27; *Ant.* 16.149; cf. Finley and Pleket 1976: 99, 111.

145. Josephus, *Ant.* 19.329.

146. Otto 1913: 55-110; Momigliano 1934b: 329-30; Jones [A.H.M.] 1938: 99-100; Robert 1938: 136-38; Schalit 1969: 412-13; Stern [M.] 1974b: 242-58; Smallwood 1976: 77-84; Netzer 1981; Braund 1984a: 75-77; Bartlett 1985: 101-110; Jacobson 1988.

147. The only benefaction of Herod to the Jews was the Temple at Jerusalem (cf. Horbury 1991; for new archaeological reconstructions, see Patrich 1988; Ritmeyer and Ritmeyer 1989; Ritmeyer 1992; and now Patrich 1994), and even this was countered with an impressive building at Hebron, as the visible architectural work of Haram el-Khalil betrays (Jacobson 1981; Miller [N.] 1985). Josephus (*Ant.* 19.329) was appalled at Herod's record: 'there was not a single city of the Jews on which he deigned to bestow even minor restoration or any gift worth mentioning'.

148. *PP* 1.931; 5.13800; cf. Antipater of Hierapolis a Chaldaean astronomer (Bowersock 1983a); *RE* lists 37 fairly well-known individuals; *LGPN* lists many from the firth century BCE in Thasos (Herodotus, 7.118) to the third century CE in Cyrene (*SEG* 26.1830).

at Demetrias—the father of Jason, and perhaps another father of Zenon.[149]

Of particular importance is 'Antipater of Ascalon, son of Aphrodisius' known from a fourth or third century BCE bilingual inscription at Athens.[150] His name is also given in Phoenician as [ר]מס (guardian?) or [ת]מס (descendant?), which is not very far from the Greek ἀντίπατρός (one who stands *in loco parentis*), while his father is called עבדעסתרת (servant of Astarte), a near equivalent of 'Αφροδίσιος.[151] Antipater was a sailor or a merchant who was killed by a lion as he disembarked from his vessel (possibly in Peiraeus), and was buried by a Sidonian friend of his in the Athenian cemetery of Kerameikos. Here we have a key illustration of the transition from Phoenician to Hellenized culture at Ascalon, already in the earliest Ptolemaic period, together with evidence for the early adoption of a Greek name, which took root in the area and happened to be glorified later by the Herodian dynasty.

The name Herod ('Ηρῴδης or 'Ηρωΐδης) is familiar in the Hellenistic period, for example in Egypt where among others an Alexandrian διοικητὴς is on record for 164 BCE, as well as a ποιητὴς ἐπιγραμμάτων, a μηχανικὸς and even a Herod ἱερόδουλος (by coincidence to the Christian tradition) of Isis.[152] A Herod appears in the Zenon papyri as τελώνης in Gaza (258 BCE), and the name persists in this city for a considerable time, as can be seen by a number of lead

149. *ID* 1723, 2599; Arvanitopoulos 1949: no. 257; Arvanitopoulos 1952–53a: no. 347; for Delos in general see Roussel 1987; for Demetrias see Milojcic and Theocharis 1976, and Hourmouziadis *et al.* 1982: 40-42.

150. *CIS* 1.115 = *IG* 2².8388 = Cooke 1903: no. 32 = *KAI* 54 = Gibson [J.C.L.] 1982: 147; cf. Lenormant 1864: 120-33, nos. 40-41; Palmer and Sandys 1872; Wolters 1888.

151. 'Abd'Ashtart (servant of Astarte) was also rendered in Greek as Straton, e.g. the Philhellene king of Sidon (see Chapter 1 n. 41). Bilingual inscriptions illustrate that the Greek names adopted by the Phoenicians were often based on a resemblance in sound to the Semitic, or a rough translation: Artemidorus for 'Abdtanit (servant of Tanit); Heliodorus for 'Abdshemesh (servant of the Sun-God); Diopeithes for Samabaal (Baal has listened)—*KAI* 53, 60; *IG* 2, Suppl. 1335b; Avi-Yonah 1978: 182; for Hebrew analogies see Cassuto 1932; cf. Ilan 1987; Mussies 1994.

152. *P. Paris* 63; *PP* 6.16543, 16690; *SB* 8142; *RE* lists 14 fairly well-known individuals outside the Herodian dynasty; *LGPN* lists 36 from the fourth century BCE in Chios (*SEG* 15.540) to the fourth or fifth century CE in Cyrene (*PLRE* 2, 551).

weights referring to an ἀγορανόμος called Herod (CE 154).[153]

A second century CE sarcophagus of a 'Herod son of Antipater' was discovered at Tyre, while another contemporary Herod (probably also a citizen of a Phoenician metropolis) was buried in the Jewish cemetery of Beth-She'arim.[154] Of particular interest is a 'Herod of Ascalon, son of Aphrodisius', whose tombstone (dated between the first century BCE and the second century CE) was found at Puteoli.[155] This Herod seems to have been a merchant conducting business in southern Italy—since he was buried at Bauli by Demetrius a steward (*vilicus*), no doubt working for a local Roman villa.[156]

5. *The Coins of Ascalon and the Herods*

Early in the century Svoronos reported an exceptional coin struck at Ascalon in the Ptolemaic period: a silver tetradrachm of the fourth year of Ptolemy IV, indicating that in 218 BCE the city was still under Egyptian control.[157] However, the first *regular* issue of Ascalonian currency (an Attic drachm depicting Apollo on the reverse) appears under Antiochus III at the beginning of the second century BCE, thus

153.   *P. Zen.* 5.59804, l. 5 (= *P. C. Zen.* 1.3 + *PSI* 6.602 + 7.863g); for the weights see Manns 1984: nos. 15, 16 (four examples); cf. Qedar 1986–87: 35, no. 7 ('five' examples). There is another weight (Wadd. 1904 = *IGRR* 3.1212; Lifshitz 1976: 168-69, no. 1) with the inscription ΚΟΛΩΝΙΑΣ ΓΑΖΗΣ ΕΠΙ ΗΡΩΔΟΥ ΔΙΟΦΑΝΤΟΥ ΙΕ, which is thought to date to CE 145 following the era of Hadrian's visit in CE 130 (Clermont-Ganneau 1896: 399 n.). Although it is tempting to identify the two *agoranomoi* named Herod (CE 145 and 154), this is not possible if Gaza became a *colonia* in the late third century CE (Glucker 1987: 78; Millar 1990a: 55-56). A weight from Azotus, which was thought to mention a Herod *agoranomos* in 69–70 CE (*SEG* 26.1665; Meimaris *et al.* 1992: 363-64, no. 49), actually refers to Herod the Great (Kushnir-Stein 1995a).

154.   Rey-Coquais 1977: no. 115; Schwabe and Lifshitz 1974: no. 56; at that period many Herods are found on inscriptions from the Hauran, for example from Sûr (Littmann [E.] *et al.* 1921: no. 7978); cf. Chapter 8 n. 128 and Chapter 10 n. 171; for an *eirēnarchos* at Smyrna, see Chapter 9 n. 42.

155.   *CIL* 10.1746; I have not examined the palaeography on the actual stone, but the ligatures it contains do not seem to exclude a date as early as the first century BCE (Gordon 1983: 95), while the text would predate the letter of the Tyrians at Puteoli in 174 CE (*OGIS* 595).

156.   This villa may even have been that of Hortensius the orator—a major establishment at Bauli, which later became the property of Antonia Augusta (Kokkinos 1992a: 153-55).

157.   Svoronos 1904: no. 1188, pl. 36.16.

confirming the fact that the city had now passed into the Seleucid hands of Syria.[158] From Antiochus IV (175–169 BCE) to Antiochus VIII (126–96 BCE) many dated bronze and silver 'royal' types (principally portrait/eagle) tell their own story about a significant mint at Ascalon.[159]

In 168/167 BCE, precisely when the great events in Jerusalem were taking place (visit of Antiochus IV and desecration of the temple), the coins of Ascalon for the first time advertized: ΑΣΚΑΛΩΝΙΤΩΝ ΔΗΜΟΥ.[160] Whether this would mean that Ascalon was granted the rights of a polis by Antiochus IV is not clear. Unfortunately the legend does not persist in later issues and no recognizable era begins at this point. If the city did receive any privileges in this year, these do not appear to have been of lasting consequence.

It may be of interest that after the end of Alexander I Balas's rule in 145 BCE, the mint of Ascalon changed its style and weight according to Phoenician standards, as can be observed in the issue of Tryphon of 140 BCE and in all subsequent coinage.[161] This was approximately when Jonathan marched to Ascalon, and when the first Herod of our dynasty (possibly born around 178 BCE) would have been among the most influential citizens of the city. If one of the historical models already proposed is correct, on this occasion Antipas the son of Herod would have been presented as a hostage to the Maccabaean leader.

In 112/111 BCE for the first time the coins advertized ἱερά and ἄσυλος.[162] This was the year of the return of Antiochus VIII Grypus

158. Brett 1950: 46, no. 1, pl. 8.1; for minting in Late Persian Ascalon, see Meshorer 1989a; Mildenberg 1994: 68.

159. The dates found on the royal issues of Ascalon according to the Seleucid Era are: 144 = 169/8 BCE; 145 = 168/7 BCE; 165 = 148/7 BCE; 166 = 147/6 BCE; 186 = 127/6 BCE; 187 = 126/5 BCE; 189 = 124/3 BCE; 190 = 123/2 BCE; 191 = 122/1 BCE; 192 = 121/0 BCE; 193 = 120/19 BCE; 195 = 118/7 BCE; 196 = 117/6 BCE; 197 = 116/5 BCE; and every year from 199 = 114/3 BCE to 20 = 104/3 BCE.

160. *BMC* Palest./Asc. no. 7, pl. 11.13 (the date has been confirmed by *RIC* 1.34, no. 2); for the events in Judaea, see *SVM* 1, 152-53 n. 32.

161. Brett 1950: 45, 48, no. 8, pl. 8.7.

162. Brett 1950: 51, nos. 20-21; Spaer 1984: nos. 18-22 and C; Although it has remained unnoticed, a coin of Demetrius II Nicator (second reign) dated to 127/6 BCE seems to read ΙΕ[ΡΑΣ] but without ΑΣΥΛΟΥ (Brett 1950: 49, no. 11, pl. 8.9; cf. *BMC* Palest./Asc. no. 13, pl. 11.15, an undated minor bronze with ΙΕΡΑΣ on the reverse). At any rate, it is only in 112/1 BCE that both epithets begin to appear regularly.

to power. The Seleucid king seems to have rewarded Ascalon, perhaps for support he received during his struggle. An unusual monogram Ⱦ, most probably belonging to the person in control of the mint, also appears for the first time.[163] If this is understood as a ligature of the initial two letters HP (as later types and other evidence suggest) of the dynastic name 'Herod', this person acting in the now 'Holy and Inviolable' city, could have been the same early Herod of our family. The monogram is also found in some subsequent pre-independence issues of Ascalon, in the following developed forms: Ⱦ (=HPΩΔ) in 110/9 BCE, Ⱦ or Ⱦ in 109/8 BCE, and Ⱦ or Ⱦ in 107/6 BCE.[164]

For many years numismatists wrestled with the question of the meaning of the symbol Ⱦ found on the famous coins (Year 3) of Herod the Great. From King, over a century ago, who compared it with a number of monograms including the Christian XP and the Roman *sigla* X denoting a denarius, or X a commander of 1000 men (χιλίαρχος), to Meyshan's interpretation that TP stands for Tyre, that is the place of minting, and to Meshorer's new idea that TP should read τετράρχης (a title possessed by Herod before he became a king), an adequate answer has always been lacking.[165] Krupp and Qedar referred to other unsuccessful interpretations:

> Cavedoni and Levy suggested that it represents a *crux ansata*, the Egyptian symbol of immortality. De Saulcy and other scholars interpreted it as a ligature of a Greek T and P, standing for τριάς (three), or τριχάλκου i.e. its value. Narkiss as well as Goodenough suggested that it stands for Trachonitis, the area given to Herod in 28 B.C. Yet another suggestion was that it stands for the name Tigranes, the name of a mint-master. Kanael put forward the theory that this ligature means τρίτῳ ἔτει ('in the third year') the same as LΓ which appears together with it on the same coins.[166]

In the light of the evidence presented above a positive answer may now be attempted: the monogram on Herod's coins is a version of the (by then) standard mint mark, denoting Herodian authority (HP). Krupp and Qedar themselves realized that the ligature 'combines a Greek H and P, the two initial letters of HP(WΔHC)'. Their claim was

---

163. Brett 1950: 51, no. 20, pl. 9.16; Spaer 1984: 233, no. 20, pl. 36.

164. Spaer 1984: 234, nos. 26-28, 30-38, pl. 36.

165. King [C.W.] 1873: 13; Meyshan 1959: 115 (on Tyre cf. Meshorer's theory, above n. 125); *AJC* 2, 10; cf. Meshorer 1990–91: 108.

166. Krupp and Qedar 1981: 18.

supported by a specimen (anchor/legend type) in which the first letter
of Herod's name is replaced by a cross.[167] Rappaport, who feels that
Herod's 'Year 3' coins were in fact struck at Ascalon, came very close
to suspecting that the Ascalonian monogram represents the Herodian
family:

> As the monogram is most probably a sign of the mintmaster it may repre-
> sent two magistrates of the same name and family, the one contemporary
> of Hyrcan I, the other of Herod.[168]

The connection of the Herods with the early coins of Ascalon, as
revealed here, continued after independence. The city became
αὐτόνομος in 103 BCE (at the beginning of the reign of Alexander
Jannaeus), a date confirmed with other evidence by the last numismatic use of the Seleucid era (Year 209 = 104/3 BCE).[169] The first
known examples of the new era (Year 6) are dated to 98 BCE and
again they show a Herodian mint mark (⚮)—perhaps in the very year
that Antipas rose to power under Alexander Jannaeus.[170] The striking
of royal silver types (at first still with Seleucid portraits and later with
Ptolemaic) continued uninterrupted until 38 BCE (when the last
portrait of Cleopatra VII appeared).[171] Curiously, Herodian authority

167. Krupp and Qedar 1981: pl. 5.3, 5; cf. a rare specimen of Herod's 'anchor'
coins with the abbreviation HP on the obverse (Kindler 1953: 240, no. 4, pl. 15.4);
this monogram also appears to have been added at the bottom of one of Herod's
inscriptions from Athens (cf. below n. 195), but this has to be discussed elsewhere.
Meshorer's (1990–91) new reference to a Chalcis coin with a similar monogram does
little to support his view of *tetrarchēs*, not only because as a symbol of authority it
could have been adopted in different contexts, but also because of the intriguing
relationship of the Herods with Chalcis (see above n. 96).

168. Rappaport 1981b: 365.

169. Spaer 1984: 234, no. 48, pl. 37; for the era see Brett 1937; *SVM* 2, 106
n. 102.

170. Spaer 1984: 235, nos. 50-51, pl. 37; note an enigmatic coin reported by
Madden (1864: 68-69 n. 5) as belonging to the reign of Alexander Jannaeus (due to
the 'star' on the reverse), depicting on the obverse an unknown portrait, a part of the
legend being read by Poole as HPΩ!

171. Spaer 1984: 239 argues (contra Brett 1937) that Seleucid portraits were
used long after independence, at least until 79 BCE, and perhaps until 49 BCE when
the Ptolemaic head of Cleopatra VII makes its debut. However, Spaer may not be
totally right since a portrait previously dated to 54 BCE (and therefore Seleucid
according to him) has now been redated to 48 BCE, i.e. after the appearance of
Cleopatra (see next note). The known autonomous dates of the 'royal' series are: 6 =
98 BCE; 8 = 96 BCE; 10 = 94 BCE; 12 = 92 BCE; 20 = 84 BCE; 21 = 83 BCE; 24 = 80

over the local mint is evident later only in vital years for the history of the Herods: Year 41 = 63 BCE (as 𝓣) after the conquest of Jerusalem by Antipater with the help of Pompey, and Year 56 = 48 BCE (as Ͱ𝓟) when Antipater became the protagonist of Caesar's victory over Egypt.[172] We have to presume that Antipater was responsible for both of these issues.

Armed with such new interpretations a search for the Herods in the Ascalonian coinage of the early Roman period is inevitable, and specifically for the reign of Herod the Great. There exists a considerable corpus of material which has yet to be properly studied. Many years ago, in his catalogue of Palestinian coins at the British Museum, Hill observed:

> The classification of the remainder of the undated coins of Ascalon, before or at the beginning of the Imperial period, presents great difficulty... The arrangement in the text of this catalogue is merely tentative. Some of the heads which are represented seem to be portraits of other people than Augustus... With regard to the types of nos. 39-45, de Saulcy has pointed out that they suggest a connexion with Herod the Great... The types of cornucopiae and caduceus are, however, so colourless that little stress can be laid on their occurrence at Ascalon as well as on Herod's coins. In any case they cannot have been struck at Herod's orders, but only out of compliment to him, and de Saulcy's further speculations about Salome and Archelaus are extremely improbable. The identification of those heads, whether portraits or not, which cannot be meant for Augustus, must remain for the present undecided, however tempting it may be to see in them Herod the Great or some other ruler of the time.[173]

BCE; 25 = 79 BCE; 30 = 74 BCE; 31 = 73 BCE; 33 = 71 BCE; 34 = 70 BCE; 35 = 69 BCE; 36 = 68 BCE; 38 = 66 BCE; 39 = 65 BCE; 40 = 64 BCE; 41 = 63 BCE; 43 = 61 BCE; 51 = 53 BCE; 55 = 49 BCE (Cleopatra); 56 = 48 BCE (Cleopatra); 66 = 38 BCE (Cleopatra).

172.   For 'Year 41' see *BMC* Palest./Asc. no. 18, pl. 12.1 = Brett 1937, no. 5, pl. 9.13; de Saulcy 1874, 181, no. 36; for 'Year 56' see *BMC* Palest./Asc. no. 19, pl. 12.2, as well as another copy (no. 803) recently sold at the Numismatic Fine Arts auction (14 Dec. 1989) of the Paul Stadler Szego collection. Note that the British Museum specimen (no. 19) is actually listed as 'Year 50' of an era beginning in 84 BCE, but this is incorrect. The era of Ascalon is now known to have begun in 103 BCE, while the year has been read as '56' by Vardaman and myself (see now comment in *RPC* 1, 724). Our reading is supported by the Szego example, and this date is further attested among the 'non-royal' coins of Ascalon (*SNG(ANS)* Palest., 661-62, pl. 20; *RIC* 1.38, no. 31).

173.   *BMC* Palest., lvi-lvii.

If the combination of historical, epigraphical and numismatic evidence explored in this part of the book has any real value, the time has surely come to decide on these portraits and attempt to identify them.

Concentrating only on the dated 'non-royal' autonomous bronze,[174] one may suggest that the portrait of Year 49 = 55 BCE (thought to illustrate a bearded Ascalus) is that of Antipater the father of Herod the Great. This was apparently the year that he was appointed *epimelētēs* of Jerusalem by Gabinius.[175] The issue, bearing an eagle on the reverse, may originally have appeared in 63 BCE (Year 41) at the conquest of Jerusalem, if such a date has been correctly read by Rosenberger.[176] Similarly, it may be suggested that the 'old bearded' Antipater appears on Year 56 = 48 BCE, upon his promotion by Caesar to the position of *epitropos* of Judaea.[177] Finally, he may also be depicted on Year 61 = 43 BCE, at the time of his death as we know from Josephus.[178]

The identification of Antipater on the coins of Ascalon is significant. Phythian-Adams in the past, without paying any attention to Hill's statements, wrote:

> ... under the Roman aegis (Ascalon) was issuing barbarous looking coins, which occasionally bear the head of Aretas III, the Nabatean King, whose defeat of the Jews appears to have been the reason for this compliment.[179]

It is astonishing that some scholars were prepared to recognize in the portraits contemporary authorities involved in the conflict between Hyrcanus and Aristobulus, but were unable to point to the obvious individual behind the battle and its outcome, as well as directly connected to Ascalon: the Herodian Antipater! Aretas III fought

174. Since Hill's time many dated examples have been published (cf. comment in *RPC* 1, 673-74). The known autonomous dates of 'non-royal' series in the first century BCE are: 33 = 71 BCE; 35 = 69 BCE; 37 = 67 BCE; 49 = 55 BCE; 51 = 53 BCE; 56 = 48 BCE; 61? = 43 BCE; 63 = 41 BCE; 64 = 40 BCE; 67 = 37 BCE; 74 = 30 BCE; 79 = 25 BCE; 100 = 4 BCE; 101 = 3 BCE—also possibly three dates following the era of Herod the Great: 3 = 37 BCE; 8? = 32 BCE; 19 = 22 BCE (see below n. 191).

175. *RIC* 1.35, no. 8; see above n. 52.

176. *RIC* 1.35, no. 9—it is unfortunate that Rosenberger's publication is of poor quality and many coins are often unclearly or wrongly described.

177. *SNG(ANS)* Palest., 661-62, pl. 20; *RIC* 1.38, no. 31; see above n. 52.

178. *RIC* 1.35, no. 6; this date is not certain, and the age of the portrait is not clear from Rosenberger's drawing—if a much younger man then he may represent Herod instead (see below).

179. Phythian-Adams 1921: 82.

Aristobulus only at the request of Antipater and in fact he lost his battle. It was Antipater with the help of the Roman forces of Pompey who won this major war.

It will further be suggested that the reasonably young portrait on Years 63 = 41 BCE and 64 = 40 BCE is that of Herod the Great. In 41 BCE, at the age of about 31, he had practically taken over Jerusalem, and in 40 BCE after the Parthian invasion and after sailing to Rome he succeeded in being appointed *de jure* king of Judaea by the Roman Senate.[180] The next dated coin of Ascalon, although carrying no human portrait (but Tyche and the prow of a galley), is highly indicative: it belongs to Year 67 = 37 BCE, when Herod defeated Antigonus in Jerusalem and became the king *de facto*.[181] Some undated portrait-issues may well have been struck during this precise year: for example one which appears to depict young Herod on the obverse and a winged caduceus (or sometimes double cornucopias) on the reverse, and another possibly depicting the 'beautiful' Mariamme on the obverse and double cornucopias on the reverse.[182] These pagan symbols are amply attested among the Judaean coins of Herod, while his marriage to Mariamme the Hasmonaean (to whom he was betrothed at Ascalon according to the theory already proposed) was contracted immediately before the fall of Jerusalem.[183]

An older, more authoritative portrait of Herod, resembling that assigned here to his father Antipater, seems to appear on Year 74 = 30 BCE. This was the crucial year in which the kingship of Judaea was reconferred on him by Augustus at Rhodes.[184] A later issue (Year 79

180. For 'Year 63' see *RIC* 1.39, no. 36; for 'Year 64' see *BMC* Palest./Asc. nos. 30-34, pl. 12.8-12; *RIC* 1.39, no. 37; de Saulcy 1874: 182 n. 43; see Josephus, *War* 1.282-85; *Ant.* 14.386-89.

181. *RIC* 1.39, no. 38; see Josephus, *War* 1.349-57; *Ant.* 14.476-81.

182. For young Herod, see *BMC* Palest./Asc. nos. 39 (pl. 12: 15) and 45 (pl. 12.19); *SNG(ANS)* Palest., nos. 659 and 666; *RIC* 1.39-40, nos. 40-44. As Trell (1982–83) argued the symbol of winged caduceus (clearly connected with Hermes and his Phoenician prototype, the son of Baal and Astarte) signified a Phoenician solar cult as well as a mark of authority (cf. Jacobson 1986: 161, 163-64); for Mariamme see *BMC* Palest./Asc. no. 42 (pl. 12.17) and *RIC* 1.39, no. 39— contra (but with admiration) de Saulcy 1869–70, who would instead have seen Salome, the sister of Herod the Great.

183. *AJC*, 2, 18-30; see Chapter 8 §2.

184. *BMC* Palest./Asc. no. 16, pl. 11.18 (*RPC* 1, 4869); de Saulcy 1874, 182, no. 38; see Josephus, *War* 1.393; *Ant.* 15.195.

= 25 BCE) depicting Tyche may have circulated on the occasion of Herod's completion of his building project at Ascalon.[185] Subsequent dated coins, to the end of the king's reign, are known only for the Years 100 = 4 BCE and 101 = 3 BCE, exactly at his death and when Salome inherited the city's palace.[186]

It must be stressed that the last-mentioned examples are imperial—almost all of them carry 'dated' portraits of Augustus. This would further indicate that Herodian chronology played an important role here. One may rightly wonder again whether the city, though influenced by Herod, was until then autonomous, or whether it was leased by him or even under his direct jurisdiction (see above nn. 101-102). Somehow the coins of Augustus from 4/3 BCE had taken up what was suddenly, and unexpectedly, left by Cleopatra VII in 38 BCE (see above n. 171). Between those two dates lies the entire reign of Herod the Great. Surely this cannot be coincidental.[187] Hill's statement above that if the coins of Ascalon depict the king they 'cannot have been struck at Herod's orders, but only out of compliment to him', can now be seriously questioned.

Attention should immediately be drawn to three dated specimens which, strangely, do not seem to follow the official era of Ascalon.[188] A 'Year ΛΓ' (Tyche/eagle type) is combined with the word ΓΑ/ΜΑ, the first part of which was sometime thought to be the abbreviation of Gaza, and the second that of the numeral 41. In fact the word seems to spell out the codified date: Year Three (γάμα or γάμμα). Following the city's era this would translate into 101 BCE, too early for this type of bronze. While a reasonably similar type (Tyche/war galley) is dated to 67 BCE, another (Tyche/figure with *chitōn*) belongs to 25 BCE.[189] Additionally, as we saw, the earliest known year of the city's era is Year 6 of the 'royal' series.

185. *BMC* Palest./Asc. no. 17, pl. 11.19 (*RPC* 1, 4871); *RIC* 1.36, no. 14; de Saulcy 1874: 182 n. 44; see above nn. 89-90.

186. de Saulcy 1874: 189 (nos. 5-7); *BMC* Palest./Asc. nos. 72-74, pls. 13.6-7 (*RPC* 1, 4877); *RIC* 1.43, no. 74; *CREAM* 1497; cf. de Saulcy 1874: 182 (nos. 39-40) without Augustus's portrait; see above n. 91.

187. Cf. the imperial coins of Gaza, which also begin only after the death of Herod (e.g. de Saulcy 1874: 213; see comment in *SVM* 2, 101-102).

188. *SNG*(*ANS*) Palest., 654-55; *RIC* 1.35-6, nos. 10-12; de Saulcy 1874: 181, no. 34.

189. For the 67 BCE, see *BMC* Palest./Asc. no. 15, pl. 11.17; for the 25 BCE, see references above n. 185.

Interestingly the only date attested among Herod's Judaean coins is the famous Year 3 (LΓ) = 37 BCE when Jerusalem fell into his hands.[190] It would make sense, given that these coins were minted at Ascalon according to Rappaport, to suggest that the Ascalonian ΓΑΜΑ type refers to the same event. The other two dates which apparently follow Herod's era, are Year 8? = 32 BCE and Year 19 = 22 BCE.[191] The latter is also attested on a coin, possibly from Sebaste, which I once attributed to Herod the Great.[192] The Ascalonian example of 22 BCE bears a countermark on the obverse, which may even be a tiny portrait of Herod himself![193]

Portraits of Philip the Tetrarch, Agrippa I and his wife Cyprus III, Herod of Chalcis, Aristobulus III of Lesser Armenia and his wife Salome, Agrippa II and possibly his elder brother Drusus, probably Tigranes I (V), and Alexander IV and his wife Jotape, are known from coins.[194] Although such currencies did not circulate in Jerusalem, or in areas where Jewish presence was overwhelming, they were common in the non-Jewish Herodian territories. A question generally avoided is why the image of Herod the Great does not

190. *AJC* 2, 235, nos. 1-6; *RPC* 1, 4901-904; Meshorer 1990–91: 118-19, nos. 1d-5a; cf. Kanael 1951–52; Jacobson 1986; Hendin 1990–91.

191. A similar case may perhaps be made for the 'unknown' era found on a few inscriptions from Tombs 1 and 8 at Marisa: LA, LB, LE (Peters and Thiersch 1905, nos. 11, 17, 27, 28; Oren and Rappaport 1984, nos. 7, 16); judging from the archaeological evidence, at least Tomb 8 could have been sealed as late as the first century BCE; but the question needs further study.

192. Kokkinos 1985—note that the anchor on this coin was interpreted as signifying the journey of Herod's sons to Rome, an event which has now been redated (Appendix 2, pt. 2); consequently, this journey may instead be seen as that of Herod himself to Greece in 22/21 BCE, to meet Marcus Agrippa and Augustus (Kokkinos forthcoming 1); moreover, the idea that the female figure and the legend are those of Korē, the goddess of Sebaste, may be combined with Augustus's daughter Julia (as Korē), who had newly married Agrippa (Dio, 54.6.5); the title of 'Sebaste' was borne unofficially by Julia in the East (Kokkinos 1992a: 103).

193. The earliest countermarks on Herodian coins are on those of Philip the Tetrarch dated to 1 BCE/CE 1 (my reckoning—see Meshorer 1990–91: 121, no. 1a; cf. *AJC* 2, 47-48, 244, no. 3a), but earlier examples exist from various Greek cities (Howgego 1982–83: 54); portrait-countermarks are also known on Augustan coins of the first century BCE (*CREAM* index 8).

194. *AJC* 2; Meshorer 1990–91; cf. Reifenberg 1935; Meyshan 1962; Meyshan 1963; Kindler 1971; Kokkinos 1986a; Burnett 1987; for Drusus see Chapter 10 §2; for Tigranes I and Alexander IV, see Chapter 9.

appear on any coins outside Judaea? Surely there is no need for the later Herods to have been so innovative in placing their heads on coinage. Would they not rather have followed an established Herodian tradition going back at least to the time of the great king?

Moreover, it is reasonable to assume that numismatic portraits did not materialize out of nothing, but were copies of existing sculpture and paintings. Statuary representing members of the Herodian family existed in public as well as in private collections. Indeed, judging from inscribed bases, we know that statues of Herod the Great stood in the temple of Baalshamin at Seeia (Si'a) in the Hauran, on the island of Cos, and on the Acropolis and possibly Agora of Athens.[195] Statues of Herod Antipas were erected on the islands of Cos and Delos, of Glaphyra in Athens, of Agrippa I in Heliopolis (Baalbek) and probably Apamea, and of Berenice II in Athens again.[196] Josephus says that a painted portrait of Mariamme (as well as one of her brother Aristobulus/Jonathan) was made and sent to Mark Antony as a gift.[197] If this was executed at Ascalon, as seems possible in view of the theory advanced above concerning the Hasmonaean movements during this period, it may even have been used as a model by the die-cutter of the coin attributed here to Mariamme.

A long-lost head originally discovered at Jerusalem (!) and now relocated at St Petersburg, and a bust from Memphis in Egypt have

195. Seeia (*OGIS* 415 = *IGRR* 3.1243); Cos (Höghammer 1993: no. 13; Jacobson 1993–94); Acropolis (*OGIS* 414, 427 = *IG* 2². 3440-41); Agora (Merritt 1952: 370, no. 14 = *SEG* 12.150; cf. a fragment from the Agora usually attributed to Herod Atticus (Pittakes 1835: 35-36 = *IG* 2².3600; see Kokkinos forthcoming 1); note also Herod's own dedication (for which he might have earned a statue) from Delos/Syros and possibly, but unlikely, from Chios (Mantzoulinou-Richards 1988); and also possibly from Paphos (*CIG* 2.2628 = *IGRR* 3.938) and Selaema (Sleim) in the Hauran (Allen 1885: 213, no. 57); for a collection of the inscriptions of Herod and bibliography, see Vardaman 1974; interesting but clearly unreliable information is provided by Moses of Chorene (*Hist. of Armen.* 1.2), who says that Herod asked for his statue to be erected by King Abgar in Armenia!

196. Cos (*OGIS* 416 = Maiuri 1925: 161-62, no. 456 = Höghammar 1993: no. 16); Delos (*OGIS* 417 = *ID* 1586 = Gabba 1958: 45-46, no. 15); Athens-Glaphyra (*OGIS* 363 = *IG* 2².3437/8; Kokkinos 1987 = *SEG* 37.148); Athens-Berenice II (*OGIS* 428 = *IG* 2². 3449); for the inscriptions of Agrippa I, see Chapter 10 nn. 124, 126.

197. Josephus, *Ant.* 15.26-27; *War* 1.439; cf. the tapestry made by Cyprus III the wife of Agrippa I (Gow and Page 1968, 300, no. 6; see *GLAJJ* 1, 375-76, no. 154).

been variously ascribed to Herod the Great.[198] Although the numismatic portraits are not of a quality capable of verifying the sculpture, the bearded head from Jerusalem may be successfully compared with the old portrait of Herod from Ascalon, and to some extent with that of Antipater presented above.

Fragments of a gigantic statue discovered at Ascalon were once attributed to Herod the Great by Garstang:

> the sandalled foot and an arm of a giant statue in marble (presumed to be that of Herod) have just come to light... the foot... measures 98 cm or almost a metre from heel to toe...[199]

This statue would have stood over 7 m in height and in the event it is unlikely to have been of the king of Judaea—in the Roman world only gods, emperors and their wives had been represented in such colossal sizes (but compare the size of the Memphis bust above).

Finally, a head from Byblus and a bust from Ostia thought in the past to be of Agrippa I, as well as a statue at Naples conjectured as belonging to Agrippa III son of Drusilla, merit re-examination, though this lies beyond the scope of the present study.[200] At any rate we do know from Josephus that Agrippa I kept statues of his daughters in his palace at Caesarea and his Hellenized Phoenician culture can thus usefully be seen in such contexts.[201]

Summing up briefly, Nicolaus's invention of a Babylonian-Jewish descent for the Herodian family was plain propaganda, as seen by Josephus. The latter himself had no doubt about Herod's general Idumaean background and wealth. But 'Idumaea' and 'Idumaeans', particularly in the Hellenistic period, meant more than one thing: the predominant position was now held by the Greek-Phoenician cities of the Shephelah and the coast. A more specific tradition, preserved by

198.   For the head from Jerusalem, see Clermont-Ganneau 1899: 259-66 (royal or imperial); Watzinger 1935, 86, taf. 31, ab. 73 (priest of Zeus); Vardaman 1974: 120-27 (Herod); Vostchinina 1974: 159-60, no. 32, pls. 50-51 (Hadrian); for the head from Memphis, see Ingholt 1963; Vardaman 1974: 114-19.

199.   Garstang 1921: 16; cf. Garstang 1922: 117.

200.   Poulsen 1960: 42-46, figs. 13-15; cf. Ingholt 1963: 140 n. 135 (Byblos); Visconti [P.E.] 1880: 31-32, no. 43 (Ostia); Eisler 1930: 35-36, pl. 6 (Naples). For a modern sculptured head of Agrippa I in the Israel Museum, produced by copying his best-preserved portrait coin, see Gitler 1995: 36.

201.   Josephus, *Ant*. 19.357, 364; cf. the statues and the εἰκόνες erected by Agrippa II at Berytus (Chapter 10 n. 199).

the Christian Church, connected the Herods with the city of Ascalon.

The historicity of the Ascalonite tradition, even with its varied details and number of generations involved, cannot be ruled out. Possible Herodian genealogies covering the second and first centuries BCE have been offered. Epigraphic evidence of the Hellenistic period shows people with the correct names from Ascalon, as do coins, emphasizing their prominence. Ascalon turns out to have had a much closer relationship with the Herodian dynasty than has previously been thought. The city, not included in the forcible Maccabaean conversion, remained a place of strong Greek culture. Herod's own culture, attitudes and building programme, seen against this background, at last make good sense. It can now be said with increased confidence that the origins of his dynasty have been rediscovered. The consequences for the understanding of the Second Temple period as a whole are significant.

Part II

THE HERODIAN FAMILY AND SOCIAL STRUCTURE

Chapter 4

PROGRAMMATIC NOTES

A brief mention of the first Herodian court established at Jerusalem in the time of Antipater I, and eventually inherited by Herod the Great, has already been made. By 41/40 BCE, even before Herod became a king, this court had a considerable size, that is some 800 people counting only women (500) and their followers. These 'Idumaean' women, led by the female members of the Herodian family *per se*, were promised to the Parthians as a bribe by Antigonus for attacking Jerusalem.[1] Thirty-five years later, at the death of Herod, this court could produce 500 male slaves and freedmen, while its wider grip upon Judaean society had reached the order of 10,000 associates, an estimate only of those who were sufficiently Hellenized ("Ελληνες).[2] In the court were to be found a remarkable variety of assistants, eunuchs, writers, tutors, bodyguards, huntsmen, doorkeepers, physicians, barbers, torturers and secretaries. The wealth of many Herodian courtiers, not only in Jerusalem but also in the offshoot palaces of Tiberias and Panias later, was notorious enough for Jesus to remark that the only places where one could find people dressed in 'fine and delicate draperies' were such palaces.[3]

Considerations of space do not allow here an examination of the development of this court, that is from the point of view of its physical

1. Josephus, *Ant.* 14.362. *Ant.* 14.379 reads: '...five hundred women, who were to be of the first families and of their own race (τοῦ γένους τοῦ αὐτῶν)...' The Loeb translator took this to be either the Jewish race or the Idumaean of Herod. But from the context is clear (cf. *War* 1.257) that the Idumaean race is meant, since the reference is made specifically to the Herodian entourage (cf. further *Ant.* 14. 331, 343, 365; *War* 1.248).

2. Josephus, *Ant.* 17.199; *War* 1.673; Nicolaus, *apud* Constantinus Porphyrogenitus (*FGrH* 90, F136; *GLAJJ* 1, 250-52, no. 97); cf. more generally the 'Hellenists' in Jewish society referred to in Acts 6.1, etc.

3. Mt. 11.8; Lk. 7.25.

existence, institutions, administration, economy, military and the like, not even a scrutiny of its lesser members and attendants, though many glimpses will appear sporadically. What will be offered instead is a broad survey of the human heart of this court, that is all the members of the Herodian dynasty (blood and marriage relatives), focusing on their domestic and foreign actions—most importantly looking at their direct impact on Jewish society. The idea is not to present a descriptive catalogue or a prosopography, but rather a compilation of brief lives running on to each other and reflecting the political history of this period, which will thus be viewed from different angles. The sources to be used will be as diverse as possible (though Josephus is inevitably constant), while attention will be paid on saying more about the people of whom we know less, and less about those of whom our knowledge is greater. Of the major figures, Archelaus, Antipas and Philip will be treated lightly, as well as the unfortunate Alexander I and Aristobulus I, not only because much has been written about them, but also due to the fact that the Agrippas deserve a closer look, belonging, as they did, to the most consequential period of Jewish history—that which sealed itself with the dramatic fall of the holy Temple.

For all purposes Herod the Great's royal court was strongly Hellenized, but at least in one aspect it seems to have followed the path of its ancient oriental counterparts: the creation of a harem, though this too was not unknown in the palace at Macedonia.[4] Herod married ten times, besides, surely, having many concubines—one was presented as a gift to Archelaus of Cappadocia—and even boy lovers (παιδικά).[5] Polygamy was permitted in the Second Temple period, and thus the possession of a large harem must have been a mark of wealth and power; since few could afford such a luxury, it was natural to become the privilege of the élite.[6] For a king the Mishna sets the limit at 18

---

4. For the Herodian court, see Schalit 1969: 403-11; Jeremias 1969: 88-92; Stern [M.] 1975a: 94-95; for its Hellenistic prototype, see Bevan 1927: 118-21, 277-81; Bikerman 1938: 33ff.; Fraser 1972: 1.101-105; for the entourage of Philip II of Macedonia, see Milns 1968: 18-19; cf. the composition of earlier Eastern courts such as those of Nebuchadnezzar II (*ANET* 307-308) and Solomon (2 Sam. 8–20; 1 Kgs 1–2; see de Vaux 1965: 115-26).

5. Josephus, *War* 1.511; *Ant.* 16.230; 17.44; cf. the number of wives of Izates in the royal court of Adiabene (*Ant.* 20.34).

6. Jeremias 1969: 90; cf. with reservations Daniel-Rops 1962: 117-18; *t. Yeb.* 1.10 on high priestly families. Archer (1990: 127 n. 1) points out that polygamy was

wives. Most of the kings of Judah, from David onwards, are reported to have married several times. Solomon is said to have had a record of 700 wives and 300 concubines, no doubt a wild exaggeration—but whatever the precise number he must have ignored the advice of Deuteronomy (had any laws from this book been current at his time), that kings should avoid excessive polygamy.[7]

Herod became the father of 15 children, and we have knowledge of some 20 of his grandchildren, 13 great-grandchildren, eight great-great-grandchildren and two great-great-great-grandchildren. The Herodian blood and marriage relatives over nine generations, known to us principally from Josephus, either by name, or anonymously, or as assumed or implied, number about 144 individuals (see Appendix 1, together with the genealogical trees, charts and tables, provided in the text). No other family of the Graeco-Roman period can be traced without interruption, and in such detail, from the second century BCE to the second century CE.

It is accepted throughout that the marriageable age in the Jewish society began soon after menstruation for the females, that is from around 12 years old, and between 18 and 20 for the males.[8] Although this may suggest a length of 20 to 25 years for a patrilineal generation, many males of the Herodian family waited to their thirties before they took a wife, and bore children from then until their late fifties. For example, Antipater I would have been around 56 when he became a father to his last child Salome I, if the estimate of her birth here is correct (see Chapter 7 §1). Herod the Great, almost certainly born in

---

not a common practice (cf. Epstein 1942: 20, 13, 17), which may be true only in reference to the majority in the Jewish society, for we now know that even in the case of Babatha, her second husband had a living undivorced wife (*P. Yadin* 26). Further, the Essenes had to denounce bigamy (*CD* 4.21) and demand monogamy even of kings (*11QTemple*[a](11Q19), col. 57.15-19; see Yadin 1985: 198-200).

7.   *m. Sanh.* 2.4; cf. Falk 1974: 514-15; for commoners were permitted to have up to four (*m. Ket.* 10.5), or five wives (*m. Ket.* 3.7); cf. Josephus, *Ant.* 17.14; Hanson 1989: 77; for references to the Hebrew kings, see de Vaux 1965: 115; for Solomon see 1 Kgs 11.3; Deut. 17.17; cf. Josephus, *Ant.* 4.224; the chronology and *basic* historicity of the early kings should not be doubted (contra Garbini 1988; see Hughes 1990; James *et al.* 1991; and now Biran and Naveh 1993; Biran and Naveh 1995).

8.   *b. Pes.* 118a; *b. Qid.* 29b-30a; *m. Ab.* 5.21; see Archer 1990: 95-96, 152-53; for the female marriageable age among the Romans, see Shaw 1987; cf. Hopkins 1964–65; for the male see Saller 1987.

72 BCE, had his last child in late 15 BCE, when he would have been 59 years old (see Chapter 8). Agrippa I, born in late 11 BCE, became a father for the last time at the age of 49 (see Chapter 10), while Herod of Chalcis around 57 (see Chapter 10).

Also the evidence for both endogamy and exogamy among the Herods is incontestable, as many female members (such as Salome I and Berenice II) remarried several times. Yet apart from Herod we do not seem to have any clear indication that other male relatives practiced polygamy or even bigamy, certainly not readily. As we shall see Joseph I may have maintained two wives (but this is only a guess—Chapter 5); Antipater II was a married man when he was betrothed to a young lady (though no wedding took place—Chapter 8); and possibly Herod of Chalcis married his second wife while his first was still alive (but this is not certain—Chapter 10). An early betrothal apparently between Agrippa I and a daughter of Antipater II, must have failed (as others did) long before he married the only wife of his known to us, Cyprus III (Chapter 10). In the case of endogamy, it appears that it formed the largest kinship chasm between the Jews and the Graeco-Roman culture in the first century CE,[9] but we must not forget that the marriage of first cousins in Athens could not have been abandoned before the first century BCE, while in Egypt and Mesopotamia close-kin marital unions continued until the third and sixth centuries CE respectively.[10] Most combinations of endogamy are observed among the Herods, the commonest being that of cross-cousins. Characteristic was uncle–niece marriages. Many Herodians married their nieces: Herod the Great (Chapter 8), Herod III (Chapter 8), Philip the Tetrarch (Chapter 8), Antipas the Tetrarch (Chapter 8) and Herod of Chalcis (Chapter 10). Also Antipater II was betrothed to his niece Mariamme IV (Chapter 8), but the girl may later have become the wife of Archelaus, another uncle of hers (Chapter 10).[11]

The nature of Josephus's text will be treated in the notes, with

9. From an anthropological point of view (based on E. Todd), see Hanson 1989: 77; on the general absence of close-kin marriage in the Roman society, see Shaw 1984.

10. For first-cousin marriages in Athens, see Thompson [W.E.] 1967; Littman 1979: 20-24; for brother–sister marriage in Egypt, see Hopkins 1980; for Mesopotamia, see Lee 1988; cf. Roth 1987; for Attic kinship terminology, see Thompson [W.E.] 1972.

11. Cf. the statistics on endogamy in Hanson 1989: 144, Table 1.

emphasis on the following: the condensing and conflating manner with which *War* operates, his style of narrative with its frequent 'flash-backs', reigns or governorships often being briefly taken to their historical conclusion only to be introduced again by noting other con-temporary events, or indeed his numerous factual mistakes. Appendix 3, in particular, will deal with the structure and sequence of the important events spanning the period 14 to 8 BCE. Various dating refinements will be necessary, beginning with the main anchors in the reign of Herod the Great (Appendix 2). Among the chronological dis-cussions the following should be stressed: the death of Agrippa I (Appendix 5), the last procurators of Judaea (Appendix 8), the com-mencement of the Jewish Revolt (Appendix 9), and the death of Agrippa II (Appendix 10). Certain aspects of the notes here are dis-cussed further in the conclusion.

Chapter 5

THE UNCLES AND COUSINS OF HEROD

Of the ancestors of Herod the Great we have already examined Herod
of Ascalon, who appears to be the founding member of this remarkable dynasty, as well as his son Antipas I who became the *stratēgos* of
Idumaea. Wives and other relatives of these early members remain
totally unknown. We have also discussed Antipater I, the son of
Antipas I and father of Herod the Great, as well as his wife Cyprus I,
a noble woman of Petra. Two brothers of Antipater I have further
emerged in Josephus—Phallion I and Joseph I—these are the only
uncles of Herod of whom we are aware. If we put the evidence for
them together, an important dimension opens up, through which one
can begin to observe the wider structure of the Herodian society and
its influence on Jewish affairs of the Second Temple period.

1. *Phallion I*

It has been briefly mentioned that in 65/64 BCE, during the Hasmonaean civil war, Phallion, the brother of Antipater I, fell in battle
(Chapter 3). The place in which he met his death is called *Papyrōn* by
Josephus, and according to Avi-Yonah it would have been located
south of Jericho, near the north shore of the Dead Sea.[1] But *War*
1.130 strongly implies that Phallion was killed not far from the territory of Philadelphia, where he was retreating with the Nabataean
forces, and thus east of the Jordan. Although the Jewish historian

---

1.   Avi-Yonah 1937: 253-54 (identifying Παπυρὼν with a marshy spot over-
grown with reeds mentioned as 'Calamos'); yet a variant reading *Capiron* is accepted
by Schalit (1969: 741-42), which if it were correct, I believe it could have indicated a
'dried-up' (καπυρὸς) place instead.

refers to this event in both main works of his, he supplies no other information in regard to Phallion.[2]

At Scythopolis (Beth-Shean) a sarcophagus of the 'Roman period', which carried an inscription with the owner's name was discovered in 1922:

> Year 86 [or 386]. (Belonging to) Antiochus (the son of) Phallion (also known as) Kaboas.[3]

Many authorities took this person to be a first cousin of Herod the Great—the argument being that Phallion is an extremely rare name, in fact known only in connection with the Herodian family.[4] Fuks legitimately questioned such an identification, but his objections are not decisive. He thought that a 'Jew' would not have been called Antiochus (the name of the hated Antiochus IV Epiphanes), an odd reason if we have to classify the Herods simply as Jews! Fuks seemed undeterred by the ample Hellenistic onomasticon adopted by the members of the Herodian dynasty. The name Antiochus is attested in Idumaean Marisa.[5]

2.   A variant reading of his name as Κεφαλλίων (*Ant.* 14. 33), accepted by Schalit (1969: endpaper), and another, Φιλλίων (*War* 1.130), which would have seemed a better restoration (incidentally known in the inscription of Antipas from Cos—Chapter 3 n. 196), must be excluded in view of the fact that Φαλλίων has been attested independently of Josephus at Scythopolis (Beth-Shean)—see below; cf. a Φαλλ... (*NB* 1922: 453), Φάλων and Φάλλας (*LGPN*, 453), Φαλλαῖος (Roussel 1987: 417, third col., l. 6) and Φαλλέος (Moutèrde 1925: 235, no. 17).

3.   Rowe 1930: 49, pl. 54.3. Vincent (1923: 435), followed by Avi-Yonah (1939: 60-61), read the date as ET Πς (86 = CE 22/23) of the Scythopolis era (beginning in 64/63 BCE—Kindler 1963), while Abel (1946: 57) followed by Fuks ([G.] 1981) and Meimaris (1992: 84-85, no. 13) as ET ΠΕ (85 = CE 21/22). *SEG* (8.46) reprinted the date as ET ΠΕΤ (an odd order for 385 = CE 73/74) of the Seleucid era. I have only seen the photograph of the sarcophagus, but it seems that the year can only be ET Πς* (86 = CE 22/23, city era) or E ΤΠς* (386 = CE 74/75, Seleucid era), depending on the abbreviation of the word 'Year' as ET or just E (both attested in Avi-Yonah 1940: 61, 65). The *digamma* is certain, and a horizontal (accidental) scratch has confused Abel, who took it as *epsilon*. Also the *digamma* seems to be followed by a sigla, separating the date from the name, which has confused the editor of *SEG* who took it as *tau*.

4.   Vincent 1923: 435; Avi-Yonah 1937: 254 n. 18; Abel 1946: 57; Lifshitz 1978: 271-72.

5.   Moulton 1915: no. 4 = Abel 1925: no. 8 = *SEG* 8.256 (Tomb 7); Josephus (*Ant.* 14.146) refers to a son of an Antiochus among the envoys of the Jews to Rome

Of course, other problems occur in the Scythopolis text. The date of Antiochus's death in CE 22/23 or 74/75 (see above n. 3), would make him at least 87 or 138 years old, if he was the son of Phallion I who died in 65/64 BCE—the latter age is simply out of the question. But the possibility that Antiochus was the son of a descendant of Phallion I with the same name, that is Phallion II, was never entertained. Such an intermediary relative, admittedly elsewhere unattested, would be adding a generation and potentially solving the chronological problem.

That Phallion II would have carried the same name as his father will not be unusual among the Herodians, if only we are to think of Herod himself, his brothers (Phasael and Joseph), his sons (Alexander and Aristobulus) and his grandson (Agrippa), all of whom had homonymous offspring. As to what a 'Herodian' might have been doing dying at Scythopolis, an independent city state, need not trouble us as it did Fuks. If the text dates to CE 22/23, Judaea was then under direct Roman rule. While the leading members of the Herodian family would have been employed in the administration of the province (contrary to previous beliefs—see Chapter 7), some lesser members could have found it profitable to move their business from Jerusalem to the Greek cities of Palestine. In the case of Antiochus, Scythopolis would have been selected. If the text dates to CE 74/75, it is even easier to explain. During the time of the Jewish Revolt, Agrippa II had a significant influence upon Scythopolis—so much so that Josephus went as far as to claim that the place was under the king's jurisdiction.[6] Lesser members of the Herodian family may well have found the Greek Decapolis an ideal refuge to protect themselves from the Jewish revolters.

That Phallion II bore the epithet 'Kaboas' should not deprive him from the chance of being identified as a Herodian. On the contrary it may be in line with a contemporary trend of adding a nickname for distinction (among other reasons) to people who carried the same name as an ancestor—for example in the high priesthood, Simon surnamed 'Cantheras' or 'Kathros', and Joseph 'Caiaphas' (see Chapter 8); or even within the Herodian circle, Alexas 'Kalleas' (see Chapter 7). We do not know what 'Kaboas' meant; a similar name 'Kabbeos'

at the time of Hyrcanus II (but apparently under Simon—cf. 1 Macc. 15.16-21), and also to an Antiochus, a Syrian Jew (but a renegade), at the time of the Jewish Revolt (*War* 7.47).

6. Josephus, *Life* 349: τῆς ὑπηκόου βασιλεῖ; cf. *SVM* 2, 145.

appears much later in Trachonitis, while we should note the nickname of another high priest, Joseph 'Kabi'.[7]

Hanson recently conjectured that Phallion I might have left a son (Achiabus) and an unnamed daughter (the cousin-wife of Herod). But this mainly suffers from the fact that Phallion died too early to be reasonably regarded as the father of these individuals, who were apparently children of the other uncle of Herod, Joseph I (see below §2). Hanson's conclusion was forced upon him as a result of his decision to denounce the historicity of Joseph I by following Schalit's imperfect Herodian tree, as well as a feeble note by Marcus in the Loeb edition of Josephus.[8] Understandably this led him to some difficulty, since the husband of Salome I, who was a 'Joseph', had to be left with an unclear background. Thus Hanson in his Herodian chart had to refer to him with a question mark—and still as brother of Herod's father![9]

2. *Joseph I (Josephus I)*

The first appearance of a Joseph connected to the Herodian family is in *War* 1.441. Here he is described as the husband of Herod's sister Salome I, 'faithful' (πιστός) towards Herod and 'well-disposed' (εὔνους) due to this marriage connection (διὰ τὸ κῆδος). Had it been only for this passage one would have thought that the sole relationship between Joseph and Herod was one of *anchisteia* (by marriage), that is through Salome's marriage. However, there existed a deeper stratum of affiliation and it is not atypical of Josephus not to have mentioned it outright. After all, the story as given in *War* in which Joseph is involved (the crisis of Mariamme I), is a literary amalgamation of two similar but different events (see Chapter 8 n. 21), and in such cases priority must always be given to the evidence of *Antiquities*.

In *Ant.* 15.65, his later work in which he deals more fully with a number of issues and in effect improves on *War*, Josephus mentions Joseph, the husband of Salome I, as being also the 'uncle' (θεῖος) of Herod. Regrettably by laying stress on *War*, Marcus (among other

---

7. Wadd. 2466; Josephus, *Ant.* 20.196.

8. Hanson 1989: 144; Schalit 1969: endpaper; Marcus in the Loeb *Josephus* vol. 8, 33, n. d.

9. Hanson 1989: 78.

5. *The Uncles and Cousins of Herod*   151

scholars) in Loeb was prompted to question this relationship, and without MS support to suggest emending *Antiquities* to read 'brother-in-law' (πενθερός)! Clearly, room cannot be found for such a hypothesis, unless it is demanded by other equally direct evidence (compare Chapter 6 n. 59). Presumably this emendation would have spared us the implication of an uncle–niece marriage, but among the Herodians who practiced endogamy such a union is entirely credible (see Chapter 4).

In his defence the Loeb editor also pointed to *Ant.* 15.169 in which a kinsman (συγγενὴς) of Joseph is mentioned, who does not seem from this context to have concurrently been related to Herod. His name was Dositheus, apparently an Idumaean, a friend and follower of Hyrcanus II. But it is possible that Joseph's affiliation to Dositheus was through marriage. For example the latter could have been his brother-in-law: given the seniority of Joseph, he may have had a wife before Salome who was a sister of Dositheus.[10]

In fact after the execution of Joseph Herod may have established a somewhat closer relationship with Dositheus by marrying Joseph's daughter (see below), who would have been the niece of Dositheus. This may explain the sudden change of heart on the part of Dositheus. At first he hated Herod whom he held responsible for the killing of his brothers in Tyre, ordered by Marcus Antonius in c. 41 BCE,[11] as well as for the death of his brother-in-law (?) Joseph in 34 BCE (see below). Later, however, he betrayed Hyrcanus II to Herod, causing his execution in 30 BCE, hoping, as Josephus puts it, for a 'greater reward from the king'.[12] Eventually Dositheus himself was executed by Herod in 26 BCE, when the details of the 36/35 BCE attempted revolt of Costobarus I became known, with which he was apparently involved together with an important clique of Idumaeans (some of whom were related by marriage to the Hasmonaeans), such as

10. Stern's reference ([M.] 1982: 44-45) to Joseph as the 'brother' of Dositheus is puzzling. Stern may not have accepted (though he does not say so) the fact that Joseph was Herod's uncle—but even then, there is no evidence that Joseph and Dositheus were brothers.

11. Josephus, *Ant.* 14.327-29; *War* 1.245-47; although probably Hellenized Idumaeans, these men remained loyal to the household of Hyrcanus II; cf. the circle of Malichus (Chapter 6 §1).

12. Josephus, *Ant.* 15.170; Dositheus's betrayal of the Hasmonaean cause is not the only known instance—Sabbion (*Ant.* 15.45) acted similarly against Alexandra.

Lysimachus, Antipater surnamed Gadias and the two unnamed sons of Baba (see Chapter 7 §1). Incidentally the name Dositheus is attested in Marisa, as is that of Baba.[13] So there is no reason to disbelieve that Joseph I was indeed Herod's uncle.

Joseph I was the only surviving male member of the Herodian dynasty known to us, who would have been older than Herod the Great when the latter became king. As a brother of Antipater I it is probable that from an earlier period he was granted some local command. It has already been suggested (Chapter 3 §2) that Joseph may have become the *stratēgos* of Idumaea when Antipater rose to power in Jerusalem. If this is so then at the beginning of Herod's reign the Idumaean post will have been reconferred on his uncle, but only for a short period in view of the promotion of Costobarus I in 37/36 BCE (see Chapter 7 n. 9). This would also have been the appropriate time for Joseph to have married his niece Salome I, the sister of Herod, but this union appears to have taken place earlier in c. 44 BCE (Chapter 7 §1). Presumably Joseph's first wife (arguably the sister of Dositheus) had by then died, unless he maintained two contemporary wives (compare Chapter 4).

In 34 BCE on the occasion of Herod's journey to Laodicea to meet Marcus Antonius, Joseph was chosen to look after the kingdom's affairs, conceivably being the most senior and capable member of the Herodian dynasty. He was designated ἐπίτροπος τῆς ἀρχῆς καὶ τῶν πραγμάτων,[14] a position which unfortunately led to his death. Joseph was assigned the protection of Mariamme I and he was given strict orders to kill her if Herod did not return. After he had made the mistake of revealing this to Mariamme, the latter did not hesitate to rebuke Herod when they were reunited. According to Josephus, the king immediately suspected that his uncle must have slept with her, for her to know such a secret, and driven by his excessive jealousy

13. Moulton 1915: no. 3 = *SEG* 8.253b; for Babas see Chapter 7 n. 11; if Dositheus is to be identified with the one who appealed to L. Lentulus Crus in support of the Jews at Ephesus, then his background was Alexandrian (Josephus, *Ant.* 14. 236). A much earlier Dositheus is also known as the father of a Simon, an envoy of Hyrcanus I (*Ant.* 13.260). It has been suggested (Stern [M.] 1982: 45) that Lysimachus may have been the son of Pausanias, known to have served also as emissary of Hyrcanus II (*Ant.* 14.222, 307).

14. Josephus, *Ant.* 15.65.

and a false testimony by Salome he ordered Joseph's execution.[15]

But there were also heavy political overtones in the episode. While Herod was away a report went round the city that the king had been put to death by Antonius, upon which Alexandra seized the opportunity to persuade Joseph to flee the palace and take refuge with a Roman legion then stationed near Jerusalem. Her persistent plan was the reinstatement of Hasmonaean rule, to which Joseph was drawn in.[16] It was Alexandra in the first place who had caused Herod to appear before Antonius to give an account for the murder of her son Aristobulus III (see Chapter 8 §2). It is no wonder that Herod in the following years did not rest until he had murdered one by one all of the remaining Hasmonaeans upon whom he could lay his hands.

Assuming that Joseph I was around 60 at his execution in 34 BCE, he would have been born, let us say, in c. 95 BCE, and thus he must have been the youngest child of Antipas I (see family tree, Chapter 3 §3). Joseph himself seems by his first wife to have had a son named Achiabus, whom Josephus mentions as a 'cousin' (ἀνεψιὸς) of Herod. His peak of activity was in the period shortly before and after the death of the king in 4 (or 5) BCE, and therefore it is difficult to see him as a son of Phallion I, who died in 65/64 BCE.[17] Although Achiabus makes his debut in Josephus in 28/27 BCE, he seems at the time to have been fairly young. He was one of the commanders of the Jerusalem garrison who warned Herod against Alexandra, eventually causing her death.[18] The fact that he was obviously on good terms with Herod, despite Herod's recent parricide, must not be seen out of context. First, Achiabus held Alexandra ultimately responsible for his father's death, hence his contribution to her downfall. Second, his sister was now the wife of Herod, which would have enhanced his present and future position in the court.

15. Josephus, *Ant.* 15.87; cf. *War* 1.443, but note that Mariamme was spared in this instance—for the correct date of her death, see Chapter 8 n. 21). *War* 1.486 clearly refers to the execution of Joseph I 'on a charge of adultery'. In *Ant.* 15.185 a Joseph, ταμίας, was left with Soaemus to guard Mariamme during Herod's journey to Augustus in 30 BCE—this person must not be confused with Joseph I, because in the same episode (*Ant.* 15.204) Mariamme remembers the time when she was under the custody of Joseph I, during Herod's journey to Marcus Antonius in 34 BCE.

16. Josephus, *Ant.* 15.72-87.

17. Contra Hanson 1989: 79; note that his name was expressly Hebrew (cf. Kasher 1988: 65) as was his father's.

18. Josephus, *Ant.* 15.250.

Indeed Achiabus's power steadily increased, and by the end of Herod's reign he is found very close to the king, as a kind of *praefectus praetorio*, if one is allowed to use the equivalent Roman equestrian appointment. Almost ironically, in 4 (or 5) BCE he saved Herod's life by preventing him from committing suicide,[19] and after his death he became instrumental in temporarily opposing the uprising of 2,000 veterans in Idumaea.[20] Later, when P. Quinctilius Varus had arrived with his army, Achiabus succeeded in persuading the leaders of the rebellion in Idumaea, which had now gathered 10,000 people, to give up before they were exterminated by the Roman army. It is of interest that among the Idumaean leaders who were sent to be tried by Augustus, there were some unnamed, lesser members of the Herodian family, 'βασιλέως συγγενῶν... κατὰ γένος'. These Augustus decided to punish for taking up arms against a sovereign who was their own kin.[21] Who might have been these condemned individuals? Of course it is difficult to know, but given their Idumaean connection a guess would be either descendants from the line of Costobarus I and Salome I, or much more likely from that of Antipater II son of Doris, who had just been executed by Herod (see Chapter 8 §1).

Also to Joseph I by his first wife there seems to belong an unnamed daughter who was taken in marriage by Herod, apparently in 34 BCE (Chapter 8 §3). If the girl was at the youngest possible age of 12 or 13, she would have been born in c. 47 BCE, but she was probably older. As a comparison Salome I—the last child of Antipater I, no doubt the eldest brother of Joseph I by more than a decade-and-a-half (Chapter 3 §3)—was born in c. 57 BCE (Chapter 7 §1).

Finally Joseph I had another unnamed daughter, this time by his second wife Salome I, who would thus have been born not earlier than c. 43 BCE. She was given to the son of Alexas I in c. 20 BCE. Her husband was also her step-brother, an affinal arrangement without precise parallel in the Herodian family (for her and Alexas, see Chapter 7 §1). Joseph I must have had his second daughter when he was in his early fifties, but still within the age range of Herodian fatherhood (see Chapter 4).

19. Josephus, *War* 1.662; *Ant.* 17.184; I do not believe that Stern ([M.] 1975a: 92) was right to think that Achiabus became governor of Judaea *per se*.
20. Josephus, *War* 2.55; *Ant.* 17.270, reads Ἰουδαία instead.
21. Josephus, *War* 2.77; *Ant.* 17.297 does not specify the place.

Family Tree: *The Uncles of Herod and their Descendants*
(c. 205 BCE–80s CE)

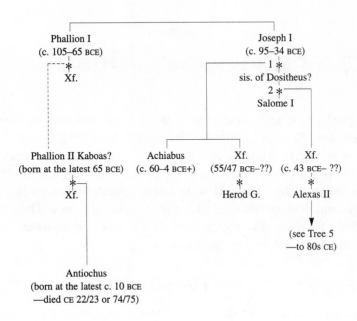

Chapter 6

THE BROTHERS, NEPHEWS AND NIECES OF HEROD

Josephus gives clear indications of the order of Antipater I's sons: the oldest was Phasael I, followed by Herod the Great, Joseph II and Pheroras. Phasael also happened to die first, either by committing suicide or by being murdered—or perhaps falling in battle. He was later followed by Joseph II who was decapitated after he had been killed, and then by Pheroras who was allegedly poisoned. Only Herod died of natural causes in old age, evidently due to his extremely strong determination, but also to good fortune.

1. *Phasael I*

The eldest brother (πρεσβύτατος) of Herod was noticeably older than the king, perhaps by at least five years.[1] Herod was born in 72 BCE and thus Phasael around 77 BCE.[2] His homonymous son was seven in 41/40 BCE, which means that Phasael became a father in 47/46 BCE (at the outset of his public career) when he was about 30 (see below). His

---

1. Josephus, *War* 1.203; *Ant.* 14.158; cf. *War* 1.181; *Ant.* 14. 121.

2. Herod seems to have celebrated his sixtieth birthday in 12 BCE on his return from Rome and at the completion of the Temple—Augustus's fiftieth birthday had fallen a year earlier, perhaps at the completion of Caesarea (cf. Kokkinos 1989: 155, 162; see Appendix 2, pt. 3). This would make Herod 68 (or 69 inclusively) on his death in 4 BCE (or 67/68 if 5 BCE), a good match to the statement that the king died σχεδὸν ἐτῶν ἑβδομήκοντα (*War* 1.647; cf. *Ant.* 17.148; contra Filmer 1966: 293). He was thus about ten years older than both Augustus (Snyder 1940: 227-30) and Nicolaus of Damascus (*FGrH* 90, F136; cf. Wacholder 1962: 16). Josephus in *Ant.* 14.158 presents Herod as 15 (instead of 25) when he became governor of Galilee in 47 BCE, but this is rejected universally (*SVM* 1, 275 n. 29; Smallwood 1976: 44; contra Otto 1913: 18). The problem should not alarm—*Ant.* 15.178 presents Hyrcanus II also as much older than he was.

name is Nabataean and it was probably given to him by his mother Cyprus I.[3]

Phasael's first major appointment in 47 BCE was that of *stratēgos* of Jerusalem and its environs, which he kept under control without abusing his authority, according to Josephus.[4] When Herod was summoned to trial in the city, Phasael with his father prevented him from attacking Hyrcanus II.[5] Later Phasael, together with Herod, led reinforcements to Apamea to help the followers of Caesar, and subsequently, following Antipater's request, he collected part of the contribution demanded by Cassius.[6]

During the time when the plot of Malichus was unravelled, that is about 44/43 BCE, we find Phasael close to all significant events. Malichus had categorically denied any involvement, defending himself under oath before Antipater, Phasael and Herod.[7] But Antipater was subsequently murdered by poisoning (43 BCE), and Phasael advised Herod not to avenge his death openly, for fear of a popular uprising. He then arranged the funeral.[8] In 42 BCE after the extermination of Malichus, craftily planned by Herod, Phasael repelled an attack by Helix, who had been left with an army in Jerusalem (apparently by Hyrcanus on his way to Tyre), and succeeded in locking him up in a tower.[9]

Malichus (Malchus) was probably an Idumaean nobleman, and possibly of Nabataean origins, as his name suggests. He and Peitholaus are first mentioned by Josephus in the service of Hyrcanus II. Peitholaus, who was a *hypostratēgos* at Jerusalem, had defected to Aristobulus II and was later killed at the instigation of Antipater.[10] The plot of Malichus presents us with an interesting complex of circumstances. His direct aim was the murder of Antipater and the effective removal of Hyrcanus II. But there also seem to have been wider political issues

3. See discussion on Antipas the Tetrarch's Nabataean wife, who, if correctly identified, shared the same name with Phasael in its feminine form (Chapter 8 §5).
4. Josephus, *War* 1.203, 206; *Ant.* 14.158, 161.
5. Josephus, *War* 1.214; *Ant.* 14.181.
6. Josephus, *War* 1.217, 220; *Ant.* 14.268, 273.
7. Josephus, *Ant.* 14.278; but cf. *War* 1.224 where Malichus approaches only Phasael and Herod.
8. Josephus, *Ant.* 14.282-83; but cf. *War* 1.228 where it is Herod who arranged the funeral.
9. Josephus, *Ant.* 14.294-95; *War* 1.236-37.
10. Josephus, *War* 1.162, 172, 180; *Ant.* 14.84, 93, 120.

involved. A little earlier Malichus had stirred a revolt in Syria, for which the Roman governor L. Statius Murcus hated him. Malichus's son was taken as a hostage in Tyre, while his brother succeeded in controlling all of Judaea's desert fortresses, including Masada. Alliances were arranged with Marion of Tyre who ruled over some cities in Galilee, and ultimately with Ptolemy of Chalcis who strongly supported Antigonus. Finally Helix, a military commander no doubt working for Malichus, waged war against the Herods as soon as the murder of his master became widely known.[11]

Early in 41 BCE an embassy of the Jews to Antonius in Bithynia accused Phasael and Herod of wielding excessive influence over Hyrcanus II, but without success due to the bribes from Herod.[12] Later in Antioch 100 Jewish officials repeated the accusation but again unsuccessfully. Even worse, disregarding the dissenting voices, Antonius promoted Phasael and Herod from *stratēgoi* to tetrarchs, an event that led to a third wave of 1,000 Jews complaining loudly to Antonius in Tyre.[13]

When the Parthians invaded and the supporters of Antigonus attacked Jerusalem, Phasael, together with Hyrcanus II and Herod, defended the city bravely.[14] Later, Phasael consented to admit into Jerusalem Pacorus, the cup-bearer of Pacorus the Parthian prince, and he was even persuaded to go with Hyrcanus to Galilee to meet Barzapharnes the satrap, despite Herod's objections.[15] When Phasael realized Barzapharnes's motives he attempted to bribe him with more money than Antigonus had offered him, but in vain—he and Hyrcanus were arrested.[16] Herod learned of the fate of his brother and quickly fled Jerusalem.

After the Parthian victory at the end of 41 (or early in 40 BCE), Antigonus was raised to the throne and the two distinguished prisoners were delivered up to him in chains.[17] While Hyrcanus lost his ears (thus being deprived of the capacity of ever becoming a high priest),

11. Josephus, *War* 1.223-24, 231, 236-39; *Ant.* 14.277-79, 290, 294-97.

12. Josephus, *Ant.* 14.302-303; *War* 1.242.

13. Josephus, *Ant.* 14.324-29; *War* 1.243-47.

14. Josephus, *War* 1.250-52; *Ant.* 14.334-36; for the chronology of the Parthian attack, see Appendix 2, pt. 1.

15. Josephus, *War* 1.254-55; *Ant.* 14.342-43.

16. Josephus, *War* 1.256-60; *Ant.* 14.345-48.

17. Josephus, *War* 1.269; *Ant.* 14.365.

Phasael, according to one account, committed suicide by dashing his head upon a rock; another account claimed that Phasael survived the blow, to be drugged to death by a physician of Antigonus.[18] But perhaps neither is correct. Josephus elsewhere strongly implies that Phasael was slain by the Parthians, a story also found in Julius Africanus most probably based on Justus of Tiberias.[19]

Herod built a tower to the memory of his brother and named it after him, as well as a city to the north of Jericho which he called Phasaelis.[20] The tower was the highest of the three on the city wall attached to the Herodian palace, and it was preserved by Titus.[21] It is believed (but not by all) to be the northeast tower of the present citadel, popularly known as 'David's tower', of which Josephus gives a detailed description:

> ... (it) was of equal length and breadth, forty cubits each way; forty cubits was also the height of its solid base (21 × 21 × 21 m). Above and around this ran a cloister, ten cubits high (5.25 m), protected by parapets and bulwarks. Over this and rising from the centre of the cloister was built another tower, apportioned into sumptuous apartments, including a bath, in order that nothing might be wanting to impart to this tower the appearance of a palace. Its summit was crowned with battlements and turrets, and its total height was about ninety cubits (47.25 m). In form it resembled the tower of Pharos that emits its beacon light to navigators approaching Alexandria, but in circumference it was much larger.[22]

The son of Phasael I, with the same name, who had been under Herod's protection during the Parthian war in 41/40 BCE, was then

18. Josephus, *War* 1.271-72; *Ant.* 14.367-69; 15.13; the Slavonic has Phasael being poisoned to death (after *War* 1.328—see the Loeb *Josephus* 3: 635-36).

19. Note the following passages in Josephus: *War* 1.484: Πάρθων... ἀναιρεθέντι; *War* 2.46: διαφθαρέντα ὑπὸ Πάρθων; *War* 5.162: ἀποβαλὼν ἐν πολέμῳ γενναίως ἀγωνισάμενον; *Ant.* 14. 379: ὑπὸ Πάρθων ἀπόλοιτο συλληφθείς; *Ant.* 17.257: τελευτῆς ὑπὸ Παρθυαίων αὐτῷ γενομένης. Remember that Hyrcanus was taken to Parthia as a prisoner (*War* 1.273; cf. *Ant.* 15.11-22). Importantly Julius Africanus has Phasael falling in battle (*Chron.* 17: ἐν τῇ μάχῃ ἀναιρεῖται)—see Syncellus [edn Dindorf 1: 581-82]; for his reliance on Justus, see Chapter 3 n. 69; cf. *SVM* 1, 280 n. 52.

20. Josephus, *War* 1.418; *Ant.* 16.144-45.

21. Josephus, *War* 2.46, 439; 5.166-69; 7.2.

22. Josephus, *War* 5.166-69; one cubit equals 52.5 cm according to the latest estimate (Ritmeyer 1992: 64 n. 14); for the archaeological evidence, see Amiran and Eitan 1970; Amiran and Eitan 1976; and now Sivan and Solar 1994; Geva (1981; cf. 1994: 160-61) argues that the 'Tower of David' should be identified with Hippicus.

seven.[23] Thus Phasael II was born in 47/46 BCE. He was given in
marriage to Salampsio, the eldest daughter of Herod, not earlier than
20 BCE, when she would have been around 14 (she was born c. 33
BCE—Chapter 8 §2, and below §3), and he would have been around
27.[24] Five children were born to them: Herod VI, Alexander III,
Antipater IV, Alexandra and Cyprus III.[25]

In *War* 1.484 Josephus erroneously refers to Phasael II as having
been killed by the Parthians 'later'. But this is evidently a confusion
with the death of his father Phasael I 'earlier'.[26] Of Phasael II's
daughters, Alexandra, who was named after a great-grandmother (the
mother of her mother's mother Mariamme I), married Timius of
Cyprus with whom she died childless. All we know of Timius is that
he was 'a man of some importance'. We may guess that his connection
with the Herodian family had something to do with the copper mines
in Cyprus (almost certainly near Soloi), half of the revenue of which,
and the management of the other half, were granted to Herod the
Great by Augustus in 13/12 BCE. Perhaps Timius, a local aristocrat,
was appointed a royal procurator of the mining operations there, and
Alexandra may eventually have settled in Cyprus.[27] The other daughter of Phasael II, Cyprus III, who was also named after a great-
grandmother (the mother of her mother's father Herod), married
Agrippa I by whom she had five children: Drusus, Agrippa II,
Berenice II, Mariamme VI and Drusilla (see Chapter 10 §2).

Of Phasael II's sons we hardly have any information. Josephus mentions that Herod VI and Alexander III died childless, which may imply
that Antipater IV had left offspring.[28] Nevertheless no names are on
record. It is perhaps just about possible to identify Antipater IV with a

23. Josephus, *War* 1.274-75; *Ant.* 14.371.

24. Josephus, *War* 1.566; *Ant.* 16.196; 17.22; 18.130.

25. Josephus, *Ant.* 18.131; the order of the boys' names in this passage is actually Antipater, Alexander and Herod, but later it is reversed (*Ant.* 18.138).

26. Moses of Chorene (*Hist. of Armen.* 1.2) has Phasael II dying in Armenia,
but this is a fantasy created around Josephus's slip in *War* 1.484. Also Moses
thought that the wife of Phasael II was previously married to Pheroras, but
Salampsio had only been engaged to him (*Ant.* 16.194).

27. For Augustus's grant see Josephus, *Ant.* 16.128; these mines were visited
later by Galen (12.220); for the archaeology see Bruce [J.L.] 1937; for a possible
inscription of Herod from Paphos, see Chapter 3 n. 195; Nicolaou (1986: 435) also
suggests that Alexandra may have gone to live in Cyprus.

28. Josephus, *Ant.* 18.138.

mysterious member of the Herodian family (τοῦ βασιλικοῦ γένους) named Antipas III, who was active during the time of the Jewish Revolt.[29] Phasael II's children were born after 20 BCE and not much later than the turn of the century (in view of Salampsio's age), though we do not know precisely when. Josephus affirms that all were alive at least up to the reign of Agrippa I (CE 37–44).[30] If Antipater IV was the same person as Antipas III, he would have had to be the last child and still not be less than 60 in the mid-60s CE.

Antipas III was one of the leading citizens of Jerusalem and in charge of the public treasury (ἐπὶ τῶν δημοσίων θησαυρῶν) when the revolt broke out.[31] He was associated with other notables (also minor members of the Herodian family), namely the brothers Saulus and Costobarus II (who would have been his first cousins if he is iden- tified with Antipater IV), and Levias and Syphas the son of Aregetas (see Chapter 7 §2). After the expulsion of king Agrippa II from the city and the capture of Masada by the rebels, a deputation consisting of Antipas, Saulus and Costobarus II was dispatched to Agrippa in Panias to plead for military help. Indeed an army of 2,000 soldiers from Auranitis, Batanaea and Trachonitis, under the general com- mand of Philip, son of Jacimus, son of Zamaris, was sent back to Jerusalem together with the Herodian delegation.[32]

Their first objective was to free the Temple which had fallen to the insurgents. This objective failed, and in trying to escape, Antipas and

29. Alternatively it is possible that he was a son of Antipas the Tetrarch (Kokkinos 1986a: 44; see Chapter 8 §5). This may remotely be reflected in the Christian tradition. We know from Josephus (*War* 4.145) that Antipas III was killed by one John 'son of Dorcas', in Aramaic 'bar Tabitha' (בר טביתא—feminine; cf. the Slavonic; see Cassuto 1932, 217, no. 10). Now the murder of a Tabitha by Antipas the Tetrarch is alluded to in the *Hist. of Joseph the Carp.* 32 (Arabic version; cf. *Apoc. of Elias*—Coptic version; see James 1924: 86). The scenario may have been that a son of a Dorcas/Tabitha avenged Antipas's murder of his mother by later killing Antipas's son. The name Dorcas/Tabitha is feminine throughout the Christian literature (*ND* 4.177-78, no. 94). In Acts 9.36 it is that of the disciple restored to life by Peter in Joppa, while in the Syriac narratives of the *Assum. of the Virgin* (2) it is that of Mary's follower, curiously 'the daughter of Archelaus (?)' (James 1924: 220). A final possibility is that Antipas III, as a close associate of Costobarus II and Saulus, himself was a descendant of Antipater III (see Chapter 7 §2).

30. Josephus, *Ant.* 18.142.

31. Josephus, *War* 4.140; cf. Goodman 1987: 148-49; see Chapter 7 n. 104.

32. Josephus, *War* 2.418-21.

his company shut themselves up in the palace of Herod the Great.[33] There they were besieged, and after a fierce battle they had to request permission to quit the grounds under treaty. Such permission was given only to the royal troops and to some notables of Jewish blood. It seems that with them also escaped a few Herodians (see Chapter 7 §2) but not Antipas.[34] He managed to be arrested, imprisoned and then savagely killed while in custody.[35]

2. *Joseph II (Josephus II)*

The first younger brother of Herod, Joseph II,[36] may have been born around 70 BCE as he was of an age to command troops in Idumaea (if Josephus is not confusing him here with Joseph I, Chapter 3 n. 59) during the period of the Parthian invasion in 41/40 BCE. When Herod made his escape to the south towards Masada, Joseph met him in a desert fortress called Rhēsa (emended to Orēsa) and offered him valuable advice on military logistics.[37] This was probably the biblical Horesh(ah), in the Wilderness of Ziph, where David was hidden during his flight from Saul 'in the strongholds at Horesh, on the hill of Hachilah, which is south of Jeshimon'.[38]

At first Joseph was entrusted with the protection of the Herodian court (including the family—see Chapter 8 §1), hidden away in Masada from the Parthians. On one occasion, due to a lack of water, he nearly fled to Nabataea, but abandoned this course of action when a

33. Josephus, *War* 2.423-29.
34. Josephus, *War* 2.437-38, 557.
35. Josephus, *War* 4.140-46.
36. Josephus, *War* 1.181; *Ant.* 14.121.
37. Josephus, *War* 1.266-67; *Ant.* 14.361. In *War* 1.294 (cf. 1. 266) Ῥῆσα or Θρῆσα is mentioned as a 'fortress' (φρούριον), while in *Ant.* 14.361 the name has been emended to Ὀρῆσα (the MSS variously have Θρῆσα or Θρῆσσα or Risa) and is given simply as a 'place' or perhaps 'fortified place' (χωρίον). In *Ant.* 14.400 the name has also been emended to Ὀρῆσα (the MSS variously have Ῥῆσα or Ῥύσσα or Ῥύσα or Ῥῆσσα or Risam) and is mentioned again as *phrourion*. The attempt by Oren (1968: 59) to identify the place with Marisa must be discounted. Both are mentioned in the same context by Josephus—one as a fortress, the other as a major town (*Ant.* 14.361, 364; *War* 1.266, 269).
38. 1 Sam. 23.19. Possibly modern Khirbet Khureisa (c. 8 miles south of Hebron), where Conder in the last century discovered some ancient ruins (Smith [G.A.] 1935: 306-307 n. 2); see *TIRIP* 98 (Caphar Orsa, 162095).

heavy rainfall filled the cisterns.[39] On Herod's return to fight Antigonus in the second half of 39 BCE, Joseph was put in charge of troops for the defending of Idumaea, while the Herodian court had to be moved from Masada to Samaria.[40]

In 38 BCE when Herod went to Samosata, Joseph encamped outside Jerusalem having been ordered not to attack the city and to stay away from Machaeras, a commander (στρατηγὸς) of five Roman auxiliary forces (σύμμαχοι), whose war tactics Herod did not approve of, and who had previously in anger murdered some followers of the Herodian dynasty (Ἡρώδειοι). Yet, after a while, Joseph decided to accept one of Machaeras's plans and accordingly led his army towards Jericho, with five newly levied Roman cohorts from Syria. The result was catastrophic. The Hasmonaean forces fell upon them and destroyed them to a man. Antigonus even abused Joseph's corpse by cutting his head off, and later sold it to young Pheroras.[41]

It is said that Herod had seen a dream warning him of his brother's death before he received the bad news.[42] As soon as he resumed his fight in Judaea he took swift revenge. In a battle in which Pappus (the *stratēgos* of Antigonus who had killed Joseph) fell, Herod decapitated his body and also sent the head to Pheroras.[43]

Joseph II was succeeded by a son, Joseph III (Josephus III),[44] and possibly by a daughter whom Herod took as his wife when he conquered Jerusalem (see Chapter 8 §3). Joseph III is correctly given in *War* 1.562 and *Ant.* 17.20 as a nephew (ἀδελφιδοῦς) of Herod, also in *War* 2.74 as a cousin (ἀνεψιὸς) of Archelaus the son of Herod, but the parallel passage in *Ant.* 17.294 is wrong in giving him as a cousin (ἀνεψιὸς), of Herod, instead of Archelaus.

Joseph III, who was probably born in the 40s BCE (certainly before 38 BCE when his father died), was given in marriage to Olympias the

39. Josephus, *War* 1.286-88; *Ant.* 14.390-91.

40. Josephus, *War* 1.303; *Ant.* 14.413; Herod's march did not begin before the later part of 39 BCE when P. Ventidius Bassus had taken possession of Palestine (Debevoise 1938: 114-16; cf. *SVM* 1, 251-52).

41. Josephus, *War* 1.323-25; cf. *Ant.* 14.438, 448-50.

42. Josephus, *War* 1.328; *Ant.* 14.451; the Slavonic (after *War* 1.328) adds that Joseph was cut down and his body dragged away without burial (see the Loeb *Josephus* 3: 635-36).

43. Josephus, *War* 1.342; *Ant.* 14.464.

44. Josephus, *Ant.* 18.134.

daughter of Herod,[45] who seems to have been born in c. 22 BCE, though a later date is also possible (Chapter 8 n. 73). Since Olympias would have been ready for a husband only after about 8 BCE, this union may have taken place on the special occasion in c. 8/7 BCE when Herod arranged many family betrothals and weddings.[46] At any rate we know that when Herod died in 4 (or 5) BCE, only the two youngest daughters, Roxane and Salome II, were still virgins (Chapter 8 §7).

Thus during the time Joseph III was active (after the death of the king, as mentioned by Josephus), he would apparently have been a married man in his forties. Joseph was in charge of a division of the royal army, and in direct communication with the most important royal troops (the Σεβαστηνοὶ) which were under the control of Herod's generals Rufus and Gratus.[47] He and these men waited for Varus outside Jerusalem when the Roman governor of Syria arrived to quell the local insurrection.

Joseph III had a daughter, Mariamme V, by Olympias. Her name may or may not reflect that of her grandmother (the wife of Joseph II), whom Josephus does not mention anywhere. Mariamme, hardly born before the beginning of the Christian era, was given in marriage to Herod of Chalcis (apparently in the late CE 20s). She eventually had a son by him, Aristobulus III of Lesser Armenia,[48] who became the husband of a Salome, whom Josephus thought to be the daughter of Herodias, the commonly identified notorious dancer of the Gospels (see Chapters 8 §5 and 10 §§1, 3).

3. *Pheroras*

Pheroras was the youngest son (τῷ νεωτάτῳ) of Antipater I, and was therefore born not much earlier than c. 65 BCE.[49] He was probably

45. Josephus, *War* 1.562; *Ant.* 17.20.

46. Josephus, *War* 1.556-61, 564-66; *Ant.* 17.12-18; none the less it is possible that Olympias had only been engaged in c. 8/7 BCE, and that she married sometime later as implied in *Ant.* 17.20 (Kokkinos 1986a: 37).

47. Josephus, *War* 2.74; *Ant* 17.294; for the Herodian army, see references in Chapter 10 n. 103; an identification of Rufus and Gratus with the later homonymous governors of Judaea will be suggested elsewhere.

48. Josephus, *Ant.* 18.134.

49. Josephus, *War* 1.264, 308; *Ant.* 14.419; cf. *War* 1.181; *Ant.* 14.121; note that his Hasmonaean wife (see below) was born in c. 50/49 BCE, prior to her father's execution in 48 BCE (Chapter 3 n. 98).

born by at least 64 BCE when his father, as Josephus specifies, entrusted his 'children' (τέκνα) to the Nabataean king.[50] Pheroras is a Greek name, apparently used by Hellenized Idumaeans/Phoenicians— it has now been discovered in a tomb at Marisa.[51] It is of interest that the inscription of the buried person carries the date LB, which, if this follows one of the eras of Herod (as tentatively suggested in Chapter 3 n. 191), would mean 39 or 37/6 BCE. In such a case the Marisan Pheroras would have been a contemporary of the Herodian Pheroras, who was apparently born in the same town (Chapter 3 §2).

In the struggle against Antigonus, beginning from late 39 BCE, Pheroras, at the age of about 25, was ordered to fortify Alexandreion. On this occasion he was either in charge of the commissariat (ἀγορὰ) of Herod's army, or was instructed to provision Silo and the Romans.[52] In 38 BCE Pheroras ransomed from Antigonus for 50 talents the head of his brother Joseph I, and later received from Herod the head of Pappus, Joseph's executioner, as a sign of revenge.[53]

When Herod went to Rhodes in 30 BCE to meet the victorious Octavian, Pheroras was entrusted with the affairs of the Judaean kingdom, as well as with the care of their mother Cyprus I, their sister Salome I and all of the family's children, who were again sent to Masada for safety.[54] From that point onwards the position of Pheroras was considerably enhanced:

> (Pheroras) shared with Herod all the honours of royalty, except the diadem. He had a private income of a hundred talents, exclusive of the revenue derived from the whole of the trans-Jordanic region, a gift from his brother, who had also, after requesting Caesar's permission, appointed him tetrarch. Herod had conferred upon him the further honour of marrying one of the royal family, by uniting him to the sister of his own wife.

50. Josephus, *Ant.* 14.122 (cf. Chapter 3 n. 39); apparently only the four sons were included, since Salome I would have been born later (Chapter 7 §1).

51. As Greek name see *WGEN*, 1612 (cf. the Suda s.v.); for the Marisan Pheroras, see Oren and Rappaport 1984: no. 16 (Tomb E.8); cf. also the property known as the 'Pherora orchard', referred to in two documents of CE 130 from the archive of Babatha (*P. Yadin* 21.10; 22.11).

52. Josephus, *War* 1.308 against *Ant.* 14.419.

53. Josephus, *War* 1.325, 342; *Ant.* 14.450, 464.

54. Josephus, *Ant.* 15.184; incidentally this was a similar situation to that when Herod in 34 BCE met M. Antonius in Laodicea and left Joseph I in charge of affairs in Judaea, and even more so to that when Herod in 40 BCE went to Rome and left Joseph II (if not confused with Joseph I) at Masada.

> On her death, he had pledged to him the eldest of his own daughters, with
> a dowry of three hundred talents; but Pheroras rejected the royal wedding
> to run after a slave-girl of whom he was enamoured.[55]

The Transjordanian region given to Pheroras was Peraea, of which he
officially became the tetrarch (at about 45) after Herod's visit to
Augustus at Antioch in 20/19 BCE.[56] The centre of his rule must have
been established in the Herodian palace (βασίλεια) at Betharamtha,[57]
later renamed Livias/Julias by Antipas the Tetrarch (see Chapter 8
§5). Pheroras's first wife was evidently a member of the Hasmonaean
family (born c. 50/49—above n. 49), a sister of Mariamme I the wife
of Herod,[58] whom he should have married after 37 BCE (marriage of
Herod; and beginning of her marriageable age) but before 26 BCE
(execution of Costobarus I).[59] It may be assumed that Pheroras's

55. Josephus, *War* 1.483-84.
56. Josephus, *Ant.* 15.362.
57. Josephus, *War* 2.59; *Ant.* 17.277; see *SVM* 2, 176-78. The site of
Betharamtha (cf. its renaming as Livias/Julias in *Ant.* 18.27) has been identified with
Tell er-Râmeh (Glueck 1943: 20-22; Glueck 1951: 389-91; Harder 1962: 60-63), in
agreement with the location given by Eusebius (Chapter 8 n. 101). However, based
on the reading in *Ant.* 17.277, Avi-Yonah (1977a: 96) claimed that the Herodian
palace was situated at Amathus (Tell 'Ammata, 208183). Unfortunately both sites
remain unexcavated, with Tell 'Ammata being archaeologically more promising (see
Ibrahim *et al.* 1976: 58).
58. Cf. Josephus, *War* 1.485 where by βασιλίδος, i.e. 'royal-wife', the sister of
Mariamme must be meant, and not Mariamme herself, as in the Loeb translation, in
which case one would have expected βασιλίσσης, i.e. 'queen' (cf. Jeremias 1969:
90, who is also in error); for the date of her birth see above n. 49.
59. Pheroras was already married to his Hasmonaean wife before Costobarus
was executed (Josephus, *War* 1.486)—in agreement with the fact that she gave birth
to three sons, and thus her marriage could not have taken place later than 26 BCE.
The first of her sons was ready for marriage in c. 14 BCE (*Ant.* 16.228), when he
was in his late teens (μειρακίῳ). Two other sons were given in marriage to the
youngest daughters of Herod by Augustus in c. 4 (or 5) BCE. (*Ant.* 17. 322; *War*
2.99), and they would also have been at least in their late teens. The wedding of her
first son in c. 14 BCE would presumably have been with Cyprus II (*Ant.* 16.228),
but Josephus is mistaken again, since Cyprus actually married Antipater III (*War*
1.566; *Ant.* 17.22; 18.130). Josephus is also inaccurate in including it within a part
of history (consisting of events occurring at two earlier periods), thought to date
from 11 to as late as c. 9/8 BCE. Yet Cyprus II, born in 30/29 BCE, would have been
ready for marriage from about 15 BCE—*not* from 11 or from as late as 9/8 BCE. The
degree of error in *Ant.* 16.228 is in fact considerable: Josephus sees Pheroras's son
as successor to the tetrarchy, and he adds that in giving him his daughter, Herod

Hasmonaean wife died around 20 BCE (if not as early as 29/28 BCE, in connection with the execution of her sister Mariamme I). This is deduced from the fact that Pheroras had already been married to his 'slave'-mistress, when she decided to pay the fine on behalf of the Pharisees, who failed to take the required oath to Augustus and Herod in 19 BCE.[60] Also 'the eldest daughter of Herod', that is Salampsio, who was offered to him upon the death of his Hasmonaean wife,[61] could not have been ready for marriage earlier than this year, since she was born in c. 33 BCE (Chapter 8 §2).

During the time when Pheroras's Hasmonaean wife was alive, and before the fall of Costobarus (26 BCE), Pheroras was accused of a plot to poison the king. Upon an investigation it was revealed that Pheroras had considered only an escape to Parthia with his mistress (the 'slave'-girl and subsequent wife), to be joined shortly by Costobarus. Since the latter finally took all the blame, Pheroras was pardoned.[62]

Around 21/20 BCE when Syllaeus of Nabataea visited Judaea and came to dinner with Salome, Pheroras was spying on the couple apparently on behalf of Herod.[63] Two or three months later, when Syllaeus

added to her dowry 100 talents (cf. Chapter 10 n. 9)!

60. In *Ant.* 17.42-43 it is clear that the 'slave' was married to Pheroras at the time of the oath—the story here being a 'flashback' among events belonging to c. 7 BCE (but generally thought to date c. 6/5 BCE). In *Ant.* 16.194 the marriage (without the oath connection) is also given as a 'flashback' to events belonging to c. 14 BCE (but generally thought to date from 11 to as late as c. 9/8 BCE). The oath story runs as follows: Augustus arrived at Syria in the spring of 20 BCE (in the consulship of M. Apuleius and P. Silius—Dio 54.7.6; and in the eighteenth year of Herod—Josephus, *Ant.* 15.354). At the end of his stay Herod escorted him to the sea (*Ant.* 15.363). The emperor went to Samos and spent time in Athens, before arriving back at Rome on 12 October 19 BCE (*Res Gest.* 11; Dio 54.10; *I.It.* 13.2, 519-20). Therefore it was either in late 20 or early 19 BCE on his return to Judaea that Herod demanded from the people an oath of loyalty to Augustus as well as to his own government. This stirred up trouble. Only two religious groups escaped: the Pharisees, who managed to pay a fine instead (the money being provided in secret by Pheroras's 'slave'-wife), and the Essenes, for whom, according to Josephus, Herod had high regard. The main event is recorded in *Ant.* 15.368-79, but more details are found in another version in *Ant.* 17.41-47 (cf. *War* 1.571; Mason 1991, 116-19), which is, as I said, a 'flashback' at the trial of Pheroras's 'slave'-wife in c. 7 BCE (see later); see also Mason 1991: 260-80, but with defective dating (276 n. 101).

61. See further Josephus, *Ant.* 16.194-95; cf. *Ant.* 17.22.

62. Josephus, *War* 1.485-87.

63. Josephus, *Ant.* 16.223; for the date see Chapter 7 n. 22.

returned to ask for Salome's hand, and was refused on the basis of his unwillingness to convert to Judaism, Pheroras accused her of misbehaviour.[64] According to *Ant.* 16.227-28 it was now that Salome asked for Cyprus II, who was born in 30/29 BCE (Chapter 8 §2), to be given to her son Antipater III, but Pheroras persuaded Herod to give the girl to his first unnamed son. Yet, this is another of Josephus's mistakes. Cyprus was offered to Pheroras only much later (χρόνου διελθόντος), in c. 14 BCE, when she would have been 15,[65] and even worse she was finally given in marriage to Antipater III not to Pheroras's son (above n. 59). On this occasion (in c. 14 BCE) Pheroras went as far as to promise to marry Herod's daughter within 30 days, putting away his 'slave'-wife and their child (*paida*). But his love for them was overwhelming and thus he had to dishonour the King for the second time.

Pheroras's role during the two major dissensions in Herod's house-hold (14/13 and 11–8 BCE) was central. But any reconstruction of the events pertaining to this period is complex and tedious, and has to assume many errors in the received sequence of events in Josephus. Unfortunately various family intrigues which took place in the first dissension have been moved forward, in some cases duplicated (as if the same events from two different sources were not recognized as such by Josephus), to fill the period of the second dissension (for which the historian might have had inadequate evidence). Together with them went many points of wider historical interest, thus creating a false chronology affecting events and people in and out of Judaea.[66]

64. Josephus, *Ant.* 16.226; cf. *War* 1.487.

65. Josephus, *Ant.* 16.196-200.

66. From 14 BCE Herodian chronology becomes increasingly entangled, and any reasonable disentaglement, i.e. by moving back many events currently thought to date between 12 and 9/8 BCE, to the period between 14 and 13 BCE (cf. Corbishley 1934; Corbishley 1935), has the effect of thinning out the history of the area after 12 BCE. Curiously the information on Syria is also scanty, and even Roman events in Dio are far from being adequate or in order. First the chronological order of key events must be appreciated: Herod's return from Pontus in c. mid-14 BCE; his recall of his son Antipater and dispatch to Augustus in c. late 14 BCE; his journey to Rome with his other sons, Alexander and Aristobulus, to press charges against them in c. mid-13 BCE; his return after reconciliation with all three sons, and the celebration of the completion of the Temple at Jerusalem in the autumn of 12 BCE. For a treatment of these points (cf. Kokkinos forthcoming 1) and the structure of Josephus's text, see Appendixes 2 and 3.

In what is said below about Pheroras, a new scheme is followed which tends to backdate many family clashes from the second dissension to the first—their natural place. This scheme is based on the detailed prosopography presented here, which provides a better understanding of the activities of all members of the Herodian family, with estimates of their ages and dates of marriages and deaths.

On Herod's return from Pontus in the second half of 14 BCE, where he had gone to fight on the side of M. Antonius, Pheroras together with Salome informed him of his sons' (Alexander's and Aristobulus's) conspiratorial tendencies.[67] Pheroras seems to have been instigated by the older son of Herod, Antipater II, who had been banished from Jerusalem (to give way to his Hasmonaean half-brothers), but who was to be recalled shortly by his father.[68] Perhaps such an instigation is consistent with Pheroras's subsequent change of tactics, when he slandered Herod by saying to Alexander that the king was in love with his wife Glaphyra. Herod at once reproached Pheroras, who had no other excuse than to blame Salome. But she promptly explained that Pheroras had implicated her only because he was upset with her for still trying to persuade him to leave his 'slave'-wife and marry Herod's daughter Cyprus II.[69]

Pheroras's intrigues did not stop there. In early 13 BCE, when Alexander had been imprisoned, he helped him to write a work in four books against Herod. Soon afterwards Archelaus of Cappadocia arrived at Judaea to support Alexander, his son-in-law.[70] Archelaus first denounced Pheroras for his deeds, but when he saw that Alexander was to be set free he helped Pheroras to overcome Herod's wrath, thus bringing a general, if only temporary, reconciliation.[71]

During the second major dissension in the Herodian family Pheroras is mentioned as helping Herod to prevent the populace of

67. Josephus, *Ant.* 16.73-74; cf. 16.68.

68. Cf. Josephus, *War* 1.475, where Antipater roused the enmity of Pheroras and Salome against Alexander and Aristobulus.

69. Josephus, *Ant.* 16.206-19; the point made by Salome is indicative of chronology, for if the event was to be dated as late as c. 9/8 BCE, Salome would hardly have been trying to persuade Pheroras to marry Cyprus II, five years after his formal rejection of the girl.

70. Josephus, *Ant.* 16.256, where the assumed date would be from c. 11 to 9/8 BCE, but *War* 1.498-99 conclusively places the writing of the work during the state visit of Archelaus of Cappadocia in early 13 BCE.

71. Josephus, *Ant.* 16.267-69; cf. *War* 1.502-508.

Jericho from stoning Alexander and Aristobulus, when these two had been imprisoned again in c. 10/9 BCE.[72] Pheroras and Salome later participated in the trial of Herod's sons at Berytus in 9/8 BCE, and apparently on their return to Caesarea, Tiro, an old soldier of Herod, accused them publicly of being directly responsible for the fate of the young men.[73]

In the special gathering of c. 8/7 BCE to restructure the royal family after the execution of his Hasmonaean sons, Herod arranged for Alexander I's homonymous son to marry the unnamed daughter of Pheroras, when she should reach the proper age.[74] If the girl was at that time about ten, she could have been the 'child' (already mentioned) of the 'slave'-wife to whom Pheroras was married from around 20 BCE (but see end of chapter). In fact since Alexander II was born in 15 BCE, the girl must have been even younger[75]—assuming that the object of Herod was to match couples of broadly similar age. At any rate the marriage of Pheroras's daughter to Alexander II did not actually take place[76]—the girl was finally given to Antipater II's unnamed son (see Chapter 8 §1).

During this period Antipater II paid court to Pheroras and vice versa, and their pact grew stronger. Many members of the royal staff, such as the eunuch Bagoas, were also drawn in to what developed into a plot against the king. Pheroras himself was totally subdued by his 'slave'-wife, who had made a league with other women, such as her unnamed mother, unnamed sister, Doris the mother of Antipater, and evidently Mariamme II the wife of Herod. All these women shared the same beliefs, heavily influenced by Pharisaism.[77] Salome I, Herod's

72. Josephus, *Ant.* 16.321—it must have been c. 10/9 BCE since it was during this time that Nicolaus was in Rome—*Ant.* 16. 299, 335ff.

73. Josephus, *War* 1.538, 545.

74. Josephus, *Ant.* 17.14, 16; cf. *War* 1.557; I take Alexander I's 'elder son' (τῷ πρεσβυτέρῳ) referred to here, to be Alexander II and not Tigranes I (see Chapter 9 §1).

75. For betrothals at an early age among the Herodians, the evidence is incontestable: for example Drusilla was six on her betrothal (Josephus, *Ant.* 19.354; see Kokkinos 1986a: 39). Pheroras's 'child' (or children, if the 'daughter' was another child) from his 'slave'-wife must have been born after 19 BCE, since apparently in that year the Pharisees foretold that the royal power would fall 'to any children that they might have' (*Ant.* 17.43: παῖδάς τε οἵ εἶεν αὐτοῖς).

76. Josephus, *Ant.* 17.18; cf. *War* 1.565.

77. Neusner's version (1971) of the pre-CE 70 history of the Pharisees must now

sister, did not hesitate to warn the king about the serious danger he was under, and his first reaction was to kill Bagoas and other members of the palace staff, as well as many Pharisees.[78]

Then Herod brought charges against Pheroras's 'slave'-wife. This he did on the pretext of her mistreatment of his youngest daughters, but in reality because he hated her for having in the past alienated his brother who refused to marry Herod's older daughters. More importantly, she had become the instrument of the Pharisees in their effort to corrupt the royal court. Herod's verdict was the banishment from Jerusalem of Pheroras's 'slave'-wife—whom Pheroras decided to follow—and the annulling of the relationship between her associates and those of Antipater II.[79] Pheroras retired to his territory, swearing that he would never return so long as his brother lived, an oath which he kept to the end. As it happened, it was Herod who went to Pheroras when the latter became seriously ill in c. 7 BCE, and as soon as he died he provided him with a burial-place in Jerusalem followed by a period of solemn mourning.[80]

Despite rumours that Pheroras had been drugged by Herod, it was later alleged by two freedmen of Pheroras that he had actually been

be abandoned (Rivkin 1978; Schwartz [D.R.] 1983; Sanders 1985: 388-89 n. 59; Masson 1991; cf. Kokkinos 1992c). Neusner (1987: 292) believes that the Pharisees functioned effectively only in the first half of the first century BCE and that: '. . . as a sect the group seems to end its political life with the advent of Herod. . .' But under Herod Pharisaism infiltrated even the royal court and took root among the female circle, a distant echo of the times of Salome-Alexandra the Hasmonaean (cf. the imperial court in CE 19 and later the court of Izates of Adiabene). No doubt Herod oppressed the Pharisees as hard as circumstances would allow, and they in turn rejected him throughout his reign (Allon 1961: 70-72), but nevertheless due to political necessity Herod showed a measured tolerance towards this sect. Already in 47 BCE, in his trial by the Sanhedrin, Herod avoided killing Samaias (or should it be Pollion?) the Pharisee leader (Josephus, *Ant.* 14.175), and in 37 BCE, when he conquered Jerusalem, he honoured Pollion and his disciple Samaias for having advised the people to admit Herod (*Ant.* 15.3). In 19 BCE on Pollion's account the king exempted the Pharisees from taking the oath of loyalty, even if only on the basis of a fine (see above n. 60). Despite Herod's executions of Pharisees in c. 7/6 (see later), Pharisaism remained influential into the next century (*SVM* 2, 402, 405 n. 7; see also Appendix 7).

78. Josephus, *Ant.* 17.32-45; cf. *War* 1.554, 567-70.

79. Josephus, *Ant.* 17.46-51; *War* 1.567-73.

80. Josephus, *Ant.* 17.58-59; *War* 1.578-81; for Pheroras's burial see Abel 1946: 62-65.

poisoned by the women of his household. A thorough new investigation began, which revealed the extent of the plot against the king himself. After persistent torture of Pheroras's women and their female Peraean entourage (slave-girls, freedwomen and ladies of rank) the truth came out. Pheroras was accused of having taken part in the conspiracy of Antipater II, having had an intimate relationship with Antipater's mother, and having had designs to fly to Petra apparently to be supported by Syllaeus the enemy of Herod. All blame was then put on Doris, who was immediately exiled for the second time, and ultimately on her son Antipater II, who had for the moment gone to Rome for safety.[81] Mariamme II was also implicated, with the result that Herod divorced her, while her son was struck out of the king's will, and her father lost his high priesthood.[82]

Other people were also exposed: Antipater from Samaria, an agent (ἐπίτροπος) of Antipater II; Antiphilus from Egypt, a friend (φίλος) or companion (ἑταῖρος) of Antipater II; some members of Antiphilus's family, such as his mother and two unnamed brothers, one of whom was a doctor (ἰατρὸς) in Alexandria; an unnamed slave of Antiphilus; Bathyllus, a freedman (ἀπελεύθερος) of Antipater II; Theudion, the brother of Doris; Acme the Jewess, a maidservant (θεραπαινὶς) of Livia, the wife of Augustus; and apparently the unnamed Hasmonaean wife of Antipater II, daughter of Antigonus.[83]

In the final analysis it is not clear whether Pheroras was really poisoned by his 'slave'-wife, though it seems likely in view of Antipater's double stance. During his trial in c. 7/6 BCE he was accused of having had affairs with the women close to Pheroras,[84] and he may have had

81. Josephus, *Ant.* 17.61-68; *War* 1.582-91.

82. Josephus, *War* 1.598-99; *Ant.* 17.78; for Mariamme II and her son, see Chapter 8 §4.

83. Josephus, *Ant.* 17.69-82; *War* 1.592-603; for Antipater II and his wife, see also Chapter 8 §1.

84. Josephus, *Ant.* 17.121; cf. *War* 1.638. The general order of events, a guess as to their duration, and Varus's dates in Syria, would suggest c. 7/6 BCE for the trial of Antipater (Chapter 7 n. 27). The news of Pheroras's death (c. 7 BCE) reached Antipater in Tarentum (*War* 1.609; *Ant.* 17.85), when he was on his way back to Judaea after an absence of over seven months (*Ant.* 17.82), which had followed the execution of Alexander and Aristobulus in c. 8 BCE. Now since Antipater was killed shortly before Herod died, apparently in 4 BCE, one would have to assume that Antipater remained in prison for almost two years! But it is possible that Herod died in 5 BCE, see Appendix 2, pt. 5.

plans to dispose of both Pheroras (despite their alliance)[85] and Herod. As for Pheroras's 'slave'-wife, Herod at first, after torture, gave her a pardon (as well as to her associates), but only because he had extracted enough evidence to condemn Doris and Antipater. Later it is said that she went through a second interrogation (or is it identical with the first?) in which she ran and fell from the roof but did not die—it is not clear whether Pheroras's 'slave'-wife was pardoned again, but it seems likely she was, since Herod had promised her freedom if she spoke the truth, which Josephus believed she did.[86]

In the events following the death of Herod in 4 (or 5) BCE many members of his family made the long journey to Rome,[87] each to claim from Augustus the lion's share of the king's wealth. Among them were the two unnamed younger sons of Pheroras (by his Hasmonaean wife) who were given in marriage to the youngest daughters of Herod (see Chapter 8 §7). We know nothing of their destiny, other than that they remained childless. Nor do we know anything about Pheroras's eldest son (also by his Hasmonaean wife), who is erroneously said by Josephus to have married Cyprus II (above n. 59), or indeed about his daughter (by his 'slave'-wife), who finally married the unnamed son of Antipater II already mentioned.

In a penetrating analysis of *Ant.* 17.43-45, prompted by the discovery of an important ossuary of an individual claiming to belong to 'the House of David', Flusser suggested that the 'slave'-wife of Pheroras may have been of Davidic descent, and that the 'Pharisees' (though in fact some religious group close to them), hoped that she would become the mother of the expected Messiah.[88] Although the suggestion

85. Cf. Antipater's envy and fear of Pheroras's tetrarchship—Josephus, *Ant.* 17.16; *War* 1.559.

86. Josephus, *Ant.* 17.71-72; *War* 1.593; curiously the manner of the attempted suicide resembles the type of death assigned to Mariamme I in rabbinic tradition (*b. B. Bat.* 3b—Chapter 8 n. 21).

87. The group which travelled to Rome (or rather groups since they arrived separately), included Herod's sons (Archelaus, Philip and Antipas), one of his wives (Malthace), his sister (Salome I) with her entire family (see Chapter 7 n. 60), his youngest daughters (Roxane and Salome II) and his 'nephews' who became also his 'sons-in-law', i.e. Pheroras's sons (Josephus, *War* 1.14-15, 20, 83, 99; *Ant.* 17.219-20, 224-25, 250, 303, 322). Herod's other 'nephews', who were also 'sons-in-law', i.e. Phasael's son and Joseph's son, would have stayed behind—the latter certainly did (*War* 2.74; cf. *Ant.* 17.294; see Chapter 6 §2).

88. Flusser 1986; the inscription found on the ossuary reads: שֶׁל בְּי דוד.

that the 'slave' may actually have had an illustrious background, real or imagined, cannot be discounted *a priori*,[89] particularly since Pheroras's first wife was Hasmonaean, implications drawn from it are difficult to substantiate. The text says that the 'Pharisees' foretold

> that by God's decree Herod's throne would be taken from him, both from himself and his descendants, and the royal power would fall to her and Pheroras and to any children that they might have... And the king put to death those of the Pharisees who were most to blame and the eunuch Bagoas... Now Bagoas had been carried away by their assurance that he would be called the father and benefactor of him who would some day be set over the people with the title of king, for all the power would belong to him and he would give Bagoas the ability to marry and to beget children of his own.

Flusser made some leaps of faith. We may, of course, reconsider whether the 'Pharisees' in this instance were indeed a different group prone to prediction, like the Essenes. This is possible if the account derives from Nicolaus of Damascus, who may not have been fully informed on all divisions in Judaism, and who was hostile towards the Pharisees. But we are said that the sect involved spoke to Pheroras's wife out of gratitude for her paying the 'oath-fine' to Herod on their behalf, and this presumably was the case with the Pharisees,[90] while the Essenes are excluded because they had been excused from the oath by Herod himself.[91] If we are to think of another sect close to the Pharisees, such as the one known later as the Fourth Philosophy, we would then have to assume that the 'fine' was imposed only on them, and it was they—not the Pharisees—that Pheroras's wife baled out. It would also have been they who corrupted the females of the royal court, they who had looked for a change in government, and they who had been killed in large numbers by Herod as a result. This requires convoluted argument.

But more to the point, it is not clear that what this religious group uttered to Pheroras's wife is to be connected with what they said to

89. Cf. Herod's family, called 'subject' or 'slave' to the Hasmonaeans (Chapter 3 n. 85); and the variety of this word's use in Gibbs and Feldman 1986; see also discussion in Chapter 8 n. 79.

90. Josephus, *War* 1.571; *Ant.* 17.42; even their leaders, Pollion and Samaias, are given by name in *Ant.* 15.370, though it is true that no 'fine' is mentioned in this context; see above n. 60.

91. Josephus, *Ant.* 15.371.

Bagoas. Although the prediction to Bagoas is apparently messianic,[92] that to Pheroras's wife need not be. The connection between the falling of the throne to a child of Pheroras's wife and the coming of the 'Messiah' does not necessarily follow, as we are lacking the evidence itself that she was of *Davidic* descent. This is the assumption. Yet one may forge a connection by raising the question: how would Bagoas be named 'father' and 'benefactor' of the future 'Messiah', without committing himself to long-term service, for example, by helping with the upbringing of the child of Pheroras's wife. Even so, the outcome of this story is murky. As we saw, Pheroras did have a 'child' by this woman, which, if a male, would presumably have been potentially dangerous to Herod, but this 'child' may have been identical to the 'daughter' mentioned later. So one has to argue again that Pheroras's wife gave birth to two children, the first being a boy, of whom we know nothing, and so on and so forth.

This is not the place to go further into this discussion, extraordinary as it is, attempting to find parallels with the story of the persecution in Matthew's Gospel, as Flusser does. Nevertheless, one has to point out that soon after Herod's death, another 'slave' emanating from the Peraean court was bold enough to claim the royal title. His name was Simon and his attempt must have been of some impact to earn him a mention even from Tacitus (see Chapter 8 n. 79)!

92. See Isa. 56.1-5.

Family Tree: *The Brothers of Herod and their Descendants*
(c. 77 BCE–CE 100)

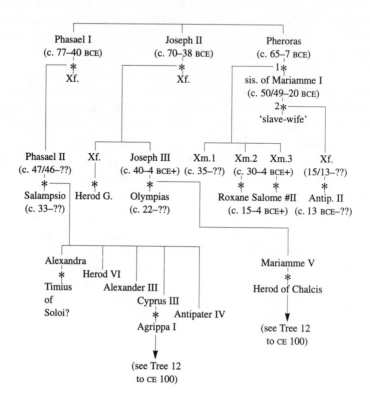

Chapter 7

THE SISTER OF HEROD AND HER OFFSPRING

Herod the Great's sister Salome was evidently the last child born to Antipater I and Cyprus I, and she also died last, some 15 years after Herod. She and her descendants played a major role in the shaping of the Herodian dynasty, and by reflection in the establishment of the royal court and the ruling class of Judaea up to the fall of Jerusalem in CE 70.

1. *Salome I*

Salome I was the only sister of Herod[1] and she would have been born in the 50s BCE, perhaps in the year 57 at the *dicennium* of the death of Queen Salome/Alexandra (the Hasmonaean patroness of Antipater I), whose name she adopted (had it not also been that of her grandmother, the unknown wife of Antipas I—see Appendix 1, no. 134). An earlier date is unlikely in view of her need to be attractive enough to Syllaeus in c. 21/20 BCE (see later). Also unlikely is a later date in view of the royal court's flight from the Parthians in 41/40 BCE, at which time she was of age, perhaps even already a mother.[2]

---

1.   Josephus, *War* 1.181; *Ant.* 14.121. If *War* 1.264 actually reads τὰς ἀδελφὰς this is a mistake (either Josephus's slip or a scribal error), since Herod had only one sister. The Jewish name 'Salome' was extremely common, and approximately 50 per cent of all women of the time were called 'Salome' or 'Mariamme' (Ilan 1989: 192). Among the many occurrences note the name in the Goliath family at Jericho (Hachlili 1979: no. 10), on a talisman from Syria (Seyrig 1985: 793-97), and an epitaph in Rome (*IGUR* 1323; cf. *ND* 4.182: no. 99); cf. Chapter 8 n. 28; see also comments on Salome III (Chapter 10 §1). Macurdy (1937: 69-77) represents Salome as more of a monster than she actually was.

2.   In *Ant.* 14.353-54 (cf. *War* 1.264) Josephus mentions the principal members of Herod's court on their way to Masada: '...his mother [Cyprus I] and sister [Salome I] and the daughter of Alexander [Mariamme I]...and her mother

If so, and since she would have been ready for marriage from about 45/44 BCE, she may have been given to her first husband—her uncle Joseph I—by her father himself, who was still alive. The unnamed daughter of Salome would then be Joseph's child (Chapter 5 §2 end), born a year or two before the events of 41/40 BCE. If the conjecture that Joseph was in charge of Idumaea since the days of Antipater I is correct (Chapter 3 §2), then Salome would have become the first lady of the region even before the destruction of Marisa. The escape of the Herodian court to Masada is the first episode in which Salome makes a debut in Josephus's narrative. The court was eventually rescued by Herod, and moved to Samaria early in 38 BCE.[3] Later, at the beginning of the king's *de facto* rule, Salome's husband would have been transferred to Jerusalem (his position was given to one Costobarus I— see below). This was perhaps due to his seniority and experience (his services were required in the capital—he was soon to be made temporary administrator of the whole kingdom), and also perhaps because Marisa, arguably the old Herodian centre, had fallen beyond repair. We hear of Salome again only in c. 35 BCE, when she and her mother Cyprus I were abused by Mariamme I, in the events following the murder of the latter's young brother. In turn Salome and Cyprus succeeded in infuriating Herod by accusing Mariamme of sending her portrait to M. Antonius.[4]

After Herod's return from his meeting with Antony in 34 BCE, when Mariamme was guarded by Joseph, Salome seized the opportunity to confirm to Herod that Joseph had seduced Mariamme. Even

[Alexandra]...his youngest brother [Pheroras] and all the servants and the rest of the crowd that was with them...' He also mentions the women leading 'their infants...', but Cyprus I had none, and Alexandra's children were not infants since Mariamme I (then bethrothed to Herod) was about 13, Aristobulus (III) about 12, and her unnamed daughter (Pheroras's future wife) about 10 (Chapter 3 n. 98). Thus Josephus may imply that Salome I (then about 18) was a mother of a child. Also at least three other women of the most immediate family, who are unmentioned, must have been present with children: the unknown wife of Phasael I, Doris the wife of Herod, and the unknown wife of Joseph II. The first's son, Phasael II, who was then seven, is actually acknowledged shortly afterwards (*Ant.* 14.371; *War* 1.275). Doris's son Antipater II would have been more or less of the same age (Chapter 8 §1). One of Joseph II's two children was even younger (Chapter 6 §2).

    3.   Josephus, *Ant.* 14.353, 396-97, 400, 408, 413; *War* 1.264, 292, 293-94, 303.

    4.   Josephus, *War* 1.438-39; cf. *Ant.* 15.27, 29.

more seriously she accused him of a political conspiracy with Alexandra.[5] This led to the execution of Joseph, though Mariamme on this occasion was pardoned (Chapters 5 §2 and 8 §2). Not fully content, Salome and her mother continued their efforts against Herod's Hasmonaean wife, and about 30 BCE, before Herod set sail to meet Augustus, they provoked the king with various slanders. By the time he returned the situation was out of control: Mariamme openly jeered at Salome's low birth, and Salome fabricated an attempt by Mariamme to poison the king, in which she implicated Herod's butler.[6] Together with other reasons Mariamme was finally condemned to death in 29/28 BCE (Chapter 8 n. 21).

Meanwhile soon after the execution of Salome's first husband late in 34 BCE, Herod arranged for his sister to marry Costobarus I.[7] Of this rich nobleman Josephus says:

> Costobarus was of Idumaean race and was one of those first in rank among them, and his ancestors had been priests of Kōze (or Kozai), whom the Idumaeans believe (νομίζουσιν) to be a god... he set no limit to his hopes, having good reason for this both in his lineage and in the wealth which he had acquired through continual and shameless profit-seeking...[8]

Costobarus was in Herod's service at least from the time of the siege of Jerusalem (38–37 BCE). After the conquest in 37 he was assigned with the guard of the city, and subsequently, possibly in 37/36 BCE, he was appointed governor (ἄρχων) of Idumaea and Gaza (perhaps due to the vacancy in this position created by Joseph's transfer, as is assumed here).[9]

5. Josephus, *War* 1.441, 443; *Ant.* 15.80-81.
6. Josephus, *Ant.* 15.213, 220, 223, 231.
7. Josephus, *War* 1.486; cf. *Ant.* 15.254; cf. Stern [M.] 1982: 43 but with inaccuracies about his descendants.
8. Josephus, *Ant.* 15.253, 257; as such the name of Costobarus does not occur elsewhere, but it seems to be equivalent to Qos-gabar (קוסגבר) or Qos-bar (קוסבר), both well-attested (Cook 1930: 203-204 n. 5; Flusser 1976: 1074; Israel 1979: 177, 186, 189). Josephus no doubt implies that in the time of Costobarus the cult of Qos still functioned in Idumaea (see Chapter 3 nn. 12 and 33).
9. The meaning of *Ant.* 15.254 is ambiguous (also noted by Smallwood 1976: 63 n. 10): it implies that Costobarus became concurrently the governor of Idumaea and the husband of Salome soon after Herod became a king in 37 BCE. But Salome's first husband was killed only in 34. Even more ambiguously, Josephus (*Ant.* 15.258) says that Salome pleaded with Herod to pardon Costobarus's involvement

From the outset Costobarus proved to be profoundly disloyal to Herod. Although he controlled the city gates he permitted the escape of the Sons of Baba, and in fact he provided for them a hiding place in his own Idumaean estates for 12 years (37–26 BCE inclusive). The Sons of Baba were serious opponents of Herod, with great influence among the people, related by marriage to the Hasmonaean family and staunch supporters of Antigonus's regime. After their disappearance Costobarus had to take an oath that he knew nothing about them, and they were eventually proclaimed outlaws by Herod, with a big reward for their capture.[10] There should be little doubt that like Costobarus the family of Baba was of Idumaean origins (compare Malichus and Peitholaus—Chapter 6 §1; and Dositheus, Lysimachus and Antipater Gadias—Chapter 5 §2) and apparently connected with Marisa, as inscriptions bearing this relatively rare name suggest.[11] A further connection, though vague, may be made with the sage Baba ben Buta known from Talmudic traditions, upon whose head, according to one such tradition, Herod placed 'a garland of hedgehog bristles and put out his eyes'.[12]

Costobarus's disloyalty continued after his appointment as governor in c. 37/36 BCE, by plotting against Herod with the endorsement of Cleopatra VII of Egypt, to whom he had offered his territory with assurances that the Idumaeans were prepared to abandon Judaism.[13] The date of this event may be confirmed by looking at wider Roman history. Cleopatra demanded extra land from M. Antonius at least from the time of their marriage in the winter of 37/36 BCE, and by late 36 she succeeded in having her children presented with portions of Ituraea, Nabataea, Phoenicia, Palestine, Crete, Cyrene and Cyprus.[14] Approximately a year later (c. late 35 BCE) Cleopatra

with the queen of Egypt, which was not a thing for her to do before the execution of Joseph. These ambiguities are not discussed by Ronen (1988: 214-20).

10.   Josephus, *Ant.* 15.260-65; cf. Schalit 1969: 142-43.

11.   Peters and Thiersch 1905: 45, nos. 10-11 (Babas brother of Babata); Oren and Rappaport 1984: 144, no. 8 (Babata), and their n. 68 for various references; cf. the famous Babatha (*P. Yadin*).

12.   *b. B. Bat.* 3b–4a; see Ronen 1988: 219-20, referring to Ben-Shalom's Hebrew thesis (to which I have no access) for a collection of all relative material on Baba ben Buta.

13.   Josephus, *Ant.* 15.255-57.

14.   Dio 49.32; Plutarch, *Anton.* 36. Unfortunately the precise character of the Palestinian portion is not specified. *SVM* (1, 298; cf. Stern [M.] 1974b, 232;

pressed on with her desire to possess more of Herod's territory, but according to Herod without success, as he triumphantly noted in his letter to Jerusalem from Laodicea dated to 34 BCE. Herod stated that in this instance she was given Coele-Syria instead.[15] Yet, the king had actually made more concessions, as Josephus subsequently discloses. Cleopatra came to Judaea in late 34 or early 33 BCE only to settle an agreement with Herod, concerning his leasing from her parts of his own territory![16] Thus Costobarus's offer to Cleopatra would have followed the trend of the period (36–35/34 BCE) in which the queen of Egypt was expanding the size of her domains.

It cannot be ignored that at this time Alexandra was also plotting against Herod via Cleopatra.[17] There seems to have been a link between Costobarus's and Alexandra's causes, though the first was ultimately seeking the wider goal (καὶ μεῖζον πράξειν) of total independence from Jewish influences.[18] This link can also be sensed in the role played by the pro-Hasmonaean Sons of Baba, and the other associates: Dositheus, Lysimachus and Antipater surnamed Gadias. At this time, in c. 34/33 BCE, Herod took drastic action neither against Alexandra nor Costobarus, because of the constant fear of Cleopatra—in the case of Costobarus and the others all particulars had yet

Smallwood 1976: 61 n. 4) dates these grants to late 37 or early 36 BCE, apparently following Plutarch who seems to suggest that they were made at the time of Cleopatra's marriage to Antony (winter 37/36 BCE). But Dio's date is clearly late 36 BCE (Stern [M.] 1974b: 305-307), which can be consistent with Eusebius's Armenian version [edn Karst 79] placing the grants in Cleopatra's sixteenth year, i.e. sometime between Oct. 37 and Oct. 36 BCE (cf. Sherk 1984: ‡10-11, no. 88).

15.   Josephus, *Ant.* 15.77-79; cf. *War* 1.359-63, where Josephus amalgamates (as is often done in this work) the events from 36 to 33 BCE. Schalit (1969: 84, 387, nos. 162, 163) correctly saw a relatively early date for the grants made to Cleopatra and the connection with Costobarus, but he seems to be wrong about Costobarus's execution in 28/27 BCE (at least not if Herod began his *de facto* rule in 37 BCE).

16.   Josephus, *Ant.* 15.96, 106, 132; cf. *War* 1.362, but see above n. 15. A brief guidance on Josephus's text is appropriate here: *Ant.* 15.87 ends with the execution of Joseph I in late 34 or early 33 BCE; followed by 15.88-95, a 'flashback' of Cleopatra's activities over some years ending with Antony's grants to her in 36 BCE; followed by 15.96-103, the aftermath (33 BCE onwards) of Cleopatra's gaining parts of Herod's land in 34 BCE.

17.   Note Alexandra's letters to Cleopatra in 36/35 BCE (*Ant.* 15.32), and twice in c. 35 BCE (*Ant.* 15.45-46; 62-63, 65), causing Herod to appear before Antony in 34 BCE.

18.   Josephus, *Ant.* 15.257.

to be unravelled.[19] However after Augustus's conquest of Egypt in 30 BCE things were different. It is indicative that the Idumaean clique of Costobarus was exterminated by Herod soon after Alexandra's execution in 28/27 BCE.[20] The main evidence which led to their downfall was contributed by Salome in 26 BCE, after she had presented to her husband an official divorce (the *get* of the rabbis), contrary to Jewish law. Evidently at some point she had learned the details of Costobarus's conspiracy, and in the first domestic quarrel she decided on the ultimate punishment for him.[21]

Salome was now a widow for the second time, but probably not for very long, if only because of her age—she was over 30. Around 21/20 BCE Syllaeus the minister of Nabataean king Obodas was to pay two official visits to the Herodian court.[22] This ambitious and crafty young man was desperately seeking to ally himself with Herod, and during his stay at Jerusalem offered to marry Salome. There were many motives for this would-be alliance. Bowersock saw that the acquisition of northern territories (Trachonitis, Batanaea, Auranitis, Ulatha and

---

19.   See above n. 9 on Josephus's ambiguity in *Ant.* 15.258, concerning the pardoning of Costobarus in a pre-34 BCE context.

20.   Josephus, *Ant.* 15.252; for the date see Chapter 8 n. 21.

21.   Josephus, *Ant.* 15.259-60.

22.   In the absence of Herod in Rome in 13/12 BCE, the people of Trachonitis revolted and Herod's generals had to subdue them. Forty chiefs escaped to Petra. Syllaeus received them, being on bad terms with Herod as a result of the Salome affair (*Ant.* 16.275)—thus the affair happened before 13 BCE. Now since this is placed close to the time when Pheroras's Hasmonaean wife was alive (*War* 1.487), it would have occurred before 20 BCE (see Chapter 6 §3). Given the expedition of Syllaeus to Arabia in 26/25 (Jameson 1968; *SVM* 1, 290 n. 8; cf. Braund 1983: 239-40), and Herod's trip to Greece in 22/21 (Otto 1913: 70; contra Reinhold 1933: 84 n. 47; Roddaz 1984: 451; see Kokkinos forthcoming 1), only the years 24/23 and 21/20 BCE seem possible, with the latter being likely for two reasons: First the grants made to Herod of the northern territories, which triggered Syllaeus's mission to Judaea, took place in late 24 and 20 BCE. Secondly Salome's resort to Livia (by writing to her in Rome) for help in marrying Syllaeus, presupposes that they knew each other, which could only have been made possible during the journey of the Herodian family in 22/21 BCE (cf. Dio 54.7.2; Suetonius *Tib.* 6.2). So Salome would not have stayed a widow for a lengthy period after 26 BCE. The affair with Syllaeus is introduced in *Ant.* 16.220-26 as a 'flashback' among events of c. 14/13 BCE concerning Pheroras (which begin in 16.206-19 and continue in 227-28). For the structure of Josephus's text concerning the first dissension in the Herodian court, see Appendix 3.

Panias) by Herod in 24 BCE and 20 BCE must have been an embarrassment to the Nabataean king, and since he was an ineffectual character a skillful plan to approach Herod (who had clearly become the
source of power in the Near East) was contrived by his minister. Kasher
realized the importance of a substantial loan taken by Syllaeus from
Herod (as well as a lease of pastureland), which would have secured
him a better standing at the court of Petra in an attempt to depose
Obodas.[23]

Thus a marriage tie with Herod's family would have meant the possibility of Salome becoming the Queen of Nabataea. She was therefore
prompt to accept Syllaeus's offer, and (as she was accused later) may
even have signed an illegal contract.[24] But there would be no wedding.
According to Josephus the agreement with Herod failed to cover religious practices. Syllaeus could not submit to being converted to
Judaism.[25] Yet, this was apparently a pretext used by Herod to avoid a
suspicious link with a dangerous man capable of creating political
problems for Judaea (as in fact he later did). At least the record of
Syllaeus in his dealings with the Romans, during their Arabian expedition of 26/25 BCE, would not have inspired much confidence, even if
it may be wrong to blame the Nabataean for the whole of the disaster.[26] Despite Salome's pleading with Herod and her recourse to the
intercession of Livia in Rome, the king stood firm in his decision.[27]

23.   Bowersock 1983b: 50; Kasher 1988: 163; Kasher follows Bowersock's
1971 conclusions, ignoring his 1983 radical changes. Nevertheless, Kasher laid particular stress on the significant loan element in the story, which has been overlooked
by Bowersock. For this loan of 60 (Josephus, *Ant.* 16.279) or 500 (*Ant.* 16.343)
talents, see also *Ant.* 16.281-82, 291, 296, 340, 348, 351, 353. The only other
study of Syllaeus which may be noticed is Negev 1978: 564-68, but with numerous
mistakes.

24.   Josephus, *War* 1.487.

25.   Josephus, *Ant.* 16.220-25.

26.   Bowersock (1983b: 47) convincingly argues that Strabo, our main source,
found Syllaeus a suitable scapegoat.

27.   Letters of Salome to Livia must have survived in Rome, if Acme later imi-
tated them on behalf of Antipater II, in order to accuse Salome of trying to kill the
king (below n. 57). After initial success in turning Augustus against Herod, and after
two trials in Rome (11/10 and 7 BCE), Syllaeus was beheaded (Strabo, 16.4.24;
Josephus *Ant.* 16.352; *FGrH* 90, F136). Stern ([M.] 1974b: 247; cf. *GLAJJ* 1, 257)
dated the execution to 4 BCE, while Bowersock (1983b: 53) to around 6, and Kasher
(1988: 172) to 6 or 5. But Syllaeus was evidently executed at the end of the trial in
which Antipater II was his main accuser (*War* 1.606, 633; *Ant.* 17.81). Since the

Josephus elsewhere relates the circumstances which followed Syllaeus's affair:

> And though Salome was eager to be married to the Arab Syllaeus, for
> whom she felt an erotic desire, Herod forced her to become the wife of
> Alexas; in this situation Julia co-operated with her, persuading Salome not
> to refuse the marriage lest open enmity be declared between them, for
> Herod had sworn that he would not be on good terms with Salome if she
> did not accept marriage with Alexas. And she took Julia's advice both
> because she was the wife of Caesar and because on other occasions she
> would give her very helpful counsel.[28]

On the same occasion and in order to strengthen this new marriage
arrangement of about 20 BCE, Herod gave Salome's unnamed daughter to the son of Alexas I by a former wife.[29] This daughter would
have been born in c. 43, certainly not later than 34, when her father
Joseph I died (Chapter 5 §2), and if she had to have reached marriageable age by c. 20.

It is peculiar that Josephus seems to mention Salome's husband as
'Calleas' in *Ant.* 17.9 (in reference to his son), but as 'Alexas' immediately afterwards in *Ant.* 17.10 and everywhere else. Perhaps 17.9
should read ἐκ τοῦ ἀνδρὸς αὐτῆς Καλλέας παῖς, instead of ἐκ τοῦ
ἀνδρὸς αὐτῆς Καλλέα παῖς, which would mean that Calleas was the
name, or in fact the epithet, of the son. This young man may have
been a homonymous son of Alexas I—that is Alexas II 'Calleas' son of
Alexas I, like the case already discussed of Phallion II 'Kaboas' son of
Phallion I (Chapter 5 §1); see also Simon II 'Cantheras' son of Simon
I (Chapter 8 §4). This is supported by the existence of a descendant of
the same lineage, half a century later, called 'Alexas Helcias son of
Alexas' (see Chapter 7 §2). The latter would probably have been
Alexas III 'Helcias' son of Alexas II 'Calleas' son of Alexas I.[30]

---

latter returned to Judaea in late 7 or early 6 BCE (Chapter 6 n. 84), in agreement with
Varus's arrival at Jerusalem (*Ant.* 17.89; *War* 1.617; *terminus post quem* mid-7 BCE,
if he held Africa in 8/7 BCE—Thomasson 1984: col. 372, no. 8), Syllaeus must have
died in 7 BCE.

    28.   *Ant.* 17.10; cf. *War* 1.566.

    29.   Josephus, *Ant.* 17.9; *War* 1.566. The reference to this wedding has been
placed by Josephus conveniently close to the mention of the Herodian group marriages of c. 8/7 BCE, but is a 'flashback' to the time Salome herself married Alexas
(cf. below n. 55).

    30.   Stern's belief ([M.] 1976: 613) that Alexas Helcias was the son of Salome I
and Alexas I cannot be accepted for two reasons: first Josephus mentions no children

The Alexas family emerged in power under the patronage of Herod the Great. Alexas I was a chief follower (ἀνδρὶ πρώτῳ) of the king, also described as one of his court friends (τινι τῶν φίλων).[31] By marrying Salome he may also have been appointed to the vacant position of governor of Idumaea left by the demise of Costobarus. Of Alexas's origins nothing is known.[32] In terms of speculation, an Alexas (ex-friend of Antony) was present at Rhodes in 30 BCE (when Herod was there), giving an account of his past hostility to the victorious Octavian. Herod sought to obtain a pardon for him but without success. Josephus does not give any hint of this Alexas's identity, nor does he explain why Herod had such an interest in him. From Plutarch we learn that he was Alexas the Laodicean, a member of Cleopatra's court, who had been sent from Alexandria to dissuade Herod from deserting to Augustus.[33] That Herod had friendly connections in the court of Cleopatra can be gathered at least from the case of Nicolaus of Damascus, who was employed by Herod after the dissolution of the palace at Alexandria.[34] Is it possible then that upon the execution of Alexas the Laodicean, Herod became patron to the surviving members of his deceased friend's family, including another Alexas, whom he brought back to Judaea?

This suggested background of the Herodian Alexas should however be seen against the fact that the name 'Helcias', equivalent to the Hebrew 'Hilkiah', is attested from an earlier period in the Ptolemaic court: Cleopatra III had a general called Chelkias, from the famous family of the Oniads.[35] In any case, whatever its origins, the Alexas

---

of Salome by Alexas (although the historian had the chance to do this on a number of occasions); second Salome would have had to give birth to a child—her fourth—in her late thirties, not physically impossible but none the less unlikely. Stern elsewhere presented Helcias as a son of Alexas I but not of Salome I ([M.] 1982: 49; followed by Rosenfeld 1988), presumably being a child of Alexas's former wife, and thus a brother of the man who married Salome's unnamed daughter. But this is equally unconvincing, for Helcias would have been too old (born some time before c. 20 BCE) for the kind of activities attributed to him by Josephus in the CE 40s.

31.   Josephus, *Ant.* 17.7; *War* 1.566.
32.   Stern [M.] 1976: 612; Stern 1982: 48-49; Goodman (1987: 42) calls Alexas's family 'Idumaean', but without citing any evidence.
33.   Josephus, *War* 1.393; *Ant.* 15.197; Plutarch, *Anton.* 72.3.
34.   Sophronius, *Narrat. mirac.* 54.
35.   Cassuto 1932: 214 (no. 1), 222 (no. 29); note Hilkiah the minister of King Hezekiah (2 Kgs 18.18; cf. Isa. 22.20); for Chelkias of Cleopatra III, see Strabo,

family took root in Palestine for over a century to come. In an important article Rosenfeld pointed out that the so-called 'Boundary of Gezer' inscriptions, which mention an Alexas ('Alexa' in the genitive), an Alkios (for Helcias) and an Archelaus, may refer to members of this family known from Josephus, who would have owned royal estates in the area, which was not far, according to Rosenfeld, from the land inherited by Salome (see later). Despite objections raised against this theory, it cannot be discounted.[36] Another property connection of some interest is the so-called 'palace of Hilkiya', in first-century CE Khirbet el-Murak in Idumaea, but this is difficult to substantiate.[37] A nobleman, Alexas, based in Lydda, at the end of the first-century CE (the time of Rabbi Tarfon) is referred to in the Tosefta: 'when Alexa[s] died in Lod, the people of the city came to eulogize him'.[38]

Coming back to Salome, when Mariamme's sons returned from Rome in the early autumn of 16 BCE, tensions began to arise between them and their aunt. It was perhaps for this reason that Herod attempted to improve domestic relationships by marriage arrangements—his sons were of marriageable age anyway.[39] Aristobulus I was united with the second daughter of his mother's accuser, that is with Salome's daughter Berenice I (see below). But Salome and her brother Pheroras were soon to be abused by the youth, and this signalled the serious trouble which lay ahead.[40] After Herod's return

Hypomn., *apud* Josephus, *Ant.* 13.284-87; Gabba 1958: 36-38, no. 11; for the Oniads cf. Chapter 8 §4.

36.   Rosenfeld 1988; see the objections of Reich (1990) and Schwartz ([J.] 1990). Nine inscriptions mention Alkios, one refers to Alexas and one to Archelaus. While it is possible that Alexas of Gezer was identical to the Herodian Alexas I (see below n. 58), Archelaus could refer to the ethnarch rather than to Julius Archelaus son of Helcias. Alkios may then be a non-Herodian individual dated to the Hasmonaean period as suggested by the original editor. Palaeography cannot be decisive, but BCE dates seem more appropriate for these texts.

37.   Damati 1982; note that the person concerned is called 'Helcias son of Simon', which, if anything, reminds us of 'Alkios son of Simon Gobar' known from the Lydda ossuary (Chapter 8 n. 63). We may simply be dealing with synonymous yet entirely different people.

38.   *t. Hag.* 2.13; see Gereboff 1979: 65; Oppenheimer 1988: 119; cf. *b. Qid.* 66b; *y. Ter.* 8.45b, 36; *t. Miq.* 1.17.

39.   Josephus, *Ant.* 16.8; for their ages and marriages, see Chapter 8 §2.

40.   Josephus, *Ant.* 15.66-72. In *War* 1.473 we read 'The king's alienation from the lads was shared by people at court, some acting of their own accord, others under orders, such as...the king's ἀδελφοί...' But since at that time c. 15/14 BCE

from Pontus in 14 BCE the first major dissension in the royal household occurred, with Salome warning the king that he was in real danger from his own sons.[41]

On being recalled to Jerusalem by the king in late 14 BCE, Antipater II roused against his brothers the further enmity of both Pheroras and Salome.[42] The latter was also irritated by Glaphyra, Alexander I's wife, who boasted of her noble ancestry (see Chapter 9 §2) and stressed the low birth of Salome. She was also aggravated by Aristobulus I, her own son-in-law, who was upbraiding his wife (Salome's daughter) for her low origin. In return Salome did not allow her daughter to show him any wifely affection and kept reporting everything to the king.[43]

Salome next quarrelled with her brother Pheroras (c. early 13 BCE) as their intrigues apparently had different aims. Although both were hostile to the youths, Pheroras was helping the cause of Antipater who was ultimately plotting against Herod. At some point Salome was implicated by Pheroras in his accusations against Herod to Alexander I.[44] Salome attributed this to the fact that she had lost her brother's favour because she was still trying to persuade him to marry Cyprus II, whom he had rejected from c. 14 BCE (Chapter 6 §3). Herod now began to distrust Salome, and the more so under pressure from his royal wives whose relationships with the king's sister varied extremely.[45] But the real hurt for Herod had been Salome's previous contact with Syllaeus, and Pheroras did not fail to keep reminding the king that she had even secretly signed a contract to marry the Nabataean. Yet finally Herod pardoned Salome, despite the claim of Alexander in the books he wrote against Pheroras and Salome, when he was imprisoned in early 13 BCE, that Salome had forced him into an immoral relationship.[46]

During the second period of dissension in the Herodian court in

(generally thought to be post-11 BCE) only Pheroras was still alive, by 'brothers' Josephus must mean 'siblings', that is to say 'brother and sister' (cf. above n. 1).

41.   Josephus, *Ant.* 15.73-77.
42.   Josephus, *War* 1.475; cf. 483; for the order of events c. 14 to 8 BCE, see Appendix 3.
43.   Josephus, *War* 1.476-79; cf. *Ant.* 16.193, 201-205.
44.   Josephus, *Ant.* 16.206, 213-14.
45.   Josephus, *Ant.* 15.219.
46.   Josephus, *War* 1.487, 498; *Ant.* 16.256.

c. 10/9 BCE, Aristobulus sent Salome a warning that the king would now kill her on the old charge previously brought against her: her affair with Syllaeus. The subject became current again, due to the Nabataean's temporarily successful attempt to destroy Herod's image in Rome. Salome ran to her brother to warn him about Aristobulus's acknowledgement of Syllaeus, and the youth was immediately arrested.[47] Later, in c. 9/8 BCE, Salome and Pheroras participated in the trial of Herod's sons at Berytus,[48] and subsequently they were accused by the soldier Tiro of being responsible for the fate of the youths.[49] After the executions of Alexander and Aristobulus (c. 8 BCE), Antipater II made gifts of great value to Salome to keep her on his side, but she could not be easily fooled.[50]

Aristobulus I left five children who were born to him by Salome's second daughter Berenice I.[51] These were Herodias, Mariamme IV, Agrippa I, Herod (V) of Chalcis and Aristobulus II (see Chapter 10). Berenice was the daughter of Costobarus I,[52] and therefore she was

47.   Josephus, *War* 1.534-35; *Ant.* 16.322-23.

48.   Josephus, *War* 1.538; not stated in *Ant.*

49.   Josephus, *War* 1.545; unnamed in *Ant.* 16.382.

50.   Josephus, *Ant.* 17.7.

51.   Josephus, *War* 1.552; *Ant.* 17.12. It must be noted that the name chosen by Idumaean Costobarus for his daughter was that of the Hellenistic patroness of Marisa, where an inscription of Berenice the mother of Ptolemy IV Philopator has been discovered (Bliss and Macalister 1902: 70); the name is also known from Tomb 4 (Peters and Thiersch 1905: no. 53).

52.   Josephus *Ant.* 18.133. The textual transmission of this passage is problematic. Niese, in his edition of Josephus (Berlin 1887–92), suspected a lacuna (cf. Kokkinos 1986a, 41). The Loeb's erroneous translation has added to the confusion. I here restore a Greek text (inevitably choosing among various readings) and give a new translation:

Κύπρῳ δ'ἐξ 'Αγρίππου μὲν ἄρρενες γίνονται δύο, θυγατέρες δὲ τρεῖς Βερενίκη Μαριάμμη Δρούσιλλα, 'Αγρίππας δὲ καὶ Δροῦσος τοῖς ἄρσεσιν ὀνόματα, ὧν ὁ Δροῦσος πρὶν ἡβῆσαι τελευτᾷ. Ὁ δὲ πατὴρ τούτων 'Αγρίππας ἐτρέφετο μετὰ καὶ ἑτέρων ἀδελφῶν 'Ηρώδου τε καὶ 'Αριστοβούλου· καὶ ἀδελφὴ [αὐτῶν] 'Ηρωδιὰς 'Αριστοβούλου, καὶ οἵδε παῖδες τοῦ υἱέος 'Ηρώδου τοῦ μεγάλου· ἡ δὲ [μήτηρ] Βερενίκη Κοστοβάρου καὶ Σαλώμης παῖς τῆς 'Ηρώδου ἀδελφῆς.

By Agrippa [I] Cyprus [III] had two sons, Agrippa [II] and Drusus, and three daughters, Berenice [II], Mariamme [VI] and Drusilla. Of these children Drusus died before reaching adolescence. Their father Agrippa [I] was raised together with his other brothers, Herod [of Chalcis] and Aristobulus [II], and their sister was Herodias [I] the daughter of Aristobulus [I], and they [all] were children of the son of Herod the Great. [Their mother] Berenice [I] of Costobarus and Salome, was the child of Herod's sister.

born between 33 and 26 BCE. In fact since she married in 16/15, she would not have been born later than 29, and a date in the 30s BCE would correlate with the age of her important friend in Rome, Antonia Minor, who was born in 36 BCE.[53] In the multiple marriages arranged by Herod in c. 8/7 BCE the young widow was given to Theudion (see Chapter 8 §1), but this decision was according to Antipater II's wishes, for he believed that he could thus conciliate his enemy Salome, since Theudion was his maternal uncle.[54] Josephus presents Salome's failure to arrange any of the marriages in her favour as similar to the occasion when she had failed to marry Syllaeus despite the intercession of Livia.[55]

In the events of c. 7/6 BCE Salome reported to Herod the suspicious dealings involved in the pact between Antipater II and Pheroras. She also made known to the king the existence of the group of women of Pheroras's house, which was conspiring against him, and its connection to the Pharisees (Chapter 6 §3). But Antipater had sensed Salome's move in advance, and with the help of friends in Rome he left Judaea in time, carrying with him his father's will in which he was named as the principal heir to the throne.[56] In his trial at Jerusalem in c. 6 BCE, at which Salome was present, it was revealed that Antipater in the past had plotted against her through letters forged by Acme, the Jewish maidservant of Livia.[57] When Herod altered his will, so that Antipater was struck out, Salome was given magnificent gifts, and in a subsequent revision of this will he even assigned to her Jamnia, Azotus and Phasaelis, along with 500,000 pieces of coined silver.[58]

---

53. *CIL* 6.2028c; see Kokkinos 1992a.

54. Josephus, *War* 1.553; *Ant* 17.9.

55. Josephus, *War* 1.566. Apart from Salome's marriage to Alexas, and the simultaneous one of her unnamed daughter to Alexas's son in c. 20 BCE (above n. 29), the marriage of Salome's son Antipater III, soon after 13 BCE (see below n. 71), is also conveniently placed here by Josephus among the wedding arrangements of c. 8/7 BCE.

56. Josephus, *Ant.* 17.36-40, 44; *War* 1.569-71, 573.

57. Josephus, *War* 1.641-46; *Ant.* 17.93, 137-42; cf. above n. 27.

58. Josephus, *War* 1.646; *Ant.* 17.147, 189. At that time (as in the Hellenistic period) the toparchy of Jamnia included the town of Azotus (Chapter 2 n. 36). This is also seen in *Ant.* 18.31 (cf. *War* 2.167) where Azotus is omitted: Ἰάμνειαν καὶ τὴν τοπαρχίαν πᾶσαν... (cf. some MSS in section VII of the ancient table of contents for book 18 of *Ant.*) The regions of Ekron and Gezer (now in decline) were

In a wave of belated violence Salome and Alexas I were summoned by Herod on his deathbed, to be asked to kill all the prisoners whom he had confined in the hippodrome of Jericho, an order they did not carry out since the king was dying. Soon afterwards Salome and Alexas let the prisoners free and read Herod's letter to the royal troops.[59] In the struggle for power which followed the death of Herod in 4 (or 5) BCE, Salome with her entire family (τὴν γενεὰν ἀγομένη τὴν αὐτῆς) accompanied Archelaus to Rome, though she had promised to support Antipas when she got there.[60] The Salome party presented its case to Caesar—her son Antipater III excelled in oratory in his multiple accusations against Archelaus.[61]

Given this fierce opposition, and the fact that Archelaus finally managed to become the ethnarch of Judaea, many of Salome's relatives would have avoided returning to Jerusalem. They would have realized the risk, since Archelaus was brutal and vindictive. Even before he set sail for Rome to claim the throne he slew about 3,000 mostly innocent people in the disturbances during the feast of the Passover following Herod's death.[62] On taking possession of his ethnarchy Archelaus did not forget to repay violently all those who had stood on his way.[63] Berenice I with her children (certainly Agrippa I)

---

probably still part of the same toparchy (Chapter 3 n. 7)—contra Rosenfeld 1988: 244 (part of Lydda) and Schwartz [J.] 1990: 53-57 (part of Emmaus). This would give strength to the identification at least of 'Alexas' (leaving out Alkios) in the Gezer inscription already discussed. The whole toparchy belonged to Salome and she was the wife of Alexas I.

59. Josephus, *War* 1.660, 666; *Ant.* 17.175-79, 193-94; some fieldwork on the Jericho hippodrome (Tell es-Samarat) has been carried out by Netzer (1980).

60. Josephus, *War* 2.15, 20; *Ant.* 17.220, 224. The members of Salome's family must have included her husband (Alexas I), her daughters (the unnamed one and Berenice I), her son-in-law (Alexas II—the other one, Theudion, was probably dead), her son (Antipater III) and daughter-in-law (Cyprus II), her grandsons (Alexas III Helcias, Agrippa I, Herod of Chalcis and Aristobulus II—Costobarus II and Saulus would not have been born yet) and her granddaughters (Herodias, Mariamme IV and Cyprus IV). Some are clearly attested in Rome: Berenice I, Antipater III, Agrippa I, and apparently Herod of Chalcis, Aristobulus II and Herodias; cf. Chapter 6 n. 87.

61. Josephus, *War* 2.24, 26-33; *Ant.* 17.230-40.

62. Josephus, *War* 2.13, 30, 32, 89; *Ant.* 17.218, 237, 239, 313; cf. Paltiel 1981: 126-27.

63. Josephus, *War* 2.111; cf. *Ant* 17.339, 342. One cannot fail to see some correspondence between Archelaus's attitude and that of the nobleman in the parable

stayed on at Rome. Strabo says that Augustus honoured Berenice.[64] Josephus records her death there in the late CE 20s (see Chapter 10 §2). Salome herself may have remained for a while at Rome—she seems to have become well known, given that Galen even mentions a medicine named after her.[65] But she must have departed later, accompanied by Antipater III and his family, and probably headed safely toward the palace at Ascalon which was now hers (Chapter 3 §4).

Apart from all that she had been granted in Herod's will—being made mistress (δεσπότις) of the Jamnian toparchy (which included Azotus) and the city of Phasaelis (in the Jordan Valley), plus 500,000 silver coins—Augustus gave Salome the royal palace at Ascalon, and altogether her revenue amounted to 60 talents. While the territory in which her property (οἶκος) was situated was placed under the jurisdiction of Archelaus,[66] her residence at Ascalon was located beyond the Ethnarch's reach. On Archelaus's banishment in CE 6 Salome may have profited further from Augustus by obtaining as a gift Archelais, a splendid village (like Phasaelis also in the Jordan Valley) built by Archelaus and famous for its high-quality dates.[67]

---

of Jesus (Lk. 19.11-27; cf. Mt. 25.14-30; Mk 13.34), who went far away to claim his kingdom and when he returned, as king, he killed all those who had previously tried to stop him from reigning (Jeremias 1972: 58-63; *SVM* 1, 333 n. 10).

64.   Strabo, 16.246; A papyrus (fragment of the so-called *Acts of the Pagan Martyrs*) contains an accusation made against Claudius that he was a cast-off son of the Jewess Salome I (*P.Cairo* 10448; *CPJ* 2, 80-81, no. 156d, col. 3, l. 11; Smallwood 1967b: no. 436; Jones and Milns 1984: no. 93; Braund 1985: no. 575), but which may mean her daughter Berenice I (Kokkinos 1986a: 41) for the following reason: Claudius was born only a few months after Berenice gave birth to Agrippa I, and Claudius's mother Antonia Minor was Berenice's close friend; the latter may have looked after Claudius as she raised Agrippa (Kokkinos 1992a: 194 n. 84). At least two freedwomen of a 'Berenice' (or 'Beronice'), known to have died in Rome, may have belonged to Berenice I (*CIL* 6.10588, 20394); cf. Chapter 10 n. 217.

65.   Galen, *De Comp. Med. per Gen.* 11.7; *GLAJJ* 2, 324, no. 387.

66.   Josephus, *War* 2.98; *Ant.* 17.321; for an explanation see Chapter 3 n. 93. Since οἶκος could also mean 'estate', 'household' or 'residence', it becomes somewhat ambiguous as to whether the reference is to her toparchy or to her palace at Ascalon, or both. But it is the toparchy, which was now part of Judaea (not Idumaea), that mattered for Archelaus. Ascalon almost certainly was placed under imperial control after the death of Herod (Chapter 3 n. 186).

67.   Josephus, *Ant.* 18.31; cf. Pliny, *Hist. Natur.* 13.44; see Otto 1913: 25; Avi-Yonah 1977a: 104; Paltiel (1981: 134 n. 121) thought that she might have acquired Archelais by purchase as the estate was liquidated by Quirinius in CE 6.

At her death during the governorship of Marcus Ambibulus in c. CE 10, aged around 67, Salome left her entire landed wealth to the Empress Livia.[68] The latter had to administer it through her imperial procurators: in Jamnia she appointed one C. Herennius Capito. After Livia's death in CE 29, Salome's estates were passed on to the Emperor Tiberius and then to Caligula, as we know from Capito's own inscription from Teate Marrucinorum (Chieti).[69]

2. *Antipater III*

In the earliest reference to a son of Salome I by Costobarus I, in *Ant.* 16.227-28, the name of the boy is not given. The episode concerns Salome's attempt to arrange her son's marriage with the second-oldest daughter of Herod, Cyprus II, who had been rejected by Pheroras in c. 14 BCE (Chapter 6 §3). According to Josephus in this passage, Herod fell under the influence of Pheroras, and gave Cyprus instead to Pheroras's son. However, as we have seen, this is a blunder (Chapter 6 n. 59). Josephus elsewhere, in *Ant.* 17.22 and *War* 1.566, clearly states that Herod's daughter (without naming her) was married to Salome's son Antipater III. Further, in *Ant.* 18.130, the Jewish historian confirms beyond any doubt (with all relevant names) that Cyprus II married her cousin Antipater III, the son of Salome.

Cyprus was born in c. 29 BCE, and she would have been fit for marriage from about 17/16 BCE (see Chapter 8 §2). She remained single until c. 14 BCE when Herod unsuccessfully offered her to Pheroras, and apparently she was still available in early 13 BCE when Salome kept trying to persuade her brother to marry the young girl.[70] It is probable that at that stage, and certainly before the arrangements of 8/7 BCE, Cyprus married Antipater.[71] As a son of Costobarus I, Antipater would have been born between 33 and 26 BCE. In c. 14 BCE, when Salome was negotiating his marriage, he was called νεανίσκος, but this is not of great help since the word is variously

68.   Josephus, *War* 2.167 gives a date after CE 6 and before CE 14; *Ant.* 18.31 narrows it down to after CE 9 and before CE 12.
69.   Josephus, *Ant.* 18.158; cf. Philo, *Legat.* 199; Smallwood 1970: 260-61; Crawford 1976: 39; for the inscription see Fraccaro 1940; on Capito see Pflaum 1960–61: 23-26, no. 9.
70.   Josephus, *Ant* 16.215.
71.   Josephus, *War* 1.566; *Ant.* 17.22.

used by Josephus for young men as early as 12 or as late as about 20.[72] Nevertheless, Antipater cannot have been older than 19 (his parents were married in 34/33 BCE) and hardly younger than 18 (male marriageable age). Thus he would have been born around 33/32 BCE, being the first child of Costobarus and older than his sister Berenice I who was born before 29 BCE (in 31 or 30). Antipater would thus have been a few years older than his wife Cyprus.

Among the members of Salome's party present in Rome in 4 BCE, Antipater III was the ablest orator, and strongly accused Archelaus.[73] The man was then in his late twenties. After his mother's probable return to Ascalon, where he may have gone himself, his footsteps disappear from history. Josephus acknowledges a daughter of his, apparently his first child (see later for his possible sons), named after her mother. Cyprus IV, born to Antipater probably a few years before the death of Herod, was married to Alexas III 'Helcias', who, as suggested above, would be the son of Alexas II 'Calleas', son of Alexas I.[74] This Helcias, born perhaps c. 15 BCE, is called 'the great' (ὁ μέγας) by Josephus, implying that a 'younger' one existed (see below). His public career as known to us begins with his participation in an embassy sent to P. Petronius the Roman legate of Syria in CE 40, when he would have been in his mid-fifties, to protest against Caligula's attempt to erect his statue in the temple of Jerusalem.[75] Helcias and some relatives, notably his cousin Aristobulus II (brother of Agrippa I), are described as the 'most powerful members' of the dynasty at that time (see Chapter 10 §4).

From the imposition of direct Roman rule in CE 6 to this embassy in CE 40, and with the exception of Salome's death in her household in CE 10 and a few of the building activities of Antipas and Philip in their own territories, Josephus has nothing to say about the status or even the existence of the Herodian family in Judaea. However, is it possible that a royal court of such magnitude, a ruling centre for over half a century, with its established political, economic and military mechanisms, lost its well-placed manpower in a spectacular overnight

72.   For a 12-year-old νεανίσκος see the case of Aristobulus (III)/Jonathan (Chapter 8 n. 19); for slightly over 20-year-old νεανίσκοι, see the cases of Alexander I and Aristobulus I (e.g. *War* 1.481).

73.   Josephus, *War* 2.26-33; *Ant.* 17.230-40, 242.

74.   Josephus, *Ant.* 18.138.

75.   Josephus, *Ant.* 18.273; on Caligula's attempt see Chapter 10 n. 87.

disintegration? Could the Romans have replaced all the people of experience, for example in local administration, with their own nominees (of which we hear nothing), or could they have filled the vacancies with a batch of unpopular priests, to whom Herod had merely allowed the role of running the Temple? In a perplexed assessment Goodman recently wrote:

> Nonetheless it was to such High Priests [i.e. of doubtful background, promoted by Herod] that Rome handed over power in A.D. 6 (*A.J.* 20.251). It might seem a little strange that the Romans desired these priests as rulers rather than Herod's Idumaean associates, especially since by the fifties A.D. the relatives both of Herod himself and of Herod's close Idumaean [*sic*] friend Alexas... did indeed become prominent in Judaean politics; it might reasonably be expected that when the province was founded such Idumaeans would already gladly have cooperated with Rome and that... the Romans would have trusted them... But Josephus does not attest any role at all for such men... and though it is possible that this silence arises from the historian's comparative ignorance about the period of the first procurators, it is more likely that they remained in political isolation on their estates in the southern part of the province until Agrippa I brought them into prominence in Judaea during his brief but popular reign.[76]

Many objections must be raised here. First of all it is questionable whether *Ant.* 20.251 has been properly understood by Goodman or those before him.[77] Josephus says that after the reigns of Herod and Archelaus, the constitution became an aristocracy (ἀριστοκρατία μὲν ἦν ἡ πολιτεία), whereas (δὲ) the protection (προστασίαν) of the nation (ἔθνους) was entrusted (ἐπεπίστευντο) to the high priests. Does this mean that the high priests were actually the sole aristocracy? Not at all. This passage can be interpreted as meaning that an aristocracy—any variety of which must have included the surviving members of the Herodian family and court (invaluable as they were to Rome)—assisted the Romans in administering the province (as was the case with other provincial upper classes of the empire),[78] while the high priests (in Judaea's special case) were particularly asked to protect the nation's heritage: the Jewish 'theocratic' culture and religion.[79]

76. Goodman 1987: 42-43; cf. McLaren 1991: 223-25; Sanders 1992: 472.
77. Smallwood 1962; *SVM* 1, 377; Rhoads 1976: 27-31; Horsley 1986: 30.
78. Millar 1967: 63; Brunt 1976; cf. Brunt 1977; Brunt 1990: 517-31.
79. Cf. Josephus, *Apion* 2.165-67; reference to the pre-Hasmonaean *status quo*

Second it is by no means strange that Josephus ignores the Herodian family from the time of Archelaus to that of Agrippa I, because the historian knows practically nothing of the period CE 6–26, and comparatively little of CE 26–36. Third no Herodian isolation should be postulated under the prefects, since the Herods would not have re-emerged so suddenly in vital positions some 30 years after they had effectively abandoned their public functions. In fact the prominence of members of the Herodian family in the Judaean society, despite Goodman, is on record well before the time of Agrippa I. Philo expressly states that under Pontius Pilate, apart from other Herodian descendants, Herod's 'four sons enjoyed prestige and rank equal to that of kings'.[80] This is in agreement with the Gospels which refer to a circle of 'Herodians' in the early 30s, probably members or aristocratic followers of the royal family.[81] Luke also implies that Antipas had some influence in Jerusalem,[82] an initial step to the political equilibrium

(*Ant.* 11.111) is irrelevant, and does nothing to support a rule of aristocratic high priests under the Roman prefects (cf. Schwartz [D.R.] 1983–84: 34-36); in any case the period after Nehemiah to the Ptolemies was as dark to Josephus as it is to us now (cf. Chapter 2 n. 10).

80.   Philo, *Legat.* 300. This was the time of the episode of the shields, possibly in the autumn of 33 CE (Kokkinos 1989: 142; cf. Lemonon 1981: 205-30; Fuks [G.] 1982; Davies [P.S.] 1986), shortly before Tiberius's birthday on 16 November (Suetonius, *Tib.* 5; Dio 57.18.2; see Snyder 1940: 235), when only a few of Herod's ten sons were still alive (Smallwood 1970: 302-304): Alexander I and Aristobulus I had been executed in c. 8 BCE, while the unnamed third son of Mariamme I had died young in c. 15 BCE (Chapter 8 §2); Antipater II was killed in 4 (or 5) BCE (Chapter 6 n. 84); Herod III of Mariamme II had been struck out of Herod's will in c. 7 BCE, divorced by Herodias in the early years CE, and probably led a private life, but he could have been alive in CE 33 and may not be excluded as a candidate (Chapter 10 §1); Archelaus had been exiled in CE 6, and if he returned to Judaea before CE 20 (as is possible) and was still alive, he would hardly have been involved in politics (Chapter 8 §5); Philip met his death between late August and early October CE 33, which means that he may or may not be one of the embassy's four (Chapter 8 §6); Antipas was alive and prosperous at that time (Chapter 8 §5); of Herod IV of Cleopatra and Phasael III of Pallas nothing is known (Chapter 8 §§6, 7). Thus the embassy of four consisted *definitely* of Antipas, *probably* of Herod IV and Phasael III, and *possibly* either Philip or Herod III.

81.   On the 'Herodians' see Chapter 3 n. 72 end; Chapter 4 n. 6; cf. Kokkinos 1990: 133 n. 49.

82.   Lk. 23.6-16; cf. *Gos. Pet.* 4–5; Jerome, *Comm. in Mt.* 7.223, with an alleged reference to Josephus on Antipas's authority over the high priesthood. Millar (1990b: 368) doubts Luke's reliability concerning the presence of Antipas in

created later, by which Herod of Chalcis and then Agrippa II were granted the right to appoint high priests and in effect control the Temple and its economic life (see Chapter 10 §§3, 5).

It could be argued that being a priest Josephus had a natural interest in the priesthood, to which he attributed as much power as possible. Having had access to hieratic lists, he would, even though he had no other knowledge about this period, have been able to record at least the names of the high priests. For example, under Gratus (CE 15–26) the only information he adduces is the succession of four high priests in the space of three years.[83] Naturally such a bare narrative gives the false impression that besides the Roman governor the power in Judaea was monopolized by the high priesthood. Although there was indeed an enhancement compared to Herod's time, the 'priestly class' as the sole ruling class in Judaea under Rome is a myth, certainly for the period before Agrippa I. The evidence known to us shows that in political disputes with the Romans the Jewish embassies dealing with the case were 'aristocratic', but headed by Herodians not high priests.

With the advent of Agrippa I's new Herodian monarchy, Helcias, the son-in-law of Antipater III, became a friend (φίλος) of the court and commander (ἔπαρχος) of the royal army (in fact 'commander-in-chief'—Chapter 10 §2). This military position had been given by Agrippa initially to one Silas, who had served the king through many hardships, especially when he had been imprisoned by Tiberius.[84] Yet

---

Jerusalem at the time of the crucifixion of Jesus, on the basis that Acts 4.25-27 seems to expose the source of this story, i.e. Ps. 2.1-2. Yet, as he admits, 'the fact that an episode in the Gospels is explained or justified in terms of a Biblical quotation does not necessarily prove that the episode concerned is invented'. That Antipas was in Jerusalem at Passover of CE 36 (my date) is perfectly conceivable—in fact it would have been exceptional for the Tetrarch not to attend this major Jewish festival in any given year (see Josephus, *Ant.* 18.122 for the following year CE 37; cf. the later Herods). But a crucial detail in Luke's story (23.12) has been overlooked: the ἔχθρα (23.12) between Antipas and Pilate, which expired with Jesus' crucifixion (cf. Soards 1985: 356-57). Antipas had wanted to arrest Jesus for some time (Lk. 13.31; 23.8; cf. Mk 3.6). The reason for this 'enmity' can now be determined from Philo: it refers back to the episode of the shields, in which evidently Antipas led a bitter opposition against the prefect (see above n. 80).

83. Josephus, *Ant.* 18.34-35; cf. Kokkinos 1986b; for the hieratic lists, see *Apion* 1.30-31; cf. *Ant.* 20.224-51; for the archives in general, see Chapter 3 n. 79. That the priestly *prostasia* is Josephus's invention has also been argued by Schwartz ([D.R.] 1983–84).

84. Josephus, *Ant.* 18.204; 19.299; for Silas see Chapter 10 n. 70.

Silas soon lost his honours, for talking too much and embarrassing the king, and was banished to his country of origin. When Agrippa I died in CE 44, and before the news reached the populace, his brother Herod of Chalcis conspired with Helcias and killed Silas.[85]

Helcias left a daughter, Cyprus V, named after her mother and maternal grandmother. Of this girl we know nothing—she is a mere cypher.[86] Helcias evidently also left two sons: Julius Archelaus, whose mother is not specified as being Cyprus IV (although this is implicit), and presumably the younger Helcias II (see below). Julius Archelaus was apparently quite a character, 'well-versed in Greek learning', figuring prominently in society even after the fall of Jerusalem in CE 70, when he was among the most significant people to whom Josephus sold a copy of his *Jewish War*.[87] Stern observed:

> The very name Julius Archelaus attests to his having been a Roman citizen. Whether he was the first member of the house of Alexas to receive Roman citizenship is uncertain. His predecessors may well have been Roman citizens... (and like them) Julius Archelaus was a distinguished figure.[88]

Yet, the fact that he was a Julius (and not a Tiberius or a Claudius) should probably indicate that his Roman citizenship was passed on to him by his ancestors, who would have gained it at the time of Herod the Great.

Julius Archelaus was betrothed to Mariamme VI by her father king Agrippa I, apparently at the end of CE 41, when she would have been about eight. Her brother Agrippa II confirmed this union, and the wedding, if correctly dated by Josephus, took place in CE 53 when she was 19.[89] Archelaus would thus have been older than 20, perhaps

---

85.   Josephus, *Ant.* 19.317-25; 353; Josephus does not explain the reason behind this murder, he only states that Silas was Herod's and Helcias's enemy (ἐχθρὸς)—cf. Kasher 1988: 190; an intriguing possibility has to be discussed elsewhere.

86.   Josephus, *Ant.* 18.138.

87.   Josephus, *Apion* 1.51.

88.   Stern [M.] 1982: 49; elsewhere, however, Stern ([M.] 1976: 613) wrote: 'We do not know to what extent Julius managed to assume an important position in the life of Jerusalem in the Second Temple period.' This was a more cautious statement, but it must not be utilized as negatively as in Schwartz ([J.] 1990: 50 n. 12).

89.   Josephus, *Ant.* 20.140—the Loeb's translation fails again here; cf. *Ant.* 19.355.

nearly 30, at his marriage—he may have been born in the early CE
20s when his father Alexas III Helcias would have been in his mid-
thirties.

Mariamme in about the mid-50s CE gave birth to a daughter,
Berenice III, and after some time she decided to divorce Archelaus.
This drastic step she took concurrently with the premature divorce by
her sister (Berenice II) of King Polemo of Cilicia, with whom Berenice stayed from c. CE 63 to 65 (see Chapter 10 §5). Mariamme may
then also have divorced Archelaus in c. 65, moving to Alexandria to
become the wife of a Hellenized Jew called Demetrius.[90] This date
agrees also with the fact that Magassarus, one of Mariamme's royal
henchmen, who would have been relieved of his duties when she left
Jerusalem, distanced himself from the Herodian court and in the ensuing Jewish War joined the rebels.[91]

According to Josephus, Demetrius the Alabarch was first in birth
and wealth (πρωτεύοντι γένει τε καὶ πλούτῳ) among the Jews of
Alexandria. His position was once held by the famous brother of
Philo, Alexander, whose social status is described by the Jewish historian in identical terms (γένει τε καὶ πλούτῳ πρωτεύσαντος).[92] It
seems possible that Demetrius was related to this family. Alexander
was the alabarch at least until CE 36, and it is unlikely that he would
have regained his position after he was released from prison in Rome
by Claudius in 41.[93] Meanwhile his son Marcus Julius Alexander may
have succeeded him in office, but he died in 44 after he had been
married to Berenice II for about three years.[94] Alexander's other son
Tiberius Julius Alexander followed a distinguished Roman military
career, being appointed procurator of Judaea from c. 46/47 to 48/49.[95]

90.   Josephus, *Ant.* 20.147.
91.   Josephus, *War* 5.474.
92.   Josephus, *Ant.* 20.100; for Demetrius see *SVM* 3.1, 136-37; on the office
of 'alabarch', see Burr 1955: 16, 87-88 n. 4; *CPJ* 1, 49 n. 4; for Alexander's family
cf. Foster 1976–77; *SVM* 3.2, 815 n. 14; the identification of Alexander with one
mentioned in *P. Ryl.* 126, 166 is incorrect (see Chapter 9 §1); note that Alexander
decorated the Temple gates (*War* 5.205), possibly by employing the artist Nicanor
(*CII* 1256).
93.   Josephus *Ant.* 18.159-60; 19.276; cf. 18.259.
94.   Josephus, *Ant.* 19.277; for Marcus see *CPJ* 2, 197-200, no. 419; and discussion in Chapter 10 n. 134.
95.   Josephus, *Ant.* 20.100-104; *War* 2.220-23; see *PIR*² A.139; *CPJ* 2, 188-
97, no. 418; cf. Kokkinos 1990: 130; for Tiberius see Turner 1954; Burr 1955;

In 65 Tiberius was made prefect of Egypt, and Agrippa II visited Alexandria to congratulate him.[96] Perhaps this was precisely the occasion when Agrippa's sister Mariamme VI was united with Demetrius, now the city's alabarch, as a renewed alliance between these two important families—if indeed Demetrius was a relative of Tiberius.

By Demetrius Mariamme had a son called Agrippinus. Josephus promises to tell the reader more about this young man's whereabouts, but either never kept his promise or an unknown work of his has not survived.[97] Mariamme's daughter by Julius Archelaus, Berenice III, would have been taken by her mother to Alexandria to live there with her stepfather Demetrius. She may tentatively be identified with a Berenice who married another Alexander, one of the wealthiest Jews of Cyrene. Following Josephus, after the fall of Masada, apparently in CE 73, many *sicarii* who had escaped to Alexandria and Cyrene continued their fight there against Rome.[98] On a false accusation of illegal co-operation with them, Catullus, the governor of the Libyan Pentapolis, implicated many of the well-to-do Jews of the area, whom he hated for other reasons, and proceeded to execute them in great numbers. His first victims were Alexander and his wife Berenice, possibly the last survivor of this line of Salome's genealogy.[99]

Barzanò 1988; for a possible third son of Alexander, called 'Lucius Julius Ph...', see Sullivan 1978b: 301.

96.   Josephus, *War* 2.309, 335; for the date see Appendix 9, pt. g.

97.   Josephus, *Ant.* 20.147; Petersen 1958: 273-74; cf. *Ant.* 20.48, 53, 96, 144.

98.   The date of the fall of Masada has yet to be decided (Eck 1970: 93-111; *SVM* 1, 512, 515; Cotton 1989), but the weight of evidence would seem to favour 73. If Josephus is right in saying that the riots at Alexandria and Cyrene took place subsequently (μετὰ ταῦτα—*War* 7.409), then the governor 'Catullus' cannot be identified with L. Valerius Catullus Messalinus who was consul in 73 (contra Schwartz [S.] 1986: 383; cf. Cotton 1989: 160). At any rate, the consul was alive up to 93 (Tacitus, *Agr.* 45), whereas 'Catullus' died not long after (*War* 7.451-53), and certainly before the completion of the *Jewish War* in c. 76–78 (Stern [M.] 1987: 78 n. 9; for *War* 7 as a later addition, see Chapter 9 n. 25). Also a point of relative chronology must be noted: Jonathan the rebel of Cyrene was sent (or taken) by 'Catullus' to the Emperor (*War* 7.449; *Life* 424) about the same time (καθ' ὅν δὴ καιρὸν) as Josephus divorced his third wife (*Life* 426), her last son being born between July 72 and June 73 (*Life* 5). The fall of Masada and the subsequent riots at Alexandria and Cyrene would hardly have taken place after 73 (cf. Bowersock 1975: 183-84; Bowersock 1991: 344; Roxan 1991: 458).

99.   Josephus, *War* 7.445; a Berenice, landowner in Egypt in the first half of the second century CE (*P. Hamb.* 8), may have been a descendant of the Berenice in

Apart from Archelaus, Helcias 'the Great' seems to have had another son, Helcias II, apparently 'the Younger'.[100] At the time of Porcius Festus, procurator of Judaea (c. CE 58–60), the Jews erected a high wall to block the view from the Herodian palace and from the western portico where the Romans used to post their guards for supervising the Temple.[101] Festus and King Agrippa II immediately ordered the demolition of this wall, but the Jews appealed to the emperor and they were allowed to sent an embassy to Rome. Ten foremost personalities were thus assembled, headed by the high priest Ishmael and the 'Herodian' treasurer (γαζοφύλαξ) Helcias II, both presumably openly or secretely supporting Agrippa's view.[102] In Rome Nero consented to leave the wall as it stood, persuaded by Poppaea Sabina who was a religious woman (θεοσεβής).[103] Subsequently Poppaea, not yet officially the wife of Nero, let the delegation return to Jerusalem, but for reasons that can only be assumed from the above, she detained Ishmael and Helcias as hostages. Since Agrippa II, when he heard the news, removed the high priesthood from Ishmael, one may guess that Helcias was also replaced as keeper of the

question, or else of Berenice II (Chapter 10 n. 217); cf. Chapter 9 n. 45.

100. Josephus, *Ant.* 20.194-95; cf. Stern [M.] 1982: 60 n. 56; Goodman 1987: 143.

101. Josephus, *Ant.* 20.189-92; for the dates of Festus see Appendix 8.

102. Josephus, *Ant.* 20.193-94. Due to the long and repressive rule of Felix, it seems that under Festus (c. 58–60) and Albinus (60–63/64) the time was ripe for social appeals and delegations to Rome. A few months before the embassy in question (of Helcias II), Paul the Apostle was sent to the Emperor (see Appendix 8). At the same time the conflicting Jewish and Syrian embassies from Caesarea were allowed journeys (*Ant.* 20.182-84). Under Albinus, late in 63 (see Appendix 9, pt. e), Josephus himself went to Rome to free a batch of priests who had been sent there by Felix (*Life* 13-16). This event is also indicative of chronology, since it suggests a short time span for Festus's tenure.

103. Josephus, *Ant.* 20.195, where Poppaea is called 'wife' of Nero loosely (and anachronistically), probably because the historian met her as such three years later (*Life* 13-16). According to Tacitus (*Ann.* 14.60) Poppaea married Nero in 62, and technically speaking Josephus should not have called her 'wife' (τῇ γυναικὶ) in c. 60, the date accepted here. At any rate Poppaea had been Nero's mistress since 58 (Tacitus, *Ann.* 13.45, 46, 47), and she was from the beginning influential at court, 'dominating him first as an adulterer [and] then as a husband' (*Ann.* 14.60). During her premarital period with Nero she helped to sharpen the discord between him and his mother and sister, which led to their executions (see Momigliano 1934c: 715-16; cf. Griffin 1984: 75, 98-99).

treasury.[104] Indeed when we next hear of this position in the period before and leading up to the Jewish Revolt, the man in charge is another Herodian, Antipas III (Chapter 6 §1). Later on the rebels took charge of the treasury—we know of two chief keepers: first Eleazar son of Simon, and then, at the destruction of the Temple, Phineas.[105]

Although the details of the fate of Helcias and Ishmael are lost to us, after the death of Poppaea, around the autumn of CE 65, they were evidently set free. Since a return to Jerusalem would have been out of the question, not only because their mission had failed, but also due to the outbreak of the Jewish Revolt, they seem to have gone to Cyrene. At least Ishmael does appear there later, where he was beheaded, no doubt in the executions ordered by Catullus (already discussed).[106] Helcias, who may have found asylum with his relative Berenice III (above), may also have been killed in Cyrene.

Finally, coming back to Antipater III the son of Salome I, it is possible that in the first decade CE he became the father of two sons, who were younger brothers of Cyprus IV, and uncles of Cyprus V, Julius Archelaus and Helcias II. They were called Costobarus II, presumably named after his Idumaean grandfather, and Saulus, a prominent Jewish name.[107] The only reference to them in *Antiquities* concerns their actions contemporary with the clashes of c. CE 62 (on my reckoning) between the followers of two high priests, Jesus son of Damnaeus and Jesus son of Gamaliel:

> Costobarus and Saulus also on their own part collected gangs of villains.
> They themselves were of royal lineage and found favour because of their

104. Josephus, *Ant* 20.196; the γαζοφύλακες are described by *SVM* (2, 281-82) as priests in charge of the Temple money, among other things. Although this was true for most periods in Jewish history, Helcias II, like Antipas III later (Chapter 6 §1), could not have been priests. Obviously under the Herods the office (next in importance to the high priest) was kept in Herodian hands. Josephus (*Ant.* 20.15) clearly states that Herod of Chalcis was granted authority not only over the Temple and the selection of high priests, but also of the ἱερὰ χρήματα.

105. Josephus, *War* 2.564, 6.390.

106. For Poppaea's death, see Tacitus, *Ann.* 16.6; Dio, 62.28.1; for Ishmael's execution, see Josephus, *War* 6.114.

107. At a popular level and by ingenious speculation, Ambelain (1972) portrayed Paul (Saulus) the Apostle, as a Herodian prince, whose identity he based on the figure of Saulus son of Antipater III; now also accepted by Eisenman (1983: 62-63; Eisenman 1986: 10 n. 22)! But despite the usual historical coincidences, evidence is lacking, while dates and motives do not match (see instead Chapter 3 n. 75).

kinship with Agrippa, but were lawless and quick to plunder the property
of those weaker than themselves.[108]

It should be noted that the attitude of Costobarus II and his brother
reminds us of Costobarus I, who acquired his wealth, as we saw,
'through continual and shameless profit-seeking'. No evidence other
than the onomastic (and tentatively that of character) can be adduced
to support their placement at this precise point of Salome's lineage.

The close associates of Costobarus and Saulus were other minor
members of the Herodian dynasty (βασιλικὸν γένος): Antipas III,
possibly also a descendant of Antipater III (but see alternatives in
Chapter 6 n. 29) whom we have already examined, and 'Levias' and
'Syphas son of Aregetas', persons otherwise totally unknown.[109] In
Josephus these are the most obscure members of the royal family.
Without any hint available it is impossible to insert them at any level
of the Herodian genealogical tree, not even approximately, though one
could conjecture that they were either husbands of Herodian females,
or close relatives of women who had married Herodian males.

Costobarus and Saulus were among the deputation sent by the
leadership of Jerusalem to Agrippa II in Panias to ask for help, at the
outbreak of the revolt in CE 65 (see Appendix 9). The king sent them
back together with his *stratēgos*, Philip son of Jacimus son of Zamaris
the Babylonian, and 2,000 horsemen.[110] Their objective was to free
the temple from the hands of the revolutionaries, before any serious
intercession from Rome. But the royalists were outnumbered and
retreated to the Herodian palace, where they locked themselves in.
Soon the rebels came after them, besieged the palace and forced them
to a conditional surrender, late in the month of August.[111]

Concerning what happened next to the royal party Josephus's account
leaves much to be desired, and his information in *War* contradicts that
in *Life*. It can be gathered, however, that since the permission to evacuate the palace specified only 'the king's troops and natives of the
country', the Herodian notables and the Romans who had joined them

108. Josephus, *Ant.* 20.214; that they were brothers is clear from *War* 2.556:
ἀδελφοί; cf. Goodman 1985: 197.

109. Josephus, *War* 4.141.

110. Josephus, *War* 2.418, 421; for the best account on Philip son of Jacimus
and the contradictory statements in Josephus, see Cohen [S.J.D.] 1979: 160-69; cf.
also Price 1991, but with reservations.

111. Josephus, *War* 2.423, 426, 429, 431, 437, 440.

were left behind. Then one would have thought that these people would eventually have been killed, and indeed elswhere we are told that Antipas III was arrested and murdered while in custody (Chapter 6 §1 end). But Josephus later, after the shocking defeat of C. Cestius Gallus at the end of November, explicitly mentions Costobarus II, Saulus and Philip son of Jacimus as being among distinguished individuals who had 'abandoned the city as swimmers desert a sinking ship' and joined the retreating Cestius beyond Antipatris—when heading toward Caesarea and Ptolemais from where he had begun his march.[112] How did they manage to do this?

War provides no explanation. *Life* which at least pays more attention to Philip's career, in an entirely different story says of him:

> ...after miraculously escaping with his life from the royal palace at Jerusalem...(he) was exposed to the further peril of being slain by Menahem and his brigands. The latter were, however, prevented from accomplishing their purpose by some Babylonian kinsmen of Philip who were then in Jerusalem. Here he remained for four days and on the fifth escaped, disguised by a wig, and reaching...the confines of the fortress of Gamala, sent orders to some of those under his command to join him...[113]

So Philip here escapes in disguise alone, not with Costobarus II and Saulus; he runs toward Gamala, not toward Ptolemais where Cestius had fled; and he does this a few days after leaving the royal palace— early in September, not early in December.

The confusion goes even further: *War* says that when Costobarus II, Saulus and Philip reached Cestius, the Roman governor of Syria dispatched them to Nero in Achaea, 'at their request' (ἀξιώσαντας), to inform him of the past catastrophe, and put all the blame on Florus the procurator of Judaea.[114] The Herodians would have reached Nero not earlier than the late spring of CE 66 (on my reckoning), and it was presumably their information that urged the Emperor to send Vespasian to quell the revolt.[115] *Life* presents Philip as being sent to Rome at the request of Vespasian, after the latter's arrival at Tyre in

112. Josephus, *War* 2.554-56.

113. Josephus, *Life* 46-47.

114. Josephus, *War* 2.558; cf. Rajak 1983: 166 n. 37. Goodman's (1987: 159-61) attempt to conflate the two accounts ('with some ingenuity' as he says) leaves many questions unanswered.

115. Josephus, *War* 3.1: 'The news of the reverses sustained in Judaea filled Nero...with...alarm'.

the early spring of CE 67 (see Chapter 10 n. 209), to give an account
of his actions to Nero. According to Josephus, Philip never had the
chance of an audience because he found the Emperor 'in extremities
owing to the prevailing disorders and the civil war...'[116]

There are major problems between the two accounts. We cannot be
sure whether Philip and his companions were sent to Nero (individually or as a group) by Cestius or by Vespasian, whether they went
to Achaea or to Rome, whether they reached their destination after the
late spring of 66 or by the early summer of 67, and whether the
reason for their journey was to inform the Emperor (by their own
volition?) or to be tried by him. These accounts also suffer from
internal chronological inconsistencies. For example in *Life* Philip goes
to Rome to see Nero in 67, but Nero returned to Rome presumably
only by the beginning of the following year.[117] A CE 68 date would
accord with the disturbances in Nero's administration mentioned by
Josephus,[118] and one therefore is tempted to see at least Philip being
sent to Rome by Vespasian at that time, for a trial that never was.[119]

In the last analysis we do not know whether these intriguing Herodians, Costobarus II and Saulus, who were almost certainly descendants of Salome I, ever made the trip to Greece or Italy, or whether
they returned to witness the bloodbath in Jerusalem at the time of the
destruction of the Temple in CE 70. But for all the obscure and contradictory statements, even at this late stage, it remains clear that
members of the Herodian dynasty—and not just Agrippa II—played
an important role and were in a crucial position between the revolutionaries and Rome.

116. *Life* 408-409.
117. Suetonius, *Nero* 50; see Bradley 1978a: 71; cf. Gallivan 1973; and
Appendix 9, pt. 3. However, Halfmann (1986: 173-77) argues that Nero returned to
Rome in the autumn of 67.
118. These disturbances led to Nero's death apparently on 9 June (Sumner 1967:
416; Bradley 1978b: 292).
119. Priority must be given to the account in *Life* (cf. now Rappaport 1994; see
also Appendix 10 end). Yet an earlier Achaean connection is also reflected in Vespasian's dispatching of 6,000 youths, captured in the battle of Tarichaeae (Sept. 67),
to work on Nero's project at the isthmus (*War* 3.540; cf. Jones [B.W.] 1984a: 38-
39); for the attempt to cut a canal through the isthmus, see Suetonius, *Nero* 19; Dio,
62.16; cf. Warmington 1969: 133-34.

Family Tree: *The Sister of Herod and her Descendants*
(c. 57 BCE–CE 100)

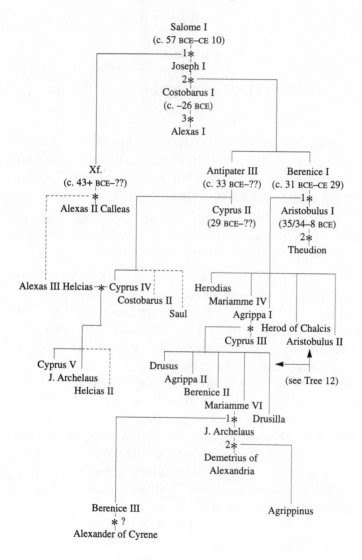

Chapter 8

THE WIVES OF HEROD AND THEIR OFFSPRING

In the introduction to the second part we have briefly discussed the Hellenized court of Herod the Great at Jerusalem, with its harem of ten wives, many concubines and boy lovers. Josephus explains how Herod came to create such a sizeable *gynaikōnitis*:

> ... (Herod's wives) had been chosen for their beauty and not for their family... (they) were numerous, since polygamy was permitted by Jewish custom and the king gladly availed himself of the privilege.[1]

Some of his marriages Herod contracted in batches: for example, he seems to have taken three wives soon after the murder of Mariamme I in 29/28 BCE, and another three on what appears to have been the occasion of the wedding of his sons by Mariamme I late in 16 BCE. That there was a gap in time between these two batches is also implied by Josephus's reference to the 'more recent wives' of Herod.[2]

Josephus provides us with two genealogical lists (one in *War* and one in *Antiquities*) concerning Herod's wives. The order of their names in *War* is simply according to their offspring: first the wives who bore sons (beginning with the elder), then those who bore daughters and finally those who remained childless. But the order in *Antiquities* is evidently arranged according to the sequence of weddings, and therefore this is the list to which we must give priority for any establishment of historical chronology.

The order in *War* 1.562-63 followed by that in *Ant.* 17.19-22 will now be tabulated for convenience (names in round brackets are implied, as is in square brackets the position of Mariamme I):

1. *War* 1.477; for the word cf. *Ant.* 17.3.
2. *War* 1.480.

War

Antipater II	~	DORIS
[Alexander I, Aristobulus I, (X-son), (Salampsio) and (Cyprus II)]	~	[MARIAMME I]
Herod III	~	MARIAMME II
Antipas II, Archelaus and Olympias	~	MALTHACE
Herod IV and Philip	~	CLEOPATRA
Phasael III	~	PALLAS
Roxane	~	PHAEDRA
Salome II	~	ELPIS
No child	~	X-COUSIN
No child	~	X-NIECE

Antiquities

(DORIS)	~	Antipater II
[(MARIAMME I)]	~	[Alexander I, Aristobulus I, (X-son), (Salampsio) and (Cyprus II)]
(MARIAMME II)	~	Herod III
X-NIECE	~	No child
X-COUSIN	~	No child
(MALTHACE)	~	Antipas II, Archelaus and Olympias
CLEOPATRA	~	Herod IV and Philip
PALLAS	~	Phasael III
PHAEDRA	~	Roxane
ELPIS	~	Salome II

X = unknown

As the discussion proceeds and individual people are examined, it will become increasingly clear that even the preferred list in *Antiquities* cannot be taken as absolutely accurate. For example, the marriages of Herod to his X-niece and X-cousin may have been the result of circumstances before the death of Mariamme I. Also a minor slip in the order could have occurred with marriages that took place during short periods of time. For example Mariamme II, Malthace and Cleopatra all became Herod's wives within a year or two. It seems certain that Mariamme II preceded the other two, on the basis of the link with the Jewish nation that Herod would have needed to re-establish after it had been broken by the murder of Mariamme I in 29/28 BCE, and of the greater age of her son Herod III. However, the order of Malthace and Cleopatra could have been either way. At any rate, the resulting chronology of the marriages, together with the ages of the children, can be better illustrated in the following tables (and charts and tree at the end of the chapter):

Wives

(1) Doris (married c. 47 BCE, sent away in 37 BCE, recalled in c. 14 BCE and sent away again in c. 7/6 BCE)
(2) Mariamme I (married from 37 BCE to 29/28 BCE—executed in 29/28 BCE)
(3) X-niece (daughter of Joseph II?—marriage c. 37 BCE)
(4) X-cousin (daughter of Joseph I?—marriage c. 34/33 BCE)
(5) Mariamme II (married in 29/28 BCE and divorced in c. 7/6 BCE)
(6) Malthace (married from 28 BCE to 4 [or 5] BCE—died in 4 [or 5] BCE)
(7) Cleopatra (marriage 28/27 BCE)
(8) Pallas (marriage c. late 16 BCE)
(9) Phaedra (marriage c. late 16 BCE)
(10) Elpis (marriage c. late 16 BCE)

Sons and Daughters

(1)	Antipater II	(born c. 46 BCE—died 4 [or 5] BCE)
(2)	Alexander I	(born 36 BCE—died c. 8 BCE)
(3)	Aristobulus I	(born 35/34 BCE—died c. 8 BCE)
(4)	Salampsio	(born c. 33 BCE—died?)
(5)	X-son of Mariamme I	(born c. 31 BCE—died c. 15 BCE?)
(6)	Cyprus II	(born 29 BCE—died?)
(7)	Herod III	(born c. 28 BCE—died post-CE 33?)
(8)	Herod IV	(born c. 27 BCE—died post-CE 33?)
(9)	Archelaus	(born c. 27 BCE—died post-CE 20?)
(10)	Philip	(born c. 26 BCE—died CE 33)
(11)	Antipas	(born c. 25 BCE—died post-CE 39)
(12)	Olympias	(born c. 22 BCE—died?)
(13)	Phasael III	(born c. 15 BCE—died post-CE 33?)
(14)	Roxane	(born c. 15 BCE—died?)
(15)	Salome II	(born c. 15 BCE—died?)

1. *Doris*

Herod's first (or what almost certainly must have been his first) wife Doris was apparently an Idumaean by origin and of Hellenized stock, as her name also suggests.[3] The marriage was contracted while Herod

---

3.   The Loeb translation in *War* 1.241 ('His first wife was a Jewess of some standing...') is too free. A literal reading is '...he had previously a wife who was not undistinguished among the natives (ἐπιχωρίων)'. The Loeb in *War* 1.432 ('...a

was still a commoner (ἰδιώτης), evidently before 40 BCE and possibly in 47 when he was appointed *stratēgos* of Galilee (Chapter 3 n. 57). Herod would have been about 26 (in c. 46) when Doris made him the father of Antipater II.[4] Doris may have belonged to one of the élite families which moved to Jerusalem from Idumaea to attach themselves to the Herodian court established there by Antipater I (Chapter 3 §2).

On ascending the Judaean throne (38/37 BCE) Herod dismissed Doris and soon after banished her son Antipater II from Jerusalem, allowing him to visit it only during the major festivals. Antipater, evidently with his mother, was recalled to the capital in late 14 BCE in order to become, even if temporarily, the sole heir to the kingdom.[5]

native of Jerusalem...') is also free. It should read '... her family (γένος) being from Jerusalem'. Otto (1913: 23 n.) suspected the last statement of Josephus, but it may only have meant that Doris's family was living in Jerusalem, although its origin was Idumaean. For example, Matthias son of Theophilus is called a 'Jerusalemite' (*Ant.* 17.78), but he was from Galilee. Also Simon son of Boethus is called 'Jerusalemite', but he was from Alexandria (*Ant.* 15.320). Thus Stern ([M.] 1982: 44) clearly stated that: 'this appellation proves only that (the person concerned) functioned in Jerusalem' (see now Cohen [S.J.D.] 1994). In any case, Josephus (*Apion* 2.38) testifies that one always took the name of the city one joined whatever one's nationality (cf. Philo, *Conf. Ling.* 78). In regard to Doris this is supported by the Loeb's own translation in *Ant.* 14.300 ('He had previously married a plebeian woman of his own nation...'), even if it actually reads 'He had previously a wife, who was a citizen (δημότις) from the nation (ἐκ τοῦ ἔθνους)', which could refer either to the Jewish or to Herod's Idumaean nation (but cf. Chapter 4 n. 1). The name Doris is Greek (Hesiod, *Theog.* 241; see *WGEN*, 328-29; *LGPN*, 144; cf. Ilan 1989: 194, no. 38) and it has been found as 'Dorothea' (in company with two Egyptian names) in Marisa (Wünsch 1902: 170, no. 29).

4.   Josephus, *War* 1.562; cf. *Ant.* 17.19. Antipater II was the eldest son of Herod (*Ant.* 14.300), born well before 40 BCE (*Ant.* 16.78), already 'grey-headed' in c. 13 BCE (*War* 1.587; cf. *Ant.* 16.233), and could have passed as 'an old man' by c. 7 BCE (*Ant.* 17.66). If born in c. 46 BCE he would have been 42 (contra Hanson 1989: 83) when he was executed in 4 (or 5) BCE. Such an age is compatible with that of his cousin Phasael II (son of Phasael I the elder brother of Herod) who was born in 47/46 BCE (Chapter 6 §1).

5.   Josephus, *War* 1.433, 448; Antipater was sent to Augustus to confirm his appointment (see Appendix 2, pt. 4), and his journey seems to have taken him through Greece, visiting Sparta on the way and introducing himself to the local monarch Eurycles (Kokkinos forthcoming 1). When the latter subsequently fled to Judaea, it is said that he stayed with Antipater whom he knew well, and who helped to conspire against his brothers (*War* 1.517; *Ant.* 16.302; see Bowersock 1961; Lindsay [H.] 1992).

After the death of Pheroras in c. 7 BCE Doris again fell out of Herod's favour, suspected of a plot to poison the king:

> ...he stripped her of all the finery which he had bestowed on her and for the second time dismissed her from court.[6]

Her brother Theudion, who had married Berenice I around 8/7 BCE after the execution of her husband Aristobulus I,[7] was also accused of the same plot. Theudion was either banished together with Doris in c. 7/6 BCE, or killed by Herod, possibly by 4 (or 5) BCE when Antipater was executed.[8] Alternatively he may have been one of the deserters of the Herodian family who caused trouble in Idumaea and were executed later by Augustus (Chapter 5 §2). At any rate after the death of Herod, Theudion's wife Berenice followed her mother Salome to Rome, apparently without a husband.[9]

As soon as Doris's son Antipater was recalled to Jerusalem and named heir to the throne, he seems to have contracted his symbolic marriage. His bride was the surviving unnamed daughter of Antigonus (see family tree, Chapter 3 n. 98), the last Hasmonaean king who was killed in 37 BCE after the conquest of Jerusalem by Herod.[10] This woman must then have been around 25, while Antipater was in his early thirties. The couple bore at least two children (a son and a daughter), all of whom remain unnamed.[11] In the dynastic ceremony of c. 8/7 BCE, a son of Antipater was promised to marry Mariamme IV, the daughter of Aristobulus I, both at the most aged seven, and a

6.   Josephus, *War* 1.590; cf. *Ant.* 17.68.
7.   Josephus, *War* 1.553; *Ant.* 17.9; Theudion is a another Greek name similar to Theudas (*WGEN*, 502; *LGPN*, 220) which might be an abbreviation of Theodorus—note that this is the reverse of Dorothea (for Doris his sister). Josephus (*Ant.* 20.14) mentions an envoy called Theudion together with a Dorotheus, while an ossuary from Jerusalem records a Theudion, father of a Salampsio (*CII* 1265).
8.   Josephus, *War* 1.592; *Ant.* 17.70, 73.
9.   Josephus, *War* 2.15; cf. *Ant.* 17.220; 18.145; Strabo, 16.246; see Chapter 7 n. 60.
10.   Josephus, *Ant.* 17.92; cf. *War* 1.619. It seems that this Hasmonaean princess had two brothers (see *Ant.* 14.489 where Antigonus's παῖδες are mentioned), who may have survived in Ituraea under the protection of their aunt Alexandra III (*War* 1.185-86; *Ant.* 14.126). The latter may have had children of her own by the deceased Ptolemy King of Chalcis (cf. Chapter 3 nn. 96 and 98).
11.   A second son of Antipater may be implied in *War* 1.588 (but cf. *Ant.* 17.67) where his τέκνα are mentioned—i.e. 'sons', since he had hopes for them to succeed him.

daughter of Antipater was promised to Aristobulus's elder son (most probably Agrippa I), both at the most aged four. This idea, however, was soon eclipsed. At least in the case of Mariamme IV, it was decided that she would be given instead to Antipater himself, while his son had to marry Pheroras's unnamed daughter (until then promised to Alexander II—Chapter 6 §3).[12]

It is worth noting that Antipater, then about 40, would have had to commit bigamy, since his Hasmonaean wife was still alive. This is one of the rare cases which provide evidence that other members of the family, apart from Herod, could have possessed more than one wife—evidently they were capable of contracting endogamous unions with females over 30 years their junior. Yet, Antipater's second wedding never actually took place. He was obliged to leave Judaea in c. 7 BCE, after multiple intrigues against his younger brothers and his father, to stay away for almost a year, and then return only to be tried, imprisoned and later executed—all before Mariamme IV had reached marriageable age.[13] But about Antipater enough has already been said under Pheroras and Salome I.

2. *Mariamme I*

Mariamme I, the ill-fated Hasmonaean wife of Herod, was the granddaughter of Hyrcanus (II) from the side of her mother Alexandra, and that of Aristobulus (II) from her father Alexander (see family tree, Chapter 3 n. 98).[14] It is possible that the idea of marriage was contrived by Herod's father Antipater at Ascalon when Mariamme was still an infant—she was born in c. 53 BCE. From its inception the motives of this arrangement would clearly have been political. Josephus later comments:

> Herod married... Mariamme, hoping to capture the goodwill of the people
> for himself, thanks to their recollection of Hyrcanus.[15]

12.   Josephus, *War* 1.557, 565, 567; *Ant.* 17.14, 26, 18.
13.   In his effort to demonstrate the errors and omissions in Schalit's genealogical tree (1969, endpaper), Hanson (1989: 78) himself erred in thinking that Antipater actually married Mariamme—but at best he was only betrothed to her.
14.   On Mariamme I see Macurdy 1937: 66-69; Deltombe 1963; Sievers 1989: 142-44. Her name, probably due to its Hasmonaean connection, was most commonly adopted in the Second Temple period. Approximately 50 per cent of all Hebrew women were named either Mariamme or Salome (Chapter 7 n. 1).
15.   *Ant.* 20.248; contra Schalit 1969: 61-66.

Something resembling a legal tie with the Hasmonaean line was thus achieved by Herod, a vital factor at the outset of his reign.[16] The betrothal took place in 42 BCE when Mariamme was about 12, and the marriage in 37 BCE (in the midst of battle) when she would have been 17.[17]

Already upon betrothal Herod must have taken the girl, together with her mother, brother and sister, to stay at the Jerusalem court, because when the Parthians attacked the city in 41/40 BCE they were among those whom Herod led to Masada for safety.[18] Mariamme's brother Aristobulus (III), also named Jonathan, was first made high priest by Herod, and then drowned in Jericho in 35 BCE by the orders of the king.[19] Mariamme's unnamed sister was given in marriage to Pheroras the brother of Herod (Chapter 6 §3).

Mariamme I brought trouble into the Herodian house, which was triggered by the murder of her brother in 35 BCE, as well as that of her grandfather Hyrcanus II in 30 BCE.[20] This led to various family

16.   Cf. Hoehner 1972: 9. Schalit (1969 n. 15) argued that the king would not have had any interest to form a legal tie with the Hasmonaeans for he presented himself as a descendant of David. But if Herod ever developed an interest in the Davidic family, this must have been later, i.e. when his kingship was mature and a messianic expectation was aired (Chapter 3 n. 72; cf. Chapter 6 end)—perhaps when Nicolaus forged a genealogy for him, and David's tomb was violated. At the beginning of Herod's reign a Hasmonaean tie was essential. If his wedding to Mariamme had no political view why would he make it an interlude of the siege of Jerusalem in 38/37 BCE (see next note)?

17.   Josephus, *War* 1.241; *Ant.* 14.300; and Josephus, *War* 1.344; *Ant.* 14.467.

18.   Josephus, *War* 1.264; *Ant.* 14.352-58; cf. *Ant.* 14.351 correcting *War* 1.262.

19.   Josephus, *War* 1.437; *Ant.* 14.388. Aristobulus died in late 35 BCE, since Herod was asked by M. Antonius to go to Laodicea in 34 BCE to clear himself of the charge—*Ant.* 15.64. The young man was 18 (*Ant.* 15.56; cf. 15.51; 15.29), and therefore he was born in 52 BCE. This is in agreement with the birth of his sister Mariamme in c. 53 BCE, as well as with the marriage of their parents in c. 55 BCE (Chapter 3 n. 98). In *Ant.* 14.388 he is called νεανίσκος in 40 BCE—the word is here applied by Josephus to one who was 12 (cf. *War* 1. 23).

20.   Josephus, *War* 1.433, 437; *Ant.* 15.173-78; Josephus in *Ant.* 15.178 is mistaken in saying that Hyrcanus II was 81 when he died, which would have placed his birth in c. 110 BCE. His mother Alexandra (*War* 1.107-109; cf. *Ant.* 15.179) married his father Alexander-Jannaeus only in 103 BCE, given that she appears to have been the same person as Salome-Alexandra, previously the wife of Aristobulus

clashes, plots and further executions, including her own death in 29/28 BCE, her mother's in 28/27 BCE and eventually that of her sons in c. 8 BCE.[21] Herod was passionately devoted to Mariamme and very jealous of her beauty, but her hatred of him was as great as was his love for her.[22] Josephus describes Herod's frame of mind after her murder:

> So consuming, indeed, was the flame of his passion that he believed she was not dead, and his affliction would address her as though she were alive; until time taught him the reality of his loss...[23]

Herod had five children by Mariamme, three sons and two daughters.[24] Josephus makes it clear that Mariamme's sons were born after Herod's accession to the throne,[25] evidently after 37 BCE when the couple's full marriage also took place. Alexander I, the eldest of the three,[26] would have been born in c. 36 BCE and Aristobulus I in c. 35

(I), Jannaeus's brother (see family tree in Chapter 3 n. 98)—but cf. now Ilan 1993.

21.   In *War* 1.441-44 Josephus has Mariamme being killed together with Joseph I in 34 BCE (after Herod's meeting with Antonius in Laodicea), but this is anachronistic and a literary amalgamation of two similar but different events for reasons of brevity, characteristic in the early part of the *War*. From *Ant.* 15.87 it is clear that Herod pardoned Mariamme in 34 BCE, although he did execute Joseph. Mariamme was put to death together with Soaemus the Ituraean, in 29/28 BCE (a year after Herod's meeting with Augustus in Rhodes), as can be seen from *Ant.* 15.229-31 (note 15.221). This date makes sense since Mariamme gave birth to five children after 37 BCE, which she could not have done by 34 BCE. It also corresponds with the fact that she died after her grandfather Hyrcanus II, who was killed at the beginning of 30 BCE. Alexandra's execution was ordered within a year after Mariamme's at the latest, i.e. in 28/27 BCE (*Ant.* 15.251; cf. Sievers 1989: 143). Mariamme's death in *b. B. Bat.* 3b is by suicide (throwing herself from the roof), whereupon Herod preserved her body in honey for seven years. The only similar story in Josephus is the suicide attempt made by Pheroras's 'slave'-wife in c. 7/6 BCE (Chapter 6 n. 86).

22.   Josephus, *War* 1.436; for the use of 'antithetic feelings' in Greek erotic literature through the ages, see Kakrides 1954: 172-73; Mariamme was famed for her beauty (*Ant.* 15.23, 25, 67, 237), and as we saw, her portrait was painted for M. Antonius (Chapter 3 n. 197).

23.   *War* 1.444.

24.   Josephus, *War* 1.435; *Ant.* 14.300; cf. *War* 1.563, 566; *Ant.* 17.22; 18.130.

25.   *War* 1.435.

26.   Josephus, *Ant.* 16.401; also because he was named first in order as successor after Antipater II (*Ant.* 16.133); the brothers were of some age in 28 BCE to be proclaimed by Alexandra as the future rulers (*Ant.* 15.249); cf. generally Feldman 1953: 80 n. 35; Smallwood 1976: 89 n. 104.

BCE, particularly if he had been named after Aristobulus (III) the brother of Mariamme who was killed in that year. This is in accordance with the fact that the boys were sent to Rome for education (and in a way semi-hostageship) when they reached approximately 12; their journey took place in 24 BCE.[27] The youngest son, whose name Josephus does not convey, seems to have been slightly separated in age from his brothers, and therefore Salampsio the eldest daughter of Herod[28] would have preceded him in birth—let us say in c. 33 BCE (for her descendants see Chapter 6 §1). If the boy was born around 31 BCE, and given that he died in the course of his training in Rome,[29] presumably between 13 and 18 years of age, he would have died after 19 and before 14 BCE. The second daughter,[30] Cyprus II, was evidently named after Herod's mother Cyprus I. She may then have been born in 29 BCE, perhaps soon after her grandmother died[31] and shortly before her mother was executed (for Cyprus II also see Chapter 7 §2).

Mariamme's sons were also ill-fated, although at the beginning of their career one would hardly have guessed at their destiny. Herod

27.   In negotiating peace treaties the Romans frequently demanded as 'hostages' the second eldest sons of client monarchs (Moscovich 1983: 299; Braund 1984a: 9-21), which Herod's sons were. But in 30 BCE, when Augustus confirmed Herod on his throne, they were too young for the task. Herod's sons were sent to Rome not later than 24 BCE (see Appendix 2, pt. 2). The identification of 'Pollio' in whose house they resided is debated (Feldman 1953; Braund 1983: 240-42; Feldman 1985). But whether Asinius, Vedius, or any other Pollio, he must have had a good connection with the senate or the palace (cf. the case of the house built for Antiochus IV Epiphanes—Asconius, *In Pison.* 13.16-17; Marshall 1985: 105-106).

28.   Josephus, *War* 1.483; cf. *War* 1.563, 566; *Ant.* 16.194; 18. 130; her name is attested in Marisa (Abel 1925: no. 2 = *SEG* 8.248; cf. Oren and Rappaport 1984: no. 18), in the archive of Babatha (*P. Yadin* 18-20), and in Jericho (Hachlili 1979: nos. 11a-c, 7a-b); it was thought to be an expansion of 'Salome' (Ilan 1989: 191; cf. Mussies 1994: 255), but the appearance now of both names together in the Aceldama ossuaries of two sisters has made this unlikely (Avni *et al.* 1994: 215-16; cf. Avni and Greenhut 1994: 43).

29.   Josephus, *War* 1.435.

30.   Josephus, *Ant.* 16.196; cf. *Ant.* 18.130; *War* 1.563, 566.

31.   Cyprus I is mentioned for the last time in 29 BCE (Josephus, *Ant.* 15.220; cf. 15.80, 184; *War* 1.438). She was certainly dead when Herod gave her name to a fortress above Jericho, the completion of which is related by Josephus among events variously dating from c. 15 to 12 BCE (*Ant.* 16.143; cf. *War* 1.407, 417, 484; cf. Appendix 3).

went to Rome himself to fetch them at the end of their stay there in mid-17 BCE,[32] and upon their return to Palestine via Greece, where they were now introduced to Greek public life and attended the Olympic Games of 16 BCE, they were given important wives for themselves and considerable wealth—it looked as if they were being prepared as candidates for the throne.[33] Yet within three years Alexander I and Aristobulus I were dragged back to Rome, in the journey of 13/12 BCE (Chapter 6 n. 66), to be accused in front of the Emperor of plotting against their father. The reconciliation that followed was short-lived and a second phase of dissension in the Herodian palace led to the ultimate trial at Berytus in c. 8 BCE, where the youths were condemned to death. Their transfer to Samaria/Sebaste, to be strangled there, and to the fortress of Alexandreion to be buried, was decided by Herod, evidently because it was at Sebaste that he married their mother Mariamme I and at Alexandreion that their Hasmonaean grandfather Alexander's dead body had been placed.[34]

Many of the activities of Mariamme I's sons, leading to their execution, have been briefly discussed here under Pheroras and Salome I. Alexander's wife was the notorious Glaphyra, the daughter of Archelaus king of Cappadocia. She bore two sons. Glaphyra remarried twice after the execution of Alexander, first to Juba II king of Mauretania and then to Archelaus the Ethnarch (Chapter 8 §5). Aristobulus's wife was Berenice I, the daughter of Salome I and Costobarus I. She bore two daughters and three sons.[35] (The remarkable line of descendants of Mariamme I's sons will be examined later in two separate chapters covering well over 100 years of history.)

32.   Josephus *Ant.* 16.6 (cf. *War* 1.445); for the date see Appendix 2, pt. 2 end.

33.   For their marriages see Josephus, *Ant.* 16.6-11; cf. *War* 1.445-46; for preparation to rule, see *Ant.* 16.97-98; cf. 133. The young men must have married as soon as they returned to Judaea (i.e. by the end of 16 BCE), being then 21 and 20 respectively. *War* 1.446 reads καὶ ἐπειδὴ γάμων ἔχοντες ὥραν, which I translate as 'and *because* they were of age for marriage', not as in the Loeb 'and *when*, on reaching an age to marry'. *Ant.* 16.11 reads καὶ γυναῖκας ἐν ἡλικία γεγονόσιν εζεύγνυεν, which may also be understood as if they had reached the proper age to take for themselves wives. Corbishley (1935: 28) dated the marriages around 15 BCE; a later date is out of the question given the age pattern of Herod's grandsons (Kokkinos 1986a: 38).

34.   Josephus, *War* 1.538-51; *Ant.* 16.356-94; cf. 14.467.

35.   Josephus, *War* 1.552; *Ant.* 18.139; cf. *War* 1.509; *Ant.* 17.12.

3. *The X-Niece and X-Cousin*

One of Herod's wives is said to have been his 'niece' (ἀδελφιδῆν), or actually as Josephus makes clear, his 'brother's child [i.e. daughter]' (ἀδελφοῦ παῖς).[36] Since we know that Herod had three brothers (Phasael I, Joseph II and Pheroras) it may be possible to determine whose daughter Herod actually took as his wife and perhaps under what circumstances. According to the order of the list in *Antiquities* the wedding took place after Herod married Mariamme II and before Malthace, which would be in c. 28 BCE, as will be revealed later. This is a useful chronological *terminus* for the discussion below, even though a slightly earlier placement (that is after Mariamme I and before Mariamme II) would seem to make better sense.

The elder brother of Herod, Phasael I, died very early in 40 BCE, and was apparently survived only by a son, who was seven at the time (Chapter 6 §1). An unrecorded daughter of Phasael might have existed, but if she was mature at her father's death, why would Herod have waited for at least a dozen years before marrying her (to follow Josephus's *terminus*)? Had she been too young, would Herod have raised her for the same length of time, before making her his wife? Perhaps this is not an impossible scenario, but none the less not very opportune for such an endogamous wedding.

The youngest brother of Herod, Pheroras, is said to have had a daughter, but she seems to have been the child of his second wife (the 'slave') and thus born after 20 BCE and most probably around 13 (Chapter 6 §3); therefore too young for the king. Further, if Pheroras's first wife (the Hasmonaean), by whom he had three sons, had an unrecorded daughter, she would have been born after 37 BCE, and would also have been too young.

36.   *War* 1.563; *Ant.* 17.19; Jeremias (1969: 366 n. 42) is wrong to think that Herod married a daughter 'of his sister Salome'; Hanson's opinion (1989: 83) that Herod's endogamous wives were married to him before Doris (i.e. before c. 47) cannot be right. For example, Herod's X-niece-wife would have had to be born at least before 60 BCE, at a time when his *eldest* brother would appear to have been only less than 17 (Chapter 6 §1). But apart from age limitations, it was really the conquest of Jerusalem in 38/37 that set Herod upon building a harem: he was now a king, and obliged to rehabilitate (endogamously) the orphans of his family which had been created by the war. Before the fall of Jerusalem Herod would have been too busy with political affairs, and quite satisfied being married to Doris and engaged to Mariamme (see above n. 17).

Joseph II is conceivably the likely candidate. We know that he left a son (Chapter 6 §2). But his daughter who may have married Herod is unrecorded as such! Joseph II lost his head to Antigonus in 38 BCE, and if he had a daughter she could have been made a queen by Herod as a tribute to the memory of his brother as soon as Jerusalem was conquered in 37 BCE. This would make Joseph II's daughter the royal wife before Mariamme II. The X-niece wife bore no children to Herod, and this is the reason why she disappeared from history.

Another of Herod's wives is said to have been his 'cousin' (ἀνεψιάν), that is daughter of his uncle (or aunt). We know that Antipater I, Herod's father, had two brothers: Phallion I and Joseph I. The first died very early, in c. 65 BCE (Chapter 5 §1), and this alone would distance any offspring of his from a marriage to Herod some 40 years later. Hence Joseph I has to be the likely candidate. By his second wife, Salome I, he did have a daughter, but the girl, who was born at the earliest c. 43 BCE, was given to Alexas II son of Alexas I in c. 20 (Chapter 5 §2 and Chapter 7 §1). By his first wife Joseph I had a son, Achiabus, as we have assumed.

Under the circumstances it would seem probable that by his first wife Joseph I also had a daughter (thus sister of Achiabus) who remained unrecorded. Joseph I was executed by Herod in 34 BCE, at which time the king may have thought it appropriate to marry his deceased uncle's daughter, who would have been of age and an orphan. We should be reminded of the endogamous marriages which Herod arranged for the orphans of his sons by Mariamme, immediately after their execution (see Chapter 9 and Chapter 10). Thus Herod's X-cousin wife should be another wife before Mariamme II. She, like his X-niece wife, bore him no children and also disappeared from history.

4. *Mariamme II*

Mariamme II was the daughter of Simon, a priest in Jerusalem, the son of an Alexandrian named Boethus. Once again Herod was initially attracted by the young lady's physical appearance, but he had to increase her father's prestige (by appointing him high priest) before he could marry her.[37] However it is possible that Mariamme's family

---

37. Josephus, *Ant.* 15.320, 322; Simon son of Boethus became a kind of *novus homo* in the Roman parlance.

was connected to the old Zadokite family of the Oniads—Josephus himself[38] draws a parallel between the two—and thus Herod would seem very cleverly to have attempted to re-establish an authority which preceded that of the Hasmonaeans, in his effort to gain popularity among the Jews. Hengel suggests the following:

> Boethus could have been a descendant of Onias IV of Leontopolis who fled to Egypt in 164 BCE: that would explain the later status of his family in Jerusalem. The successful Simon, son of Boethus, who married a daughter, Mariamme, to Herod, succeeded in founding the richest high priestly family after the clan of Annas and at the same time a particular group among the Sadducees, the Boethusians, who were evidently close to the Herodian rulers.[39]

All of Mariamme's brothers became high priests, although their identification and exact relationship have been a matter of intense dispute. My reconstruction of the Boethus family[40] is shown in the following genealogical tree:

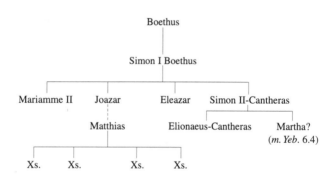

38.   *Ant.* 19.298.

39.   Hengel 1989: 14.

40.   Largely agreeing with Stern [M.] 1982; the name Simon Boethus (given as שמעון בוטון) is found on an ossuary from Jerusalem (*CII* 1246); the family of Cantheras (Kantheras-Kithairus) is in all probability mentioned in *b. Pes.* 57a as Kathros (Neusner 1970: 62-63; cf. *t. Min.* 13.21); a 'son of QTRS' (בר קתרס) was recently found inscribed on a stone weight from Jerusalem (Avigad 1983: 129-31; cf. Jaros 1982: 105, no. 95), and it is possible that it refers to the high priest Elionaeus son of Simon II-Cantheras; a 'daughter of Qatra' (בת קתרא) is mentioned on an ostracon from Masada (Yadin and Naveh 1989: 22, no. 405); an Ἰούλιος Κάνθουρος is known from an inscription on the Hermon (Moutèrde 1951–52: 24); cf. Julius Pant[h]era from Sidon (*CIL* 13.7514).

D. Schwartz's reconstruction, which may be schematically sum-
marized below, I must reject.[41]

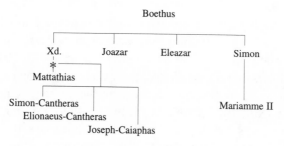

The idea (taken from Smallwood)[42] that Joazar was the brother of the
wife of Mattathias cannot stand. The plain meaning of *Ant.* 17.164 is
that Joazar was the brother of the wife of Herod (Mariamme II), and
it follows from *Ant.* 17.339 that Eleazar was her second brother.[43]
That Mariamme had 'brothers' is clearly revealed in *War* 1.599, a
passage unknown to Schwartz and Smallwood, as well as to Stern. In
fact this passage can explain why Herod, even though he divorced his
wife and struck her son out of his will, later entrusted the high priesthood to a brother (Joazar) of hers: Mariamme's brothers had flatly
denounced her.

Schwartz's argument,[44] is based on a peculiar interpretation of an
ambiguous statement in *Ant.* 19.297 (translation and elucidations in
square brackets are mine):

> Agrippa removed Theophilus son of Ananus from the High Priesthood
> and bestowed his high office on Simon [II] son of [Simon I] Boethus,
> surnamed Cantheras. Simon [II] had two brothers and [it was] his father
> [Simon I] Boethus whose daughter was married to king Herod, as I
> explained earlier. Simon [II] accordingly, as did his brothers [Joazar and
> Eleazar] and father [Simon I Boethus], obtained the High Priesthood...

It is clear from Josephus's reference to his previous account of the
marriage of the high priest's daughter to Herod, that by 'Boethus' he

41.   Schwartz [D.R.] 1990: 185-89.
42.   Smallwood 1962: 33-34; Mattathias had no connection with the Boethus
family (contra Smallwood and Schwartz); if anything his relationship lay with the
family of Ananus—see Appendix 7.
43.   Stern [M.] 1982: 61 nn. 83, 88; cf. Goodman 1987: 43-44, 139-40.
44.   Refuting Feldman (in the Loeb *Josephus*, IX, 355-57 n.d) and Stern ([M.]
1982): 49-55.

actually means 'Simon Boethus'. Nowhere does the historian say that the wife of Herod was the daughter of Boethus, but explicitly of Simon son of Boethus.[45]

'Boethus' here is intended simply as the name of the family, the relevant member of which (Simon I) had already been clearly mentioned in the appropriate place (when Mariamme's marriage to Herod was related). It follows that Simon II-Cantheras was not the son of Boethus but of Simon I son of Boethus. Indeed, as the passage states, Cantheras's father (Simon I) as well as his brothers (Joazar and Eleazar) became high priests, while his sister (Mariamme) was the wife of Herod. Joazar in *Ant.* 17.339 and 18.3 is likewise called simply 'the son of Boethus', instead of 'son of Simon Boethus', another such general use of the family's name. Finally, a later high priest Matthias, who in *War* 5.527 is said to be 'the son of Boethus', should be seen as 'son of Joazar, son of Simon Boethus' (although of course he could instead have been the son of Eleazar, or even another son of Simon II-Cantheras). This Matthias was slaughtered together with three of his sons by Simon bar Gioras. *War* 6.114 refers to a fourth son of Matthias who managed to escape Jerusalem.

According to Schwartz, one of Simon-Cantheras's brothers was Elionaeus-Cantheras, presumably a son of Mattathias. But Josephus states that the high priest Elionaeus was 'the *son* of [Simon II] Cantheras'—apparently himself called Cantheras—while in turn Simon II-Cantheras was the son of [Simon I] Boethus.[46] Further, there is no evidence that Mattathias was ever known as Cantheras. As to Elionaeus the son of Haqqayyaph (Caiaphas), referred to in the Mishna,[47] again he is mentioned neither as the son of Mattathias or that the latter was also known as Haqqayyaph. In fact the Mishna's Elionaeus may be placed chronologically before the Herodian period and he could have been a different person from Josephus's Elionaeus.[48] Schwartz's theory that the high priest Joseph-Caiaphas was the second brother of

---

45. Josephus, *Ant.* 15.320; 17.78; 18.109, 136; cf. *War* 1.557, 562, 573, 599; *Ant.* 17.14, 19, 53.

46. Josephus, *Ant.* 19.342; 20.16; 19.297.

47. *m. Parah.* 3.5.

48. Cf. *SVM* 2, 229 n. 5; the order, although not necessarily chronological, is nevertheless Elihoenai ben ha-Qayyaph (Hellenistic?), Hanamel the Egyptian (who seems to be a corruption for Ananel the Babylonian, 37–36 BCE; cf. Chapter 3 n. 66), and Ishmael ben Phiabi (c. CE 15–16, or c. CE 58–59).

Simon-Cantheras is even more extreme, and the philological argument suggesting that the names Cantheras and Caiaphas are equivalent is hypothetical to say the least. And even if this onomastic equation were to be accepted, one could have been able to argue only that Elionaeus was the son of Joseph-Caiaphas *not* his brother.[49] At all events, it is possible that Elionaeus Haqqayyaph was a predecessor of Joseph-Caiaphas but this is as far the evidence can go.

The most appropriate time for Herod to marry Mariamme II (as well as Cleopatra and Malthace—see later) would have been immediately after the death of Mariamme I, that is 29/28 BCE, when his tie with the Hasmonaean dynasty was suddenly broken and when no Jewish wife (and in fact no wife at all) was to be accounted for in his harem. The marriage may have been the result of the psychological depression he went through, during the time of which according to Josephus: 'He would...devise all kinds of distraction possible, and arrange banquets and parties for himself, and yet none of these would help'.[50]

However an uncritical reading of *Ant.* 15.317-19 would seem to place the event around 23 BCE,[51] which is too late a date on many considerations. For example this would presuppose that Herod remained without a wife from 29/28 to 23 BCE (see charts 1–2), an eventful period in which the king was very active particularly with a number of building projects. It would also mean that his son by Mariamme II would have been designated heir to the throne in c. 7 BCE when he was only a minor (about 15),[52] whereas he would have been around 20 in the earlier dating. The same problem will be encountered later with the ages of Herod's sons by Cleopatra and Malthace. It therefore seems probable that Josephus connected the marriage of Mariamme II with the completion of the palace at Jerusalem in 23 BCE,[53] whereas it had actually occurred when the work began in

49.   E.g. see Goodman 1987: 144. The discovery of a group of ossuaries in the North Talpiyot belonging to a family of קפא or קיפא (Reich 1992; 1994), almost certainly have nothing to do with Joseph Caiaphas (Horbury 1994), and in any case they throw no light on the present question.

50.   Josephus, *Ant.* 15.241.

51.   Otto 1913: 71 n. 131; *SVM* 1, 320: 'about 24 B.C.'; Smallwood 1976: 91 n. 109: 'c. 23'; cf. Stern [M.] 1974b: 263.

52.   Josephus, *War* 1.573, 588, 600; *Ant.* 17.53, 78; cf. Chapter 10 §1.

53.   Josephus, *Ant.* 15.318-20; the key point is the naming of one of the rooms after Marcus Agrippa, who received *imperium proconsulare* (later *imperium maius*)

c. 29/28. This conclusion is supported by an earlier statement of Josephus in which he says that the palace began to be built before the work at the city of Sebaste, named after Augustus (Σεβαστὸς) in 27 BCE, had commenced.[54] Josephus's point in *Ant.* 15.319 might simply have been a 'flashback' (familiar in his narrative) giving the false impression that the marriage of Mariamme took place as late as 23 BCE.

The question of age-limits in my reconstruction of the Boethus family may now be clarified. Mariamme must have been at least 13 when she married Herod in 29/28 BCE, and born at the latest by c. 41/40 BCE. Her father Simon I Boethus could himself have been born as late as c. 61/60, if for example he had her as a first child when he was as young as 20. The question then is whether it is possible for him to have had a son, Simon II Cantheras, who became high priest 100 years later in CE 41 (see Chapter 10 §2). The answer to that is that it is not impossible: if Cantheras was 50 on his appointment, his father would have had him when he was 50. Childbearing in advanced age is demonstrable in the Herodian age patterns (see Chapter 4). But it can also be illustrated from within the high priestly circle. Ananus became high priest in CE 6, and if he was then even 45 he would have been born in c. 39 BCE.[55] Now since his youngest son Ananus became high priest in c. CE 60 (see Chapter 10 §5), this would have happened some 100 years later. These rough calculations must not be taken as real proposals; they only serve to show the feasibility of the argument presented here.

Mariamme II's only son Herod III would have been born in c. 28

over the eastern part of the empire in that year (Reinhold 1933: 167-75; Roddaz 1984: 339-51; cf. Thomasson 1984: 205, no. 3); for Herod's close (and diplomatic) friendship with Agrippa, see *War* 1.400; *Ant.* 15.361; Herod also gave the name of Agrippa to the city of Anthedon (*War* 1.87, 118, 416; *Ant.* 13.357), to a reception hall at Jericho (*War* 1.407), to a gate in the Temple area (*War* 1.416), and to one of his grandsons (Chapter 10 §2).

54.   *Ant.* 15.292—instead of the more usual βασίλειον, Josephus here mentions the palace as αὐλή (also see *War* 2.431; 5.176; Mk 15.6; cf. Acts 23.35). The period 28–21 BCE needs further investigation: events include the institution of pagan games in Jerusalem, the beginning of work at Sebaste and Caesarea-on-the-coast (cf. Appendix 2, pt. 3), the drought and the Sabbatical Year (Vardaman 1975: 45; Flusser 1987), the expedition of Aelius Gallus (cf. Chapter 7 n. 22), and Herod's journey to Greece (Kokkinos forthcoming 1).

55.   Josephus, *Ant.* 18.26; Ananus was alive at least until CE 37 (Acts 4.6—my date), when in the present hypothesis he would have been around 75.

BCE, and thus he must have been the next in line to the throne after Antipater II. Indeed Herod the Great's will of c. 7 BCE included him instead of any other of the king's sons, who were evidently younger at the time.[56] The stubborn insistence of many theologians on referring to Herod III as 'Herod-Philip' is without any value.[57] No such person ever existed—he is an illusion created to account for an *apparent* contradiction between the Synoptic Gospels and Josephus. The reference to 'Philip' in Mark, Matthew and Luke is inevitably to Philip the Tetrarch.[58]

For the life of Herod III we can only say that he was alive probably at the beginning of the first century CE, when Herodias divorced him after she had borne him a daughter, Salome III (see Chapter 10 §1). It is possible that he survived among the Herodian notables—in fact being one of 'four' major figures—who dominated Judaean life through the time of the Roman *praefecti*, from CE 6 to the arrival of King Agrippa I in CE 41. This may be gathered from Philo's testimony, as has already been discussed (Chapter 7 n. 80). In the 30s CE Herod III would have been in his late fifties.

5. *Malthace*

Josephus calls Malthace a 'Samaritan', and the impression is that she would have been a Samaritan Jewess, like for example the woman who conversed with Jesus in Sychar according to John's Gospel.[59] However this is merely an impression. Josephus is frequently imprecise about ethnic origins, and unless qualification is provided, terms such as 'Idumaean' or 'Jerusalemite' (compare above n. 3) mean nothing more than the geographical area in which a person concerned was born, lived or simply functioned. Malthace's *genos* is not specified by the

56.   See above n. 52; the fact that in a later will (Josephus, *War* 1.646; *Ant.* 17.146) Herod skipped two older sons (Archelaus and Philip) in favour of a younger one (Antipas), does not mean anything other than that on this occasion there were special circumstances (rightly Hoehner 1972: 11 n. 4; contra Otto 1913: 131-32, 200). No reason at all why one should suspect that in the case of Mariamme II's son, older brothers had been passed over.

57.   Hoehner 1972: 133-36; Hanson 1989: 79; but cf. Taylor [V.] 1966: 312.

58.   Mk 6.17; Mt. 14.3; partly Lk. 3.19; cf. 3.1; see Kokkinos 1986a; cf. Stap 1859.

59.   Josephus, *War* 1.562: τῆς Σαμαρείτιδος; *Ant.* 17.20: τοῦ Σαμαρέων ἔθνους; Jn 4.7.

historian, and in Samaria, as in Idumaea, a variety of *ethnē* were to be found. Strabo refers to the majority of the Samaritan population as being Jews, Arabs and Phoenicians.[60] If one is to begin from the distant past, Malthace could theoretically have been of native Israelite origins, since such remnants must have existed despite their alleged *total* exile in the eighth century BCE, or she could have been of foreign 'Chuthaean' stock, implanted into Samaria by the Assyrians, and by her day thoroughly Israelized.[61] But it is more likely that she belonged to an important family of colonists, such as the Macedonians at Samaria, or better, those who were believed to have descended from the Phoenicians at Shechem.[62] In fact her name may suggest a Hellenized Phoenician background, which would be perfectly compatible with Herod's own origins.[63]

Herod had strong connections with Samaria. In 47/46 BCE Sextus Caesar had appointed him *stratēgos* of Coele Syria and Samaria.[64] In

60. Strabo, 16.2.34; for the reason the geographer refers to the Jews as 'Egyptians' and to the Idumaeans as 'Nabataeans', see Chapter 1 n. 34; also note Luke's description of a 'Samaritan' as ἀλλογενής (17.18), a term often used to describe the racial status of Herod himself (Chapter 3 n. 81).

61. 2 Kgs 17.24; Josephus, *Ant.* 9.288-91; 12.257; Mor 1989: 2 n. 5; if Assyrian cuneiform evidence is clear about the transfer to Samaria by Sargon II of 'foreigner populations' and particularly 'Arabs' (*ANET* 284-86; see Oded 1979: 29), little of 2 Kings is a late elaboration (cf. Dexinger 1981: 90; Coggins 1987: 259); the fact that there were people in c. 100 BCE still calling themselves 'Israelites' is shown by inscriptional evidence from Delos (Bruneau 1982: 465ff.; cf. White 1987).

62. See Chapter 2 n. 49; cf. Montgomery 1907: 156, 319; contra Coggins 1987: 266; Schwartz [S.] 1993: 20 n. 4; also the rabbinical accusation of a dove cult at Shechem (*b. Hul.* 6a), which may hint at a Phoenician background (cf. Chapter 3 n. 115); further note that at about the time of his marriage to Malthace, Herod settled at Samaria some 6,000 pagan colonists (Josephus, *War* 1.403; *Ant.* 15.296).

63. Malthace is a Greek name (Athenaeus, 13.587-88; see *WGEN*, 848; *LGPN*, 296; cf. Ilan 1989: 195, nos. 72-73) and it has been found in Lydda on the Samaritan border (*CII* 1173; cf. Clermont-Ganneau 1896: 341-49), though this example is probably masculine (Μαλθάκης). Further the name has been restored in one of the limestone inscriptions from Marisa: [Μαλ]θάκ[η] (Wünsch 1902: 161, no. 9).

64. Josephus, *War* 1.213; cf. *Ant.* 14.180 where Samaria is omitted; see Gilboa 1979–80. In *War* 1.225 it is said that Cassius in 43 BCE upgraded Herod to ἐπιμελητής of the whole of Syria and even promised to make him King of Judaea. Yet, in *Ant.* 14.280 the position given to Herod in 43 BCE is only that of στρατηγὸς of Coele Syria, which however he already had from c. 47/46 (*SVM* 1, 277). Although Otto (1913: 22) doubted the *epimelētēs* appointment, on the basis of

43 BCE Herod restored order and repaired damage in the city, which had been the result of sedition, and in 39/38 BCE he installed his entire family and other members of the Herodian court there for safety.[65] In 37 BCE Herod married Mariamme I in Samaria, and in 30 BCE the city was granted to him by the victorious Octavian.[66] After the death of Mariamme in 29/28 BCE Herod suffered from his illness at Samaria, and it was probably during his recovery (c. 28 BCE) that he met and married Malthace.[67] This would have been seen as a tribute to the city where his wedding with Mariamme, his loved one, had taken place. It was also then that he began the large-scale rebuilding of the city, which was renamed 'Sebaste' after Augustus in 27/26 BCE.[68]

Malthace gave birth to three children: two sons and one daughter.[69] Archelaus, who later became ethnarch of Judaea, Idumaea and Samaria (his mother's land of origin), was the eldest son,[70] apparently born in 27 BCE. Antipas, who was appointed tetrarch over Galilee and Peraea, was younger than Archelaus[71] and seems to have been born around 25 BCE, especially if it was his sixtieth birthday that was celebrated in CE 35, when he ordered the decapitation of John the Baptist.[72] Olympias was probably the youngest child, and she may have been born in 22/21 BCE, during the visit of Herod the Great to the Peloponnese accompanying Augustus, and thus the girl may have

Appian (*Bell. Civ.* 4.63) who refers to the nephew of Cassius as the recipient of this position, it is almost certain that Herod's power was enhanced by Cassius.

65. Josephus, *War* 1.229 = *Ant.* 14.284; *War* 1.303 = *Ant.* 14.413.

66. Josephus, *War* 1.344; *Ant.* 14.467; *War* 1.396 = *Ant.* 15.217.

67. Josephus, *Ant.* 15.246.

68. Josephus, *War* 1.403; *Ant.* 15.293, 296-98; for the date see Appendix 2, pt. 2.

69. Josephus, *War* 1.562; *Ant.* 17.20.

70. Josephus, *War* 1.646: τῶν πρεσβυτάτων Ἀρχελάου καὶ Φιλίππου; *War* 1.664: τὸν πρεσβύτατον υἱόν; for the older dating of Archelaus's birth see Otto 1913: 165; Rees 1951: 348.

71. Josephus, *Ant.* 17.146: τῷ νεωτάτῳ; if it was not for this reference (and those above n. 70) we would have had to assume that Antipas was older than Archelaus, since both family lists of Josephus (*War* 1.562; *Ant.* 17.20) mention Antipas first; this is a salutary warning for placing too much faith in the order of Josephus's lists (my own rule throughout has been to follow *Ant.*, in lack of other evidence).

72. Mk 6.21 τοῖς γενεσίοις αὐτοῦ δεῖπνον ἐποίησεν; cf. Mt. 14.6; see Josephus, *Ant.* 18.119; contra Hoehner 1972: 12, who dates Antipas's birth 'not...earlier than 20 B.C.'

carried the name of the city of Olympia where she would have been born.[73] Olympias's marriageable age seems to have been reached by c. 8/7 BCE, at the time when Herod was arranging many endogamous unions—she was certainly either still engaged or married before her father's death in 4 (or 5) BCE; the King left only two virgin daughters and Olympias was not one of them (for her marriage and descendants see Chapter 6 §2).

When Archelaus went to Rome in the early summer of 4 (or 5) BCE to claim the throne of Judaea he took his mother Malthace with him for support; presumably she knew Livia well—they would have met in the journeys of Herod to Greece and Rome and of Augustus to Greece and Syria.[74] But Malthace was soon persuaded to side with her younger son Antipas.[75] The Samaritan lady never returned to Palestine—she died in the Roman capital before the legal proceedings had ended.[76]

On his return to Judaea as ethnarch, Archelaus was quick to settle old scores, crushing all remaining trouble[77] (after Varus's suppression of the revolt in the aftermath of Herod's death), and to exercise his power of appointing high priests and minting his own coins.[78] Once

---

73. Cf. Josephus, *Ant.* 15.350; however, it is also possible that Olympias was born later, when Herod attended the Olympic Games of 16 BCE (see Chapter 3 n. 144). Alternatively the Greek name Olympias (*WGEN*, 1051-52; *LGPN*, 348; cf. Ilan 1989: 197, no. 149) may simply have been chosen in commemoration of the mother of Alexander the Great. Note that the names of the father (Philip), mother (Olympias), sister (Cleopatra) and wife (Roxane) of Alexander the Great (see Milns 1968: 18-19), were all to be found among Herod's immediate family.

74. Josephus, *War* 2.14; *Ant.* 17.219; cf. Chapter 7 n. 22.

75. Josephus, *War* 2.21; *Ant.* 17.225.

76. Josephus, *War* 2.40; *Ant.* 17.250.

77. Josephus, *War* 2.64, 111; *Ant.* 17.284—Archelaus took some considerable time to capture the last two rebel brothers of Athronges (cf. Farmer 1958); for the trouble after Herod's death see Chapter 7 n. 62.

78. Josephus, *Ant.* 17.339, 341; 20.249, 251; the two recorded high priests appointed by Archelaus are Eleazarus son of [Simon I] Boethus (above §4) and Jesus son of Se[th], possibly a brother of Ananus (Appendix 7); cf. Derenbourg 1867: 193-204; for Archelaus's coins, see *AJC* 2, 239-41, nos. 1-7; Meshorer 1990–91: 119-20. The numismatic evidence makes it clear that when Archelaus became ethnarch, he dropped his name and officially adopted the dynastic title 'Herod', exactly as Antipas did after his brother's deposition in CE 6 (*War* 2.167—for the reading see below n. 102). Thus Dio (55.27.6) is justified in calling Archelaus simply 'Herod'. On this basis it is *perfectly* possible that Luke's reference to 'Herod the King of Judaea' (1.5) may not after all be to Herod the Great but to Archelaus

Archelaus had fully prevailed, possibly by the end of the first century BCE, he began to enjoy his rule in a leisurely way as his father had done. Like Herod he undertook building projects, his main work being at Jericho, which had been devastated by Simon of Peraea. The royal winter palace there was restored and enlarged, and the plain (πεδίον) to the north was enriched by palm groves for which abundant water had to be brought in from other areas. Halfway from Jericho to Phasaelis, a whole village was created and named after him: Archelais.[79]

Archelaus's first wife was called 'Mariamme', and she is probably to be identified with his niece, Mariamme IV, daughter of Aristobulus I and sister of Agrippa I (see Chapter 10 §1). If so, and considering her date of birth, the wedding would not have taken place earlier than 1 BCE/CE 1 (though the couple may have been engaged from c. 7 BCE when Archelaus had completed his education). All we know is that this girl was abruptly divorced by Archelaus, the only reason being his desire to marry Glaphyra (daughter of King Archelaus of Cappadocia), his ex-sister-in-law and mother of two sons of Hasmonaean descent by Alexander I. This union caused serious concern among the Jewish people who seem to have condemned it on the basis of levirate law.[80] Archelaus is said to have fallen in love with Glaphyra, when he 'saw her at her father's' (παρὰ τῷ πατρὶ θεασάμενος), probably in the Cilician palace at Elaeussa/Sebaste (see Chapter 9 §1). We have no information of this journey of Archelaus—its ultimate destination may have either been Greece or Rome. As for its date, it must have been

---

(cf. Derrett 1975: 82-85). The fact that he calls him 'king' instead of 'ethnarch' is not a problem—at Luke's time this was a popular trend and other examples can be adduced (see Chapter 10 n. 60), even Josephus occasionally refers to Archelaus as king (*Ant.* 18. 93; *Life* 5). In effect this makes Luke's dating of Jesus' birth *internally* consistent (i.e. in CE 6: census of Quirinius, 'about 30 years old', etc.), but it remains *externally* wrong (Kokkinos 1989).

79.   Josephus, *Ant.* 17.340; for the archaeological work at the Herodian palace-complex in Tulul Abu el-Alayik (south of Jericho), see Netzer 1975; Netzer 1977; cf. Netzer 1993; Hachlili 1988; and on the baths, Small 1987: 71; for Simon's burning of the palace, see *War* 2.57; *Ant.* 17.274; cf. Tacitus, *Hist.* 5.9; by δοῦλος βασιλέως we may not take Simon merely as 'slave' of Herod (cf. Chapter 6 n. 89), for he could have held an important position in Peraea—cf. the official title 'servant of the King' for governors of the Transjordan from the Persian period onwards (Bright 1981: 382 n. 18; Chapter 2 n. 79); for Archelais (Khirbet Beiyudat 194152), see *SVM* 1, 355 n. 12; *TIRIP* 67.

80.   Josephus, *Ant.* 17.341; on Mariamme see *Ant.* 17.350; *War* 2. 115.

around CE 4/5, for Glaphyra meanwhile had married and divorced Juba II of Mauretania, who seems to have met her in 1 BCE and have taken her to his kingdom in CE 1 (or not later than CE 4).[81] Glaphyra's second stay in Judaea was brief—after a while (μετ' ὀλίγον) she allegedly saw a dream and died.[82]

According to Josephus a dream was also seen later by Archelaus, heralding the end of his rule within days. After a reign of ten years, and after being accused in front of the emperor by Jewish and Samaritan embassies, he was banished to Vienna in Gaul in CE 6.[83] Strabo has Archelaus's brothers (Antipas and Philip) being present at Rome, and narrowly escaping punishment themselves. In a similar context Dio describes the brothers as actually being the accusers of the ethnarch.[84]

Archelaus may not have died in exile. Strabo in his *Geography*, completed around 20 CE, says ἐν φυγῇ διετέλει (imperfect tense)—

81.   Josephus, *War* 2.115; on Glaphyra see Pani 1972: 114-40; Sullivan 1980: 1161-66; for a reconstruction of her inscription from Athens, see Kokkinos 1987. Josephus (*War* 2.115; *Ant.* 17.350) believed that Glaphyra's second marriage came to an end when Juba II died (i.e. before CE 6), but he was wrong because the king did not die before CE 23 (Strabo 17.3.7; Mazard 1955: 87, no. 187; see Kokkinos 1986a: 41). Glaphyra must have divorced Juba after a brief stay in Mauretania, and if we judge from her attitude at the Herodian court, she may have found herself in conflict with Cleopatra Selene, Juba's first wife (Braund 1984c), who appears to have been still alive (contra Macurdy 1932: 224-28; Macurdy 1937: 51-62; cf. Kokkinos 1990: 126 n. 2; 138 n. 83).

82.   Josephus, *War* 2.116; *Ant.* 17.351-3.

83.   Josephus, *War* 2.111-3; *Ant.* 17.342-48; *Life* 5. The length of Archelaus's reign in *War* is given as nine years, but is corrected to ten (i.e. Tishri CE 5 to Tishri CE 6) in both of Josephus's later works. It took place in the consulate of Aemilius Lepidus and Lucius Arruntius in CE 6 (Dio 55.27.6). A coin of the first Roman prefect Coponius dates to 'Year 36' of the Actian Era, i.e. between Sept. CE 5 and Sept. CE 6 (*AJC* 2, 281, nos. 1-2; *RPC* 1, 4954). But the census of Quirinius is dated by Josephus (*Ant.* 18.26) to 'Year 37' of the Actian Era, i.e. Sept. CE 6 to Sept. CE 7. If all the events took place in CE 6, there is no discrepancy among the sources: for example, Archelaus may have died in June (*Ant.*, *Life*, Dio), Coponius may have been appointed in August (coin), and the census may have begun in Oct. (*Ant.*).

84.   The fact that Josephus does not mention the involvement of Archelaus's brothers in his banishment, is not a good reason for discounting the evidence of both Strabo (16.2.46) and Dio (55.27.6); see Otto 1913: 178-79; Hoehner 1972: 103; cf. *GLAJJ* 1, 311; 2, 365; also at least the inscription of Antipas from Delos (Chapter 3 n. 196), seems to date to CE 6, supporting a journey of his to Rome at this time (Kokkinos forthcoming 1).

meaning that until recently he was in exile.[85] It thus seems possible that Archelaus was released from Gaul under Tiberius and probably returned to Palestine. By then he would have been about 47. Given his previous misconduct, it is unlikely that he would have involved himself in politics,[86] but none the less he could have retired to Judaea and died in the CE 20s or 30s. He may even have resided in the general area of Herodium built by his father, if the '*tumulus* of Archelaus' near Bethlehem, pointed out as a royal tomb to Jerome at the end of the fourth century CE, bore an inscription or was correctly identified from tradition.[87] (Archelaus is discussed further in Chapter 7 §1 and Chapter 10 §1).

As far as Antipas is concerned, he returned to Judaea, together with his elder brothers Archelaus and Philip, after the completion of their Roman education in c. 7/6 BCE.[88] At that time the trial and imprisonment of Antipater II meant that Herod the Great had to name a new heir to his throne, and because of uncertainty regarding the qualities of Archelaus and Philip (arising from Antipater II's calumnies), the king decided to appoint his younger son Antipas as his successor.[89] The occasion would have required a celebration, not only because the second phase of dissension in the Herodian court had come to an end, but also due to the fact that Syllaeus, the enemy of Herod, had now been executed in Rome (Chapter 7 n. 27), making the recultivation of a friendly relationship between Judaea and Nabataea imminent. Now was the time for the arrangement of an intermarriage between the two client kingdoms, and indeed this is what must have happened when Herod's heir Antipas (then around 19) took as his wife a daughter of Aretas IV king of Petra.[90]

85.   Strabo, 16.2.46. Note that the text does not say ἐν φυγῇ διατελεῖ ('he continues to be in exile') or ἐν φυγῇ διετέλεσεν ('he lived in exile', i.e. he died there). Also by 'one of Herod's sons', Strabo must mean Archelaus; at that time no other son of Herod had been banished.

86.   It is obviously hardly possible that Archelaus was one of the 'four sons of Herod' dominating Judaean politics under the *praefecti* (CE 6–41), as has been argued from Philo and other evidence (Chapter 7 n. 80).

87.   Jerome, *Onom.* [edn Klostermann 45]; see Abel 1946: 70; Rees 1951: 354; *SVM* 1, 356 n. 13.

88.   Josephus, *War* 1.602-603; *Ant.* 17.20-21, 80-81; for Antipas in general see Hoehner 1972; *SVM* 1, 340-53.

89.   Josephus, *War* 1.646; *Ant.* 17.146.

90.   Josephus, *Ant.* 18.109-12. Her story is related by Josephus retrospectively,

The identification of this Nabataean young lady (the first to enter
the Herodian dynasty since Cyprus I, the mother of Herod) is an interesting problem, which may be solved here with the aid of epigraphical
and numismatic evidence tied to our new chronological framework.
The children of Aretas IV are reasonably well known: he had three
sons Obodas, Malichus II and Rabbel, and five daughters, Phasaelis,
Sha'dat, Hagaru I, Shaqilat II and Gamilat I.[91] The last two daughters
were probably born shortly after CE 18 and thus cannot be considered
as candidates—in any case Shaqilat II died in CE 75/76 after marrying
Malichus II. Hagaru I, who seems also too young for Antipas, would
have been born not later than the beginning of the Christian Era, and
she is known in inscriptions from Petra (CE 18/19) and the Wadi
Musa–Petra main road (probably CE 23/24), as being the mother of a
child called Aretas (V). The name of her husband in the Wadi Musa
text is not legible, but it has been suggested that it might read
'Han'aktabs'—ironically not Herod Antipas.[92] Also Sha'dat is known to
have had a son and a grandson, both named Qashma, mentioned in an
inscription from the end of the reign of Rabbel II (c. CE 100–106),
with the real possibility that she had been the first 'sister-wife' of
Malichus II, before Shaqilat II.[93] Thus we are left with Phasaelis, and
under the circumstances we have to conclude that she is the person we

i.e. only in CE 33/34. This was the time when Antipas divorced her, evidently after
some 40 years of marriage (improving on Kokkinos 1989: 134). Note that this
lengthy period has to be reflected in the words συνῆν χρόνον ἤδη πολύν (109). No
wonder Aretas reacted in the way he did after Antipas broke such an old alliance,
contrived by Herod and possibly Augustus himself (cf. Suetonius, *Aug.* 48)—see
Chapter 10 §1.

91.   On Aretas IV in general see Starcky 1960: 913-16; *SVM* 1, 582-83; Negev
1978, 567-70; and now Wenning 1994: 35-36; cf. Bowersock 1983b: 51ff.; and
Chapter 3 n. 46; for a reconstruction of his family tree with evidence for the order of
his children, see Appendix 4.

92.   In an additional note to Khairy (1981: 25-26), Milik has attempted to read
the name of Hagaru I's husband as הן אכתבס, a proper name according to him related
to the Lihyanite god 'the great Scribe' or Han-'Aktab.

93.   For the inscription see Dalman 1912: 103, no. 92; *RES* 1434; cf. a
Nabataean document from the archive of Babatha (Yadin 1962: 239-41; Yadin 1971,
235); note another inscription which mentions Sha'dat as the sister (אחתה) of Malichus
(Zayadine 1981: 354-55, pl. 102). Starcky's (1960: 914) identification of Sha'dat
(שעדת or שעודת) with the wife of Antipas has no evidence to support it, and cannot
correlate with the text in Dalman. Meshorer's (1975: 79) understanding of Sha'dat as
a sister of Aretas IV is surely untenable.

are looking for, particularly since she was almost certainly the eldest daughter of Aretas IV.

Her name is both masculine, like Phasael the brother of Herod, and feminine, like Phasaelis found in inscriptions from the Hauran.[94] In the context of the Nabataean royal family, פצאל has often been taken to refer to a son of Aretas IV, but only because in the three main texts in which it appears, it is listed together with brothers and sisters, all being qualified as Aretas's בנוהי (בניהם or בני) and it is thus impossible to determine individual sexes. But separate graffiti of Phasaelis have been discovered, referring to her as a Nabataean 'queen' (מלכת), and her name also followed by the title 'queen' is restored in the inscription of Rabbel II mentioned above.[95]

Phasaelis was the only child of Aretas IV to have had her name mentioned on his coins.[96] These examples were minted in the fifth year of Aretas, that is in 7/6 BCE (by the new reckoning followed here—compare Appendix 3), or in other words exactly at the time proposed for Antipas's marriage. Meshorer, who takes the name to be masculine, thought that this coin commemorated the birth of a fourth son of Aretas—his first after he became king.[97] But the commemoration obviously concerns the elder daughter of Aretas, and it seems to advertize not her birth but her wedding to Antipas, precisely in that year. A closer look at the design of this coin would support this conclusion. The special emblem of the palm branch, alongside parallel *cornucopiae*, symbolizes an important and joyful event, such as a royal wedding—as observed by Meshorer himself. Clearly there is only one other instance in which the palm branch is depicted on Nabataean coinage, and this is minted in the days of Shaqilat I, Aretas's second wife, and is associated with their marriage.[98]

Phasaelis must have been at least 12 in 7/6 BCE, which means that she would have lived with Antipas until she was divorced at 50 in

94.   Wadd. 1928: Φασήελης; 2445: Οὔλπια Φασαίελις; see Negev 1991b: 55, no. 970, who gives some 16 occurrences of the name פצאל, but who takes them all as male.

95.   For the rock graffiti see Milik and Starcky 1975: 112-15; for Rabbel II's genealogical text, see above n. 93, together with Meshorer's restoration (1975: 79).

96.   Meshorer 1975: 97, nos. 60-64A; note that only one specimen carries the full name of פצאל (pl. 4.61); cf. Schmitt-Korte 1990: 115, nos. 47-49.

97.   Meshorer 1975: 48-49.

98.   Meshorer 1975: 103, no. 97, pl. 6.97; cf. Schmitt-Korte 1990: 119-20, nos. 66-69.

CE 33/34. Despite its long duration this marital union produced no children who are explicitly recorded, but possibly a son and a daughter may have existed. We have already discussed the case of Antipas III, a leading member of the Herodian family, who was in charge of the public treasury of Jerusalem at the outbreak of the revolt. An attempt was there made for him to be identified with Antipater IV son of Phasael II, which would mean that this person was at a minimum 60 years old in CE 65. This was reckoned not to be impossible for the position he held, but none the less two alternative identifications were presented, in one of which Antipas III was seen as a son of Antipas the Tetrarch, and therefore a younger man at the time of his murder at the hands of the Jewish rebels (Chapter 6 n. 29). If the latter is to be preferred, then Antipas III may have been a son of the Nabataean Phasaelis.

The existence of a daughter of Antipas the Tetrarch is documented only in the Gospel of Mark. Here in the famous story of the dancing κοράσιον, the girl is said to have been 'a daughter of Antipas' called 'Herodias [II]'.[99] As argued elsewhere, this story associated with John the Baptist's death was not created by a simple process of legend making, and it seems to supplement Josephus's information. Herodias II (perhaps known as Herodias-Salome?) is the best candidate for identification with 'Salome' the wife of Aristobulus III of Lesser Armenia, mentioned on coins (see Chapter 10 §3). Aristobulus's Salome—who was married in the 50s CE, attested in 56/57, became mother of three children, and died possibly in the 90s—cannot have been identical to Salome III daughter of Herodias I, who was born at the beginning of the century. Further, the existence of yet another, unknown, Salome is unlikely. However we should note that if Antipas's daughter was by Phasaelis, and if she was a κοράσιον in the early 30s (that is born not earlier than CE 20), the Nabataean lady

99.   Mk 6.22: τῆς θυγατρὸς αὐτοῦ Ἡρωδιάδος (best MSS); see Kokkinos 1986a: 43-45, where evidence from apocryphal and patristic sources is given; cf. my omission of Speyer 1967; and add Eusebius, Athanasius and John Chrysostom, all of whom refer to the daughter of Antipas as 'Herodias', as does Salomon of Basra in his Syriac *Book of the Bee* (Budge 1886: 91; cf. Metzger 1970: 96; *OTP* 1, xxvi); further, an allusion to the 'dancing' episode in *Sib. Or.* 1.342 has been suggested by Herrmann (1973: 62); and yet another parallel to the 'dancing-girl' motif omitted from my article (and perhaps never pointed out before) is in Josephus, *Ant.* 12.186-89; cf. Chapter 10 §1.

would have had to have given birth to her at the age of 40. Perhaps not impossible but a constraint to remember when pronouncing Phasaelis as the mother of Herodias II.

The reign of Antipas over Galilee and Peraea lasted 43 years, a span slightly exceeded among all rulers of Herodian stock only by Agrippa II (Chapter 10 §5).[100] At first Antipas seems to have centred his activities (4 [or 3] BCE–CE 6) at Betharamphtha in Peraea—Pheroras's former seat of power (Chapter 6 n. 57)—where he would have rebuilt the palace, recently burned down by a body of Peraean insurgents (compare above n. 79). We know for certain that he fortified this city, which should initially have been renamed 'Livias', after the wife of Augustus, that is before she was adopted into the Julian gens (CE 14). Later the city was mainly called 'Julias', at least until the time of Agrippa II, but the name must finally have reverted to 'Livias' as we find it in the Babatha Archive and later Eusebius.[101] It also makes sense that at the beginning of his rule Antipas would stay close to Judaea, opposite Jericho where Archelaus had enthroned himself amidst his new buildings, as well as near the borders of Nabataea from where his wife had come.

After his return from Rome in CE 6 (above n. 84), when Judaea became a Roman province, Antipas, now adopting the dynastic name 'Herod' previously held by Archelaus, seems to have moved to Galilee.[102] Here he fortified Sepphoris, which was refounded in

---

100. Josephus, *War* 2.94-95; *Ant.* 17.318. Antipas was a late starter in minting coins (*AJC* 2, 242-43, nos. 1-19; Meshorer 1990–91: 120-21). His first example is dated to Year 24 (CE 19/20, on the occasion of the founding of Tiberias), then follow Years 33 and 34 (CE 28–30, in the heyday of Sejanus), Year 37 (CE 32/33, possibly on the Emperor's birthday) and 43 (CE 38/39, the last year of the Tetrarch). A lead weight is also known from Tiberias dated to Year 34 of Antipas (CE 29/30, possibly on the *decennium* of the founding of the city—see Qedar 1986–87: 29-30, no. 1 = *SEG* 38, 1646). I cannot subscribe to Stein's (1992) date and interpretation of this weight: it is not possible to refer to Agrippa I whose *praenomen* was almost certainly a Marcus (Chapter 10 n. 26; cf. above n. 53), and who was still in Rome at this time (Chapter 10 §2).

101. *P. Yadin* 37.4; Eusebius, *Onom.* [edn Klostermann 48]; see Jones [A.H.M.] 1971: 275; cf. Hoehner 1972: 88; *SVM* 2, 177 nn. 504-505; for Antipas in Betharamphtha/Livias/Julias, see Josephus, *War* 2.168; *Ant.* 18.27.

102. Josephus, *War* 2.167: but read Ἀντίπας ὁ κληθεὶς Ἡρώδης; cf. Hoehner 1972: 109. Sepphoris already possessed a Herodian palace (*War* 2.56; *Ant.* 17.271; cf. *Life* 38).

honour of Augustus, evidently in gratitude for his reconfirmation of Antipas's position. As it appears, the official celebration fell sometime after CE 6 and before CE 9, and this would be supported by the name given to the city: Αὐτοκρατορὶς (that is *Imperatoria*). It was precisely in CE 6 (and then again in CE 9) that Augustus was hailed 'imperator' for the eighteenth (and nineteenth) times, in a turbulent period, which also combined the important event of the emperor's seventieth birthday (23/24 September CE 7, inclusively).[103] Another project of Antipas at Sepphoris may have been the building of the theatre excavated there, which he could have undertaken in imitation of his father's theatres at Jerusalem, Jericho and Caesarea, but the matter is disputed. Archaeology has yet to prove such an early date for the theatre at Sepphoris, and its construction in the second century CE would seem more likely.[104]

After the accession of Tiberius, Antipas gained a closer relationship with Rome, which made it necessary for him to express his appreciation more vigorously than before. A totally new city was created on the Sea of Galilee, named directly after the emperor: 'Tiberias'. Its official foundation date fell shortly before CE 19/20 (as Antipas's coins now show the *terminus ante quem*), no doubt at or soon after the celebration of Tiberius's sixtieth birthday on 16 November CE 18 (inclusively). Because the site chosen lay on what had previously been burial ground, most Jews refused to settle on it, and Antipas had great

103. Josephus, *Ant.* 18.23; for Sepphoris see Hoehner 1972: 84-87; *SVM* 2, 172-76; Miller [S.] 1984; *TIRIP* 227-28; for excavations see Waterman 1937; Meyers 1986; Batey 1992; Weiss 1993; coins were struck for the first time during Vespasian's campaigns in CE 67/68 (*AJC* 2, 279, nos. 8-9; but ignore no. 10 which is not of Sepphoris, and Agrippa II had little to do with this city [Chapter 10 n. 246]—also contra Meshorer 1985: 36; Meshorer 1990–91: 110); a lead weight recently unearthed at Sepphoris (Meshorer in Meyers, *et al.* 1986: 16-17, with wrong transcription; cf. *SEG* 36, 1342) with the names of the *agoranomoi* (Simon son of Aianus; Justus son of Ju[das]), would also belong to a later period, since there is no mention of Antipas (cf. lead weight from Tiberias, above n. 100); for Augustus's IMP. XVIII and XIX, see Kokkinos 1995a: 33; Kokkinos forthcoming 3, where relevant references; for his birthday, see Snyder 1940: 227-30; cf. Gellius, *Attic Nights* 15.7.3; Josephus gives the new name of Sepphoris according to the Loeb edition as Αὐτοκρατορίδα not Αὐτοκρατίδα (*SVM* 2, 174 n. 485).

104. Strange and Longstaff 1984; cf. Batey 1984: 566, 573 n. 11; Segal [A.] 1989: 149.

difficulty in populating the place. Many Galilaeans had to be moved in both by force and by the offering of expensive gifts, and the majority had to be made up of mixed foreign people from the surrounding territories.[105] A lavishly decorated palace (including animal representations apparently on frescoes) was built by Antipas at Tiberias, which became the central seat of power in Galilee, and to which Sepphoris was made subordinate. The building was later destroyed in a massive conflagration started by the rebel Jesus bar Sapphias in the first half of CE 66 (in the chronology followed here). Antipas was also probably responsible for the construction of a stadium here, as well as a hippodrome at Tarichaea to the north.[106]

Despite its longevity, Antipas's rule itself ended in disgrace, when under Caligula in CE 39 he was banished to Gaul. The verdict came after a series of dramatic episodes which followed the death of Philip the Tetrarch in CE 33, and involved Antipas's divorce of Phasaelis, marriage to Herodias, war with the Nabataeans, conflict with Agrippa I and a final, fatal journey to Rome (see Chapter 10 §§1, 2).

6. *Cleopatra*

The information we have for Cleopatra is meagre. She is said to have been a 'Jerusalemite', but as with Doris her family may have been living in the capital, possibly working for the Herodian court, although being of Hellenized Idumaean/Phoenician origins (see above n. 3). Without relying on the onomastic argument, her name certainly supports this view, and would be expected in places such as Marisa and Ascalon closer to Egypt, or in Syria/Phoenicia in the north.[107]

105. Josephus, *War* 2.168; *Ant.* 18.36-38; for Tiberias see Hoehner 1972: 91-102; *SVM* 2, 178-82; Hirschfeld 1991; *TIRIP* 249-50; cf. Avi-Yonah 1950; Rajak 1973; Rajak 1987; for the excavation of the city gate, see Foerster 1978; 1993; for the coins and a lead weight issued at Tiberias by Antipas, see above n. 100 (cf. Chapter 10 n. 250); Hoehner (1972: 95) wrongly dated the founding of the city to CE 23 (Kokkinos 1986a: 40); for Tiberius's birthday see Snyder 1940: 235; for chronological 'elasticity' in keeping Roman anniversaries, see Grant 1950: 10.

106. For the palace see Josephus, *Life* 37, 65-67; for the stadium see e.g. *Life* 92; for the hippodrome at Tarichaea see e.g. *Life* 132; for Tarichaea/Magdala (Mejdel 198247) see *TIRIP* 173.

107. Cleopatra is of course a Greek name (Apollodorus, *Bibl.*, 2.1.5; see *WGEN*, 675-76; *LGPN*, 265; cf. Ilan 1989: 194, nos. 28-29; at Marisa is known from Tomb 2 (Peters and Thiersch 1905: no. 36).

The fact that her son Philip was presented with Ituraean territory may suggest that his mother's roots sprang from the Syro-Phoenician environment. It must be stressed that although Cleopatra is thought to have been a very common name, no Jewish woman called thus is mentioned by Josephus. Furthermore in the entire corpus of evidence from the Second Temple and Mishnaic periods, only one other woman is known from an ossuary to have borne this name.[108]

Cleopatra gave birth to two sons, Herod IV and Philip. Of Herod, apparently born in c. 27 BCE (see beginning of Chapter 8), we know nothing at all. He may have died young. He took part in no event recorded in Josephus or elsewhere, with the possible exception of the embassy referred to by Philo (Chapter 7 n. 80), and at the death of his father he made no claim to the throne. But there is no reason to doubt his historicity. Josephus explicitly mentions Cleopatra as having had two 'sons' (παῖδες).[109] Also at least one other son of Herod the Great is known simply and only by name: Phasael III (see Chapter 8 §7).

Cleopatra's son Philip was the famous tetrarch, born approximately in 26 BCE. He was younger than Archelaus (born c. 27 BCE) and·older than Antipas (born c. 25 BCE).[110] If this is so, Philip, together with his brothers, would have been sent to Rome for his education around 14 BCE.[111] Indeed, although previously unnoticed, from a fragment of Nicolaus's history we learn that when Herod sailed to Pontus in 14 BCE, his 'sons' (υἱεῖς) were left at Rhodes, later to be seen off to Italy by Nicolaus.[112] This piece of evidence clearly supports the earlier

108. Apart from the Hellenistic queens, the only other Cleopatra in Josephus is the wife of Gessius Florus from Asia Minor (*Ant.* 20.252); for the ossuary of a Cleopatra (if a Jewess, then Hellenized), see Figueras 1983, no. 15.

109. *Ant.* 17.21; cf. *War* 1.562.

110. See above nn. 70-71; cf. Nicolaus, *apud* Constantinus Porphyrogenitus (*FGrH* 90, F136): τοὺς δὲ μετ' αὐτῶν ἀδελφοὺς Φίλιππον καὶ ᾿Αντίπαν; for Philip in general see *SVM* 1, 336-40, with the important omission of the 'Nabataean' inscription referring to his rule (below n. 125)—but see now Millar 1993b: 393.

111. Josephus, *Ant.* 17.20-21 says that his brothers, as well as he, were being brought up in Rome, evidently all παρά τινι ἰδίῳ. The last word has been emended to ᾿Ιουδαίῳ, meaning 'a certain Jew', or to ἰδιώτῃ, 'a certain private person' (see recently Braund 1983: 240; Feldman 1985: 242). But surely it means 'one of their own', i.e. either a 'relative' or 'friend' (see Latin version *familiarem*; and cf. modern Greek δικός = 'friend' or 'relative').

112. Nicolaus, *apud* Constantinus Porphyrogenitus (*FGrH* 90, F134; *GLAJJ* 1, 246-48, no. 95). There is no question that these 'sons' were Archelaus, Philip and

dating proposed here for Herod's marriages with Malthace and
Cleopatra. It is also in agreement with the fact that the young men
were summoned back to Judaea at the completion of their studies in
7/6 BCE, at the time of Antipater II's trial.[113]

According to *Ant.* 18.137, Philip married Salome III. But this does
not seem to be right. For him to able to do that he should have stayed
celibate up to the age of at least 40—uniquely among the Herods
(Salome could not have married before c. CE 13). From other evidence we may actually deduce that Philip's wife (during the first three
decades of the Christian Era) was Salome III's mother, Herodias I,
who had divorced her first husband, Herod III, and later also resorted
to marrying Antipas after the death of Philip (see Chapter 10 §1).
Josephus twice tells us that Philip died childless, and this must be
accurate because the succession to his tetrarchy became a matter of
dispute.[114] The date of Philip's death can be calculated with confidence. He died 'in the twentieth year of Tiberius's reign and after
thirty-seven years of his own rule'. Year 20 of Tiberius ran from 19
August CE 33 to 18 August CE 34—thus it is commonly held that
Philip died in 33/34. But greater precision is now possible. His rule of
37 years is confirmed by coin evidence, and since the 'Tishri' reckoning for Herodian reigns is now accepted (that is Philip's rule began in
October 5 BCE), Philip died between October 32 and October 33. The
only overlap allowed between this reckoning and Tiberius's twentieth
year is from late August to October CE 33; thus the death of Philip
must have occurred around September CE 33.[115]

Antipas. The other sons, Alexander I and Aristobulus I, who were now newly-weds
and fathers, had stayed behind in Jerusalem. As soon as Herod returned (in the
autumn of 14 BCE) his brother Pheroras and sister Salome informed him of Alexander's and Aristobulus's bad behaviour in his absence (Josephus, *Ant.* 16.73-74; cf.
War 1.447); see Appendix 3.

113. Josephus, *Ant.* 17.80; cf. *War* 1.602.

114. Josephus, *Ant.* 18.108, 137; a late and worthless gloss in the Slavonic
Josephus (after *War* 2.168) has Philip leaving four children (see Eisler 1931: 230
n. 4).

115. Josephus, *Ant.* 18.106; for Tiberius's date see Schillinger-Häfele 1986: 52;
for Philip's coins of Year 37, see *AJC* 2, 246, nos. 13-14 (but different reckoning
there); the first serious attempt to employ the 'Tishri' reckoning for the Herodian
reigns (including that of Philip), was made by van Bruggen (1978: 12); see Chapter
10 n. 76.

Philip ruled successfully over a large kingdom comprised of a substantial part of Ituraea, the whole of Panias, Gaulanitis, Batanaea, Trachonitis and the northern part of Auranitis.[116] (For Philip's kingdom see discussions under Agrippa I and II.) He first seems to have raised to the status of a city Bethsaida, a village in Gaulanitis to the north of the Sea of Galilee, which he enlarged and fortified by early 2 BCE at the latest. This is inferred from the fact that he renamed it 'Julias', after the daughter of Augustus who was banished in that year.[117] The new name could not have lasted, and it soon reverted to what it was called originally—thus known to the Gospels unanimously as 'Bethsaida'.[118] Work at Panias, the capital of Philip's territory, would have begun before 1 BCE/CE 1, if the temple depicted on his earliest dated coins is that built by his father near the Paneion (and apparently now improved by him), while further evidence sets the beginning of the city's era at 3/2 BCE.[119] Panias was renamed 'Caesarea' in honour of Augustus (known as Caesarea Philippi to be distinguished from Caesarea-on-the-coast),[120] and it is possible that Philip was imitating Augustus's Mausoleum at Rome, when he ordered the erection of his own monumental tomb apparently at Panias.[121] He further seems to have been occupied with the improvement of the

116.   Josephus, *War* 2.95, 247; *Ant.* 17.189, 319; 18.106; 20.138.

117.   Josephus, *War* 2.168; *Ant.* 18.28; for Julia see Velleius, 2.100.3; Dio, 55.10.4; cf. Tacitus, *Ann.* 1.53; Julia may have returned in CE 4, but she was never accepted by her father until his death (Suetonius, *Aug.* 65.3-4; 101.3); if Bethsaida's dedication preceded that of Panias (below n. 119), then this should have happened not later than 3 BCE; for Bethsaida (et Tell 208257 and 'Araj 208255) see *SVM* 2, 171-72; Pixner 1985; *TIRIP* 85; and now Urman 1995: 519-22.

118.   Mk 6.45; 8.22; Mt. 11.21; Lk. 9.10; 10.13; Jn 1.44; 12.12.

119.   For coins of Year 5 depicting the facade of the Temple, see *AJC* 2, 244, no. 2; for Herod's building of it, see Josephus, *Ant.* 15.363-64; *War* 1.404; for its current excavation, see Ma'oz 1988–89; Ma'oz 1993: 140; for numismatic and inscriptional evidence of the Era of Panias, see Meshorer (1984–85) and cautiously Meimaris, *et al.* (1992: 142-45).

120.   Mk 8.27; Mt. 16.13; Josephus, *War* 2.168; *Ant.* 18.28; for Panias see *SVM* 2, 169-71; *TIRIP* 199; for excavations there, see Tzaferis and Peleg 1988–89; Tzaferis and Avner 1989–90.

121.   Josephus (*Ant.* 18.108) says that Philip died in Julias and that his body was transferred to the μνημεῖον that he had previously built. This need not imply that his tomb was also at Bethsaida, where he happened to die (contra Pixner 1985: 211; cf. Abel 1946: 71). It would seem more likely that he was brought back and buried at Panias.

water system in the area, if the story of his attempt to discover the sources of the river Jordan is to be believed.[122] Philip's founding of cities and his general building activity was advertized when he assumed a title that not even Herod the Great had adopted outside his Jewish territory: ΚΤΙΣ(ΤΗΣ).[123]

Josephus describes the rule of Philip as being just, so much so that the tetrarch in all of his excursions is said to have taken his throne with him for judging any cases that might be brought to his attention on the way. But he was known to have imposed unwelcome taxes at least on the Babylonian military colony at Batanaea, though this did not prevent him from having loyal supporters among his army, members of which after his death defected to Nabataea in order not to submit to Philip's brother Antipas.[124] A celebrated inscription from Sî'a in Auranitis, written in Nabataean (or perhaps 'Gentile' Aramaic), cut on a decorated altar which once carried a statue of a local dignitary, גלסו son of בנתו, mentions that the work was dedicated 'in the Year 33 of our Lord (למרנע) Philippus (פלפס)', that is in CE 28/29.[125] Also two Safaitic inscriptions are thought to mention Philip, but it is impossible to be certain. The first was found in a recent survey of the Basalt Desert in northern Jordan, and contains the dating formula: 'the year the people of the Hauran (*Hrn*) complained to Caesar (*qṣr*) about Philippus (*Flfṣ*)'. Josephus does not record any such complaint under Philip the Tetrarch, and although this is not a reason for rejecting this identification, the circumstances may better suit Philip son of Jacimus

---

122. Josephus, *War* 3.509-15; for the episode and geography, see *SVM* 1, 339 n. 6.

123. *AJC* 2, 246, no. 11; see Jacobson 1988: 396-97, where parallels are drawn with another κτίστης, Archelaus of Cappadocia, etc. Philip's coins, apart from his portrait, depict Augustus, Tiberius and Livia. Tiberius's mother appears together with her son on one type (*AJC* 2, 245, 6-6a; corrected in Meshorer 1990–91: 132), and on her own on another (*AJC* 2, 278, no. 1; corrected in Meshorer 1990–91: 108-109). The latter carries Philip's regnal 'Year 34', i.e. CE 29/30, which is significant in that it must commemorate Livia's death (see Kokkinos 1992a: 91-93). As we now know, the same type was reissued later, in 32/33 CE (Meshorer 1990–91: 127, Suppl. III, no. 1a; with wrong reckoning).

124. Josephus, *Ant.* 17.27; 18.114.

125. Littmann 1914, no. 101; cf. Offord 1919; Starcky (1985: 174-75) argues that the script is not precisely Nabataean but 'Gentile' Aramaic; for the epithet מרא as the equivalent to κύριος (so common in the Bible), cf. Chapter 10 n. 92.

(see Chapter 7 §2 and Chapter 10 §5).[126] The second Safaitic text was discovered in the Burqu' region of northeastern Jordan, containing the dating formula: 'the year Caesar's son (*bn qṣr*) died; and he heard that Philippus (*Flfṣ*) had been killed'. Macdonald argues that this refers to Philip the Tetrarch and that the son of Caesar would be Germanicus, the adopted son of Tiberius. However Germanicus died in CE 19 and Philip in 33, so that Macdonald has to take the latter's reported demise in 19 only as a baseless rumour and unknown to Josephus. The death of Drusus, the natural son of Tiberius, in CE 23, would have brought this argument closer to Philip's death, but still not close enough. On balance it might instead be wiser to adopt the interpretation, also mentioned by Macdonald, that the text refers to the Emperor Philip the Arab and his son, both of whom died in CE 249.[127]

The name Philip, adopted by numerous subjects of the tetrarch, persisted in the area for centuries, as is revealed particularly from inscriptions. From one example at Panias we learn that in the second century CE the local *boulē* and the *dēmos* set up statues of one 'Philip [II] son of Antipater' and of his father 'Antipater son of Philip [I]', for having served the local priesthood and the gymnasiarchy, and for having provided allowances (ἐπιδόσεις) to the city. Thus three generations of this important family are on record, and if, for argument's sake, we take Philip II as having flourished c. CE 75–145, his father Antipater c. CE 50–120, and his grandfather Philip I c. CE 25–95, the latter would have been born under Philip the Tetrarch and obviously named after him.[128]

7. Pallas, Phaedra and Elpis

His 'recent wives', as Josephus describes them, Herod the Great seems to have married at the same moment, probably on the occasion of the

126. Macdonald 1995: 288-89; for the survey see King [G.] 1990.

127. Macdonald 1995: 286-88; cf. here the interesting confusion of Malalas (*Chron.* 10.13), allegedly on the authority of Clement of Alexandria: 'The King Herod son of Philip (!), became plethoric and was ill in bed for eight months. He was slain in his bed-chamber after the end of those eight months, with his wife's complicity...' Josephus testifies that Philip died while at Julias, apparently suddenly (see above n. 121).

128. Haussoullier and Ingholt 1924: 331-33, no. 7; for other examples, see from al-Hît: 'Herod son of Herod' and 'Philip son of Malchus' (Wadd. 2115); cf. Chapter 10 n. 171.

double wedding of his Hasmonaean sons at the close of 16 BCE. Their names, Pallas, Phaedra and Elpis, are purely Greek,[129] and the women may have been brought to Judaea by Herod from his journey to Greece and Rome in 17/16 BCE. Alternatively, like Doris, Malthace and Cleopatra, they may also have been Hellenized Idumaean/ Phoenician ladies attached to the Herodian court.

Pallas was a traditional name among the Arcadians and it is not impossible that she was from the Peloponnese. She bore one son, Phasael III, probably around late 15 BCE, but of whom Josephus knows nothing at all. Like Herod IV son of Cleopatra, he is a mere cipher. The name given to the boy is obviously that of Herod's brother Phasael I, who was killed early in 40 BCE (Chapter 6 §1). But no assumption can be made that he was born as early as this (that is that Pallas was an early wife of Herod despite the order in the list of *Antiquities*), because there would then be a problem with the succession to the Judaean throne. We would have expected Phasael III to be mentioned by Josephus as the candidate following Antipater II son of Doris. Also it would be far-fetched to imagine that he was banished with his mother (like the Doris-Antipater pair), and that he never returned to Jerusalem to reclaim his rights as an heir of Herod.

Therefore the estimate of his birth in late 15 BCE must be sustained. His naming after his uncle does not seem to have related to any apparent anniversary, although it may have coincided with the completion of the great tower which Herod dedicated to Phasael approximately at that time.[130] The fact that we hear of no claim made by him in 4 (or 5) BCE when Herod died, would be explained by the fact that he was only a minor and for the next few years he remained under the control of Archelaus. When Judaea became a Roman province in CE 6 he could have joined the Herodian aristocracy which dominated the local

129. Pallas (*Iliad* 1.200), Phaedra (*Odys.* 11.321) and Elpis (Sophocles, *Oedip.* 157); see *WGEN*, 355, 1113, 1592; *LGPN* 357, 150-51; cf. Ilan 1989: 194 (no. 42), 197 (nos. 150, 153); Cassuto 1932: 227, no. 64. The name 'Phadris' (if it was read correctly) appears at Marisa (McCown 1921–22), and it has been compared with a Phoenician name in *CIS* 220 (l. 5); the masculine form Phaedrus (*LGPN* 452) is known from an ossuary in Jerusalem (*CII* 1283b).

130. Josephus, *War* 1.418; 2.46, 439; 5.166-69; 7.1; *Ant.* 16.144; 17.257; Josephus speaks of Phasael's tower immediately after the completion of Caesarea in 13 BCE, but the details are part of a summary list (with 'flashbacks') of building achievements which would have been finished sometime before and up to the foundation of Caesarea.

political affairs until the 30s, probably being one of the 'four' protagonists mentioned by Philo (Chapter 7 n. 80), or, if not, he may have emigrated to Greece if his mother was really Greek. When Agrippa I became the next Herodian king of Judaea in CE 41, Phasael III would either have lost his prestige or perhaps died.

Phaedra and Elpis bore one child each. Roxane the daughter of the former may have been named after one of her mother's ancestors (possibly her grandmother),[131] while Salome II the daughter of the latter was evidently named after Herod's sister. Both these girls were born about the same time as Phasael III. They were the youngest daughters of Herod, and the only ones who were still virgin when the king died.[132] Thus they were conceivably under 12 in 4 (or 5) BCE, which fits well with my estimate of their birth late in 15 or slightly later.

In one episode dated c. 7 BCE Roxane and Salome II are said to have been insulted in the Herodian palace by a group of women related to Pheroras (his unnamed 'slave'-wife, her mother and sister), and Herod made this a pretext for arresting these women whom he hated anyway (Chapter 6 §3).[133] Ironically, after the death of Herod, his youngest daughters were given in marriage by Augustus to two unnamed sons of Pheroras. Besides what their father had left them in his will, the emperor made each of them an additional gift of 250,000 pieces of silver.[134] As it happened Roxane and Salome II both died without progeny, and thus disappeared from history.[135]

131. If so, the family of Phaedra's mother may have been of oriental origin, since Roxane is a Persian name (Arrian, *Anab.* 4.19.5; cf. Ilan 1989: 198, no. 156). But, the name had become familiar to the Greeks from the history of Alexander the Great, whose wife was a Roxane (Curtius, 8.4. 23; see Milns 1968: 183).

132. Josephus, *Ant.* 17.322; *War* 2.99.

133. Josephus, *War* 1.568, 571; *Ant.* 17.34, 46.

134. Josephus, *Ant.* 17.322; *War* 2.99 says 500,000 for both.

135. Josephus, *Ant.* 18.141.

Chart 1: *The Wives of Herod (Old Chronology)*
Hoehner's dating of marriages 2, 3, 6, 7, following Josephus' order of wives in Antiquities (Note in this scheme Herod had no wife between 29 and 23 BCE)

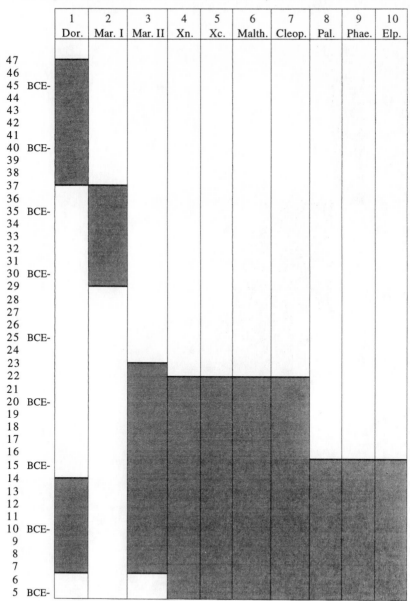

Chart 2: *The Wives of Herod (New Chronology)*
A new dating of the marriages following Josephus' order of wives
in Antiquities, with Xn. and Xc. before not after Mar. II
(note in this scheme there are no gaps in Herod's married life)

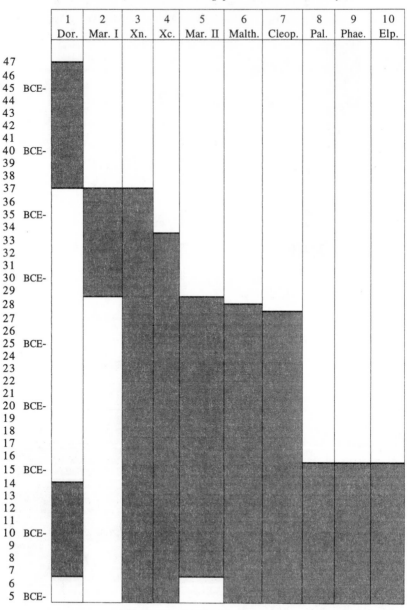

Family Tree: *The Wives of Herod and their Offspring*

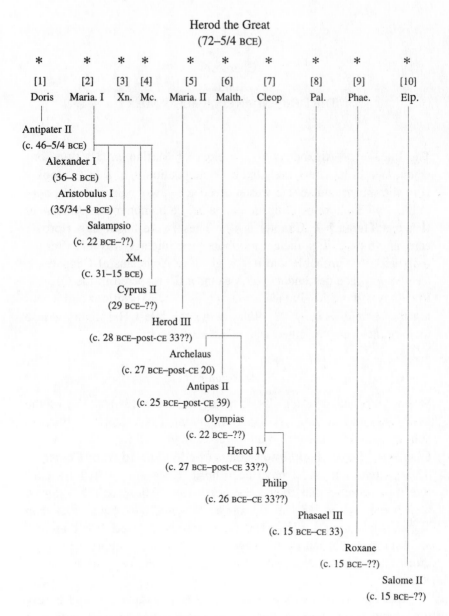

Herod the Great
(72–5/4 BCE)

*	*	*	*	*	*	*	*	*	*
[1]	[2]	[3]	[4]	[5]	[6]	[7]	[8]	[9]	[10]
Doris	Maria. I	Xn.	Mc.	Maria. II	Malth.	Cleop	Pal.	Phae.	Elp.

Antipater II
(c. 46–5/4 BCE)

Alexander I
(36–8 BCE)

Aristobulus I
(35/34 –8 BCE)

Salampsio
(c. 22 BCE–??)

XM.
(C. 31–15 BCE)

Cyprus II
(29 BCE–??)

Herod III
(c. 28 BCE–post-CE 33??)

Archelaus
(c. 27 BCE–post-CE 20)

Antipas II
(c. 25 BCE–post-CE 39)

Olympias
(c. 22 BCE–??)

Herod IV
(c. 27 BCE–post-CE 33??)

Philip
(c. 26 BCE–CE 33??)

Phasael III
(c. 15 BCE–CE 33)

Roxane
(c. 15 BCE–??)

Salome II
(c. 15 BCE–??)

See further: Tree 2 (Antipater II)
Tree 4 (Salampsio; Olympias; Roxane; Salome II)
Tree 5 (Aristobulus I; Cyprus II)
Tree 10 (Alexander I)

Chapter 9

THE DESCENDANTS OF ALEXANDER I

The lineage of Alexander I—the elder of Mariamme I's two sons whom Herod the Great executed by strangulation in c. 8 BCE—took a very significant course. He was succeeded by two male children, born to him by Glaphyra of Cappadocia, namely a homonymous Alexander II and a Tigranes I (Chapter 8 §2). These were taken into Herod's care, and though it is unclear to whom their tutelage was left after the king died, it is probable that it was given to Archelaus of Cappadocia (see below). The descendants of Alexander II prospered in the Graeco-Roman world outside Judaea, attaining high social positions and reaching the second century CE—thus being the latest Herodians whose identity may be determined with some confidence.

1. *Alexander II*

When Archelaus of Cappadocia visited Judaea in 13 BCE, during the first dissension in the Herodian court (compare Chapter 6 n. 66), his son-in-law Alexander I had already had children (τέκνα) by Glaphyra.[1] Since Herod's son was married in late 16 BCE (Chapter 8 §2), his two sons must have been born in 15 and 14 BCE respectively—assuming that they were not twins. Following the order of their names in *Ant.* 18.139, Alexander II would have been older than Tigranes I—though in *War* 1.552 the order is reversed. It is therefore an assumption, based on the superiority (as often accepted) of *Antiquities* in such matters, that Alexander II was the first child, born in 15 BCE.

When his father was killed in c. 8 BCE, Alexander II was hardly more than seven, and unlikely to have had any clear recollection of this tragic loss. A marriage arrangement in the following year by

1. Josephus, *War* 1.509.

Herod, apparently between this young man and the unnamed daughter of Pheroras, was soon to be abandoned (Chapter 6 §3 and n. 74 there). His future wife is unknown to us, but she may have been given to him elsewhere than Judaea, either in Cappadocia or Rome. It looks probable that after Herod's death Alexander II and his brother were taken under the care of king Archelaus, first in Cappadocia, and later in Rome for the usual education provided for most client-princes (compare their father and uncles). This may be deduced from three factors:

a) the fear of Antipater II that his quasi-Hasmonaean young nephews would soon be acquiring royal protection from their Cappadocian grandfather.[2]

b) The fact that their mother Glaphyra had been sent back to her father's domain from c. 8 BCE;[3] although later she returned to Judaea and died there in c. CE 5 (Chapter 8 §5).

c) The subsequent history of Alexander's descendants, who were established in non-Jewish environments, particularly in Rome and southern Asia Minor (see below).

Nothing much can be said about Alexander's life, other than that he may have acquired some land in Egypt—he seems to be mentioned in a few papyri from the Arsinoite nome. A lease dated to CE 54 informs us that two estates (situated perhaps in the village of Euhemeria), one belonging to Antonia Minor and another jointly shared with Livia, passed to Claudius after Antonia's death; but it also records that initially they had been inherited from one G. Iulios [Alexandros].[4] This person died probably between CE 26 and 28, as can be determined from two other papyri, and his identity has caused some trouble.[5]

Rostovtzeff suggested that he was C. Julius Alexander I, the son of Herod and Mariamme I, but this was rejected by Fuks on the grounds that Herod's son had been executed in c. 8 BCE. Fuks instead proposed Alexander the Alabarch (Antonia's ἐπίτροπος), but he was also rejected by Parassoglou on the grounds that Philo's brother was alive under Claudius.[6] A closer look at the papyri may partly justify

2. Josephus, *Ant.* 17.16; *War* 1.561.
3. Josephus, *Ant.* 17.11; *War* 1.553.
4. *P. Vin. T.* 10; see Kokkinos 1992a: 73.
5. *P. Ryl.* 126, 166.
6. Rostovtzeff 1957: 672 n. 45.VI; *PIR*[2] J.137; *CPJ* 2, 200-203, no. 420;

Rostovtzeff. If the word after 'Alexandros', in the seventh line of
P. Ryl. 166 is read as 'of royal descent' ([βα]σι[λικοῦ]), he could
after all have been a member of the Herodian family. Now since
Alexander I cannot qualify, the obvious alternative would be his homonymous son under discussion, C. Julius Alexander II. This grandson
of Herod the Great could have died between CE 26 and 28 (when he
would have been in his forties), and he could have bequeathed part, or
all, of his wealth to Livia and Antonia (compare the wills of Herod,
Salome I and Berenice I). This can especially be true if the orphan
Alexander had spent his teenage years in Rome, supervised by the
great ladies of the imperial court (for example, compare Agrippa I).

Alexander II left one son, Tigranes II, whom he evidently named
after his brother (see later). This young man, like his uncle, was destined to become king of Greater Armenia—now known as 'Tigranes
VI'.[7] His selection for this position was made by the Emperor Nero,
after he remained as a royal 'hostage' in Rome for some considerable
time. According to Tacitus, Tigranes's long residence in the capital,
reduced him to a slave-like docility (*ad servilem patientiam demis-
sus*).[8] If his father had died shortly before CE 30, Tigranes, who
would, in any case, have been born not later than in the early 20s
(when his father was already in his mid-thirties),[9] might have stayed
in Rome for his entire life. In CE 60 on his Armenian appointment he
would have been almost 40.

Tigranes II (VI) was sent to Greater Armenia as a result of Cn.
Domitius Corbulo's victories there and the ousting of the Parthians.
His reception by the natives was anything but enthusiastic, and for the
preservation of order he was allowed a garrison of 1,000 legionaries,
three auxiliary cohorts, and two *alae*. Moreover, rulers of the neighbouring districts gained some kind of jurisdiction over Armenian
border crossings, so that they would be on the alert to support
Tigranes militarily. These rulers certainly included Aristobulus III of

Josephus, *Ant.* 16.394; Parassoglou 1978: 17 n. 12; cf. Josephus, *Ant.* 19.276.

7. Josephus, *War* 2.222; *Ant.* 18.140; see Sullivan 1978d: 924 n. 72; Sullivan
1980, 1165.

8. Tacitus, *Ann.* 14.26; also cf. 15.1: *per annos inter mancipia habiti.*

9. One must compare here Alexander II's first cousin, Agrippa I, who was born
in late 11 BCE, and was only four years younger than Alexander. Agrippa I had his
children in c. CE 24, 27/8, 28/9, 34/5 and 38/9, i.e. from when he was around 35 to
50 (see Chapter 10 §2).

Lesser Armenia (a Herodian second cousin of Tigranes—Chapter 10 §3) and Antiochus IV of Commagene, and possibly Polemo II of Pontus, Pharasmanes of Iberia, and Sohaemus of Sophene.[10]

In the following year Tigranes, either out of political inexperience, or seeking local recognition by winning a war beyond his realm, or more likely following a Roman plan of diverting Parthian military attention, began ravaging the neighbouring kingdom of Adiabene. Its king, Monobazus II, immediately complained to Vologaeses I, king of Parthia, who sent Monaeses, one of his nobles, with an army commissioned to attack Tigranes and, with Monobazus's help, ejected him from Armenia.[11] The ensuing battle and siege of Tigranocerta, a well-defended town occupied by Tigranes and his forces,[12] failed to accomplish its goal, and Tigranes ultimately emerged as the victor. However, quite unexpectedly, after the full retreat of the Partho-Adiabenians, Tigranes and the two Roman legions, which had been sent to his rescue, also withdrew from the scene. The Romans spent the following winter (CE 61/2) in a temporary camp on the verge of Cappadocia, and local rumour had it that Tigranes himself was preparing his exit from the country.[13]

In CE 62, when L. Caesennius Paetus was sent by Nero, apparently with the intention of annexing Armenia,[14] it became clear that Rome regarded Tigranes's position as useless—he was reckoned to be a

10. Tacitus, *Ann.* 14.26. Barrett (1979) is right to criticize the orthodox view that parts of Greater Armenia were actually handed over to the neighbouring kings (contra Anderson 1934a: 765; Chaumont 1976: 107 and n. 197; cf. *GLAJJ* 2, 84 n. 2). He is also right that the names of Pharasmanes and Polemo are not to be found in Tacitus's MSS, but are a modern emendation of *pars nipulique*! Yet both kings, as well as Sohaemus, may be implied by the circumstances. Further, Barrett (1977) is probably correct in identifing Sohaemus of Sophene (Tacitus, *Ann.* 13.7; *Hist.* 2.81; 5.1), with Soemus/Soaemus of Emesa (Josephus, *Ant.* 20.158; cf. Frankfort 1963: 188; Sullivan 1978a: 216).

11. Tacitus, *Ann.* 15.1-2; Dio, 62.20.2-3.

12. Due to conflicting data in Strabo, Pliny and Tacitus, the location of Tigranocerta is disputed. Syme (1983) has shown that Tacitus is wrong in saying that it was anywhere near Nisibis. Syme (1958: 1.396 n. 4; cf. Syme 1995: 58-65) has always considered it to be 'somewhere in the upper valley of the Tigris', possibly Byzantine Martyropolis (cf. Jones [A.H.M.] 1971: 225 [Maipherqat]; and Chaumont 1976: 105 [Farqin]). Bivar (1983: 45-46) ignores Syme.

13. Tacitus, *Ann.* 15.4-6.

14. Tacitus, *Ann.* 15.6; Anderson 1934a: 768; cf. Chaumont 1976: 111; Bivar 1983: 84; but see Dio, 62.20.4.

'phantom king'. Paetus, nevertheless, was attacked with disastrous effect by the Parthians and eventually driven out of the country, having had to take an oath that Armenia must be restored to its former Parthian king, Tiridates.[15] Either at this point or a little later, when Paetus was deposed from his command by a furious Nero,[16] Tigranes also lost his throne. In CE 63 Armenia was handed back to Tiridates (officially confirmed in 66), but not before another campaign by Corbulo, for which he entrusted as a commissioner Tiberius Alexander, the famous Alexandrian nephew of Philo.[17]

Tigranes II's fate after his brief but adventurous kingship is unrecorded. His potentially valuable claim to Armenia, no doubt following the precedent of his homonymous uncle, will be discussed later. We should note here that Monobazus II of Adiabene, against whom Tigranes conducted probably the only military operation of his life, ironically was a convert to Judaism. His brother Izates and mother Helena, both staunch supporters of the Jewish faith, had recently been buried in Jerusalem.[18] We should also note the mention of Aristobulus III—for the entire region of Armenia (Lesser and Greater) was from CE 60 to c. 62 held by two Herodian cousins—and lastly, the Jewish background of Tiberius Alexander in Corbulo's last campaign.

Tigranes II was succeeded by a son Alexander IV, the great-great-grandson of King Herod, and perhaps by a daughter called Julia, since an inscription from Falerii in Etruria, apparently dated to the first century CE, refers to a *[I]ulia Tigranis regis f(ilia) Ammia*.[19] With Alexander IV we enter a new phase in the history of the Herods, extending beyond the date of death (CE 100) of the famous Agrippa II, usually thought to mark the end of the Herodian dynasty (see Chapter 10 §5 and Appendix 10).

15. Dio, 62.21.2; Tacitus, *Ann.* 15.16.

16. Dio, 62.22.4; Tacitus, *Ann.* 15.24-25.

17. Tacitus, *Ann.* 15.28; see Chapter 7 n. 95.

18. Josephus, *Ant.* 20.75-76, 95; on the conversion see Neusner 1964a; Oppenheimer *et al.* 1983, 14-17; and Schiffman 1987; on the archaeology see Vincent and Stève 1954, 346-62; Finegan 1992, 314-18; cf. Clarke 1938.

19. *CIL* 11.380 = *ILS* 850; Braund (1984a: 50 n. 29) is right to criticise Mommsen's emendation, making the girl the king's freedwoman, but wrong to think that she would have been a daughter of either Tigranes II (VI) or his uncle Tigranes I (V), because the latter died childless (see below §2); the name Ammia appears in a Jewish context (אמיה) at Scythopolis (*CII* 1372), but it is Greek (*WGEN*, 74).

If my estimate of Tigranes II (VI)'s birth in the early CE 20s is approximately correct, then Alexander IV would have been born not later than the early 50s (for Tigranes's marriage possibly in CE 53, see Chapter 10 §3)—presumably less than a decade before his father was sent to Armenia as king. This date would not seem to conflict with Alexander's consulship at the end of the century (see below), given that at this time the normal age limit was 42.[20] Further he would have been at his marriageable age in the 70s, which can agree with his wife's chronology, as it will now be explored.

Alexander IV married Jotape III (VII) the daughter of Antiochus IV Epiphanes, king of Commagene.[21] This woman had Median blood in her veins. She was a great-granddaughter of the princess Jotape of Atropatene, who had first been fiancée of M. Antonius's and Cleopatra's son, and then wife of Mithridates III of Commagene.[22] Jotape III (VII) was cousin once removed of Jotape I (IV) of Emesa, the wife of Agrippa I's younger brother Aristobulus II (Chapter 10 §4). Also she was sister of Epiphanes, who had been promised to Drusilla, the daughter of Agrippa I, before the girl was given to Azizus of Emesa, another cousin once removed of Jotape (Chapter 10 §5). An elementary genealogical tree showing the intermarriages between the royal houses of Commagene, Emesa and Judaea will be of help here:

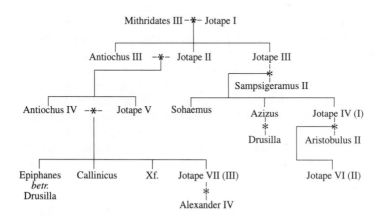

20. For the senatorial *cursus*, see Birley 1981: 4-35; and Talbert 1984.

21. Josephus, *Ant.* 18.140; Sullivan 1978c: 794-95.

22. Plutarch, *Anton.* 53.6; Dio, 49.40.2; 49.44.1-2; Macurdy 1936: 40; cf. Grosso 1957.

Jotape's father, Antiochus IV, was a close friend of Agrippa I, as is evident in the joint influence they had on Caligula in Rome, and in the unprecedented dynastic summit conference at Tiberias.[23] Antiochus, who had at least two sons and two daughters, was deposed from his kingdom in CE 72/73, after a prosperous and long life (ἐπὶ γήρως).[24] His son Epiphanes would have been born in the early 30s CE, if he were to be united to Drusilla (born in CE 38), and mature enough to refuse her in the early 50s (see Chapter 10 §5). Epiphanes went on to marry a woman, probably from the family of Ti. Claudius Balbillus the prefect of Egypt, with whom he had a son, C. Julius Philopappus, a distinguished citizen of Athens and a consul in Rome in CE 109 (thus born c. CE 67). Jotape must have been the youngest child of Antiochus, and one that he had when around 50. She seems to have been born in the middle 50s CE, approximately matching the age of her husband Alexander IV. Jotape must be one of the 'daughters' (θυγατέρας) mentioned in *War* 7.234, and therefore still under her father's control at his deposition.

The marriage with Alexander, who, as we saw, would have been of age in the 70s, might have taken place in c. CE 75, after the royal family of Commagene had settled in Rome,[25] and a little before the publication of Josephus's *War*. In that case it is possible that Agrippa II and his sister Berenice II were present on the occasion, for they

23. Dio, 59.24.1; Josephus, *Ant.* 19.338-42; by 'unprecedented' I mean to exclude occasions when client-kings met to welcome the emperor in the provinces, and/or dedicate joint building projects to him (e.g. Suetonius, *Aug.* 60).

24. Josephus, *War* 5.461; cf. Tacitus, *Hist.* 2.81.1. Antiochus's grandfather, Mithridates III, was a παιδίσκος in 20 BCE (Dio, 54.9.3), and unlikely to have had Antiochus's father before 15 BCE (see Chapter 10 n. 175). So Antiochus could scarcely have been born before CE 5, and thus he would have been up to 15 years younger than Agrippa I (born late 11 BCE), and over 65 years old when he was deposed. Hence he may have died around 75, a few years after the completion of Josephus's *War* in c. CE 76-78 (see next note).

25. Josephus, *War* 7.238-43. The fact that Josephus reports this marriage only in *Antiquities* (above n. 21), may not be taken as indicative of the time in which *War* was completed, unless this happened as early as CE 75! The completion of *War* is dated by Stern 'towards the end of Vespasian's life' (Chapter 7 n. 98). I cannot see the evidence that Book 7 was written under Domitian or Trajan (contra Cohen [S.J.D.] 1979: 87; Schwartz [S.] 1986: 381). Schwartz ([S.] 1986: 374) thinks that Commagene is irrelevant to Jewish history, but one should consider the intermarriage with the Herodian dynasty, and the fact that in Antiochus's deposition there was at least one Herodian involved: Aristobulus III (see Chapter 10 §3).

were in Rome in that year, apparently for the completion of the Temple of Peace, in which the spoils from Jerusalem were deposited (see Chapter 10 §5). Their involvement in this marital arrangement may even be reflected in the names which Alexander gave to his children (see below). The young couple received what would have been a most valuable wedding present from the Emperor Vespasian: a kingdom to rule. Josephus tells us that Alexander was assigned a part of Cilicia.[26]

The name of the place ἡσίοδος as given in the MSS is evidently corrupt and has been emended to νησίδος (that is 'the island'), which is thought to be Elaeussa/Sebaste, where Archelaus of Cappadocia had built an island palace.[27] However, it is difficult to suppose that a kingdom was formed out of such a small place and perhaps the word Κιητίδος may be more accurately restored, to include the land of the tribe of Cietae in Rough Cilicia.[28]

Vespasian's choice was well thought out, but somewhat predictable.[29] Alexander's great-great-grandfather Archelaus I, king of Cappadocia, had ruled over two parts of Cilicia between 20 BCE and CE 17: in the north, the country south of Cybistra to Derbe (that is northern Rough Cilicia); and in the south, the coastal area around Elaeussa.[30] Archelaus's son, Archelaus II, was also given a part of Cilicia between c. CE 18 and 37: in the south, the coastal area around Elaeussa; together with a region in the west, which included Cietis (Kiētis) of Rough Cilicia.[31] Further, Jotape's father Antiochus IV had ruled over part of Cilicia between CE 37 and probably 72/73: the

---

26. Josephus, *Ant.* 18.140. Other Herodians who might have been present in Rome at this time include: Drusilla, her husband Felix, and their son Agrippa III with his unnamed wife, both of whom died at Pompeii in CE 79 (see Chapter 10 §5); possibly Julius Archelaus, to whom Josephus sold a copy of his work (Chapter 7 §2); and perhaps some members of the household of Aristobulus III—for example Herod VII, if he is the same person with 'the *semnotatos* Herod' to whom Josephus also sold a copy of his work (see Chapter 10 §3).

27. Strabo, 14.671; Josephus, *Ant.* 16.332; cf. 131.

28. Wilhelm 1894: 5-6; cf. Jones [A.H.M.] 1971: 439 n. 30.

29. Sullivan 1978d: 924; 1978c: 786, 794-95; 1979: 19; 1980: 1165.

30. Strabo, 12.540, 555; cf. 535; Dio, 54.9.2; *OGIS* 357; see Sherk 1980: 958-59; Sullivan 1980: 1155-56.

31. Strabo, 12.540; 14.671; Tacitus, *Ann.* 6.41.1; cf. 2.78.2; 2.80.1; on Archelaus II see Sullivan 1980: 1167-68; cf. Pani 1970.

coastal strip of Elaeussa and the region of Cietis.[32]

By the end of Domitian's rule this small kingdom had been lost to Alexander IV and Jotape III (VII), apparently as part of a Roman policy of annexation, initiated by Vespasian and dramatically concluded by Trajan. Given that by CE 93 Aristobulus III's kingdom may have been taken away from him (see Chapter 10 §3), as was the case with a part of Agrippa II's (see Chapter 10 §5), it is possible that around this time Alexander IV was deprived of his. For posterity the royal couple seems to have left a coin type of local mint, depicting the king on the obverse and the queen on the reverse.[33] If the portrait is indeed that of Alexander, then he is the last member of the dynasty to have gained a numismatic commemoration.

Beyond kingship, and as regards what it might have been expected that the Herodians could achieve by the end of the first century CE, Alexander IV was the first member of the family to serve the Roman senate in the highest position, and in non-titular fashion. The bestowal of senatorial rights (*ornamenta* or τιμαί) on non-senators is first encountered in the time of Tiberius, but it was a matter simply of the right to sit among the senators on public occasions and to appear in the *insignia* of their respective ranks. From the time of Caligula senatorial rights began to be bestowed upon confederate kings.[34] For example, Agrippa I was given a titular praetorian rank, and later consular rank. Herod of Chalcis was also given praetorian rank, and likewise Agrippa II.[35] The case of King Alexander was different, for he became an actual *consul suffectus* sometime between CE 94 and 110; possibly in 103 according to Halfmann, but more likely at the beginning of this period, considering his age.[36]

---

32. Dio, 59.8.2; 60.8.1; Josephus, *Ant.* 19.276; Tacitus (*Ann.* 12.55) confirms Antiochus's holding of Cietis at least until CE 52, and Suetonius (*Vesp.* 8.4) must mean 'Antiochus IV', when he says that 'Rough Cilicia' was taken away from its 'king' by Vespasian; the coins of Antiochus clearly support this geographical allocation—for the position of Lacanatis in the western *not* eastern Cilicia (*RPC* 1, 3864-67), see Honigmann 1950: 44-46.

33. Visconti [E.Q.] 1811: 310-11, pl. 57.13; Mionnet 1835: 297, no. 570; Babelon 1890, ccxvi, fig. 47; cf. Forrer 1938: 53, no. 175.

34. Remy 1976–77; cf. Braund 1984a: 29.

35. Philo, *Flacc.* 40; Dio, 60.8.2; 60.8.3; 66.15.4

36. *OGIS* 544 = *IGRR* 3.173; see Halfmann 1979: 119, no. 25. Syme (1953: 154) stated that Alexander was not only a Trajanic consul, but one who served before CE 109 (cf. Syme 1958: 2.510 n. 6). He also thought (Syme 1968: 139) that [Fabius

Of course, by this time the Herodian power had been totally shifted away from Syria-Palestine, and with Alexander's descendants, who also enjoyed high offices, we come to deal with people who regarded themselves as fully Hellenized Romans. Josephus, carefully avoiding giving their names, remarks:

> (they) abandoned from birth the observance of the ways of the Jewish land and ranged themselves with the Greek tradition.[37]

Had it not been for epigraphical evidence we would not have known the names of King Alexander's sons. One called Caius Julius Agrippa, βασιλέως Ἀλεξάνδρου υἱός, is referred to as being ταμίας and ἀντιστράτηγος (*quaestor pro praetore*) of Asia, in an inscription found at Ephesus and now kept in the British Museum.[38] He may be the same person who had as 'tutor' Babrius, the writer of fables from Syria or Asia Minor (active at the beginning of the second century CE). Babrius dedicated the second part of his work to 'the son of King Alexander'.[39]

Caius Julius Agrippa, evidently named after his father's second cousin Agrippa II, may or may not have worked his career up to the point mentioned in our inscription before his father's consulship.[40]

Ap]er, rather than [Julius Alexand]er, might be the *suffectus* of CE 103 (contra Halfmann). Indeed, if Alexander was born in the mid-50s as is suggested here, he would have been consul by CE 97. Further, Bowersock (1982: 656 n. 21) stressed that what counts is the city from which one enters the senate, and thus Alexander and his descendants should not be reckoned by Halfmann as 'Judaean' senators. The origins of the Herodian family from the city of Ascalon suggested here, may now also bear on this question.

37. Josephus, *Ant.* 18.141. If the Loeb translation is right, then Stern (in *GLAJJ* 2, 84 n. 1) would be wrong in thinking that Judaism had been given up already by Alexander I's sons. Josephus refers to an abandonment 'from birth', which cannot be applied to them, since they had been raised in Judaea by Herod until about the age of ten. Thus it has to mean Alexander IV and his descendants. Yet, if the Loeb is wrong (which is not unusual), and by εὐθὺς ἅμα τῷ φυῆναι we understand 'as soon as they were physically developed', then Stern may be right—though he avoided giving his personal translation.

38. *OGIS* 429 = *ILS* 8823 = *IBM* 537 = *IK* 15.1537; Magie 1950: 1439 n. 26; 1590; cf. Desideri 1991; Hopwood 1991.

39. Babrius, *Fab.* 2.1.

40. Because Alexander is mentioned in this text as 'king', it must not be assumed that Agrippa became quaestor before his father was raised to the position of consul— Alexander was known as 'king' even after his consulship (*OGIS* 544 = *IGRR* 3.173).

For example, he would not have been able to become public *quaestor* to the proconsul of Asia (in fact endowed with military power, *pro praetore*; perhaps due to an early departure or death of the then *proconsul provinciae*), before he was 24, that is to say in c. CE 100 had he been born around 76. One can only speculate on whether King Alexander's career in the Senate progressed any further, perhaps being chosen to a proconsulship, or whether Agrippa reached the consulship as *suffectus*.[41]

Another son of Alexander IV was probably Caius Julius Alexander Berenicianus, who, like his father, ascended to the position of *consul suffectus*, and went on, indeed, to become ἀνθύπατος (*proconsul*) of Asia under the Emperor Hadrian in CE 132/33. His later position is testified by two inscriptions: one copied in Ephesus by the important fifteenth-century traveller Cyriaco de Pizicolli, and another discovered in 1891 near the temple of Apollo at Clarus.[42] As has been shown by Halfmann, 'Julius Alexander' the ὑποστράτηγος (*legatus Augusti pro praetore*) of Trajan in the Parthian War, is likely to have been the same person as our Caius Julius Alexander Berenicianus—rather than with Ti. Julius Alexander Julianus, presumably *consul suffectus* in CE 117 as supposed by Syme.[43] Dio, therefore, seems to relate how a

41. The list of the proconsuls of Asia under Trajan is by no means settled or without difficulties (Eck 1982; Thomasson 1984: 220-22, nos. 87-102), not to mention the list of the Roman suffect consuls. We may note that the 'Lucius Julius Agrippa', son of a 'Caius Julius Agrippa', known from an inscription in Syrian Apamea (*IGLS* 4.1314), may have been thought to be a grandson of King Alexander—the text even refers to 'illustrious ancestors' who had been honoured by Augustus. But no less than eight inscriptions mentioning Lucius have been discovered, the longest of which (Rey-Coquais 1973: 42), dated to the beginning of the second century CE, names Lucius's main illustrious ancestor as *Dexandros*, ironically not *Alexandros*! Thus no direct connection with the Herods is possible. Yet, the name 'Agrippa' in such a close geographical and chronological proximity (including the discovery at Apamea of an inscription of Agrippa I—Chapter 10 n. 126), may suggest some relationship. However, as Bowersock (1982: 656 n. 21) said, 'we do not know what it is' (cf. Braund 1983).

42. Riemann 1877: 292, no. 80; Chamonard and Legrand 1894: no. 3 = *IGRR* 4.1587; Thomasson 1984: 226, no. 120. In terms of speculation, one would wonder whether a Herodian grip on Asia may remotely be traced to a Herod, who was police magistrate (εἰρήναρχος) at Smyrna in c. CE 155, when the Christian martyr Polycarp was questioned (*Mart. Pol.* 6.2; cf. Eusebius, *Hist. Eccl.* 4.15.15).

43. Halfmann 1979: 141, no. 47; Syme 1958: 511 n. 2; cf. Magie 1950: 1479 n. 30; *SVM* 1, 458 n. 9; Sullivan 1978b: 304; *PIR²* J.142. Note that Halfmann

distant member of the Herodian family captured and burned Seleucia following the orders of Trajan. As an ex-*praetor* at the time, Alexander Berenicianus was apparently awarded the consulship for the period October–December CE 116.[44]

Alexander Berenicianus would have taken the name of Agrippa II's sister, Berenice II, as his brother probably did of Agrippa II. Or else, his name might betray that of his grandmother or great-grandmother; as we saw, we do not know the names of the wives of Tigranes VI or Alexander II. In such a case the question would be whether this Berenice was also a Herodian princess. The only known person who would fit, at least chronologically, is Berenice III, daughter of Mariamme VI and Julius Archelaus (see Chapter 10 §5), but, as has already been assumed, she would have married Alexander of Cyrene (see Chapter 7 §2). Thus, unless an unknown 'fourth' Berenice existed in the Herodian family, it is more likely that Berenice II lies behind the naming of Alexander Berenicianus.[45]

A remote descendant of Caius Julius Alexander Berenicianus may tentatively be conjectured from an inscription of Heliopolis/Baalbek, possibly dated to the second half of the second century CE. It refers to a Tiberius Claudius Antoninus Calpurnius Atticus Julius Berenicianus, who was apparently an important benefactor of this famous Syrian place (within the territory of Berytus, but a separate *colonia* from the 190s CE).[46]

Two other relatives of King Alexander of Rough Cilicia may be found in inscriptions. First, an unnamed female cousin (ἀνεψιὰν) from Perge, but the text remains unpublished.[47] Second, a male cousin ([ἀν]ε[ψ]ιὸν) called [Caius] Julius Severus referred to in a monument from ancient Ancyra, claiming kinship also with other royals including the kings Amyntas and Deiotarus I of Galatia. This Severus must be the consul of CE 155, who became *legatus Augusti pro praetore* of

(1979: 143, no. 53), gives Ti. Julius Alexander Julianus as *suffectus* in CE 126, after he had been *legatus* of Arabia between 123 and 126 (cf. Thomasson 1984: 327, no. 3).

44. Dio, 68.30.2; see Lepper 1948: 85-86 n. 3.

45. A Julia Berenice (*PIR*[2] J.653), priestess of Artemis in the Syrian city of Laodicea-ad-Mare in CE 116/17, who claims royal descent (*IGLS* 1264), does not seem to have had any link with the Herodian dynasty—her claim was probably Seleucid. For a Julia Berenice known from a papyrus, see Chapter 7 n. 99.

46. *IGLS* 6.2784; for the status of Heliopolis, see Chapter 10 n. 124.

47. See Sullivan 1978c: 795 n. 261.

Syria Palaestina in the last years of Antoninus Pius.[48] Surprisingly, therefore, Herodian authority returned to Judaea a century later, in the Antonine period, in the form of Roman governorship, by a remote descendant of the royal family.

Finally, the recent attempt by Astarita to link the genealogy of C. Avidius Cassius (the Roman governor of Syria in c. CE 165) with that of King Alexander (and thus by implication stretch the Herods into the third century CE), is difficult to substantiate.[49] Many of her assumptions are speculative. Thus from the evidence at our disposal, one should be content to trace Herodian blood up to the middle of the second century CE.

2. *Tigranes I (V)*

Since Tigranes I, like his brother Alexander II, was an 'infant' when Archelaus of Cappadocia visited Judaea in 13 BCE,[50] and since his brother would have been born around 15 (see above), Tigranes's birth date has to be calculated as 14 BCE.

48. For the Ancyra text, see *OGIS* 544 = *IGRR* 3.173; cf. Sullivan 1978d: 936-37; for Severus (*PIR*[2] I.574) in Syria Palaestina, see Thomasson 1984: 325, no. 33; cf. Smallwood 1976: 479. It is of interest that an inscription from the tomb of a 'King Deiotarus' excavated at Karalar (about 40 km northwest of Ancyra), refers to him as being the son of another 'King Deiotarus' and a 'Queen Berenice' (Arik and Coupry 1935: 141-42, fig. 10). The buried king has been identified with Deiotarus I's son, Deiotarus II, who would have died by c. 40 BCE, despite a confusion in our sources over his mother's name (Arik and Coupry 1935: 145-46; Magie 1950: 1249 n. 40; 1266 n. 29; 1276 n. 60; Sullivan 1990: 167-69). Berenice is a well-known Hellenistic name, but also one frequently used among the Herods. Although this queen of Galatia, apparently of the first century BCE, would hardly have had Judaean origins, an intermarriage between the two dynasties would explain the future relationship of Severus with King Alexander. In any case, it must be noted that although Galatia proper became a Roman province in 25 BCE upon the death of King Amyntas (Dio, 53.26.3), the fate of various districts attached to it (e.g. Paphlagonia in the north and Pamphylia and Pisidia in the south) is not clear around this period (Magie 1950: 1304-1306, nn. 4-5; Jones [A.H.M.] 1971: 132-33; Mitchell [S.] 1993: 1.63, 91-2; 2.151f.; cf. Ramsay 1893: 13-15, 111).

49. Astarita 1983: 16-18; her conjecture is that Alexander IV may have had a daughter (*sic*), who could have married a Cassius (*sic*) and had a daughter by him called Cassia Alexandria (*sic*), who would have been the mother of C. Avidius Cassius.

50. Josephus, *War* 1.509; on Tigranes I (V) see particularly *RE* 6, 980; and Pani 1972: 55-64.

Josephus maintains that Tigranes's mother Glaphyra boasted Persian ancestry (ἀπὸ Δαρείου τοῦ Ὑστάσπεως) on her mother's side.[51] This woman must had been the first wife of King Archelaus, and probably an Armenian princess—thus explaining how a potentially valuable claim to the Armenian throne was passed on to Glaphyra's sons.[52] Upon this claim, Tigranes (who even bore an important royal name from the region) made an attempt on the throne, as mentioned by Josephus (βασιλεύων Ἀρμενίας) and partly by Tacitus[53] (*Armenia potitus*)—and evidently with Roman support, as testified by Augustus at the end of his personal account of Armenia:

> In the case of Greater Armenia, though I might have made it a province after the assassination of its King Artaxes, I preferred, following the precedent of our fathers, to hand that kingdom over to Tigranes [III], the son of King Artavasdes, and grandson of King Tigranes [II], through Tiberius Nero who was then my stepson. And later, when the same people revolted and rebelled, and was subdued by my son Gaius, I gave it over to King Ariobarzanes the son of Artabazus, King of the Medes, to rule, and after his death to his son Artavasdes. When he was murdered I sent into that kingdom Tigranes [I/V], who was sprung from the royal family of the Armenians.[54]

Since there appears to be no allusion in the *Res Gestae* to provincial and foreign affairs after CE 6,[55] it is unlikely that Tigranes's appointment took place after that year. If this is so, it will be assumed that he would have become a king at the age of about 20. It should be noted that Tigranes was actually 'sent' by Augustus, which might suggest

51. Josephus, *War* 1.476.

52. From another perspective the presence of Jews in Armenia and Nisibis under Adiabenian rule is intriguing (see Neusner 1964b; Neusner 1976; and above n. 18). Faustus of Byzantium (4.55) alleges that a large number of Jews were transported there by Tigranes II during his domination of Syria (83-69 BCE). As we saw by Nero's time the whole of Armenia (Lesser and Greater) fell into the hands of the Herodian Aristobulus III and Tigranes II (VI), and even Corbulo's adviser in the campaign, Tiberius Alexander was of Jewish background. In view of the existence of Jewish communities in the area, there might have been a purpose behind these arrangements (cf. Smallwood 1976: 416-17).

53. Josephus, *Ant.* 18.139; cf. *War* 2.222; Tacitus, *Ann.* 6.40.

54. *Res Gestae* 27. Note that Augustus had to stress that the last Tigranes had not been put forward gratuitously, but *ex regio genere Armeniorum*. It is unfortunate that his Herodian background was left out by Augustus, even though the circumstances together with the evidence of Josephus and Tacitus make it certain.

55. See Brunt and Moore 1967: 6 n. 1; Gagé 1977, 16-23; but cf. Ramage 1987: 13.

that he had been staying in Rome. No doubt his presence there is to be seen in terms of his course of education, which, judging from his age, must recently have been completed. But his reign must have been short. The history of Greater Armenia during this period is obscure.[56]

For our purpose here a bare outline will be useful (complementing *Res Gestae* above), which may run as follows. Tiberius (the future Emperor) was sent by Augustus in 20 BCE to restore the throne of Armenia to Tigranes III, brother of King Artaxes, who had meanwhile been assassinated.[57] Despite Tacitus, who says that 'Tigranes's period of rule was brief', the king died only shortly before 6 BCE.[58] His throne was assumed by his son Tigranes IV and daughter Erato, but without Rome's consent, as can be gathered from their omission in Augustus's account.[59] According to Tacitus, Augustus appointed his own king, an 'Artavasdes', possibly the younger brother of Tigranes III, Artavasdes III.[60] This ruler seems to have lost power in c. 2 BCE, when Armenia came under intense Parthian influence exerted by Phraataces; and because it happened that he died in CE 1, Rome was forced to confirm Tigranes IV.[61] But Tigranes was killed in the same year and his sister-wife Erato resigned; thus the crown was then given by Gaius to Ariobarzanes of Media.[62]

56. Anderson 1934b: 273-79; Pani 1972: 36-64; Chaumont 1976: 76-84; Bivar 1983: 67-69; for the coins see Langlois 1859; Babelon 1890: 215-16, 230, cciv-ccvi; *BMC* Gal., xlii, 101; Newell 1937: 48-50; Forrer 1938: 47; Seyrig 1955; Bedoukian 1968; Bedoukian 1971; Sullivan 1973; Bedoukian 1978; and Toynbee 1978: 132-33.

57. *Res Gestae* 27; Tacitus, *Ann.* 2.3; Suetonius, *Tib.* 9.1 (cf. *Aug.* 21.3); Dio, 54.9.4-5. Velleius (2.94) by confusion mentions Tigranes with his father's name 'Artavasdes'; unless this is a reference to a second appointment by Tiberius after 6 BCE (Dio), when an Artavasdes (III) was made king (below n. 60).

58. Tacitus, *Ann.* 2.3; see Dio, 55.9.4.

59. Tacitus, *Ann.* 2.3, Dio, 55.10a.5.

60. Tacitus, *Ann.* 2.4; see silver coin with reverse legend ΒΑΣΙΛΕΩΣ ΜΕΓΑΛΟΥ ΑΡΤΑΥΑΖΔΟΥ (Gardner 1872: 9; Bedoukian 1971: 138, nos. 4-5; Toynbee 1978: 133, no. 258)—wrongly assumed, I believe, by Babelon (1890: ccvi), Head (1911: 755), Wroth (in *BMC* Gal., xlii, 101, pl. XIV.3) and Bedoukian 1978: nos. 163-64, to be Artavasdes the son of Ariobarzanes the Mede; see now *RPC* 1, 3843, also pointing out that the reference to Augustus as 'benefactor' fits Artavasdes III.

61. Dio, 55.10.20; though here Artavasdes is called 'Artabazus', i.e. as per the Median—yet cf. Strabo 11.15, who also calls 'Artabazus' the native king Artavasdes II.

62. Dio, 55.10a.5; *Res Gestae* 27; Tacitus, *Ann.* 2.4.

Again despite Tacitus, who says that the natives 'raised no objection' to this king, the Armenians refused to accept him and in CE 2 broke in revolt.[63] It was during its suppression (CE 3), that Gaius received a wound from which he eventually died on 21 February CE 4.[64] Before long Ariobarzanes also died, and he was succeeded by his son Artavasdes,[65] whose rule must have been very short, if Armenia was handed over to Tigranes V by CE 6. Tacitus, apparently omitting the reign of Artavasdes the Mede and certainly omitting that of the Herodian Tigranes V (although elsewhere he acknowledges his existence), refers to a brief comeback by Erato, after which time the country passed into an interregnum lasting essentially until CE 18, when Germanicus placed the emblem of royalty on the head of Zeno-Artaxias.[66]

To summarise, it will also be useful to give here a genealogical tree, with the reigns of at least the last members of the native Armenian dynasty, the kingdom of which was held by our Herodian Tigranes:

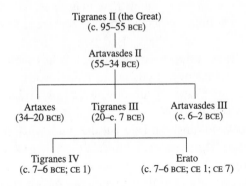

Tigranes II (the Great)
(c. 95–55 BCE)

Artavasdes II
(55–34 BCE)

Artaxes
(34–20 BCE)

Tigranes III
(20–c. 7 BCE)

Artavasdes III
(c. 6–2 BCE)

Tigranes IV
(c. 7–6 BCE; CE 1)

Erato
(c. 7–6 BCE; CE 1; CE 7)

The conclusion must be that Tigranes I (V) became king around CE 6, ruled jointly with Erato in CE 7 (compare below coin discussion),

63. Tacitus, *Ann.* 2.4; Dio, 55.10a.5.

64. Dio, 55.10.19, 10a.6; Velleius, 2.102; *ILS* 140; cf. Romer 1978; 1979.

65. *Res Gestae* 27; Dio 55.10a.7, where he calls him 'Artabazus', the name of his grandfather.

66. Tacitus, *Ann.* 2.4, 56; Suetonius, *Gal.* 1; Strabo, 12.555. In c. CE 12, the Parthian Vonones fled to Armenia and assumed the throne perhaps for a couple of years before he escaped to Syria (Josephus, *Ant.* 18.50; Tacitus, *Ann.* 2.4, 58, 68). Between c. 14 and 18 Armenia may have been supervised by Orodes the son of Artabanus III (recently reclassified as Artabanus II—Bivar 1983: 99), as mentioned solely by Josephus, *Ant.* 18.52.

and was deposed at the latest by CE 12 when the Parthian Vonones assumed for a while the throne of Armenia (see above n. 66). We do not know what happened to Tigranes after his failure to retain his kingdom. Much later we find him in Rome under Tiberius, where he was accused of some kind of a plot against the state (κατηγοριῶν αὐτοῦ ἐπὶ Ῥώμης γενομένων) for which he was executed in CE 36, at the age of about 50.[67] Stern's interpretation of Tigranes's conviction, as 'under the charge of *maiestas*', must be technically correct.[68] It seems that the events of CE 34–36, which included the death of King Zeno-Artaxias (18–35) and the Parthian invasion of Armenia, played some vital role in the execution of Tigranes.[69] According to Josephus, he died childless.[70]

In recent years a few coins have been attributed to Tigranes I (V), but not without criticism. Among the issues usually thought to belong to Tigranes IV, Bedoukian distinguished three types depicting a beardless king, two of which carry the additional word: NEOC. He argued that these coins must represent a 'new' Tigranes, and thus Tigranes V is called for.[71] Sullivan objected to this, for according to him it was not unusual for a king to have used two different portraits, and the word NEOC may refer to a 'restored' rule, such as the one of Tigranes IV.[72] Other objections could have been raised, one serious: the appearance of Erato on the obverse of two of these types—one with and one without NEOC.

None the less, nothing can rule out the possibility that we are dealing with coins of Tigranes V, and in fact there is much to commend it. The honouring of Erato, the last member of the local royal family, would have nicely placated the Armenians. As we saw, a brief return to power by her around the time of the Herodian Tigranes is attested by Tacitus. One of the coins also bears the portrait of Augustus (otherwise appearing only on Artavasdes III's issue), and this depiction would

67. Josephus, *Ant.* 18.139; Tacitus, *Ann.* 6.40; thus Tigranes I (V) was the exact contemporary of Jesus, having been born only two years earlier and executed in the same year as he—see Kokkinos 1989.

68. In *GLAJJ* 2, 73; for a definition of *maiestas*, see Jones [A.H.M.] 1972: 106-107.

69. Cf. Tacitus, *Ann.* 6.31; see Sullivan 1980: 1164-65.

70. Josephus, *Ant.* 18.139.

71. Bedoukian 1971: 138-39, nos. 6-8; Bedoukian 1978: nos. 165-67; see now *RPC* 1, 3841-42.

72. Sullivan 1973: 24, 25 n. 21.

have had to be authorized by a pro-Roman king, which Tigranes IV hardly was. The word NEOC would represent not only a 'new' Tigranes, but also one who was much younger in age. Tigranes V was barely 20, whereas Tigranes IV never ruled long enough to have had the choice to use younger (unbearded) and older (bearded) portraits on his coins.

Finally it is worth making the contrast between the two Herodian kings of Armenia: Tigranes I (V) and Tigranes II (VI). The first, a younger ruler, almost achieved a really central and important status in this remote country, as the *Res Gestae* also claims—but then it all came to nothing; not even one descendant of his (if ever existed) attained any recognition. The second Tigranes, a more mature individual, failed totally as king of Armenia—and yet his family flourished for a long period of time, becoming the only Herodian branch, known to us, to have carried the dynasty well into the second century CE.

Family Tree: *The Descendants of Alexander I*
(36 BCE–c. 150 CE)

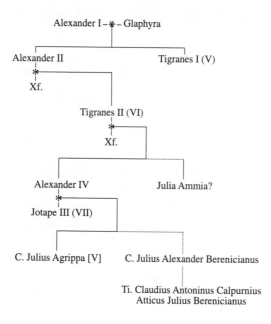

Chapter 10

THE DESCENDANTS OF ARISTOBULUS I

Aristobulus I, Mariamme I's second son by Herod the Great, left five children, born to him by Berenice I, Salome I's second daughter (Chapter 7 §1). These were Herodias (I), Mariamme IV, Agrippa I, Herod (V) of Chalcis and Aristobulus II. In the history of the Herodian dynasty during the first century CE, Aristobulus I's descendants played a leading role, first in line among them being the kings Agrippa I and his son Agrippa II. As noted in the introduction individuals about whom whole books have been published need not be discussed extensively here. Agrippa I will thus be treated fairly lightly, focusing on points where I can offer new ideas, or where I disagree with previous reconstructions.

1. *Herodias (I) and Mariamme IV*

Of the five children of Aristobulus I, who died in c. 8 BCE, we know the precise date of Agrippa I's birth: late 11 BCE (below §2). Since he was apparently older than his two brothers, his two sisters would have had to be born before 11, though obviously not before mid-15 (their parents married in late 16—Chapter 8 §2). The order of the girls in *War* 1.552 has Herodias first, and we are obliged to adopt this view, since unfortunately *Ant.* 17.12 gives no names. Thus Herodias would have been born as early as 15 BCE, and Mariamme perhaps in 14/13 BCE (their father was away in 13/12 BCE).[1]

Aristobulus I's second daughter was evidently named after her famous Hasmonaean grandmother. Mariamme IV is a very little-known figure. In Herod's special family gathering in c. 8/7 BC—in

---

1.   The view that Herodias was the eldest child (contra Hoehner 1972: 154-55) I already took in my article on Salome III (largely written in 1982, but published in 1986); this is now also supported by Schwartz ([D.R.] 1990: 40 n. 5).

which new marital unions were forged—she, then about only six, was promised to an anonymous son of Antipater II of the same age. This idea, however, was soon eclipsed when it was decided that the girl should be given to Antipater himself.[2] Yet even this union must eventually also have failed, since Antipater left Judaea in c. 7 BCE, to return after almost a year to be tried, imprisoned and later executed (Chapter 8 §1).

After the death of Herod one may assume that Mariamme IV was taken to Rome by her mother Berenice I (Chapter 7 §1), where she would have reached marriageable age shortly after the beginning of Archelaus's rule in 4/3 (or 5/4) BCE. We are not informed as to whether she ever returned to Judaea, but if she is to be identified with the enigmatic Mariamme III, then she is certainly the one who married Archelaus.[3] In that case, Mariamme's misfortune will have continued: the ethnarch soon divorced her to marry the notorious Glaphyra, ex-wife of his deceased half-brother Alexander I. This created a great scandal in the Jewish nation at the time (Chapter 8 §5).

If there were anything else in Mariamme's life important enough to be recorded, it would presumably have been mentioned by Josephus in his general account of the house of Aristobulus I in *Ant.* 18.132-37 (despite textual problems—Chapter 7 n. 52). Suprisingly or not, the only member of this family whom the historian chose to ignore here was Mariamme. Nothing more is known of her life.

Herodias will have been about eight when her grandfather Herod promised her to his homonymous son by Mariamme II, the daughter of Simon Boethus (Chapter 8 §4). Herod regarded this union as enhancing the future of Herodias, because she would be marrying the grandson of a high priest (which Simon was); or at least this is what Josephus tells us, interested as he was in the question of priestly descent.[4] From the time of her betrothal in 8/7 BCE, Herodias had to wait until she reached marriageable age in about 1 BCE (ὁπότε ἀφικοίατο εἰς ὥραν τὴν ἐπ᾽ αὐτῷ), for her wedding with Herod III, who would have been by then around 27.

Despite its potential merits, as claimed by Josephus, this union did not last. Herod III was struck out of his father's will (in c. 7 BCE), after he had been named second in line to the throne behind Antipater

2. Josephus, *War* 1.557, 565, 567; *Ant.* 17.14, 18.
3. Josephus, *War* 2.115; *Ant.* 17.350.
4. Josephus, *War* 1.557; *Ant.* 17.14.

II,[5] and Herodias, an extremely ambitious young woman, could not have tolerated living a private life with a commoner.[6] Indeed, as soon as she gave birth to Salome III (μεθ' ἧς τὰς γονάς)—apparently at the beginning of the Christian era—she took it into her head to flout the way of the Jews, and she parted from a living husband.[7]

Josephus's inability—evidently due to the lack of sources—to relate almost anything about the Herods in the period roughly between Archelaus and Agrippa I (Chapter 7 §2), is here laid bare. The historian did not know who the person was whom Herodias married in the early years CE, and he seems to have assumed that he must have been Antipas, because it was with him that Herodias ended her life. But her marriage to Antipas took place only in CE 34 (for its outcome culminated in the war with Aretas of Petra in CE 36), and by having to present Herodias as divorcing Herod III at this time Josephus created an internal problem for his narrative. For centuries this has led scholars to a historical and chronological impasse.[8]

As I have argued elsewhere, we are fortunate to learn from the Gospels that the second husband of Herodias was Philip the Tetrarch (no illusory Herod-Philip ever existed—Chapter 8 §4), whom Josephus then had to make the husband of Salome, Herodias's own daughter:

> The Gospels do state clearly that Herodias' former husband was Philip (Mk. 6:17; Mt. 14:3), that is to say that before she married Antipas, with whom she ended her life, she was the wife of his half-brother Philip the Tetrarch. Luke may omit the name (3:19), none the less the name "Philip" is included in A C K W Ψ 33 565 1424 al sy[p,h] sa[m.ss] bo, and also Luke

5. Josephus, *War* 1.573, 588, 600; *Ant.* 17.53, 67, 78.
6. Cf. Josephus, *War* 2.182; *Ant.* 18.242 and see below.
7. Josephus, *Ant.* 18.136; about the same time also Archelaus unlawfully divorced Mariamme III, possibly identical with Herodias's sister, as mentioned above.
8. For reasons why the two statements of Josephus (*Ant.* 18.136-37 and 18.109-15) cannot be reconciled, see Kokkinos 1986a: 40; cf. Kokkinos 1989: 133-37; for examples of puzzlement over chronology, see selectively Macurdy 1937: 79; Herrmann 1973: 52-54; Schenk 1983; Saulnier 1984; my dating position here has been accepted by Lane Fox (1991: 32-36); cf. references in Millar 1990b: 380 n. 1; Finegan 1992: xliii-xliv, 193; Brown [R.E.] 1994: 1375 n. 49; a reply to Sanders's concern (1993: 286-90) over the order in Josephus's narrative (a problem that needs to be explained further to scholars of theological background) has to be given elsewhere—about the way the historian operates, cf. Chapter 4 end; Appendix 3, etc.

3:1 immediately before makes it implicit that the tetrarch Philip is intended (cf. Origen, *Com. in Mat.* X, 21)... Herodias left her first husband Herod...while he was living, soon after her marriage [in 1 B.C.] and her daughter's birth...to go and live with Philip the Tetrarch, her real second husband. This story caused a deviation from the tradition, and made Salome, rather than Herodias herself, the wife of Philip. The general opinion that Salome married Philip rests solely on a single statement (*Ant.* XVIII, 137), which the present writer considers incorrect... That there should have been confusion, even in the first century, is not surprising, given the genealogical complexities of the Herodian house. The present writer is able to show many similar mistakes in Josephus...[9]

The events around the time of Herodias's marriage to Antipas, as narrated in *Ant.* 18.109-26, have hitherto being poorly understood, mainly due to Josephus's own lack of cohesion, based on his faulty identification of Herodias's second husband. These events, involving Roman, Ituraean, Nabataean and Jewish history (notably including the death of John the Baptist and the crucifixion of Jesus), are immensely important to interpret with accuracy. Josephus begins by presenting Antipas (clearly after the death of Philip in late CE 33) as preparing a journey to Rome, while paying a visit to his half-brother Herod III's house, where he met Herodias, fell in love with her, and asked her to marry him when he returned. His motives are left unexplained and the story at this level does not make sense. What was the purpose of Antipas's journey at this time?[10] Why would he need to visit his brother before departing for Rome? How could he abuse his brother's hospitality by suddenly falling in love with his sister-in-law (then about 48), whom Herod should have divorced some 35 years before, as we have been led to believe elsewhere? Why would Antipas need to wait after the outcome of his Roman journey before he could confirm

9. Kokkinos 1986a: 40-41; for other blunders in Josephus already mentioned, see e.g. *War* 1.264; 1.473; 1.484; *Ant.* 16. 228; 17.294; cf. *Ant.* 15.407 where Josephus by 'Vitellius' must mean 'Longinus'. It should be noted that the Slavonic version (after *War* 2.168) has Herodias as the wife of Philip the Tetrarch (see Creed 1932: 307; cf. Kokkinos 1989: 136).

10. Hoehner's (1972: 130) theory that Antipas would have gone to Rome in the late 20s to ask for permission to mint coins, has been refuted (Kokkinos 1986a: 40). Schwartz ([D.R.] 1990: 47 n. 35) ignoring my refutation—and thus the numismatic evidence—agrees with Hoehner. Saulnier's (1984: 366-71) theory that Antipas went to Rome in 21 or 22 is unsubstantiated, and based on the erroneous assumption that Agrippa I left Rome in 23 (cf. below n. 31). From the evidence at our disposal a previous journey of Antipas can be found only back in CE 6 (Chapter 8 n. 84).

his agreement with Herodias, and what was the position of Herod in all this?

Now, given that according to the Gospels Herodias's husband was Philip the Tetrarch, who had just died childless, the story immediately gains in plausibility. Antipas envisaged the acquisition of his deceased brother's possessions.[11] Tiberius had annexed Philip's tetrarchy to the province of Syria, but only as a temporary measure. He was apparently open to negotiations with any claimant party, as can be understood by his order for the tribute to be held on deposit.[12] Antipas ventured on a trip to Rome (in CE 34) to make his claim, and for his argument to carry weight he felt that he should first strike a deal with his brother's widow at Panias. Herodias readily agreed, but demanded of him that he should divorce his Nabataean wife, a condition which he had to accept.[13] The Nabataean wife learnt of his plans and promptly made her way to her father, who had his own interest in a part of the disputed territory.[14] This is further evident in the action taken by what appears to have been a pro-Nabataean party from the tetrarchy of Philip, which defected to Aretas and betrayed Antipas at a crucial time (in CE 36) when the latter was attacked by the former.[15]

11. Josephus, *Ant.* 18.106. For a confused account of the war between Aretas and Antipas, with my interpretation of Antipas's role (as published in 1980, 1986 and 1989), see Kasher (1988: 177-83).

12. Josephus, *Ant.* 18.108.

13. Josephus, *Ant.* 18.110. The motive of the imprisonment of John the Baptist was no doubt the fear of political unrest, but John may well have given a pretext, by condemning Antipas's marriage with Herodias (Kokkinos 1986a: 45). From the point of view of Jewish Law, it would seem that Herodias was not digressing on this occasion, since she was being married to her husband's brother, having had no children with the deceased. But in the process Antipas divorced his Nabataean wife, and it was this act that John rebuked (Mk 6.18; Mt. 14.4). Herodias had already committed an unlawful marriage, when she divorced Herod III, with whom she had a daughter. As to whether Jewish law would have permitted Antipas to divorce his wife (cf. Jeremias 1969: 370-71), evidently this was not how John and Jesus interpreted it (Mk 10.11; Mt. 19.9).

14. Josephus, *Ant.* 18.111-13 n. περί τε ὅρων ἐν γῇ τῇ Γαμαλίτιδι. Jones's emendation ([A.H.M.] 1971: 449-50 n. 19; cf. *SVM* 1, 350 n. 33; Negev 1978: 568-69) of Γαβαλίτιδι, which I have momentarily trusted in the past, is certainly wrong (Starcky 1960: 914). The correct place, as written in the MSS of Josephus, is the region of Gamala (see Bowersock 1983b: 65-66 nn. 24-5).

15. Josephus, *Ant.* 18.114; cf. previous defections to Nabataea in 22/21 BCE (*Ant.* 15.353) and 13/12 BCE (*Ant.* 16.275).

Meanwhile, in Rome, it seems that the emperor had provisionally approved of Antipas's claim, and this is why he was angered when he was later informed by Antipas of Aretas's victory. At once he ordered the governor of Syria, L. Vitellius (*cos.* CE 34), to capture Petra, but before this mission was completed, Tiberius died (on 16 March CE 37).[16] Reversing the policies of Tiberius, Caligula would have relaxed the tension with the Nabataeans by giving Philip's tetrarchy to Agrippa I, an enemy of Antipas, and probably by offering Damascus to Aretas.[17] Two years later, Herodias, who had now lost her original domain to her younger brother, instigated Antipas to make another journey to Rome for a fresh claim. This proved to be a disaster, for the couple lost all of their possessions and were exiled to Gaul.[18] Herodias thus played a vital part at an important moment in the history of the family.

16. Josephus, *Ant.* 18.115, 120-26; for Tiberius's date of death, see Tacitus, *Ann.* 6.50; Suetonius, *Tib.* 73; Schillinger-Häfele 1986: 52-53; cf. Dio, 58.28.5.

17. Josephus, *Ant.* 18.237; *War* 2.181; Philo, *Flacc.* 25; cf. Dio, 59.8.2; Tacitus, *Ann.* 12.23. Dated imperial coins of Damascus with the head of Tiberius were struck in CE 16/17, 23/24 and 33/34, to be followed by coins of Nero in 62/63, 63/64 and 64/65 (Mionnet 1811: 286, nos. 28-33; Mionnet 1837: 195-96, nos. 12-13; de Saulcy 1874: 36-37; *BMC* Syr., 283, nos. 6-7; cf. now *RPC* 1, 4797-806). Rightly *SVM* (1, 582 n. 25; cf. 2, 129-30) stated that 'in the interim Damascus may have belonged to the Nabataean kingdom' (cf. Peters 1977: 271; Taylor [J.S.M.] 1992). Bowersock (1983b: 68-69), evaluating 2 Corinthians 11.32-33, concluded that Aretas seems to have taken Damascus by force immediately before the death of Tiberius (CE 37) and kept it for 'perhaps less than a year'. Although this does not conflict with my chronology of Paul, who would have been in Damascus in 37 (Kokkinos 1989: 145, 148; cf. Jewett 1979: 30-33), it appears incredible that Vitellius did nothing about Aretas's violent occupation of the city, and that when he marched from Antioch against Nabataea he did not liberate Damascus on the way, but proceeded to Judaea via Ptolemais (*Ant.* 18.120-24). Also why would not imperial coins be struck under Caligula and Claudius, as in other cities of the Decapolis, e.g. Kanatha just to the south (*RPC* 1, 4836-7)?

18. Josephus, *War* 2.182-83; *Ant.* 18.240-55. The journey must have taken place around August in CE 39, since Gaius was at Baiae (Dio, 59.13.7; 59.17; see conclusively *SVM* 1, 352-53 n. 42). The place of exile would have been Lugdunum (Lyons) in Gaul as in *Antiquities* (Braund 1983: 241-42) and not Lugdunum Convenarum on the border with Spain as in *War* (Crouzel 1970; Crouzel 1971; Hoehner 1972: 262 n. 1). The fact that Antipas's brother Archelaus had been exiled to Vienne, the neighbour and rival of Lyons, would have been appropriate: neighbours in ruling, neighbours in exile (but Archelaus may have been freed some 20 years earlier—Chapter 8 n. 85).

We are simply unaware of the destiny of Herodias's daughter, Salome III. As argued above, she would not have been the wife of Philip the Tetrarch, as assumed by Josephus. Nor would she have become the wife of Aristobulus III, if this marriage, which produced three sons, was arranged in the mid-50s CE, at a time when Salome III was probably an old woman (see below §3). Nor, indeed, could she have been the 'young dancer' of the Gospels, as confused in popular imagination, for this girl must have been a younger princess called Herodias II or perhaps 'Herodias II-Salome' (Chapter 8 §5).

The Gospel of Mark mentions a Salome among the female followers of Jesus, who was important enough to be listed together with his mother Maria[mme], and Maria[mme] Magdalene (his κοινωνός according to the Gospel of Philip).[19] In Christian Gnostic tradition, this Salome was seen as one of the most important female disciples,[20] but the name was very common in Jewish society (Chapter 7 n. 1), and no identification with the Herodian princess is possible. Such a connection, however, must not be regarded as totally unthinkable, if only because of the mention of Joanna (Yohannah) the wife of Chuza (Kuza), 'the ἐπίτροπος of Herod' among Jesus' followers; or the βασιλικός (royal official) from Capernaum of Galilee whose house believed in Jesus; or Manaen (Menahem), 'the σύντροφος of Herod the Tetrarch' among the earliest members of the Christian movement; or even 'Herodion', conceivably from the house 'of Aristobulus', whom Paul calls his συγγενής.[21] The New Testament presents extremely

19. Mk 15.40, 16.1; cf. *Gos. Phil.*, Cod. II, 59.7-10; Salome was possibly identical with the wife of Zebedee as in Mt. 27.56, but not necessarily with the sister of Jesus' mother, or the wife (or daughter?) of Clopas as in Jn 19.25, or even with Jesus' own sister as in Epiphanius (*Panar.* 78.8.1; 78.9.6); cf. Meyer and Bauer 1963: 426; Kokkinos 1980, 153-54; and now Bauckham 1990: 44.

20. *Gos. Thom.*, Cod. II, 43.25-34; *1 Apoc. James*, Cod. V, 40.25; also in *Pistis Sophia*; *Gos. Eg.* (*apud* Clement, *Strom.* 3.6.5); *Book Res. by Bartholomew*; and *Gos. Nic.*, Greek B (James 1924: 116); cf. Origen, *Contra Celsum* 5.62.

21. For Joanna and Chuza see Lk. 8.3; and cf. Burkitt 1899; Cadbury 1933: 53-54. For βασιλικός see Jn 4.46-55; cf. the followers of Herod in Galilee (Josephus, *War* 1.326; *Ant.* 14. 450), and the βασιλικοί of Agrippa II from Tarichaea (Josephus, *Life* 149); and contra Mead 1985. For Manaean see Acts 13.1; and cf. Deissmann 1901: 310-12; Lake and Cadbury 1933: 4.141-42; Finegan 1992: 368; his mother may be mentioned by Papias (Hengel 1989: 17, 75 n. 93). For Herodion see Rom. 16.10-11; cf. Chapter 3 n. 75 and below n. 169. Cf. generally the connection of the Pharisees to the female circle of the Herodian court (Chapter 6 n. 77); and

important evidence for the position of the wider Herodian house in Jewish society (compare Chapter 7 §2).

2. *Agrippa I*

In *War* 1.552 Aristobulus I's sons are listed in the following order: Herod (V) of Chalcis, Agrippa I and Aristobulus II. However, as we have seen time and again, it is in *Antiquities*, which focuses on marriage arrangements, that we should place more faith. *Ant.* 18.133-34 mentions Agrippa first (see reconstruction of this passage in Chapter 7 n. 52). That he was older than Herod of Chalcis can also be inferred from a comparison of his and Herod's portraits, as depicted on their coins,[22] and from the ages of their wives and their sons Agrippa II and Aristobulus III (see below §3). Furthermore Agrippa's seniority over both of his brothers may have been suggested from the fact that the three died in this order: first Agrippa, then Herod, followed by Aristobulus—but it is uncertain whether Agrippa actually died by natural causes.[23] Clear proof could have been obtained from *Ant.* 17.14 (omitted in *War* 1.557), had Josephus mentioned the name of the evidently 'older' (πρεσβύτερος) son of Aristobulus I, or had even the projected marital union reported there—between this son and an unnamed daughter of Antipater II—occurred. As it happened, no son of Aristobulus I ever married a daughter of Antipater II, and this early arrangement seems to have been abandoned when many others were.[24]

Josephus informs us that when Agrippa I died in the summer of CE 44 (see later) he was in his fifty-fourth year. Assuming that his fifty-fourth year began late in CE 43, we can fix his birth in late 11 BCE.[25] This date accords well with the fact that his father, Aristobulus I, had returned from Rome only late in 12 BCE, after the important (though short-lived) reconciliation with Herod the Great (Chapter 8 §2). Moreover it accords well with his being named after the famous M. Agrippa,

the discussions on Tabitha (Chapter 6 n. 29) and Saulus (Chapter 7 n. 107).

22. Cf. *AJC* 2, 170.

23. Josephus, *War* 2.219-21; Schwartz ([D.R.] 1990: 39-40) does not consider any of these points, and places Agrippa's birth after that of Herod simply on the basis of *War*.

24. Josephus, *Ant.* 17.18; *War* 1.565.

25. Josephus, *Ant.* 19.350; for this kind of retrocalculation, see Sumner 1967.

who had died in Rome in 12 BCE.[26] We are in position to conclude
that Herod of Chalcis would have been born in 10 or 9 BCE, and
Aristobulus II in c. 8 BCE; the latter was obviously named after their
father, who was executed in this year. Josephus says that the boys
were left νήπιοι.[27]

At the beginning of the history of Agrippa I, as narrated by Josephus, we are told that shortly before the death of Herod the Great he
was being brought up in Rome.[28] This would mean in c. 5 BCE (or 6).
But the boy would surely have been too young for a proper Roman
education. From what we can gather, his father and his many uncles
all went to Rome after the age of 12 approximately, let us say, when
in later Judaism they would have become 'Bar Mitzva'. Also we know
that Agrippa's grandmother, Salome I, together with his mother,
Berenice I, and their entire family, set off for Rome immediately
after the death of Herod (Chapter 7 n. 60). This would seem to be a
more appropriate time for Agrippa to have arrived at the Roman
capital. At any rate, once he was there, he lived very close to the seat
of power, under the supervision of Antonia Minor, and in association
particularly with the son of Tiberius, Drusus (born at the latest 7
October 13 BCE).[29]

The question of how long Agrippa I stayed at Rome is significant
for an understanding of the early part of his career, and it needs to be
addressed properly here. Josephus clearly tells us that Agrippa left
Rome only after he was reduced to poverty, as a result of recklessly
spending the fortune left to him by his mother on her death.[30] Hence
our primary question must be the year in which Berenice I died. Any
other chronological hints given by the historian will be of interest, but

26. Agrippa I's full name must have been 'Marcus Julius Agrippa' (contra Stein
1992: 147-48), identical to the known *tria nomina* of his son Agrippa II (*SEG* 7, no.
970; Puchstein *et al.* 1902, 107 n. 43; cf. *SEG* 7, no. 216; *OGIS* 420; *AJC* 2, 250,
nos. 6 and 6BN). For the close friendship of Herod the Great with M. Agrippa and
the naming of a city and various buildings after him, see Chapter 8 n. 53. Agrippa I's
nomen 'Julius' is attested epigraphically (*OGIS* 428; cf. probably *OGIS* 421), as of
course it ran in the family since the time of Antipater I, the father of Herod (Chapter 3
n. 54; cf. C. Julius Herodes; C. Julius Alexander II, Julius Archelaus and Julia
Berenice II; see further *SVM* 1, 452 n. 41).

27. Josephus, *Ant.* 18.134.
28. Josephus, *Ant.* 18.143.
29. Cf. Sumner 1967: 428; for Antonia's court see Kokkinos 1992a: 59ff.
30. Josephus, *Ant.* 18.145-46.

nevertheless they have to be viewed as secondary material. Indeed Josephus goes on to say:

> Also Tiberius forbade the friends of his deceased son to pay him visits because the sight of them stirred him to grief by recalling the memory of his son.

No real indication is given here as to whether this state of affairs was imposed on Agrippa before or after Berenice I's death. Yet despite this uncertainty, most scholars have automatically assumed that he left Rome in CE 23, in the year when Drusus died.[31] This is a seriously uncritical assumption, the date provides only a *terminus post quem*.

First of all Drusus's funeral took place on 14 September CE 23.[32] Any departure by Agrippa after this event—assuming that his mother had already died and he had already spent all her money—would not have taken place earlier than CE 24. But the point made by Josephus concerns chronology only in a broad sense. His actual intention was to present another obstacle to Agrippa's stay in Rome, that is to say, a long-term one: Agrippa had lost influence in the imperial court since the death of Drusus in CE 23. As for motives ascribed to Tiberius by Josephus, we are not compelled to believe them, certainly not verbatim. Contrast what Suetonius says about Tiberius's mourning:

> He had a father's affection neither for his own son Drusus nor his adopted son Germanicus... even when (Drusus) died, Tiberius was not greatly affected, but almost immediately after the funeral returned to his usual routine, forbidding a longer period of mourning. Nay, more, when a deputation from Ilium offered him somewhat belated condolences, he replied with a smile, as if the memory of his bereavement had faded from his mind...[33]

Now, since upon his arrival at Palestine Agrippa withdrew to Idumaea, and since all subsequent events relating to him belong to the early 30s CE, Smallwood could not find the means to explain why, had he returned in CE 23, Agrippa's life stood still for almost a decade.[34] Would he have locked himself up in the tower of Malatha, contemplating suicide for some ten years? In its effort to avoid this artificial

31. For example, Stern [M.] 1974b: 288; Smallwood 1976: 188; cf. Schwartz [D. R.] 1990: 45; such a misconception can give rise to all kinds of useless theories (e.g. above n. 10).
32. *I. It.* 13.1, 329; *CIL* 6.32493; Tacitus, *Ann.* 4.8-9; Dio, 57.22.1-4.
33. Suetonius, *Tib.* 52; cf. Tacitus, *Ann.* 4.8.
34. Josephus, *Ant.* 18.147-48; Smallwood 1970: 251; 1976: 188 n. 29.

vacuum the new Schürer admitted that Wieseler was 'more or less correct' to place the journey of Agrippa from Rome to Palestine in CE 29 or CE 30.[35] An even later date is surely called for.

Schürer continued by pointing out that the return of Agrippa could not have occurred before the marriage of Antipas to Herodias, an event dated here to CE 34 (above §1). Although a short period (perhaps up to a year) elapsing between Agrippa's withdrawal to Idumaea and his wife's appeal to Herodias in 34, is not excluded by *Ant.* 18.147-48, the implication nevertheless is that he would not have returned before c. 32/33. Such a date can illuminate many points raised here for the first time:

a. C. Herennius Capito, who had been commissioned to recover from Agrippa some considerable debts incurred to the imperial treasury in Rome, began dunning him for the repayment only in late CE 35. Clearly this debt, which baffled Smallwood, is not likely to have been owing since before CE 23, the year when Agrippa left Rome according to the majority opinion![36]

b. Consider what Josephus says about Tiberius Gemellus, the son of Drusus and grandson of the Emperor Tiberius. Agrippa 'had helped bring him up'.[37] But Gemellus was born only in CE 19, he was still regarded as 'a mere child' in 33, and had yet to enter puberty early in 37—in fact he became *princeps iuventutis* only later in that year.[38] Certainly Agrippa did not help bring Gemellus up before CE 23!

c. The involvement of Antonia Minor in the uncovering of Sejanus's conspiracy is reported solely by Josephus. What was his source? On the basis that such a source could not have existed, because presumably Agrippa I would have left Rome in CE 23, Nicols dismissed Josephus's testimony![39] But a source, sprang directly from inside

35. *SVM* 1, 443 n. 4; cf. Hoehner 1972: 259 n. 1; and now Schwartz [D.R.] 1990: 47.

36. Josephus, *Ant.* 18.158; note in 18.163: ἐκλιπὼν χρόνον τὸν συγκείμενον; cf. Smallwood 1976: 189; Millar 1977: 178 n. 19.

37. Josephus, *Ant.* 18.191; cf. 206, 211.

38. Tacitus, *Ann.* 2.84; Dio, 58.23.2: ἔτι γὰρ παιδίον; Tacitus, *Ann.* 6.46; Dio, 59.1.2; Josephus, *Ant.* 18.212; Philo, *Legat.* 23; Suetonius, *Cal.* 15.2; Dio, 59.8.1; on the date of Ti. Gemellus's death (before 24 May 38), see Barrett 1989: 75.

39. Josephus, *Ant.* 18.181-82; Nicols 1975: 53; for supportive evidence on Antonia's involvement, see Kokkinos 1992a.

Antonia's court, can be found in Agrippa I and his slave Thaumastus (ex-slave of Caligula), who later served Agrippa II, until 'old age'. Josephus could have received information from both—he almost certainly did so from Agrippa II.[40] We may confidently conclude that Agrippa I did not leave Rome before CE 32—Sejanus was executed on 31 October CE 31.[41]

As stressed at the beginning, what needs to be determined is the year of Berenice I's death. Considering all of the above, this would hardly have fallen before the very end of the 20s. Would such a dating be compatible with any other indications we may possess? Let us consider a number of points:

a. When in CE 35 on behalf of Agrippa his freedman Marsyas visited Protos, the freedman of Berenice, the latter's transfer to the service of Antonia Minor (after the death of Berenice) seemed relatively recent. Even in CE 36 Berenice's death was still 'fresh' in the memory of Antonia.[42]

b. Berenice had been honoured by Augustus himself, and her mother's property had been left to Livia (Chapter 7 §1). One would have expected Berenice to follow her mother's example, or at least to share her property between both great imperial ladies, Livia and Antonia Minor. Yet among the beneficiaries of her will, we hear only of Antonia.[43] Whatever the circumstances, this would make perfect sense after the death of Livia at the beginning of CE 29.[44]

40. Josephus, *Ant.* 18.194; see *Life* 364-66; cf. Feldman 1962: 333; in the analysis of Schwartz ([D.R.] 1990: 10 n. 13) this source is termed *Vita Agrippae*, for which it is conjectured that Protos may have been responsible. But Protos was a freedman (ἀπελεύθερος) of Berenice I left to Antonia, apparently with some land in Ptolemais, which he would have been looking after, when Marsyas, Agrippa's freedman, met him. Protos would have been serving Antonia (probably as *epitropos*) from Ptolemais not Rome (Josephus, *Ant.* 18.155-57; cf. Kokkinos 1992a: 194). By the same token but the other way round, Thaumastus, slave of Caligula and *apeleutheros* of Agrippa I, served Agrippa I (and later Agrippa II and Berenice II) as *epitropos* of his estate (οὐσία) no doubt in Rome.

41. *I. It.* 13.1, 186-87; *ILS* 158; cf. Josephus, *Ant.* 18.250-51, where Agrippa is said to have known about a conspiracy of Antipas with Sejanus (see below n. 51).

42. Josephus, *Ant.* 18.155-57, 165.

43. Josephus, *Ant.* 18.143, 156, 165.

44. Tacitus, *Ann.* 5.1; Dio, 58.2.1.

c. One of the daughters of Agrippa I, the notorious Berenice II, was born in CE 28/29 (see below), and, as her name betrays, she would have been called after her grandmother—possibly immediately after the latter's death. It may then well be the case that a few months after the death of Livia in January(?) CE 29, Berenice I died, to be followed shortly by the birth of her granddaughter. Berenice I would have been around 60 at that time (Chapter 7 §1).

As mentioned earlier, it seems that when Agrippa I was only four, it was arranged for him to marry an unnamed daughter of Antipater II. This marriage does not seem to have materialized, but if it did we have no information as to its outcome or for how long it lasted. In the 20s CE we find Agrippa being married to, and having children by, Cyprus III, the daughter of Salampsio and Phasael II. This Herodian lady was certainly born after 20 BCE (the year of her parent's wedding), most probably after 11 BCE (Agrippa's birth year), and possibly as late as the end of the first century BCE (Chapter 6 §1). Since it is unlikely that Salampsio and Phasael II went to Rome in the 'exodus' of the royal court which followed Herod the Great's death (Chapter 6 n. 87), Cyprus III may have been sent to Rome later, probably for her education. There she would have met and become the wife of her cousin Agrippa I.

The first child of this marriage, a male, was not born until the early 20s CE. This was probably in c. CE 24, because he was named after the deceased friend of Agrippa, Drusus the son of Tiberius. The Herodian Drusus died πρὶν ἡβῆσαι, so perhaps at around 15.[45] The second child was Agrippa II, born in Rome in CE 27/28, followed by Berenice II in CE 28/29, as we have seen. They were 17 and 16 respectively when their father died in CE 44 (see below).[46] Agrippa I's life at the beginning of the 30s was too unsettled and in sharp decline, thus hardly appropriate for enlarging his family. Indeed his next child, called Mariamme VI after his Hasmonaean grandmother, was born only in

45. Josephus, *Ant.* 18.132; Drusus is omitted in *War* 2.220; he died possibly in 38 (see below). Drusus is mentioned in *Antiquities* after Agrippa II, but he must have been relegated to this position because he died young (cf. ground rule in Chapter 8 n. 71). Drusus would have been older than Agrippa II, not only due to his name, but also due to the fact that there is no space appropriately vacant in Agrippa I's life after the birth of Agrippa II for him to be born.

46. Josephus, *Ant.* 19.354; cf. *War* 2.220.

CE 34/35, when Agrippa was being offered employment at Tiberias (she was ten when he died). Lastly, in CE 38/39, after Agrippa's return to Syro-Palestine to receive the kingdom granted to him by Caligula, he became the father of his youngest daughter Drusilla (she was six when he died). This girl was probably born at Panias, and no doubt she would have been named after Caligula's sister, who died in that year.[47] It may also have happened that Agrippa's son Drusus died in CE 38 (then being about 14), which would have given another reason for naming the last child Drusilla. Thus the dates of birth of his children bear important witness to his movements and chronology. Also it must be underlined that Agrippa had his last child when he was 49, in line with Herodian patterns of becoming a father in a relatively advanced age.

With the marriage of Herodias to Antipas in CE 34, a chance of economic recovery was sensed by Cyprus III, who was supporting her husband in his withdrawal to Idumaea from CE 32/33. Cyprus wrote to Herodias asking for help, and the elder sister of Agrippa responded by arranging for him to become *agoranomos* at Tiberias. But Agrippa soon (οὐ μὴν ἐπὶ πλεῖον) fell out with Antipas one day at Tyre, and by CE 35 he was forced to move to Antioch, that is to the headquarters of his friend L. Pomponius Flaccus, the then governor of Syria.[48] After a disagreement with Flaccus as well, Agrippa resorted to borrowing money to make his way back to Italy early in 36 (ἐνιαυτῷ πρότερον ἢ τελευτῆσαι Τιβέριον).[49]

Agrippa already had hopes of political power from when he was in Rome at the beginning of the 30s—he had spent a lot of money for achieving this goal (ἐλπίδι πράξεως), though in vain.[50] Philip the Tetrarch's death in late 33 found Agrippa penniless in Idumaea. No doubt he would have realized the possibility of advancing a claim over Philip's possessions, but at that time his return to Rome was out of the question. His role under Antipas in 34 would have given him a new impetus for a claim, particularly since Antipas was himself bidding for the disputed territory. Agrippa may also have collected important

47. Dio, 59.11.2; cf. Suetonius, *Cal.* 24.2; also note Agrippa I's coin dated between Oct. 40 and Jan. 41, commemorating both Caligula's sister and grandmother (Kokkinos 1992a: 101-103; contra Burnett 1987: 29-30, no. 6)—see below n. 88.

48. Josephus, *Ant.* 18.148-50.

49. Josephus, *Ant.* 18.126, 151-60.

50. Josephus, *Ant.* 18.145.

information from inside the palace of Tiberias, which could be used against Antipas.[51] The latter must have suspected the former, seeing in him a capable adversary, and this is perhaps why in CE 35 he provoked him into leaving. With the protection of Flaccus, Agrippa may have wished to promote his personal interests, but when he fell out with the Roman too, he was left with only one option: to borrow money, repay his debtors, and hasten to the emperor with his claim— πράξων τι παρὰ τῷ αὐτοκράτορι δυνάμεώς τινος αὐτῷ παραγενομένης.[52] His claim now had been strengthened with an accusation against Antipas, but his attempt in CE 36 was largely unsuccessful, since Tiberius could not be persuaded.[53] Agrippa must have then known that it would only be Caligula who could support him, if and when he succeeded Tiberius. So he openly encouraged the young man. This of course led Agrippa to prison, from which after six months (μῆνας ἕξ) he emerged as a king, upon the accession of Caligula in CE 37.[54] Agrippa was indeed granted Philip's territory (see below).

Schwartz in his recent monograph has attempted to rearrange the events of Agrippa's life, convinced by a source-critical analysis of Josephus's text for this period.[55] In my opinion his chronology fails in cardinal points, creating conflicts with internal data and with no external evidence to support it. Schwartz's claim that Agrippa's return to Rome in CE 36 was not the main one (contrary to what Josephus says), requires independent substantiation, not resort to unwarranted, and in fact wrong, translations. Agrippa arrived in Rome 'a year before the death of Tiberius'—there is no other way to perceive ἐνιαυτῷ πρότερον![56] Tacitus cannot yield support for an earlier

51. Cf. Josephus, *Ant.* 18.250-51—perhaps a letter by Sejanus dating back to CE 31, in combination with the existence of Antipas's excessive armoury; cf. Hoehner 1972: 261; or would Agrippa know about Sejanus directly from Antonia's court, where he was in 31?

52. Josephus, *Ant.* 18.126—the Loeb translation is inadequate; I would freely translate: 'to negotiate some advantage in the presence of the emperor, having found the power to do so'. Professor Millar renders it: 'as some (divine) power was assisting him'. At any rate cf. *Ant.* 18.160, where Alexander the Alabarch lent a large sum of money to Agrippa, presumably having been persuaded of the good chance that Agrippa had to rule over Philip's tetrarchy.

53. Josephus, *War* 2.178; *Ant.* 18.250-51.

54. Josephus, *Ant.* 18.166-204; cf. *War* 2.178-80.

55. See Kokkinos's review 1992d.

56. Schwartz [D.R.] 1990: 50. *Ant.* 18.126 is supported by *War* 2.178, where

journey: the Roman historian will either need (as is familiar by now) to be understood in the light of Josephus or be proved wrong by numismatics or epigraphy.[57] Schwartz ignores the fact that Flaccus struck coins in Syria between October 33 and October 34, at which time according to one understanding of Tacitus he should have been dead.[58] Approval from Syme at this level cannot impress. Despite Syme's defence of Tacitus and objection to the new Schürer (even in a more recent article not mentioned by Schwartz), the evidence as set out here is overall against him.

Agrippa's rule effectively began in the early summer of CE 38 when he set sail for Syro-Palestine to assume control over the lands granted to him in the previous year:

Agrippa's return is placed right at the end of Pilate's prefecture. There is no evidence for Schwartz's awkward model of Agrippa's return to Rome in 33/34, and comeback to Palestine in 36 to collect his family and return to Rome again. This only creates a hiatus in the history of Agrippa between 34 and 36, as admitted by Schwartz ([D.R.] 1990: 53), at a time when information is otherwise abundant in Josephus. Moreover there is direct evidence against this model: Agrippa became the father of Mariamme VI in 34/35!

57. E.g. see recently Kokkinos 1990; 1992a: 37-39.

58. *BMC* Syr., 170, nos. 161-62; see *RPC* 1, 4274-75; for the well-established Caesarean Era, see Downey 1961: 157-58. Flaccus's coin 'Year 82' was struck probably around early summer of CE 34—*note* that 'Year 60' of this era is equated with 'Year 42' of the Actian Era (= CE 11/12; *BMC, ibid.*, no. 149 = *RPC* 1, 4159), and that 'Year 29' of Actium (= 3/2 BCE; *BMC, ibid.*, no. 140 = *RPC* 1, 4155) is equated with Augustus's thirteenth consulship, which began only in January 2 BCE. Tacitus (*Ann.* 6.27) places Flaccus's death after (*exim*) that of Aelius Lamia, who died at the very end of CE 33 (*extremo anni*). This surely implies that Flaccus would have died either in 34 or 35, and that Tacitus due to the nature of his discussion, mentioned him together with Lamia despite the fact that his information had thus to be included under the year 33. Frequently Tacitus functions in this way—the nearest determinable example is in 35-36 (*Ann.* 6.38); cf. also his placement of Agrippa I's death in 49 when Sohaemus of Ituraea died (*Ann.* 12.23)! According to Josephus, Flaccus was still alive in early 35, and this accords perfectly with the fact that L. Vitellius (*cos.* 34) was appointed governor of Syria only in 35 (Tacitus, *Ann.* 6.32; Josephus, *Ant.* 18.96; cf. 18. 88; Suetonius, *Vit.* 2.4). Another argument pointing in the same direction would be L. Arruntius's governorship of Tarraconensis (apparently CE 25–35), but Syme (1956: 20-21; cf. 1981: 129) has managed to neutralize it for the moment. Flaccus was governor of Syria from 32 (cf. Dio, 58.19.5) to 35 (*SVM* 1, 262; cf. Smaliwood 1976: 188-89 n. 30; contra Schwartz [D.R.] 1990: 47, 183-84).

Gaius Caesar gave to Agrippa, the grandson of King Herod, the kingship
over that third part of his grandfather's territory, the revenues of which
were taken by Philip the tetrarch, Agrippa's paternal uncle.

This is what our contemporary source Philo states, together with the
comment that Agrippa received not only the title of 'king', but also
that of 'friend of Caesar', as well as 'praetorian rank' (compare Chapter 9 §1 and below §5).[59]

Josephus in *Antiquities* initially refers to Agrippa's kingdom as
consisting of two tetrarchies, the second being that of 'Lysanias', but
later he mentions 'Abilene' (demonstrably the same tetrarchy) as
having being added (προσετίθει) by Claudius, together with all of his
own (or of Lysanias's?) property in the mountainous region of
Lebanon.[60] This is a problem that has not been recognized, even if
legitimate assumptions can be made. On the one hand, it may be that
Josephus was eager to assign an extended territory to Agrippa at the
earliest stage after his release from prison by Caligula, and that he
was careless in repeating the same information under Claudius. In
favour of this would be *War*, where the grant of Lysanias's territory
is indeed reserved for the time of Claudius.[61] On the other hand, Josephus may be repeating the acquisition of Lysanias's Abilene under
Claudius, only by way of 'confirmation'.[62] With both alternatives
Lysanias could have died shortly before either CE 41 or 37, and the
notorious passage in Luke 3.1 would correctly be referring to the
same tetrarch, as still being alive in 28/29.

59. Philo, *Flacc.* 25, 40.

60. Josephus, *Ant.* 18.237; 19.275; cf. 17.28—for these territories see below
Sections 3 and 5. This tetrarch Lysanias appears to be a younger individual of such
name and title from the time of Tiberius (*SVM* 1, 567-69; cf. Cronin 1917). It could
be argued that the elder Lysanias (40–36 BCE) is unanimously mentioned by our
ancient historians as 'King' (Josephus, *War* 1.440; Dio, 49.32.5; Porphyry, *apud*
Eusebius, *Chron.* [edn Schoene 1.170]), but coin evidence officially calls him (as
well as his father Ptolemy and his son Zenodorus) 'Tetrarch and High Priest' (*BMC*
Syr., 279-81, nos. 2-7; Kindler 1987–89; *RPC* 1, 4768-70, 4774-76)—a good
example of popular use of the title 'King' (cf. Chapter 8 n. 78). So both men named
'Lysanias' must have been tetrarchs.

61. Josephus, *War* 2.181; 2.215; cf. the error in Dio, 59.8.2 where the whole
kingdom of Herod the Great is assigned to Agrippa at this stage!

62. See *SVM* 1, 568 n. 40; followed by Schwartz ([D.R.] 1990: 60, 112) who
takes this possibility for granted, and when he comments on *Ant.* 19.275 he makes
the property in the mountainous region of Lebanon that of Claudius.

But the case may be more complicated, and perhaps very instructive. When Agrippa obtained Philip's territory this may have included Abilene anyway. About Philip we know from *Ant.* 17.319 that he inherited 'a certain portion of the so-called Zenodorus's domain', the latter being a substantial part (conceivably most) of the old kingdom of Ituraea, last ruled by the elder Lysanias who was executed by M. Antonius.[63] The 'portion' received by Philip, evidently consisted of Ulatha, Panias and Mt Hermon,[64] and possibly the attached Abilene, which was also possessed by Zenodorus (Chapter 8).[65] The Hermon and Abilene may well be meant by the extra land of Lysanias (rather than of the emperor) 'on the mountainous region of Lebanon', said by Josephus to have been given to Agrippa by Claudius.

If this Ituraean portion did belong to Philip before it was granted to Agrippa, it will, for the first time, be understood why *Ant.* 18.152-54 says that after the death of Philip a serious argument broke out between Damascus and Sidon, concerning border questions. While Philip was alive, he would have occupied 'a great wall', as it were, south to north, separating the territories of the two cities, that is Mt Hermon (from Panias on the southern slopes to Abila in the saddle to its north). With his demise the two cities were brought face to face, and control over the Hermon passes must have been important for their respective trade routes. Luke's mention of Philip as ruling over 'Ituraea' would also be better explained, although the tetrarch could only have taken over Abilene between c. CE 30 and 33, presumably after the death of the younger Lysanias.

---

63. Josephus, *Ant.* 15.92; *War* 1.440; Dio, 49.32.5; see *SVM* 1, 565; cf. below §3. According to an inscription from Heliopolis Zenodorus seems to have been the son of Lysanias of Ituraea (*IGLS* 2851; see *SVM* 1, 566; cf. Kasher 1988: 157).

64. Josephus, *Ant.* 17.189; *War* 2.95 specifies that this 'portion' was in the neighbourhood (τὰ περὶ) of 'Innanō' (or Inan), emended to 'Panias'; cf. *War* 1.400; *Ant.* 15.359-60, noting τὴν πέριξ χώραν; for the Hermon see Dar 1988; Dar 1993; cf. Dar and Kokkinos 1992. Kasher (1988: 157) is mistaken in thinking that 'all Mount Hermon' was under the control of the Herods, because an inscription of Agrippa I was found at 'El-Mushnaf' in Auranitis. The inscription from al-Mushannaf (Nila or Nelae) on the Jebel Hauran (below n. 92; cf. Smith [G.A.] 1935: 649) has nothing to do with the Hermon.

65. Josephus, *Ant.* 15.344; *War* 1.398-99; Zenodorus had to pay taxes for Abila to Cleopatra, in a similar way Herod was paying for Jericho, etc. (Chapter 3 n. 101 and Chapter 7 §1).

In his source criticism of Josephus, Schwartz has attempted to move *Ant.* 19.293-99 *en bloc* from the time of Claudius back to that of Caligula. This part of Agrippa's history concerns his inaugural acts in Jerusalem: offering sacrifices, sponsoring a considerable number of Nazirites, presenting to the Temple the 'golden chain' received from Caligula, appointing Simon-Cantheras as high priest, remitting local taxes, and naming Silas as commander-in-chief of his army. But Josephus does not mention Agrippa as having been granted from Caligula such powers over the Temple and the administration of Judaea, nor does he even indicate that Agrippa passed through Jerusalem on his way to his kingdom (via Alexandria) in the early summer of CE 38. Worse still Philo, presents Agrippa as ready to sail directly from Alexandria to Syria.[66] Further, rabbinical evidence seems to attest to Agrippa's return to Jerusalem around October 41, on the important occasion on which he read the Torah at the public ceremony during the Feast of Tabernacles at the end of a Sabbatical Year.[67]

Theoretically it is possible for Agrippa to have controlled the religious life of the Jews without possessing Judaea, had this been ordered by Caligula. Later examples of Herod of Chalcis and Agrippa II, who

66. Josephus, *Ant.* 18.238-39, 241; *War* 2.181; Philo, *Legat.* 179.

67. *m. Sotah* 7.8. Schwartz ([D.R.] 1990: 106; cf. 159-62) is far too sceptical about this passage (for rabbinical evidence on Agrippa, see also Derenbourg 1867: 205-19; Goodblatt 1987a; Schwartz [S.] 1990: 160-68). He thinks that questions of identity and chronology cannot be answered. But the main reason for his hesitation is obvious: his chronological rearrangement of Josephus will be ruined, if the Mishnah refers to Agrippa I dealing with the Temple in 41, as does Josephus. The Sabbatical Cycle has been fixed firmly, with only *one* year's difference between the two existing schools of thought (Wacholder 1973; Wacholder 1983; Blosser 1981; cf. Grabbe 1991, 60-63). It is highly probable that Oct. 41 saw the end of a Sabbatical year (Kokkinos 1989: 138-39), and thus it has to be Agrippa I who is meant in the Mishnah. The following Sabbatical year ending in Oct. 48, does not conform with Agrippa II, who remained in Rome until 53, nor do those ending in Oct. 55 and 62, and no important 'return' of his from Rome is on record before the destruction of the Temple in 70 (see below §5). A return of his can be assumed when he appointed a new high priest, Ishmael son of Phiabi (*Ant.* 20.179). This is conventionally dated to c. 59 (but read 58), and significantly interlocks with Agrippa's visit to Caesarea when Paul was kept there (see Appendix 8). Of course Schwartz ([D.R.] 1992: 238) elsewhere puts Ishmael's appointment as early as 49, but he is mistaken again: for example when Paul is arrested in Jerusalem in c. 56 (no earlier than 55 on any historical chronology), the high priest is still Ananias son of Nebedaeus (Acts 23.1-5; 24.1; contra Goodman 1987: 142 n. 5; 146).

were so empowered, are very clear (see later). We have also seen how Antipas was a leading protector of the Temple's interests at the time of Pilate (Chapter 7 nn. 80 and 82). Schwartz's move even has apparent attractions.[68] The golden chain, which had been given to Agrippa by Caligula, would have had to be dedicated to the Temple in CE 41— somewhat oddly after the hurtful experience of the emperor's attempt to erect his statue therein. Simon-Cantheras the high priest might be identified with 'Simon the Just' of the rabbinical sources, who announced Caligula's death, and thus his appointment by Agrippa would have been made before CE 41.[69] Silas, who had nursed Agrippa while he was imprisoned, would have been rewarded with a military command as soon as the latter was released and assumed royalty, rather than several years after.

Yet the golden chain of Caligula may adequately be explained as a kind of 'compensation' offered by Agrippa for the ex-emperor's attempted evil deed. Also even if there were a way to identify Simon-Cantheras with 'Simon the Just', it is not clear that the latter was high priest at the time of the episode related in the rabbinical sources. Furthermore, Agrippa's military machine would have become substantial enough only after his acquisition of Judaea in CE 41, and Silas, who may already have enjoyed the position of *eparchos* at Panias, would then have been promoted to the *eparchia* of Agrippa's 'entire' (παντὸς) army.[70]

Again Agrippa's serious concern about Caligula's idea of erecting his statue in the Temple in CE 40, would seem to favour Schwartz's thesis about Agrippa's association with Jerusalem at an early stage.[71]

68. Schwartz [D.R.] 1990: 12-13.

69. *b. Sotah* 13.6; *y. Sotah* 9.14 (24b); *Meg. Ta'an., scholion* on 22 Shebat (Lichtenstein 1931–32, 344-45; cf. Zeitlin 1919–20: 260-61).

70. See Kokkinos 1990, *passim*. Silas is thought to be from the Babylonian colony in Batanaea (Schwartz [D.R.] 1990: 70—reference to Applebaum); cf. 'Silas the Babylonian', a deserter from Agrippa II's army (below n. 241). Kasher (1988: 187-92) argues that our Silas was 'Ituraean'. His choice would be limited to Mt Hermon and Abilene, because Silas's consignment to captivity was 'to his homeland' (πατρὶς), which was under the control of Agrippa I (Josephus, *Ant*. 19.320). Cf. Paul's companion (Acts 15.22-41; 16.37-38; 1 Thess. 1.1; Mussies 1994: 249-51); and that of Josephus (*War* 2.616; *Life* 89-90, 272).

71. Josephus, *Ant*. 18.296-97; cf. 15.405 where stress is laid on the priestly vestments. Nevertheless Agrippa's detailed acquaintance with the Temple and its functions as represented by the letter attributed to him by Philo (*Legat*. 276-329),

But since Agrippa did not actually become king of Judaea before CE 41, he would surely have been unable to interfere with the political administration of the country, namely the remission of taxes in a Roman province. Schwartz's reply is that Judaea was not a Roman province under Caligula.[72] But what was it then? Even if it had temporarily been left leaderless, the area would legally have been attached to Syria, and would hence have been subject to Roman rule—like Philip's tetrarchy between 33 and 37 (despite a provisional approval of Antipas's plan by Tiberius discussed above). Remission and collection of taxes (as well as the minting of coins) would have continued to be the prerogative of Rome, regardless of whether, like Philip's tetrarchy, the tribute could have been held 'on deposit'—Agrippa could simply not intervene. Moreover, Josephus supplies us with the names of two Roman officers responsible for Judaea in the period CE 37–41. Whatever one may say about Marcellus (ἐπιμελητὴς) and Maryllus (ἱππάρχης), whether they are two different people or one, whether one was a temporary governor and the other his replacement or subordinate, or even if they are little more than cyphers, the fact remains that one cannot make them disappear, as Schwartz tries to.[73]

In conclusion, Agrippa I's association with Judaea under Caligula seems to have been negligible. In any case the king did not stay in

---

cannot be taken seriously, since it does not represent Agrippa's but Philo's own knowledge, as accepted by Schwartz ([D.R.] 1990: 178-80, 200-202; cf. Zeitlin 1965–66). Philo had visited Jerusalem around that time (Chapter 3 and n. 112).

72. Schwartz [D.R.] 1990: 63, cf. 65.

73. Josephus, *Ant.* 18.89, 237; Schwartz [D.R.] 1990: 62-66; Marcellus will be discussed elsewhere. Support for a leaderless state of Judaea under Caligula cannot be gained by Schwartz's rearrangement of Acts 6–7 (cf. Scharlemann 1968: 109-12), even if these chapters are actually misplaced. Paul was converted to Christianity in the midsummer of 37 (above n. 17), and normal understanding would place Stephen's death slightly before that date. Schwartz ([D.R.] 1990: 72 n. 21) resorts to the disassociation of Paul from the episode of Stephen, but if one is allowed to do this (is Acts 22.20 also redactional?), then Stephen may be dated to any time before Herod of Chalcis died (cf. a 'Stephen' under Cumanus in *War* 2.228; *Ant.* 20.113) and not only between 39-41, where Schwartz wants him. He states (1990: 72) that Acts provides only a general chronology between chapters 1 and 12, i.e. from Jesus' death to Agrippa's. But its framework seems to be narrowed down in 4.6, where at least three 'past' high priests are mentioned: Annas, Caiaphas and John/Jonathan (cf. Barag and Flusser 1986: 42-43). The latter was in office between Dec. 36 and Apr. 37, in harmony with a late date for the crucifixion and conversion of Paul.

Syro-Palestine for more than a year, that is from CE 38 to 39.[74] During this period he concentrated on establishing his rule at Panias, exactly where he minted his first coins.[75] Since there is now consensus on the typically Hellenistic 'Tishri' reckoning of regnal years by the Herods, we may readily date the four types of Agrippa's 'Year 2' coins sometime between October 37 and October 38.[76] No reason here to assume that the minting would have been made *in absentia* of the

74. When Agrippa left Rome at the beginning of June CE 38 (below n. 81), he promised to return as soon as his kingdom had been organized (Josephus, *Ant.* 18.238). When Antipas with Herodias met Caligula around Aug. 39 (above n. 18), according to *War* 2.183 Agrippa also went to Rome to accuse the couple, but according to *Ant.* 18.247 he sent his freedman Fortunatus while promising again to come personally in a short while. Did Agrippa go to Rome in Aug. 39 or did he go later? Schwartz ([D.R.] 1990: 57) resorts to *Ant.* 19.351 (a problematic verse) which he misinterprets: if anything Josephus there puts the acquisition of Antipas's territory by Agrippa some time after 18 March 40. But Dio (59.24.1) mentions Agrippa being with Caligula in the winter of 39/40, and since Suetonius (*Cal.* 17) testifies that the emperor entered the consulship in Jan. 40 at Lugdunum, then the obvious conclusion would be that Agrippa followed Caligula in Gaul. Antipas and Herodias will have been escorted to the place of their exile! Agrippa may well be among the emperor's *amici* mentioned by Suetonius in this expedition (*Cal.* 45.1; cf. Dio, 59.21.2). SVM (1, 395 n. 70; 397 n. 180) doubts Dio on the basis that Philo (*Legat.* 261) has Agrippa apparently in the late summer of 40 knowing nothing about Caligula's order to raise his statue in the Temple at Jerusalem. Unless one discounts Philo (as does Schwartz) the explanation would be that the outrageous plan was concealed from Agrippa while at Gaul (for reasons easy to understand). Caligula's order would have been issued upon departure from Italy in the autumn of 39 (Philo, *Legat.* 189-90; Josephus, *Ant.* 18. 261-62), in time for Agrippa to be unaware until they returned in the late summer of the following year. It must be noted that Agrippa was not in Palestine at the close of 39 or early in 40 when Petronius sent a letter from Antioch to inform the Jews of Caligula's plan (Philo, *Legat.* 222-24), and he was certainly absent in the spring (ἔαρ) of 40 when the Herodian delegation met with Petronius at Tiberias (*Ant.* 18.270, 273-76; cf. Smallwood 1970: 288). At any rate, Agrippa stayed at Rome until the late summer of 41, many months after Caligula's death and the accession of Claudius (Josephus, *Ant.* 19.236ff.; 19.286; *War* 2.206ff.; cf. Dio, 60.8.2). Incidentally, Agrippa's journey to Italy and Gaul (39/40) may be reflected in the curious information of Philip of Thessalonica concerning the tapestry (depicting the lands and seas of the Roman Empire), made for Caesar by Queen Cyprus III (Gow and Page 1968: 300, no. VI; see *GLAJJ* 1, 375-76, no. 154).

75. *AJC* 2, 52; Meshorer 1990–91: 121-22, nos. 1-4; cf. Burnett 1987: 27-28, nos. 1-3; *RPC* 4980; for two claimed sculptural portraits of Agrippa, see Chapter 3 n. 200.

76. See van Bruggen 1978; Stein 1981; Edwards 1982; *AJC* 2; Burnett 1987.

king,[77] because he could have authorized it as soon as he arrived at his kingdom in c. mid-July 38—and still within his second year. Of the three types which carry effigies, the first depicts Caligula and his three sisters, Julia Livilla, Drusilla and Agrippina the Younger. The second type shows on the obverse the crowned portrait of Agrippa, and on the reverse, as is generally accepted, his young son Agrippa II (about 11 at the time) riding a horse. The third displays Agrippa's wife, Queen Cyprus III. Obviously this is a series of heavily Romanized coins minted by a grateful client king, which serves to underline not only how flattery towards the emperor for his choice to grant a throne had to be made visible, but also how Agrippa's personal background was tightly bound to Rome. Burnett has recently pointed out that these coins are actually adaptations of Roman *sestertii* and *dupondii* struck in Rome in CE 37/38, and never circulated east of the Adriatic.[78] Indeed it looks as if Agrippa had brought with him some newly minted specimens, which he copied at the first available moment.

These coins represent important evidence and it may be of benefit to register a couple of ideas here. How certain is the depiction of the young Agrippa II riding a horse? The accompanying legend according to its editors read in the genitive ΑΓΡΙΠΠΑ ΥΙΟΥ ΒΑΣΙΛΕΩΣ, in contrast to the nominative on the obverse, ΒΑΣΙΛΕΥΣ ΑΓΡΙΠΠΑΣ. Evidently the coin meant to 'belong' to the son. The *dupondius* upon which this type is based shows two young men riding horses, commemorating Caligula's dead brothers, Nero Caesar and Drusus Caesar.[79] But it is possible for the inscription on the Panias coin to be understood as referring to the dead son of Agrippa I, who may have died at around the age of 14 precisely in CE 38 (see above). His name was Drusus too. The inscription must surely be accepted as reading ΥΙΟΥ ΒΑΣΙΛΕΩΣ ΑΓΡΙΠΠΑ, and thus the name of the son would not have been included. The order of words in such a tiny circular legend has to be flexible—in fact the order suggested here is a better grammatical construction, as well as beginning directly above the head of the young man in whose honour the coin was struck. Of course Agrippa II was depicted on later coins of his father when, after the

77. Stein 1981: 25; followed by Schwartz [D.R.] 1990: 73; but cf. Burnett 1987: 28.

78. Burnett 1987: 28.

79. *CRE* Cal., no. 44; cf. nos. 70-71.

death of the misfortuned Drusus, he became the sole heir to the throne (see below).

Should not Agrippa I on this occasion have commemorated Drusilla in a more distinct way, being the most 'beloved' sister of Caligula who happened to die on 10 June CE 38?[80] The news of her death must have reached Alexandria by between 20 and 23 June. Mourning for her was still current (presumably at the beginning of July) when the riots that followed Agrippa's visit had spread all over the city. The king would have arrived in Egypt, and stayed there for a few days, around mid-June.[81] He must have been informed about Drusilla, at the latest by the time he came to his kingdom. Did Agrippa choose not to represent her individually, but among her sisters (following the Roman *sestertius*), thus avoiding stressing her demise out of consideration for Caligula who was apparently greatly hurt by it? Of course Drusilla together with Antonia Minor (who died in 37), appears on a later coin of Agrippa I (see below).

The prime aim which seems to have occupied Agrippa's mind in CE 38/39 was the enforcement of civil order in the areas under his jurisdiction. A fragmentary inscription found at Kanatha (al-Qanawât) on the western slopes of Jebel Hauran, the only settlement of Auranitis in the Herodian period enjoying city status, is a part of a proclamation issued by Agrippa I (rather than by his son) in his effort to take steps against brigandage. It suggests that there had been considerable local disturbances (apparently during the interregnum which followed Philip's death) by robbers with 'beastly habits' who 'lurked in dens'.[82] The implied topography hints particularly at the area called Trachonitis immediately to the north of Kanatha. This lava plateau, modern El-Leja (translated as 'a refuge'), which is full of caves, was used as a hiding place by various gangs not only in antiquity (the reason why

80. *PIR*[2] J.664.

81. Philo, *Flacc.* 56. Agrippa left Rome in the second year of Caligula, which began on 18 March 38 (Josephus, *Ant.* 18.238; Schillinger-Häfele 1986: 53). The shipping season had started from 10 March, but the Emperor advised Agrippa to wait for the Etesians (ἐτησίαι), modern *meltemia* (in Greek/ Turkish), the yearly Mediterranean northerly winds from June to September (violent in August), which would have taken him to Alexandria within two weeks (Philo, *Flacc.* 26; see Casson 1971: 272-73, 297-99; Rathbone 1986: 103; cf. Kokkinos 1992a: 198-99; contra Smallwood 1970: 17, 283-84; Schwartz [D.R.] 1990: 55 n. 66).

82. *OGIS* 424 = *IGRR* 3.1223; cf. Jones [A.H.M.] 1931b: 269; Isaac 1984: 181; for Kanatha see *SVM* 2, 140-42; Sartre 1981.

Herod the Great had settled an Idumaean army there—see below
n. 224) but also in modern times. A handbook of the 1920s quoted by
Isaac describes it well:

> The passes, fissures, and caverns in this black and desolate region are so
> inaccessible that the Bedouin robbers by which El-Leja has been infested
> for centuries, continue to find secure refuge from the law... The secrets
> of internal communication are carefully guarded by the inhabitants...[83]

Strabo referring to Ituraea and Arabia, mentions the help needed by
the farmers living in the plains (such as in Batanaea), when they were
harassed by the Arabian brigands who used strongholds (such as in
Auranitis and Trachonitis) as bases of operation (see further, below
§5).[84]

Another inscription from Auranitis which may be attributed to
Agrippa I is a block of basalt found in the forecourt of the temple of
Baalshamin at Seeia (Si'a).[85] Unfortunately only his name and title
have been preserved, but nevertheless it is important for being the
only semitic text on stone for that king. Further it illustrates a continuous Herodian presence in this area from the time of Herod the Great
and that of Philip the Tetrarch, both of whom are attested epigraphically at Si'a (Chapter 3 n. 195 and Chapter 8 n. 125).

Upon Antipas's and Herodias's exile in CE 39, Agrippa I's domain
was substantially enlarged. The addition to it of Galilee and Peraea
must for the first time have made Agrippa realize that control over
the entire territory once held by his grandfather, Herod the Great,
was a possibility within his reach.[86] If Agrippa joined Caligula's
expedition to Gaul in the autumn of CE 39 to late summer CE 40, and
if indeed during this period he was kept uninformed about the
emperor's sacrilegious plan against the Jewish Temple (above n. 74),
his hopes for further advancement would have been kept high. Such
hopes, however, must have been shattered when the truth was revealed
to him. But Agrippa did not give up entirely, since in the autumn of
40 he seems to have succeeded in either averting or simply postponing

---

83. Isaac 1984: 176 n. 19.

84. Strabo 16.2.18; cf. 16.2.20; also *SVM* 1, 563 n. 17; Shatzman 1991: 170-
74, 293-8; Isaac 1992a: 62-66; Millar 1993b: 36-37.

85. Littmann 1914: 81, no. 102.

86. Josephus, *War* 2.183; cf. 2.95; *Ant.* 18.252; cf. 17.188, 318; further cf.
Philo, *Legat.* 326.

Caligula's original intention.[87] His success may be reflected in the order which he gave from Rome to the authorities in Palestine (at Panias or Tiberias which was now also under his rule) to issue new coins on his behalf as a further compliment to Caligula. Agrippa's 'Year 5' coins were minted between October 40 and January 41. One type depicts the emperor on the obverse and his father Germanicus on the reverse. A second type commemorates Antonia Minor, the grandmother of Caligula and 'second mother' of Agrippa, and Drusilla the emperor's sister. A third type carries the portrait of Agrippa on the obverse, and his wife Cyprus surprisingly *standing* to front on the reverse. A fourth type was dedicated especially to Agrippa's homonymous young son, now about 14, and probably when his formal education began in Rome (see below §5).[88]

The murder of Caligula on 24 January CE 41 and the crucial involvement of Agrippa in the accession of Claudius, created the right circumstances for Agrippa to obtain all that he had ever wished for.[89] Claudius's donation to him was announced by an edict, which was engraved on bronze tablets and deposited in the Capitol. Josephus says of Claudius:

> ...he both confirmed the rule of Agrippa, which Gaius had presented to him, and delivered a panegyric on the king. He also added to Agrippa's dominions all the other lands that had been ruled by King Herod, his grandfather, namely Judaea and Samaria... and he celebrated a treaty with Agrippa in the middle of the Forum in the city of Rome.[90]

Dio adds that Claudius bestowed consular status on Agrippa and he invited him (together with his brother—see below §3) to enter the

87. On Caligula and the Temple, see Smallwood 1957; *SVM* 1, 394-97; Bilde (1978); Schwartz ([D.R.] 1990: 77-89).

88. Meshorer 1990–91: 122, nos. 5-8; cf. Burnett 1987: 28-31, nos. 4-7; cf. above n. 47. Burnett (1987: 30) thinks that these coins were minted at Panias, while Meshorer (*AJC* 2, 54, 63) feels that they should belong to Tiberias on the basis of their weight. Burnett (1987: 26 n. 4) is right that two other issues thought by Meshorer (*AJC*, 278, nos. 2-3) to have been struck under Agrippa I are Thracian in origin and should be excluded (cf. Meshorer 1990–91: 132). Further the coin thought by Meshorer (*AJC* 2, 278-79, no. 4) to have been minted by the city of Tiberias under Agrippa I, has now correctly been attributed to Agrippa II (Qedar 1989).

89. Josephus, *Ant.* 19.236ff.; *War* 2.206-13; Dio, 60.8.2; cf. Schwartz [D.R.] 1990: 91-92.

90. Josephus, *Ant.* 19.274-75, 362; *War* 2.215-16.

senate and express his thanks in the Greek language.[91]

Agrippa's reorganization of Antipas's territory would thus have coincided with that undertaken in Judaea and Samaria, on his return to Palestine in the early autumn of CE 41. This return was marked by what can be described as a triumphal entry into Jerusalem, followed by the various activities already discussed. The event also came to fulfil certain vows which would have been taken by political followers of the Herodian dynasty, particularly outside Judaea. One such follower (his name is not preserved) from al-Mushannaf (Nila or Nelae) in Auranitis, set up an inscription to express his gratitude to Zeus and to Apollo for bringing Agrippa back safely.[92] The mention of πάτριος θεὸς ᾿Απόλλων (if this reading is accepted) is interesting, in that it might suggest that the dedicator knew that his and Agrippa's progenitors shared the same god (Chapter 3 §4).

91. Dio, 60.8.2; see Chapter 9, nn. 34-35. According to Josephus (*Ant.* 19.278-91), Agrippa also played an important role in the issuing of two edicts (CE 41 and 42) by Claudius protecting the rights of the Jews in Alexandria and the Diaspora at large (see Kasher 1985: 310-26; cf. Kucharczak 1980; also below n. 95). Schwartz ([D.R.] 1990: 99-106) declares them inauthentic, the first more than the second. While he may be right about the first, since it seems to be an 'abstract' edition of Claudius's famous letter to Alexandria (*CPJ* 2, 36-55, no. 153), he is wrong about the second, which he does not realize dates to 42. There is of course no implication that Agrippa stayed in Rome until the second edict was circulated. When Josephus says of him that μετὰ τάχους ὑπέστρεψεν (*Ant.* 19.293), it can only mean immediately after the issuing of the first edict in the late summer of 41 (which should approximately also be the date of Claudius's letter—cf. Bell 1924: 19). One can sense the urgency on the part of Schwartz to minimize Claudius's friendliness towards the Jews at the beginning of his reign, because Schwartz had just accepted Luedemann's (1984: 164-71) untenable argument that Claudius expelled the Jews from Rome in 41. Our primary source, Acts 18.2, decisively dates this event to 49/50 (see Jewett 1979: 36-38).

92. *OGIS* 418; cf. Prentice 1908: 298, no. 380. Some doubt may remain as to whether this text actually refers to Agrippa I, because there are two other ὑπὲρ σωτηρίας inscriptions, clearly connected with Agrippa II (below n. 214). But this is not decisive. Also κύριος does not necessarily indicate Agrippa II (even though common in his texts), since it is also found in connection with Herod the Great (*OGIS* 415) and Philip the Tetrarch (למרנא—Chapter 8 n. 125) from the general area. On balance, and due to the emphasis on the ἐπάνοδος, the al-Mushannaf inscription has as good a chance of belonging to Agrippa I as any of the seven attributed here to that king. This text determines how far east the *meris* of Auranitis went.

As has been rightly noted by Schwartz, there is no good reason for modern scholars to portray Agrippa I as having had strong Jewish inclinations.[93] Perhaps it may be allowed that he appeared to be more Jewish than his predecessors, largely due to the burden he carried of having descended from the Hasmonaeans through his father's mother's side. This fact, together with Agrippa's clear support at Rome of the Jewish cause, would have given the initiative to Josephus in *Ant.* 19.331 to proclaim him as a practising Jew. But the Hellenized non-Jewish roots which Agrippa inherited, both from his father's father's side and directly from his own mother, dominated his life. This 'foreign' background of his, was heavily blended with his totally Roman upbringing, as well as his relentless focus on Italy throughout his life.

Agrippa may look as if he understood Hebrew when the news of the death of Tiberius was brought to him in his Roman prison, and even knew how to read Hebrew in the Temple, but this would have been a formal and elementary step taken by all Herodian princes. His specific education was undoubtedly in Latin and Greek, which he spoke in the Senate when he thanked Claudius.[94] Agrippa is also represented as being castigated by his accuser Isidorus as a 'cheap Jew' (Ἰουδαίου τριωβολείου) for supporting the despised Jews of Alexandria, but Agrippa was a king over Jews and Isidorus's speech was merely polemical. Isidorus did not hesitate to accuse Claudius himself of being the cast-off son ([ἀπό]βλητος) of Salome I (or Berenice I?).[95] By contrast one must note that even Carabas, a lunatic in Alexandria, and his troublemakers, knew the king's real background: Agrippa was 'Syrian by birth' (καὶ γένει Σύρον), that is of Syro-Phoenician ancestry, as has already been put forward here.[96]

93. Schwartz [D.R.] 1990: 170-71, cf. 130-34.
94. Josephus, *Ant.* 18.228; *m. Soṭ.* 7.8; Dio, 60.8.3.
95. *P. Cairo* 10448; for references and discussion see Chapter 7 n. 64. The theory that the trial of Isidorus and Lampo dates to 52/53 and refers to Agrippa II (as argued by von Premerstein 1932, and followed by many—e.g. Garzetti 1974: 141; Jones and Milns 1984, no. 93), can hardly be correct (*CPJ* 2, 68-69; cf. Schwartz [D.R.] 1990: 97).
96. Philo, *Flacc.* 39; to match further the ancestral origin of the Herods argued here, see a Σύρος Ἀσκαλωνείτης (*IBM* 1072); cf. Vaggi 1937; Feldman 1990: 13-14; and Chapter 3 n. 62.

Agrippa's remission of taxes and reform of the economy in Judaea would be reflected in a new issue of coins and especially in the release of new standard weights for the local market. The *prutot* coins of 'Year 6' were minted between autumn 41 and autumn 42, and as one would have expected they are clearly of Jewish orientation, though of course with Greek inscriptions. On the obverse they depict a canopy, the king's companion in all of his excursions, a fitting substitute for Agrippa's portrait which symbolized royalty without offending the Jews. On the reverse there appear three ears of grain which signified the fertility of the land.[97] No less than ten inscribed stone weights of Agrippa I are known today, eight from Jerusalem, one from Ain-Feshkha and one from Machaerus; the most ambitious one reading: 'Year 5 of King A(grippa) F(riend of the) R(omans), (One) Libra' (LE ΒΑΣΙΛΕΩΣ Α. ΦΡ. ΜΝΑ).[98]

As regards military affairs after the fall of Silas in the late autumn of 41 (see above), the position of commander-in-chief of the royal army was almost certainly granted to Helcias (that is Alexas III Helcias, son of Alexas II Calleas, son of Alexas I—Chapter 7 §2), even though he is mentioned as ἔπαρχος rather than ἔπαρχος παντὸς στρατεύματος.[99] But Josephus is often imprecise when using such titles, and sometimes he calls Silas himself simply ἔπαρχος.[100] The person in charge of the royal cavalry, the specialized Babylonian horsemen of Batanaea founded by Zamaris on behalf of Herod the Great, continued to be Jacimus son of Zamaris, whose service must have begun under Philip the Tetrarch (compare the name of Jacimus's son Philip serving under Agrippa II).[101] Jacimus was a distinguished (ἐπίσημος) and illustrious (ἐπιφανὴς) man according to Josephus, but

97. *AJC* 2, 58-60, 249, nos. 11-11j; Meshorer 1990–91: 122-23, nos. 9-9L.

98. From Jerusalem see Mazar ([B.] 1969: 15, pl. XI.B13-14; 1971: 17, 21, pl. XXIII.2-4), Avigad (1983: 203, no. 246) and Tushingham (1986: 203, no. 76; 432, fig. 80.10); from Ain-Feshkha see De Vaux (1973: 67-68, pl. XXXVb—correcting his earlier view); from Machaerus see photo in *Southwestern News* (Ft. Worth, Texas), April 1987, p. 8—Vardaman *per litt.*

99. Josephus, *Ant.* 19.353; cf. 299.

100. Josephus, *Ant.* 19.317, 320.

101. Josephus, *Ant.* 17.29-30. It is possible that Jacimus and Silas were related; the latter's name is attested in the Babylonian military colony of Batanaea (above n. 70).

again instead of ἱππάρχης he is variously given as ἔπαρχος, or even as στρατάρχης, field marshal![102]

In an article on Ti. Claudius Felix, the procurator of Judaea, I have argued that [Ti]tus Mucius Clemens was an *eparchos* of an infantry cohort of Agrippa I, based in Caesarea-on-the-coast between CE 41 and 44. In this work more can be found regarding the composition of the Herodian army, a subject that has not been sufficiently studied.[103] Moreover another *eparchos* of Agrippa I is known from Josephus. His name was Crispus son of Compsus; he had a sphere of influence around Tiberias, and was the owner of private estates 'beyond the Jordan' (no doubt in Peraea and of Herodian origin).[104] This individual may potentially be of historical interest, in view of the recent publication of the Greek documents from the archive of Babatha. Here we find a Julia Crispina, a powerful woman mentioned as ἐπίσκοπος, who first supported (CE 130) and then represented at court (CE 131) the guardian of Babatha's young relatives. Crispina was a Roman citizen of Hellenized background, and may be identified with Julia Crispina recorded between CE 131 and 133 as a notable absentee owner of two houses in Egypt.[105] Could she have been a descendant of our Crispus, who was alive at least until CE 66? If Lewis's restoration of her name as daughter (θυγάτηρ) of a 'Berenicianus' in *P. Yadin*

102. Josephus, *Life* 46; *War* 4.81; for the Zamarid colony see Cohen [G.M.] 1972; Applebaum 1989a: 47-65.

103. Kokkinos 1990; cf. Broughton 1933; Speidel 1982–83; Gracey 1986; and now Shatzman 1991 (but only of Herod the Great).

104. Josephus, *Life* 33.

105. *P. Yadin* 20.5, 24, 43; 25.2, 24, 59; cf. Goodman 1991: 172; for Crispina in Egypt see *BGU* 53; cf. Polotsky 1962: 261-62; Yadin 1971: 247-48. Ilan (1993) has now suggested that Julia Crispina may have been the daughter of Berenicianus son of Berenice II, an identification that I abandoned in an earlier stage of my research. In view of Herodian age patterns chronology is not a problem— Berenicianus was born in CE 46 (below n. 170), while Crispina probably in the late 90s, so he could have become her father at about 50 years of age (even though he must have married before the fall of Jerusalem). But another Crispina, wife of Berenicianus, has to be created to be the mother of Julia Crispina—otherwise her name will be a curio in the Herodian onomasticon. Also, the background of such a woman, a daughter of an *eparchos* of Agrippa I, though adequate in a local context, would hardly have been appropriate for Queen Berenice II's son, especially at a time when she was related to Titus, Roman Emperor from 79 to 81. Moreover, the name Berenicianus is not uncommon in this area for a long period of time, no doubt due to the Herodian legacy (see below n. 171).

25.2 is correct, then a Herodian connection is increasingly possible. Assuming that like Babatha she was born in the late 90s, her father may have been a son of Crispus, who may have been named after Berenice II, or better her son Berenicianus, born in CE 46 (see below §3). Hence Babatha's archive may confront us with an aspect of the fragmentation of the Idumaean aristocracy after the eclipse of the Herods; but this is not the place to elaborate.[106]

In late CE 41, after the enthronement of Agrippa in Jerusalem, the time was ripe for a more general celebration, particularly since Agrippa's birthday (γενέθλιον) came round at this time of the year. Although he was then 52, this would have been a specially extended half-centenary birthday—during the two previous winters he had been away in the West.[107] For the festivities Agrippa invited all the prominent figures among his subjects, and he even recalled Silas, who had recently been cast into confinement in Batanaea, but the latter refused to attend.[108] It seems that this was the appropriate occasion for Agrippa to arrange husbands for his daughters. Only his eldest was actually of age to marry, while for the others a mere promise at the time would have sufficed. Berenice II was now 12 (or 13 in inclusive counting), and indeed she was given as παρθένος to Marcus Julius Alexander the son of Alexander the alabarch of Alexandria.[109] It may be assumed that Alexander had been invited to Jerusalem for the

106. It should be noted here that the case of Babatha has an unavoidable link with Idumaea. Her home town was Maōza in Nabataea (near the Idumaean border), but only because her father had moved there after buying a considerable plot of land (cf. Kokkinos 1994a). There is evidence (in the form of Qos-worship) of Idumaeans in Nabataea at that time (Chapter 1 n. 33). While it is not clear that Babatha was a Jewess by faith, she may have been an Idumaean Jewess—her name is attested solely in Marisa (Chapter 7 n. 11), and she was capable of swearing by 'the Tyche of Lord Caesar' (but see Cotton 1991: 266-67; Cotton 1993). It was by marriage to a Jew from En-Gedi (a town sometime belonging to Idumaea) that she developed Judaean connections (see generally Bowersock 1991; Goodman 1991; Isaac 1992b).

107. Josephus, *Ant.* 19.321; for chronological elasticity in celebrating anniversaries, see Chapter 8 n. 105; 'round-numbered' birthday parties seem to have been keenly observed by the Herods (cf. Chapter 6 n. 2 and Chapter 8 n. 72).

108. Josephus, *Ant.* 19.322-25.

109. Josephus, *Ant.* 19.277; an early promise of this union may already have been conceived in 38 when Agrippa as a king passed through Alexandria (above n. 81), or even earlier in 36 when Cyprus III (with her children) 'fell at the feet', as it were, of Alexander for money on behalf of her husband (above n. 52 end).

wedding, before the couple could depart for Egypt. As we saw, there were strong bonds between the two families: Alexander had saved Agrippa's life in the past by lending large sums of money to him (above n. 52); but also Agrippa in return, when Claudius became emperor, would have helped with Alexander's liberation from prison, where Caligula had put him (Chapter 7 n. 93). Mariamme VI was about eight, and hence she was only promised in marriage to Julius Archelaus, the son of Helcias, the new commander-in-chief of Agrippa's army (for Mariamme VI see Chapter 7 §2). Drusilla was about four, and any decision concerning her destiny waited for a couple of years, when apparently at the meeting of Tiberias (see below), Agrippa promised her to Epiphanes, son of Antiochus IV of Commagene. But this wedding did not materialize, because the prince later refused to be circumcised (for Drusilla see below §5).

It would also then have been the right time for Agrippa to announce his building projects, which, apart from having practical value, would have provided needed employment to a multitude of local people. The Herodian palace had fallen into decay, and part of its podium had collapsed outwards (as has been shown by archaeology), and Agrippa undertook to reconstruct it, as he did with an apartment in the Hasmonaean palace which was to command a view of the interior of the Temple.[110] The upper-level aqueduct of Jerusalem (apparently began by Herod the Great and continued by Pilate) had still to be completed, so that the city would benefit by a better water supply from the spring at Bir ed-Daraj (c. 20 km away); while numerous houses which had been built beyond the north ramparts of the city, as a result of encroachment, required to be protected by a new enclosing wall. Agrippa's ambitious venture of erecting a massive wall to enclose the northern side of the city, the so-called 'Third Wall', was later cut short when C. Vibius Marsus, the Roman governor of Syria (CE 42–44), firmly objected to it and informed the emperor.[111] This was the beginning of

110. Tushingham 1986: 25, 45; on the palace see Josephus, *War* 5. 176-82; Philo, *Legat.* 299; Tacitus, *Hist.* 5.8.1; Simons 1952: 265ff.; cf. Chapter 6 n. 22; for the apartment in the Hasmonaean palace, see Josephus, *Ant.* 20.189-90).

111. On the water supply, see Wilkinson 1974: 50; Mackowski 1980: 87; Patrich 1982; cf. Goodman 1987: 54; on the Third Wall, see Josephus, *War* 2.218-19; 5.147-55; *Ant.* 19.326-27; Tacitus, *Hist.* 5.12.2; for the differences between these accounts and the historical perspective, see Schwartz [D.R.] 1990: 140-44; on the archaeological question, see Hamrick in Tushingham 1986: 215-32; Kloner 1986;

serious animosity between Marsus and Agrippa, to the development of which we shall return below.

With the various constructions at Jerusalem went the organization of royal estates. The evidence at our disposal is tenuous but perhaps adequate to illuminate our path. We know that in CE 6 Quirinius had liquidated Archelaus's property (Chapter 8 §5),[112] and it is conceivable that Agrippa would have repossessed most of the previously royal land (certainly that which had meanwhile been transformed into imperial) and not only in the vicinity of Jerusalem, but also in other places such as Jericho and En-Gedi, as well as Western Idumaea, the Jamnian territory and Samaria.[113] In a pseudepigraphon of the Old Testament, a Hebrew text in its original, commonly known as *4 Baruch* and dated from the time of Agrippa I (though some believe it to be as late as the time of Bar Kokhba), we read:

> And the Lord said to Jeremiah, "Send him (i.e. Abimelech the Ethiopian) to the vineyard of Agrippa and in the shadow of the mountain I will shelter him until I return the people to the city..." And when it was morning Jeremiah sent Abimelech away, saying, "Take the basket and go out to the farm of Agrippa by the mountain road and get a few figs to give to the sick among the people, for the delight of the Lord (rests) upon you.[114]

and Wightman 1993: 159ff.; Tzaferis *et al.* 1994: 287-88; on the opposition of the Roman government to the building of walls by client-kings, see Lawrence 1979: 111; for the northern quarter of the city called 'Bezetha', and named after a Herodian building with five porticoes housing a twin pool (Jn 5.2, Βηθζαθὰ) see Jeremias 1966: 13; cf. Finegan 1992: 228-29.

112. Note the wording in Josephus, *Ant.* 17.355 (οἶκος); 18.2 (χρήματα); Dio, 55.27.6 (μέρος).

113. Pliny (*Hist. Natur.* 12.111) explicitly refers to royal land (i.e. Herodian) in the two areas of Palestine where balsam grew. We know that these were Jericho (Strabo, 16.2.41; Pompeius Trogus *apud* Justinus, 36.3.2-3; Josephus, *War* 4.469) and En-Gedi (Josephus, *Ant.* 9.7; Galen, *De Antid.* 1.4; Eusebius, *Onom.* [edn Klostermann 86]; Jerome, *Comm. in Hiez.* 27.17; cf. *b. Šab.* 26a); for imperial Jericho, cf. below n. 187; possible activity under Agrippa I in the Herodian palace there, may now be indicated by a graffito on a column, which seems to mention 'King Agrippa', found in the garden excavations (Gleason 1987–88, 38 n. 45); for the Jamnian territory, cf. Avi-Yonah 1977a: 106; note that no successor is known of C. Herennius Capito, the procurator of Jamnia (Chapter 7 n. 69).

114. *4 Bar.* 3.14-22; see Harris [J.R.] 1889: 33-34; and Robinson [S.E.] 1985. It is possible that in the original Hebrew part we are dealing with a cryptic Judaeo-Pharisaic document of Christian aspiration. The '66 years' from a conquest of Jerusalem (5.30), may refer back to Herod's conquest in 38/37 BCE—so that the year

The existence of rural property of Agrippa around Jerusalem seems to be historical, and the reference would not be to Agrippa II, whose association with the city was of a different kind (below §5), though he could have inherited local land from his father.[115] The evidence of *4 Baruch* serves to underline how much we do not know about land exploitation by the Herods in Judaea. But it may go some way to provide an answer to Goodman's statement that 'no Herodian lands in the hills around Jerusalem are recorded'.[116]

With such settlements and a decision to replace the high priest Simon-Cantheras with Matthias son of Ananus,[117] Agrippa saw fit to move on to other areas of his kingdom, and specifically to the less Jewish territory, where he could express himself in a more pagan way. The overdue commemoration of his latest achievements in Rome was still to materialize. In the autumn of CE 42, after a delay of over a year and a half (apparently due to his obligations towards Jerusalem), Agrippa struck at Caesarea four types of coin, summarizing the important Roman events concerning his accession, and thus offering us hard evidence for checking Josephus. The first type depicts the crowning of Claudius with a wreath by Agrippa who stands on the left, and Herod of Chalcis on the right. As the inscription on the reverse makes clear (cut around a pair of clasped hands), the scene represents part of the ceremony in the Forum where the imperial treaty (Josephus's ὅρκια) was made with Agrippa:

ΟΡΚΙΑ ΒΑΣ (ΙΛΕΩΣ) ΜΕ (ΓΑΛΟΥ) ΑΓΡΙΠΠΑ ΠΡ(ΟΣ) ΣΕΒ(ΑΣΤΟΝ)
ΚΑΙΣΑΡ[Α Κ(ΑΙ)] ΣΥΝΚΛΗΤΟΝ ΣΥΝΚΛΗΤΟΝ Κ(ΑΙ) ΔΗΜΟ(Ν)
ΡΩΜ(ΑΙΩΝ) ΦΙΛΙ(ΑΣ) Κ(ΑΙ) ΣΥΝΜΑΧΙ(ΑΣ) ΑΥΤΟΥ.[118]

specified would be CE 28/29, when John the Baptist began to preach (cf. 6.25). If so, the doctrine of the resurrection (6.6-10) may allude to Jesus, and thus it may have been composed a few years after the crucifixion, under or shortly after Agrippa I. This would agree with the fact that it was readily taken over and interpolated later by Christians (8.12-9.32).

115. An echo of the fact that this portion of the Judaean Hills belonged to Agrippa I may be found in the הר המלך tradition, see *t. Men.* 9.13; remember that Agrippa II was not king of Judaea.

116. Goodman 1987: 37 n. 13; 58-59; cf. Chapter 2 n. 24; for imperial land cf. below n. 187.

117. Josephus, *Ant.* 19.313-16.

118. Burnett 1987: 32-35, no. 8; cf. Meshorer 1990–91: 123, nos. 10-10a; *AJC* 2, 248, nos. 5-5b; Kraay 1980: 53-56; see Josephus, *Ant.* 19.275. The date of the

The second type, as interpreted by Burnett, seems to depict the consecration of the treaty in a Roman temple, with Agrippa standing next to
Claudius in the role of a priest, wearing his toga pulled over his head.
A kneeling figure in the foreground appears to be killing a pig
(mentioned by Suetonius), to which Agrippa obviously did not object
or even care to omit from the scene when the coin was minted at Caesarea![119] The third type of coin is a kind of ἐνκώμιον to king
Agrippa, who is depicted on the obverse, and to the city of Caesarea
(specified as being the one by the harbour Σεβαστὸς) represented by
its Tyche on the reverse, while the fourth type, which carries the like-
ness of young Agrippa II, reminds us again of the existence of the heir
to the throne.[120] The second and third issues (and perhaps all four)
were restruck in the following year with the date 'Year 8', that is
October 43 to October 44, during which Agrippa died (see below).

It appears that Agrippa's move to Caesarea in CE 42 coincided (or
initiated?) the episode at Dora, about 12 km to the north. A band of
youths of Hellenized Phoenician background,[121] recklessly put an
image of Claudius into the Jewish synagogue, imitating in effect Caligula's attempt against the temple at Jerusalem two years earlier. This
act infuriated Agrippa, who had recently secured the emperor's edicts
safeguarding Jewish rights, and drove him to Syria to register a formal
complaint with Publius Petronius, the then Roman governor.[122]

first type is not preserved but from comparison with a new coin of Herod of Chalcis,
Burnett succeeded in dating it to 'Year 7', i.e. between Oct. 42 and Oct. 43 (even
though Herod's coin may date a little later, see below n. 154).

119. Burnett 1987: 35-37, no. 10; cf. Meshorer 1990–91: 124, nos. 11-11a, 14-
14a; *AJC* 2, 248, nos. 8-8a, 10-10a; Suetonius, *Claud.* 25.5.

120. Meshorer 1990–91: 124, nos. 12-13, 15-15a; cf. *AJC* 2, 248, nos. 6-7, 9-
9a; 250, nos. 4-4a (previously classified under Agrippa II with a wrong date).

121. That these *Dōritai* would have been Hellenized Phoenicians, see in combination Josephus, *Ant.* 19.306 (Ἕλλησιν) and *Life* 31 (Φοινίκης)—cf. Caesarea's
case, Chapter 3 n. 62. They would have been of exactly the same culture as the
Tyrian woman mentioned in Mk 7.26 as Ἑλληνὶς Συροφοινίκισσα τῷ γένει. The
story shows that Dora was in the province of Syria (see now Gera and Cotton 1991:
261). Claudius Iolaus (*apud* Stephanus) in the first century CE refers to the inhabitants of Dora as Phoenicians (*FGrH* 788, F2). For Dora see *SVM* 2, 118-20; for
Hellenized Phoenician archaeology at Tel Dor, see Stern [E.] 1988; cf. 1989; 1993.

122. Josephus, *Ant.* 19.300-12; Petronius was still governor in 42, since he
struck coins dated to Oct. 41–Oct. 42 (Mionnet 1811: 167, no. 173; Dieudonné
1927: 38; see *RPC* 1, 4276); he was apparently replaced by Marsus late in this year
(Josephus, *Ant.* 19.316; cf. Thomasson 1984: 306, no. 21).

Petronius issued a decree rebuking the people of Dora, and Agrippa's effort was fully justified.

While in Syria Agrippa took the opportunity to become a royal benefactor to Gentile cities, in marked resemblance to his grandfather Herod the Great. Josephus mentions that Agrippa built in many cities, but his account is restricted to the most significant of the king's contributions: that to the Roman colony of Berytus. Agrippa's programme was lavish. To the halls, porticoes, temples and market-places built by Herod he added a theatre of remarkable beauty, an amphitheatre of great expense, as well as baths and extra porticoes.[123] According to Josephus the gladiatorial spectacles of purely Roman fashion that Agrippa staged in the theatre at one time (after its completion, or in an older structure which was about to be renovated?), involved the annihilation of 1,400 men. Ironically Berytus was the city where Agrippa's father, Aristobulus I, had been condemned to death (Chapter 8 §2).

In an inscription from Heliopolis/Baalbek, Agrippa is referred to as having been made *patronus coloniae*,[124] that is of Berytus, since the territory of Heliopolis at that time belonged to it.[125] The honour needs to be attributed to Agrippa I, not only because Agrippa II was not as great a benefactor of Berytus as his father was, but also because in texts of the latter from this area he is paired with his sister, Berenice II (see below §5). We may also assume that a Latin inscription from

123. Josephus, *War* 1.422; *Ant.* 19.328, 335-37; cf. Agrippa II's and Berenice II's benefactions (below n. 200); also cf. Herod's building at another Roman colony: Nicopolis near Actium (Kokkinos forthcoming 1).

124. *CIL* 3.14387 = *ILS* 8957 = *IGLS* 6.2759; the title *pius* (Greek εὐσεβής) should not favour Agrippa II (*SEG* 7.129; *OGIS* 419; *IGLS* 5.2707; cf. Josephus, *Ant.* 20.12), because it is also attested for his father (*OGIS* 419; *SEG* 7.216); cf. also for Herod the Great (below n. 152).

125. See Millar 1990a: 18-19: 'inscriptions from this period which refer to the *colonia* must be taken as an allusion to the city of Berytus'. To Millar's thorough discussion I would add the fact that we know one of the earliest magistrates (a retired Roman officer) of the colony on record—around CE 10–20. His name as stated in his *cursus honorum* (*CIL* 3.6687 = *ILS* 2683; Gabba 1958: 52-61, no. 18; Braund 1985: no. 446) was Q. Aemilius Secundus, famous for having served under Quirinius, the governor of Syria (from CE 6). Berytus is not mentioned by name, but at that time there was only one *colonia* in this part of the world, from which the inscription is reported to have come to Venice (thus known as Lapis Venetus); cf. below n. 234.

Apamea will reflect Agrippa I, and although very fragmentary (even his name is missing) it seems from the title (*regi magno philo* [*romano*]) to be similar to that from Heliopolis.[126] If this identification is accepted Agrippa may have visited Apamea, and the city (being one of those mentioned anonymously by Josephus) would have gained by his benefactions.

On his return Agrippa went to Tiberias, which he continued to regard as the capital of Galilee, and there he held a most remarkable conference of Eastern client-kings.[127] Among known figures attending were Antiochus IV of Commagene, the then richest king of the Roman Empire (Chapter 9 §1), Sampsigeramus II of Emesa, Cotys of Armenia Minor, Polemo of Pontus and Herod of Chalcis. Such a display of friendship and alliance (but also of power), together with the fact that at Jerusalem a massive wall was being built, brought Marsus in haste to Tiberias. The Roman governor broke up the meeting and ordered the kings to depart at once, each to his own domain. The building of the wall, as we saw, had to stop without question. But Marsus's suspicions cannot have been well founded, for Agrippa was highly unlikely to have been planning an open revolt against Rome.[128] It is safer to imagine that he had been affected by acute megalomania, seeing himself as the leader of all the client-kings, and somehow divinely inspired, as his behaviour later shows at Caesarea. Such a disease not only endangered his career, but it heralded his approaching fall, which cut his reign short exactly like that of Caligula (see below).

Back in Jerusalem in the second half of CE 43, Agrippa stayed continuously until about the summer of 44, so that Josephus may be justified in pronouncing the city as his permanent residence.[129] One of the first things that the king had to do was to appoint a new high priest—this time entrusting the office to Elionaeus son of Cantheras.[130] Such frequent replacements at the highest level of Jewish authority

126. Balty 1981: 203, no. 16, pl. 225.

127. Josephus, *Life* 37; *Ant.* 19.338-42.

128. Schwartz [D.R.] 1990: 137-40; cf. Brandon 1967: 96; affairs in Parthia may have been worrying but no connection can be made (Tacitus, *Ann.* 11.8-10)—cf. below n. 161.

129. Josephus, *Ant.* 19.331.

130. Josephus, *Ant.* 19.342—see Chapter 8 §4; it is possible that this son of Simon-Cantheras is meant on a stone weight excavated in Jerusalem (Chapter 8 n. 40).

(three times within a space of two years) would suggest some religious tensions. Perhaps during Agrippa's absence the trouble which was generated since the crucifixion of Jesus in 36 (on my chronology) had intensified. To add to this, it must have been during the winter of 43/44 that the 'Apostolic Council' (in which the abolition of circumcision as a prerequisite for Gentiles wishing to become Christians was discussed) would have taken place in Jerusalem, perhaps exacerbating the situation further.[131] Indeed at the beginning of 44, Agrippa took drastic steps against the Christian leaders. Evidently his real motive was the fear of political unrest, which could have transmitted the wrong signals to Rome. This is proved by the fact that he killed James son of Zebedee by the sword (μαχαίρῃ), exactly as Antipas had done to John the Baptist less than a decade before. Note that no stoning is attested. Agrippa was next prompted to arrest Simon/Peter, whom he put into prison, intending also to execute him after the then approaching Passover. The escape of Peter by 'divine' intervention is advocated with pride by Acts. Agrippa is said to have searched for him in vain, while he punished his guards.[132] But this is a vast topic,

---

131. Acts 15.1-35; Gal. 2.1-9; for the date see Kokkinos 1989: 148. The latest serious attempt of dating this event to the autumn of 51 (Jewett 1979: 100), runs into difficulties. A simple point never explained is how the burning issue of circumcision managed to remain unraised for a whole decade after Paul had begun proselytizing Gentiles? Another point is that if Silas was assigned to Paul for the first time by the Council of 51, how could he be Paul's secretary in 50 when 1 Thessalonians was written at Corinth? Note that by dating the Council in 43/4, James son of Zebedee can still be alive—if he is the one meant in 15.13, for the other James (Jesus' brother) was also involved from the beginning (Gal. 1.39; Acts 12.17). It is possible that James was killed together with his brother John (Papias, *Log. Kyriak. Exēg.*, *apud* Philip Sidetes, *Chron.* [edn de Boor 170], and George Hamartolos, *Chron.* 3.134.1; Syriac *Martyrol.* 27 Dec.; cf. Rev. 11.1-13), despite the criticism that Papias's lost work has received (see Bruce [F.F.] 1979: 137-38). Some stories related by Papias were disliked by the Early Church. For example, Clement of Alexandria in his *Hypotypōseis* (*apud* Eusebius, *Hist. Eccl.* 2.8.3), unable to accept Papias's testimony (cf. *Strom.* 6.5), introduced in the place of John an unnamed Christian follower who was decapitated with James! If it is true that the sons of Zebedee fell together before Agrippa I, then the identity of John who died in Ephesus, apparently after becoming the author of the Fourth Gospel, needs to be sought in John Mark (see Parker [P.] 1960; Cullmann 1976: 76-77; cf. now Hengel 1989c).

132. Acts 12; Lake 1933; Bruce [F.F.] 1982: 105-28; see discussion and bibliography in Schwartz [D.R.] 1990: 119-24, 208-16. It is noticeable that Agrippa, in

concerning the very beginnings of Christianity, and this is not the place to expand. It is important to stress, however, that Josephus ignored this event and related instead an enigmatic story about a Jew also called Simon, a religious fanatic, who despite openly denouncing Agrippa was kindly pardoned by him and was even presented with a gift before he was let free![133]

During this troublesome period in the early months of CE 44 Marcus Julius Alexander, the husband of Agrippa's elder daughter Berenice II, died in Alexandria.[134] The young woman (still only 15) had to return to Judaea, and her father, as testified by Josephus, lived long enough to see her marrying his brother Herod of Chalcis.[135] The new arrangement would have been made at the feast of Passover, when Herod must have visited Jerusalem (we find him immediately afterwards with Agrippa at Caesarea—see below).

Following the narrative in Acts, sometime after Passover of 44 and probably at the end of July, Agrippa moved down to Caesarea-on-the-coast. His intention was to contribute spectacles to the festival which was to be celebrated by the city for the safety of the emperor, apparently for Claudius's recent return from Britain. It would have been convenient for the games to have occurred in the summer period, and possibly to have coincided with Claudius's *dies natalis* of 1 August.

Once more we are in debt to Acts for another episode shortly before the beginning of the festival, which Josephus again ignores. An embassy of Tyrians and Sidonians arrived at Caesarea to plead with the king for a reconciliation:

contrast to Herod the Great and Antipas, does not appear as 'persecutor' (in fact he does not appear at all) in the entire apocryphal literature (Greek, Syriac, Armenian, Coptic, Ethiopic or Arabic). Should one have expected him to be mentioned in the *Acts of Peter*? An exception is the Ethiopic *Martyrdom of St James*, where the son of Zebedee falls victim to a Herod [Agrippa] under Nero (Budge 1935: 255-56)!

133. Josephus, *Ant.* 19.332-34; cf. Baumgarten [J.M.] 1983; Schwartz [D.R.] 1990: 124-30.

134. The evidence is quite explicit and invalidates at a stroke the lengthy argument of Schwartz ([D.R.] 1990: 107-11, 203-207), who attempted to move Agrippa's death back to the end of Sept. 43. Marcus was alive at least until after 25 Jan. CE 44, when the fourth year of Claudius had commenced, referred to in *O. Petr.* 271: (ἔτους) δ´ Τιβερίου Κλαυδίου Καίσαρος (cf. *CPJ* 2, 199, no. 419d, but with wrong absolute reckoning).

135. Josephus, *Ant.* 19.277, 354; cf. Kokkinos 1986a: 37-38 with references.

Now he (Herod—read Agrippa) was angry with the people of Tyre and Sidon; and they came to him in a body, and having persuaded Blastus, the king's chamberlain, they asked for peace (εἰρήνη), because their country depended on the king's country for food. On an appointed day Herod put on his royal robes, took his seat upon the tribunal, and made an oration to them.[136]

We are not told why these Phoenician cities were on bad terms with Agrippa, to the extent of his cutting their food supply and presumably boycotting their trade, and of their talking about 'peace' as if a war had been threatened. We are also left in the dark on the outcome of this hearing, though it appears that Agrippa remained intractable. Theologians and historians alike have wrestled with this story without being able to understand it.[137]

On the second day of the festival at Caesarea, Agrippa entered the theatre extravagantly dressed, performed a kind of self-apotheosis, which stunned the populace, and suddenly fell fatally ill under mysterious circumstances.[138] From the medical point of view the first modern retrodiagnosis was of the opinion that Agrippa died of peritonitis.[139] Recently it has been suggested that it might instead have been a myocardial infarction or a gastric or duodenal ulcer.[140] But it has also been argued that Agrippa was poisoned.[141] Josephus offers us only the symptoms of his illness (Acts merely follows the familiar scenario of σκωληκόβρωτος),[142] which modern medicine interprets in different ways, including poisoning. Although it is certainly true that

136. Acts 12.20-21; Rawlinson 1889: 543-44; Jidejian 1969: 89-90; for Luke's popular use of the dynastic name 'Herod' for Agrippa, cf. Chapter 8 n. 78 and above n. 60.

137. Haenchen 1971: 386; Schwartz [D.R.] 1990: 144 n. 157; the latter calls it 'obscure' and with 'no Christian connection' (147)—possible clues will have to be discussed elsewhere.

138. Josephus, *Ant.* 19.343-50; cf. cautiously Morgenstern 1947: 90-91.

139. Bennet 1896: 86; Merrins 1904: 561-62; Masterman 1920: 55.

140. Schwartz [D.R.] 1990: 218 (consulting S. Adler); cf. Short 1953: 66ff.; and now Kottek 1994: 35.

141. Meyshan 1958–59; Meyshan 1968: 106 n. 2; cf. Madden 1881: 130 n. 5.

142. The punishing scenario of 'eaten by worms' in Acts 12.23 (i.e. *phthiriasis* according to Africa 1982), only serves to place Agrippa in the worse possible company, that of Herod the Great (Josephus, *Ant.* 17.169) and of Antiochus Epiphanes (Josephus, *Ant.* 17.169; 2 Macc. 9.9; see Schwartz [D.R.] 1990: 148 n. 9). Yet the circumstances and deaths of these kings were totally different (Merrins 1904; Sandison 1967; Kottek 1994: 189-90; also cf. Ladouceur 1981).

rumours of this type of death were circulated for almost every dying Julio-Claudian, it is equally true that a few of them do seem to have died in this way, for example Germanicus or Drusus the son of Tiberius.[143] As far as Herodian history is concerned, the deaths of Antipater I and Pheroras, and the attempt against Herod the Great himself, might suffice as examples (Chapter 6 §1, 2). No rumours here but two different lots of poison (in the cases of Pheroras and Herod) which were seized, the second being brought into a law court in the trial of Antipater II and used on a prisoner under the sentence of death, who died instantly of an overdose.[144]

Since the description of Agrippa's death by Josephus allows poisoning as an explanation, this view seems possible on other grounds: the king's relatively young age (54), his brief reign, and his character. Agrippa had managed to make enemies on all sides. Without repeating here the early events of his life (especially his quarrel with Antipas), only lately he had made an enemy of Silas, his right-hand man and the troops' favourite, and of the Roman Marsus for competing with him, by building a defensive wall and by creating a dangerous alliance between most eastern client-kings. Agrippa had been in conflict with Hellenized cities such as Alexandria, Dora, Tyre and Sidon, and while he persecuted the leaders of the Christians he annoyed the Jews by his double stance, spending heavily on pagan communities and gradually seeing himself as a god. It may be indicative that his own troops from Caesarea and Sebaste celebrated his death by wearing garlands, hurling insults, pouring libations to Charon, and abusing the statues of his daughters which they carried to local brothels![145]

3. Herod (V) of Chalcis

It has already been inferred that Herod (V) of Chalcis was second in line after Agrippa I among the sons of Aristobulus I and Berenice I, and that he would have been born in 10 or 9 BCE (above §1). The pattern of events in Herod's life very much resembles that of his elder brother. He was taken to Rome, evidently after the death of Herod the Great, when the entire family of Salome I moved there, and

143. See Kokkinos 1992a: 16, 22, 26, 28.
144. Josephus, *Ant.* 17.77, 79, 132.
145. Josephus, *Ant.* 19.356-59; cf. Grottanelli 1983.

he was raised, educated and settled in the Roman capital for as long as and even longer than Agrippa I.[146]

Apparently in the late 20s CE, a few years after Agrippa, Herod also contracted a marriage to a Herodian princess and likewise cousin of his, Mariamme V. While Agrippa's wife was a daughter of Salampsio (born c. 33 BCE) daughter of Herod the Great, Herod's wife was the daughter of Olympias (born c. 22 BCE), also daughter of Herod the Great. Olympias, sister of Antipas the Tetrarch, was betrothed to Joseph III sometime between 8 and 5 BCE (and married possibly later—Chapter 6 n. 46), which means that Mariamme V (her only recorded child) would have hardly been born before the beginning of the Christian Era. In that respect Mariamme would have been slightly younger than Cyprus III—in agreement with the fact that her mother was a full decade younger than the mother of Agrippa I's wife.

Like Cyprus, Mariamme would have been sent to Rome for education in the early part of the reign of Tiberius (her parents stayed in Judaea in the aftermath of Herod's death), and she must have lived in Italy until she married Herod. Their son, Aristobulus III, being younger than his cousin Agrippa II (apparently by three to five years), would have been born at the beginning of the 30s CE.[147] We do not know how well Herod's family did socially through that difficult period in Agrippa I's life (32/33–37), but in contrast to his brother there is no indication that Herod was driven either to poverty or to prison.

When Agrippa in 38 set sail to take up the kingdom granted to him by Caligula, Herod was not invited to participate, evidently having received no benefit from his brother at this time. Even in 40 Herod had yet to pursue any activity in the East, for he is significantly missing from the important Herodian embassy (in which we would have expected him to be) which encountered Petronius at Tiberias appealing against Caligula's statue (see below §4). Only in 41 does Herod

146. Josephus, *Ant.* 18.133 (see the reconstruction in Chapter 7 n. 52). Herod stayed longer than Agrippa in Rome, since the latter was absent during the periods 32/33–36 and 38–39. Both left Italy in 41.

147. Josephus, *War* 2.221; *Ant.* 18.134; 20.104; see Kokkinos 1986a: 34-36, where a correlative examination of Agrippa II's and Aristobulus III's lives, has indicated that the latter would have been some five years younger, born about 32/33. I believe that this may now be clarified as 'from three to five years', and since Agrippa was born in 27/28, Aristobulus could have been born as early as 30.

make his debut in political history, when—evidently after assisting Agrippa in helping Claudius to the throne—he was presented with the kingdom of Chalcis at the instigation of his brother. As Dio informs us, the emperor further bestowed upon Herod praetorian status together with the honour of entering the Senate and expressing his thanks in Greek.[148] Herod also played a part in influencing the issuing of the edicts for the protection of Jewish rights (above n. 91), and according to Josephus in his second edict Claudius directly referred to both Agrippa and Herod as 'my dearest friends'.[149]

Concurrently with Agrippa's departure for Judaea to assume his extended kingship in late CE 41, Herod must have moved to his own principality. He was now about 50 years old, and for the first time was established not far from his country of origin. The history of what we may call Chalcidice South (over a part of western Anti-Lebanon and the Beqâ'), with its centre at Chalcis (previously the capital of the entire Ituraean kingdom), is basically unknown between the death of Cleopatra (30 BCE) and the accession of Claudius (CE 41).[150] It is not easy to uncover the actual circumstances that led to the need for an independent ruler in this central part of Ituraea at that time, and especially for one of Herodian stock. A vacancy could have occurred in the seat of power at Chalcis, but this is unlikely because the area seems to have remained under the direct control of the governor of Syria—at least from the time of P. Sulpicius Quirinius (from CE 6) and probably from the death of Herod the Great 4 (or 5) BCE.[151]

148. Josephus, *Ant.* 19.277; *War* 2.217; Dio, 60.8.2-3; in its typically condensed manner *War* in this juncture mentions Herod's further relationship to Agrippa as his son-in-law, giving the wrong impression that Herod might have married Berenice II (Agrippa's daughter) as early as 41 (*SVM* 1, 572: n. 59; followed by Kasher 1988: 186 n. 149)—but this happened only in 44, as is clear from *Antiquities* and the ostraca of Nicanor (above n. 134).

149. Josephus, *Ant.* 19.279, 288; cf. later the letter of Claudius to Jerusalem (below n. 156).

150. *SVM* 1, 571-73; Schmitt 1982; Will 1983; cf. Schottroff 1982.

151. I am assuming that in 40 BCE Chalcis was passed on to Lysanias from his father Ptolemy son of Mennaeus, and that after his murder in 36 BCE (cf. Chapter 7 n. 14) his son Zenodorus (*IGRR* 3.1085; *IGLS* 2851; *SVM* 1, 566; cf. Seyrig 1970) leased the area from Cleopatra (note Porphyry, *apud* Eusebius, *Chron.* [edn Schoene 1.170]), which he kept until his death in 20 BCE, when *all* of his possessions were awarded to Herod the Great by Augustus. So I believe that Chalcis (and in fact most of Ituraea, and thus southern Syria—cf. Josephus, *War* 1.399) became Herodian

Therefore Chalcidice was granted perhaps as a kind of *dōrea* by the Emperor Claudius, grateful as he was towards Agrippa and Herod, following the trend begun by Caligula of handing Ituraea back to client-kingship, portion by portion. Presumably Claudius also based himself on a potential claim (of Herodian-Hasmonaean nature) advanced by the two brothers (compare Chapter 3 n. 96).

No inscriptions of Herod of Chalcis are known to us,[152] but there are two types of coins struck by him which are found mainly in the Lebanon. The first type, in three denominations, depicts on the obverse his portrait, name and official title ΒΑΣΙΛΕΥΣ ΗΡΩΔΗΣ ΦΙΛΟΚΛΑΥΔΙΟΣ, while on the reverse appears the name of Claudius surrounded by a wreath. The second type has the same reverse, but its obverse is basically identical to one of Agrippa I's coins, depicting the Herodian brothers (now mentioning Herod first) crowning the emperor at the conclusion of the ceremony in the Roman Forum where their treaty was made.[153] Since the coins from Chalcis carry the date 'Year 3' in association with the name of the emperor (in contrast to other Herodian issues), they may need to be reckoned according to Claudius's reign (January 43/January 44) and not to Herod's (October 42/October 43).[154] This suggests that the original ceremonial design (no dated specimen of which survives) was minted at Caesarea sometime before 43, the year in which the copy of it was ordered at Chalcis. Indeed it now appears probable that Agrippa's prototype was initially struck at the beginning of 'Year 7' of that king, that is in the

between 20 and 4 (or 5) BCE (not realized by Jones [A.H.M.] 1971: 270, or Avi-Yonah 1977a: 93); this will have to be discussed elsewhere.

152. An inscribed base of a now-lost statue found on the Acropolis at Athens in 1860 by Pittakes (*AEph* 1860: 1935, no. 3768), and sometimes thought to refer to Herod of Chalcis (*OGIS* 427 = *IG*.2².3441; Graindor 1927, 82-83; cf. *SVM* 1, 572 n. 64), actually belongs to Herod the Great (Chapter 3 n. 195). The title εὐσεβὴς καὶ φιλόκαισαρ of the Athenian text is attested for Herod the Great on a stone weight from Jerusalem dated to Oct. 9/Oct. 8 BCE (*AE* 1972, 672; Meshorer 1970, but with wrong restoration—now also noted by Kushnir-Stein 1995a: 83-84). The known title of Herod of Chalcis was φιλοκλαύδιος (as on his coins). No other Herodian candidate can qualify for this inscription.

153. *AJC* 2, 280, nos. 1-3; Burnett 1987: 34-35; Meshorer 1990–91: 127, A; for Agrippa's coin see above n. 118.

154. Contra Burnett 1987: 34. It should be remembered that, based on 'Tishri' reckoning, Herod's reign would have entered its second year in Sep./Oct. 41—his first lasting only a few months.

autumn of 42, and hence several months or even a year before Herod's own coin. It is possible that Herod became acquainted with it during his participation (around the summer CE 43) in the notorious conference of client-kings at Tiberias, where he was of course invited (above §2).

The ties between the two Herodian kings continued to be close, and they would have met at least twice a year at the major Jewish festivals, when Herod must have visited Jerusalem. As we saw, it must have been at Passover of 44 that Agrippa arranged for his daughter Berenice II, then a young widow, to marry Herod of Chalcis (above §2). We do not know whether Herod's first wife Mariamme V had been divorced or had died, or whether he committed an endogamous bigamy (with a cousin and a niece), but such unions—at least in reference to endogamy—were common in the Herodian dynasty. It is worth noting that Berenice II, Princess of Judaea, who was first married to a private (but wealthy) individual from Alexandria, now became Queen of Chalcis.

At Caesarea-on-the-coast Herod stood by the side of Agrippa through the last dramatic days in the life of the King of Judaea, who died unexpectedly in August 44. At this time Herod gave orders to Ariston, his best attendant, to execute the imprisoned Silas (Chapter 7 n. 85). But the ugly scenes which followed, staged in the city by the army, Herod does not seem to have been able to avert, and he may have been responsible for informing Claudius about them (above n. 145).

The death of Agrippa brought some advantage to Herod's sphere of power. Although Judaea and the rest of the kingdom reverted to direct Roman rule (since Agrippa II was too young for such an appointment), Herod managed to claim authority over the Temple at Jerusalem, the treasury, and the selection of the high priests. This must have helped to preserve the considerable Herodian interests in Judaea (in terms of influence and assets), and it must have suited both Rome, which would have avoided dealing directly with any internal religious strife, and the high priestly (mainly Sadducean) families, which were regularly benefitted by the Herods. Josephus says that this authority 'passed to his (Herod's) descendants alone until the end of the war (in AD 70)', but this cannot be accurate as stated.[155] None of

155. Josephus, *Ant.* 20.15-16.

his own children are known to have been involved with the Temple, a power solely reserved for Agrippa II (see below §5).

The new appointment of Herod of Chalcis would have been conferred on him in late 44 or early in 45, because Claudius in his letter to the Jews of Jerusalem (28 June CE 45), by which he restored to them the right to guard the high priest's sacred robe, wrote:

> ...I know that in doing so I shall give great pleasure to King Herod himself and to Aristobulus the Younger—excellent men for whom I have high regard, men of whose devotion to me and zeal for your interest I am aware and with whom I have very many ties of friendship...[156]

It must have been around this time that Herod exercised his power over the Temple by replacing the high priest 'Cantheras' (Elionaeus-Cantheras son of Simon II-Cantheras, see Chapter 8 §2), with Joseph son of 'Camei' (read Camith or Camis). Within his lifetime only once did Herod select another high priest, Ananias son of Nedebaeus (or Nebedaeus). This happened around Passover of 48, shortly before his death, apparently as a result of the crucifixion of James and Simon, sons of Judas the Galilaean, who like their father would have objected to Roman taxation (the Sabbatical year 47/48 had probably overlapped with a Roman Census year in 48/49, once more raising the tensions).[157]

The 'young' Aristobulus in the above-mentioned letter, cannot have been Aristobulus II, Herod's younger brother (then over 50), who had settled in Syria from earlier on and who does not seem to have had any special dealings with Claudius in the last 15 years (see below §4); it must rather be Aristobulus III, Herod's son by Mariamme V (then about 15—see above). This young man grew up in Rome together with his cousin, Agrippa II, and thus would have been looked after by Claudius, though it is possible that at the time the letter was written he was temporarily present at Chalcis. The fact that he was a minor, and younger than his cousin, explains why at his father's death late in 48 (below n. 184) he could not succeed him on the throne: he was then

156. Josephus, *Ant.* 20.13.

157. Josephus, *Ant.* 20.16, 102-103; on Nedebaeus see below n. 201; on the probability of Roman censuses in Judaea after CE 6/7 (i.e. in 20/21, 34/35, 48/49, 62/63), see Kokkinos 1989: 139-41, and add there the Ituraean revolt in CE 6/7 (*CIL* 3. 6687 = *ILS* 2683; above n. 125) and further allusions to the census of 62/63 (*War* 6.422-27, and *t. Pes.* end of ch. 4; *b. Pes.* 64b; *Lam. R.* 1.1); cf. Kokkinos forthcoming 2, appendix; on censuses in Egypt, see now Bagnall and Frier 1994.

about 18. Chalcis was given instead to Agrippa II (then approaching 22), who had previously also been left out of office when his father Agrippa I died, for he was then seventeen and thus 'quite young' (see below §5).

When Agrippa II took over Chalcis (early in 49), Aristobulus III must have returned to Rome and resided there, while apparently associating himself with the young Nero (born 15 December CE 36 or 37), the adopted son of Claudius (in c. 50) and future emperor.[158] This may safely be assumed from the honour that Nero was soon to bestow upon him (see below). Nero's early marriage (at 16) to Octavia in 53 would have triggered several royal weddings among client-princes living in Rome,[159] and Aristobulus was certainly at the right age for such a commitment (then in his early twenties). We have already discussed Tigranes II (VI), second cousin of Aristobulus III, who seems to have married around this time (Chapter 9 §1). He too was soon to be honoured by Nero. In the same year Agrippa II, who was still in Rome, would have attended the imperial and royal weddings, and his kingdom was enlarged by Claudius (see below §5; and compare his presence at another possible Herodian wedding in CE 75—Chapter 9 §1). It was also precisely now that Agrippa II decided to arrange his sisters' marriages, as testified by Josephus (see below §5).

In the case of Aristobulus III, the Jewish historian tells us that his bride was Salome III, the daughter of Herod III and Herodias (I), who was at once his father's cousin (being the daughter of his father's uncle) and his own cousin (being the daughter of his father's sister). But we have already criticized this uncorroborated statement of *Ant.* 18.137, which seems to be based on Josephus's own misconception (above §1). Salome III was apparently born at the beginning of the century, and she was too old for Aristobulus. A woman over 50 cannot have given birth to three sons, as Aristobulus's wife did. That he did marry a Herodian princess called Salome, however, is a fact confirmed by coin evidence (she was reigning in CE 56/57, and was possibly alive up to the early 90s). As I have argued elsewhere, this younger princess (born not earlier than the 20s CE) would have been

158. For the date of Nero's birth, see Suetonius, *Nero* 6.1; Sumner 1967: 416-18; for his adoption by Claudius, see Tacitus, *Ann.* 12.26; Suetonius, *Nero* 7.1; cf. Dio, 61.32.2.

159. Tacitus, *Ann.* 12.58; cf. Suetonius, *Nero* 7.2; Dio, 61.33.11.

the 'dancer' of the Gospels, or κοράσιον—a daughter of Antipas possibly called Herodias (II) Salome (Chapter 8 §5). This princess may have settled in Rome after her father's and stepmother's exile to Gaul in 39. Her destiny was to become a queen, when after her wedding (one year later on the present chronology), Aristobulus was made king of Lesser Armenia by Nero. Both Tacitus and Josephus agree that the appointment took place at the end of 54, but they do not explain on what basis Nero decided to send a member of the Herodian family to rule over part of Armenia.[160] It may simply have been a decision of a new and extremely young emperor, who wanted to see his friend awarded with any royal position available at the time; for it is difficult to think of a potential claim—unlike in the case of Tigranes II—that Aristobulus III could have put forward. Lesser Armenia had previously been ruled by Cotys (son of the homonymous king of Thrace), who had taken it up in 38 and who was still active in 42 and 43.[161] Presumably his reign continued for several years, but he must either have been deposed or died shortly before 54.[162]

In retrospect—and again unlike Tigranes II's career in Greater Armenia—Aristobulus's rule over Lesser Armenia was quite successful, at least if we judge from the fact that he held his throne for 17 years. At Nicopolis-ad-Lycum, the capital of his kingdom, Aristobulus minted an interesting series of coins (although their style is more Syrian than Armenian). The first type featuring his queen on the reverse has now been dated to 'Year 3', CE 56/57, confirming the existence of a new royal house in the area. The second type depicting Aristobulus's portrait on the obverse and a dedication to Nero on the reverse, is dated to 'Year 8', CE 61/62. The purpose of this issue may have been twofold. It would have been in line with that of his cousin Agrippa II, who in 60/61 inaugurated a new era at Panias (now called

160. Josephus, *War* 2.252; *Ant.* 18.158 says τῷ πρώτῳ τῆς Νέρωνος ἀρχῆς, i.e. between 13 Oct. 54 and 12 Oct. 55 (Schillinger-Häfele 1986: 55); Tacitus, *Ann.* 13.7 specifies *fine anni*, i.e. before 31 Dec. 54.

161. For his accession in 38, see Dio, 59.12.2; for his activities in 42, see Tacitus, *Ann.* 11.9 (this was the year in which Mithridates repossessed Greater Armenia, starting the civil war between Gotarzes and Vardanes); and in 43, see Josephus, *Ant.* 19.338 (participation at the conference in Tiberias).

162. On Lesser Armenia, Cotys and Aristobulus III, see Reinach 1914; Magie 1950: 1.574; Jones [A.H.M.] 1971: 170 and n. 44; Bosworth 1976: 66-67; Sullivan 1978b: 319-21; Mitford 1980: 1174; Kokkinos 1986a; Mitchell 1993: 2.154; Syme 1995: 137-43.

Neronias), in honour of Nero's shaving of his beard in 60 (see below §5). But it may also have reflected local events. In 60 Greater Armenia was granted to Tigranes II, and Aristobulus (among other client-kings) had gained jurisdiction over the border crossings of the two Armenias, so that he would be able in time of war to assist without delay his newly installed second cousin (Chapter 9 §1). The third type, dated to 'Year 17' (70/71), after the fall of Jerusalem, is a dedication to the new Emperor Vespasian who is mentioned on the reverse, and must have been minted shortly before the annexation of Lesser Armenia around mid-71 (rather than 72 as was previously thought). This is demonstrable by the era of Nicopolis which began in 71/72.[163]

As a compensation Aristobulus was presented with his father's old kingdom of Chalcis,[164] where we find him in 72/73 setting out with an army to support the invasion of Commagene. The annexation of Lesser Armenia was followed within a year by that of neighbouring Commagene (Chapter 9 §1), as part of Vespasian's plan to strengthen the Syrian frontier.[165] Aristobulus's knowledge of the region and the fact that he was related to Antiochus IV King of Commagene (nephew-in-law of Jotape I (IV), cousin of Antiochus IV—see below §4), must have been the reason for his selection by Paetus, the governor of Syria. No more evidence concerning Aristobulus's reign at Chalcis is available, but if a new era did commence in this region in CE 93, we would have to assume that he lost his kingdom under

163. For the coins see *AJC* 2, 280, nos. 4-6a; *RPC* 1, 3839-40; and now Meshorer 1990–91: 112, 127, no. 5BN, with the corrected date; cf. Kokkinos 1986a: 33, 36, 47 n. 1. To my bibliography of Salome's coin add: Hennin 1830: 2.261; Macler 1907: 621-62, 625; Kahrstedt 1910: 304; Reifenberg 1950: 82-83; Reifenberg 1953: 27, no. 16; Sear 1982: 552, no. 5605. To the three copies mentioned there (Paris, Munich, Haifa) add a fourth at St Petersburg (Golicov 1930; Golicov 1931), and possibly a fifth in the collection of A. Sofaer in New York (Qedar *pers com.*). For the date of the annexation and Nicopolis's new era, see Mitford 1980: 1180 n. 15.

164. Josephus, *War* 7.226; there should be little doubt that 'Aristobulus of Chalcidice' was the son of Herod of Chalcis (Kokkinos 1986a: 36; cf. Bosworth 1976: 66 n. 27)—the fact that he was selected to support the invasion of Commagene, a kingdom close to Lesser Armenia, which Aristobulus III had surrendered only a year before, is indicative.

165. Josephus, *War* 7.219-43; Suetonius, *Vesp.* 8.3; see Cumont 1936: 608; Bowersock 1973: 135; Rey-Coquais 1978: 50; and now Millar 1993b: 81-82; for numismatic evidence cf. Kokkinos 1986a: 48 n. 3.

Domitian.[166] At that time he was slightly over 60, and he may either have been deposed or died (compare below §5).

Aristobulus III had three sons: a Herod VII, an Agrippa IV, and another Aristobulus IV, apparently born from the early 50s onwards.[167] We have no information as to their whereabouts, but they would probably have been brought up in Rome. Herod VII (the last member of the dynasty known to us to carry this name) seems to be the person acknowledged by Josephus as having bought a copy of *War*, evidently at the end of the 70s or the early 80s.[168] Josephus comments on his Hellenic wisdom (ἑλληνικὴ σοφία), and gives an unusual epithet to him: σεμνότατος ('the most modest' or 'the most decent'). In terms of speculation, Paul in his epistle to the Romans sent his greetings to 'those in the household of Aristobulus', conceivably mentioning a member of it: 'Herodion'—the diminutive of the name Herod, that is 'the young Herod' or 'the small Herod'—presumably a mere boy for whom Paul had an affection.[169] Of course no positive identification can be made with Herod the son of Aristobulus and Salome, the so-called later 'most modest', but this is another intriguing example of possible first-hand information on the Herodian family to be found in the New Testament (above §1).

Herod of Chalcis, the father of Aristobulus III and grandfather of Herod VII, left two more sons by Berenice II, who were born not earlier than CE 45 (one year after Herod's marriage to Berenice) or later than 48 (the year when Herod died)—let us say in 46 and 47. We must note that Herod of Chalcis was around 56 and 57 years old respectively when he became their father. The first was named Berenicianus after his mother (or should he have been Herod Berenicianus?),

---

166. The evidence for a new era is numismatic, beginning from CE 93 (not 92, as in Reinach 1914: 156; Jones [A.H.M.] 1971: 461 n. 60; Sullivan 1978b: 321)— 'Year 25' must equal CE 117, since on coins of Trajan and Hadrian. However, it is not certain whether ΧΑΛΚΙΔΕΩΝ refers to Chalcis ad Libanum or Chalcis ad Belum (*BMC* Syr., liv-v, 147-48, nos. 1-9), as rightly observed by *SVM* 1, 573 n. 68.

167. Josephus, *Ant.* 18.137.

168. Josephus, Apion 1.51.

169. Rom. 16.10-11; cf. Phil. 4.22, referring to those of the House of Caesar. Noy (in *JIWE* 2, no. 292) reads the name Ἡροδίων in a fragmentary inscription from Rome (cf. *CII* 173; rejected in Kokkinos 1990: 133 n. 49), but he cannot justify its context (purely Jewish), date (third/fourth century CE) or orthography (*omicron*). Even if the badly preserved letter is an *ēta*, could it not belong to the end of the previous word?

while the second took the name Hyrcanus, reviving his remote Has-monaean descent.[170] We have no knowledge as to what became of these children, but a guess may suffice. It is conceivable that after their father's death they were brought up by their mother at Chalcis, which had now been taken over by their uncle Agrippa II *in absentia*, and that after the latter's appointment to a larger kingdom (in CE 53), the boys followed her mother to her brother's new residence at Panias. Berenice later remarried (c. CE 63) and went on to live in Cilicia for a while, but only when her sons would have been old enough to be sent to Rome for their education (see below §5). On their return (assuming that they did return) Berenice had also come back to Agrippa's palace, and the now young men may have been employed by their uncle in his administration.

An inscribed lintel from a temple (?) at Saura (Sûr) in Trachonitis, possibly dating to the end of the first century CE, mentions a Ἡρώδης Βερενικιάνος (or 'Herod son of Berenicianus?') who seems to have been a very distinguished individual. The inscription is another ὑπὲρ σωτηρίας text (frequently connected with ruling figures), dedicated by an architect, Heracleides son of Alaphalus, apparently fulfilling his vow for the 'safety' or 'safe return' of his master. Although it is difficult to make a direct identification, since Herodian names abounded there for centuries, and the inscription carries no date, if it could be shown on palaeographical grounds to belong to the end of the first century CE, then it could be of some importance for the last stage in the history of the Herodian family in that area.[171]

4. *Aristobulus II*

The younger brother of Agrippa I and Herod of Chalcis is an interest-ing if shadowy figure. Aristobulus II, born in c. 8 BCE (above §2),

170. Josephus, *War* 2.221; *Ant.* 20.104; see Kokkinos 1986a: 37-38. Josephus named his eldest son 'Hyrcanus' in c. CE 72 (*Life* 5, 426), but the name also appears in an Egyptian inscription of the first century BCE (*OGIS* 182.19), as well as in a text from Jerusalem (*CII* 1297).

171. Littmann, *et al.* 1921: no. 797[8] (cf. letter forms with no. 797[1] dated to 74/75); for a 'Berenicianus' father of Julia Crispina, see above n. 105; cf. a son of Symmachos from Lubbên (Littmann, *et al.* 1921: no. 793[4]); a son of Alexander from Babiska (Prentice 1922: no. 1092); also in a much later text (a list of *dioikētai*) from Oumm-ez-Zeitoun, which records several names of Herodian origin (Wadd. 2547); cf. Chapter 8 n. 128.

was the only son of Aristobulus I not to become a king, though the private life he led was not in isolation or even far from royalty. Taken to Rome after the death of Herod the Great, his early years would have been spent together with his brothers, educating himself in the usual manner of client-princes.[172]

Apparently at the beginning of the 30s CE, after the death of his mother Berenice I, Aristobulus II contracted his marriage. Unlike Agrippa I (in the early 20s) and Herod of Chalcis (in the late 20s), Aristobulus did not take as wife a Herodian princess, but a princess of another dynasty who would then have been resident in Rome. Her name was Jotape I (IV), and she was the daughter of Sampsigeramus II of Emesa and Jotape III of Commagene (see family tree in Chapter 9 §1). Since Sampsigeramus II was already ruling from about CE 17, Aristobulus after the wedding must have made the right decision to join the kingdom of his father-in-law.[173] Good relationships between Emesa and the Herods of Judaea had been cultivated since the time of Aristobulus II's great-grandfather Antipater I, who in 47 BCE exerted influence upon Iamblichus I, possibly the great-grandfather of Sampsigeramus II.[174]

Jotape I (IV) is unlikely to have been born before CE 5 at the earliest, and thus to have been ready for marriage before 20, for her mother (Jotape III) is unlikely to have been born before 10 BCE. Note

172. Josephus, *War* 1.552; *Ant.* 17.12-13; 18.133 (see the reconstruction in Chapter 7 n. 52).

173. Josephus, *Ant.* 18.135; Cantineau 1931: 139-41, no. 18; see Sullivan 1978a: 212-14, who conjectures that his reign may have begun in CE 5/6, but this seems too early—cf. the following two notes.

174. Josephus, *War* 1.188; *Ant.* 14.129. According to Sullivan (1978a: 212-13) Iamblichus I was the grandfather of Sampsigeramus II, but we may or may not be missing a generation, i.e. between Iamblichus II and Sampsigeramus II—see the following comparative list between the ages of the Herods and the floruit of the Emesenes:

Antipater I (c. 112—43 BCE)	~	Iamblichus I (floruit 50s BCE—30s BCE)
Herod the Great (73/72—5/4 BCE)	~	Iamblichus II (floruit 20 BCE)
Aristobulus I (c. 35–8 BCE)	~	??
Aristobulus II (c. 8 BC—AD 50s?)	~	Sampsigeramus II (floruit 17 CE—40s CE)

that the latter's father (Mithridates III) was still a παιδίσκος ('a young boy') in 20 BCE![175] The role she played in the court of Emesa when she returned with her husband there is not known to us, but Aristobulus, as displayed in his later activities, seems to have developed a great reputation among the aristocracy of Syria. It may have been in the mid-30s CE that Jotape gave birth to the only recorded child of Aristobulus, a girl also named Jotape II (VI). Josephus notes the fact that she was deaf mute (κωφή).[176]

In CE 35, when Agrippa I broke with Antipas at Tyre, and had to make his way to Flaccus at Antioch (above §2), it is revealed to us that Aristobulus was on very bad terms with his brother. Their disagreement might have sprung from Rome, where Agrippa carelessly spent large sums of their mother's money. Perhaps Aristobulus, who seems to have been the first to leave Italy, establishing himself at Emesa, was not keen to know that his penniless closest relative was now circulating in Syro-Palestine causing further trouble. Also Aristobulus almost certainly kept strong ties with Antipas and the Jews of Galilee, and therefore he would not have wanted to be seen supporting Agrippa at that stage. However, as Josephus tells us, their enmity for a while was not allowed to become apparent to Flaccus, the most important Roman authority in the Near East. Nevertheless it was not long before their differences injured Agrippa, for when he was bribed by the Damascenes in their conflict with the Sidonians (above §2), Aristobulus felt that it would be best if Flaccus learned the details and ousted Agrippa. His older brother had become a nuisance and a threat to his stability among the élite of Syrian society.[177]

Aristobulus's career advanced in the following years, and even after Agrippa became king over Galilee (CE 39), his influence in the region was not diminished—though the new king assumed direct control only

175. Dio, 54.9.4; cf. Chapter 9 n. 24. Sullivan (1978a: 212-13) rightly disagrees with Macurdy (1936; Macurdy 1937: 96-99), who would have dated the marriage of Aristobulus's mother-in-law as early as 5 BCE, and thus the possibility that our Jotape was born ten years earlier. But even Sullivan's own conjectured date of CE 5/6 for this marriage, should be taken only as a *terminus post quem*. Although Sullivan (1978c: 780-83) is in a basic agreement with Macurdy's general reconstruction and chronology of the royal family of Commagene from Mithridates III onwards, a fresh investigation of the problem seems to be needed.

176. Josephus, *Ant.* 18.135; *War* 2.221.

177. Josephus, *Ant.* 18.151-54.

after his return from Italy in the second half of 41. In the episode of Petronius with the statue of Caligula in 40, the embassy supporting the Jews of Galilee was headed by Aristobulus, Helcias the Elder and other Herods (a situation familiar from earlier and later such delegations).[178] Helcias himself no doubt represented the Jews of Judaea (who had been notified by Petronius), exactly where we find him a short time later under Agrippa I. As has been put forward earlier, in contrast to previous interpretations, Judaea under Roman rule (CE 6–41) possessed an aristocratic government led by the surviving members of the Herodian dynasty (Chapter 7 §2). The plea of Aristobulus and others to Petronius was successful, at least in that it delayed the execution of Caligula's plan, which could have changed history by bringing Jerusalem's fall some 30 years before its time.

No role in the administration of Agrippa, nor any other benefit, is recorded as coming Aristobulus's way, after Agrippa had established himself over the entire kingdom once ruled by Herod the Great. We may assume that their bad relationship had not changed. All the more because Agrippa through his imprisonment had become hard and vindictive, even to people who had helped him in the past (such as Silas). Yet early in 43 a truce might have been achieved in the spirit of the conference at Tiberias, where among other kings Agrippa invited Sampsigeramus II. It is possible that the King of Emesa saw the chance to bring with him his son-in-law (particularly since Herod of Chalcis also participated), and put an end to this 'improper' argument between the brothers, which must have affected his personal dealings with the now powerful King of the Jews.[179] Aristobulus II would have outlived both Agrippa and Herod, dying 'in private station' in the CE 50s or 60s. Josephus knew of his death in *War* 2.221, which means that Aristobulus died before the publication of this work in the late 70s (Chapter 7 n. 98).

5. *Agrippa II*

As we saw, Agrippa II, the famous son of Agrippa I, was born in Rome in CE 27/28. His first acquaintance with Palestine was at the age of five, when he must have been taken there by his father, who was

178. Josephus, *Ant.* 18.273-78; for other known embassies led by members of the Herodian family, see Chapter 7 nn. 80, 102, 114.

179. Josephus, *Ant.* 19.338.

forced to leave Italy after spending his entire fortune. For a year or so Agrippa II stayed on a Herodian estate at Malatha or Malathai (Tel Malḥata), on the southern border of Idumaea, from where he was briefly moved to Tiberias, on the Sea of Galilee, and then to Antioch in Syria and Alexandria in Egypt following the changing circumstances in his father's career. After Agrippa I's return to Rome in CE 36, however, Agrippa II followed his mother, Cyprus III, back to Judaea.[180]

We do not know whether Agrippa I took his son with him on his journey to Gaul (CE 39–40) accompanying Caligula (as is assumed here), but by the time this was over Agrippa II had reached 14, and thus he would have needed to settle in Rome for his education (compare coin, above n. 88). Josephus underlines the fact that Agrippa II was thoroughly conversant with Hellenic culture (ἑλληνικὴ παιδεία).[181] Four years later, at the death of Agrippa I, he was still in Rome and 'too young' for the throne of Judaea, which was reckoned to be of importance.[182] Claudius in his letter dated to 28 June CE 45 confirmed that the Herodian prince was being brought up at the imperial court, and that it had been mainly due to his influence that a Jewish delegation sent to Rome had achieved its goal of gaining possession of the then disputed priestly robes. We must note that from very early on Agrippa II showed an interest in the affairs of Jerusalem and the Temple.[183]

When Herod of Chalcis, the brother of Agrippa I, died in late 48, Claudius assigned his kingdom to his nephew,[184] Agrippa II—Herod's

---

180. Josephus, *Ant.* 18.160—note μετὰ τῶν τέκνων, which must refer to Drusus (13), Agrippa II (9), Berenice II (8) and Mariamme VI (2); Drusilla had yet to be born.

181. Josephus, *Life* 359; on Agrippa II's reign in general, see Frankfort 1962; *SVM* 1, 471-83; Stern [M.] 1974b: 300-305; Stern 1975b: 176-78; Sullivan 1978b: 329-45; on his kingdom see now Dentzer 1986; MacAdam 1986: 47-67.

182. Josephus, *Ant.* 19.360-62; cf. *War* 2.220; also cf. Suetonius, *Aug.* 48, for those too young to rule.

183. Josephus, *Ant.* 20.9-12; cf. 15.407.

184. Josephus, *Ant.* 20.104; *War* 2.223. Herod's death is said to have occurred in Claudius's eighth year, i.e. sometime between 25 Jan. 48 and 24 Jan. 49 (cf. Appendix 9, pt. a). But the precise time will have been around the autumn of CE 48, so that there is no reason to postulate that Chalcis remained unassigned for a whole year (contra Smallwood 1976: 262 n. 22). This is broadly in agreement with Tacitus (*Ann.* 12.23), who although he confused Herod with Agrippa I (*GLAJJ* 2, 75),

own son evidently being under aged (above §3). Conceivably at this time Agrippa II was given, in addition to Chalcis, the authority (enjoyed by his uncle) over the Temple at Jerusalem.[185] This carried the right of selecting the high priests, and later Agrippa (from about CE 58) exercised it frequently, by appointing and deposing six of them (see below). The control of the Temple, not only kept him in direct touch with Jerusalem but also added a significant aspect to his wider rule, since the Temple apart from being the religious centre of the Jews, was the social and economic heart of Judaea. In effect Agrippa could interfere in the internal affairs of this otherwise Roman province, and no doubt often profit from it.

But Agrippa did not leave Rome immediately upon his appointment over Chalcis in 48/49. It appears that he stayed with Claudius at least until c. 51/52, when the trial concerning the conflict between Cumanus, the Jews and the Samaritans took place.[186] His influence again saved

found it expedient (see above n. 58) to mention his death early in the consulship of Q. Veranius and C. Pompeius (CE 49).

185. Cf. Josephus, *Ant.* 20.15-16; and 20.222 where it is said that the ἐπιμέλεια of the temple was left with Agrippa by Claudius (i.e. before 54); cf. below n. 189.

186. Cumanus became procurator of Judaea in the summer of 48. *War* 2.223 puts his arrival immediately *after* the death of Herod of Chalcis in the autumn of 48 (above n. 184), but the fuller *Ant.* 20.103 puts it immediately *before*. Thus his arrival must have taken place after the disturbances (perhaps connected with them) leading to the crucifixion of the sons of Judas under Tiberius Alexander, apparently during Passover of this year. Now since at least two other Passovers are attested in the governorship of Cumanus (*Ant.* 20.106 = *War* 2.224; *Ant.* 20.133 = *War* 2.244), the second cannot be earlier than CE 50. This is in agreement with the presence of C. Ummidius Durmius Quadratus, who cannot have arrived in Syria as governor earlier than late 49—the last coins of Longinus date between Oct. 47 and Oct. 48 (Mionnet 1811: 167, no. 175; see now *RPC* 1, 4278), and Tacitus, *Ann.* 12. 11-12 refers to him as still in the post in 49 (*SVM* 1, 264; contra Schwartz [D.R.] 1992: 239). But if Thomasson (1984: 306, no. 24; cf. Syme 1981: 131-32) is right that Longinus may have been succeeded by a L. Papillius Balbus between 49/51, then Quadratus did not arrive in Syria earlier than 51, when he is first attested by Tacitus, *Ann.* 12.45. So the episode between the Jews and the Samaritans under Cumanus which was tried in Rome (*Ant.* 20.135; *War* 2.245), could hardly date before 51, and thus Felix would not have become the new procurator of Judaea before 52, in the twelfth year of Claudius (*Ant.* 20.137; cf. *War* 2.247-48). Tacitus (*Ann.* 12. 54.1) does refer to Felix in 52, even though he is confused over the area in which Felix had been active previously (perhaps in Samaria and not Judaea), and Acts 24.10 would

the Jews, by ensuring the intercession of Agrippina the Younger, wife of Claudius. It should be noted that the relationship of Agrippa II with Agrippina is an important reminiscence of that between Agrippa I and Antonia Augusta, the empress's grandmother.[187] Even in 53 Agrippa II may still have been resident at Rome. Josephus tells us that Claudius, 'after the completion of his twelfth regnal year' (that is in his thirteenth year beginning in January 53), deprived him of Chalcis and granted him a larger domain consisting of the old tetrarchies of Philip and Lysanias (compare above §2).[188] Agrippa, at the age of 26, must then have found it necessary to move to his new territory (he was certainly in Syria at the end of 54 when Nero asked him to prepare his forces for a possible crossing of the Parthian frontier).[189] *War* 2.247 implies that the tetrarchy of Varus in Arca was also presented to Agrippa on this occasion, but this actually happened later, under Vespasian (see below).

As soon as he arrived in his kingdom, Agrippa arranged for his sisters' weddings, which were long overdue. Mariamme VI, now 19,

imply the same by saying that he was known to the Jews for many years (Kokkinos 1990: 137 n. 74).

187. Like Antonia (and Livia before her), Agrippina will have inherited some landed wealth in Palestine, which may be traced to the time of Agrippa II. The more striking evidence is the recently published ossuary of Theodotus, a freedman of βασίλισσα Ἀγριππείνα, who was based at Jericho, an area rich in plantations (Hachlili 1979: 33 [no. 3], 46; Piattelli 1990). The wife of Claudius is also commemorated on the coins struck in Judaea by Felix in 54 (*AJC* 2, 284, nos. 32-34), as well as in Caesarea-on-the-coast (*RPC* 4859; cf. under Nero 4845, 4860-61; cf. also Kindler 1983–84), and her name survived in the fortress 'Agrippina' (*m. Ro Haš.* 2.4), identified with Kokhav ha-Yarden (Kaukab el Hawa 199223) east of Mt Tabor in Lower Galilee (Bar-Kochva 1974: 111; *TIRIP* 168-69). Cf. the presence of Stephanos, a Claudian slave, at Bethhoron northwest of Jerusalem in c. 49 (*War* 2.228; *Ant.* 20.113).

188. Josephus, *Ant.* 20.138; cf. *War* 2.421. The coins struck by the city of Tiberias in 53/54 (*AJC* 2, 279, nos. 5-7a; see now *RPC* 1, 4851-54) do not show the coming of Agrippa II, because the city was then out of his jurisdiction (cf. below n. 193; Freyne 1980: 76-78). These issues heralded those of Jerusalem and Caesarea struck by Felix (see previous note). Nevertheless, Agrippa eventually did take over Tiberias's mint, using the same designs (see above n. 88 end).

189. Tacitus, *Ann.* 13.7. If Meshorer (1990–91: 113) is right that stone weights from Jerusalem refer to Agrippa II as 'king' in CE 50 (cf. Agrippa I's weights, above n. 98), then this proves that he inherited the authority of Herod of Chalcis in the city (above n. 185), but it had to be *in absentia*.

had been promised by their father to Julius Archelaus son of Helcias. But her marriage, which produced a daughter, Berenice III, did not last. In the early 60s CE, she left Archelaus and married Demetrius of Alexandria from whom she had a son called Agrippinus (for Mariamme and her descendants see Chapter 7 §2). Drusilla, now 15, had also been promised to Epiphanes, son of king Antiochus IV (above §2). Yet the Commagenean prince changed his mind, in spite of her beauty, being unwilling to convert to Judaism (compare Syllaeus in Chapter 7 §1), and Agrippa gave her instead to Azizus king of Emesa, who was nephew-in-law of his uncle Aristobulus II. Not long after, evidently in 54 (Azizus died between October 54 and October 55), Drusilla was seduced by the notorious [Ti.] Claudius Felix, and like a typical Herodian lady defiling Jewish law she parted from a living husband to marry the procurator of Judaea.[190] By Felix she had a son, another Agrippa—[Ti. Claudius] Agrippa III—of whom Josephus had extensive knowledge, but which he unfortunately either forgot to include in his later work or it has not survived:

> How this youth and his wife disappeared at the time of the eruption of Mount Vesuvius in the times of Titus Caesar (in CE 79), I shall describe later.[191]

The young couple obviously lived in Campania, possibly at Pompeii, where they may have owned a villa. Agrippa III must have been less than 25 when he and his unnamed wife were swept away by the volcano.

Berenice II, the elder among the sisters of Agrippa II, widow of Marcus Alexander (from 44) and of Herod of Chalcis (from 48) and mother of two children, moved into her brother's palace at Panias

---

190. On Azizus see Josephus, *Ant.* 20.139, 141, 158; Sullivan 1978a: 215-16. It is not clear how Drusilla would have escaped 'the malice of her sister Berenice II' by divorcing Azizus and marrying Felix. Presumably Agrippa II's kingdom (where Berenice resided) seriously overpowered Azizus's (the home of Drusilla). The bad relationship between the sisters may explain the apparent lack of contact between Agrippa II and Felix, once sensed by Smallwood (1976: 273-74) and now followed by Goodman (1987: 148). But this point may be deceptive, considering that we have no history for this area from c. 55 to 58 (see below n. 194). On Felix see Kokkinos 1990; also Kokkinos 1992a: 31-32, for a claimed royal background—consistent with his marriages to three princesses.

191. Josephus, *Ant.* 20.144; cf. Petersen 1958: 273-74, where the general problem of unfulfilled promises for information in Josephus is also treated.

(above §§2 and 3). In c. 63 Berenice decided to remarry, allegedly because of rumours that she was living incestuously with Agrippa.[192] Her third husband was a 'Polemo king of Cilicia', probably [C.] Julius Polemo king of Pontus and [Eastern] Cilicia [Pedias] (see Appendix 6), but the union failed and by 65 at the latest she returned to her brother (see below).

Josephus apparently implies that in the first year of Nero (54/55) the territory of Agrippa II was enlarged by the addition of a portion of Galilee (including the cities of Tiberias and Tarichaea) and a portion of Peraea.[193] *Ant.* 20.159 has Agrippa receiving in Peraea only the city of Julias (as renamed by Antipas, and former capital of Pheroras's territory) with its attached 14 villages, but *War* 2.252 maintains that he was also given the city of Abila with its own district. However it appears that this grant was made in the second year of Nero (despite its being conveniently placed by Josephus together with that of Aristobulus III at the end of 54—above §3), because it was in 55/56 that a new era of his commenced, which we may thus call Agrippa's Era of Tiberias (see Appendix 10, pt. d). We may observe that the allotment of Peraea was of double importance. Not only was the region very fertile, but it also held a strategic position. It now constituted the southernmost point that Agrippa could reach—within walking distance, as it were, from Judaea and the Temple on the one side, or the cities of Nabataea on the other.

Between c. 58 and the outbreak of the Revolt in 65 (see Appendix 9) Agrippa's presence in Judaea became increasingly powerful, especially towards the end of that period, when it was as if the Herodian king, who lived almost permanently at Jerusalem, ran the province hand in hand with its Roman governors. In c. 58 we find Agrippa together with Berenice at Caesarea-on-the-coast, paying their respects to the newly arrived Porcius Festus. This was a momentous occasion in the history of early Christianity, perhaps the last direct encounter of the new faith with the Herods, since Paul (who was about to be sent to Rome after two years of imprisonment under Felix) had the opportunity to converse with Agrippa and his sister, and presumably 'preach' to them.[194] Subsequently Agrippa went up to Jerusalem

192. Juvenal, *Sat.* 6.157-58; Josephus, *Ant.* 20.145-46.

193. Josephus, *Ant.* 20.159; cf. *Life* 38; we know now that one of the 14 villages attached to Peraean Julias must have been 'Soffathe..' (*P. Yadin* 37.4, 11).

194. Acts 25.13-27; 26.1-32; Luke's literary construction of Paul's speech before

where he appointed his first high priest, Ishmael son of Phiabi (compare the episode of Helcias II—Chapter 7 §2), and within a year another, Joseph Kabi son of Simon.[195] There he initiated an ambitious building programme of enlarging the Herodian palace and renovating the Temple (a work completed some five or six years later), by bringing a great quantity of precious cedar from Mount Lebanon (like Solomon and evidently Herod the Great).[196]

The sudden death of Festus in c. 59/60 found Agrippa again selecting a new high priest, Ananus son of Ananus, before departing to his kingdom, where he undertook the enlargement of Panias (Caesarea Philippi), which he renamed Neronias. Agrippa's Era of Neronias—as has been worked out from numismatic evidence—began in the year 60/61, almost certainly as a response to Nero's celebration of the first shaving of his beard, followed by the institution of the 'Neronia'.[197] Meanwhile at Jerusalem, without Roman or Herodian supervision, Ananus was able to take fresh action against the leaders of the Christian congregation. This time James, the brother of Jesus, was hastily tried on an alleged religious offence and stoned to death. Agrippa was immediately informed of this misdeed, and shortly before the arrival of the new procurator Lucceius Albinus, he replaced Ananus (after only three months in office) with Jesus son of Damnaeus.[198]

Agrippa is of course open to criticism (see e.g. Kilgallen 1988), but the event itself cannot be doubted; that Luke does not refer to Berenice as 'Queen' should not be taken as an error, because strictly speaking between 49 and c. 63 she was not (cf. Appendix 6), and later her title (particularly after the Titus affair) became honorary; for the date of Festus and Paul's journey to Rome, see Appendix 8. As with other instances (e.g. Appendix 9, pt. e end), it is odd that Josephus ignores Paul. Josephus's history for the period between Passover 55 and c. 58 is totally blank. This is exactly the time of the arrest and imprisonment of Paul (56–58). Josephus, 19 in 55/56 (Appendix 9, pt. e), and studying under the Pharisees, must have been present in Jerusalem. He had recently returned to the city, after spending three years in the wilderness instructed by Bannus, a type of John the Baptist (*Life* 11–12).

195. Josephus, *Ant.* 20.179, 196; for convenient lists of the high priests, see Smallwood 1962: 31-32; *SVM* 2, 229-32.

196. Josephus, *Ant.* 20.189, 219; cf. *Ant.* 15.391; *War* 5.36.

197. Josephus, *Ant.* 20.211; *War* 3.513; for coin evidence see Appendix 10, pt. d; the refoundation of Panias seems to have been celebrated by Agrippa with the issue of a coin (*AJC* 2, 250, nos. 1-3; contra Meshorer 1990–91: 110), which however carries no date (Stein 1984–85); for Nero see Dio, 62.19.1-21.2; Suetonius, *Nero* 12.3-4; cf. Tacitus, *Ann.* 14.20-21.

198. Josephus, *Ant.* 20.197, 203; cf. Eusebius, *Hist. Eccl.* 2.23.11-18.

324

The Herodian Dynasty

Agrippa's plans for building continued in c. 61/62 with benefactions to the non-Jewish communities of Syria beyond his realm, following the tradition established by his famous predecessors, Herod the Great and Agrippa I. The Roman *colonia* of Berytus was embellished, by the addition of another theatre, and by many statues (ἀνδριάντες) and what appear to have been sculptured panels (εἰκόνες). Agrippa even instituted annual spectacles in which he distributed grain and olive oil, conceivably by the way of *tesserae* thrown to the crowd.[199] It is probably from this period that the celebrated Latin inscription found at Berytus comes, testifying to the reconstruction of a building, originally built by Herod the Great, to which marble dressing and six columns were added by 'Queen Berenice' and 'King Agrippa' II.[200]

Back in Jerusalem in c. 62, the appointment by Agrippa of yet another high priest, Jesus son of Gamaliel, created a feud between his supporters and those of the previous high priest. This led to internal strife, because among the latter was a powerful ex-high priest, Ananias son of Nedebaeus, who had recently been the target of the *sicarii*, and who now decided to break away with his followers.[201] As a consequence, two important members of Agrippa's family, Saulus and Costobarus II, organized their own gang, no doubt to protect Herodian interests (Chapter 7 §2). Thus near the end of Albinus's procuratorship, a serious division occurred in the upper class of Jerusalem

199. Josephus, *Ant.* 20.211-12; on the question of Herodian see εἰκόνες Millar 1990a: 14; cf. Diplock 1971; on Herodian *tesserae* see the interesting collection from Caesarea-on-the-Coast published by Hamburger [A.] 1986.

200. *AE* 1928, no. 82; Gabba 1958: 102-103, no. 30; for the inscription and archaeology, see Moutèrde and Lauffray 1952: 8-9; Lauffray 1978.

201. Ananias son of Nedebaeus had a recently career beginning from 48, when he was appointed high priest by Herod of Chalcis (above n. 157; cf. Stern [M.] 1971). Ananias survived a trial in Rome under Claudius (c. 51), ordered Paul to be struck on the mouth and accused him in front of Felix (c. 56), strongly opposed the *sicarii* (c. 60–62), and was finally killed by the rebels of Menahem the grandson of Judas from Gamala in 65. Ananias had a brother (Josephus, *War* 2.429), and apparently five sons (*War* 2.243; *Ant.* 20.131; *War* 2.409, 566; *Ant.* 20.208; *War* 2.418, 568; and a Hebrew ostracon from Masada—Yadin and Naveh 1989: 37-38, no. 461). A brief family tree might help:

society, in conjunction with increased rebellious activities among the oppressed lower class.[202]

With every other incident, minor or major, the situation worsened, as for example when Agrippa allowed the Levite hymn singers to wear linen robes on equal terms with the priests, or when the completion of the work on the Temple in c. 63, left a mass of people unemployed. This serious problem Agrippa failed to solve, unable to undertake another large project for the creation of jobs. The timing was particularly bad, since this was a post-Sabbatical year, when shortages of food became critical, as it probably was also a Roman Census year, after which new and conceivably inflated taxes were to be collected (above n. 157). Agrippa's further appointment of a high priest, Matthias III, son of Theophilus II, indicates the continuing religio-political tension and the king's inability to deal with it, which was now to be escalated by the arrival early in 64 of Gessius Florus as procurator of Judaea. According to Josephus this man's character and actions broke the camel's back—in the second year of his rule the situation was violently concluded by a general uprising against Rome.[203]

At the early stage of the Jewish Revolt Agrippa was absent from Judaea, having gone to Alexandria (c. May 65 on my reckoning), to offer his congratulations to Tiberius Alexander, ex-procurator of Judaea and new *praefectus Aegypti*.[204] His sister Berenice II, however, who had come to Jerusalem in discharge of a vow, witnessed the atrocities associated with the slaughter ordered by Florus. But being unable to avert it, even when barefooted (due to her vow) she pleaded with the procurator, she wrote to Cestius the governor of Syria, seeking refuge in the palace after her own life was endangered by the troops from Caesarea.[205]

---

202. Josephus, *Ant.* 212-13; see analyses by Horsley (1986: 45-48) and Goodman (1987: 137-51), with which I agree on some points—but the role of the Herodians has been extremely minimized. For the wider question of the causes of the Revolt, see Bilde 1979; Rappaport 1981; Parente 1984–85; Goodman 1987 (cf. Goodman 1990); Nikiprowetzky 1989; Applebaum 1989b; Kreissig 1989; Brunt 1990: 517-31; and Price 1992.

203. Josephus, *Ant.* 20.216-23, 252-58; *War* 2.277-79 and following.

204. Josephus, *War* 2.309.

205. Josephus, *War* 2.310-14, 333; remember the abuse of her and her sister's statues by these same troops at Caesarea when her father died (below n. 145).

Upon his return, after meeting on the way with dispatches from Cestius and various Jewish sides, Agrippa gave his famous speech in an effort to dissuade the people from rebellion. The main points, as set out at length by Josephus, are instructive: why should all suffer for the view of some who have an 'unreflecting hope of independence' (ἀλόγιστος ἐλπὶς ἐλευθερίας); procurators can be intolerably harsh (ἀνηκέστως χαλεποί), but they come and go; you cannot win a war against Rome—greater nations have failed; do understand that all pay their taxes (φόροι)—Alexandria pays 12 times more than Jerusalem; stop expecting help either from humans (for example from beyond the Euphrates) or from God (θεός), because it is not going to come; thus submit at once your unpaid tribute (εἰσφορά) to Caesar. It is interesting that during the speech, Agrippa's sister Berenice was placed in a commanding position on the roof of the Hasmonaean palace, perhaps symbolizing royal authority. But the whole effort came to nothing, since the rebels soon expelled Agrippa from the city and stones were even thrown at him.[206]

Subsequently at Panias Agrippa received a delegation of Herodian family members asking for a military force, which he made available to them (Chapter 7 §2), but which did not prevent the burning of his palace at Jerusalem. He himself visited Cestius either at Antioch or Berytus, to join him in a campaign which ended in disaster for the Romans on 25 Nov. CE 65.[207] Meanwhile Agrippa's kingdom was left under the management of his friend Varus (Noarus), apparently the then tetrarch of Arca and a descendant of king Soaemus of northern Ituraea. Varus betrayed Agrippa's trust and after serious misconduct against the Babylonian colony of Batanaea and Philip son of Jacimus (compare Chapter 7 §2), was deprived of his position—even his

206. Josephus, *War* 2.335-407. In spite of invention (common in the speeches of classical literature), this particular speech is important, having presumably being read and approved by Agrippa himself (cf. below n. 219)—and as pointed out by Brunt (1990: 529): '(it) doubtless represents much of what was thought and said at the time'; cf. Paul 1990; Schwartz [S.] 1990: 133-36; Rajak 1991; coins dated to 65/66 minted by Agrippa probably at Panias (*AJC* 2, 250, nos. 5-6), may reflect his retirement to his kingdom at that time; these are the earliest inscribed examples on which the double era of Agrippa was used (Year 16 = 6).

207. Josephus, *War* 2.418, 421, 426, 481, 500, 502, 523-26, 554-55; cf. *Life* 24; for 'Berytus' instead of 'Antioch' before Cestius's defeat, see *Life* 49; also cf. *Life* 182, 357 but here 'Berytus' would be after Cestius's defeat; for the campaign of Cestius, see Gichon 1981.

tetrarchy was later taken away from him. To deal with the situation at home Agrippa sent one Aequus Modius, an old comrade of Philip. This helped the latter, who was then hiding in Gamala (while keeping it pro-Roman), to move to Panias and wait for his master. Sometime after Cestius's defeat, when Agrippa returned to Berytus, the news of the uprising of Gaulanitis must have come. This prompted Agrippa, possibly by the spring of 66, to send both Modius and Philip to recapture Gamala, but without success even after a siege of seven months. The destruction of this important hilltop town had to wait for the following year, when a formidable Roman army was brought on to the scene.[208] At the very beginning of 67 Agrippa welcomed Vespasian at Antioch and with his army followed him to the city of Tyre and then Ptolemais, ready to assist in his mission.[209] After the first victories of Vespasian, Agrippa invited the future emperor to rest at Panias before further campaigns. It was Agrippa's mediation that saved the city of Tiberias, as well as some of the people of Tarichaea, from destruction, but the king in his effort to parley with the defenders of Gamala was wounded—around September 67 he was struck on the right elbow with a stone by one of the slingers.[210]

When Vespasian later—on hearing of the death of Nero (9 June CE 68)—sent his son Titus to salute the new Emperor Galba and receive orders, Agrippa accompanied him. Berenice may have participated in

208. Josephus, *War* 2.481-83; 4.4; *Life* 46-61, 114, 177-87. As already noted (Chapter 7 n. 110) there are conflicts in the accounts of *War* and *Life* concerning Philip son of Jacimus; the different factions in Gamala are of interest, as is the fact that the place came between two hostile sides: the Hellenized Phoenicians of Panias and the Jewish-Babylonian colony in Batanea; note that it must have been during the siege of Gamala that Tiberias also asked Agrippa for help (*War* 2.632; *Life* 154-55); to grasp this complicated issue, a detailed chronology for the outbreak of the revolt and Josephus's career in Galilee (cf. Cohen [S.J.D.] 1979: 181-231) is essential (see Appendix 9); for the archaeology at Gamala (es Salam 219256), see Syon 1992; Gutman 1993; *TIRIP* 128; and now Urman 1995: 513-18; a Safaitic inscription found by the Basalt Desert Rescue Survey (King [G.] 1990: 62, KR 3, pl. IIa), alluding to a revolt under a 'King Agrippa' (*mlk grfṣ*), may refer to this uprising of Gaulanitis in 65/66 (*Life* 187), in which many people from Trachonitis participated (*War* 3.542).

209. Josephus, *War* 3.29, 68; *Life* 407; cf. Suetonius, *Vesp.* 4.5; Jones [B.W.] 1984a: 36, says that Vespasian arrived 'in February', but all we may know is that the campaign began around 'March' (cf. Jones [B.W.] 1989: 127 n. 1).

210. Josephus, *War* 3.443, 453-61, 540; 4.14; cf. *Life* 352.

this journey via Greece (Titus was now her lover), from which time her celebrated inscription from Athens may date.[211] As it happened, when they reached Corinth and learned of Galba's death (15 January CE 69), Titus decided to return to his father, while Agrippa continued the journey to Rome. There he experienced the dramatic events of 69, which involved the rapid successions of Otho and Vitellius. Eventually it was in the Roman capital that the news from Palestine of Vespasian's proclamation as Emperor reached Agrippa, who hastened back home.[212]

At the age of 43 Agrippa with his entire army followed Titus in the fatal attack on Jerusalem in CE 70.[213] Among other events he therefore must have witnessed the total destruction of the Temple, built by his great-grandfather and renovated by himself. We have no way of knowing the reactions and personal feelings of Agrippa during the massacre that followed—it would have been interesting to know what effect such a catastrophe had on him. The crushing of Judaea and the triumph of Titus was celebrated with splendour in the capital of Agrippa's kingdom, with 2,500 Jewish prisoners slaughtered in the wild-beast fights and gladiatorial spectacles. Since celebrations were also held by Titus at the *colonia* of Berytus, it is reasonable to assume that Agrippa was also there—he and his sister had recently contributed to its public adornment (see above). The 'safety' or perhaps 'safe return' of the Herodian couple was noted within the Roman colony's territory, by a dedication to Atargatis at the temple in Qalaat Fakra, which may belong to this time. This ὑπὲρ σωτηρίας inscription was set up by one, Strabo, with the help of the high priest and ἐπιμελητὴς of the temple, Gaius Mansouētos.[214]

211. Tacitus, *Hist.* 2.1; Josephus, *War* 4.498; for the inscription see Chapter 3 n. 196; for discussion see Kokkinos forthcoming 1; for the date of Nero's death, cf. Sumner 1967: 416; Tacitus (*Hist.* 2.2) says that *fuerunt qui accensum desiderio Berenices reginae vertisse iter crederent*, which implies that Berenice was in Judaea, but this is not historical rumour—it is Tacitus's own way of introducing Titus's love affair (cf. Braund 1984b: 122 n. 6). The decision by Titus to return to Judaea was political, and its itinerary may even imply that Berenice was with him (cf. Jones [B.W.] 1984a: 45).

212. Josephus, *War* 4.500; Tacitus, *Hist.* 2.81.1; for the date of Galba's death cf. Sumner 1967: 418.

213. Tacitus, *Hist.* 5.1.2.

214. Josephus, *War* 7.23, 37-40; Puchstein *et al.* 1902: 107 n. 43; for Qalaat Fakra and its temple, see Krencker and Zschietzschmann 1938: 1.46-47; cf. Collart

Although Agrippa did not follow Titus to Rome, where the magnificent triumphal procession took place—as depicted on the Arch of Titus in the Roman Forum—he did visit the Roman capital with his sister in 75. This was most probably on the occasion of the completion of the Temple of Peace, where the spoils from the Jerusalem Temple were deposited.[215] According to Dio, Agrippa was awarded the titular rank of *praetor*, and it must have been then that his territory was increased by Vespasian, as Photius testifies on the authority of Justus of Tiberias. Any attempt to determine the nature of this increase must include Arca (Arcea) the tetrarchy of Varus referred to above. In describing Agrippa's kingdom at the beginning of the revolt Josephus clearly omits Arca, but he does mention it as belonging to Agrippa after the end of the war.[216]

Berenice stayed in Rome in the palace of Titus as his mistress, no doubt giving the impression of the arrival of a new Cleopatra to the Roman political life. According to Braund she seems to have remained there until 79, when Titus became emperor. Quintilian tells us that during this period she behaved as an empress. It was thought, but probably unreliably, that Titus was so jealous of her that he ordered the assassination of a Roman general, Caecina, whom he suspected of wishing to share Berenice's favours. It has even been suggested that Berenice may lie behind Maternus's 'Medea' in the *Dialogus* of Tacitus.[217] However under social and political pressure Titus was

1973; on Atargatis in the general area note Millar 1990a: 21; for Berenice's part in the Flavian victory, see Tacitus, *Hist.* 2.2. Another text (recorded in Batanaea at Deir Ayûb, 4 km south of Nawâ) may refer to Agrippa II, and perhaps dating to the same period, but it is very fragmentary: ὑπὲρ σω[τηρίας βασιλέως μεγάλου] κυρίου Μά[ρκου Ἰουλίου Ἀγρίππα]... ιους τὴν θύρ[αν]... (Fossey 1897: 39-40, no. 2).

215. Dio, 66.15.3 (in Rome in CE 75); cf. Suetonius, *Tit.* 7.1; Josephus, *War* 7.158-62 (Templum Pacis).

216. Dio, 66.15.4; Photius, *Bibl.* 33; Josephus, *War* 3.57; 7.97; for Arca see Starcky 1971–72; cf. Thalmann 1990.

217. Dio, 66.16.1; Quintilian, *Inst. Orat.* 4.1; Victor, *Epit. de Caes.* 10.4; Tacitus, *Dial.* 3 (Haywood 1942–43); on Berenice II see Macurdy 1935; Macurdy 1937: 84-91; Mireaux 1951; Crook 1951; Jordan 1974; Sullivan 1978b: 310-13; McDermott and Orentzel 1979: 32-38; Rogers [P.M.] 1980; Braund 1984b; a bust in Naples attributed to Berenice by McDermott and Orentzel (1979: 161 in reference to Maiuri) is a confusion with a Hellenistic queen; for a possible freedwoman of Berenice II from Apulum in Dacia, see Jung 1900: 182-86, no. 9; cf. Chapter 7 n. 64 end.

obliged to send Berenice away from Rome, perhaps to a secret location in the countryside, from where she made a brief comeback only
to be dismissed again. After the death of Titus in 81, Berenice, now
53, would have left Italy to return to her brother's kingdom. We hear
nothing more of her.[218]

Our literary information about Agrippa II also largely ceases at this
point, though a further few facts emerge from Josephus's *Life* and
Against Apion. Agrippa promoted Justus of Tiberias and made him
his private secretary, but then banished him on a charge of fraud
(above n. 218). The king wrote 62 letters to Josephus (two of which
are quoted by the Jewish historian) in order to verify some aspects of
the latter's history of the Jewish War. One should be appended here:

> King Agrippa to dearest Josephus, greeting. From what you have written
> you appear to stand in no need of instruction, to enable us all to learn
> (everything from you) from the beginning. But when you meet me, I will
> myself by word of mouth inform you of much that is not generally
> known.[219]

Agrippa later bought a copy of the complete work of Josephus, which
was available from the late 70s or early 80s, and the historian even
named his youngest son after the king.[220]

On the strength of a rabbinical passage a few scholars have suggested that Agrippa II may have left a family. The evidence is vague
and cannot be taken seriously. Here is what the Babylonian Talmud
says concerning the Feast of Tabernacles:

218. Dio, 66.18.1. Berenice II was unpopular in Italy and although she would
have had the means to stay there until she died, no reason can be found, especially
after Titus's death (cf. Jones [B.W.] 1984a: 93, 210). That she fell victim to Domitian (Applebaum 1974: 117) is a misunderstanding of Quintilian (*GLAJJ* 1, 514).
Life 343 relates how Berenice in 67 saved the life of Justus of Tiberias by begging
her brother not to execute him, after Vespasian had empowered Agrippa to do so.
Now, in *Life* 355 Josephus says that Justus later acquired wealth from Agrippa, but
he was subsequently (ὕστερον) cast 'twice' into prison, ordered 'twice' to leave his
place of origin, and he was 'once' condemned to death—pardoned by Berenice. Is
this a second time that Berenice intervened? Josephus's statement is ambiguous and
polemical (cf. Rajak 1987: 92), but it may refer to a later occasion, because it continues by saying that Justus finally became a secretary of Agrippa until he was banished
on a fraud charge. If this is so, Berenice's second involvement would date to the 80s
and thus present evidence for her return from Italy.

219. Josephus, *Life* 364-66.

220. Josephus, *Apion* 1.51; *Life* 428.

> The steward of King Agrippa asked R. Eliezer...: (A man) such as I who
> have two wives, one in Tiberias and one in Sepphoris, and two *sukkot*
> (booths), one in Tiberias and one in Sepphoris, may I go from one
> *sukkah* to the other (during the seven days of the feast) and thus be free
> from my obligation (to stay in the booth for seven days)? (R. Eliezer)
> answered him: No! For I say that he who goes from one *sukkah* to
> another annuls the good deed of dwelling in the first one.[221]

It has been assumed that the *epitropos* asked the question on behalf of
Agrippa II, and that therefore the latter had two wives and thus probably children. But this is mere speculation. The only point (and irrelevant to this discussion) that can be accepted is that the *epitropos* was
serving Agrippa II and not Agrippa I. The source is R. Eliezer, who
is reckoned to belong to the second generation of rabbinical teachers
(c. CE 80–120).[222]

A few more facts have emerged from the ground, as it were, by the
discovery of inscriptions. But before we examine them we must
briefly discuss Agrippa II's territory and its population. As we saw,
the main part of his kingdom, the old tetrarchies of Philip and Lysanias, consisted of the districts of Abilene (extending over the Anti-
Lebanon), the Hermon, Panias, Ulatha (perhaps separated from Panias),
Gaulanitis, Batanaea, Trachonitis and northern Auranitis. Josephus
describes the limits of this main part as follows:

> ...beginning at Mount Libanus and the sources of the Jordan, (it) extends
> in breadth (from north to south) to the lake of Tiberias, and in length
> (from east to west) from a village called Arpha (unidentified, but to the
> east of Trachonitis towards As-Sapha) to Julias (Bethsaida-Julias at the
> head of the Sea of Galilee); it contains a mixed population of Jews and
> Syrians (Σύροι). [223]

Σύροι here is used as a general term for non-Jews. Some of them
would have been Aramaeans, like the people who first worshipped
Baalshamin at Seeia (Si'a) in Auranitis. Others (as Σύροι often means

---

221. *b. Suk.* 27a; cf. Derenbourg 1867: 252-54.
222. Danby 1933: 799. Jeremias (1969: 94 n. 24) thought that this passage
referred to Agrippa I, but this is not so (see Schwartz [D.R.] 1990: 168-69). It must
be stressed that the majority of rabbinical references to a King Agrippa are likely to
refer to Agrippa II. Also being of late date and of relatively obscure meaning, their
value for historical inquiry is not great (cf. Goodblatt 1987a: 10, 25 n. 18)—thus my
reluctance to use many (cf. above §2).
223. Josephus, *War* 3.57-58.

in Josephus) may have been Hellenized Phoenician settlers, perhaps
reflected in the interest which those from Panias had in Batanaea (see
above, the episode of Varus). Such people would have been at home at
least among the Idumaeans (many of Hellenized Phoenician background) established in Trachonitis by Herod the Great.[224] However
among the Aramaic speakers must also have been included a considerable number of Jews from Babylonia, who were brought to Batanaea
again by Herod the Great, and who built Bathyra and Ecbatana.[225] A
strong Jewish element in both Gaulanitis and Batanaea is of course
evident from Josephus's fortifications at Gamala, Soganaea (or
Soganē) and Seleucia, and from the archaeological evidence, notably
the remains of Neve (Nawâ).[226] Further, according to early Christian
tradition, a community of Jewish Christians (of Nazarene or Ebionite
stock) lived in the area, and along the road to Damascus where Paul
was converted.[227] But the majority of the population was clearly composed of Arabs: Ituraean Arabs in Abilene and the Hermon, Nabataean
Arabs in southern Auranitis (like the worshippers of Dushara/

224. The 3,000 Idumaeans sent to Trachonitis in c. 11 BCE (Josephus, *Ant.*
16.285) are said to have been ravaged later by the Nabataeans (*Ant.* 16.292), but this
does not mean that they were totally exterminated (contra MacAdam 1986: 65 n. 65;
cf. now Shatzman 1994: 134-35). Some may have moved to Batanaea and may be
included in 'the Trachonites living in Batanaea', with whom Varus and the Hellenized Phoenicians from Panias wanted to unite against the Batanaean-Babylonian
Jews (*Life* 54). MacAdam's objection to the fact that Idumaeans settled *in* Trachonitis, by understanding ἐπὶ τῇ Τραχωνίτιδι only as 'in order to monitor Trachonitis',
is not right (*loc. cit.*). The phrase could have meant 'in charge of Trachonitis'—i.e.
not necessarily stationed there—but not in a context followed by κατοικίσας and
ἐκεῖ.

225. Josephus, *Ant.* 17.23-30; *Life* 54, 58; see Applebaum 1989a: 53-54; cf. an
Aramaic inscription from El-Mal in Batanaea dated to 7/6 BCE (Naveh 1975).

226. For Josephus's fortifications, see *War* 2.574; *Life* 9, 187; for archaeological
evidence in general, see Kochavi 1972; Dar 1977; Ma'oz 1981; Dauphin 1982;
Urman 1995; for Nawâ see Schumacher 1886: 167-80; cf. Eusebius, *Onom.* [edn
Klostermann 136].

227. Julius Aphricanus, *apud* Eusebius, *Hist. Eccl.* 1.7; Epiphanius, *Panar.* 30.2;
Acts 9; cf. Pritz 1988: 108-10, 120-21; Taylor [J.E.] 1993: 36-38; the main site
mentioned is Κωχάβα in 'Basanitis' (Epiphanius, *Panar.* 29.7.7), which may be
identified with Kûkab (235250) on the border of Gaulanitis with Batanaea (Schumacher 1886: 83; cf. Avi-Yonah 1976: 107). If ever the circumstances were right
(but they have never been since the inception of archaeology!), the excavation of the
ruins seen by Schumacher would be of interest.

Dionysos in the city of Dionysias/Soueida) and the unnamed Arabs of Trachonitis. What is certainly undeniable is that this highly mixed population of diverse cults and cultures (compare with these Idumaea), had gone through a uniform process: a degree of Hellenization, as proved by a formidable corpus of Greek inscriptions found in the area, even from village contexts.[228]

Concerning Abilene, an interesting inscription, though fragmentary, came from Iabruda (see Map 3).[229] It mentions a Samsigeramus son of S[oaemus], possibly connected to the royal family of Arca or Emesa, who seems to have usurped the position of priest and defrauded the city of a large amount of money. Agrippa II, when the area was put under his jurisdiction, ordered the immediate liquidation of the priest's property to recover the money on behalf of the citizens. The inscription from Iabruda can set the northern limit of Abilene, while a fragmentary text, believed to have originated from Shafuniyeh (northeast of Damascus) and dated probably by the era of Agrippa II (but the year is missing), may indicate the southern limit of the tetrarchy bordering Damascus.[230] It must be stressed that no less than four different fragmentary inscriptions from Helbon (Halbûn) testify to some considerable construction work during Agrippa's rule of Abilene.[231]

Epigraphical evidence from Batanaea (Aqraba, CE 72/73), Trachonitis (Nēgrân, CE 76/77; as-Sanamein, CE 91/92), Auranitis (Seeia), and Peraea (Wâdî al-Kittar, under Nerva?), also bears witness to private building projects in the reign of Agrippa.[232] But most interesting is

228. Cf. Millar's statement in Chapter 2 n. 128; for a convenient introduction to the epigraphical material, see MacAdam (1983: 103-105), who gives an estimate of over 2000 inscriptions; for a guide, see Bérard *et al.* 1989: 66-70; for an index to the American expeditions, see now Kennedy 1995; for another analysis of village administration, see Grainger 1995; cf. Macdonald 1993; for a recent survey in Auranitis, see Dentzer 1986; cf. Graf 1992; also cf. the inscriptions from Senaim, Mt. Hermon in Dar and Kokkinos 1992 (= *SEG* 42, 1408-16), where there are references to archaeological work in the general area.

229. *IGLS* 5.2707.

230. Clermont-Ganneau 1901: 52 n. 1.

231. *OGIS* 420; *IGRR* 3.1090; *SEG* 7.216, 218; for Helbon see Abel and Barrois 1933.

232. *OGIS* 419 (Seeia), 423 (Aqraba), 426 (as-Sanamein = cf. Smith [G.A.] 1935: 652 n. 4); Littmann, *et al.* 1921: 37, no. 785 (Nēgrân); Clermont-Ganneau 1899: 499-501 (Wâdî al-Kittar); but for the latter see comment below n. 250.

the case it provides for the army at Trachonitis. In Saura (Sûr) a text dated to CE 74/75, a dedication (probably funerary) of an Agrippa to his father Herod son of Aumus, mentions the latter as στρατηγὸς of the king, and στρατοπεδάρχης of what appears to be a mixed unit of *coloni* (ἱππεῖς κολωνεῖται καὶ στρατιῶται).[233] If the reference is indeed to soldiers from a formal *colonia*, at that time it can only be Berytus (15 BCE), Ptolemais (CE 52/54) or Caesarea-on-the-coast (CE 69-71). Herod may then have received his last appointment a few years earlier, during the Jewish Revolt, when Agrippa and his war cabinet spent a long period in these *coloniae*, particularly in the region of Berytus.[234] An inscription referring to Lucius Oboulnius, a centurion (ἑκατοντάρχης) of a σπ(ε)ῖρα Αὐγούστα, may offer us the name of this unit, since it was only a year after the Saura text that this man (in 75/76 and apparently until 82/83) supervised some construction work on the Jebel Hauran under Agrippa.[235] No doubt the same σπεῖρα Αὐ[γούστα] is intended in the essentially contemporary inscription from Eitha (see below), and it may thus be possible to trace its origins back to the *cohors I Aug(usta)* around CE 6, in the notorious text of Q. Aemilius Secundus from Berytus (above n. 125).[236]

The inscription from Eitha (al-Hît), on the eastern side of the lava lands, is of particular importance. The surviving part mentioning Agrippa, also refers to ...Χαρητος επα..., and most commentators have taken this to be an ἔπαρχος of the king called Charētos (Harith). But the text only gives the patronymic in the genitive of the name Charēs. The man's name is supplied to us by another inscription found

233. *OGIS* 425; the ideas in *IGRR* 3.114 and Littmann, *et al.* 1921: 424-25, no. 797[1], that we are dealing with an *ala colonorum*, or with people from a region called Kolōnos are not convincing; also Applebaum's position (1989a: 60 n. 88) of *coloni* referring to the Zamarid settlers on the basis of the word found in *Mid. R.* (Num. 4.20) seems of late and doubtful character.

234. Millar 1990a: 12, 24, 26; cf. Isaac 1980–81; see Josephus, *Life* 49, 181, 357; this text should be added to the discussion of Millar (cf. above n. 125).

235. *SEG* 7.970; cf. 1100; the commencement of the work is determined by the double dating 'Year 21 = 16' (see Chart 3 in Appendix 10), while its end would be represented by the 'Year 28' which follows after a break in the text—incorrectly interpreted by Speidel 1982–83: 238.

236. Another connection has been suggested with the cohort called Σεβαστὴ in Acts 27.1 (Speidel 1982–83: 237-40; cf. MacAdam 1986: 65) which is also possible; but see criticism by Gracey 1986: 320-21.

in close proximity, at al-Hayat, where he is called Δ[ι]ομήδης (Χ)άρη(τ)ος the ἔπαρχος of King Agrippa.[237] Diomedes also had dealings with the Bedouin population in the area (νομάδες), and he seems to have been engaged in two other regions, ...ης και Χαλ... (last line of the text), which may perhaps be restored as ['Αβιλην] ἧς καὶ Χαλ[κίδος] (or Χαλκιδικῆς)[238] According to MacAdam Eitha would have been the military base of Trachonitis under Agrippa II, and the headquarters of the *cohors Augusta*, operating in the east of the general area as Bathyra was in the west.[239] This is an attractive hypothesis which however has to wait for a more explicit text, or better the excavation of the site. On the other hand if Diomedes had connections with a leading family of Batanaea, there may not have been a reason to create a second military base. To this possibility we must now turn.

The reference to Diomedes's father, Charēs, raises an intriguing question. Josephus refers to an individual with this name, with whom it is tempting to identify him, despite the fact that he appears in the problematic saga of Philip son of Jacimus (above and Chapter 7 §2). In *War* 4.18 and 68, Charēs together with a Joseph (Joses) are

237. *OGIS* 421; 422; see Peters 1978: 323; MacAdam 1986: 62; Applebaum 1989a: 55, 57. Gracey (1986: 320), realizes that it might be 'son of Charēs', while Kasher (1988: 188) is here correct to attribute both inscriptions to Diomedes, even if he calls his father 'Aretos' (cf. cautiously Paltiel 1991: 216 n. 23). The second inscription was initially recorded as from 'Deir-esh-Schaʿîr' (Wadd. 2135), but it was later rediscovered in al-Hayat (Prentice 1908: 287-88, no. 362), to where it had apparently been moved (cf. comments in Graf 1992: 456). Some have assumed that the two places are identical: MacAdam (1986: 64 n. 62) places it 'just 5 km northeast of al-Hît', while Applebaum (1989a: 55) says 'northeast of the village of Taille'. But Deir ash-Shaʿîr lies about 45 km southeast of Bostra, within Nabataean territory! The southern limit of Auranitis is thought to have run in a line north of Bostra. It is al-Hayat which is close to al-Hît, but about 3 km northwest (cf. Dentzer 1986: 284, fig. 1).

238. The *eparchoi* of Agrippa's army were probably modelled on the earlier auxiliary *praefecti* of the Roman army, and thus they may have been chiefs of their tribes (cf. Webster 1985: 146). Such then would have been Diomedes's background. His connection with the nomads is however based on a restoration [στρατηγ]ὸς νομάδων. Peters (1978: 323), who takes *stratēgos* for granted, sees Diomedes as a kind of a Bedouin sheikh or a phylarch (but cf. Macdonald 1993: 368-82). In any case the background, status and function of the royal military *stratēgoi* are not always clear (see Bengston 1964: 2.265-70; Allon 1977; *SVM* 2, 97).

239. MacAdam 1986: 62, 64 n. 62.

presented as *anti-Roman* leaders of Gamala, repulsing the attack of the armies of Vespasian, Titus and Agrippa. Joseph (Joses) is killed by the Romans, while Charēs dies of an illness shortly before the fall of the fortress, survived only by two women, daughters of the sister of Philip son of Jacimus. By contrast in *Life* 177-78 and 186, Charēs and his 'brother' Jesus (rather than Joseph or Joses), husband of the sister of Justus of Tiberias, are 'relatives' of Philip and evidently *pro-Roman*. Here they were killed by the people of Gamala, led by a Josephus son of a midwife, in an uprising first against the followers of Philip and then against Agrippa and Rome.[240] Once again our preference must lie with the later account of Josephus. We may safely assume that some stories related in the *War* came under attack with the publication of Justus's work, and that despite all the rhetoric Josephus was actually compelled to rectify some in *Life*. The precise relationship of Charēs with Philip is not spelt out, but it could have been a kinship through marriage, like that of Charēs with Justus of Tiberias. Although no clear proof can be found, would not this relationship—given the military background of the leading Jewish/Babylonian family of Batanaea—be in favour of identifying Charēs the father of Diomedes at al-Hît, with Charēs the relative of Philip at Gamala?

The military personnel of Agrippa is extensively attested. Apart from those already mentioned (Philip, Modius, Herod, Oboulnius, Diomedes) we know of another Babylonian called Silas. This man must have held a significant post in Agrippa's army, since as a deserter he became attached to the royal family of Adiabene, some members of which were among the leaders of the rebel forces in Jerusalem. Silas met a hero's death at the hands of the Romans, and Josephus called him κορυφαῖος.[241] We also know of yet another, evidently Babylonian, called Darius, a subordinate of Philip serving as ἱππάρχης, and the same origins must be claimed for one, 'Syllas' (or also Silas?), the

240. The conflict between *War* and *Life* is massive (despite Goodman 1987: 161-62 n. 9), but there are no necessary inconsistencies between *Life* 177-78 and *Life* 186 (contra Price 1991); examination of the details will have to be made elsewhere. There should be no question that Charēs of *War* and *Life* is the same person (cf. indexes of Niese, Feldman and Schalit). Price (1991: 92, 56) glosses over this fact (which does not fit his view) by adhering to two different individuals of the same name, because Cohen suggested it! But Cohen ([S.J.D.] 1979: 167) only raised a question without been convinced by it.

241. Josephus, *War* 2.520; 3.11, 19; cf. Silas under Agrippa I, above n. 70.

captain of Agrippa's bodyguard (ἐπὶ τῶν σωματοφυλάκων).[242] Lastly, while at least one unnamed general of Agrippa is attested in rabbinic sources, an inscription from the Jebel Hauran refers to Archieus, a centurion (κεντυρίων) who served Agrippa in the last 18 years of his reign (see Appendix 10, pt. b).[243]

The lands under his jurisdiction must have yielded Agrippa a substantial income. Josephus does not state the figure, but if we judge from what Philip the Tetrarch received from a smaller territory, Agrippa's revenue would have been at least three times as much—about 300 talents per year. We should underline his possessions in the fertile land of Peraea, the important region round the sea of Galilee, and the area near the Mediterranean coast at Arca. Since one talent was worth 6,000 drachmas, such an income would have equalled 1,800,000 drachmas—or in other words, approximately the full year's wage of 9,000 labourers.[244] Many fragments of evidence indicate that Agrippa's landholdings were considerable. For example, together with his sister Berenice, the king owned property near Mt Tabor administered by Ptolemy the *epitropos*, and elsewhere by Thaumastus—the latter being a probable source of information for Josephus, as we have seen.[245] We have also seen another *epitropos* of Agrippa at Tiberias, referred to in the Talmud, which also acknowledges royal property at Sepphoris.[246] This connection with certain parts of Galilee is clear throughout: it was at Besara towards Ptolemais in the West that Berenice held stocks of corn, and in the Jezreel Valley further south

242. Josephus, *War* 2.421; *Life* 398.

243. *b. 'Abod. Zar.* 55a; Seyrig 1965 = *AE* 1966: 493; a possible *eparchos* of Agrippa, himself called 'Agrippa', is recorded in a text from Deir al-Kahf in southern Auranitis, within Nabataean territory (Littmann, *et al.* 1921, no. 230).

244. Josephus, *War* 2.95; *Ant.* 17.319; my calculation assumes that one drachma or denarius was the ordinary day-wage, and follows the Talmudic view that a labourer would scarcely work more than 200 days per year (cf. generally Sperber 1974); on the Herodian economy, see Schalit 1969: 262-98; Hoehner 1972: 70-79; Gabba 1979 = Gabba 1990; Broshi 1987; Schwartz [D.R.] 1990: 112-13; Kokkinos forthcoming 2, appendix.

245. Josephus, *War* 2.595; *Life* 126-27; *Ant.* 18.194; with Ptolemy of Agrippa II compare Ptolemy the friend of Herod and Archelaus, who possessed land in Arous of Samaria (*War* 2.69); for Herodian property in the general area, cf. Applebaum 1989a: 97-110.

246. *t. Šab.* 13.9, etc. (see Miller 1984).

that royal land was later transferred to imperial control.[247]

As regards the various parts of his kingdom Agrippa seems to have lost Batanaea about CE 93.[248] Since apparently in the same year his cousin Aristobulus III lost Chalcidice (above §3), and his cousin once removed, Alexander IV, probably lost Cilicia (Chapter 9 §1), we may guess that Agrippa also handed back to the Romans Abilene, Trachonitis and Auranitis. Trachonitis is still attested as his in 91/92 (above inscription from as-Sanamein), but not in 96/97, while Auranitis was clearly taken away from him by 96.[249] However the king must have held his other territories, namely Panias, Ulatha, Gaulanitis, and the portions of Galilee and Peraea. Galilee was certainly under his jurisdiction at least until 97/98, and Peraea possibly until under Nerva.[250]

As testified by Justus of Tiberias (*apud* Photius) and now supported by numismatic and other evidence, Agrippa II died in CE 100 (see Appendix 10), when all his remaining possessions became provincial. He was 73. In the words of Barag, Agrippa lived in an eventful and

247. Josephus, *Life* 119; cf. the imperial σῖτος in Upper Galilee (*Life* 71); for the Jezreel valley, see Isaac and Roll, 1982: 1.104-108. We may also know of royal land in Batanaea. An unfortunately fragmentary inscription from Nawâ (Moutèrde 1957), which could have been important, refers to three or four generations of a distinguished family, ending with a Caius Julius Aelia[nus] possibly of the time of Hadrian. The [πρό]γονος was one Philip (died 73), whose son Tiberius Claudius [...] (died 53) had fought against the [φυ]γάδες and ἐπιτρόπευσεν β[ασιλέως μεγάλου Ἀγρίππα] (my restoration). The name 'Berenice' seems to be that of his wife, while one of his sons was 'Tiberius Claudius Philippus'. I am unable even to speculate on any connection with the family of Philip son of Jacimus.

248. Josephus, *Ant.* 17.28—i.e. just before the completion of *Antiquities* (20.267) in 93/94; this reference may not be taken as implying that Agrippa himself was dead (see Appendix 10).

249. *IGRR* 3.1176 from Aerita dated to the first year of Nerva; Dunand 1934: 49, no. 75 (now in Dionysias/Soueida) dated to the sixteenth year of Domitian.

250. Qedar 1986-87: 30-32, no. 2 (= *SEG* 38, 1647)—in publishing this lead weight from Tiberias, Qedar followed my interpretation (no credit appears), but ironically it was only later that I understood the meaning of this text, i.e. as referring to the forty-third year of Agrippa II by his Era of Tiberias (see Appendix 10, pt. c). The Peraean inscription (see above n. 232), refers to one 'Cocceius', the family name of Nerva. But, it must be noted that Clermont-Ganneau's restoration... φιλο[ρ]ώ[μαιου]... [Ἰου]λίου Ἀγρίπ[πα]... Κοκκηίου Ἀκ... is very uncertain. I fear that we may be dealing with Κοκκήιος Ἀγριππεῖνος son of Κοκκήιος Ἀκρίσιος, known from a text in Amman (Abel 1908: 567-68, no. 1).

often stormy period. He managed to retain his kingdom through the reigns of Claudius, Nero, the three emperors of 68/69, of the three Flavian emperors, as well as of Nerva and a part of that of Trajan—in all ten emperors! Neither the Jewish War nor the love affair of his sister Berenice with Titus shook his reign. The fact that he held power for almost half a century (30 years of which were after the fall of Jerusalem), over a variegated and geographically discontinuous kingdom, proves his ability to survive and overcome difficult and dangerous conditions. Nevertheless, his record regarding the Jews and the Temple was far from satisfactory, even if he is not to be directly blamed for the revolt. We need not exaggerate his responsibility: Agrippa happened to be present at the countdown of an exploding political situation, which had been brewing for several decades before his arrival. Yet Agrippa clearly failed to control the high priesthood, and his actions together with those of close members of his family contributed to the sharp division of the upper class in Jerusalem, giving further impetus among the religious fanatics and the lower class to the idea of theocracy and independence.

With the exception of Nabataea, Agrippa's was the last major kingdom within the Roman Empire to survive. Its incorporation into the province of Syria in CE 100, may have made Trajan realize how wide his annexation programme could now be. His takeover of Nabataea might have come earlier than 106, had it not been for the conquest of Dacia on the other side of the Empire, completed in 106. Then it was only a matter of time for the subjugation of Greater Armenia in 114 and the extraordinary invasion even of Parthia in 115.

Looking back at the surviving Eastern kingdoms of the first century CE, we see Cappadocia being annexed in the 40s, Thrace in the 50s and Pontus in the 60s. In the early 70s, following Vespasian's campaigns, came the Flavian wave of incorporations, at which time Lesser Armenia, Commagene and Emesa were taken over. This only left Chalcidice of Aristobulus III and the kingdom of Agrippa II still in operation. Obviously the Herodian kings were appreciated as the most able and trustworthy friends of Rome, so much so that a third king, Alexander IV, was by contrast now to commence his rule over a part of Cilicia. However Domitian seems to have taken back Chalcidice in 93 (perhaps upon Aristobulus's death), and about the same time he may have claimed a large part of Agrippa's kingdom and Alexander's Cilicia. But it was really the death of the most famous great-grandson of Herod the Great in CE 100, perhaps in combination with the fact that he left no children, which signalled the ultimate change in the Near Eastern political *status quo*. There were never to be any future 'client'-kingdoms west of the Euphrates.

Family Tree: *The Descendants of Aristobulus I*
(c. 35 BCE–CE 100)

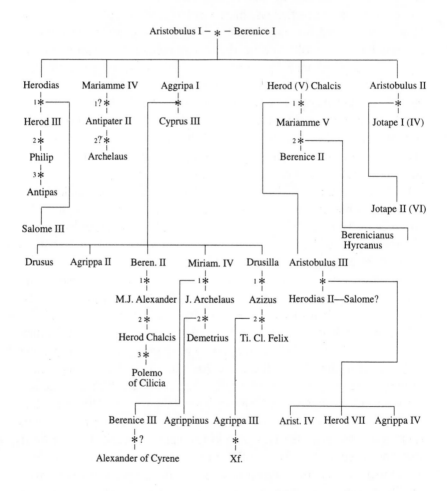

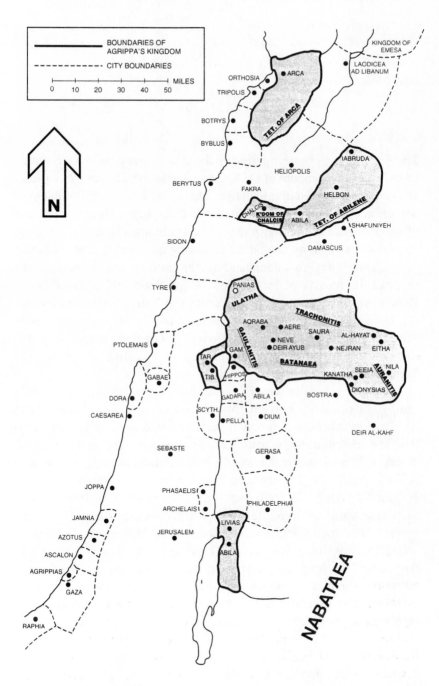

The Kingdom of Agrippa II, c. CE 48–100

CONCLUSION

The first thing to be recognized is the fragmentary and varied nature of the enormous amount of evidence available, which inevitably makes any overall interpretation tentative. The second is the real problem of definition of ethnicities and cultural identities in the Near Eastern part of the Roman Empire. With these two difficulties in mind, the Conclusion must begin by raising the following question: is it possible that an important key to understanding the culture and politics of the remarkable dynasty of the Herods, which flourished in the Graeco-Roman world between the second century BCE and the second century CE, lies in its social and geographical origins? This book sets out to discover the ethnic affiliation of Herod the Great, as a necessary preliminary to any writing of the history of Palestine in the Second Temple Period.

The only generally known indication of the origins of Herod's family, as primarily derived from Josephus, was that it came from 'the land of Idumaea', on which very little had previously been written. The examination of historical, documentary and archaeological evidence from Idumaea has resulted in an understanding of the geopolitical background of the area from the neo-Babylonian to the late Hellenistic period. The movements and settlements of different groups of people were explored, leading to a distribution-map of majority groups: Jews and Edomites on the eastern side; Hellenized Phoenicians and Philistines in the west and along the coast; Arabs and Edomites in the south. The 'Idumaean' origins of the Herods were now realized to be no more than a geographical pointer, offering no precise definition of ethnic identity, especially since in the Maccabaean period this highly mixed population was converted to Judaism by force.

Circumstantial evidence suggested that Herod's home town was the Idumaean capital Marisa, even if his ancestors may have come from elsewhere. An important tradition preserved by the Christian Church (essentially by Justin Martyr, Julius Africanus and Epiphanius), but until now generally discounted, firmly connected the Herods with the coastal city of Ascalon. Both Marisa and Ascalon were centres of Hellenized Phoenician culture, particularly the latter, which was renowned as a centre of Greek *paideia*, and boasted philosophers, grammarians and historians. An investigation of the material evidence from Ascalon has shown that people with the right 'Herodian' names originated there, and coins suggested that the family would have been prominent. Other details in Josephus then fell into place.

Such a Hellenized background for the Herodian dynasty connected well with the neglected testimony of Ptolemy, who wrote a biography of Herod. He was most probably the grammarian of Ascalon around the end of the first century BCE, but in any case he is quoted in a work composed not later than the end of the first century CE and attributed to Ammonius. Ptolemy in his *first* book, in which he would evidently have discussed the origins of his subject, set out to explain the 'Idumaean' connection of Herod by distinguishing between Jews and Idumaeans, and pointing to the fact that most of the latter (no doubt as far as Herod's ethnicity was concerned) were Phoenicians and Syrians (Chapter 3 n. 22):

> Jews and Idumaeans differ... Jews are those who are so by origin and nature. The Idumaeans, on the other hand, were not originally Jews, but *Phoenicians and Syrians*; having been subjugated by the Jews and having been forced to undergo circumcision, so as to be counted among the Jewish nation and keep the same customs, they were called Jews.

The objections of Antigonus, the last Hasmonaean king, to Herod's claiming the kingship, can now be seen from a different angle, and in clear agreement with the description of Ptolemy. Antigonus totally excluded the possibility of 'an Idumaean', according to him one that is 'a half-Jew', becoming king of Judaea (Josephus, *Ant.* 14.403).

Starting therefore from an entirely new context for the Herods, we can afford to treat their Hellenized Phoenician background as offering a hypothesis: does it not make sense that their relation to Judaism remained always ambivalent, while their attraction to the wider Hellenized Near East stands out as a more important factor in the lives of most of them? To take the best example, Herod's personal culture, as displayed in his education (Greek philosophy, support of gymnasia, and writing of memoirs), prowess and love of theatre and sport (construction of hippodromes, institution of festivals and patronage of the Olympic games), journeys to Greece and benefactions there, patronage of architecture and art, and indeed interest in non-Jewish cults (Apollo, Aphrodite, the Dioscuri and Korē), perfectly matched that of Hellenized Phoenician Ascalon.

Herod's Hellenistic royal ideology was exemplified as much by his imposition of the celebration of the anniversary of his accession (Josephus, *Ant.* 15.423), and his assumption, among other titles, of that of εὐσεβής (Chapter 10 n. 152), as by his numerous foundations of *poleis*, villages and fortresses. Even the onomasticon which he chose for some of his children—Philip, Olympias, Alexander and Roxane—recalled directly the royal family at Macedonia; so did the Greek names of most of his wives: Doris, Malthace, Cleopatra, Pallas, Phaedra and Elpis. We should have expected that Herod would have admitted feeling much 'closer to the Greeks than to the Jews', as Josephus has it (*Ant.* 19.329).

Such a Hellenized culture can be traced in the lives and behaviour of Herod's descendants, allowing, of course, for a variety of choices by individuals (not all members of the family followed exactly the same path), and for the development of manifold identities (as different degrees of Jewish and Roman influence played their part in subsequent generations). But the principal Hellenized elements continue to be apparent in their education, journeys and building programmes. His sons Alexander I and Aristobulus I were carefully instructed in Greek studies by, among others, a court tutor, Andromachus, evidently even before they were sent to Rome. Alexander I was capable of composing books, and his Aegean friends included a prominent priest of Apollo at Cos. Antipater II also had a close associate in Greece, in the person of Caius Julius Eurycles the dynast of Sparta. Antipas and Philip became founders of *poleis*, and great builders in the Greek style, the latter assuming the title of κτίστης on coins depicting his portrait. Antipas's projects included most probably a stadium at Tiberias and a hippodrome at Tarichaea (Chapter 8 n. 106), and possibly a theatre at Sepphoris (Chapter 8 n. 104). We know that Antipas had had connections not only with Cos, but also with a community worshipping at the Temple of Apollo on Delos; both were islands noted for the presence of groups of wealthy Hellenized Phoenicians. Hellenic training had been received by Herod's nephew, Antipater III, son of Salome I, who excelled in oratory during the hearing of 4 (or 5) BCE at Rome, in which various members of the family struggled for power after Herod's death (Chapter 7 §2).

Herod's grandchildren, Agrippa I and Herod of Chalcis, both of whom had allowed their images to be placed on coins, must have been fluent in Greek, since they were asked to address the emperor in this language in the Senate—although a degree of Romanization had already gradually entered the evolution of the family. Nevertheless Agrippa I's benefactions to Gentile cities, and his role as president at Greek games, closely followed his grandfather's example. Interestingly, he arranged for the image of his wife and his son(s) to appear on coins, erected statues of his daughters at Caesarea-on-the-coast, and one of his followers from Auranitis seems to refer to his master's ancestral god as Apollo (Chapter 10 n. 92). Agrippa II and Berenice II, Agrippa I's children, also built extensively at Berytus and Athens, as well as fostering pagan spectacles, while a supporter of theirs, Strabo, made a dedication in their name to Atargatis at Qalaat Fakra (Chapter 10 n. 214). Again, while he too was noticeably Romanized, Agrippa II was known to Josephus as being 'thoroughly conversant with Hellenic culture'. The Jewish historian assures us that among the post-CE 70 survivors of the Herodian dynasty, Julius Archelaus, great-great-nephew of Herod, was markedly 'well-versed in Greek learning', while Herod VII, great-great-grandson of Herod, was noted for his 'Greek wisdom'. The descendants of Alexander I later in the first century CE, according to Josephus, not only 'ranged themselves with the Greek tradition', but actually decided 'to abandon' Judaism (Chapter 9 n. 37).

Having launched the hypothesis of a Hellenized *Phoenician* background for the Herods, which was ignited by the evidence set out at the beginning, it will be worth stressing that other local Hellenized backgrounds, such as the Arab or the Jewish, are inefficacious in offering alternative hypotheses. No specific evidence can lead to this direction (in fact all indications are directly to the contrary—see below), and in any case there is no appropriate example of any Jewish family—that is to say biologically and religio-culturally Jewish—living *in* Judaea *before* the Herods, showing a degree of Hellenization even a quarter as high (compare the remarks on Hellenized native cultures in the introduction). Comparing the Hellenization of the Hasmonaeans to that of the Herods is like comparing the distance from Judaea to Galilee with that from Judaea to Gaul! Mendels (1992: 62, 64) is absolutely right to warn that we must not overestimate Hasmonaean Hellenization (compare Rajak 1994: 296-97). The adoption of a few Greek names, arguably not earlier than the end of the second century BCE, a functional reaction which never overwhelmed the Jewish names (compare Ilan 1987), and the few architectural affinities which had become practical by that time, show an expected *minimum* degree of Hellenization. For example, the most vocative evidence, the numismatic, remained throughout image-free, inscribed in its vast majority and right to the end in Hebrew characters (*AJC* 1). By contrast Herodian coins without a single exception were written in Greek. This commitment could not have materialized out of nothing. There must have been a strongly Hellenized 'non-Jewish' tradition behind Herod the Great's ancestry.

The fact that Josephus evidently chose not to say anything explicit about the origins of the family (though he certainly hints at an Ascalonite relationship) needs to be seen in context, because many other vital themes in Josephus were never made as explicit as modern scholars would have liked. On the one hand, had the Ascalonite tradition (as known to us from the Christian sources) been available in the work on Herod by Ptolemy of *Ascalon* (itself a remarkable piece of evidence, if accurate) before the time of Josephus, the latter might have ignored it, particularly if it had already been adopted by Christian circles—and the Jewish historian was writing under a serious constraint: Agrippa II was still alive. On the other hand, if this tradition circulated only in the work of Justus of Tiberias after the death of Agrippa II, Josephus may not have known all the details—and of course later he would not have endorsed information advocated by his main rival, even though, as Agrippa II's private secretary, Justus may have had good sources at his disposal.

But the truth remains that Josephus essentially knew of Herod's 'non-Jewish' biological background (compare Chapter 3 n. 41, and highlight *War* 1.521: βασιλεύσας ἐν ἀλλοτρίοις, 'he reigned over a kingdom in which he was an alien'), and most of Josephus's contemporaries in Judaea would also have been aware of this fact, despite an apparent attempt by the king to conceal it at home. Although such an attempt cannot be proved, it is clearly suggestive that Herod allowed his court historian, Nicolaus, to invent a Jewish genealogy for him. As we find it in Josephus, Nicolaus frivolously claimed that the family 'belonged to the leading Jews who came to Judaea from Babylon'! (Since current local roots were obviously impossible to claim, Jewish ancestors had to be sought far and away. But even so, and in contrast to the Hasmonaeans, Herod never dared to claim the priesthood! And why not if he really had descended from a *leading* Jewish family from Babylon?) We may reasonably assume that this then represented the official version that the palace wanted the people to believe in. Of course such a ludicrous invention (dismissed categorically by Josephus—Chapter 3 nn: 62-63) would neither have convinced the populace, nor have condemned them to amnesia; but nevertheless it would have made it very dangerous for anyone to argue against it openly or raise the question in public. Significantly, Hebrew apocryphal and rabbinical evidence did conserve echoes of the dynasty's 'foreign' as well as 'Hellenized' stock. The *Psalms of Solomon*, almost certainly referring to Herod, speak of him as 'a man alien to our race', while the Babylonian Talmud's tractate *Baba Qamma* tacitly attests to his father Antipater I's 'Grecian wisdom' (Chapter 3 n. 41). *Baba Batra* relates how Herod killed the sages who expounded Deut. 17.15, prohibiting a 'foreigner' from being appointed as king (Chapter 3 n. 79). The origins of Agrippa I were still a handicap in the first century CE, as seen in the episode recorded in the Mishnaic tractate *Soṭah*, in which he shed tears when he read Deut. 17.15 in the Temple, and the Jews had to assure him that he was their 'brother'. An aspect of the same episode, concerning his alien ancestry (he was not one of the natives—ἐγγενεῖς in Codex Vaticanus), would have been the denunciation of Agrippa I by Simon, a pietist in Jerusalem, as recorded in Josephus's *Antiquities* (Chapter 3 n. 64). As far as Christian tradition down the ages is concerned, there is total and formidable unanimity in calling Agrippa I's grandfather Herod, an ἀλλόφυλος or ἀλλογενής (Chapter 3 n. 81). Millar's approval now (1994: 202) of Mendel's assertion that no Herodians were ever seen as potentially fulfilling popular aspirations for a truly Jewish *basileia*, should be earnestly received.

In the Hellenized world, however, Herod's origins must have been freely recognized. Indeed at Ascalon they may have been common knowledge (especially if the hard evidence of the local coins depicting Herod have been correctly assigned here), and it seems that the Ascalonite biographer of the king did not overlook it. The Hellenized Phoenicians (Ἕλληνες-Σύροι) of Caesarea-on-the-coast could strongly claim priority as citizens over the Jewish inhabitants, countering the latter's argument that the founder of the city was a 'Jewish' king, no doubt, with the argument of Herod's real ethnic origins, as now understood (Chapter 3 n. 62; compare Chapter 10 n. 121). At Alexandria even a lunatic called Carabas could proclaim Agrippa I's real background: καὶ γένει Σύρον (Chapter 10 n. 96), in close agreement with the Φοίνικες καὶ Σύροι of Herod's biographer, as we have seen. The wider Graeco-Roman world and its aristocracy, which welcomed and honoured the Herods as friends and benefactors, would not have been in the dark, even if their origins were not particularly advertized (especially in those areas where there was a substantial Jewish population).

Recourse to the evidence in the Latin and Greek pagan sources of the Roman period, brings no further enlightment on this question. The Herods are mentioned in Latin by Horace, Persius, Pliny the Elder, Quintilian, Tacitus, Juvenal, Suetonius, Victor, Ammianus and Macrobius; and in Greek by Strabo, Isidorus of Alexandria, Philip of Thessalonica, Plutarch, Appian, Celsus, Galen, Dio and Aelian. Most of these writers make only brief allusions, and the contexts of their reference are not pertinent for stressing the dynasty's ethnic origins—had anyone happened really to know, given the relatively late date of most of them.

A cursory reading of a few passages has created to some the impression that the Herods were seen abroad as more 'Jewish' than they are portrayed in the present reconstruction. But this is only an impression and a simplistic one. To identify someone as 'Jewish' was (as it always has been) to risk blurring the distinction between ethnic origins and religion. The Jewish view of the Herods was ambivalent as to whether they could really be called 'Jews', as seen, for example, in the position taken by Antigonus the Hasmonaean. Pagan views could similarly be ambivalent, as the case of Ptolemy has shown. Since the Herods were mostly identified by the pagans as 'kings of Judaea', Jewish customs upon occasion were inevitably attributed to them. It is important to remember that religious classification with the Jews does not prove a biological Jewish background (see below).

Strabo (Chapter 3 n. 62) refers to Herod as ἀνὴρ ἐπιχώριος, which says little, especially when combined with Strabo's confusion of Herod with Hyrcanus II in the same passage! The geographer elsewhere (*apud* Josephus, *Ant.* 15.8-10) underlined how hated Herod really was by the Jews. The Alexandrian Isidorus (Chapter 10 n. 95) may have called Agrippa I a Ἰουδαῖος τριωβολεῖος, but this is merely polemical, since Claudius also is castigated by Isidorus as [ἀπό]βλητος of

Salome I. Plutarch (*Anton.* 61.3; 71.1) mentions Herod as Ἰουδαῖος, only as an indication of the geographical location of his kingdom—in a similar way to Dio (55.27.6), who calls Archelaus Παλαιστῖνος. (Compare the variety of meanings of such terms in Kraemer 1989; Feldman 1990; Cohen [S.J.D.] 1994.)

Persius (*Sat.* 5.176-84) refers to the *Herodis dies*, but not without qualifying it with *recutitaque sabbata*. The context is poetical, and the 'day of Herod' is nothing more than 'the day of the Jewish people *ruled* by Herod'—thus 'the Sabbath of the circumcised'. Other Roman writers discussed the Jewish Sabbath, including Seneca and Juvenal, but without involving any of the Herodian family. Juvenal (*Sat.* 6.153-60) calls Agrippa II *barbarus*, but again the context is poetical, and what follows makes it clear that it refers more generally to the barbaric 'country where kings celebrated festal Sabbaths with bare feet, and where a long-established clemency suffers pigs to attain old age'. In fact Agrippa II, although pictured here as king of a barbaric nation, and although he had ruled over a part of Syro-Palestine where Jews lived, had not even been king of Judaea! Had Juvenal been personal, and meant it literally in calling him 'barbarian' or 'non-Greek', based either on his outlook or behaviour, it would have been extraordinary that Tacitus was unfamiliar with it, and that Josephus had specified that Agrippa II was heavily Hellenized. Juvenal's satyrical allusion to this king, written more than two decades after his death, is definitely no evidence of Agrippa's personal culture.

Finally the later writer Macrobius (*Saturn.* 2.4.11) records the familiar saying *melius est Herodis porcum esse quam filium*, which, if it goes back to Augustus's own lips, may well be indicative of Herod's abstinence from pork; a habit, in any case, which he would have maintained as King of Judaea and officially a Jew by religion. But also as a descendant of a Phoenician family, Herod's diet would not have been dissimilar. Although circumcision had been abandoned by the Phoenicians under Greek influence (Chapter 3 n. 24; Hellenized Phoenicians in Idumaea had been recircumcised), there is no evidence that such Semitic peoples had dropped the habit of not eating pork (on the contrary, see Porphyry, *De Abstinentia* 1.14). However, we must be firmly warned that Macrobius's phrase may well be interpreted simply as a stronger way of saying 'I'd rather be Herod's dog than Herod's son', based on the play of the Greek words υἱός and ὕς (see *GLAJJ* 2, 666). Further, the context of Macrobius is highly suspect, mixing, as it does, Augustus's alleged quotation with the theme of Herod's 'Massacre of the Innocents'!

It will now be necessary to define briefly the term 'Jew'. By far the most important element of 'Jewishness' was the fundamental belief in a single God and his law (Josephus, *Apion* 2.165-66). Judaisation, unlike Hellenization, primarily involved a religious commitment. To become Judaised was to sympathize with the Jewish God. To become a Jew was to convert to Judaism by submitting to circumcision, besides adopting all other Jewish customs, and thus entering the status of the proselyte. But being a proselyte was to be seen by fellow Jews as a peculiar Jew, one missing the biological connection, and thus by no means equal to the native-born. This peculiarity was inherited, though until which generation was a moot point—one's original ethnicity and future marital arrangements seem to have played a significant role. For example, assuming that all 'Idumaeans' fell under the religious category of 'Edomites' (Deut. 23.7-8), a 'third generation' Idumaean convert should have been accepted (halakhically speaking) as a full Jew. On the basis of rabbinical law, the son of a proselyte had the legal status of his father (*t. Qid.* 4.15), unless his mother was a native-born Jewess (compare Cohen [S.J.D.] 1989: 30).

Herod the Great's family had clearly shared in the general conversion of Idumaea to Judaism in the late second century BCE. This must have occurred under Antipas I, father of Antipater I and grandfather of Herod. We do not know the ethnic background of Antipas I's wife, although she may have been a native-born Jewess, if she was called 'Salome', the name Antipater I gave to his only daughter (Chapter 7 §1). Had this been the case, the legal status of Antipater I may have been strengthened, but presumably only to become ambiguous again when his son Herod was born to a Nabataean mother.

Herod's degree of subscription to Judaism has thus to be seen in perspective. Living in Jerusalem, as a 'third generation' convert, potentially a full Jew, but doubted by Antigonus (even if polemically) as ἡμιιουδαῖος, Herod's birth could only be traced back to Idumaea, his citizenship to Rome, and his biology to the Phoenician coast, while his culture remained extremely Hellenized. There should be no wonder then that his official Jewish religion was evidently practised only for the sake of his relations with the Jewish people. Perhaps the best example is at the completion of the Temple in Jerusalem (his only contribution to Jewish religious life), when he is reported to have said: τὸ θεῖον (rather than τὸν θεὸν) τεθεραπεύκαμεν (Josephus, *War* 1.462). But this did not prevent him from displaying his pagan beliefs on coins (albeit cryptically), and from building temples and shrines to other deities, such as Apollo (Rhodes), evidently Korē (Samaria) and possibly Qos (Idumaean Mamre), and several *Sebasteia*, such as in Sebaste, Caesarea-on-the-coast and Panias. Josephus was appalled at Herod's general home record, notwithstanding the provision by the king, at least in an emergency, of relief to his subjects during the great famine of c. 25 BCE (Josephus, *Ant.* 15.299-316). The historian lamented that: 'there was not a single city of the Jews on which he deigned to bestow even minor restoration or any gift worth mentioning' (Chapter 3 n. 147).

Given that Herod in the present hypothesis is being presented with the complex identity of *Phoenician* by descent, *Hellenized* by culture, *Idumaean* by place of birth, *Jewish* by official religion, *Jerusalemite* by place of residence, and *Roman* by citizenship, a number of questions may be raised concerning the relationship of his dynasty to the native Jewish *status quo*. How far, for example, do we find that Herodian members conformed to Jewish law in their private lives? In the case of Syllaeus of Petra, the condition put to him by Herod, that he must be circumcised if he wished to marry Salome I, may be understood as sincere support for this Jewish custom; but, as we have seen (Chapter 7 §1), it would also have served as a pretext to avoid a dangerous adventurer. Nevertheless, Salome I, as was later discovered, had already signed a document accepting Syllaeus without concern for Judaism. Salome I, Herodias I and later female members of the family including Drusilla, became notorious for flouting the marital customs of the Jews. But also Archelaus and Antipas failed in handling with responsibility this delicate religious area, as both transgressed levirate law (Deut. 25.5-10) in marrying former sisters-in-law who had children from their previous husbands (Chapter 8 §5).

Herod's grandson, Agrippa I, may appear to have adhered to Judaism more seriously than any other member of the family, but even in his case it has been argued that diplomacy was the prime driving force. Since he descended partly from the Hasmonaeans (his father's mother being Mariamme I), it is natural that he felt more obligation towards the Jewish religion, not only in insisting on circumcision, as he must have done in the subsequently failed betrothal of his daughter Drusilla to Epiphanes of Commagene, but also in defending Judaism in Rome itself. Yet Agrippa I's Hellenized roots, combined with his totally Roman upbringing, clearly governed his entire life, and the very style of apotheosis in which he ended it is the best illustration of his alien character.

One may point to the fact that Herod's fortresses, such as Herodium or Masada, are devoid of iconography, conforming with the second commandment of the Mosaic law which forbade human and animal representations (Josephus, *Apion* 2.75). Yet, this only shows that Herod was careful in the forms of artistic expression which he could allow within his kingdom. Otherwise why did he not object to (in fact he craved for—*Ant.* 16.157-58) the erection of his statues in places beyond Jewish territory, such as in the Temple of Baalshamin at Seeia, on the island of Cos, or the Acropolis and Agora of Athens? Antipas, the son of Herod, statues of whom existed in the Aegean islands, must have ignored his father's example when he permitted the walls of his palace at Tiberias to be adorned with frescoes showing animals (Chapter 8 n. 106). Agrippa I also had statues erected in Heliopolis and probably Apamea (not to mention the statues of his daughters and the portraits of his wife and sons), as had Berenice II at Athens, despite the fact that she could come to the Temple at Jerusalem in discharge of vows at the time of the outbreak of the Jewish Revolt; and other members of the family living abroad, such as Aristobulus III and his wife Salome, and probably Tigranes I (V) and Alexander IV, readily had their portraits depicted on coins (cf. Philip the Tetrarch and Herod of Chalcis). Furthermore, we must not forget that even Herod's careful conduct at home suffered a number of lapses, most of which resulted in serious confrontations with the Jews: for example when he introduced into Jerusalem pagan athletic contests and trophies containing images (*Ant.* 15.268-91), plundered the tomb of David (*Ant.* 16.179-83), and placed a stone eagle at the gate of the Temple (*War* 1.648-55; 2.5; *Ant.* 17.151).

In tracing the history of the Herodian family down the generations, a wide analysis of all known members of the dynasty has been undertaken. Herod, husband of ten wives, was father of 15 children, and we have knowledge of some 20 of his grandchildren, 13 great-grandchildren, eight great-great-grandchildren and two great-great-great-grandchildren. A complex genealogy of endogamous and exogamous unions has been worked out, arriving at a total of around 144 individuals. The impact of all these people on Jewish society and the eastern

Graeco-Roman world was considerable. The lineages of Herod's sister, Salome I, and of Herod's son, Aristobulus I, proved to be of crucial importance in the development of events leading to the fall of Jerusalem in CE 70, and the descendants of Herod's son, Alexander I, played a vital role in the eastern policies of the Roman Emperors.

One may ask whether polygamy and endogamy constitute a characteristic pattern, and whether this makes any difference to the proposed new understanding of the origins and attitude of the Herods. Do Herodian marriages conform to Jewish rules or do they not? First let us take polygamy. As discussed in Chapter 4, polygamy was permitted among the Jews, and denounced only by the Essenes. However, since few could afford such a luxury it became the privilege of the élite. While a few individuals who practised bigamy may be attested (for example the second husband of Babatha—Chapter 4 n. 6), the only polygamous person from the Second Temple period known to us by name is Herod the Great! Further, there is no *clear* indication that any other member of his family practised polygamy or even bigamy, certainly not readily. So Herod's *gynaikōnitis* would not have contradicted Jewish law, but nevertheless it was an extremely uncommon, if not unique, phenomenon.

For good measure this conclusion on polygamy must be balanced against the Hellenized background of Herod. Although it is true to say that the creation of a 'harem' was oriental in character, the 'harem' was not unknown at least in the palace at Macedonia (Chapter 4 n. 4). Philip II, the father of Alexander the Great, was a notorious womaniser who could boast of seven wives, many concubines and numerous children. His wives were all of princely and aristocratic stock: two Macedonian (Phila and Cleopatra), two Thessalian (Philinna and Nicesipolis), one Molossian (Olympias), one Illyrian (Audata), and one Danubian (Meda). The Hellenized habits and practices of the Herodian dynasty clearly grew from Semitic roots and bore fruits on Semitic ground. Herod's court may well have been styled in Ptolemaic/Seleucid fashion, but there was nothing to stop it also from incorporating local Phoenician tradition. It would have been decisive to know the precise marital arrangements of the royal courts in early Hellenistic Phoenicia itself, and whether Herod was in a way reviving them. Unfortunately the evidence is scanty, but nevertheless it is striking to point out that from the little we know about general court functions, for example from Theopompus (*apud* Athenaeus, *Deipn.*

12.531A), Aelian (*Var. Hist.* 7.2) and other sources, the description of luxury and display of Straton I of Sidon, his licentious life surrounded by women from the Peloponnese, his hiring of Greek entertainers, benefactions to Athens, celebrations of games, and Phoenician sacred embassies of his time to Apollo on Delos, are very much like the picture drawn here of Herod of Jerusalem. Of course a notable link between Herod and Straton is provided by Straton's famous Tower, the old town which was lavishly rebuilt by Herod and renamed 'Caesarea'.

Turning now to endogamy, it was regularly practised by the Jewish society at large, and since the law prohibited incestuous unions (Lev. 18.6-18), the types preferred were those of first-cousin and uncle-niece (again with objections for the latter only from the Essenes—*CD* 5). But although endogamy would have formed the largest kinship chasm between the Jews and the Graeco-Roman culture, we must remember that close-kin unions were practised in Athens (in the form of first-cousin marriage) at least until the first century BCE; and importantly they continued in Egypt (in the form of brother-sister marriage) to the third century CE (Chapter 4 n. 10). Besides the marriage of cousins was legalized even in Rome by the time of Claudius, who ventured himself to marry his niece Agrippina the Younger (Tacitus, *Ann.* 12.5-8). Therefore unions between cross-cousins and uncle-nieces, as observed among the Herodian family, and certainly conforming with Jewish law, cannot be taken as being peculiar if the Herods' culture was particularly Hellenized. On the contrary, what overturns the argument completely, is that the Herods, in accord with their Hellenization, had to devise a clear mixture of endogamy and exogamy. In fact their exogamous weddings, in terms of statistics, exceeded overall the number of their endogamous ones (Chapter 4 n. 11). Of Herod's ten wives only *two* were relatives!

Now since marriages could be contracted both 'outside the family' and 'outside the Jewish community', we may further need to define exogamy in its Herodian context. The question then is how often did the members of the dynasty marry Jews/Jewish women, and how often Gentiles? Again in terms of statistics, the evidence is clear: weddings to Gentiles exceeded the number of those with Jews/Jewish women. Of Herod's ten wives only *two* were definitely Jewish, that is by blood and religion! Pheroras, the brother of Herod, also married a Jewess, and so did Antipater II, the son of Herod. But it is extraordinary and at the same time revealing, that once the dynasty had been established, no further effort was ever made for any marital connection with the Jewish community of Judaea. To the end of the family's history, we have no record of any member of the Herodian family after Antipater II (at the latest by 14 BCE) contracting an exogamous marriage with a Jew or a Jewess from Palestine! While three unions are later acknowledged with Hellenized Jews living in Alexandria and Cyrene (Marcus, Demetrius and Alexander), and possibly four unions had involved individuals who may, but *only* may, have been converts to Judaism already before marriage (Doris, Costobarus I, Malthace, Cleopatra), no less than some 13 other exogamous Herodian weddings, were incontestably to Gentiles (see below).

Can it be determined whether the marriages to Gentiles were made only on condition of conversion? From the two examples of doomed betrothals that we know, which failed to cover religious practices (Syllaeus and Epiphanes, already mentioned), one might wish to assume that all successful unions therefore imply that the Gentile husband or wife were fully converted to Judaism: the male being circumcised and the female purified by immersion. But this must remain doubtful. Without recourse to the fact that members of the family often abused Jewish law in questions of marriage, which we discussed earlier, it is very unlikely that *all* of the Gentiles who entered the family would have been made to accept Jewish faith. For one thing, Jotape III of Commagene married Alexander IV in Rome, at a time when the latter, according to one interpretation (Chapter 9 n. 37), had already abandoned Judaism. We may take it for granted that Alexas I (possibly of Alexandria/Laodicea), was fully converted, particularly since his descendants subsequently played an important role in the Jewish society, and we may also assume the same for Glaphyra of Cappadocia, who married twice into the Herodian family (even though the second time controversially). Further, Polemo the King of Pontus and [Eastern] Cilicia [Pedias], who married Berenice II, seems to have become briefly a Jew by religion as Josephus suggests (*Ant.* 20.145-46). But can we imagine, for example, that Ti. Claudius Felix, the Roman procurator who married Drusilla, had actually been circumcised?

Another question may be posed. What were the reasons for, and influences on, the exogamous marriages of the Herods, and could such marriages alone account for the family's growth to prominence?

Although dynastic intermarriages most certainly added dimension and prestige, it is difficult to imagine how the Herods could have succeeded in associating themselves effectively with the other rulers of the eastern Graeco-Roman world, had they not in the first place been able to demonstrate their Hellenic views, to them as much as to Rome. Origins from the Phoenician coast must have been highly attractive, simply because no other area, except parts of Syria and Egypt, could have impressed with its degree of Hellenized tradition a ruler, let us say, from Commagene, Cappadocia or Pontus.

The reasons for the exogamous weddings (to Hellenized Jews and non-Jews) were indeed largely political, but what has not been recognized is that in many cases it was the interests of the other dynasts and aristocrats that were better served in connecting themselves with the Herods, rather than the other way round—particularly when Herodian females were involved in the union: for example when Salome I was given to Costobarus I of Idumaea (and later to Alexas I possibly of Alexandria/Laodicea), Alexandra to Timius of Cyprus, Berenice II to M. Julius Alexander of Alexandria (and later to Polemo of Pontus and Cilicia), Drusilla to Azizus of Emesa, Mariamme VI to Demetrius of Alexandria, and Berenice III to Alexander of Cyrene. Other exogamous marriages (to Gentiles) were more mutually beneficial: for example that of Antipater I to Cyprus I of Nabataea, Alexander I (and later Archelaus) to Glaphyra of Cappadocia, Antipas to Phasaelis the daughter of Aretas IV of Petra, Aristobulus II to Jotape I of Emesa, Drusilla to the procurator Ti. Claudius Felix, and Alexander IV to Jotape III of Commagene.

But on balance the most important exogamous 'political' marriages were those of Herod to Mariamme I the Hasmonaean (37 BCE), Pheroras to Mariamme I's sister (c. 37 to before 26 BCE), and Antipater II to a daughter of Antigonus II (at the latest by 14 BCE). Here the Herods were clearly seeking legitimacy in their immediate environment, and it is interesting that when such a tie was broken in the case of Herod, he quickly realigned himself with a Jewish family by marrying Mariamme II the daughter of one Simon-Boethus, whose status he had to raise (Chapter 8 §4).

So there does not seem to be any proof that can be adduced to contradict the position explored, that the origins of the family from a Hellenized environment are essential for understanding the views and attitudes of most of its members. A question which may reasonably be asked, however, is how significant such a background was for the subsequent development of the dynasty, and its ultimate destiny of reaching the Roman Senate. The foundation was laid by Antipater I, father of Herod, who succeeded in gaining a grant of Roman citizenship. But what really earned him this honour was not just his bravery in war: it was his far-reaching diplomacy in relations with neighbouring rulers, all of whom had to be persuaded to contribute to Caesar's victory. *Precisely* such diplomacy (shown also by his father Antipas I before him) was a characteristic of the political life of Hellenized Syro-Palestine in the late Hellenistic period, as also illustrated by Nicolaus's father Antipater in defence of the interests of Damascus (*FGrH* 90, F.131). It is striking that Caesar deposited his decrees in favour of Hyrcanus II (obviously due to Antipater I, who also benefitted by them), *precisely* at the Hellenized Phoenician cities of Ascalon, Tyre and Sidon (Chapter 3 n. 88).

Herod's Hellenized background, together with the privilege of the Roman citizenship extended to him and his offspring, played a vital role in his achievement in Rome of being appointed King of Judaea, and this is confirmed by his subsequent establishment of an even more strongly Hellenized court at Jerusalem. From then an important avenue had opened, leading eventually to the Senate: Hellenization and royal lineage were to become valuable qualifications for entry. Agrippa I was given praetorian and later consular rank, while Herod of Chalcis gained praetorian rank, as did likewise Agrippa II. But the first member of the Herodian dynasty to serve the Senate in the highest position and in *non-titular* fashion was Alexander IV at the end of the first century CE. His sons Caius Julius Agrippa (V) and Caius Julius Alexander Berenicianus, both worked their way up the senatorial career, the latter becoming *consul suffectus* for the period October–December CE 116. When we remember, with Bowersock (1982: 651, 658), that Roman policy seems deliberately to have excluded Palestinian Jews and non-Syrian Arabs from the Senate, and that Roman senators were never admitted from the cities of Judaea, Arabia and Mesopotamia, the Hellenized Phoenician origins of the Herods, as disclosed here, would seem strikingly relevant. We may conclude with confidence that their Hellenized origins must have assisted the members of the family not only in their dealings and exchanges with the other client-kingdoms and the wider Greek world, but also in the important claims they made on Rome, notably when they were accepted as a coherent aristocratic family, to represent Judaean society even when under direct Roman rule (see below).

In the course of this study numerous subjects of political, religious and chronological interest have been tackled. For the purpose of the conclusion we must briefly recall and distinguish two things: a) general strife within the Herodian court, that is complicated dynastic conflicts (mainly under Herod the Great), which betray an unsettled internal environment; and b) episodes of political/religious popular resistance, illustrating the external pressures exerted upon the dynasty in its struggle to gain acceptance.

Significant dynastic conflicts which have been examined from the point of view of family history include the following: the failure of Syllaeus to infiltrate the Herodian family by marrying Salome I in c. 21/20 BCE; the two major dissensions in the royal court involving the sons of Mariamme I the Hasmonaean, in c. 14–13 BCE and again in c. 11–8 BCE; the intrigues surrounding the death of Pheroras in his Peraean tetrarchy in c. 7 BCE, which triggered repeated trials and executions, including those of many Pharisees; the belated execution of Antipater II in 4 (or 5) BCE, followed by the struggle for succession after Herod's death; and the dramatic contribution to the downfall of Antipas in Galilee by his wife Herodias in CE 39. These crucial episodes clearly show the fragility of the family's position, constantly balanced between external and internal difficulties.

As regards political/religious popular resistance, from the inception of his real power in 37 BCE, and despite Roman recognition, Herod the Great encountered serious opposition. The defeated Hasmonaeans, together with a clique of Jewish and some Idumaean collaborators, continued their anti-Herodian activities at least up to the death of Cleopatra VII of Egypt in 30 BCE—political adversaries were still being executed by Herod in 26 BCE, while a curfew and an oath of loyalty were imposed on the citizens in 20/19 BCE (Josephus, *Ant.* 15.366-70; 17.41-43). Although both Judaea and Idumaea revolted openly again only after the death of the king in 4 (or 5) BCE, a number of religiously motivated uprisings and assassination attempts, did take place during the reign of Herod: for example, as mentioned earlier, on the introduction of athletic contests, trophies, and the eagle over the Temple gate. The harsh rule of Herod's successor, Archelaus, resulted in serious trouble, which led not only to his exile to Gaul in CE 6, but also to direct Roman rule for the first time. Popular rejection of Herodian influence and control reached unprecedentedly high levels again under Agrippa II, when he was expelled from Jerusalem at the outbreak of the Jewish Revolt.

None the less, in the case of certain members of the family a different pattern of relationship with the Jews has also been observed—one created out of necessity in response to important circumstances, that is the imposition twice of direct Roman rule (the 'prefectorial' and the 'procuratorial' periods). If we follow Josephus uncritically, after the exile of Archelaus in CE 6, the Herodian family apparently regained power in Judaea only at the time of Agrippa I in CE 41. But, as has been argued here, the fact is that in the interim the Romans governed the province with the aid of surviving members of the dynasty. The evidence known to us from Philo and the Gospels (corroborated by a critical understanding of Josephus) clearly shows that the leading aristocracy under Rome continued to be comprised, to a significant degree, of Herodian stock.

This group of individuals (many of whom can be surmised with confidence—for example descendants of Salome I, Pheroras and Phasael I) was headed by 'four sons' of Herod the Great, who, in the words of Philo, 'enjoyed prestige and rank equal to that of kings'. As spokesmen of the Jewish community in Jerusalem, they defended the Jewish position against Pontius Pilate (most probably in CE 33), who had set up aniconic, yet somehow offensive, gilded shields. Herod's sons appealed to be sent to the emperor as an embassy, and later they wrote a letter to Tiberius, by which they succeeded in defeating Pilate. Analysis has demonstrated that these Herodian leaders could only have been: *definitely* Antipas the Tetrarch, *probably* Herod IV and Phasael III, and *possibly* either Philip the Tetrarch or Herod III (Chapter 7 n. 80). Lower in rank to these 'four' at that time, must have been Helcias I, grandson of Salome I, who later (in CE 40) represented the Jews of Judaea (while Aristobulus II, brother of Agrippa I, supported the Jews of Galilee), in the embassy to Petronius concerning Caligula's statue (Chapter 10 §4).

Antipas's influence in Jerusalem was an initial step to the political equilibrium created later (in the second 'provincial' period or that of the procurators), by which Herod of Chalcis and then Agrippa II were granted authority over the Temple. This authority encompassed not only the right of selecting high priests, but also the control of the treasury (Chapter 7 n. 104). In effect the religious and economic life of the Jews was thoroughly monitored by the Herods. Under Agrippa II, we find two Herodians in charge of the 'sacred money' of the Temple: Helcias II and later Antipas III. We must assume that the position of treasurer, at least in the 'procuratorial' period, had become a non-priestly one. It is interesting that Helcias II (arguably son of Helcias I), holding the second most powerful office after that of the high priest, was sent (around CE 58–60) on an embassy to Nero. Even at the late stage when the Jewish Revolt had begun, it was Herodians who were in a crucial position as intermediaries between the revolutionaries and Rome. Costobarus II and Saulus, also descendants of Salome I, formed a deputation dispatched to Nero to inform him of the catastrophe (Chapter 7 §2). This continuous involvement in Judaean affairs on the part of the Herodian family, perfectly reflects both the varying degrees of attachment to Judaism (for many of those members who played an integral part in Jewish communal politics in the 'provincial' periods, must one way or another have been looked upon as Jews), and the vested interest in maintaining at all costs power and control over a kingdom established by Herod the Great, and briefly revived by Agrippa I.

Although, of course, there are many things of which we cannot be sure, and there are some problems that cannot be solved instantly, from the present examination of the Herodian dynasty from beginning to end as a whole, a coherent picture has emerged of a complex and evolving identity. The Hellenized roots of the family stand out, throughout, and form the background to its development and achievement of prominence down to the earlier part of the second century of our common era. The family only came to be Jewish by the accident of the forced conversion of the Idumaeans. Balancing on the edge of Judaism, some members tipped one way and some the other. Those who were kings had to show greater respect for the cult of the Temple, while others moved freely into the multi-regional, Hellenized environment of the Roman Near East. Similarly, their 'Roman' identities, which for some became stronger with time, remained essentially superficial. Antipater I's and Herod's generations show little Roman influence in comparison with those of Agrippa I and Agrippa II. Herod's personal 'Roman' identity was very feeble: he was a Roman citizen, but practised polygamy, which was forbidden under Roman law.

In sum, the hypothesis has been advanced that the Herodian dynasty originated from Hellenized Phoenician Ascalon, but, as a power which influenced the surrounding territories, it emerged in Maccabaean Idumaea of the second and first centuries BCE, then newly converted to Judaism. Its members by descent and marriage soon came to represent a political/ideological Hellenized élite, whose leaders reigned over Judaea, much of Palestine and southern Syria, struggled with various groups in Jewish society, maintained an important position through the 'provincial' periods in Judaean history, were partly responsible for the fall of Jerusalem in CE 70, enjoyed an illustrious afterglow in the person of Agrippa II, managed to rule in Ituraea, southern Asia Minor and the two Armenias, entered the Roman Senate, even returned later to govern Syria Palaestina with Julius Severus as a Roman appointee under Antoninus Pius, and finally faced eclipse in the rapidly transforming Greek world of the late second century CE.

Looking ahead, one may wish to enquire whether there are even wider consequences based on the proposed rediscovery of the origins of the Herods. The case of the Hellenized Phoenician background of the dynasty certainly leads to further explorations. The Herods as a family, albeit the largest and most important, remain only one prominent example. Other families, groups or individuals, described without qualification simply as 'Idumaeans', 'Judaeans', 'Samaritans' or 'Galilaeans', in numerous significant episodes narrated in Josephus and other sources, now need to be carefully examined. We must recall that Hyrcanus's anti-pagan campaigns had affected not only Idumaea, but also Samaria and Scythopolis, while Aristobulus I had enforced 'Judaisation' upon Ituraeans, apparently then occupying northern Galilee (Chapter 3 n. 27).

Questions of communal identity, or 'ethnicity', in this region continue to be elusive and intractable. The ethnic definitions of people living in Syria-Palestine as a whole, have to be refocused more sharply. It might prove possible to draw an ethnic profile, with individual territories shared between majorities and minorities of various distinct groups. The political views and religious beliefs that such sections of the society had in common and those in which they differed, must be separately evaluated.

But this complicated evolution of personal and communal identities was taking place in a period which saw profound changes that influenced the history of the Near East, and indeed gradually the rest of the world. The development of Judaism and its offshoot branch Christianity have much to benefit from such an investigation. The emergence

of a group of people identifying themselves as Χριστιανοί, itself a
question of great difficulty, needs to be seen against this highly
complex profile of local society—it was precisely such a society from
which the earliest Christians arose, and which was the very first to
feel their impact. What effects would a then 'fresh' reinterpretation of
Judaism have had on such a spectrum of distinct ethnic groups,
whether Jews, converts, semi-Jews, sympathisers or non-Jews? What
were the really important social (and political) contexts for the spread
of Christianity in its varying forms in its original homeland, marked
by such manifold patterns of ethnic, communal and religious identity?
Answers to these questions must await a future work.

APPENDIX 1

HERODIAN PROSOPOGRAPHY

To avoid confusion the names are listed in familiar forms, if inconsistently, disregarding the proper Greek, Latin or Hebrew onomasticon. In some cases titles have been added for easier distinction.

Mentioned by name
1) Achiabus (s. of Joseph I?)
2) Agrippa I, [M.] Julius (s. of Aristobulus I and Berenice I)
3) Agrippa II, M. Julius (s. of Agrippa I and Cyprus III)
4) Agrippa III, [Ti. Claudius] (s. of Drusilla and [Ti.] Claudius Felix)
5) Agrippa IV (s. of Aristobulus III and Herodias-Salome?)
6) Agrippa (V), C. Julius Agrippa (s. of Alexander IV and Jotape III)
7) Agrippinus (s. of Mariamme VI and Demetrius)
8) Alexander I (s. of Herod G. and Mariamme I)
9) Alexander II, [C. Julius] (s. of Alexander I and Glaphyra)
10) Alexander III (s. of Salampsio and Phasael II)
11) Alexander IV (βασιλεὺς—s. of Tigranes II)
12) Alexander, M. Julius (from Alexandria—h. of Berenice II)
13) Alexander? (from Cyrene?—h. of Berenice III?)
14) Alexandra (m. of Mariamme I)
15) Alexandra (d. of Salampsio and Phasael II)
16) Alexas I (from Laodicea/Alexandria?)
17) Alexas II Calleas? (s. of Alexas I)
18) Alexas III Helcias ('Helcias the Great', s. of Xd. of Salome I and Alexas II)
19) Ammia, Julia? (d. of Tigranes II)
20) Antiochus? (s. of Phallion II?)
21) Antipas I (στρατηγὸς—s. of Herod of Ascalon)
22) Antipas II (τετράρχης—s. of Herod G. and Malthace)
23) Antipas III (ἐπὶ τῶν δημοσίων θησαυρῶν) = Antipater IV, no. 27?
24) Antipater I (s. of Antipas I)
25) Antipater II (s. of Herod G. and Doris)
26) Antipater III (s. of Salome I and of Costobarus I)
27) Antipater IV (s. of Salampsio and Phasael II)
28) Archelaus (s. of Herod G. and Malthace)

29) Archelaus, Julius (s. of Cyprus IV and Alexas III-Helcias)
30) Aregetas? (f. of Syphas?)
31) Aristobulus-Jonathan (b. of Mariamme I)
32) Aristobulus I (s. of Herod G. and Mariamme I)
33) Aristobulus II (b. of Agrippa I, s. of Aristobulus I and Berenice I)
34) Aristobulus III (s. of Herod of Chalcis and Mariamme V)
35) Aristobulus IV (s. of Aristobulus III and Herodias-Salome?)
36) Azizus (from Emesa—h. of Drusilla)
37) Berenice I (d. of Salome I and Costobarus I)
38) Berenice II, Julia (βασίλισσα—d. of Agrippa I and Cyprus III)
39) Berenice III (d. of Mariamme VI and Julius Archelaus) = Berenice
    w. of Alexander from Cyrene?
40) Berenicianus (s. of Herod of Chalcis and Berenice II)
41) Berenicianus, C. Julius Alexander (s. of Alexander IV and Jotape III?)
42) Berenicianus, Ti. Claudius Antoninus Calpurnius Atticus Julius
    (desc. of C. Julius Alexander Berenicianus?)
43) Cleopatra (w. of Herod G.)
44) Costobarus I (h. of Salome I)
45) Costobarus II (b. of Saulus, s. of Antipater III and Cyprus II?)
46) Cyprus I (from Petra—w. of Antipater I)
47) Cyprus II (d. of Herod G. and Mariamme I)
48) Cyprus III (w. of Agrippa I, d. of Salampsio and Phasael II)
49) Cyprus IV (d. of Cyprus II and Antipater III)
50) Cyprus V (d. of Cyprus IV and Alexas III-Helcias)
51) Demetrius (from Alexandria—h. of Mariamme VI)
52) Doris (w. of Herod G.)
53) Dositheus (1st h. of Xd. of Joseph I?)
54) Drusilla (d. of Agrippa I and Cyprus III)
55) Drusus (s. of Agrippa I and Cyprus III)
56) Eleazarus (b. of Mariamme II)
57) Elpis (w. of Herod G.)
58) Epiphanes (from Commagene—fiancé of Drusilla)
59) Felix, [Ti.] Claudius (*procurator*—h. of Drusilla)
60) Glaphyra (from Cappadocia—w. of Alexander I and of Archelaus)
61) Helcias II? (s. of Alexas III Helcias and Cyprus IV?)
62) Herod (I) of Ascalon
63) Herod (II), C. Julius, the Great (s. of Antipater I and Cyprus I)
64) Herod III (s. of Herod G. and Mariamme II)
65) Herod IV (s. of Herod G. and Cleopatra)
66) Herod (V) of Chalcis (b. of Agrippa I, s. of Aristobulus I and Berenice I)
67) Herod VI (s. of Salampsio and Phasael II)
68) Herod VII (s. of Aristobulus III and Herodias-Salome?)
69) Herod VIII (σεμνότατος) = Herod VII, no. 68? = 'Herodion'?
70) Herodias (sis. of Agrippa I, d. of Aristobulus I and Berenice I)
71) Herodias-Salome? (d. of Antipas II)

72) Hyrcanus (s. of Herod of Chalcis and Berenice II)

73) Joazarus (b. of Mariamme II)

74) Joseph I (b. of Antipater I, s. of Antipas I)

75) Joseph II (b. of Herod G., s. of Antipater I and Cyprus I)

76) Joseph III (s. of Joseph II)

77) Jotape I (from Emesa—w. of Aristobulus II)

78) Jotape II (d. of Aristobulus II and Jotape I)

79) Jotape III (from Commagene—w. of Alexander IV)

80) Levias?

81) Malthace (w. of Herod G.)

82) Mariamme I (Hasmonaean w. of Herod G.)

83) Mariamme II (Priestly w. of Herod G.)

84) Mariamme III (w. of Archelaus) = Mariamme IV, no. 85?

85) Mariamme IV (sis. of Agrippa I, d. of Aristobulus I and Berenice I)

86) Mariamme V (d. of Olympias and Joseph III)

87) Mariamme VI (d. of Agrippa I and Cyprus III)

88) Olympias (d. of Herod G. and Malthace)

89) Pallas (w. of Herod G.)

90) Phaedra (w. of Herod G.)

91) Phallion I (b. of Antipater I, s. of Antipas I)

92) Phallion II Kaboas? (s. of Phallion I?)

93) Phasael I (b. of Herod G., s. of Antipater I and Cyprus I)

94) Phasael II (s. of Phasael I)

95) Phasael III (s. of Herod G. and Pallas)

96) Pheroras (b. of Herod G., s. of Antipater I and Cyprus I)

97) Philip (s. of Herod G. and Cleopatra)

98) Polemo (from Pontus and Cilicia—h. of Berenice II)

99) Roxane (d. of Herod G. and Phaedra)

100) Salampsio (d. of Herod G. and Mariamme I)

101) Salome I (sis. of Herod G., d. of Antipater I and Cyprus I)

102) Salome II (d. of Herod G. and Elpis)

103) Salome III (d. of Herodias and Herod III)

104) Saulus (b. of Costobarus II, s. of Antipater III and Cyprus II?)

105) Severus, [C.] Julius (desc. of Alexander IV)

106) Syllaeus (from Petra—temp. fiancé of Salome I)

107) Syphas? (s. of Aregetas?)

108) Theudion (b. of Doris)

109) Tigranes I (V of Armenia—s. of Alexander I and Glaphyra)

110) Tigranes II, [Julius] (VI of Armenia—s. of Alexander II)

111) Timius (from Cyprus—h. of Alexandra)

Mentioned without name

112) X-cousin-wife of Herod G. (d. of Joseph I?—*Ant.* 17.19; *War* 1.563)

113) X-niece-wife of Herod G. (d. of Joseph II?—*Ant.* 17.19; *War* 1.563)

114) X-son of Herod G. (third s. of Mariamme I—*War* 1.435; *Ant.* 14.300)

115) X-daughter of Salome I and Joseph I (*Ant.* 17.9; *War* 1. 566)
116) X-royal-wife of Pheroras (sis. of Mariamme I—*War* 1. 483)
117) X-'slave'-wife of Pheroras
118) X-mother of 'slave'-wife of Pheroras
119) X-sister of 'slave'-wife of Pheroras
120) X-child of Pheroras from his 'slave'-wife (*Ant.* 16.198) = Xd. of Pheroras, no. 121?
121) X-daughter of Pheroras (*War* 1.557, 565; *Ant.* 17.14, 16, 18)
122) X1-son of Pheroras (*Ant.* 16.228)
123) X2-son of Pheroras (*War* 2.99)
124) X3-son of Pheroras (*War* 2.99)
125) X-wife of Antipater II (d. of Antigonus—*Ant.* 17.92; cf. *War* 1.619)
126) X1-son of Antipater II (*War* 1.557, 565; *Ant.* 17.14, 18)
127) X2-son of Antipater II (*War* 1.588; but cf. *Ant.* 17.67) = X1 son of Antipater II, no. 126?
128) X-daughter of Antipater II (*Ant.* 17.14)
129) X-wife of Antipas (d. of Aretas IV of Petra—apparently 'Phasaelis')
130) X-wife of Antipater IV (*Ant.* 18.138?)
131) X-wife of Agrippa III (*Ant.* 20.144)
132) X-cousin of Alexander IV (from Perge—unpublished inscription)

Assumed or implied
133) X-wife of Herod of Ascalon
134) X-wife of Antipas I (στρατηγὸς)
135) X-wife of Phallion I?
136) X1-wife of Joseph I (sis. of Dositheus?)
137) X-wife of Phallion II Kaboas?
138) X-wife of Phasael I
139) X-wife of Joseph II
140) X-wife of Tigranes I (V)
141) X-wife of Alexander II
142) X-wife of Herod VI
143) X-wife of Alexander III
144) X-wife of Tigranes II (VI)

ABBR.: b. = brother; d. = daughter; desc. = descendant; f. = father; h. = husband; m. = mother; s. = son; sis. = sister; w. = wife; X = unknown

APPENDIX 2

MAIN POINTS IN THE CHRONOLOGY OF HEROD

1. The very first time Herod visited Rome was on the occasion of his crowning as king of Judaea by Antonius, Octavian and the Roman Senate. The year was clearly that of the second consulship of Cn. Domitius Calvinus and of C. Asinius Pollio, 40 BCE (Josephus, *Ant.* 14.389; see Stern [M.] 1974a: 63-64). Since some ambiguity exists as to the precise month of this year, it is hoped that a brief examination here may help to avert the creation of paradoxes (e.g. Filmer 1966; Edwards 1982; Martin 1989).

Herod's journey was meant to be directly from Egypt, but because of the winter season (i.e. before 11 March—see below) which prevented a crossing to Sicily, the ship followed the coast towards Pamphylia and reached Rhodes with great difficulty. There Herod built his own trireme, while he had to delay his departure due to strained political circumstances in Italy during this period. Apparently only after several months did he sail to Brundisium (Josephus *War* 1. 278-81; *Ant.* 14.375-78). *SVM* (1, 281-82 n. 3) thought that Herod took ship at Alexandria in 'late autumn' (i.e. November 40 BCE), but this cannot be accepted for the following reasons:

a) It is stated that χειμῶνος τε ὄντος, and even ἀκμὴν τοῦ χειμῶνος.

b) There was a disorder in Italy (already resolved by the beginning of October with the Treaty of Brundisium—see Tarn and Charlesworth 1934: 44).

c) There would not be enough time for Herod to stay in Rhodes, raise funds, build a trireme and get to Rome before the end of the year (or rather by 1 December when new consuls *suffecti* were suddenly appointed—Dio, 48.32.2; Tarn and Charlesworth 1934: 46 n. 3).

d) Herod would hardly have gone to Brundisium to find Antony and Octavian, who were now in Rome.

Therefore the only possible 'winter' is that of 41/40 BCE and since the 'mid-winter' had passed Herod must have left Alexandria around mid-February 40 BCE. No doubt the disturbances in Italy refer to those leading to the Perusine War, which ended at the close of the same month after Antony's brother Lucius surrendered (Charlesworth 1934: 29). Shortly before Herod's arrival at Alexandria Antony must have left for Tyre—Cleopatra welcomed Herod alone. Antony was informed of the war's outcome when he reached Asia Minor in c. April (Appian, *Bell. Civ.* 5.52; cf. 5.76; Dio, 48.27; Plutarch, *Anton.* 30.3). Herod would have stayed on at Rhodes, sailing to Italy in early autumn on receiving the news of the pact between Antony and Caeasar at Brundisium. By the time he arrived there, however, the Roman rulers had moved to the capital. Herod left Rome in a great hurry, one of the reasons being the approaching closure of the shipping season on 11 November (Vegetius, *De Re Milit.* 4.39; Pliny *Hist. Natur.* 2.47, 125; see Casson 1971: 270-99; cf. *Gen. R.* 6.5, 44-45; Sperber 1986: 99-101)—he would not risk his life twice in the same year! So the first year of Herod's reign, in standard Hellenistic fashion, should have been officially counted from autumn 40 to autumn 39 BCE.

There are two remaining difficulties with Josephus's text, which can be explained: First, is the parallel dating of the appointment of Herod in the 184th Olympiad, which ended in June 40 BCE. But similar problems exist in Josephus, for example in the capture of Jerusalem by Pompey in 63 BCE (*Ant.* 14.66; cf. *War* 1.149). The Jewish historian may have carelessly combined information about Herod's prolonged stay in Rhodes during the last months of this Olympiad with Herod's royal appointment later in the same year (even though the next Olympiad had officially begun). More likely, however, Josephus need not have followed the standard Greek dating of the Olympic Cycle (July to June), but the Syro-Macedonian (October to September) as displayed in Julius Africanus, or even the Roman (January to December) of Eusebius (see Finegan 1964: 142, 165).

The other problem is that Josephus says that it was at 'Pentecost' that Phasael defended the walls and Herod the palace of Jerusalem, when Antigonus and the Parthians attacked (*War* 1.253; *Ant.* 14.337-39). But Pentecost (in c. May) is too early for the events of 41 BCE, since the Parthians had invaded Syria only around October (Buchheim 1960: 75, 118 n. 188; contra Debevoise 1938: 109), and too late for those of 40 BCE, since Herod left Alexandria for Rome around mid-February as argued here. Thus if a festival indeed was involved, it might have been the feast of Hanukkah in December 41 BCE (1 Macc. 4.59; *Ant.* 12.325; Jn 10.22). This is not the only time that Josephus misidentifies festivals (e.g. *Ant.* 18.90 with the notorious first visit of Vitellius to Jerusalem; see Kokkinos 1980: 254-56; contra Schwartz [D.R.] 1992: 202-17).

In his attempt to defend the Herodian reckoning of regnal years from Tishri to Elul (now demonstrable by numismatics, certainly for the later Herods, see Chapter 10, no. 76), Van Bruggen (1978: 11-12, 14-15) thought that Josephus placed Herod's appointment as king *before* June 40 BCE. However, as we saw, this need not have been Josephus's position. In any case, the corollary of van Bruggen's argument would be that according to Josephus (following the 'Tishri' reckoning) Herod's first year was Tishri 41 to Elul 40—since the king died in his thirty-seventh year (Josephus) and in Nisan 4 BCE (*communis opinio*—see later). Otherwise a first year of Tishri 40 to Elul 39 (as shown above) would cause the thirty-seventh year to commence in Tishri 4 BCE, long after the demise of the king. This corollary could have been accepted on either of two presuppositions:

a) Herod was appointed in Rome a little before 1 Tishri (a few days could have been celebrated as his first year, *Ant.* 14.389). But this requires a somewhat earlier date for the Brundisium pact (see above point b).

b) Josephus wrongly thought that Herod was appointed in Rome shortly before 1 Tishri, assigning one extra year to his reign. But, assuming consistency in Josephus, this requires to understand the 'Year 3' in which Herod attacked Jerusalem (*War* 1.343; *Ant.* 14.465) as Tishri 39 to Elul 38—yet the Roman date he gives is 37 BCE (*Ant.* 14.487).

However, it must be stressed that Josephus in his accounts followed various reckonings (Hebrew = Nisan, Syro-Macedonian = Dius or Herodian = Tishri, and occasionally Roman = January) often leading to confusing results. Since the beginning of *both* Eras of Herod are given in the 'consular' dating (*Ant.* 14.389, 487), the end of them could *in this case* have been calculated from 'January' to 'December'. So Nisan 4 BCE, when Herod died, indeed fell in his thirty-seventh year (40 BCE being the first), which was also his thirty-fourth year (37 BCE being the first). But when Josephus mentions the *famous* 'Year 3', he had no choice but to follow 'royal' chronology (due to his source), and thus Tishri 38 to Elul 37 BCE (in agreement with the conclusion above). Of course in reality, and in terms of coins, Nisan 4 BCE could only have fallen in the thirty-sixth year of the king, which would also have been probably the thirty-fourth (assuming that Jerusalem fell before Tishri 37 BCE; see *Test. of Moses* 6.5-6). This can be proved only partly, because unfortunately Herod's coins are almost all undated! Nevertheless, his 'troublesome' first issue dated to 'Year 3', which was apparently struck upon his entrance to Jerusalem late in summer 37 BCE, would consistently read Tishri 38 to Elul 37. No other scheme can do justice here. Roman chronology would mint this coin in 38 BCE, the old 'Nisan' reckoning between Nisan 38 and Adar 37, while van Bruggen's interpretation of Josephus places the date between Tishri 39 and Elul 38! Such distinctions have yet to be fully realized (e.g. theory of Rappaport 1981b: 363-66, though the Ascalon approach is worth considering; theory of Meshorer in *AJC* 2, 9-11; Meshorer 1990–91: 108; cf. Jacobson 1986).

2. While I had previously accepted (1985; 1986b; cf. Chapter 3 n. 192) that the departure of Herod's Hasmonaean sons from Judaea was in 22 BCE (Otto 1913: 70-71; Hoehner 1972: 9), closer examination forced me to abandon this date. Primary evidence, i.e. the coins of Sebaste, suggest an era beginning from 26 BCE (*BMC Palest.*, xxxviii-xxxix, 78-81; Hill's dating ranged from 27 to 25, with the latter being preferred by a circular argument based on Josephus; see Barag 1993: 16 n. 6), and since the sons left shortly after the city was completed (πεπολισμένης), it could not have been later than 24 BCE. This agrees with the fact that Augustus added the northern territories to Herod's kingdom after the close of 'the first period of the Actian Era' (*War* 1.398), i.e. after September 24 BCE, when the sons were already at Rome (*Ant.* 15. 343).

The journey of Herod to fetch his son from Rome (Josephus *Ant.* 16.6; cf. *War* 1.445) took place about two years (*Ant.* 15.421) after the beginning of the work in the Temple early in 19 BCE (Kokkinos 1989: 154-55). Since Augustus was away from Rome before late 19 and after early 16 BCE (*Res Gestae* 12; Dio, 54. 19), Korach (1894: 530) placed the journey between 18/17 BCE (cf. *SVM* 1, 292). But Corbishley (1935: 27-29) was right that 17/16 BCE is a better date (cf. *GLAJJ* 1, 250). The occasion was carefully planned, since it coincided with events of marked importance. Early in 17 BCE Augustus adopted the young Gaius and Lucius, and Herod would have wanted to congratulate the emperor for now possessing his own sons (Dio, 54.18.1). The Ludi Saeculares were celebrated in June, a momentous event for Rome and the empire (cf. Lewis and Reinhold 1955: 55 and n. 158), while in Greece the 191st Olympiad was held in 16 BCE (see Kokkinos forthcoming 1).

3. Caesarea-on-the-coast was built either between 24 and 12 BCE (in 12 years—*Ant.* 15.341) or more likely between 23 and 13 BCE (in ten years—*Ant.* 16.136); cf. the ages and journey of Herod's sons by Mariamme I (Chapter 8 §2), and the dating of Herod's marriage to Mariamme II (Chapter 8 §4). In connection with its completion, Josephus refers to the twenty-eighth year of the king, which must have been reckoned (due to a Roman source) from Herod's *de jure* appointment in 40 BCE (discussed above). It would thus seem that the city's foundation was celebrated in 13 BCE (see Avi-Yonah 1950: 169, who gives, however, a wrong date for the Olympiad; Foerster 1975: 11, 19 n. 12, with reservations; cf. Kokkinos 1989: 162). This would be the only time *during* the king's reign that Josephus calculated by this system. But the fact may well be reflected in the use of the word ἀρχῆς, instead of the constant βασιλείας (e.g. *Ant.* 15.121 = *War* 1.370; *Ant.* 15. 299; *Ant.* 15.354 = *War* 1.401; *Ant.* 15.380). The parallel reference to the 192nd Olympiad, which in all counts gives a date not earlier than 12 BCE, would have to be slightly inaccurate (cf. thus *Chron. Pasch.* 1.367 where the founding of the city is placed both in 13 and 12 BCE; cf. Chapter 6 n. 2). An early beginning for the work agrees much better with Philo's statement (*Legat.* 297) that its harbour was shown to M. Agrippa, who sailed from it already in 15 BCE (cf. *Ant.* 16.13—λιμένα... κατασκευασμένον; for harbour archaeology there, see Raban 1989). Also, a 13 BCE foundation harmonizes with the quinquennial games instituted by Herod at Caesarea (*War* 1.415; *Ant.* 16.137-41), that came around again in CE 44 in the last year of Agrippa I (see Appendix 5)—the next possible date could only have been 9 BCE.

Levine (1975: 11, 149-50 n. 53; cf. Oestreicher 1962) argues that a commemorative medal from Caesarea bearing the numeral 'KA', must be dated by the Actium Era (31 BCE) from the founding of the city in 10/9 BCE. But apart from the fact that an Actium date would actually be 11/10 BCE, there is no guarantee that this is the Era in question, or even that the medal was cut on the foundation of the city. On such uncertain grounds the Era of 'Sebastos' (27 BCE) could have been suggested, giving a date of 7 BCE. But the strongest case is surely to regard the Era as being that of the city itself (13 BCE), as is common in the coinage of Greek cities, which would then date the medal to CE 8. It is significant that in this year the Roman Empire was celebrating Augustus's seventieth birthday, and that Caesarea with its harbour had been dedicated to him (cf. foundation of Sepphoris in CE 8, Chapter 8 n. 103).

4. When Antipater II, the eldest son of Herod, was recalled to be named heir to the throne, he was sent to Augustus to ratify his position, and presumably passed from Greece where he acquainted himself with King Eurycles (see Chapter 8 n. 5). In *War* 1.451 Josephus indicates that he left in late 14 BCE, and returned with his father when the latter visited Rome next (*War* 1.455). In *Ant.* 16.86 Josephus presents Herod as sailing to Lesbos with Antipater in 13 BCE to hand him over to M. Agrippa, who would have taken him to Rome (Agrippa returned to Italy in the early summer of that year—see below), and then coming back to Judaea only to sail again to Rome with his two other sons, apparently in the same year (*Ant.* 16.90). In *Ant.* 16.273 Josephus has Antipater being taken to Rome by his father on the occasion that Herod dragged Alexander and Aristobulus to the emperor. The conclusion from these contradictions must be that Antipater (for his own reason) went to Rome in late 14 BCE (no escort necessary for a man of c. 33), followed by his father and two brothers (for a different reason) in mid-13 BCE, who had joined M. Agrippa in Lesbos on the way. Herod and his three sons returned to Judaea in the autumn of 12 BCE. The question then that needs to be answered is why in the *communis opinio* Herod's *third* and *last* journey to Rome (cf. Appendix 3), is given as 12 BCE, rather than more precisely 13/12 BCE.

The conventional date of 12 BCE for this journey is based on two points, neither of which stand scrutiny:

a) A reading of Josephus (*Ant.* 16.128) mentions 'spectacles and doles (διανομαὶ) provided by Augustus for the people of Rome', and it is assumed that these were the *congiaria* referred to in *Res Gestae* for the second half of 12 BCE (Korach 1894: 531; Corbishley 1935: 30-32; *GLAJJ* 1, 250). We should note that the actual date in the Monumentum Ancyranum is any time between 26 June 12 BCE and 25 June 11 BCE (*Trib. Pot. XII*; cf. Schillinger-Häfele 1986: 51), while the nature of the occasion of the emperor's *liberalitas* is not specified. A festival (involving spectacles) may not be a bad guess, but looking at Dio the only event that might fit is the one held for the praetorship of Drusus presumably in 11 BCE (54.34.1; cf. Kokkinos 1992a: 13)—too late a date for Herod's visit.

b) Josephus (*Ant.* 16.91) refers to the fact that Herod met Augustus in Aquileia, but, as *SVM* (1, 293 n.16) admits, there is no evidence that Augustus went to this city in 12 BCE (or in 11 for that matter). The suggestion that he might have gone there accompanying Tiberius, who was heading towards Pannonia, is another unprovable guess.

But all this is not necessary. An alternative reading of Josephus mentions 'spectacles and doles provided by Herod for the people of Rome', and this makes sense because the king also made a personal present of 300 talents to Augustus himself. We know that many such gains came to the way of the emperor and the people of Rome in the second half of 13 BCE. Augustus had returned from the western provinces and Germany in July of that year, apparently via Aquileia—on the fourth day of the month the Senate ordered the consecration of the Ara Pacis (*Res Gest.* 12; *I. It.* 13.2, 476; cf. Kienast 1982: 101). On 23 September, Iullus, the son of M. Antonius, gave games in the Circus for the birthday of Augustus (Dio, 54.26.2;

Snyder 1940: 227-30). The celebration was particularly special because the emperor
was exactly half a century old, a unique moment for Herod's gift. Also Tiberius
organized a festival for the return of Augustus, probably coinciding with the
'Augustalia' on 12 October, a day commemorating his earlier return from the East in
19 BCE (Dio, 54.27.1). Furthermore, Augustus himself after making payments to his
soldiers and offering free baths and haircuts to all citizens (Dio, 54.25.5-6), dedicated the theatre of Marcellus with exotic spectacles (Dio, 54.26.1).

A case then can be made in which Herod (and his two sons—*Ant*. 16.91 against
War 1.452), joining Agrippa in the early summer of 13 BCE at Lesbos (after escort-
ing king Archelaus to Antioch—*Ant*. 16.270; cf. *War* 1.510), sailed to Rome (where
he met his son Antipater), but he arrived before Augustus's arrival (*Ant*. 16.86; Dio,
54.28.1-2; see Reinhold 1933: 124 n. 1). Eager, as always, to be among the first to
welcome the emperor Herod proceeded to Aquileia. Later in Rome (*Ant*. 16. 106) the
reconciliation with his sons was achieved (*Ant*. 16. 91-126). On Augustus's fiftieth
birthday he presented him with his valuable gift and went on to stage a show for the
people of Rome in which donations were offered. 10 September to 10 November
was considered a doubtful period for sailing, and perhaps the weather conditions in
that year were adverse (cf. Dio, 54.25. 2). At any rate, intentionally or not, Herod
missed the official closure of the shipping season on 11 November—he had to wait
until the spring of 12 BCE (11 March at the earliest or as late as 26 May—cf. previous
journey of 17/16 BCE). Meanwhile, Lepidus died (Dio, 54.27.2) and not long after
Augustus assumed the position of Pontifex Maximus (*Res Gest*. 10), Herod would
have shared in the magnificent gathering of 6 March (Snyder 1940: 233) for which
Augustus said: '. . . from all Italy a multitude flocked to my election such as had never
previously been recorded at Rome.' If Herod did not sail before May he would have
attended the contests of Panathenaic fashion (Dio, 54.28.3 mistakenly implies that
they were held at Athens—see Reinhold 1933: 126) in the name of Augustus's sons
between 20 and 23 March, during which the news arrived of the death of Agrippa
(Dio, 54.28.3; Velleius 2.96.1; Tacitus, *Ann*. 3.56.3; Livy 138). Fortunately or
unfortunately the King of Judaea may have also been present at the funeral of his
great Roman friend (cf. Chapter 8 n. 53).

5. This is not the place to engage in the complicated issue of the year of Herod's
death, for which even a lengthy chapter may be inadequate. In this book the *communis opinio* of Nisan 4 BCE (represented by *SVM* 1, 326-28 n. 165; van Bruggen
1978; Bernegger 1983; Hoehner 1989) has been employed, with the strongest alternative of Kislev 5 BCE (represented by Barnes 1968) given in brackets.

The main complaint against the conventional date has long been the fact that it
compresses too many events between the lunar eclipse (Josephus, *Ant*. 17.167), presumably that of 13 March 4 BCE, and the Passover (astronomical full moon 11 April)
which came about after Herod's death (*Ant*. 17.213; *War* 2.10). It became necessary
to suggest the previous eclipse of 15 September 5 BCE, with the death of Herod
being placed late in the same year (Barnes 1968) or early in 4 BCE (Smallwood 1976:
104 n. 158). Now the question seemed to arise as to whether the respective time span
has been overstreched instead. However, a recent study by Schwartz ([D.R.] 1992:

159-66), revived an older, ingenious observation that 'the night' of the lunar eclipse may not be connected with the occasion on which Herod killed the sages, but with an earlier 'night' when Matthias, the high priest, saw his fateful dream. If this is true, the problem is solved, since considerable time can separate the eclipse from the following Passover. But admittedly *Ant.* 17.165-67 is ambiguous, and the eclipse may also be taken as referring to the night of the killings. In such a case, it would simply have to be assumed that Josephus brought two events separated by many months as close as possible, in order to serve his purpose of presenting Herod's painful death as a punishment for (among other reasons) the recent killing of Jewish sages.

An even more recent study by Kushnir-Stein (1995b), rightly agonizing over the compression of the conventional chronology, suggests that we should retain the eclipse of 13 March 4 BCE, and instead move Herod's death to the winter of 4/3 prior to Passover of 3 BCE. This seems a bold move in the wrong direction. Although it still falls within the margin of Herod's regnal years in the 'Nisan' reckoning, it is impossible in the 'Tishri' reckoning as explained above. Also, it creates new problems. For example, it will be difficult to understand how the fomentors of disorder were mourning for the dead sages at the Passover of 3 BCE (*Ant.* 17. 214), when the killings took place at the eclipse before the Passover of 4 BCE! The implication will be to adopt Schwartz's solution with all its ambiguity, i.e. disassociating the eclipse from the killing of the sages. But even if such a stretch were to be allowed (involving an eclipse, followed by a Passover, followed by the death of Herod, followed by another Passover), why not instead tranfer the whole story a year earlier? Although almost never mentioned before, there was yet another eclipse (total) on 23 March 5 BCE (Ginzel 1911: 541). In Kushnir-Stein's scenario, Herod would have died in the winter of 5/4 prior to Passover 4 BCE, and we are back to square one.

My own analysis of Herodian court history post-14 BCE (cf. Appendix 3) leads to the conclusion that the death of Herod must be placed as early as possible (see Chapter 6 n. 84). Had it not been for the constraint of the overall length of his reign, which seems to place his last year between Tishri 5 and Elul 4 (discussed above), one could have gone as far as to suggest that Herod died before the Passover of 5 BCE! For the first time the best synchronization with Roman history at our disposal would have been fully justified. In 5 BCE Gaius Caesar received the *toga virilis* and was designated as consul, to hold office after the interval of five years (*IGRR* 4.1756; Velleius, 2.99.2; Tacitus, *Ann.* 1.3; Suetonius, *Aug.* 26; Dio, 55.9.9). Augustus himself assumed the consulship in order to introduce him to public life. As he proudly stated in *Res Gestae* 14, the Senate decreed that from that day Gaius should take part (*interessent*) in the counsels of state (*consiliis publicis*). Now, Augustus called his own *consilium* to hear the case of the Judaean princes after the death of Herod, and as Josephus testifies it was made the occasion for Gaius to sit for the *first* time (*War* 2.25; *Ant.* 17.229). It is absolutely incredible that this young man, who was virtually heaped with honours from the first day he became *princeps iuventutis*, was not offered this predetermined privilege by his adopted father in the whole of 5 BCE, but only in 4 BCE (or even in 3)! Gaius may anyway have been away from Rome during much of 4/3 BCE (and then again from 2 BCE—see references in Chapter 9 n. 64), though this argument has to be made elsewhere.

STRUCTURE OF THE JOSEPHUS TEXT 14–8 BCE

The events narrated from *War* 1.455 to 472 belong to 12 and 11 BCE, i.e. after the return of Herod and his sons from Rome. However the events from *War* 1.473 to 512 date back to 14/13 BCE, i.e. before the journey to Rome, with a few even earlier 'flashes'. One point needs to be argued. *War* 1.481-2 reads:

> Just before setting sail for Rome (but *read* Pontus) he sent for them (Alexander and Aristobulus)... exhorting them to love their brothers and promising to pardon their past offences if they would amend their ways for the future. For their part, they repudiated the charges... and assured their father that their actions (i.e. while he is away) would vindicate their statement...

Since Herod made no journey to Rome after that of 13/12 BCE (when he took his sons there—see Appendix 2, pt. 4), Josephus is either factually wrong here, or he has amalgamated different events for reasons of brevity which serve the early part of *War*'s narrative (as particularly in Mariamme's death—Chapter 8 n. 21). The trip mentioned must be that to Pontus in 14 BCE, since it follows from the discussion that when Herod returned he was briefed by his brother and sister on his sons' bad behaviour during his absence (see *Ant.* 16.73-74 dated to late 14 BCE).

In a similar way the events narrated from *Ant.* 16.78 to 135 begin in late 14 BCE (when Antipater was recalled to Jerusalem) and end with the speech of Herod at the Temple in late 12 BCE after his return from Rome (without the details which led to the journey to Rome, but with a full account of the circumstances in Italy). From *Ant.* 16.136 to 187 Josephus looks back at some of Herod's achievements and projects variously dating from c. 15 to 12 BCE. Then from *Ant.* 16.188 to 270 the full (and until now reserved) details are given for the first dissension in the Herodian court from 14 BCE to 12 BCE (with some even earlier 'flashes', but this time without the full account of the events in Rome, already given earlier). From *Ant.* 16.271 onwards the narrative resumes its chronological order after 12 BCE.

Once this scheme in Josephus is perceived the following observation must be made without reservations: *Ant.* 16.270 mentions M. Titius (*cos.* 31 BCE) as being the Roman governor of Syria when Herod was on his way to Rome in mid-13 BCE. Only Corbishley (1934) managed to come close to observing this, but his work has been largely ignored (cf. Roos 1941: 311-13; Smallwood 1976: 101 n. 145): the prime reason being Corbishley's unfortunate attempt to find vacant space between 12 and 6 BCE (once Titius had been backdated), to accommodate an assumed earlier governorship by P. Sulpicius Quirinius (*cos.* 12 BCE), and thus restore faith in Luke's account of the Nativity.

However, what has not been realized is that ironically Corbishley's conclusion (partly also mine) destroys forever any effort to find vacant space for Quirinius. Following the new order of events, in *Ant.* 16.277 we come across the earliest reference to C. Sentius Saturninus (*cos.* 19 BCE) as governor of Syria. (As soon as Herod had returned from Rome in the early autumn of 12 BCE, he found himself at war with the Arabs, for which he came into contact with Saturninus.) Thus, as with Titius, Saturninus had been appointed to the Syrian command earlier than current scholarship allows (*SVM* 1, 257; Thomasson 1984: 304, no. 8). Further, since Saturninus was still governor until after the trial of Herod's sons in c. 8 BCE, his tenure of office would have lasted from mid-12 to 8/7 BCE. His successor P. Quinctilius Varus (*cos.* 13 BCE) would have held this position from c. mid-7 to about 3/2 BCE (his coins begin in 7/6 BCE—*BMC* Syr., 158, no. 57 = *RPC* 1, 4242; cf. Chapter 7 n. 27). For replies to the two extremes concerning Quirinius and the Nativity, i.e. that of Corbishley (1936) and that of Syme (1973), see Kokkinos 1989; 1995; forthcoming 2; forthcoming 3.

There are major consequences here. A number of events, in and out of Judaea, will have to be redated, altering our understanding of the period. For example, Aretas IV king of Petra began his reign in 11/10 BCE (this year also being the twenty-first, and last, of Obodas 'III'; read II, see Chapter 3 n. 40), and *not* in 9 BCE as currently believed (Meshorer 1975: 41; Schmitt-Korte 1990: 129; Schmitt-Korte and Price 1994: 103). New suggestions put forward by Bowersock (1983b: 55-57) for Aretas's reign, based on coins and following the accepted dating system, will now have to be rejected (cf. Millar 1993b: 44 n. 1). The king appears not to have minted coins in his seventh, eighth and ninth years, which would be 5/4, 4/3 and 3/2 BCE (rather than 3/2, 2/1 and 1 BCE/CE 1 as reckoned by Bowersock), i.e. before Gaius Caesar's arrival in Syria and thus unconnected with this event. (In any case, Bowersock had overlooked an inscription mentioning Aretas's ninth year (*CIS* 2.197), and so there was not much point in imagining a brief takeover of Aretas's kingdom by the Romans.) I intend to comment on Nabataean chronology elsewhere.

APPENDIX 4

THE FAMILY OF ARETAS IV

I presume that Aretas IV's eight children were born in the following order: Obodas, Phasaelis, Sha'dat, Malichus II, Rabbel, Hagaru I, Shaqilat II and Gamilat I. This I base on the fact that apparently the earliest inscription referring to Aretas's children, possibly dating from the beginning of his reign, mentions only the first three (Negev 1961: 127-28, no. 1). The second inscription dated to his twenty-ninth year (i.e. CE 18/19; my reckoning throughout—see Appendix 3, end) adds the next three children, though not in order in relation to the first three (*CIS* 2.354; Cooke 1903: 244-46, no. 95). The third inscription most probably dated to his thirty-fourth year (i.e. CE 23/24) adds the last two children (Khairy 1981).

If this analysis is correct then we may conclude the following: The elder son Obodas, who was born before Aretas began his reign in 11/10 BCE, would either have lost his right of succession, or have died after CE 23/24 (last time mentioned) and before 38/39 (when Malichus II became king of Nabataea). Obodas's early birth is supported by the fact that his first sister, Phasaelis, was probably already at marriageable age in the fifth year of Aretas (7/6 BCE), when she is mentioned on coins (Chapter 8 n. 96). Also the fact that Malichus II died in CE 70 (Meshorer 1975: 70; cf. Josephus, *War* 3.68) indicates that he would have been born after his father became king. He and his brother Rabbel and sister Hagaru II had been born long before CE 18/19 (first time mentioned), and in fact before the twenty-fourth year of Aretas (i.e. CE 13/14) when Huldu, evidently their mother, died (Meshorer 1975: 55, 103, no. 95). Indeed, since by CE 18/19 Hagaru II was a mother of a child (second inscription above), she could hardly have been born later than the beginning of the century. The last two children of Aretas would have been born after CE 18/19 and before 23/24 (third inscription above). This is in broad agreement with the name given to Shaqilat II, adopted from her mother Shaqilat I, who could have married Aretas as late as CE 16—her earliest coin is now known to be 'Year 26' (CE 15/16 in my reckoning; see Schmitt-Korte 1990: 120, no. 70)—or in any case not earlier than CE 14 (Schmitt-Korte 1990: 129-30 suggests 'Year 25' for the wedding). Shaqilat II died in CE 75/76 (Meshorer 1975: 72) after becoming the 'sister-wife' of Malichus II and the mother of Rabbel II, the last Nabataean king (Meshorer 1975: 106-108, nos. 123-39; 108-109, nos. 142-46). Gamilat I is called 'queen' ([ת]מלכ) in CE 23/24, quite prematurely if she was only up to five years old in the present reconstruction, and in any case this is impossible if she was a daughter of the reigning king. Thus we have to understand 'queen' only as 'princess'. The meaning of this title (like those of 'brother' and 'sister') in Nabataea is not always clear, and it may sometimes be honorary, or a technical term (Bowersock 1983b: 63, 74). All five daughters of Aretas are known to have been called 'queens', and yet only two (Shaqilat II and probably Sha'dat) had become 'sister-wives' of Malichus II, and thus 'queens'.

From the inscriptions, papyri and coins mentioned here, and in Chapter 8 nn. 92-98, I shall attempt to draw a genealogical tree of Aretas IV's family:

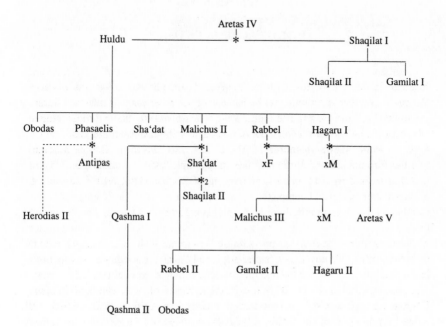

APPENDIX 5

DATE OF AGRIPPA I'S DEATH

Josephus in *Ant.* 19.343 (cf. *War* 2.219) gives the time at which Agrippa moved to Caesarea-on-the-coast. It was after he had completed three years of rule over Judaea, i.e. sometime during his fourth regnal year, when his last coins were also minted: October CE 43–October CE 44 (see *AJC* 2, 248, nos. 9-9a; Burnett 1987: 35, no. 10; *RPC* 1, 4984, 4986; Meshorer 1990–91: 124, nos. 14-15a). This is a known 'elastic' formula used by Josephus, like, for example, when he refers (*Ant.* 15.354) to Augustus's arrival at Syria in the spring of 20 BCE (Dio, 54.7.6) as having occurred after Herod had completed his *de facto* seventeenth year (October 22 BCE– October 21 BCE), or in other words during his eighteenth (October 21–October 20 BCE).

The precise point within Agrippa's fourth year for his visit to Caesarea is fixed by the evidence of *O. Petr.* 271 (Chapter 10 n. 134), which provides a *terminus ante quem* of 25 January 44 for the death of Marcus Julius Alexander (predating that of Agrippa—Josephus, *Ant.* 19.277), and by the evidence of Acts 12.3-5, which testifies that Agrippa was still in Jerusalem at Passover in April 44 (astronomical full moon 1 April—see Nicklin 1950: 149; Goldstine 1973: 88). So the death of Agrippa cannot have occurred earlier than the beginning of the summer of that year.

Can we be more specific? Josephus correlates the event with a festival, the identification of which has been hopelessly confused in previous studies. But the crucial passage (*Ant.* 19.343) should be translated here as follows:

> There he then exhibited shows (θεωρίαι) in honour of Caesar (i.e. Claudius), being informed (ἐπιστάμενος) that there would be a certain festival (ἑορτὴ) for his (i.e. the Emperor's) safety (σωτηρία).

From the point of view of Roman history, it is clear that this *hyper sōtērias* festival signifies a major return of the emperor from a campaign. Under the circumstances it has to be Claudius's return from Britain in the spring of 44, which was celebrated extensively in Rome, and no doubt subsequently in the provinces (Dio, 60.23.4-5; cf. Suetonius, *Cl.* 17.3; Syncellus [edn Dindorf 332C-333A]; see conclusively *SVM* 1, 453 n. 43; Kokkinos 1986a: 38). The earliest possible time for such spectacles to be organized, given that the news must have reached Palestine after the openning of the shipping season (see Appendix 2, pt. 1), would have been the summer of 44. Claudius's *dies natalis* on 1 August (Suetonius, *Cl.* 2.1), might have presented the most ideal coincidence.

A professional athletic association operating in the eastern provinces, and apparently originally based at Antioch, was very busy in this and the following year. Their earnings, thanks to Claudius's 'safe return', would have been substantial enough for them to send to the emperor a golden crown as a gift for his victory in Britain. We do not know whether Agrippa employed these athletes for his contribution to the shows at Caesarea, but they were certainly employed later by two of his best friends, client-kings Antiochus IV and Julius Polemo. In two letters dated to CE 46 and 47 (the second a more belated reply), Claudius extended his gratitude to the association and to the kings (*P. Lond.* 3.1178; Braund 1985: 210-11, no. 581; cf. Lewis and Reinhold 1955: 232-33; Jones and Milns 1984: 129-30, no. 81).

Considering the above, and since Agrippa fell ill on the second day of the festival (Josephus, *Ant.* 19.344), suffering for five days (*Ant.* 19.350), he may well have died on 6 August CE 44. It is commonly assumed that Agrippa died during the games of the city of Caesarea, the *quinquennalia*, instituted in the name of Augustus (thus evidently *Kaisareioi Agōnes*) by Herod the Great when he founded the city (Josephus, *War* 1.415; *Ant.* 16.137-41; see Smallwood 1976: 80 n. 62; cf. Lake and Cadbury 1933: 5.446-52). But Agrippa's spectacles simply cannot be equated with the Caesarean Games, because according to Eusebius these were held on 5 March (*Mart. Palest.* 2.30).

Schwartz's thesis ([D.R.] 1990: 108-11, 203-207; cf. Schwartz 1992: 167-81) that Agrippa would have died in the autumn of 43 is basically absurd, as it is the connection with Herodian games based on the Augustan Actia (and yet not coincidental with them) that Agrippa would have celebrated in Caesarea-on-the coast. Even if Herod the Great when instituting the Games of Caesarea wished them to imitate the Actia of Nicopolis (calling them *Isaktion* and celebrating them in September), no reason can be found why he would not have matched the two chronologically—other than the fact that the Cycle of the Actia (whether they commenced in 28 or 27 BCE) unfortunately does not fall on the foundation of Caesarea in 10/9 BCE as proposed by Schwartz! The closest coincidence would have been in 11 BCE, with the games repeated in CE 42—two years before Agrippa's death (Lämmer 1981–82). Also, it cannot be shown that the 'Isactium of Caesarea' (*IGLS* 4.1265, line 11) were games held at Caesarea-on-the-coast rather than Caesarea Philippi. Despite Schwartz's confidence in his own logic, it is perfectly logical that the second is meant in this inscription. The distinction between the two is served both by the mention of Caesarea-on-the-coast in a previous line (it would have been common knowledge that in this part of the world there was only one other Caesarea), and by the very mention of *Isaktion*, unique as games in antiquity, and conceivably *then* known to be exclusively connected with Caesarea Philippi (cf. suggestion of Gatier in *BE* 1993: 629 on Dar and Kokkinos 1992, no. 2). But this discussion is futile because Caesarea-on-the-coast would have been founded in 13 BCE (see Appendix 2, pt. 3), and so its games would have been held, as testified by Eusebius, on 5 March CE 44, when Agrippa was still in Jerusalem. Moreover, even for those who wish to reckon the twenty-eighth year of Herod (when Caesarea was founded—*Ant.* 16.136) in his *de facto* reign (i.e. October 11 BCE–October 10 BCE), the games would have been staged on

5 March 10 BCE for the first time, and then again in the spring of CE 43, but still more than a year earlier than Agrippa's death.

Agrippa I must have died about mid-44 for other reasons. *Ant.* 20.1-2 makes it clear that Marsus was replaced almost immediately after the death of Agrippa, as a kind of a tribute paid to him by the emperor, who knew of the friction that existed between the two men. Indeed not long after the death of Agrippa we find C. Cassius Longinus as governor of Syria (*Ant.* 15.406). In any case the *terminus ante quem* for Marsus's deposition is fixed by a letter of Claudius dated to 28 June 45 in which Longinus is mentioned (Josephus, *Ant.* 20.11-4; see Kokkinos 1986a: 48 n. 2). That the replacement would have taken place at the end of 44 is supported by the fact that Marsus threatened an attack on Vardanes shortly before the death of the Parthian king (Tacitus, *Ann.* 11.10). We know that Vardanes was alive at least until the autumn of 44 when he struck his last coins ('Year 356' = October 44–October 45; see Sellwood 1980: 209, nos. 64.28-30; 212, no. 64.45). This sets the *terminus post quem* for Marsus's deposition in the autumn of 44. Thus Agrippa would not have died a whole year earlier (Schwartz), but only a few months before.

Finally we should note that no festival or games of any kind are mentioned in the scene described in Acts 12.21-23, which have Agrippa seating on his βῆμα and performing his legal duties. Although the hearing of the Tyrian/Sidonian embassies would have taken place shortly before the beginning of the festival, one may understand the appropriation for the Christian view, which by moving Agrippa's death a few days earlier, presented a badly judging king being fatally judged himself from above.

APPENDIX 6

IDENTITY OF POLEMO, HUSBAND OF BERENICE II

Polemo's identity, mentioned in Josephus's *Ant.* 20.145-46, is complex and problematic. Of recent studies, see *SVM* (1, 449-51 n. 4), Barrett (1978a), Sullivan (1979) and Braund (1984a: 42, 49-50 n. 22), where documentation for all synonymous individuals need not be repeated here. Each study has a good point to make (underlined below) but none presents a generally satisfactory solution.

SVM identified 'Polemo of Cilicia' (from Claudius to Nero), with Polemo II of Pontus (from Caligula to Nero), M. Antonius Polemo husband of Mammaia (under Nero?) and M. Antonius Polemo (under Galba), while they made M. Antonius Polemo of Olba (under Tiberius) his descendant. Barrett followed the same line but presented the last mentioned as a predecessor. Sullivan identified 'Polemo of Cilicia' with: Polemo II of Pontus, M. Antonius Polemo of Olba, Julius Polemo of Pontus (under Claudius), M. Antonius Polemo (under Nero), M. Antonius Polemo husband of Mammaia, M. Antonius Polemo (under Galba), and Polemo of Olba (from Vespasian to Domitian?). Braund distinguished between 'Polemo of Cilicia' and 'Polemo II of Pontus', identifying the first with M. Antonius Polemo (under Nero), M. Antonius Polemo husband of Mammaia, M. Antonius Polemo (under Galba) and Polemo of Olba (from Vespasian to Domitian?), while identifying the second with Julius Polemo of Pontus.

But there are some facts which cannot simply be discounted. Dio (60.8.2) testifies that in CE 41 a part of Cilicia was granted to Polemo II of Pontus. Like his father, Cotys VIII, the full name of the king of Pontus would have been Caius Julius Polemo, *as seen by Braund*. In effect under Claudius the larger part of Cilicia (to exclude free cities, any territory under Roman supervision, and the kingdom of Olba) would have been shared between two kings: Antiochus IV of Commagene holding Rough Cilicia and the coastal area of Elaeussa (Chapter 9 n. 32), and Polemo II of Pontus thus holding Eastern Cilicia Pedias. The fact that a papyrus (see Appendix 5) refers to these two kings acting together under Claudius, and naming both as Julii, is clear evidence, *as partly seen by Sullivan*. In the early CE 43, Josephus (*Ant.* 19.338) refers to Polemo, mentioning only his major holding of Pontus, which is understandable in the context of the international conference he reports (Chapter 10 n. 127). In CE 63, after Polemo had lost Pontus, Josephus (*Ant.* 20.145) referred to him only as king of Cilicia, *as seen by SVM*. Even if at that time another Polemo (M. Antonius Polemo) was also ruling in Cilicia, it would be remarkable that a 'high priest-dynast of Olba' (as his homonymous predecessor was) would have been converted to Judaism, *as seen by Barrett*.

Therefore Berenice II would have married [Caius] Julius Polemo II of Pontus and [Eastern] Cilicia [Pedias]. Two other Polemos existed: M. Antonius Polemo of Olba (under Tiberius); and a probable descendant of his, M. Antonius Polemo of Olba husband of Mammaea (from Nero to Domitian?). My dating of Berenice II's marriage is an important factor for this identification, missed by all except *SVM* (who on p. 450 gives the date as 'after CE 63', and on p. 474 as 'after CE 64'). Berenice stayed as a widow (after CE 48) for a long time, πολὺν χρόνον, and she also lived with Agrippa long enough (after CE 53 when he came to Syro-Palestine) before the rumours of incest were circulated, making her marry Polemo to become a 'queen' again. The early 60s CE is the right period, and also in agreement with the fact that she still accompanied her brother in c. CE 58 (Acts 25.13, 23). The fact that Josephus places her marriage to Polemo together with events before the death of Claudius (in CE 54) means nothing (contra Smallwood 1976: 385; Barrett 1978a: 439). This is a typical Josephan grouping of weddings. The last coin of Polemo in Pontus is dated to CE 62/63 (*RPC* 1, 3836), and thus Berenice would have stayed in Cilicia between 63 and 64—at any rate she was divorced by 65 when she moved to Jerusalem (*War* 2.310). The question of Polemo's Cilician holdings, his capital city and his general area of influence—thus the realm briefly shared with him by Berenice—has to be dealt with elsewhere (cf. Kokkinos forthcoming 3).

APPENDIX 7

SADDUCEAN HIGH PRIESTS AND THE ANANUS FAMILY

It is significant that Josephus (*Ant.* 20.199) reveals that Ananus II son of Ananus I was a Sadducee. This interlocks with Acts 4.6 and 5.17, which refers to Ananus I, as well as to his son-in-law Caiaphas and to his son John/Jonathan, at the time of the persecution of Jesus' disciples, as being Sadducees (cf. Chapter 10 n. 73). In the episode which led to the killing of James by Agrippa I, the replaced high priest was almost certainly Matthias II, another son of Ananus (Chapter 10 nn. 130-32).

Thus it has to be noted that the high priests at the time of the crucifixion of Jesus (CE 36), the persecution of the disciples (CE 37), the beheading of James son of Zebedee (CE 43/44), and the stoning of James brother of Jesus (CE 59/60), were all members of the Ananus family and Sadducees. Indeed as the sect of the upper class (*Ant.* 13.298; 18.17), regular beneficiaries of the Herods, and those disbelieving in life after death (Lk. 20.27; Josephus, *War* 2.165), the Sadducees must have been the primary opponents of the new faith (cf. Schwartz [D.R.] 1990: 117).

Since the Ananus family possibly produced up to 11 high priests in the Herodian period (an attempted reconstruction is appended below), and two other families (that of Boethus and Phiabi), both arguably of Sadducean background (Jeremias 1969: 228-30; Baumbach 1989: 184), produced another nine, then about *twenty* out of *twenty-eight* known high priests between c. 37 BCE and CE 66 would have been Sadducees (*Ant.* 20.250; cf. Smallwood 1962: 15; Stern [M.] 1976: 609-12; Schwartz [S.] 1990: 58ff.).

This of course does not exclude the possibility that a Pharisee high priest might have existed, preferably in the later period, though this may have created a stir. Perhaps Jesus son of Gamaliel, whose appointment led to an explosion of violence between high priests, was a Pharisee (*Ant.* 20.213—cf. Chapter 10 n. 202; see Rajak 1983: 31; contra Stern [M.] 1986: 325). Although soon he too (cf. Caiaphas) married into a Sadducean house (*m. Yeb.* 6.4), the union may have been contrived for reconciliation.

At any rate lesser priesthoods and the vast majority of the populace seems to have followed Pharisaism (*SVM* 2, 235, 404-14; cf. Mason 1991; contra Neusner see Chapter 6 n. 77), especially if Flusser is right that the sect involved in Herod's massive persecution in the episode of the 'oath-fine' was not Pharisees (Chapter 6 nn. 88-92).

Family Tree: *Ananus*

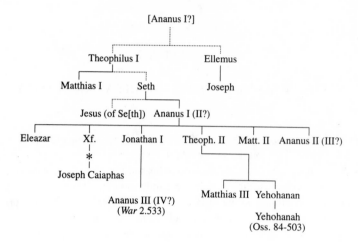

APPENDIX 8

REDATING THE LAST PROCURATORS
AND THE BROTHER OF JESUS

The dates of the procuratorships of Felix and Festus have long been in dispute (Saumagne 1966; *SVM* 1, 460 n. 17 and 465-66 n. 42; Stern [M.] 1974a: 74-76; Smallwood 1976: 269 n. 40; Robinson [J.A.T.] 1976: 43-52; Jewett 1979: 40-44; Kindler 1981: 20-21; *AJC* 2, 180-83; Bruce [F.F.] 1986: 284-87; see Schwartz [D.R.] 1992: 218-42).

Yet the question of the year in which Festus succeeded Felix, may reasonably be resolved on the evidence of procuratorial coins. Examples dated to the fourteenth year of Claudius, i.e. from January 54 to October 54, must belong to Felix (*AJC* 2, 284-85, nos. 29-34; *RPC* 1, 4970-71; Meshorer 1990–91: 128, 29c-32f). The arrival of Felix (see Chapter 10 n. 186) and the episode of the Egyptian prophet in Acts (21.38) and Josephus (*War* 2.261-63; *Ant.* 20.169-72) make it certain. Note that 54/55 was a Sabbatical year (Chapter 10 n. 67). Also note that Felix became procurator up to two years before he struck his first coins (cf. Kokkinos 1986b). Coins dated to the fifth year of Nero, i.e. from October 58 to October 59, should have been minted by Festus (*AJC* 2, 285-86, nos. 35-35q; *RPC* 1, 4972; Meshorer 1990–91: 128, nos. 35r-35s). Assuming that these types circulated at the beginning of this time span, Festus would have arrived in the summer of 58 *at the latest*. A year or two earlier (cf. Felix's case) cannot be excluded by the evidence in Josephus, whose narrative lacks the period 55–58 (Chapter 10 n. 194), but this is purely theoretical. Thus Paul's journey to Rome (Acts 25.12, 21, 25) should date to the winter of 58/59.

On conventional reckoning this would place Festus's term from c. 58 to 62, followed by Albinus from 62 to 64. However, the only evidence cited for the commencement of Albinus's rule is *War* 6.300, 308, which demonstrates that he was in Judaea in 62—i.e. four years before the revolt erupted and seven-and-a-half before the siege of Jerusalem (*SVM* 1, 468 n. 50). But this does not mean that Albinus had just arrived, it provides only a *terminus ante quem*—see Appendix 9, pt. c.

A much shorter tenure will be argued here for Festus, who died suddenly in office, and of whom Josephus has little to say (*Ant.* 20.182-97; *War* 2.271). It is during the time of Albinus that Josephus puts the enlargement of Panias/Caeasarea Philippi by Agrippa II, a city then renamed Neronias (*Ant.* 20.211). In the standard chronology this event has to date between 62 and 64. Yet a reassessment of Agrippa II's coins show beyond doubt that the era of Neronias began in 60/61, immediately after Nero's celebration of the first shaving of his beard, followed by the institution of the 'Neronia' in 60 (Chapter 10 n. 197 and Appendix 10, pt. d). Thus, since this was done under Albinus, the procurator must have arrived at Judaea in 59/60 and stayed there until 63/64, leaving for Festus the short but adequate period from c. 58 to 59/60.

A major implication of this new dating is the death of James the brother of Jesus, an event which took place according to Josephus (*Ant.* 20.200-203) in the interval between the procuratorships of Festus and Albinus (i.e. 59/60), assumed unanimously to date to 62 (Meyer and Bauer 1963: 420; Brandon 1967: 115-28; Rhoads 1976: 89; Bruce [F.F.] 1979: 110; Bauckham 1990: 87). The event is also described by Eusebius, but the only chronological indication he gives is the placement of a different event which he dates to 61/62 eighth year of Nero) *subsequently* to his material on James (*Hist. Eccl.* 2.24). If anything this would imply that James died before 61 and not in 62. In fact Eusebius begins by saying that James's ordeal closely followed the sending of Paul to Rome by Festus, and that during the time of James's interrogation by the Jewish authorities Festus died, thus presenting the Jews with the chance to kill James before the arrival of a new procurator (*Hist. Eccl.* 2.23.1-3). Since Paul, as proposed here, was on his way to Rome in the 'autumn' 58 (Acts 27.9-12), Eusebius cannot have meant to place the murder of James three (or four?) years later.

But it has to be noted that the enigmatic primary source of Eusebius, Hegesippus (cf. *2 Apoc. James* from Nag Hammadi—v. 4, 61-62), had eagerly placed James's death immediately before Vespasian began to besiege Jerusalem, i.e. in 69 (*Hist. Eccl.* 2.23.18). So Eusebius later, despite his previous dating which no doubt was based on an interpretation of Josephus, felt obliged to follow Hegesippus in claiming that the Jews were rapidly punished by God for killing James (*Hist. Eccl.* 3.7.8; 3.11; cf. Origen, *Contra Celsum* 1.47; 2.13; Jerome, *De Viris Illust.* 13; see Barnes 1984: 472; Hardwick 1989: 83-84).

In conclusion, the dates of the last procurators of Judaea are proposed here to be as follows: Felix (52–c. 58), Festus (c. 58–59/60), Albinus (59/60–63/64), Florus (63/64–65)—with the death of James the brother of Jesus consequently occurring in c. CE 59/60.

Appendix 9

Dating the First Jewish Revolt

It will not be possible here to examine in detail the arguments pertaining to the complex question of dating precisely the various stages of the First Jewish Revolt. However the foundations may be laid by assessing the validity of the standard chronology and suggesting an alternative year for the outbreak of this major uprising against Rome.

A brief look at Tacitus's statement in *Hist*. 5.10 would seem adequate to date this event. Nero sent out Vespasian, who, 'within two summers', conquered the whole of the country except Jerusalem. 'The next year was taken up with civil war (i.e. CE 69), and thus was passed in inactivity so far as the Jews were concerned'. In the following year Titus 'pitched his camp before the walls of Jerusalem', and this eventually led to the destruction of the city and its famous temple. Thus according to Tacitus the whole affair extended from CE 67 to 70.

The only reason contemplated for looking at Josephus, who spent years witnessing and writing about the war, is for details substantiating the framework already obtained from Tacitus. Yet it is these details which, paradoxically, instead of providing confirmation, create difficulty in dating the event with confidence.

The first direct date is in *War* 2.284 (cf. 284-315), where Josephus says that the outbreak was triggered by the strife at Caesarea, in combination with Florus's violation of the Temple treasury, which led to a slaughter: 'in the twelfth year' of Nero, 'on the sixteenth of the month of Artemisius [c. May]'. Later, in *War* 2.555, Josephus also dates the defeat of Cestius 'on the eighth of the month Dius [c. November] in the twelfth year' of Nero. But both events cannot have taken place in the same year of the emperor, for his 'twelfth' ran from 13 October 65 to 12 October 66 (Schillinger-Häfele 1986: 55). A few may argue that the event of November fell shortly after the end of Nero's twelfth year, but this is certainly not a substitute for saying that it had actually occurred *in* his thirteenth year. For example, the Temple was destroyed at the end of July 70 and Josephus carefully places it in Vespasian's second year, which had commenced only at the beginning of the same month (*War* 6.250, 269).

The standard opinion, therefore, concedes that one of the two year dates at the early stage of the revolt is incorrect, opting for a 'slip' on Josephus's part in his second mention of '12', which it emends into '13' (*SVM* 1, 488-89 n. 16). In conclusion the events that marked the outbreak are dated to c. May 66 (Nero's twelfth year), while Cestius's defeat to c. November 66 (Nero's thirteenth year)—cf. Gichon 1981.

But what reassurance are we given for this emendation? Presumably it is absolutely necessary. Is it though the only possible one? May we not equally well have emended the first year date of '12' into '11'? This would have dated the outbreak to c. May 65 and Cestius's defeat to c. November 65. Might not this alternative be preferable? Only an analysis of the available historical evidence may illustrate whether such a date can work. But first we must immediately note four apparent difficulties for the year 65:

1) The same 'slip' assumed in *War* 2.284 ('eleventh' instead of 'twelfth') would need to be assumed for *War* 1.20; *Ant*. 20. 257 and 159, where the outbreak is also given as the 'twelfth' year of Nero. But the question must be whether the starting point in Josephus is always clearly the beginning of the *revolt* (i.e. the Jerusalem uprising), and not the beginning of the *war* (i.e. the campaigns of Vespasian). For the latter does indeed date to the 'twelfth' year of Nero (see later pt. 3).

2) When we note the successive dates by months provided by Josephus for the first year of the Roman campaigns after the defeat of Cestius in c. November (e.g. *War* 3.142–c. May; *War* 3. 282, 306, 315–c. June), it becomes clear that we have entered a new calendar year, apparently the one that followed the outbreak. In the case of 65 this ought to have been the actual 'twelfth' year of Nero, but it is not. By July when Jotapata was taken Josephus mentions Nero's 'thirteenth' year, which ran from 13 October 66 to 12 October 67 (*War* 3.339). More 'slips' cannot be assumed, not only due to feebleness, but also to Tacitus's framework (verified by Josephus): i.e. campaigns in 67 and 68 (cf. the Sepphoris coins—Meshorer 1979: 160-62; *AJC* 2, 279, nos. 8-9), inactivity in 69, fall of Jerusalem in 70. The only way out here would seem to be the interposition of a whole year between Cestius's defeat at the end of 65 and the arrival of Vespasian at the beginning of 67.

3) Sometime after the defeat of Cestius (25 November in the Tyrian calendar), Costobarus II and Saulus escaped from Jerusalem and joined the Roman governor, perhaps at Ptolemais (*War* 2.556). This may have been achieved by the close of the year, i.e. theoretically of 65. Cestius then dispatched the Herodian party to Nero 'in Achaea', to bring the bad news to him and blame Florus for the disaster (*War* 2.558). Although this story cannot be fully trusted (see Chapter 7 §2 end), it is nevertheless useful to determine exactly when Nero was in Achaea. Dio (63.22.11) refers to the Jews revolting when the emperor was in Greece, but this may only mean the place where Nero learned about it. Tacitus (*Ann*. 15.33; cf. 34, 36) says that the emperor was contemplating crossing to Achaea to win contests from as early as 64, though he missed even 65 (start of the 211th Olympiad). Unfortunately Tacitus breaks off in 66 (*Ann*. 16.35), before Nero set sail for Greece. It is thought that the surviving text covers half of the year, but it may be less to match Dio (62.8.2), though he is also fragmentary. Momigliano (1934c: 735; cf. Gallivan 1974: 307; Griffin 1984: 160-63) dated Nero's departure for Greece as late as 25 September, based on an inference from the prayer of the Arval Brothers (*CIL* 6.2044), while Bradley (1978a: 71) opted for early August. But the spring or early summer would

be more appropriate for a journey with a heavy programme of games and contests—especially if Nero's 'liberation' of Greece is now to be dated to 28 November 66 (Halfmann 1986: 173-77; cf. Barnes 1989: 252-53). Thus if the Herodians set out from Palestine early in 66, on a mid-winter journey overland, it could have taken them three months to reach Achaea, by which time Nero was about to arrive. As a parallel, when Vespasian was informed in Palestine (*War* 4.491) of Galba's enthronement (9 June 68), he sent Titus to congratulate the new emperor (*War* 4.498), but his journey was cut short in Achaea (*War* 4. 499; Tacitus, *Hist.* 2.1; cf. Jones [B.W.] 1984a: 44-45), when the news arrived of Galba's death (15 January 69). Moreover, Nero's decision to send Vespasian to Judaea may not have been swift (*War* 3.3), and this is also borne out from Tacitus (*Hist.* 5.10.1) who refers to the decision being taken on Cestius's death, which cannot have been earlier than the end of 66 (*BMC* Syr., 175, no. 202 = *RPC* 1, 4303; cf. Syme 1981: 132); the army, which crossed the Hellespont (*War* 3.8), may have taken months to move to Palestine (*War* 3.29); the waiting for Titus to come from Egypt (contra Jones [B.W.] 1984b) may not have been short (*War* 3.64); the detention at Ptolemais may have been prolonged (*War* 3.110); Vespasian's impatience to invade Galilee may well be justified (*War* 3.116). Gabara, the first city to fall, was attacked at the end of spring 67 (*War* 3.132; cf. 142). Thus the whole of 66 could have been spent in journeys, decision making and preparations, before the beginning of the campaigns. The fact that Tacitus does not mention the Jewish uprising in 65 is not a problem, for he would have stored all references to Judaea until late 66 when Vespasian was appointed to the job (cf. *Hist.* 5.10). The Roman historian does something similar with the revolt of Boudicca (*Ann.* 14.31-32) for example.

4) Among portents claimed to have foretold the coming desolation of Jerusalem in 70, Josephus refers to a star, 'resembling a sword', which stood over the city, and to a comet 'which continued for a year' (*War* 6.289). Though the impression is given that these heavenly bodies were seen shortly before the outbreak of the revolt, the list to which they belong is not strictly chronological (*War* 6.288-315). The next portent, that of 'the light round the altar', is clearly said to have preceded the revolt in c. April, as it seems was 'the celestial armies' in c. June, but then 'the cries of Jesus son of Ananias' began four years earlier and continued until the siege in 70. Astronomically we do know that Halley's comet passed the earth in January/February 66 (Yeomans and Kiang 1981: 643), and it was recorded in China (Peng-Yoke 1962: 150, no. 78). One could hasten to argue that Josephus refers to this comet, seen at Jerusalem a few months before the revolt in 66. But Tacitus (*Ann.* 15.47) conveniently mentions another comet at the end of 64 (cf. Suetonius, *Nero* 36; Rogers [R.S.] 1953: 242), and the Chinese also recorded comets on 3 March 64 and 29 July 65 (Peng-Yoke 1962: 149-50, nos. 75-76; cf. Schove 1984: 286)—not to mention the one of 69 in Dio 64.8.1 (cf. Barrett 1978b: 100-101).

This is not the first time that 65 has been proposed as the year for the beginning of the revolt—it had already been suspected several centuries ago, as mentioned by Zeitlin (1919: 76-77 n. 129)! While working on his edition of the *Megillath Ta'anith*,

Zeitlin became convinced that only by assuming the use of the Tyrian calendar can its
dates agree with those in *War*. The case of Vitellius is of course outstanding. Josephus (*War* 4.654) records his death 'on the third day of Apellaeus [c. December]',
and in no calendar but the Tyrian may this be translated into 20 December when the
emperor was actually killed (Tacitus, *Hist.* 3.85). With the help of the Tyrian calendar imposed on Josephus, Zeitlin concluded that the revolt must have started in 65,
since only in this year can *Megillath*'s Hebrew dates be coordinated. The calendrical
argument will be avoided here (even if it could prove the case of 65), because fresh
astronomical computations are needed—the mathematical tables used by Zeitlin are
antiquated (cf. Price 1992: 210-13). At any rate, his way of arguing for the precise
year was definitely wrong, as it was his assignment of the first year's Roman campaigns to 66.

Zeitlin (1919: 76; cf. 1950–51: 244) tried to avoid emendation of either *War* 2.284
or 2.555 (above), by adopting a different reckoning for Nero's reign—i.e. not by
accession day but by tribunician power. He thought that both months (May and
November) can be accommodated in the same year of Nero, i.e. in 65. Zeitlin
believed that Nero's first TR.P. ran from October to December 54, his second from
December 54 to December 55, and thus his 'twelfth' from December 64 to December
65. At Zeitlin's time, given some confusion over the precise TR.P. of Nero, such a
theory could be sustained. But now coins show that Nero's first TR.P. ran from
December 54 to December 55 and thus his twelfth from December 65 to December
66. The crucial evidence is *BMCRE* 1, Nero no. 7, which has TR.P.[I] (December
54 to December 55) overlapping with COS [I] (January to December 55), whereas in
Zeitlin's scheme TR.P.[I] would have ended in December 54 before Nero's consulship. Another coin further illustrates the argument. *BMCRE* 1, Nero no. 21, has
TR.P. VI (December 59 to December 60) together with COS IIII (January to
December 60), whereas Zeitlin would have had TR.P VI running from December 58
to December 59, again before Nero's consulship.

In retrospect it is unfortunate for Zeitlin's position, since if we were to reckon
Nero's reign by TR.P. the year 66, and not 65, would have been capable of accom-
modating both months under discussion! Nero's 'twelfth' year would have extended
from December 65 to December 66, a period that includes both a May and a Nov.
But Josephus calculated the emperors by accession days. An example is the brief
reign of Galba. The historian says that he was assassinated after being in power for
'seven months and as many days' (*War* 4.499). Now since Nero died on 9 June 68
and Galba on 15 January 69, the latter's reign was indeed seven months and seven
days. There would have been no exception for Nero, for Josephus says (although his
text seems to suffer here of *homoioteleuton*—Niese) that he was emperor for
'thirteen years, [eight months] and eight days' (*War* 4.491). Dio (63.29) also gives
'thirteen years and eight months'—the actual reign being thirteen years, seven
months and 28 days (from 13 October 54 to 9 June 68). So in the case of the Jewish
Revolt, emendation in Josephus is necessary.

Let us now examine the evidence which seems to agree with the outbreak in 65
rather than in 66:

a) Usefully Josephus in *War* 2.284 backs up his reference to the 'twelfth' year of Nero (which has to be emended into 'eleventh' for the case of 65) with a double dating: the 'seventeenth' year of Agrippa II. Josephus's reckoning must go back to his rule in Chalcis, because Agrippa's Eras of Tiberias and Neronias, clearly determined by coins, began much later (see Appendix 10, pt. d). Now this kingdom was presented to Agrippa upon his uncle Herod's death, 'in the eighth year of the reign of Claudius' (*Ant.* 20.104; cf. *War* 2.223). Since Claudius's eighth year ran from 25 January 48 to 24 January 49 (Schillinger-Häfele 1986: 54), and Herod died around the autumn of 48 (see Chapter 10 n. 184), Agrippa would have been given control of Chalcis late in 48 or better early in 49 (Kokkinos 1986a: 35). This is confirmed by another statement of Josephus (*Ant.* 20.138), according to which after the completion of Claudius's 'twelfth' year (i.e. after 24 January 53), Agrippa was upgraded to Philip's tetrarchy, having spent 'four' years at Chalcis (49–52). Thus his 'seventeenth' year fell in 65, when Nero was in his 'eleventh' year and not 'twelfth'. The outbreak of the revolt by using the chronology of Agrippa's reign was in 65 not in 66.

b) According to *Ant.* 20.257 the revolt began in the 'second' year of Florus (cf. Tacitus, *Hist.* 5.10). Since it is assumed that Florus took office in 64 (*SVM* 1, 470 n. 62), his second year began in 65. However, this is a circular argument which should not be pressed, for the date of Florus's accession itself depends on the date of the beginning of the revolt. Similarly, when *Seder Olam* 30 (cf. *b. 'Abod. Zar.* 8b) mentions the Herodian dynasty as lasting 103 years, this depends on whether one counts Herod's reign from 38 BCE (giving CE 65 as the last year) or from 37 BCE (giving CE 66). Nonetheless the first would be supported by Josephus's 107 years from the destruction of the Temple in August CE 70, back to the beginning of Herod's reign (*Ant.* 20.250), i.e. mathematically back to August 38 BCE (cf. Appendix 2, pt. 1).

c) Josephus implies that the length of the war, up to the time of the siege (not the conquest) of Jerusalem, was three years and five months. This is deduced from the story of a 'wretched individual' (ἄγροικος ἰδιώτης) called Jesus son of Ananias, who started his lamentations over Jerusalem 'four years before the war' and continued to cry for 'seven years and five months', until he was killed by a stone during the Roman siege (*War* 6.300, 308). Since the siege began around May 70 (*War* 5.302), counting backwards three years and five months we arrive at the beginning of 67! Surely this is not the year the *revolt* broke out in anyone's reckoning. What Josephus means is that the outset of the *war*, as determined by the action taken by Vespasian's army, was in early 67 (and by the way in the 'twelfth' year of Nero). As we saw this is also Tacitus's rough estimate. So there is no inhibition on the part of Josephus, in fact there is willingness, to adopt two different starting points: the second being the Roman campaigns of 67. This is confirmed by Simon son of Gioras who became master of Jerusalem in c. May 69, 'in the third year of the war' according to Josephus (*War* 4.577), which has to be reckoned again from 67! But then surely there is nothing to prevent us from assuming a break of more than one

year between the two starting points, and other evidence points to 65 as the year
in which the trouble began. Incidentally, 'four years' before 67, would place the
appearance of Jesus in 63, and since the episode (at the feast of Tabernacles) took
place under Albinus (*War* 6.305), this year is a *terminus ante quem* for this procurator's arrival at Judaea. The episode cannot be used to date the beginning of Albinus's
term, and certainly not in 62 (*SVM* 1, 468 n. 50). Albinus may have arrived some
considerable time earlier (see Appendix 8).

d) Very near the end of Felix's career in Judaea (c. 52–58), a quarrel arose about
equal civic rights (ἰσοπολιτεία—see Kasher 1977) between the Hellenized Phoenicians and the Jews of Caesarea (Chapter 3 n. 62 and Chapter 10 n. 121). Felix over-
came the trouble by brutally suppressing the Jews (*Ant.* 20.173-8). When Festus (c.
58–59/60) succeeded him, carrying out a contrary policy to Felix in allowing
embassies and individual appeals to reach the emperor (e.g. Ishmael and Helcias II,
Paul etc.), he also gave permission to both Phoenician and Jewish deputations from
Caesarea to solve their problem in Rome (*Ant.* 20.182-84). In *War* 2.266-70 Josephus typically amalgamates the two phases of the episode, with the result of the Caesarean embassies being sent to Nero under Felix, but this is obviously not so (contra
SVM 1, 467 n. 45). We do not know how long it took the Caesareans to be heard by
the emperor—Paul had to wait at least two years, c. 59–60 (Acts 28.30). However a
hearing certainly took place before 62, since Pallas who protected his brother Felix
(*Ant.* 20.182) died in this year (Tacitus, *Ann.* 14.65). The Hellenized Phoenicians
won the trial and brought back to Caesarea the rescript which gave them greater
authority than the Jews. In *Ant.* 20.184 Josephus says that this rescript created further trouble which led to the Jewish revolt. Presumably some time elapsed. The
troops from Caesarea added to the tension, evidently by indiscriminate attacks on the
Jews, and probably by the slaughter they carried out at Jerusalem on Florus's orders
(*War* 2.296, 305-308, 312, 332)—Josephus elsewhere says that they became the
source of disaster 'by sowing the seed of the war in Florus's time' (*Ant.* 19.366; cf.
20.176, *War* 2. 268). However, Josephus in *War* 2.284, seems again to have condensed his timescale, placing the arrival of the imperial rescript in the same year as
the outbreak! If the embassies set sail for Rome roughly in 58, and if a decision was
taken shortly before 62, one would have expected their return to Caesarea by 63 or at
the very latest by 64. The eruption of the revolt in 65 (already by stretching the
chronology), would certainly agree better than 66.

e) In his *Life* (13-16) Josephus relates a journey he made to Rome, for the purpose
of freeing some fellow priests who had been imprisoned there from the time of Felix.
He says (in a familiar formula) that he left Judaea *after* he had completed his 'twenty-
sixth' year of age, i.e. sometime within his 'twenty-seventh' year. This can be calculated fairly accurately. Counting forward from the 'first' year of Caligula (18 March
37 to 17 March 38—Schillinger-Häfele 1986: 53) in which Josephus was born (*Life*
5), his twenty-seventh year would have fallen between 18 March 63 and 17 March
64. It is during this period that he went to Rome, and if we adopt a middle point
(around September/October 63), we must be making the right decision for two

reasons: The shipping season was essentially closed from November to March (see Appendix 2, pt. 1), and Josephus sailed near the end of autumn as reflected in his jeopardy at sea (*Life* 14-15)—similar to that of Paul in the winter of 58/59 (Acts 27.9). Josephus's stay in Rome would not have lasted more than a year or two. He says that he found a way to bypass the imperial appointment waiting list (*Life* 16), by forming a friendship with Aliturus who introduced him to Poppaea, through whom he achieved his purpose as quickly as possible (ὡς τάχιστα). So he would have returned to Jerusalem at the latest by 65. It must now be noted that when Josephus came back the revolt had already begun (*Life* 17, 21; cf. Hata 1994). Given the nature of his account it is difficult to imagine Josephus staying in Rome from 63 to 66. It is absolutely remarkable, incidentally, that he has nothing to say about the great fire of Rome in 64 (July), or about the persecution in which the majority of executed Christians would have been Jews.

f) The year 61/62 was Sabbatical (see 68/69 deduced from *Seder Olam R.* 30, 74-75a; cf. *War* 4.420-22; Chapter 10 n. 67), and 62/63 possibly a Roman census year—with 63/64 being the first year in which *new*, and no doubt inflated, taxes were to be collected (Kokkinos 1989: 141; cf. Chapter 10 n. 157). This was a time of potential trouble in Judaea, given the record of previous taxation assessments. The presence of Menahem the grandson of Judas the Galilaean during the first stage of the revolt serves as a reminder (*War* 2.433). The increased number of tax collectors is evident (*War* 2.287). A project on the Temple which had finished in c. 63 left many people jobless, and the king was urged to provide them with work, for they could not pay their dues (*Ant.* 20.219-20; cf. Rajak 1983: 125-26). The king pleaded with them to pay the tribute, which was by then seriously in arrears (*War* 2.403, 404; cf. 405-407). Deadlines had passed when Florus decided to take the money instead from the Temple treasury (*War* 2.293). The uprising was instant. If there is any value in this fresh calculation, then the year 65 is again called for.

g) At the outbreak of trouble Agrippa II was absent from Jerusalem. Josephus informs us that the King had gone to Alexandria to congratulate Tiberius Alexander, who had newly been appointed *praefectus Aegypti* (*War* 2.309, cf. 335). Given the rich finds of papyri from Egypt, one would have thought that the accepted date of 66 may here be proved right. Yet this is not the case. The date of Alexander itself depends on the visit of Agrippa! The last time we hear of Alexander before his governorship of Egypt, is in 63 when he was Corbulo's adviser in Armenia (Tacitus, *Ann.* 15.28; Turner 1954: 59; Burr 1955; see Barzanò 1988). It is assumed that his whereabouts in 64 and 65 are unknown. The last prefect of Egypt before Alexander was C. Caecina Tuscus, accounted for in the period from 2 September 63 to 25 July 64 (*P. Mich.* 179; Bastianini 1988: 505). This man later seems to have followed Nero to Greece, from where he was banished (Suetonius, *Nero* 35.5; Dio, 63.18.1) when the emperor learned that while in office at Alexandria he had bathed in some baths built for Nero's intended visit in 64 (Tacitus, *Ann.* 15. 36; Suetonius, *Nero* 19.1; cf. Jones [B.W.] 1984b: 282). If Alexander took office only in 66, then we are ignorant of who governed Egypt in 65. But if he arrived there early in 65, when

Agrippa visited him shortly before the outbreak of the revolt, then continuity in our record of prefects is restored (see Bureth 1988: 479; Bastianini 1988: 506; older lists in Kokkinos 1990: 139 n. 88).

h) Since Josephus was appointed to his command in Galilee after the defeat of Cestius at the end of a November (*War* 2.556, 568; *Life* 28), presently believed to be that of 66 (see Price 1992; Jossa 1994), and since by c. May 67 he was besieged at Jotapata (*War* 3.142; *Life* 412), his general activities are confined within a maximum period of *five* months, or even only *three* considering that Vespasian was close by from around February 67 (Chapter 10 n. 209). If one can evade the question by the limited account of Josephus in *War* 2.569-646, one certainly cannot escape from the detailed narrative of the entire *Life*! Josephus was forced by Justus to say more about his anti-Roman activities in Galilee (cf. Rappaport 1983; and now Rappaport 1994)—a chronic embarrassment—and this simply cannot fit within the allowed time of three to five months. It was in Josephus's interest to minimize the length of this period (cf. Appendix 10 end), and nowhere does he state exactly how long it was, but from several points we may now gather that it lasted well over a year (essentially the whole of 66). If it took Josephus 40 days to fortify Mt. Tabor (*War* 4.56), it is naive to think that in the remaining 50 to 100 days, he could have 'personally super-vised' the fortification of another 20 sites mentioned in *War* 2.573-76 and *Life* 187-88 (see Har-El 1972; Bar-Kochva 1974). It is even more naive to believe that at the same time he could have managed to defeat the 'surrounding cities' of Syria, and to take 'Sepphoris twice by storm, Tiberias four times, and Gabara once' (*Life* 81-82)! There is no reason to go into detail but another example may destroy the accepted view: Modius (*Life* 114), evidently with Philip (*Life* 183; cf. *War* 4.81; contra Price 1991: 80-81), was sent against Gamala on a mission which failed after a siege of 'seven months' (*War* 4.4, 19). This happened before Vespasian's arrival at Tyre around February 67, at which time Philip was ordered to go to Rome (*Life* 407-409). The beginning of the siege *must* then date back to July 66 at the latest, but for the conventional chronology this is impossible because Philip escaped from Jerusalem only either in September (*Life* 46-47) or in December 66 (*War* 2.555-56). The seven-month siege of Gamala can only be true if the revolt began in 65.

i) An examination of the numismatic evidence for the war casts more doubt on 66. The excavation in Jerusalem of coins dated to 'Year 5' of the revolt has been a conundrum. On the assumption that the striking authority counted the year from Nisan (March/April) to Adar (February/March), the five years in question are con-ventionally dated as follows (*AJC* 2, 259-63; Meshorer 1989b; Meshorer 1990–91, 111; cf. Roth 1962):

Year 1:	c.	May 66	—	March 67
Year 2:		April 67	—	March 68
Year 3:		April 68	—	March 69
Year 4:		April 69	—	March 70
Year 5:		April 70	—	August 70

If we remember that the first wall of Jerusalem had already fallen to the Romans by May 70 (*War* 5.302), the last issue of rebel coins will have lasted only about four months and must have circulated while the city was being destroyed. This is very peculiar. Meshorer's (*AJC* 2, 123; cf. Meshorer 1989b: 73) remarks reflect his puzzlement:

> The motivations behind the minting... are unknown... The several different dies indicated that the quantity of coins struck in the last four months of the war was not small. Suprisingly these issues are not among the most rare in Jewish coinage.

A different way of reckoning could have eased the tension, for example by counting the year from Tishri (September/October) to Elul (August/September), and thus 'Year 5' would have lasted from c. October 69 to August 70. But the rebels must have avoided such a reckoning because it had been adopted by the Hellenized Herodian court. Now if the outbreak of the revolt occurred in 65, the following dates are to be attached to these coins:

Year 1:	c. May 65	—	March 66
Year 2:	April 66	—	March 67
Year 3:	April 67	—	March 68
Year 4:	April 68	—	March 69
Year 5:	April 69	—	March 70

There would have been no reason for a new currency to have been minted after April 70 when the siege began. The Era of the Revolution continued only at Masada, where we find a document dated to 'Year 6' (Yadin 1971: 188-89; *DJD* 2, 104-109, no. 19; cf. Yadin and Naveh 1989: 9-11), which would mean sometime between April 70 and March 71 (but between April 71 and March 72 if the war began in 66). The recent discovery of the Gamala coin (*AJC* 2, 129-31) is another problem for 66. Six examples are known (Syon 1992: 34) and these must have been struck before c. October 67 when Gamala fell (*War* 4.83; Jones [B.W.] 1984a: 42), yet they have copied the legend ('for the redemption of Zion') depicted for the first time on the Jerusalem issues of 'Year 4', i.e. after c. April 69 on accepted chronology! Now if the outbreak is to be dated to 65, then the gap between the Gamala and the Jerusalem types is considerably reduced, and we need to assume that the motto circulated only a few months earlier (perhaps on coins of 'Year 3' still to be discovered). Finally, Meshorer's theory that the Tyrian silver shekels ceased to be minted in 65/66 for no apparent reason other than the outbreak of the Jewish Revolt (see Chapter 3 n. 125), does not support 66 better than 65. At any rate, this theory is based on debatable readings. The latest clear date on a shekel is actually 58/59 (*RPC* 1, 4680), with only half-shekels presumably continuing to 65/66 (*RPC* 1, 4706), and in the opinion of some numismatists (including the late Martin Price—*pers. comm.*) perhaps even to 69/70 (*RPC* 1, 4690). This would disprove Meshorer anyway. In conclusion, it seems that the most famous revolt agaist Rome, that of the Jews, which ended in the Jerusalem disaster of CE 70 and then in the Masada suicide of CE 73 (see Chapter 7 n. 98), should be reckoned to have begun in CE 65—one year earlier than hitherto realized.

APPENDIX 10

DATE OF AGRIPPA II'S DEATH

Josephus dates the closing stage of his *Antiquities* (20.267) to the thirteenth year of Domitian and the fifty-sixth of his own life. This is taken to mean that this work was completed and published in CE 93/94. Further Josephus's *Life* seems to have been originally appended to *Antiquities* (20.266), and since *Life* 429 mentions no emperor after Domitian, it is thought that both works appeared at the same time. As a consequence, since *Life* 359-60 announces the death of Agrippa II, it has been argued that the king died before 93/94 (see Frankfort 1961; *SVM* 1, 480-83; Smallwood 1976: 572-74; Barish 1978; Cohen [S.J.D.] 1979: 170-80; Rajak 1983: 237-38; Attridge 1984: 210; Rajak 1987: 83, 93 n. 10; Mason 1991: 311-24; and less strongly Stern [M.] 1974: 304 n. 4; Schwartz [D.R.] 1982: 243)—but see Schwartz [S.] 1990: 119 and Schwartz [D.R.] 1992: 272-75!

Other points claimed to support Agrippa's death before 93/94, do not carry weight. For example, it is believed that *Ant.* 17.28, where Josephus speaks of Batanaea as having been taken over by the Romans, implies that Agrippa was already dead. But this passage may only show that by 93 Batanaea had been lost to Agrippa (Chapter 10 n. 248). His rule could have continued elsewhere, in agreement with earlier (*Ant.* 16. 187) and later passages (*Ant.* 18.128: ἑκατὸν ἐτῶν), which apparently refer to him as still being alive. The same is the verdict for the inscriptions from Auranitis, dated to the last year of Domitian (96) and the first of Nerva (96/97) without mentioning the king. These texts may only show that by 96 Auranitis had been taken over by the Romans—*not* that Agrippa had died (Chapter 10 n. 249).

Yet the main assumptions stated at the beginning seem watertight. But are they? Before resorting to new evidence, a few questions must be raised: Josephus began to write *Life* after he had finished the *Antiquities* in 93/94. Do we know how long it took him to complete it? Not really, but presumably it would have been ready before the death of Domitian in 96. Did he meanwhile delay the publication of *Antiquites*? We cannot be sure. If the final version of *Life* was appended to *Antiquities*, and published in 93/94, why would Josephus need to produce two endings for *Antiquities* (20.259, 267)—as stressed by Laqueur (1920: 1-6) and Thackeray (1929: 16-19) in their '2nd edition' theory. Further, although Domitian is the last emperor mentioned in *Life* 429, Josephus refers to Domitia as having continued to confer favours upon him (διετέλεσεν εὐεργετοῦσα), apparently after the death of Domitian. That Nerva and Trajan are not mentioned, may simply suggest that Josephus had no connection to the gens Cocceia or Ulpia. At all events, how well does the circulation of his *magnum opus* fit in the years of Terror (CE 93-96) of Domitian's reign? Not very well, but we have to assume it. Yet we must remember that the emperor was ill-disposed towards intellectuals. In the early 90s he banished all philosophers (Charlesworth 1936: 27-29; Jones [B.W.] 1992: 119-24). In 93 (the end date of *Antiquities*) he banned the book *Paris and Oenone* and executed its author Helvidius Priscus (Suetonius, *Dom*. 10.4; Dio, 67.13.2; cf. Tacitus, *Agric*. 45). Writers such as Tacitus, Pliny and Juvenal remained silent. More importantly in 95 it seems that conversion to Judaism or Christianity became a punishable political offense (Dio, 67.14; Smallwood 1956: 5; Applebaum 1974: 116; cf. Sordi 1983: 43-53). Despite all this, we are to accept that Josephus, who praises Domitian and Domitia, was free to circulate in Rome a major history of Judaism.

Now the conventional dating for the death of Agrippa II is flatly contradicted by evidence external to Josephus:

a) Justus of Tiberias in his Χρονικὸν Ἰουδαίων Βασιλέων τῶν ἐν τοῖς στέμμασιν, as transmitted to us by Photius (*Bibl*. 33; see *FHJA* 1, 375 n. 17), explicitly dated Agrippa's death to the third year of Trajan, i.e. CE 100. No question as to whether Photius actually read *this* work of Justus (Cohen [S.J.D.] 1979: 142; Mendels 1986: 203 n. 32; contra Rajak 1983: 237), and the Patriarch is reckoned to be the best of the Byzantine scholars. His invaluable Βιβλιοθήκη or Μυριόβιβλον, a brief review of 280 books available to him, was commissioned by his brother, and represented a ninth-century collection to be found in one of the four great libraries of Constantinople (see Wilson 1967: 61-62; cf. Halkin 1963).

b) An inscription found in the Hauran (but presently in Beirut) strongly suggests that Agrippa's reign ran into Trajan's (Chapter 10 n. 243). This text, which has not been translated or carefully analysed, reads:

Ἀρχιεὺς ὁ ἐπὶ Ἀγρίππου βασιλέος [read βασιλέως] γενόμενος κεντυρίων δεκαοκτὼ ἔτους [read ἐτῶν] Τραϊανοῦ στρατηγὸν [read στρατηγὸς] δέκα.

Archieus who served King Agrippa as centurion for eighteen years, and Trajan as general for ten [years].

Evidently Archieus served Agrippa in the last 18 years of his reign (i.e. CE 83–100), whence he was transferred to Trajan's command (i.e. CE 100–109). This inscription may thus date to 109/110. Had Agrippa died before 93/94, Archieus would have had to remain unemployed for over five years (no mention of Domitian or Nerva) before joining Trajan who became emperor in 98. But no such reason can be found, especially since the centurion had an 18-year experience. Also Archieus's overall career of 28 years is close to the maximum length of service for normal auxiliary soldiers (Webster 1985: 143), and it may indicate that Archieus died shortly before retirement.

c) A recent discovery of an inscribed lead weight from the area of Tiberias is more decisive (see Chapter 10 n. 250):

LMΓ ΒΑΣΙΛΕΩΣ ΜΕΓΑΛΟΥ ΑΓΡΙΠΠΑ ΚΥΡΙΟΥ—ΑΓΟΡΑΝΟΜΟΥΝΤΩΝ
ΙΑΕΣΑΙΟΥ ΜΑΘΙΟΥ ΚΑΙ ΑΝΙΜΟΣ [read ΑΝΙΜΟΥ] ΜΟΝΙΜΟΥ.

Year 43 of the Great King Agrippa [our] Lord—during the term of office of the *agora-nomoi*, Iaesaios son of Mathias, and Animos son of Monimos.

This text, mentioning the *agoranomoi* of the city, clearly refers to the 'forty-third year' of King Agrippa, too high a year to be coordinated with the conventional chronology for his death. Agrippa's Era of Tiberias began in 55/56 (see Chapter 10 §5 and next pt.), and the weight therefore dates to 97/98. Agrippa's Era of Panias (see next pt.) does not come into question, because it started only in 60/61, and in any case the weight belongs to the city of Tiberias. Also the city's own era, begin-ning in 19/20, does not come into question, because it would not have been used under the jurisdiction of Agrippa (contra myself in Qedar), and in any case the text *clearly* specifies whose era it follows. The only time in its history that Tiberias could have enjoyed its own era was between 44 and 55 (*Life* 38; see Chapter 10 n. 188), and again as soon as Agrippa died, as shown by the coins struck under Trajan, evi-dently in CE 100 (*BMC* Palest., xiv; Meshorer 1985: 34).

d) The existence of an era beginning in 60/61 has now been established beyond doubt by the bilingual (Latin–Greek) coins of Agrippa, bearing his regnal years 25 and 26 together with the years of Domitian's consulship: COS X and COS XII, i.e. between CE 84 and 86. As has been suggested, this was a response to Nero's cele-bration of the first shaving of his beard, followed by the institution of the 'Neronia' in CE 60 (Chapter 10 n. 197). The existence of another era commencing in 55/56 is also established on the basis of a coin of Agrippa bearing the double dating 'Year 11 which is also Year 6' (*AJC* 2, 250, nos. 5-6BN; Meshorer 1990–91: 125, no. 6a). Inscriptions support this double dating by offering us pairs of dates: 'Year 21 which is also Year 16' (*SEG* 7. 970), and 'Year 37 which is also Year 32' (*OGIS* 426—see Chart 3).

Consequently all other dated material relating to Agrippa II must fall within the framework of these two eras. The majority of the coins are Greek, belonging to the Flavian period and depicting the portraits of Vespasian, Titus and Domitian. These coins also mention Agrippa's regnal years, ranging from the fourteenth to the thirty-fifth (*AJC* 2, 251-58, nos. 7-56; Meshorer 1990–91: 125-26). Until recently it was not clear which of the two eras is to be followed in regard to these Flavian coins. For example historians preferred the Era of 55/56, thus making Agrippa's fourteenth to thirty-fifth year equal CE 69 to CE 90. This presented an apparent agreement between the last numismatically attested date and that accepted for the king's death before 93/94. However, in two neglected articles Barag (1978 and 1981) has shown that the era followed by the Flavian coins must be that of 60/61, which makes the reign of Agrippa extend at least to 94/95.

Many points made by Barag are conclusive, two of which should be mentioned here:

a) The coins of 'Year 14' if dated as early as CE 69 (i.e. following the Era of 55/56) will have to become the prototypes used by the Flavian emperors to mint their own Roman *Judaea Capta* series, which bears the same designs. This is impossible, given that earlier issues show that it is the Jewish coins which use Roman prototypes and not the other way round.

b) The coins of 'Year 24' which mention Domitian as ΓΕΡΜΑΝ[ΙΚΟΣ], if dated as early as CE 79 (i.e. following the Era of 55/56) would conflict with Roman history, which has Domitian named 'Germanicus' only in CE 84.

Therefore the latest known coin of Agrippa II makes it certain that the king was alive at least until 94/95, already a year beyond the date of Josephus's completion of the *Antiquities*. This revelation is further supported by the weight from Tiberias, which shows that Agrippa was alive at least until 97/98, and by the inscription of Archieus, which suggests that the king's reign ran into that of Trajan's beginning in 98. This evidence combined, gives the strongest support to the date of Justus (*apud* Photius) for Agrippa's death—i.e. CE 100. One may now marvel at the comment of Attridge (1984: 210), who said of Justus's date that it 'is not supported by numismatic and epigraphical evidence for Agrippa's reign, which ends in 94'!

The new dating (accepted by the original work of Schürer 1890: 205-206) has many repercussions. We are here prompted to conclude that: although *Antiquities* was completed in 93/94, it would not have been published before 100, or if it was, it would not have incorporated *Life* in the first edition, or if it did, *Life* was re-edited at a later stage. The latter seems preferable, because the key reference—Agrippa's death—belongs to the section (*Life* 336-67) known as the 'long digression' (Cohen [S.J.D.] 1979: 114-20). It appears that this section was added after CE 100, despite Schalit (1933). Alternatively, as suggested by Hölscher (1916: 1941-42), the first edition of *Life*, which was appended to *Antiquities*, may have contained only the biographical material about Josephus (1-27, 414-30), without his critical reply to Justus. It must be stressed that Josephus had previously avoided discussing in detail his activities in Galilee (*War* 2.569-646), and there does not seem to be any reason why he should have done so now, unless, of course, Justus's criticism had meanwhile appeared. In the second edition of *Life* Josephus could admit to be breaking his silence (see *Life* 338). What he then forgot, was to add to the title of *Life* the subtitle: *At the instigation of and against Justus*.

Chart 3. *The Chronology of Agrippa II*

```
                          48/49 — Chalcis        (Oct. to Oct. reckoning)
                          49/50
            Claudius      50/51
                          51/52
                          52/53 — Panias
                          53/54
13 Oct. 54 ─────────────  54/55
13 Oct. 54
                          55/56  =  1 ─── Era of Tiberias
                          56/57  =  2
                          57/58  =  3
                          58/59  =  4
                          59/60  =  5
            Nero          60/61  =  6  ≡  1 ──────── Era of Neronias
                          61/62  =  7  =  2
                          62/63  =  8  =  3
                          63/64  =  9  =  4
                          64/65  = 10  =  5
                         │65/66  = 11  =  6│········· Coin (AJC 5-6)
                          66/67  = 12  =  7
9 June 68 ∨∨∨∨∨∨∨∨∨∨∨∨∨   67/68  = 13  =  8
1 July 69                 68/69  = 14  =  9
                         │69/70  = 15│ = 10 ·········· Coin (Qedar 1989)
                          70/71  = 16  = 11
                          71/72  = 17  = 12
                         │72/73  = 18│ = 13 ·········· Ins. (OGIS 423)
            Vespasian    │73/74  = 19│=│14│··········· Coin (AJC 7-11)
                         │74/75  = 20│=│15│··········· Ins. (OGIS 425) and Coin (AJC 12-13)
                         │75/76  = 21│=│16│··········· Ins. (SEG 7.970)
                         │76/77  = 22│ = 17 ·········· Ins. (RB 1905, 96)
23 June 79               │77/78  = 23│=│18│··········· Coin (AJC 14-16)
24 June 79               │78/79  = 24│=│19│··········· Coin (AJC 17-21)
            Titus         79/80  = 25  = 20
13 Sept. 81              80/81  = 26  = 21
14 Sept. 81              81/82  = 27  = 22
                         │82/83  = 28│ = 23 ·········· Ins. (SEG 7.970)
                         │83/84  = 29│=│24│··········· Coin (AJC 22-24)
cos x–xii =              │84/85  = 30│=│25│··········· Coin (AJC 25-29)
  = 84–86                │85/86  = 31│=│26│··········· Coin (AJC 30-37)
                         │86/87  = 32│=│27│··········· Coin (AJC 38-43)
            Domitian      87/88  = 33  = 28
                         │88/89  = 34│=│29│··········· Coin (AJC 44-48)
                         │89/90  = 35│=│30│··········· Coin (AJC 49-50)
                          90/91  = 36  = 31
                         │91/92  = 37  = 32│·········· Ins. (OGIS 426)
                          92/93  = 38  = 33
                         │93/94  = 39│=│34│··········· Coin (AJC 51-52)
18 Sept. 96              │94/95  = 40│=│35│··········· Coin (AJC 53-56)
18 Sept. 96               95/96  = 41  = 36
            Nerva         96/97  = 42  = 37
27 Jan. 98               │97/98  = 43│ = 38 ·········· Lead Weight (Qedar 1986–7, no. 2)
28 Jan. 98
            Trajan        98/99  = 44  = 39
                          99/100 = 45  = 40
```

BIBLIOGRAPHY

Abel, F.-M.
1908   'Inscriptions de Transjordane et de Haute Galilée', *RB* 17: 567-78.
1925   'Tombeaux récemment découverts à Marisa', *RB* 34: 267-75.
1935   'La Syrie et la Palestine au temps de Ptolémée Ier Soter', *RB* 44: 559-81.
1938   *Géographie de la Palestine*. II. *Géographie Politique: Les Villes* (Paris: Librairie Lecoffre).
1946   'Exils et Tombeaux des Hérodes', *RB* 53: 56-74.
1952   *Histoire de la Palestine depuis la conquête d'Alexandre jusqu'à l'invasion arabe*, I (Paris: Gabalda).
Abel, F.-M., and A. Barrois
1933   'Chronique: Helbon et ses Environs', *RB* 42: 255-62.
Aberbach, M.
1950–51   'The Historical Allusions of Chapters IV, XI, XIII of the Psalms of Solomon', *JQR* 41: 379-96.
Ackroyd, P.R.
1968   *Exile and Restoration* (London: SCM Press).
Africa, T.
1982   'Worms and the Death of Kings: A Cautionary Note on Disease and History', *CA* 1: 1-17.
Aharoni, Y.
1958   'The Negeb of Judah', *IEJ* 8: 26-38.
1966   *The Land of the Bible: A Historical Geography* (ET A.F. Rainey; London: Burns & Oates).
1975a   'Tel Beersheba', in *EAEHL*: I, 160-68.
1975b   'Excavations at Tel Beer-Sheba: Preliminary Report of the Fifth and Six Seasons, 1973–1974', *TA* 2: 146-68.
1982   *The Archaeology of the Land of Israel* (ET A.F. Rainey; Philadelphia, PA: Westminster Press).
Aharoni, Y. (ed.)
1973   *Beer-sheba I, 1969–1971 Seasons* (Tel Aviv: Institute of Archaeology).
1975   *Investigations at Lachish: The Sanctuary and the Residency (Lachish V)* (Tel Aviv: Gateway).
1981   *Arad Inscriptions* (ET J. Ben-Or; Jerusalem: IES).
Albright, W.F.
1920–21   'A Colony of Cretan Mercenaries on the Coast of the Negeb', *JPOS* 1: 187-94.
1941   'Ostracon No. 6043 from Ezion-Geber', *BASOR* 82: 11-15.

1953   *Archaeology and the Religion of Israel* (Baltimore, MD: The Johns Hopkins University Press, 3rd edn).

1955   'Some Canaanite-Phoenician Sources of Hebrew Wisdom', in M. Noth and D.W. Thomas (eds.), *Wisdom in Israel and in the Ancient Near East* (Festschrift H.H. Rowley; Leiden: Brill): 1-15.

Allen, F.D.
1885   'Greek and Latin Inscriptions from Palestine', *AJP* 6: 190-216.

Allon, G.
1961   'The Attitude of the Pharisees to the Roman Government and the House of Herod', *SH* 7: 53-78.

1977   'The *strategoi* in the Palestinian Cities During the Roman Epoch', in *idem*, *Jews, Judaism and the Classical World* (ET I. Abrahams; Jerusalem: Magnes Press): 458-75.

Alt, A.
1953   *Kleine Schriften zur Geschichte des Volkes Israel*, II (Munich: Beck).

Ambelain, R.
1972   *La Vie Secréte de Saint Paul* (Paris: Laffont).

Amiran, R., and A. Eitan
1970   'Excavations in the Courtyard of the Citadel, Jerusalem, 1968–1969: Preliminary Report', *IEJ* 20: 9-17.

1976   'Excavations in the Jerusalem Citadel', in Yadin (ed.) 1976: 52-54.

Amiran, R., and G.W. van Beek
1976   'Tell Jemmeh', in *EAEHL*: II, 545-48.

Anderson, J.G.C.
1934a   'The Armenian War of Nero's Reign: The First Phase' and 'The Parthian Intervention and its Results', in *CAH* 10: 758-70.

1934b   'The Revolt of Armenia and the Mission of Gaius Caesar' and 'The Eclipse of Roman Influence in Armenia', in *CAH* 10: 273-79.

Anderson-Stojanovic, V.R.
1987   'The Chronology and Function of Ceramic Unguentaria', *AJA* 91: 105-22.

Ap-Thomas, D.R.
1973   'The Phoenicians', in Wiseman (ed.) 1973: 259-86.

Applebaum, S.
1974   'Domitian's Assassination: The Jewish Aspect', *SCI* 1: 116-23.

1977   'Mamre', in *EAEHL*: III, 776-78.

1979–80   'Jewish Urban Communities and Greek Influences', *SCI* 5: 158-77.

1989a   *Judaea in Hellenistic and Roman Times: Historical and Archaeological Essays* (Leiden: Brill).

1989b   'Josephus and the Economic Causes of the Jewish War', in Feldman and Hata (eds.) 1989: 237-64.

Applebaum, S., S. Dar, and Z. Safrai
1978   'The Towers of Samaria', *PEQ* 110: 91-100.

Applebaum, S., B. Isaac, and Y. Landau
1981–82   'Varia Epigraphica', *SCI* 6: 98-112.

Arav, R.
1989a   *Hellenistic Palestine: Settlement Patterns and City Planning, 337–31 B.C.E.* (BAR International Series, 485; Oxford: BAR]).

1989b	'Some Notes on the Foundation of Straton's Tower', *PEQ* 121: 144-48.

Archer, L.J.

1990   *Her Price is Beyond Rubies: The Jewish Woman in Graeco-Roman Palestine* (JSOTSup, 60; Sheffield: Sheffield Academic Press).

Ariel, D.T.

1982   'A Survey of Coin Finds in Jerusalem (until the End of the Byzantine Period)', *LA* 32: 273-326.

Ariel, D.T. (ed.)

1990   *Excavations at the City of David 1978–1985*, II (Qedem, 30; Jerusalem: Institute of Archaeology, Hebrew University).

Ariel, D.T., I. Sharon, J. Gunneweg, and I. Perlman

1985   'A Group of Stamped Hellenistic Storage Jar Handles from Dor', *IEJ* 35: 135-52.

Arik, R.O., and J. Coupry

1935   'Les Tumuli de Karalar et la Sêpulture du Roi Déiotaros II', *RA* 6: 133-51.

Arvanitopoulos, A.S.

1909   Θεσσαλικὰ Μνημεῖα: Περιγραφὴ τῶν ἐν τῷ Ἀθανασάκειῳ Μουσείῳ Βόλου γραπτῶν στηλῶν τῶν Παγασῶν (Athens: Hestia).

1949   'Περιγραφὴ γραπτῶν στηλῶν', *Polemōn* 4: 1-9, 81-92, 153-68.

1952–53a   'Περιγραφὴ γραπτῶν στηλῶν', *Polemōn* 5: 5-18.

1952–53b   'Θεσσαλικὰ Μνημεῖα: Προσωπογραφία', *Polemōn* 5: 33-58.

Astarita, M.L.

1983   *Avidio Cassio* (Rome: Edizioni di Storia e Letteratura).

Astour, M.C.

1967   *Hellenosemitica* (Leiden: Brill).

Attridge, H.W.

1984   'Josephus and his Works', CRINT 2.2: 185-232.

Aubet, M.E.

1993   *The Phoenicians and the West: Politics, Colonies and Trade* (ET M. Turton; Cambridge: Cambridge University Press).

Auscher, D.

1967   'Les relations entre la Grèce et la Palestine avant la conquête d'Alexandre', *VT* 17: 8-30.

Austin, M.M.

1981   *The Hellenistic World from Alexander to the Roman Conquest: A Selection of Ancient Sources in Translation* (Cambridge: Cambridge University Press).

Avi-Yonah, M.

1937   'Two Notes on the Jordan Valley', *JPOS* 17: 252-54.

1939   'Greek and Latin Inscriptions from Jerusalem and Beisân', *QDAP* 8: 54-61.

1946   'Newly Discovered Latin and Greek Inscriptions', *QDAP* 12: 84-102.

1950   'The Foundation of Tiberias', *IEJ* 1: 160-69.

1959   'Syrian Gods at Ptolemais—Accho', *IEJ* 9: 1-12.

1974   'Abbreviations in Greek Inscriptions', in A.N. Oikonomides (ed.), *A Manual of Abbreviations in Greek Inscriptions, Papyri, Manuscripts and Early Printed Books* (Chicago, IL: Ares Publishers): 1-125.

1977a   *The Holy Land from the Persian to the Arab Conquests (536 B.C. to A.D. 640): A Historical Geography* (Grand Rapids, MI: Baker Book House, rev. edn).
1977b   'Mareshah (Marisa)', in *EAEHL*: III, 782-90.
1978   *Hellenism and the East* (Ann Arbor, MI: University Microfilms International).

Avi-Yonah, M., and Y. Eph'al
1975   'Ashkelon', in *EAEHL*: I, 121-30.

Avigad, N.
1976   *Bullae and Seals from a Post-Exilic Judean Archive* (Qedem, 4; Jerusalem: The Hebrew University).
1978   'Samaria', in *EAEHL*: IV, 1032-50.
1983   *Discovering Jerusalem* (Nashville, TN: Thomas Nelson Publishers).

Aviram, J., G. Foerster, and E. Netzer (eds.)
1989a   *Masada 1* (Jerusalem: IES).
1989b   *Masada 2* (Jerusalem: IES).

Avni, G., and Z. Greenhut
1994   'Akeldama: Resting Place of the Rich and Famous', *BARev* 20: 6, 36-46.

Avni, G., Z. Greenhut, and T. Ilan
1994   'Three Burial Caves of the Second Temple Period in Aceldama (Kidron Valley)', in Geva (ed.) 1994: 206-18.

Babelon, E.
1890   *Les rois de Syrie, d'Arménie et de Commagène* (Paris: C. Rollin & Feuardent).

Bagnall, R.S.
1976   *The Administration of the Ptolemaic Possessions Outside of Egypt* (Leiden: Brill).

Bagnall, R.S., and B.W. Frier
1994   *The Demography of Roman Egypt* (Cambridge: Cambridge University Press).

Balty, J.C.
1981   *Guide d'Apamée* (Brussels: Musées royaux d'art et d'histoire).

Bar-Kochva, B.
1974   'Notes on the Fortresses of Josephus in Galilee', *IEJ* 24: 108-16.
1989   *Judas Maccabaeus: The Jewish Struggle Against the Seleucids* (Cambridge: Cambridge University Press).

Barag, D.
1966   'The Effects of the Tenes Rebellion on Palestine', *BASOR* 183: 6-12.
1976   'En-Gedi', in *EAEHL*: II, 370-80.
1978   'The Palestinian "Judaea Capta" Coins of Vespasian and Titus and the Era on the Coins of Agrippa II minted under the Flavians', *NC* 138: 14-23.
1981   'Studies on the Coinage of Agrippa II', *INJ* 5: 27-32.
1985   'Some Notes on a Silver Coin of Johanan the High Priest', *BA* 48: 166-68.
1986-87   'A Silver Coin of Yohanan the High Priest and the Coinage of Judaea in the Fourth Century B.C.', *INJ* 9: 4-21.

1993   'King Herod's Royal Castle at Samaria-Sebaste', *PEQ* 125: 3-18.

Barag, D., and D. Flusser
1986   'The Ossuary of Yehohanah Granddaughter of the High Priest
                Theophilus', *IEJ* 36: 39-44.

Barag, D., and S. Qedar
1980   'The Beginning of Hasmonean Coinage', *INJ* 4: 8-21.

Baramki, D.
1961   *Phoenicia and the Phoenicians* (Beirut: Khayats).

Barghouti, A.N.
1982   'Urbanization of Palestine and Jordan in Hellenistic and Roman
                Times', in A. Hadidi (ed.), *Studies in the History and Archaeology of
                Jordan*, I (Amman: Department of Antiquities): 209-29.

Barish, D.A.
1978   'The *Autobiography* of Josephus and the Hypothesis of a Second
                Edition of his *Antiquities*', *HTR* 71: 61-75.

Barnard, L.W.
1967   *Justin Martyr: His Life and Thought* (Cambridge: Cambridge Univer-
                sity Press).

Barnes, T.D.
1968   'The Date of Herod's Death', *JTS* 19: 204-209.
1984   'Some Inconsistencies in Eusebius', *JTS* 35: 470-75.
1989   'Emperors on the Move', *JRA* 2: 247-61.

Barrett, A.A.
1977   'Sohaemus, King of Emesa and Sophene', *AJP* 98: 153-59.
1978a   'Polemo II of Pontus and M. Antonius Polemo', *Historia* 27: 437-48.
1978b   'Observations of Comets in Greek and Roman Sources before A.D.
                410', *JRASC* 72: 81-106.
1979   '*Annales* 14.26 and the Armenian Settlement of A.D. 60', *ClQ* 29:
                465-69.
1989   *Caligula: The Corruption of Power* (London: B.T. Batsford).

Barstad, H.M.
1988   'On the History and Archaeology of Judah during the Exilic Period',
                OLP 19: 25-36.

Bartlett, J.R.
1969   'The Land of Seir and the Brotherhood of Edom', *JTS* 20: 1-20.
1972   'The Rise and Fall of the Kingdom of Edom', *PEQ* 104: 26-37.
1973   'The Moabites and Edomites', in Wiseman (ed.) 1973: 229-58.
1977   'The Brotherhood of Edom', *JSOT* 4: 2-27.
1979   'From Edomites to Nabataeans: A Study in Continuity', *PEQ* 111: 53-
                66.
1982   'Edom and the Fall of Jerusalem 587 B.C.', *PEQ* 114: 13-24.
1983   'The "United" Campaign against Moab in 2 Kings 3.4-27', in J.F.A.
                Sawyer and D.J.A. Clines (eds.), *Midian, Moab and Edom* (JSOTSup,
                24; Sheffield: Sheffield Academic Press): 135-46.
1985   *Jews in the Hellenistic World: Josephus, Aristeas, The Sibylline Ora-
                cles, Eupolemus* (Cambridge Commentaries 1.1; Cambridge: Cam-
                bridge University Press).

1989   *Edom and the Edomites* (JSOTSup, 77; Sheffield: Sheffield Academic Press).

Barzanò, A.
1988   'Tiberio Giulio Alessandro, Prefetto d'Egitto (66–70)', *ANRW* 2.10.1: 518-80.

Baslez, M.-F.
1986   'Cultes et dévotions des Phéniciens en Grèce: les divinités marines', in C. Bonnet *et al.* (eds.), *Studia Phoenicia IV: Religio Phoenicia* (Namur: Sociéte des Etudes Classiques): 289-305.

Bastianini, G.
1988   'Il prefeto d'Egitto (30 a.C.–297 d.C.): Addenda (1973–1985)', *ANRW* 2.10.1: 503-17.

Batey, R.A.
1984   'Jesus and the Theatre', *NTS* 30: 563-74.
1992   'Sepphoris—An Urban Portrait of Jesus', *BARev* 18.3: 50-62.

Bauckham, R.
1990   *Jude and the Relatives of Jesus in the Early Church* (Edinburgh: T. & T. Clark).

Baumbach, G.
1989   'The Sadducees in Josephus', in Feldman and Hata (eds.) 1989: 173-95.

Baumgarten, A.I.
1981   *The Phoenician History of Philo of Byblos: A Commentary* (Leiden: Brill).

Baumgarten, J.M.
1983   'Exclusions from the Temple: Proselytes and Agrippa I', in G. Vermes and J. Neusner (eds.), *Essays in Honour of Y. Yadin* (Totowa, NJ: Allanheld Osmus & Co.): 215-25.

Beck, P.
1993   'Transjordanian and Levantine Elements in the Iconography of Qiṭmiṭ', in Biran and Aviram (eds.) 1993: 231-36.

Bedoukian, P.Z.
1968   'Classification of the Coins of the Artaxiad Dynasty of Armenia', *ANSMN* 14: 41-66.
1971   'Coinage of the Later Artaxiads', *ANSMN* 17: 137-39.
1978   *Coinage of the Artaxiads of Armenia* (London: Royal Numismatic Society [publ. 1980]).

Beek, G.W. van
1972   'Tel Gamma', *IEJ* 22: 245-46.
1993   'Jemmeh, Tell', in *NEAEHL*: II, 667-74.

Beit-Arieh, I.
1981   'Tell 'Ira, 1980', *IEJ* 31: 243-45.
1984   'Ḥorvat 'Uza—1984', *ESI* 3: 105 (publ. 1985).
1988   'New Light on the Edomites', *BARev* 14.2: 29-41.
1989   'New Data on the Relationship between Judah and Edom toward the End of the Iron Age', in S. Gitin and W.G. Dever (eds.), *Recent Excavations in Israel: Studies in Iron Age Archaeology* (AASOR, 49; Winona Lake, IN: Eisenbrauns): 125-31.

1993a	"Uza, Ḥorvat', in *NEAEHL*: IV, 1495-97.
1993b	"Ira, Tel', in *NEAEHL*: II, 642-46.
1995a	'The Edomites in Cisjordan', in Vikander Edelman (ed.) 1995: 33-40.
1995b	*Ḥorvat Qiṭmiṭ: An Edomite Shrine in the Biblical Negev* (Monograph Series of the Institute of Archaeology, 11; Tel Aviv: Tel Aviv University Publications).

Beit-Arieh, I., and P. Beck
| 1987 | *Edomite Shrine: Discoveries from Qiṭmiṭ in the Negev* (Jerusalem: The Israel Museum). |

Beit-Arieh, I., and B. Cresson
1982	'Ḥorvat 'Uza, 1982', *IEJ* 32: 262-63.
1983	'Ḥorvat 'Uza, 1983', *IEJ* 33: 271-72.
1985	'An Edomite Ostracon from Ḥorvat 'Uza', *TA* 12: 96-101.

Bell, H.I.
| 1924 | *Jews and Christians in Egypt* (London: B.M. Publications). |

Ben-Arieh, S., and E. Netzer
| 1974 | 'Excavations Along the Third Wall of Jerusalem, 1972–1974', *IEJ* 24: 97-107. |

Ben-Arieh, Y.
| 1962 | 'Caves and Ruins in the Beth Govrin Area', *IEJ* 12: 47-61. |

Bengston, H.
| 1964 | *Die Strategie in der hellenistischen Zeit: Ein Beitrag zum antiken Staatsrecht*, I-III (Munich: Beck, 2nd edn). |

Bennet, R.
| 1896 | *The Diseases of the Bible* (London: Religious Tract Society). |

Bennett, C.M.
1966	'Fouilles d'Umm el-Biyara, Rapport Préliminaire', *RB* 73: 372-403.
1977	'Excavations at Buseirah, Southern Jordan', *Levant* 9: 1-10.
1984	'Excavations at Tawilan in Southern Jordan, 1982', *Levant* 16: 1-23.

Bérard, F., D. Feissel, P. Petitmengin, and M. Séve (eds.)
| 1989 | *Guide de L'Epigraphiste* (Paris: Presses de l'Ecole Normale Supérieure, 2nd edn). |

Bernegger, P.M.
| 1983 | 'Affirmation of Herod's Death in 4 B.C.', *JTS* 34: 526-31. |

Bertrand, J.M.
| 1982 | 'Sur l'inscription d'Hefzibah', *ZPE* 46: 167-74. |

Betlyon, J.W.
| 1982 | *The Coinage and Mints of Phoenicia: The Pre-Alexandrine Period* (HSM, 26; Chico, CA: Scholars Press). |
| 1986 | 'The Provincial Government of Persian Period Judea and the Yehud Coins', *JBL* 105: 633-42. |

Bevan, E.
| 1927 | *A History of Egypt Under the Ptolemaic Dynasty* (London: Methuen). |

Bickermann, E.J.
1937	*Der Gott der Makkabäer* (Berlin: Schocken Verlag).
1938	*Institutions des Séleucides* (Paris: Librairie Orientaliste Paul Geuthner).
1962	*From Ezra to the Last of the Maccabees* (New York: Schocken Books).
1976	*Studies in Jewish and Christian History*, I (Leiden: Brill).

1986   *Studies in Jewish and Christian History*, III (Leiden: Brill).

Bienkowski, P.

1992a   'The Beginning of the Iron Age in Edom: A Reply to Finkelstein', *Levant* 24: 167-69.

1992b   'The Date of Sedentary Occupation in Edom: Evidence from Umm el-Biyara, Tawilan and Buseirah', in P. Bienkowski (ed.), *Early Edom and Moab: The Beginning of the Iron Age in Southern Jordan* (Sheffield Archaeological Monographs, 7; Sheffield: J.R. Collis): 99-112.

Bierling, N.

1992   *Giving Goliath His Due: New Archaeological Light on the Philistines* (Grand Rapids, MI: Baker Book House).

Bikai, P.M.

1990   'The Phoenicians: A Bibliography', *BASOR* 279: 65-66.

Bikerman *see* Bickermann.

Bilde, P.

1978   'The Roman Emperor Gaius's Attempt to Erect his Statue in the Temple of Jerusalem', *STS* 32: 67-93.

1979   'The Causes of the Jewish War according to Josephus', *JSJ* 10: 189-202.

Bilde, P., T. Engberg-Pedersen, L. Hannestad, and J. Zahle (eds.)

1990   *Religion and Religious Practice in the Seleucid Kingdom* (Studies in Hellenistic Civilization, 1; Aarhus: University Press).

Bimson, J.J.

1981   'King Solomon's Mines? A Re-assessment of Finds in the Arabah', *TynBul* 32: 123-49.

Biran, A.

1982   'Aroer, 1981', *IEJ* 32: 161-3.

1983   'And David Sent Spoils...to the Elders in Aroer', *BARev* 9: 2, 28-37.

1993   'Aroer', in *NEAEHL*: I, 89-92.

Biran, A., and J. Aviram (eds.)

1993   *Biblical Archaeology Today 1990* (Proceedings of the Second International Congress on Biblical Archaeology, Jerusalem, June–July 1990; Jerusalem: IES).

Biran, A., and R. Cohen

1976   'Aroer, 1976', *IEJ* 26: 139-40.

1979   'Tel 'Ira', *IEJ* 29: 124-25.

Biran, A., and J. Naveh

1993   'An Aramaic Stele Fragment from Tel Dan', *IEJ* 43: 81-98.

1995   'The Tel Dan Inscription: A New Fragment', *IEJ* 45: 1-18.

Birley, A.R.

1981   *The Fasti of Roman Britain* (Oxford: Clarendon Press).

Bivar, A.D.H.

1983   'The Political History of Iran Under the Arsacids', in *CHI* 3.1: 21-99.

Bliss, F.J.

1894   *A Mount of Many Cities: or Tell el Hesy Excavated* (London: A.P. Watt & Son).

1902   'The Excavations at Tell Sandahannah', in Bliss and Macalister 1902: 52-61.

Bliss, F.J., and R.A.S. Macalister
1902   *Excavations in Palestine during the Years 1898–1900* (London: P.E.F).
Blosser, D.
1981   'The Sabbath Year Cycle in Josephus', *HUCA* 52: 129-39.
Boardman, J.
1980   *The Greeks Overseas: Their Early Colonies and Trade* (London: Thames & Hudson, 3rd edn).
1982   'An Inscribed Sherd from Al Mina', *OJA* 1: 365-67.
1990   'Al Mina and History', *OJA* 9: 169-90.
Bosworth, A.B.
1974   'The Government of Syria under Alexander the Great', *ClQ* 24: 46-64.
1976   'Vespasian's Reorganization of the North-East Frontier', *Antichthon* 10: 63-78.
Bouché-Leclerq, A.
1913–14   *Histoire des Séleucides*, I–II (Paris: Ernest Leroux).
Bowersock, G.W.
1961   'Eurycles of Sparta', *JRS* 51: 112-18.
1971   'A Report on Arabia Provincia', *JRS* 61: 219-42.
1973   'Syria under Vespasian', *JRS* 63: 133-40.
1975   'Old and New in the History of Judaea', *JRS* 65: 180-85.
1982   'Roman Senators from the Near East: Syria, Judaea, Arabia, Mesopotamia', in *Epigraphia e Ordine Senatorio*, II (Rome: Edizioni di Storia e Litteratura): 651-68.
1983a   'Antipater Chaldaeus', *ClQ* 33: 491.
1983b   *Roman Arabia* (Cambridge, MA: Harvard University Press).
1991   'The Babatha Papyri, Masada, and Rome', *JRA* 4: 336-44.
Bowman, S.
1987   'Josephus in Byzantium', in Feldman and Hata (eds.) 1987: 362-85.
Bradley, K.R.
1978a   'The Chronology of Nero's Visit to Greece A.D. 66/67', *Latomus* 37: 61-72.
1978b   *Suetonius' Life of Nero: An Historical Commentary* (Collection Latomus, 157; Brussels: Latomus).
Brandon, S.G.F.
1967   *Jesus and the Zealots* (Manchester: Manchester University Press).
Braun, W.
1989   'Were the New Testament Herodians Essenes? A Critique of an Hypothesis', *RevQ* 14: 75-88.
Braund, D.C.
1983   'Four Notes on the Herods', *ClQ* 33: 239-42.
1984a   *Rome and the Friendly King* (London and Canberra: Croom Helm).
1984b   'Berenice in Rome', *Historia* 33: 120-23.
1984c   '*Ant. Pal.* 9.235: Juba II, Cleopatra Selene and the Course of the Nile', *ClQ* 34: 175-78.
1985   *Augustus to Nero: A Sourcebook on Roman History 31 BC—AD 68* (London and Sydney: Croom Helm).

Brett, A.B.
1937	'A New Cleopatra Tetradrachm of Ascalon', *AJA* 41: 452-63.
Bright, J.
1981	*A History of Israel* (London: SCM Press, 3rd edn).
Bron, F.
1988	'Les Phéniciens et l'Arabie', *DHA* 132: 25.
Broome, E.C.
1973	'Nabaiati, Nebaioth and the Nabataeans: The Linguistic Problem', *JSS* 18: 1-16.
Broshi, M.
1977	'Tel Megadim', in *EAEHL*: III, 823-26.
1980	'The Population of Western Palestine in the Roman-Byzantine Period', *BASOR* 236: 1-10.
1984	'Wine in Ancient Palestine—Introductory Notes', *IMJ* 3: 21-40.
1986	'The Diet of Palestine in the Roman Period—Introductory Notes', *IMJ* 5: 41-56.
1987	'The Role of the Temple in the Herodian Economy', *JJS* 38: 31-37.
Broughton, T.R.S.
1933	'The Roman Army in Syria and Palestine', in Lake and Cadbury (eds.) 1933: V, 441-44.
Brown, P.J.
1969	*The Lebanon and Phoenicia, I (Ancient Texts)* (Beirut: The American University).
Brown, R.E.
1994	*The Death of the Messiah*, II (London: Geoffrey Chapman).
Bruce, F.F.
1979	*Men and Movements in the Primitive Church* (Exeter: The Paternoster Press).
1982	*The Epistle of Paul to the Galatians* (Exeter: The Paternoster Press).
1986	'Chronological Questions in the Acts of the Apostles', *BJRL* 68: 284-87.
Bruce, J.L.
1937	'Antiquites in the Mines of Cyprus', in E. Gjerstad (ed.), *The Swedish Cyprus Expedition*, III (Stockholm: SCE): 639-71.
Brug, J.F.
1985	*A Literary and Archaeological Study of the Philistines* (BAR International Series, 265; Oxford: BAR).
Bruggen, J. van
1978	'The Year of the Death of Herod the Great', in T. Baarda *et al.* (eds.), *Miscellanea Neotestamentica*, II (NovTSup, 48; Leiden: Brill): 1-15.
Bruneau, P.
1970	*Recherches sur les cultes de Délos a l'Epoque Hellénistique et a l'Epoque Impériale* (Paris: de Boccard).
1982	'Les Israélites de Délos et la Juiverie Délienne', *BCH* 106: 465-504.
Brunt, P.A.
1971	*Italian Manpower 225 B.C.–A.D. 14* (Oxford: Clarendon Press).
1976	'The Romanization of the Local Ruling Classes in the Roman Empire', in D.M. Pippidi (ed.), *Assimilation et résistance à la culture*

gréco-romaine dans le monde ancien (Congrès, Madrid 1974) (Bucharest: Editura Academiei; Paris: Société d'Edition 'Les Belles Lettres'): 161-73.

1977 'Josephus on Social Conflicts in Roman Judaea', *Klio* 59: 149-53.

1990 *Roman Imperial Themes* (Oxford: Clarendon Press).

Brunt, P.A., and J.M. Moore

1967 *Res Gestae Divi Augusti* (Oxford: Oxford University Press).

Buchheim, H.

1960 *Die Orientpolitik des Triumvirn M. Antonius* (Heidelberg: Carl Winter).

Budge, E.A.W.

1886 *Salomon of Basra's Book of the Bee* (Anecdota Oxoniensia, Semitic Series 1.2; Oxford: Clarendon Press).

1935 *The Contendings of the Apostles* (Oxford: Oxford University Press).

Bureth, P.

1988 'Le préfet d' Egypte (30 av.J.C.–297 ap.J.C.): Etat présent de la documentation en 1973', *ANRW* 2.10.1: 472-502.

Burkitt, F.C.

1899 'Chuza', *Expositor* 9: 118-22.

Burnett, A.

1987 'The Coinage of King Agrippa I of Judaea and a New Coin of King Herod of Chalcis', in H. Huvelin *et al.* (eds.), *Mélanges P. Bastien* (Wetteren: Numismatique Romaine): 25-38.

Burr, V.

1955 *Tiberius Julius Alexander* (Bonn: Rudolf Habelt).

Byatt, A.

1973 'Josephus and Population Numbers in First Century Palestine', *PEQ* 105: 51-60.

Cadbury, H.J.

1933 'Some Semitic Personal Names in Luke–Acts', in H.G. Wood (ed.), *Amicitiae Corolla: A Volume of Essays Presented to James Rendel Harris* (London: London University Press): 45-56.

Campbell, E.F.

1965 'Hebron', *BA* 28: 30-32.

1979 'Jewish Shrines of the Hellenistic and Persian Periods', in F.M. Cross (ed.), *Symposia* (Cambridge, MA: ASOR): 159-67.

Cantineau, J.

1931 'Textes Palmyréniens provenant de la fouille du temple de Bèl', *Syria* 12: 116-41.

Cartledge, P.

1995 ' "We Are All Greeks?" Ancient (Especially Herodotean) and Modern Contestations of Hellenism', *BICS* 40: 75-82.

Casson, L.

1971 *Ships and Seamanship in the Ancient World* (Princeton, NJ: Princeton University Press).

Cassuto, M.

1932 'La corrispondenza tra nomi Ebraici e Greci nell'onomastica Giudaica', *GSAI* 2: 209-30.

Chamonard, J., and E. Legrand
1894   'Inscriptions de Notion', *BCH* 18: 216-21.
Charlesworth, M.P.
1934   'The Avenging of Caesar', in *CAH* 10: 1-29.
1936   'Domitian: The Court and the Aristocracy', in *CAH* 11: 22-33.
Chaumont, M.-L.
1976   'L'Arménie entre Rome et l'Iran. I. De l'avènement d'Auguste a
            l'avènement de Dioclétien', in *ANRW* 2.9.1: 71-194.
Clarke, N.P.
1938   'Helena's Pyramids', *PEQ* 70: 84-104.
Clermont-Ganneau, Ch.
1899, 1896 *Archaeological Researches in Palestine during the Years 1873–1874*,
            I–II (London: PEF).
1901   'Jean le Hierapolite, evenque d'Abila de Lysanias', *RAO* 4: 51-53.
Coggins, R.J.
1987   'The Samaritans in Josephus', in Feldman and Hata (eds.) 1987: 257-
            73.
Cohen, G.D.
1967   'Esau as a Symbol in Early Medieval Thought' in A. Altmann (ed.),
            Jewish Medieval and Renaissance Studies (Cambridge, MA: Harvard
            University Press): 19-48.
Cohen, G.M.
1972   'The Hellenistic Military Colony: A Herodian Example', *TAPA* 103:
            83-95.
Cohen, N.G.
1990   'Agrippa I and *De Specialibus Legibus IV* 151-159', *SPA* 2: 72-85.
Cohen, R.
1982   'New Light on the Date of the Petra-Gaza Road', *BA* 45: 240-47.
Cohen, S.J.D.
1979   *Josephus in Galilee and Rome: His Vita and Development as a Histo-
            rian* (Columbia Studies in the Classical Tradition, 8; Leiden: Brill).
1982–83   'Alexander the Great and Jaddus the High Priest According to Jose-
            phus', *AJSR* 7–8: 41-68.
1989   'Crossing the Boundary and Becoming a Jew', *HTR* 82: 13-33.
1990   'Religion, Ethnicity and "Hellenism" in the Emergence of Jewish
            Identity in Maccabean Palestine', in Bilde *et al.* (eds.) 1990: 204-23.
1994   'Ἰουδαῖς τὸ γένος and Related Expressions in Josephus', in Parente
            and Sievers (eds.) 1994: 23-38.
Coldstream, J.N.
1982   'Greeks and Phoenicians in the Aegean', in Niemeyer (ed.) 1982:
            261-72.
Coldstream, J.N., and P.M. Bikai
1988   'Early Greek Pottery in Tyre and Cyprus', *RDAC* (2nd part): 35-44.
Collart, P.
1973   'La tour de Qalaat Fakra', *Syria* 50: 137-61.
Colledge, M.
1987   'Greek and non-Greek Interaction in the Art and Architecture of the
            Hellenistic East', in Kuhrt and Sherwin-White (eds.) 1987: 134-62.

Collins, J.J.
1980   'The Epic of Theodotus and the Hellenism of the Hasmoneans', *HTR* 73: 91-104.
1983   'Sibylline Oracles', in *OTP* 1: 317-472.

Cook, S.A.
1930   *The Religion of Ancient Palestine in the Light of Archaeology* (London: The British Academy).

Cooke, G.A.
1903   *A Text-Book of North-Semitic Inscriptions* (Oxford: Clarendon Press).

Corbishley, T.
1934   'A Note on the Date of the Syrian Governorship of M. Titius', *JRS* 24: 43-49.
1935   'The Chronology of the Reign of Herod the Great', *JTS* 36: 22-32.
1936   'Quirinius and the Census: A Re-study of the Evidence', *Klio* 29: 81-93.

Cotton, H.M.
1989   'The Date of the Fall of Masada: The Evidence of the Masada Papyri', *ZPE* 78: 157-62.
1991   'Fragments of a Declaration of Landed Property from the Province of Arabia', *ZPE* 85: 263-67.

Cotton, H.M., and J. Geiger
1989   'The Latin and Greek Documents', in Aviram *et al.* (eds.) 1989b (whole volume).

Courtils, J. des, J.-C. Moretti, and F. Planet (eds.)
1991   *De Anatolia Antiqua*, I (Bibliothèque de l'Institut Français d'Etudes Annatoliennes d'Istanbul, 32; Paris: Librairie d'Amérique et d'Orient Adrien Maisonneuve).

Cowley, A.E.
1923   *Aramaic Papyri of the Fifth Century B.C.* (Oxford: Clarendon Press).
1929   'Two Aramaic Ostraka', *JRAS*: 107-12.

Crawford (see also Thompson), D.J.
1976   'Imperial Estates', in M.I. Finley (ed.), *Studies in Roman Property* (Cambridge: Cambridge University Press): 35-70 and nn. 173-80.

Creed, J.M.
1932   'The Slavonic Version of Josephus' History of the Jewish War', *HTR* 25: 277-319.

Cronin, H.S.
1917   'Abilene, the Jewish Herods and St Luke', *JTS* 18: 147-51.

Crook, J.A.
1951   'Titus and Berenice', *AJP* 72 (1951): 162-75.

Cross, F.M.
1955a   'Geshem the Arabian, Enemy of Nehemiah', *BA* 18: 46-47.
1955b   'The Oldest Manuscripts from Qumran', *JBL* 74: 147-72.
1961   'The Development of the Jewish Scripts', in G.E. Wright (ed.), *The Bible and the Ancient Near East: Essays in Honor of W.F. Albright* (Garden City, NY: Doubleday): 132-202.
1963   'The Discovery of the Samaria Papyri', *BA* 26: 110-21.
1964   'An Ostracon from Nebî Yûnis', *IEJ* 14 (1964): 185-86.

1966   'Aspects of Samaritan and Jewish History in Late Persian and Hel-
            lenistic Times', *HTR* 59: 201-11.
1968   'Jar Inscriptions from Shiqmona', *IEJ* 18: 226-33.
1969   'Two Notes on Palestinian Inscriptions of the Persian Age', *BASOR*
            193: 19-24.
1971   'Papyri of the Fourth Century B.C. from Daliyeh: A Preliminary
            Report on their Discovery and Significance', in D.N. Freedman and
            J.C. Greenfield (eds.), *New Directions in Biblical Archaeology* (Garden
            City, NY: Doubleday): 41-62.
1973   'Heshbon Ostracon II', *AUSS* 11: 126-31.
1975a   'Ammonite Ostraca from Heshbon: Heshbon Ostraca IV-VII', *AUSS*
            13: 1-19.
1975b   'A Reconstruction of the Judaean Restoration', *JBL* 94: 4-18.
1979   'Two Offering Dishes with Phoenician Inscriptions from the Sanctuary
            of 'Arad', *BASOR* 235: 75-77.
1981   'An Aramaic Ostracon of the Third Century BC from Jerusalem', *EI*
            15: 67-69*.
1985   'Samaria Papyrus 1: An Aramaic Slave Conveyance of 335 B.C.E.
            found in the Wâdi ed-Dâliyeh', *EI* 18: 1-17*.
1986   'An Unpublished Ammonite Ostracon from Hesbân', in L.T. Geraty
            and L.G. Herr (eds.), *The Archaeology of Jordan and other Studies
            Presented to S.H. Horn* (Berrien Springs, MI: Andrews University
            Press): 475-89.
1988   'A Report on the Samaria Papyri', in J.A. Emerton (ed.), *Congress
            Volume, Jerusalem 1986* (Leiden: Brill): 17-26.
Crouzel, H.
1970   'Le lieu d'exil d'Hérode Antipas et d'Hérodiade selon Flavius Josèphe',
            in F.L. Cross (ed.), *Studia Patristica* (TU, 107; Berlin) 10: 275-80.
1971   'L'exil d'Hérode Antipas et d'Hérodiade à Lugdunum Convenarum',
            BLE 3: 224-25.
Crowfoot, J.W., G.M. Crowfoot, and K.M. Kenyon
1957   *Samaria-Sebaste, 3: The Objects from Samaria* (London: PEF).
Culican, W.
1991   'Phoenicia and Phoenician Colonization', in *CAH* 3.2 (2nd edn): 461-
            546.
Cullmann, O.
1976   *The Johannine Circle* (ET J. Bowden; London: SCM Press).
Cumont, F.
1936   'The Frontier Provinces of the East', in *CAH* 11: 606-47.
Dahood, M.J.
1958   'Ancient Semitic Deities in Syria and Palestine', in S. Moscati (ed.), *La
            Antiche Divinità Semitiche* (Rome: Centro di Studi Semitici): 65-94.
Dalley, S.
1984   'The Cuneiform Tablet from Tell Tawilan', *Levant* 16: 19-22.
Dalman, G.
1912   *Neue Petra-Forschungen* (Leipzig: J.C. Hinrichs).
Dalven, R.
1961   *The Complete Poems of Cavafy* (London: The Hogarth Press).

Damati, E.
1982   'The Palace of Hilkiya', *Qadmoniot* 15: 117-21 (in Hebrew).
Danby, H.
1933   *The Mishnah* (Oxford: Oxford University Press).
Daniel, C.
1970   'Nouveaux arguments en faveur de l'identification des Hérodiens et des Esséniens', *RevQ* 7: 397-402.
Daniel-Rops, H.
1962   *Daily Life in Palestine at the Time of Christ* (ET P. O'Brian; London: Weidenfeld and Nicolson).
Dar, S.
1977   'The Villages of Bashan and the Foothills of Hermon', in M. Broshi (ed.), *Between Hermon and Sinai* (Jerusalem: French Publishers): 247-61 (in Hebrew).
1988   'The History of the Hermon Settlements', *PEQ* 120: 26-44.
1993   *Settlements and Cult Sites on Mount Hermon, Israel: Ituraean Culture in the Hellenistic and Roman Periods* (BAR International Series, 589; Oxford: Tempus Reparatum).
Dar, S., and N. Kokkinos
1992   'The Greek Inscriptions from Senaim on Mount Hermon', *PEQ* 124: 9-25.
Dauphin, C.M.
1982   'Jewish and Christian Communities in the Roman and Byzantine Gaulanitis: A Study of Evidence from Archaeological Surveys', *PEQ* 114: 129-42.
Davies, G.I.
1979   'The Significance of Deuteronomy 1.2 for the Location of Mount Horeb', *PEQ* 111: 87-101.
Davies, P.R., and R.T. White (eds.)
1990   *A Tribute to Geza Vermes: Essays on Jewish and Christian Literature and History* (JSOTSup, 100; Sheffield: Sheffield Academic Press).
Davies, P.S.
1986   'The Meaning of Philo's Text about the Gilded Shields', *JTS* 37: 109-14.
Dearman, J.A.
1995   'Edomite Religion: A Survey and an Examination of Some Recent Contributions', in Vikander Edelman (ed.) 1995: 119-36.
Debevoise, N.C.
1938   *A Political History of Parthia* (Chicago, IL: Chicago University Press).
Deissman, G.A.
1901   *Bible Studies* (Edinburgh: T. & T. Clark).
Delavault, B., and A. Lemaire
1979   'Les Inscriptions phéniciennes de Palestine', *RSF* 7: 1-39.
Delcor, M.
1951   'Les allusions à Alexandre le Grand dans Zach. IX, 1-8', *VT* 1: 110-24.
1962   'Von Sichem der hellenistischen epoch zum Sychar des Neuen Testaments', *ZDPV* 78: 34-48.

1978   'Les Kerethim et les Crétois', *VT* 28: 409-22.
Deltombe, F.L.
1963   'Mariamme, femme d'Hérode', *BTS* 60: 21-23.
Dentzer, J.M.
1986   'Développement et Culture de la Syrie du Sud dans la Période Préprovinciale', in J.M. Dentzer (ed.), *Hauran* 1.2 (Paris: Librairie Orientaliste Paul Geuthner): 387-420.
Dentzer, J.-M., F.M. Villeneuve, and F. Larché
1983   'The Monumental Gateway and the Princely Estate of 'Araq el-Emir', in N.L. Lapp (ed.) 1983: 133-48.
Derenbourg, J.
1867   *Essai sur l'Histoire et la Géographie de la Palestine*, I (Paris: Imprimerie Impériale).
Derfler, S.
1981   'A Terracotta Figurine from the Hellenistic Temple at Tel Beer-sheba', *IEJ* 31: 97-99.
1993   *The Hellenistic Temple at Tel Beersheva* (Lewiston, NY: Edwin Mellen Press).
Derrett, J.D.M.
1975   'Further Light on the Narratives of the Nativity', *NovT* 17: 81-108.
Desideri, P.
1991   'Strabo's Cilicians', in des Courtils *et al.* (eds.) 1991: 299-304.
Dever, W.G.
1976   'Gezer', in *EAEHL*: II, 428-43.
1993   'Gezer', in *NEAEHL*: II, 496-506.
Dexinger, F.
1981   'Limits of Tolerance in Judaism: The Samaritan Example', in E.P. Sanders *et al.* (eds.), *Jewish and Christian Self-Definition*, II (London: SCM Press): 88-114.
Dicou, B.
1984   *Edom, Israel's Brother and Antagonist: The Role of Edom in Biblical Prophecy and Story* (JSOTSup, 169; Sheffield: Sheffield Academic Press).
Dieudonné, A.
1927   'Les monnaies Grecques de Syrie au Cabinet des Médailles', *RN* 30: 1-50.
Diplock, P.R.
1971   'The Date of Askalon's Sculptured Panels and an Identification of the Caesarea Statues', *PEQ* 103: 13-16.
Doran, R.
1989   'The Non-dating of Jubilees: Jub. 34-8, 23.14-32 in Narrative Context', *JSJ* 20: 1-11.
Dothan, M.
1952   'An Archaeological Survey of the Lower Rubin River', *IEJ* 2: 104-17.
1975   'Ashdod', in *EAEHL*: I, 103-19.
1993   'Ashdod', in *NEAEHL*: I, 93-102.

Dothan, M., D.N. Freedman, and J.L. Swauger
1971 *Ashdod II–III: The Second and Third Seasons of Excavations, 1963, 1965* ('Atiqot, 9–10 Eng.; Jerusalem: The Department of Antiquities).

Dothan, T.
1982 *The Philistines and their Material Culture* (Jerusalem: IES)

Dothan, T., and M. Dothan
1992 *People of the Sea: The Search for the Philistines* (New York: Macmillan).

Dothan, T., and S. Gitin
1982 'Tel Miqne (Ekron) 1981', *IEJ* 32: 150-53.
1993 'Miqne, Tel (Ekron)', in *NEAEHL*: III, 1051-59.

Downey, G.
1961 *A History of Antioch in Syria: From Seleucus to the Arab Conquest* (Princeton: Princeton University Press).

Driver, G.R.
1957 *Aramaic Documents of the Fifth Century B.C.* (Oxford: Clarendon Press, 2nd edn).

Drougou, S., and G. Touratsoglou
1980 Ἑλληνιστικοὶ Λαξευτοὶ Τάφοι Βέροιας (Publication of the Archaiologikon Deltion, 28; Athens: Ministry of Culture).

Droysen, J.G.
1878 *Geschichte des Hellenismus*, II (Gotha: F.A. Berthes).

Dumbrell, W.J.
1971 'The Tell el-Maskhuta bowls and the Kingdom of Qedar in the Persian Period', *BASOR* 203: 33-44.

Dunand, M.
1934 *Mission archéologique au Djebel Druze: le musée de Soueïda* (Paris: Librairie Orientaliste Paul Geuthner).

Dussaud, R.
1904 'Représentations figurées d'Atargatis et des déesses assimilées', *RA* 4: 240-50.

Eck, W.
1970 *Senatoren von Vespasian bis Hadrian* (Munich: Beck).
1982 'Prokonsuln von Asia der Flavisch-Traianischen Zeit', *ZPE* 45: 139-53.

Edwards, O.
1982 'Herodian Chronology', *PEQ* 114: 29-42.

Efron, J.
1987 *Studies on the Hasmonean Period* (Leiden: Brill).
1990 'The Deed of Simeon ben Shatah in Ascalon', in Kasher 1990: 318-41.

Eisenman, R.H.
1983 *Maccabees, Zadokites, Christians and Qumran* (Leiden: Brill).
1986 *James the Just in the Habakkuk Pesher* (Leiden: Brill).

Eisler, R.
1930 'Deux Sculptures de l'Antiquité Classique représentant des Juifs', *Arethuse* 7.1: 29-38.
1931 *The Messiah Jesus and John the Baptist* (London: Methuen).

Elayi, J.
1982   'Studies in Phoenician Geography during the Persian Period', *JNES*
            41: 83-110.
Elgavish, J.
1978   'Tel Shiqmona', in *EAEHL*: IV, 1101-19.
Eph'al, I.
1982   *The Ancient Arabs: Nomads on the Borders of the Fertile Crescent*
            9th–5th Centuries B.C. (Jerusalem: Magnes Press).
1988   'Syria-Palestine under Achaemenid Rule', in *CAH* 4 (2nd edn): 139-
            64.
Epstein, L.M.
1942   *Marriage Laws in the Bible and the Talmud* (Harvard Semitic Series,
            12; Cambridge, MA: Harvard University Press).
Eshel, E., and H. Kloner
1994   'An Aramaic Ostracon of an Edomite Marriage Document from
            Maresha, Dated to 176 B.C.E.', *Tarbiz* 63: 485-502 (in Hebrew).
Evenari, M., Y. Aharoni, L. Shanan, and N.H. Tadmor
1958   'The Ancient Desert Agriculture of the Negev', *IEJ* 8: 231-68.
Ewing, W.
1895   'Greek and Other Inscriptions Collected in the Hauran', *PEFQS*: 41-
            60, 131-60, 265-80, 346-54.
Falk, Z.W.
1974   'Jewish Private Law', in CRINT 1.1: 504-34.
Fallon, F.
1985   'Theodotus', in *OTP* 2: 785-93.
Farmer, W.R.
1958   'Jesus, Simon, and Athronges', *NTS* 4: 147-55.
Feldman, L.H.
1953   'Asinius Pollio and his Jewish Interests', *TAPA* 84: 73-80.
1962   'The Sources of Josephus' *Antiquities*, Book 19', *Latomus* 21: 320-
            33.
1984   *Josephus and Modern Scholarship (1937–1980)* (Berlin: de Gruyter).
1985   'Asinius Pollio and Herod's Sons', *ClQ* 35: 240-43.
1986   'How Much Hellenism in Jewish Palestine?', *HUCA* 57: 83-111.
1993   *Jew and Gentile in the Ancient World* (Princeton, NJ: University Press).
1994   'Josephus' Portrayal of the Hasmoneans Compared with 1 Mac-
            cabees', in Parente and Sievers (eds.) 1994: 41-68.
Feldman, L.H., and G. Hata (eds.)
1987   *Josephus, Judaism, and Christianity* (Detroit, MI: Wayne State Uni-
            versity Press).
1989   *Josephus, the Bible, and History* (Detroit, MI: Wayne State University
            Press).
Fiema, Z.T., and R.N. Jones
1990   'The Nabataean King-List Revised: Further Observations on the
            Second Nabataean Inscription from Tell esh-Shuqafiya, Egypt', *ADAJ*
            34: 239- 48.
Figueras, P.
1983   *Decorated Jewish Ossuaries* (Leiden: Brill).

Filmer, W.E.
1966   'The Chronology of the Reign of Herod the Great', *JTS* 17: 283-98.
Finegan, J.
1964   *Handbook of Biblical Chronology: Principles of Time Reckoning in the Ancient World and Problems of Chronology in the Bible* (Princeton, NJ: Princeton University Press).
1992   *The Archaeology of the New Testament* (Princeton, NJ: Princeton University Press, 2nd edn).
Finkelstein, I.
1992a   'Edom in the Iron I', *Levant* 24: 159-66.
1992b   'Stratigraphy, Pottery and Parallels: A Reply to Bienkowski', *Levant* 24: 171-72.
Finley, M.I., and H.W. Pleket
1976   *The Olympic Games: The First Thousand Years* (London: Chatto & Windus).
Fitzmyer, J.A.
1970   'The Languages of Palestine in the First Century A.D.', *CBQ* 30: 501-31.
Fletcher, J.B.
1922   'Herod in Drama', *SPh* 19: 292-307.
Flusser, D.
1975   'The Great Goddess of Samaria', *IEJ* 25: 13-20.
1976   'Paganism in Palestine', in CRINT 1.2: 1065-100.
1986   'The House of David on an Ossuary', *IMJ* 5: 37-40.
1987   'Qumran and the Famine during the Reign of Herod', *IMJ* 6: 7-16.
Foerster, G.
1975   'The Early History of Caesarea', in C.T. Fritsch (ed.), *The Joint Expedition to Caesarea Maritima*, I (BASORSup, 19: Missoula, MT: Scholars Press): 9-22.
1978   'Tiberias', in *EAEHL*: IV, 1171-77.
1993   'Tiberias', in *NEAEHL*: IV, 1470-73.
Forrer, L.
1938   *Portraits of Royal Ladies on Greek Coins* (Chicago: Argonaut [repr. 1969]).
Forte, M.
1967   'Sull'origine di alcuni tipi di altarini sud-arabici', *AION* 17: 97-120.
Fossey, C.
1897   'Inscriptions de Syrie', *BCH* 21: 39-65.
Foster, S.S.
1976–77   'A Note on the "Note" of J. Schwartz', *SP* 4: 25-32.
Fraccaro, P.
1940   'C. Herennius Capito di Teate Procurator di Livia, di Tiberio e di Gaio', *Athenaeum* 18: 136-44.
Frankfort, T.
1961   'La date de l'autobiographie de Flavius Josèphe et des oeuvres de Justus de Tibériade', *RBPH* 39: 52-58.

1962   'Le royaume d'Agrippa II et son annexion par Domitien', in M.
               Renard (ed.), *Hommages à Albert Grenier* (Brussels: Latomus): 659-
               72.

1963   'La Sophène et Rome', *Latomus* 22: 181-90.
Fraser, P.M.
1970   'Greek-Phoenician Bilingual Inscriptions from Rhodes', *ABSA* 65:
               31-36.

1972   *Ptolemaic Alexandria*, I–III (Oxford: Oxford University Press).
Freyne, S.
1980   *Galilee from Alexander the Great to Hadrian, 323 B.C.E. to 135 C.E.*
               (Wilmington, DE: Michael Glazier).

Friedman, J.
1990   'Notes on Culture and Identity in Imperial Worlds', in Bilde *et al.*
               (eds.), 1990: 14-39.

Fritz, V.
1983   'Tel Masos: A Biblical Site in the Negev', *Archaeology* 36.5 (1983):
               30-37.

Fuks, A.
1974   'Patterns and Types of Social-Economic Revolution in Greece from
               the Fourth to the Second Century B.C.', *AS* 5: 51-81.

Fuks, G.
1981   'Antiochus Son of Phallion', *IEJ* 31: 237-38.
1982   'Again on the Episode of the Gilded Roman Shields at Jerusalem',
               HTR 75: 503-507.

1990   'Josephus and the Hasmoneans', *JJS* 41: 166-76.
Gabba, E.
1958   *Iscrizioni greche e latine per lo studio della Bibbia* (Milan: Marietti).
1979   'Le Finanze del Re Erode', *Clio* 15: 5-15.
1990   'The Finances of King Herod', in Kasher *et al.* (eds.) 1990: 160-68.
Gagé, J.
1977   *Res Gestae Divi Augusti* (Paris: Société d'Edition 'Les Belles Lettres',
               3rd edn).

Gallivan, P.A.
1973   'Nero's Liberation of Greece', *Hermes* 101: 230-34.
1974   'Suetonius and Chronology in the *De Vita Neronis*', *Historia* 23: 297-
               318.

Garbini, G.
1962   'The Dating of Post-Exilic Stamps', in Y. Aharoni (ed.), *Excavations
               at Ramat Raḥel: Seasons 1959 and 1960* (Rome: Centro di Studi
               Semitici): 61-68.

1988   *History & Ideology in Ancient Israel* (ET J. Bowden; London: SCM
               Press).

Gardner, P.
1872   'On an Unpublished Coin of Artavasdes II, King of Armenia', *NC* 12:
               6-15.

Garfinkel, Y.
1988   'MLS HKRSYM in Phoenician Inscriptions from Cyprus, the QRSY in
               Arad, HKRSYM in Egypt, and BNY QRS in the Bible', *JNES* 47: 27-34.

Garstang, J.

1921 'The Funds Excavation of Askalon', *PEFQS*: 12-16.

1922 'The Excavations at Askalon', *PEFQS*: 112-19.

1924 'Askalon', *PEFQS* 1924: 24-35.

Garzetti, A.

1974 *From Tiberius to the Antonines: A History of the Roman Empire AD 14–192* (London: Methuen).

Geiger, J.

1990 'Local Patriotism in the Hellenistic Cities of Palestine', in Kasher *et al.* (eds.) 1990: 141-50.

1991–92 'Euenus of Ascalon', *SCI* 11: 114-22.

1992 'Julian of Ascalon', *JHS* 112: 31-43.

Gelzer, H.

1880 *Sextus Africanus und die byzantinische Chronographie*, I (Leipzig: B.G. Teubner).

Gera, D.

1990 'On the Credibility of the History of the Tobiads', in Kasher *et al.* (eds.) 1990: 21-38.

Gera, D., and H.M. Cotton

1991 'A Dedication from Dor to a Governor of Syria', *IEJ* 41: 258-66.

Geraty, L.T.

1975 'The Khirbet el-Kôm Bilingual Ostracon', *BASOR* 220: 55-61.

1981 'Recent Suggestions on the Bilingual Ostracon from Khirbet El-Kôm', *AUSS* 19: 137-40.

1983 'The Historical, Linguistic and Biblical Significance of Khirbet El-Kôm Ostraca', in C.M. Meyers and M. O'Connor (eds.), *The Word of the Lord Shall Go Forth* (Festschrift D.N. Freedman; Winona Lake, IN: Eisenbrauns): 545-48.

Gereboff, J.

1979 *Rabbi Tarfon: The Tradition, the Man, and Early Rabbinic Judaism* (BJS, 7; Missoula, MT: Scholars Press.)

Gersht, R.

1983–84 'A Fragmentary Statue from Caesarea Maritima', *SCI* 7: 53-57.

Geus, C.H.J. de

1979–80 'Idumaea', *JEOL* 26: 53-74.

Geva, H.

1981 'The "Tower of David"—Phasael or Hippicus?', *IEJ* 31: 57-65.

1994 'Excavations at the Citadel of Jerusalem', in Geva (ed.) 1994: 156-67.

Geva, H. (ed.)

1994 *Ancient Jerusalem Revealed* (Jerusalem: IES).

Gibbs, J.G., and L.H. Feldman

1986 'Josephus' Vocabulary for Slavery', *JQR* 76: 281-310.

Gibson, J.C.L.

1982 *Textbook of Syrian Semitic Inscriptions*, III (Oxford: Clarendon Press).

Gibson, S.

1982 'Jerusalem (North-East) Archaeological Survey', *IEJ* 32: 156-57.

Gichon, M.

1967 'Idumaea and the Herodian Limes', *IEJ* 17: 27-42.

1976   "En Boqeq', in *EAEHL*: II, 365-70.
1981   'Cestius Gallus's Campaign in Judaea', *PEQ* 113: 39-62.
1993   *'En Boqeq: Ausgrabungen in einer oase am Toten Meer*, I (Mainz am Rhein: Philipp von Zabern).

Gil, M.
1970   'Land Ownership in Palestine under Roman Rule', *RIDA* 17: 11-53.

Gilboa, A.
1972   'L'octroi de la citoyenneté romaine et de l'immunité à Antipater, père d'Hérode', *RHD* 4: 609-14.
1979–80   'The Intervention of Sextus Julius Caesar, Governor of Syria in the Affair of Herod's Trial', *SCI* 5: 185-94.

Ginzel, F.K.
1911   *Handbuch der Mathematischen und Technischen Chronologie*, II (Leipzig: J.C. Hinrichs).

Gitler, H.
1995   'Numismatics and Museology—A New Outlook', *IMJ* 13: 29-36.

Gjerstad, E.
1979   'The Phoenician Colonization and Expansion in Cyprus', *RDAC*: 230-54.

Glazier-McDonald, B.
1995   'Edom in the Prophetical Corpus', in Vikander Edelman (ed.) 1995: 23-32.

Gleason, K.L.
1987–88   'Garden Excavations at the Herodian Winter Palace in Jericho, 1985–87', *BAIAS* 7: 21-39.

Glucker, C.A.M.
1987   *The City of Gaza in the Roman and Byzantine Periods* (BAR International Series, 325; Oxford: BAR).

Glueck, N.
1936   'The Boundaries of Edom', *HUCA* 11: 141-57.
1937   'A Newly Discovered Nabataean Temple of Atargatis and Hadad at Khirbet Et-Tannur, Transjordania', *AJA* 41: 361-75.
1943   'Some Ancient Towns in the Plains of Moab', *BASOR* 91: 7-26.
1951   *Explorations in Eastern Palestine*, IV (AASOR, 25–8; New Haven, CT: ASOR).
1965   'Ezion-geber', *BA* 28: 70-87.
1967a   'Transjordan', in D.W. Thomas (ed.), *Archaeology and Old Testament Study* (Oxford: Clarendon Press): 428-53.
1967b   'Some Edomite Pottery from Tell el-Kheleifeh', in *BASOR* 188: 8-38.
1971   'Tell el-Kheleifeh Inscriptions', in Goedicke (ed.) 1971: 225-42.
1993   'Tannur, Khirbet et-', in *NEAEHL*: IV, 1441-46.

Goedicke, H. (ed.)
1971   *Near Eastern Studies in Honor of W.F. Albright* (Baltimore, MD: The Johns Hopkins University Press).

Golan, D.
1982   'Josephus, Alexander's Visit to Jerusalem, and Modern Historiography', in U. Rappaport (ed.), *Josephus Flavius, Historian of Eretz-*

Israel in the Hellenistic-Roman Period (Jerusalem: Yad Izhak Ben Zvi): 29-55 (in Hebrew).

Goldstein, J.A.
1975 'The Tales of the Tobiads', in J. Neusner (ed.), *Christianity, Judaism and other Greco-Roman Cults*, III (Leiden: Brill): 85-123.

Goldstine, H.H.
1973 *New and Full Moons, 1001 B.C. to A.D. 1651* (Philadelphia, PA: American Philosophical Society).

Golikov, A.G.
1930 'The Armenian Copper Coin of King Aristobulus and his wife Salome', *SK* 4–5: 116-17 (in Russian).
1931 'Monnaie Arménienne de cuivre du roi Aristobule et de sa femme Salomé', *RN* 34: 8-10.

Gomme, A.W.
1933 *The Population of Athens in the Fifth and Fourth Centuries B.C.* (Oxford: Basil Blackwell).

Goodblatt, D.
1987a 'Agrippa I and Palestinian Judaism in the First Century', *JH* 2: 7-32.
1987b 'Josephus on Parthian Babylonia (Antiquities XVIII, 310-379)', *JAOS* 107: 605-22.

Goodenough, E.R.
1953 *Jewish Symbols in the Greco-Roman Period*, I (Bollingen, 37; New York: Pantheon Books).

Goodman, M.
1985 'A Bad Joke in Josephus', *JJS* 36: 195-99.
1987 *The Ruling Class of Judaea* (Cambridge: Cambridge University Press).
1990 'The Origins of the Great Revolt: A Conflict of Status Criteria', in Kasher *et al.* (eds.) 1990: 39-53.
1991 'Babatha's Story', *JRS* 81: 169-75.
1992 'Jewish Proselytizing in the First Century', in Lieu *et al.* (eds.) 1992: 53-78.
1994 'Josephus as Roman Citizen', in Parente and Sievers (eds.) 1994: 329-38.

Gordon, A.E.
1983 *Illustrated Introduction to Latin Epigraphy* (Berkeley, CA: California University Press).

Goudriaan, K.
1988 *Ethnicity in Ptolemaic Egypt* (Dutch Monographs on Ancient History and Archaeology, 5; Amsterdam: J.C. Gieben).

Gow, A.S.F., and D.L. Page
1968 *The Greek Anthology: The Garland of Philip and some Contemporary Epigrams*, I (Cambridge: Cambridge University Press).

Grabbe, L.L.
1991 'Maccabean Chronology: 167–164 or 168–165 BCE', *JBL* 110: 59-74.

Gracey, M.H.
1986 'The Armies of the Judaean Client Kings', in P. Freeman and D. Kennedy (eds.), *The Defence of the Roman and Byzantine East*, I (BAR International Series, 297; Oxford: BAR): 311-23.

Graf, D.F.
1992   'The Syrian Hauran', *JRA* 5: 450-67.
Graindor, P.
1927   *Athènes sous Auguste* (Cairo: Imprimerie Misr).
Grainger, J.D.
1991   *Hellenistic Phoenicia* (Oxford: Clarendon Press).
1995   'Village Government in Roman Syria and Arabia', *Levant* 27: 179-95.
Grant, M.
1950   *Roman Anniversary Issues: An Exploratory Study of the Numismatic and Medallic Commemoration of Anniversary Years 49 B.C.–A.D. 375* (Cambridge: Cambridge University Press).
Grayson, A.K.
1975   *Assyrian and Babylonian Chronicles* (Texts from Cuneiform Sources, 5; New York: J.J. Augustin).
Griffin, M.T.
1984   *Nero: The End of a Dynasty* (London: B.T. Batsford).
Groom, N.
1981   *Frankincense and Myrrh: A Study of the Arabian Incense Trade* (London: Longman).
Grosso, F.
1957   'La Media Atropatene e la Politica di Augusto', *Athenaeum* 35: 240-56.
Grottanelli, C.
1983   'Le donne di Biblo e le figlie di Agrippa I: un rito regale Siriano e le Adonie Gublite', *RSO* 57: 53-60.
Gutman, S.
1993   'Gamala', in *NEAEHL*: II, 459-63.
Guttmann, J.
1961   'The Second Commandment and the Image of God', *HUCA* 32: 161-74.
Habas, E.
1994   'The Jewish Origin of Julius Africanus', *JJS* 45: 86-91.
Hachlili, R.
1979   'The Goliath Family in Jericho: Funerary Inscriptions from the First-Century A.D. Jewish Monumental Tomb', *BASOR* 235: 31-66.
1988   *Ancient Jewish Art and Archaeology* (Handbuch der Orientalistik, 7.1; Leiden: Brill).
Haenchen, E.
1971   *The Acts of the Apostles* (ET R. McL. Wilson; Oxford: Basil Blackwell).
Halfmann, H.
1979   *Die Senatoren aus dem östlichen Teil des Imperium Romanun* (Göttingen: Vandenhoeck & Ruprecht).
1986   *Itinera Principium: Geschichte und typologie der Kaiserreisen im Römischen reich* (Heidelberger Althistorische Beiträge und Epigraphische Studien, 2 2; Stuttgart: Franz Steiner).
Halkin, F.
1963   'La date de composition de la *Bibliothèque* de Photius remise en question', *AnBoll* 81: 414-17.

Hamburger, A.
1986   'Surface-Finds from Caesarea Maritima—*Tesserae*', in L.I. Levine and
            E. Netzer (eds.), *Excavations at Caesarea 1975, 1976, 1979—Final
            Report* (Qedem, 21; Jerusalem: The Hebrew University): 187-204.
Hamburger, H.
1954   'A Hoard of Syrian Tetradrachms and Tyrian Bronze Coins from
            Gush Halav', *IEJ* 4: 201-26.
Hammond, P.C.
1959   'The Nabataean Bitumen Industry at the Dead Sea', *BA* 22: 40-48.
1968   'Hébron', *RB* 75: 253-58.
1973   *The Nabataeans—Their History, Culture and Archaeology* (Studies in
            Mediterranean Archaeology, 37; Gothenburg: Paul Åström).
1991   'Nabataean Settlement Patterns Inside Petra', *AHB* 5.1-2: 36-46.
Hamrick, E.V.
1981   'The Fourth North Wall of Jerusalem: A Barrier Wall of the First Cen-
            tury A.D.', *Levant* 13: 262-66.
Hanson, K.C.
1989   'The Herodians and Mediterranean Kinship' (pts. 1-2), *BTB* 19: 75-
            84, 142-51.
Har-El, M.
1972   'The Zealots' Fortresses in Galilee', *IEJ* 22: 123-30.
Harden, D
1963   *The Phoenicians* (London: Thames & Hudson, 2nd edn).
Harder, G.
1962   'Herodes-Burgen und Herodes-Städte im Jordangraben', *ZDPV* 78:
            49-63.
Hardwick, M.E.
1989   *Josephus as an Historical Source in Patristic Literature through
            Eusebius* (BJS, 128; Atlanta, GA: Scholars Press).
Harris, H.A.
1976   *Greek Athletics and the Jews* (Cardiff: University of Wales Press).
Harris, J.R.
1889   *The Rest of the Words of Baruch* (London: C.J. Clay and Sons).
Hart, S., and R.K. Falkner
1985   'Preliminary Report on a Survey in Edom, 1984', *ADAJ* 29: 255-77.
Hatta, G.
1994   'Imagining Some Dark Periods in Josephus' Life', in Parente and
            Sievers (eds.) 1994: 309-28.
Haussoullier, B., and H. Ingholt
1924   'Inscriptions Grecques de Syrie', *Syria* 5: 316-41.
Haywood, R.M.
1942–43   'A Note on the *Dialogus* of Tacitus', *CW* 36: 255.
Head, B.V.
1911   *Historia Numorum: A Manual of Greek Numismatics* (Oxford: Claren-
            don Press, 2nd edn).
Healey, J. F.
1989   'Were the Nabataeans Arabs?', *Aram* 1: 38-44.

Heinen, H.
1984   'The Syrian–Egyptian Wars and the New Kingdoms of Asia Minor',
                in *CAH* 7.1 (2nd edn): 412-45.
Hellström, P.
1965   *Labraunda II.1: Pottery of Classical and Later Date* (Lund: Gleerup).
Hendin, D.
1990–91   'New Discovery on a Coin of Herod I', *INJ* 11: 32.
Hengel, M.
1974   *Judaism and Hellenism*, I–II (ET J. Bowden; London: SCM Press).
1980   *Jews, Greeks and Barbarians* (ET J. Bowden; London: SCM Press).
1984   *Rabbinische Legende und frühpharisäische Geschichte: Schimeon b.
                Schetach und die achtzig Hexen von Askalon* (Abhandlungen der
                Heidelberger Akademie der Wissenschaften, Philosophisch-historische
                Klasse, 2; Heidelberg: C. Winter).
1989a   'The Political and Social History of Palestine from Alexander to Anti-
                ochus III (333-187 B.C.E.)', in *CHJ* 2: 35-78.
1989b   *The Hellenization of Judaea in the First Century after Christ* (ET J.
                Bowden; London: SCM Press).
1989c   *The Johannine Question* (London: SCM Press).
1992   'The Pre-Christian Paul', in Lieu *et al.* (eds.) 1992: 29-52.
Hennin, M.
1830   *Manuel de Numismatique Ancienne*, I–II (Paris: Merlin).
Herbert, S.C.
1993   'The Greco-Phoenician Settlement at Tel Anafa: A Case Study in the
                Limits of Hellenization', in Biran and Aviram (eds.) 1993: 118-25.
1994   *Tel Anafa I: Final Report on Ten Years of Excavation at a Hellenistic
                and Roman Settlement in Northern Israel*, parts 1-2 (JRASup, 10; Ann
                Arbor, MI: Kelsey Museum of the University of Michigan).
Herrmann, L.
1973   'Hérodiade', *REJ* 132: 49-63.
Herz, J.
1928   'Grossgrundbesitz in Palästina in Zeitalter Jesu', *PJ* 24: 98-113.
Herzog, Z., M. Aharoni, A.F. Rainey, and S. Moshkovitz
1984   'The Israelite Fortress at Arad', *BASOR* 254: 1-34.
Hill, G.F.
1911   'Some Graeco-Phoenician Shrines', *JHS* 31: 56-64.
1912   'Some Palestinian Cults in the Graeco-Roman Age', *PBA*: 1-17.
1913   *Mark Deacon: The Life of Porphyry Bishop of Gaza* (Oxford: Claren-
                don Press).
Hirschfeld, Y.
1991   'Tiberias: Preview of Coming Attractions', *BARev* 17.2: 44-51.
Hoehner, H.W.
1972   *Herod Antipas* (Cambridge: Cambridge University Press).
1989   'The Date of the Death of Herod the Great', in Vardaman and
                Yamauchi (eds.) 1989: 101-11.

Höghammar, K.
1993   *Sculpture and Society: A Study of the Connection Between the Free-Standing Sculpture and Society on Kos in the Hellenistic and Augustan Periods* (Boreas, 23; Uppsala: Acta Universitatis Upsaliensis).

Hölscher, G.
1916   'Josephus', *RE* 9: 1934-2000.

Honigmann, E.
1950   'Neronias-Irenopolis in Eastern Cilicia', *Byzantion* 20: 39-61.

Hopkins, K.
1964–65   'The Age of Roman Girls at Marriage', *PS* 18: 309-27.
1980   'Brother-Sister Marriage in Roman Egypt', *CSSH* 22: 303-54.

Hopwood, K.
1991   'The Links between the Coastal Cities of Western Rough Cilicia and the Interior during the Roman Period', in des Courtils *et al.* (eds.) 1991: 305-309.

Horbury, W.
1991   'Herod's Temple and "Herod's Days"', in W. Horbury (ed.), *Templum Amicitiae: Essays on the Second Temple Presented to Ernst Bammel* (JSNTSup, 48; Sheffield: Sheffield Academic Press): 103-49.
1994   'The "Caiaphas" Ossuaries and Joseph Caiaphas', *PEQ* 126: 32-48.

Horowitz, G.
1980   'Town Planning of Hellenistic Marisa: A Reappraisal of the Excavations after Eighty Years', *PEQ* 112: 93-111.

Horsley, R.A.
1986   'High Priests and the Politics of Roman Palestine: A Contextual Analysis of the Evidence in Josephus', *JSJ* 17: 23-55.

Horst, P.W. van der
1988   'The Jews of Ancient Crete', *JJS* 39: 183-200.

Houghton, A., S. Hurter, P. Erhart Mottahedeh, and J. Ayer Scott (eds.)
1984   *Studies in Honor of Leo Mildenberg: Numismatics, Art History, Archaeology* (Wetteren: Numismatique Romaine).

Hourmouziadis, G., P. Asimakopoulou Atzaka, and K.A. Makris
1982   *Magnesia: The Story of a Civilization* (Athens: M. & R. Capon).

Howgego, Ch.
1982–83   'The Behaviour and Function of Greek Imperial Countermarks', *INJ* 6–7: 47-58.

Hughes, J.
1990   *Secrets of the Times: Myth and History in Biblical Chronology* (JSOTSup, 66; Sheffield: Sheffield Academic Press).

Hunkin, J.W.
1919   'St. Luke and Josephus', *CQR* 88: 89-108.

Hussey, S.S.
1964   'How Many Herods in the Middle English Drama?', *Neophilologus* 48: 252-59.

Ibrahim, M., J.A. Sauer, and K. Yassine
1976   'The East Jordan Valley Survey, 1975', *BASOR* 222: 41-66.

Ilan, T.
1987   'The Greek Names of the Hasmoneans', *JQR* 78: 1-20.

1989	'Notes on the Distribution of Jewish Women's Names in Palestine in the Second Temple and Mishnaic Periods', *JJS* 40: 186-200.
1992	'Julia Crispina, Daughter of Berenicianus, a Herodian Princess in the Babatha Archive: A Case Study in Historical Identification', *JQR* 82: 361-81.
1993	'Queen Salamzion Alexandra and Judas Aristobulus I's Widow: Did Jannaeus Alexander Contract a Levirate Marriage?', *JSJ* 24: 181-90.

Iliffe, J. H.
1931	'An Inscribed Epitaph from Gaza', *QDAP* 1: 155-56.
1933	'Pre-Hellenistic Greek Pottery in Palestine', *QDAP* 2: 15-26.

Ingholt, H.
1963	'A Colossal Head from Memphis, Severan or Augustan?', *JARCE* 2: 125-45.

Irvine, A.K.
1973	'The Arabs and Ethiopians', in Wiseman (ed.) 1973: 289-311.

Isaac, B.
1980–81	'Roman Colonies in Judaea: The Foundation of Aelia Capitolina', *Talanta* 12–3: 31-54.
1984	'Bandits in Judaea and Arabia', *HSCP* 88: 171-203.
1991	'A Seleucid Inscription from Jamnia-on-the-Sea: Antiochus V Eupator and the Sidonians', *IEJ* 41: 132-44.
1992a	*The Limits of Empire: The Roman Army in the East* (Oxford: Clarendon Press, rev. edn).
1992b	'The Babatha Archive: A Review Article', *IEJ* 42: 62-75.

Isaac, B., and I. Roll
1982	*Roman Roads in Judaea*. I. *The Legio-Scythopolis Road* (BAR International Series, 141; Oxford: BAR).

Israel, F.
1979	'Miscellanea Idumea', *RivB* 27: 171-203.

Jacobson, D.M.
1981	'The Plan of the Ancient Haram el-Khalil in Hebron', *PEQ* 113: 73-80.
1986	'A New Interpretation of the Reverse of Herod's Largest Coin', *ANSMN* 31: 145-65.
1988	'King Herod's "Heroic" Public Image', *RB* 95: 386- 403.
1993–94	'King Herod, Roman Citizen and Benefactor of Kos', *BAIAS* 13: 31-35.

Jalabert, L.
1904	'Nouvelles stèles peintes de Sidon', *RA* 4: 1-16.

James, M.R.
1924	*The Apocryphal New Testament* (Oxford: Clarendon Press).

James, P.J., I.J. Thorpe, N. Kokkinos, and J.A. Frankish
1987	*Bronze to Iron Age Chronology in the Old World: Time for a Reassessment?* (Studies in Ancient Chronology, 1; London: Institute of Archaeology).

James, P.J., I.J. Thorpe, N. Kokkinos, R. Morkot, and J.A. Frankish
1991	*Centuries of Darkness* (London: J. Cape).
1992	'Centuries of Darkness: A Reply to Critics', *CAJ* 2.1: 127-30.

Jameson, S.
1968   'Chronology of the Campaigns of Aelius Gallus and C. Petronius',
              JRS 58: 71-84.
Jaros, K.
1982   *Hundert Inschriften aus Kanaan und Israel* (Fribourg/Schweiz:
              Schweiz. Kath. Bibelwerk).
Jeremias, J.
1966   *The Rediscovery of Bethesda* (New Testament Archaeological Mono-
              graphs, 1; Louisville, KY: Southern Baptist Theological Seminary).
1969   *Jerusalem in the Time of Jesus* (ET F.H. and C.H. Cave; London: SCM
              Press).
1972   *The Parables of Jesus* (London: SCM Press, 3rd rev. edn).
Jeselsohn, D.
1974   'A New Coin Type with Hebrew Inscription', *IEJ* 24: 73-76.
Jewett, R.
1979   *Dating Paul's Life* (London: SCM Press).
Jidejian, N.
1968   *Byblos through the Ages* (Beirut: Dar el-Machreq).
1969   *Tyre through the Ages* (Beirut: Dar el-Machreq).
1971   *Sidon through the Ages* (Beirut: Dar el-Machreq).
Jones, A.H.M.
1931a   'The Urbanization of Palestine', *JRS* 21: 78-85.
1931b   'The Urbanization of the Ituraean Principality', *JRS* 21: 265-75.
1938   *The Herods of Judaea* (Oxford: Oxford University Press).
1971   *The Cities of the Eastern Roman Provinces* (Oxford: Oxford Univer-
              sity Press, 2nd edn).
1972   *The Criminal Courts of the Roman Republic and Principate* (Oxford:
              Basil Blackwell).
Jones, B.W.
1984a   *The Emperor Titus* (London and Sydney: Croom Helm).
1984b   'Which Alexandria?', *Athenaeum* 62: 281-85.
1989   'Titus in Judaea, A.D. 67', *Latomus* 48: 127-34.
1992   *The Emperor Domitian* (London: Routledge).
Jones, B.W., and R.D. Milns
1984   *The Use of Documentary Evidence in the Study of Roman Imperial
              History* (Sydney: Sydney University Press).
Jones, C.P., and C. Habicht
1989   'A Hellenistic Inscription from Arsinoe in Cilicia', *Phoenix* 43: 317-
              46.
Jones, R.N., D.J. Johnson, P.C. Hammond, and Z.T. Fiema
1988   'A Second Nabataean Inscription from Tell esh-Shuqafiya, Egypt',
              BASOR 269: 47-57.
Jordan, R.
1974   *Berenice* (London: Constable).
Jossa, G.
1994   'Josephus' Action in Galilee During the Jewish War', in Parente and
              Sievers (eds.) 1994: 265-78.

Jung, J.
1900   'Mittheilungen aus Apulum', *JOAI* 3: 181-94 (Beiblatt).
Kahane, P.
1952   'Pottery Types from the Jewish Ossuary-Tombs around Jerusalem', *IEJ* 2: 125-39, 176-82.
Kahrstedt, U.
1910   'Frauen auf antiken Münzen', *Klio* 10: 261-314.
Kajava, M.
1990   'Roman Senatorial Women and the Greek East: Epigraphic Evidence from the Republican and Augustan Period', in Solin and Kajava (eds.) 1990: 59-124.
Kakrides, I.Th.
1954   'Ποικίλα Ἑλληνικά', *Hellēnika* 13: 165-74.
Kanael, B.
1951–52   'The Coins of King Herod of the Third Year', *JQR* 42: 261-64.
1952   'The Greek Letters and Monograms on the Coins of Jehohanan the High Priest', *IEJ* 2: 190-94.
1957   'The Partition of Judea by Gabinius', *IEJ* 7: 98-106.
Kantzia, Ch.
1980   'Μιὰ Δίγλωσση Ἑλληνικὴ-Φοινικικὴ Ἐπιγραφὴ ἀπὸ τὴν Κῶ', *AD* 35: 1-16 [publ. 1987].
Kasher, A.
1977   'The *isopoliteia* Question in Caesarea Maritima', *JQR* 68: 16-27.
1982   'Gaza during the Greco-Roman Era', in *JC* 2: 63-78.
1985   *The Jews in Hellenistic and Roman Egypt: The Struggle for Equal Rights* (TSAJ, 7; Tübingen: J.C.B. Mohr).
1988   *Jews, Idumaeans, and Ancient Arabs* (TSAJ, 18; Tübingen: J.C.B. Mohr).
1990   *Jews and Hellenistic Cities in Eretz-Israel* (TSAJ, 21; Tübingen: J.C.B. Mohr).
Kasher, A., U. Rappaport, and G. Fuks (eds.)
1990   *Greece and Rome in Eretz Israel: Collected Essays* (Jerusalem: Yad Izhak Ben-Zvi).
Kashtan, N.
1988   'Akko-Ptolemais: A Maritime Metropolis in Hellenistic and Early Roman Times, 332 BCE–70 CE, as seen through the Literary Sources', *MHR* 3: 37-53.
Katzenstein, H.J.
1973   *The History of Tyre* (Jerusalem: The Schocken Institute for Jewish Research).
1989   'Gaza, the Persian Period (538–322 B.C.E.)', *Transeuphratène* 1: 67-86.
1994   'Gaza in the Neo-Babylonian Period (626–539 B.C.E.)', *Transeuphratène* 7: 35-49.
Kee, H.C.
1983   'Testaments of the Twelve Patriarchs', in *OTP* 1: 775-828.

Kelly, T.
1987   'Herodotus and the Chronology of the Kings of Sidon', *BASOR* 268: 39-56.
Kempinski, A.
1977   'Tel Masos' in *EAEHL*: III, 816-19.
1993   'Masos, Tel', in *NEAEHL*: III, 986-89.
Kennedy, D.
1995   'The Publications of the Princeton University Archaeological Expeditions to Syria in 1904-05 and 1909 relating to Southern Syria', *PEQ* 127: 21-32.
Khairy, N.I.
1980   'Nabataean Piriform Unguentaria', *BASOR* 240: 85-91.
1981   'A New Dedicatory Nabataean Inscription', *PEQ* 113: 19-26.
Kienast, D.
1982   *Augustus Prinzeps und Monarch* (Darmstadt: Wissenschaftliche Buchgesellschaft).
Kilgallen, J.J.
1988   'Paul before Agrippa (Acts 26, 2-23): Some Considerations', *Bib* 69: 170-95.
Kindler, A.
1953   'Some Unpublished Coins of King Herod', *IEJ* 3: 239-41.
1963   'An Unpublished Coin-Type of Nysa-Scythopolis and the Problem of the Eras of the City', *INJ* 1: 55-56.
1971   'A Coin of Herod Philip—the Earliest Portrait of a Herodian Ruler', *IEJ* 21: 161-63.
1974   'Silver Coins Bearing the Name of Judaea from the Early Hellenistic Period', *IEJ* 24: 73-76.
1981   'A Re-Assessment of the Dates of Some Coins of the Roman Procurators of Judaea', *INJ* 5: 19-21.
1983–84   'The Status and Relations of the Herodian Kings Agrippa I and II to the Roman Imperial Court as Reflected by their Coin Issues', *IPL* 1: 67-84 (in Hebrew).
1985–86   'The Coinage of Joppe (Jaffa)', *IPL* 2–3: 21-36 (in Hebrew).
1987–89   'Coins of the Ituraeans', *IPL* 5–6: 37-46 (in Hebrew).
King, C.W.
1873   *Early Christian Numismatics and Other Antiquarian Tracts* (London: Bell & Daldy).
King, G.
1990   'The Basalt Desert Rescue Survey and Some Preliminary Remarks on the Safaitic Inscriptions and Rock Drawings', *PSAS* 20: 55-78.
Kitchen, K.A.
1973   'The Philistines', in Wiseman (ed.) 1973: 53-78.
Kloner, A.
1985   'Maresha', *ESI* 4: 64 [publ. 1986].
1986   'The Third Wall in Jerusalem and the Cave of the Kings', *Levant* 19: 121-29.
1987–88   'Maresha', *ESI* 6: 79-81 [publ. 1988].
1991   'Maresha', *Qadmoniot* 24: 70-85 (in Hebrew).

1993a   'Beth Guvrin', in *NEAEHL*: I, 195-97, 198-201.

1993b   'Mareshah (Marisa)', in *NEAEHL*: III, 951-57.

Kloner, A., and O. Hess

1985   'A Columbarium in Complex 21 at Maresha', *'Atiqot* 17: 122-33.

Kloner, A., D. Regev, and U. Rappaport

1992   'A Hellenistic Burial Cave in the Judaean Shephelah', *'Atiqot* 21: 27-50* (in Hebrew).

Kochavi, M.

1977   'Tel Malḥata', in *EAEHL*: III, 771-75.

1993   'Malḥata, Tel', in *NEAEHL*: III, 934-36.

Kochavi, M. (ed.)

1972   *Judaea, Samaria and the Golan: Archaeological Survey 1967–1968* (Jerusalem: Carta [in Hebrew]).

Kokkinos, N.

1980   *Tò Aἴνιγμα τοῦ Ἰνσοῦ τῆς Γαγιγαίας* (Athens: Chrysē Tomē).

1985   'A Coin of Herod the Great Commemorating the City of Sebaste', *LA* 35: 303-306.

1986a   'Which Salome Did Aristobulus Marry?', *PEQ* 118: 33-50.

1986b   'A Retouched New Date on a Coin of Valerius Gratus', *LA* 36: 241-46.

1987   'Re-Assembling the Inscription of Glaphyra from Athens', *ZPE* 68: 288-90.

1989   'Crucifixion in A.D. 36: The Keystone for Dating the Birth of Jesus', in Vardaman and Yamauchi (eds.) 1989: 133-63.

1990   'A Fresh Look at the *gentilicium* of Felix Procurator of Judaea', *Latomus* 49: 126-41.

1991   'Review of M. E. Hardwick, *Josephus*', *JRS* 81: 227-28.

1992a   *Antonia Augusta: Portrait of a Great Roman Lady* (London: Routledge).

1992b   'Review of J. McKenzie, *Petra*', *JRS* 82: 249.

1992c   'Review of S. Mason, *Pharisees*', *JRS* 82: 249-50.

1992d   'Review of D. R. Schwartz, *Agrippa I*', *JRS* 82: 250-51.

1994a   'Review of N. Lewis, *P. Yadin*', *PEQ* 126: 175-76.

1994b   'Review of S. Schwartz, *Josephus*', *JRS* 84: 263-64.

1995a   'The Honorand of the Titulus Tiburtinus: C. Sentius Saturninus?', *ZPE* 105: 21-36.

1995b   'Review of Y. E. Meimaris, *Inscriptions*', *PEQ* 127: 77-78.

1996   'Review of J. Elsner & J. Masters, *Nero*', *JRS* 86: 211-12.

forthcoming 1 *The Herods in Greece* (Colloquenda Mediterranea A/4; Bradford: Loid Publishing).

forthcoming 2 'The Relative Chronology of the Nativity in Tertullian', in J. Vardaman (ed.), *Chronos, Kairos, Christos*, II (Macon, GA: Mercer University Press).

forthcoming 3 'The Titulus Tiburtinus, Syme's Piso and the Province of Syria: A Rejoinder', *ZPE*.

Korach, L.

1894   'Die Reisen des Königs Herodes nach Rom', *MGWJ* 38: 529-35.

Kottek, S.S.
1994   *Medicine and Hygiene in the Works of Flavius Josephus* (Studies in
            Ancient Medicine, 9; Leiden: Brill).
Koukoule-Chrysanthake, C.
1979   ''Ανατολικὴ Μακεδονία: 'Εφορεία Προϊστορικῶν 'Αρχαιοτήτων
            Καλάλας', *AD* 34 (B.2): 322-35 [publ. 1987].
Kraay, C.M.
1980   'Jewish Friends and Allies of Rome', *ANSMN* 25: 53-57.
Kraeling, E.G.
1953   *The Brooklyn Museum Aramaic Papyri: New Documents of the Fifth
            Century B.C. from the Jewish Colony at Elephantine* (New Haven, CT:
            Yale University Press).
Kraemer, R.S.
1989   'On the Meaning of the Term "Jew" in Greco-Roman Inscriptions',
            HTR 82: 35-53.
Kreissig, H.
1989   'A Marxist View of Josephus' Account of the Jewish War', in Feld-
            man and Hata (eds.) 1989: 265-77.
Krencker, D., and W. Zschietzschmann
1938   *Römische Tempel in Syrien* (Denkmäler Antiker Architektur 5, I-II;
            Berlin: de Gruyter).
Krupp, M., and S. Qedar
1981   'The Cross on the Coins of King Herod', *INJ* 5: 17-18.
Kucharczak, T.
1980   'The Problem of the Integration of Judaea in the Roman Empire at the
            Time of Agrippa I', *Meander* 35: 45-57 (in Polish).
Kuhnen, H.-P.
1990   *Palästina in Griechish-Römischer Zeit* (Handbuch der Archäologie
            Vorderasien II.2; Munich: Beck).
Kuhrt, A., and S. Sherwin-White (eds.)
1987   *Hellenism in the East* (London: Gerald Duckworth).
Kushnir-Stein (see also Stein), A.
1995a   'An Inscribed Lead Weight from Ashdod: A Reconsideration', *ZPE*
            105: 81-84.
1995b   'Another Look at Josephus' Evidence for the Date of Herod's Death',
            SCI 14: 73-86.
Ladouceur, D.J.
1981   'The Death of Herod the Great', *CP* 76: 25-34.
Lake, K.
1933   'The Apostolic Council of Jerusalem', in Lake and Cadbury (eds.)
            1933: V, 195-212.
Lake, K., and H.J. Cadbury (eds.)
1933   *The Beginnings of Christianity*, IV–V (London: Macmillan).
Lämmer, M.
1981–82   'Griechische Agone und Römische Spiele unter der Regierung des
            judischen Königs Agrippa I', *KBS* 10–1: 199-237.
Landau, Y.H.
1961   'A Greek Inscription from Acre', *IEJ* 11: 118-26.

1966   'A Greek Inscription Found Near Hefzibah', *IEJ* 16: 54-70.
Lane Fox, R.
1991   *The Unauthorized Version: Truth and Fiction in the Bible* (London: Viking).
Langlois, V.
1859   *Numismatique de L'Arménie* (Paris: C. Rollin and A. Durand).
Laperrousaz, E.-M.
1989   'Hérod le Grand est-il "l'ennemi (qui) a agi en étranger" des Psaumes de Salomon?', in D. Tollet (ed.), *Politique et religion dans le judaïsme ancien et médiéval* (Paris: Desclée): 29-32.
Lapp, N.L. (ed.)
1983   *The Excavations at 'Araq el-Emir*, I (AASOR, 47; Cambridge, MA: ASOR)
Lapp, P.W.
1961   *Palestinian Ceramic Chronology 200 B.C.–A.D. 70* (New Haven, CT: ASOR).
1976   ' 'Iraq el-Emir', in *EAEHL*: II, 527-31.
Lapp, P.W., and N.L. Lapp
1974   *Discoveries in the Wâdi ed-Dâliyeh* (AASOR, 41; Cambridge, MA: ASOR).
1993   ' 'Iraq el-Emir', in *NEAEHL*: II, 646-49.
Laqueur, R.
1920   *Der jüdische Historiker Flavius Josephus* (Giessen: von Münchow).
Lauffray, J.
1978   'Beyrouth Archéologie et Histoire, époques gréco-romaines. I. Période hellénistique et Haut-Empire romain', *ANRW* 2.8: 135-63.
Launey, M.
1949–50   *Recherches sur les armées hellénistiques* (Bibliothèque des Ecoles Françaises d'Athènes et de Rome, 169, I-II; Paris: de Boccard).
Lawrence, A.W.
1979   *Greek Aims in Fortification* (Oxford: Clarendon Press).
Lee, A.D.
1988   'Close-Kin Marriage in Late Antique Mesopotamia', *GRBS* 29: 403-13.
Leiwo, M.
1989   'Philostratus of Ascalon, his Bank, his Connections and Naples in c. 130–90 B.C.', *Athenaeum* 67: 575-84.
Lemaire, A.
1974   'Un nouveau roi Arabe de Qedar dans l'inscription de l'autel à encens de Lakish', *RB* 81: 63-72.
1988   'Inscriptions phéniciennes de Palestine', *DHA* 132: 23.
1989   'Les inscriptions d'époque perse: un bilan provisoire', *Transeuphratène* 1: 87-105.
1990   'Populations et territoires de la Palestine à l'époque perse', *Transeuphratène* 3: 31-74.
Lémonon, J.-P.
1981   *Pilate et le gouvernement de la Judée: textes et monuments* (Paris: Gabalda).

Lenormant, F.
1864   *Monographie de la voie sacrée eleusinienne*, I (Paris: Librairie de L. Hachette et cie).
Lepper, F.A.
1948   *Trajan's Parthian War* (Oxford: Oxford University Press).
Levine, L.I.
1973   'A propos de la fondation de la Tour de Straton', *RB* 80: 75-81.
1975   *Caesarea under Roman Rule* (Leiden: Brill).
Lewis, N., and M. Reinhold
1955   *Roman Civilization*, II (New York: Columbia University Press).
Lichtenstein, H.
1931-32   'Die Fastenrolle. Eine Untersuchung zur jüdisch-hellenistischen Geschichte', *HUCA* 8-9: 257-351.
Lichtheim, M.
1976   *Ancient Egyptian Literature*, II (The New Kingdom; Berkeley, CA: University of California Press).
Lidzbarski, M.
1912   *Phönizische und aramäische Krugaufschriften aus Elephantine* (Berlin: Königl. Academie der Wissenschaften).
Liebesny, H.
1936   'Ein Erlass des Königs Ptolemaios II Philadelphos über die Deklaration von Vieh und Sklaven in Syrien und Phönikien (PER Inv. Nr. 24.552 gr.)', *Aegyptus* 16: 257-91.
Lieu, J., J. North, and T. Rajak (eds.)
1992   *The Jews among Pagans and Christians in the Roman Empire* (London: Routledge).
Lifshitz, B.
1962a   'Beiträge zur palästinischen Epigraphik', *ZDPV* 78: 64-88.
1962b   'Papyrus grecs du désert de Juda', *Aegyptus* 42: 240-56.
1976   'Bleigewichte aus Palästine und Syrien', *ZDPV* 92: 168-87.
1978   'Scythopolis. L'histoire, les institutions et les cultes de la ville à l'époque hellénistique et impériale', in *ANRW* 2.8: 262-94.
1981   'The Greek Inscriptions', in Aharoni (ed.) 1981: 177.
Lindsay, H.
1992   'Augustus and Eurycles', *RMP* 135: 290-97.
Lindsay, J.
1976   'The Babylonian Kings and Edom', *PEQ* 108: 23-39.
Lipinski, E. (ed.)
1991   *Studia Phoenicia XI: Phoenicia and the Bible* (Leuven: Peeters).
Littman, R.J.
1979   'Kinship in Athens', *AS* 10: 5-31.
Littmann, E.
1914   *The Princeton University Archaeological Expeditions to Syria in 1904-5 and 1909, IV.A: Semitic Inscriptions, Nabataean* (Leiden: Brill).
Littmann, E., D. Magie, and D.R. Stuart
1921   *The Princeton University Archaeological Expeditions to Syria in 1904-5 and 1909, III.A: Greek and Latin Inscriptions, Southern Syria* (Leiden: Brill).

Luedemann, G.
1984   *Paul, Apostle to the Gentiles: Studies in Chronology* (ET F.S. Jones;
                Philadelphia: PA: Fortress Press).
Lund, J.
1993   'The Archaeological Evidence for the Transition from the Persian to
                the Hellenistic Age in Northwestern Syria', *Transeuphratène* 6: 27-45.
Ma'oz, Z.U.
1981   'Synagogues of the Golan', in L.I. Levine (ed.), *Ancient Synagogues
                Revealed* (Jerusalem: IES): 98-115.
1988–89   'Banias 1988—Temple of Pan', *ESI* 7–8: 11 [publ. 1990].
1993   'Banias', in *NEAEHL*: I, 136-43.
MacAdam, H.I.
1983   'Epigraphy and Village Life in Southern Syria during the Roman and
                Early Byzantine Periods', *Berytus* 31: 103-15.
1986   *Studies in the History of the Roman Province of Arabia* (BAR Interna-
                tional Series, 295; Oxford: BAR).
Macalister, R.A.S.
1913   *The Philistines: Their History and Civilisation* (London: The British
                Academy).
Macdonald, M.C.A.
1993   'Nomads and the Hawrân in the Late Hellenistic and Roman Periods:
                A Reassessment of the Epigraphic Evidence', *Syria* 70: 303-413.
1995   'Herodian Echoes in the Syrian Desert', in S. Bourke and J.-P. Des-
                coeudres (eds.), *Trade, Contact, and the Movement of Peoples in the
                Eastern Mediterranean: Studies in Honour of J.B. Hennessy*
                (Mediterranean Archaeology Supplement, 3; Sydney: Meditarch):
                285-90.
Mackowski, R.M.
1980   *Jerusalem, City of Jesus* (Grand Rapids, MI: Eerdmans).
Macler, F.
1907   'Notes d'histoire sur Salomé la Danseuse', *MM* (15 June): 615-25.
Macurdy, G.H.
1932   *Hellenistic Queens: A Study of Woman-Power in Macedonia, Seleucid
                Syria, and Ptolemaic Egypt* (Baltimore, MD: The Johns Hopkins Uni-
                versity Press).
1935   'Julia Berenice', *AJP* 56: 246-53.
1936   'Iotape', *JRS* 26: 40-42.
1937   *Vassal-Queens and Some Other Contemporary Women in the Roman
                Empire* (The Johns Hopkins University Studies in Archaeology, 22;
                Baltimore, MD: The Johns Hopkins University Press).
Madden, F.W.
1864   *History of Jewish Coinage and of Money in the Old and New Testa-
                ment* (London [repr.; San Diego, CA: Pegasus, 1967]).
1881   *Coins of the Jews* (London: Trübner [repr. Hildesheim: G. Olms,
                1976]).
Magen, Y.
1986   'A Fortified Town of the Hellenistic Period on Mount Gerizim', *Qad-
                moniot* 19: 91-101 (in Hebrew).

1990	'Mount Gerizim: A Temple-City', *Qadmoniot* 23: 70-96 (in Hebrew).
1993a	'Gerizim, Mount', in *NEAEHL*: II, 484-92.
1993b	'Mamre', in *NEAEHL*: III, 939-42.

Magie, D.
1950   *Roman Rule in Asia Minor to the End of the Third Century after Christ*, I–II (Princeton, NJ: Princeton University Press).

Maiuri, A.
1925   *Nuova Silloge Epigraphica di Rodi e Cos* (Florence: Felice le Monnier).

Malamat, A.
1982   'How Inferior Israelite Forces Conquered Fortified Canaanite Cities', *BARev* 8.2: 24-35.

Mancinetti-Santamaria, G.
1982   'Filostrato di Ascalona, Banchiere in Delo', in F. Coarelli *et al.* (eds.), *Delo e l'Italia* (Rome: Bardi Editore): 79-89.

Mandelaras, V.G.
1986   Οἱ Μίμοι τοῦ Ἡρώνδα (Athens: Kardamitsa, 2nd edn).

Manns, F.
1984   *Some Weights of the Hellenistic, Roman and Byzantine Periods* (ET G. Kloetzli; Jerusalem: Studium Biblicum Franciscanum).

Mantzoulinou-Richards, E.
1988   'From Syros: A Dedicatory Inscription of Herodes the Great from an Unknown Building', *AW* 18.3-4: 87-99.

Marshall, B.A.
1985   *A Historical Commentary on Asconius* (Columbia, MO: Columbia University Press).

Martin, E.L.
1989   'The Nativity and Herod's Death', in Vardaman and Yamauchi (eds.) 1989: 85-92.

Mason, S.
1991   *Flavius Josephus on the Pharisees: A Composition Critical Study* (SPB, 39; Leiden: Brill).

Masson, O.
1969   'Recherches sur les phéniciens dans le monde hellénistique', *BCH* 93: 679-700.

Masterman, E.W.G.
1920   *Hygiene and Disease in Palestine in Modern and in Biblical Times* (London: PEF).

Mayerson, P.
1992   'The Gaza "Wine" Jar (*Gazition*) and the "Lost" Ashkelon Jar (*Askalōnion*)', *IEJ* 42: 76-80.
1993   'The Use of Ascalon Wine in the Medical Writers of the Fourth to the Seventh Centuries', *IEJ* 43: 169-73.

Mazar, A.
1985   'The Emergence of the Philistine Material Culture', *IEJ* 35: 95-107.

Mazar, B.
1957   'The Tobiads', *IEJ* 7: 137-45; 229-38.
1960   'The Cities of the Territory of Dan', *IEJ* 10: 65-77.

1964	*The Philistines and the Rise of Israel and Tyre* (Jerusalem: Israel Academy of Sciences and Humanities; *PIASH* 1.7 [1967]).
1969	*The Excavations in the Old City of Jerusalem: Preliminary Report of the First Season, 1968* (Jerusalem: IES).

Mazar, B., T. Dothan, and I. Dunayevsky
| 1966 | *En-Gedi: The First and Second Seasons of Excavations 1961–1962* ('Atiqot, 5 Eng.; Jerusalem: The Department of Antiquities). |

Mazar, E.
| 1985 | 'Edomite Pottery at the End of the Iron Age', *IEJ* 35: 253-69. |

Mazard, J.
| 1955 | *Corpus nummorum Numidiae Mauretaniaeque* (Paris: Arts et Métiers Graphiques). |

McCarter, P.K.
| 1976 | 'Obadiah 7 and the Fall of Edom', *BASOR* 221: 87-92. |

McCown, C.C.
1921–22	'A Tomb at Marissa—Beit Jibrin', in AASOR 2–3: 111-12.
1947	*Tell en Nasbeh*, I (Berkeley, CA: The Palestine Institute).
1957	'The 'Araq el-Emir and the Tobiads', *BA* 20: 63-80.

McDermott, W.C., and A.E. Orentzel
| 1979 | *Roman Portraits: The Flavian-Trajanic Period* (Columbia, MO: University of Missouri Press). |

McEvenue, S.E.
| 1981 | 'The Political Structure in Judah from Cyrus to Nehemiah', *CQR* 43: 353-64. |

McKenzie, J.
| 1990 | *The Architecture of Petra* (British Academy Monographs in Archaeology, 1; Oxford: Oxford University Press). |

McLaren, J.S.
| 1991 | *Power and Politics in Palestine: The Jews and the Governing of their Land 100 BC–AD 70* (JSNTSup, 63; Sheffield: Sheffield Academic Press). |

Mead, A.H.
| 1985 | 'The *basilikos* in John 4.46-53', *JSNT* 23: 69-72. |

Meiggs, R., and D. Lewis
| 1969 | *A Selection of Greek Historical Inscriptions* (Oxford: Clarendon Press). |

Meimaris, Y.E., K. Kritikakou, and P. Bougia
| 1992 | *Chronological Systems in Roman-Byzantine Palestine and Arabia: The Evidence of the Dated Greek Inscriptions* (Meletêmata, 17; Athens: Research Centre for Greek and Roman Antiquity). |

Mendels, D.
1986	'Greek and Roman History in the *Bibliotheca* of Photius—A Note', *Byzantion* 56: 196-206.
1987	*The Land of Israel as a Political Concept in Hasmonean Literature* (TSAJ, 15; Tübingen: Mohr).
1992	*The Rise and Fall of Jewish Nationalism: Jewish and Christian Ethnicity in Ancient Palestine* (Garden City, NY: Doubleday).

Merkel, H.
| 1988 | 'Herodes', in *RAC* 14: 815-30. |

Merrins, E.M.
1904   'The Deaths of Antiochus IV, Herod the Great, and Herod Agrippa I',
        BSac 61: 548-62.

Merritt, B.
1952   'Greek Inscriptions', *Hesperia* 21: 340-80.

Meshel, Z.
1978   *Kuntillet 'Ajrud: A Religious Centre from the Time of the Monarchy on
        the Border of Sinai* (Jerusalem: The Israel Museum).

Meshel, Z., and C. Meyers
1976   'The Name of God in the Wilderness of Zin', *BA* 39: 6-10.

Meshorer, Y.
1970   'A Stone Weight from the Reign of Herod', *IEJ* 20: 97-98.
1974   'The Beginning of the Hasmonean Coinage', *IEJ* 24: 59-61.
1975   *Nabataean Coins* (Qedem, 3; Jerusalem: The Hebrew University).
1979   'Sepphoris and Rome', in Mørkholm and Waggoner (eds.) 1979:
        159-71.
1981   'Again the Beginning of the Hasmonean Coinage', *INJ* 5: 11-16.
1984   'One Hundred Ninety Years of Tyrian Shekels', in Houghton *et al.*
        (eds.) 1984: 171-79.
1984–85 'The Coins of Caesarea Paneas', *INJ* 8: 37-58.
1985   *City-Coins of Eretz-Israel and the Decapolis in the Roman Period*
        (Jerusalem: The Israel Museum).
1989a   'The Mints of Ashdod and Ascalon during the Late Persian Period',
        EI 20: 287-91 (in Hebrew).
1989b   'The Coins of Masada', in Aviram *et al.* (eds.) 1989a: 71-132.
1990–91 'Ancient Jewish Coinage. Addendum I', *INJ* 11: 104-32.

Meshorer, Y., and S. Qedar
1991   *The Coinage of Samaria in the Fourth Century B.C.E.* (Jerusalem:
        Numismatic Fine Arts International).

Metzger, B.M.
1970   'Names for the Nameless in the New Testament', in P. Granfield
        and J.A. Jungmann (eds.), *Kyriakon: Festschrift Johannes Quasten*
        (Münster: Verlag Aschendorf): 79-99.

Meyer, A., and W. Bauer
1963   'The Relatives of Jesus', in E. Hennecke (ed.), *New Testament Apo-
        crypha*, I (ET R.McL. Wilson; London: SCM Press): 418-32.

Meyers, E.M.
1993   'Identifying Religious and Ethnic Groups through Archaeology', in
        Biran and Amiram (eds.) 1993: 738-45.

Meyers, E.M., C.L. Meyers, and E. Netzer
1986   'Sepphoris (Ornament of All Galilee)', *BA* 49: 4-19.

Meyshan, J.
1958–59 'The Disease of Agrippa I, King of Judaea', *HaRefuah* 56: 118-19 (in
        Hebrew).
1959   'The Symbols on the Coinage of Herod the Great and their Meaning',
        PEQ 91: 109-21.
1962   'A Hitherto Unknown Coin with the Portrait of King Agrippa II', *INB*
        1: 8-9.

1963   'An Unknown Portrait Coin of Agrippa I', *INJ* 1: 66-67.
1968   *Essays in Jewish Numismatics* (Numismatic Studies and Researches, 6; Jerusalem: Israel Numismatic Society).
Mildenberg, L.
1979   'Yehud: A Preliminary Study of the Provincial Coinage of Judea', in Mørkholm & Waggoner (eds.) 1979: 183-96.
1990   'Gaza Mint Authorities in Persian Times', *Transeuphratène* 2: 137-46.
1994   'On the Money Circulation in Palestine from Artaxerxes II till Ptolemy I. Preliminary Studies of the Local Coinage in the Fifth Persian Satrapy. Part 5', *Transeuphratène* 7: 63-71.
Milik, J.T., and J. Starcky
1975   'Inscriptions récemment découvertes à Pétra', *ADAJ* 20: 111-30.
Millar, F.G.B.
1967   *The Roman Empire and its Neighbours* (London: Weidenfeld and Nicolson).
1977   *The Emperor in the Roman World (31 B.C.–A.D. 337)* (London: Gerald Duckworth).
1978   'The Background to the Maccabean Revolution: Reflections on Martin Hengel's "Judaism and Hellenism"', *JJS* 29: 1-21.
1983   'The Phoenician Cities: A Case-Study of Hellenisation', *PCPS* 29: 55-71.
1987   'The Problem of Hellenistic Syria', in Kuhrt and Sherwin-White (eds.) 1987: 110-84.
1990a   'The Roman *Coloniae* of the Near East: a Study of Cultural Relations', in Solin and Kajava (eds.) 1990: 7-58.
1990b   'Reflections on the Trials of Jesus', in Davies and White (eds.) 1990: 355-81.
1993a   'Hagar, Ishmael, Josephus and the Origins of Islam', *JJS* 44: 23-45.
1993b   *The Roman Near East 31 BC–AD 337* (Cambridge, MA: Harvard University Press).
1994   'Review of D. Mendels, *Nationalism*', *SCI* 13: 201-203.
Miller, N.
1985   'Patriarchal Burial Site Explored for the First Time in 700 Years', *BARev* 11.3: 26-43.
Miller, S.S.
1984   *Studies in the History and Traditions of Sepphoris* (Leiden: Brill).
Milns, R.D.
1968   *Alexander the Great* (London: Robert Hale).
Milojcic, V., and D. Theocharis (eds.)
1976   *Demetrias I* (Bonn: Rudolf Habelt).
Mionnet, T.E.
1811   *Description de médailles antiques grecques et romaines*, V (Paris: Imprimerie de Testu).
1835   *Description de médailles antiques grecques et romaines*, Suppl. 7 (Paris: Imprimerie Royal).
1837   *Description de médailles antiques grecques et romaines*, Suppl. 8 (Paris: Imprimerie de Crapelet).

Mireaux, E.
1951   *La Reine Bérénice* (Paris: A. Michel).
Misgav, H.
1990   'Two Notes on the Ostraca from Horvat 'Uza', *IEJ* 40: 215-17.
Mitchell, S.
1993   *Anatolia: Land, Men and Gods in Asia Minor*, I–II (Oxford: Claren-
            don Press).
Mitchell, T.C.
1991   'The Babylonian Exile and the Restoration of the Jews in Palestine
            (586–c. 500 B.C.)', in *CAH* 3.2 (2nd edn): 410-60.
Mitford, T.B.
1980   'Cappadocia and Armenia Minor', in *ANRW* 2.7.2: 1169-228.
Mittwoch, A.
1955   'Tribute and Land Tax in Seleucid Judaea', *Bib* 36: 352-61.
Momigliano, A.
1934a   'Ricerche sull'organizzazione della Giudea sotto il dominio romano',
            ARSP (ser. 2): III, 183-221, 347-96.
1934b   'Herod of Judaea', in *CAH* 10: 316-39.
1934c   'Nero', in *CAH* 10: 702-42.
1979   'Flavius Josephus and Alexander's Visit to Jerusalem', *Athenaeum* 57:
            442-48.
1981   'Greek Culture and the Jews', in M.I. Finley (ed.), *The Legacy of
            Greece: A New Appraisal* (Oxford: Clarendon Press): 325-46.
Montgomery, J.A.
1907   *The Samaritans: The Earliest Jewish Sect* (New York: Ktav [repr. 1968]).
Mor, M.
1989   'Samaritan History: The Persian, Hellenistic and Hasmonaean Period',
            in A.D. Crown (ed.), *The Samaritans* (Tübingen: Mohr): 1-18.
Morelli, D.
1956   'Gli Stranieri in Rodi', *SCO* 5: 126-90.
Morgenstern, J.
1947   'The Chanukah Festival and the Calendar of Ancient Israel', *HUCA*
            20: 1-136.
1956   'Jerusalem 485 B.C.', *HUCA* 27: 101-79 (pt. 1).
Mørkholm, O.
1966   *Antiochus IV of Syria* (Classica et Mediaevalia, 8; Copenhagen:
            Gyldendalske Boghandel).
Mørkholm, O., and N.M. Waggoner (eds.)
1979   *Greek Numismatics and Archaeology: Essays in Honor of Margaret
            Thompson* (Wetteren: Numismatique Romaine).
Moscati, S.
1968   *The World of the Phoenicians* (ET A. Hamilton; London: Weidenfeld
            & Nicolson).
Moscati, S. (ed)
1988   *The Phoenicians* (Milan: Bompiani).
Moscovich, M.J.
1983   'Hostage Princes and Roman Imperialism in the Second Century
            B.C.', *EMC* 27: 297-309.

Moulton, W.J.
1915   'An Inscribed Tomb at Beit Jibrin', *AJA* 19: 63-70.

Moutèrde, R.
1925   'Inscriptions grecques conservées a l'Institut Français de Damas', *Syria* 6: 215-52.
1951–52   'Antiquités de l'Hermon et de la Beqâ'', *MUSJ* 29: 21-89.
1957   'Note sur une inscription monumentale de Nawa', *AAS* 7: 31-33.
1964   'Regards sur Beyrouth phénicienne, hellénistique et romaine', *MUSJ* 40: 145-90.

Moutèrde, R., and J. Lauffray
1952   *Beyrouth ville romaine: histoire et monuments* (Beirut: Publications de la Direction des Antiquités).

Murray, O.
1987   'The Letter of Aristeas', in B. Virgilio (ed.), *Studi Ellenistici II* (Pisa: Giardini): 15-29.

Mussies, G.
1990   'Marnas God of Gaza', in *ANRW* 2.18.4: 2412-57.
1994   'Jewish Personal Names in Some Non-Literary Sources', in J.W. van Henten and P.W. van der Horst (eds.), *Studies in Early Epigraphy* (Leiden: Brill): 242-76.

Myers, J.M.
1971   'Edom and Judah in the Sixth and Fifth Centuries B.C.', in Goedicke (ed.) 1971: 377-92.

Na'aman, N.
1979   'The Brook of Egypt and Assyrian Policy on the Border of Egypt', *TA* 6: 68-90.

Naveh, J.
1966   'The Scripts of Two Ostraca from Elath', *BASOR* 183: 27-30.
1971a   'Hebrew Texts in Aramaic Script in the Persian Period?', *BASOR* 203: 27-32.
1971b   'An Aramaic Ostracon from Ashdod', in M. Dothan, *et al*. 1971: 200-201.
1973   'The Aramaic Ostraca', in Aharoni (ed.) 1973: 79-82.
1975   'An Aramaic Inscription from el-Mal—A Survival of "Seleucid Aramaic" Script', *IEJ* 25: 117-23.
1976   'A New Tomb-Inscription from Giv'at Hamivtar', in Yadin (ed.) 1976: 73-74.
1979   'The Aramaic Ostraca from Tel Beer-Sheba (Seasons 1971–1976)', *TA* 6: 182-98.
1981   'The Aramaic Ostraca from Tel Arad', in Aharoni (ed.) 1981: 153-76.
1982   *Early History of the Alphabet: An Introduction to West Semitic Epigraphy and Palaeography* (Jerusalem: Magnes Press).
1985a   'Writing and Scripts in Seventh-Century B.C.E. Philistia: The New Evidence from Tell Jemmeh', *IEJ* 35: 8-21.
1985b   'Published and Unpublished Aramaic Ostraca', *'Atiqot* 17: 114-21.
1987   'Unpublished Phoenician Inscriptions from Palestine', *IEJ* 37: 25-30.
1992a   'Aramaic Ostraca and Jar Inscriptions from Tell Jemmeh', *'Atiqot* 21: 49-53.

1992b	'The Numbers of Bat in the Arad Ostraca', *IEJ* 42: 52-54.

Negbi, O.

1964	'A Contribution of Mineralogy and Palaeontology to an Archaeological Study of Terracottas', *IEJ* 14: 187-89.
1992	'Early Phoenician Presence in the Mediterranean Islands: A Reappraisal', *AJA* 96: 599-615.

Negev, A.

1961	'Nabatean Inscriptions from 'Avdat (Oboda)', *IEJ* 11: 127-38.
1976a	'The Early Beginnings of the Nabataean Realm', *PEQ* 108: 125-33.
1976b	'Eboda', in *EAEHL*: II, 345-55.
1978	'The Nabataeans and the Provincia Arabia', in *ANRW* 2.8: 520-686.
1981	*The Greek Inscriptions from the Negev* (Collectio Minor, 25; Jerusalem: Studium Biblicum Franciscanum).
1986a	*Nabataean Archaeology Today* (New York: University Press).
1986b	'Obodas the God', *IEJ* 36: 56-60.
1988	'Understanding the Nabateans', *BARev* 14.6: 26-45.
1991a	'The Temple of Obodas: Excavations at Oboda in July 1989', *IEJ* 41: 62-80.
1991b	*Personal Names in the Nabatean Realm* (Qedem, 32; Jerusalem: The Hebrew University).

Netzer, E.

1975	'The Hasmonean and Herodian Winter Palaces at Jericho', *IEJ* 25: 89-100.
1977	'The Winter Palaces of the Judean Kings at Jericho at the End of the Second Temple Period', *BASOR* 228: 1-13.
1980	'The Hippodrome Built by Herod at Jericho', *Qadmoniot* 51–2: 104-107 (in Hebrew).
1981	'Herod's Building Projects: State Necessity or Personal Need?', in *JC* 1: 48-61, 73-80.
1987a	'Herod the Great's Contribution to Nicopolis in the Light of his Building Activity in Judea', in E. Chrysos (ed.), *Nicopolis 1* (Preveza: Dēmos): 121-28.
1987b	'The Augusteum at Sebaste-Samaria: A New Outlook', *EI* 19: 97-105* (in Hebrew).
1993	'The Hasmonean Palaces in Eretz-Israel', in Biran and Amiram (eds.) 1993: 126-36.

Neusner, J.

1964a	'The Conversion of Adiabene to Judaism', *JBL* 83: 60-66.
1964b	'The Jews in Pagan Armenia', *JAOS* 84: 230-40.
1970	*A Life of Yohanan ben Zakkai, ca. 1–80 C.E.* (Leiden: Brill).
1971	*Rabbinic Traditions about the Pharisees before 70*, I–III (Leiden: Brill).
1976	'The Jews East of the Euphrates and the Roman Empire. I. 1st–3rd Centuries A.D.', *ANRW* 2.9.1: 46-69.
1987	'Josephus' Pharisees: A Complete Repertoire', in Feldman and Hata (eds.) 1987: 274-92.

Neusner, J., and A.J. Avery-Peck
1982   'The Quest for the Historical Hillel: Theory and Practice', in J. Neusner (ed.), *Formative Judaism: Religious, Historical, and Literary Studies* (BJS, 37; Atlanta, GA: Scholars Press): 45-63.

Newell, E.T.
1937   *Royal Greek Portrait Coins* (New York: Wayte Raymond).

Nicklin, T.
1950   *Gospel Gleanings* (London: Longmans).

Nicolaou, I.
1986   'Cypriots in the East and West: Foreigners in Cyprus', in V. Karageorghis (ed.), *Cyprus Between the Orient and the Occident* (Nicosia: Department of Antiquities of Cyprus): 423-38.

Nicols, J.
1975   'Antonia and Sejanus', *Historia* 24: 48-58.

Niemeyer, H.G. (ed.)
1982   *Phönizier im Westen* (Madrider Beiträge, 8; Madrid: Deutsches Archäologisches Institut).

Nikiprowetzky, V.
1989   'Josephus and the Revolutionary Parties', in Feldman and Hata (eds.), 1989: 216-36.

Noth, M.
1956   *Geschichte Israels* (Göttingen: Vandenhoeck & Ruprecht).

Oakeshott, M.F.
1983   'The Edomite Pottery' in J.F.A. Sawyer and D.J.A. Clines (eds.), *Midian, Moab and Edom* (JSOTSup, 24; Sheffield: Sheffield Academic Press): 53-63.

Obbink, D.
1991   'Bilingual Literacy and Syrian Greek', *BASP* 28: 51-57.

Oded, B.
1979   *Mass Deportations and Deportees in the Neo-Assurian Empire* (Wiesbaden: Ludwig Richert Verlag).

Oden, R.A.
1976   *Studies in Lucian's De Syria Dea* (Atlanta, GA: Scholars Press).

Oestreicher, B.
1962   'A Contemporary Picture of Caesarea's Ancient Harbour', *INB* 2: 44-47.

Ofer, A.
1986   'Tell Rumeideh (Hebron)—1985', *ESI* 5: 92-93 [publ. 1987].
1993   'Hebron', in *NEAEHL*: II, 606-609.

Offord, J.
1919   'A Nabataean Inscription Concerning Philip, Tetrarch of Auranitis', *PEFQS*: 82-85.

Oppenheimer, A., B. Isaac, and M. Lecker
1983   *Babylonia Judaica in the Talmudic Period* (Beihilfe zum Tübingen Atlas des Vorderasien Orients, Reihe B 47; Wiesbaden: L. Reichert).
1988   'Jewish Lydda in the Roman Era', *HUCA* 59: 115-36.

Oren, E.D.
1965   'The Caves of the Palestinian Shephelah', *Archaeology* 18: 218-24.

1968 'The "Herodian Doves" in the Light of Recent Archaeological Discoveries', *PEQ* 100: 54-61.

1982 'Ziglag—A Biblical City on the Edge of the Negev', *BA* 45: 155-66.

Oren, E.D., and U. Rappaport

1984 'The Necropolis of Maresha—Beth Govrin', *IEJ* 34: 114-53.

Østergård, U.

1992 'What is National and Ethnic Identity?', in P. Bilde *et al.* (eds.), *Ethnicity in Hellenistic Egypt* (Studies in Hellenistic Civilization, 3; Aarhus: Aarhus University Press): 16-38.

Otto, W.

1913 *Herodes* (Stuttgart: J.B. Metzler).

Palmer, E.H., and J.E. Sandys

1872 'Athenian Bilingual Inscription', *JP* 4: 48-54.

Paltiel, E.

1981 'War in Judaea: After Herod's Death', *RBPH* 59: 107-36.

1991 *Vassals and Rebels in the Roman Empire: Julio-Claudian Policies in Judaea and the Kingdoms of the East* (Collection Latomus, 212; Brussels: Latomus).

Pani, M.

1970 'Archelao II e la fine della dinastia dei Teucridi di Olba', *Athenaeum* 48: 327-34.

1972 *Roma e i Re d'Oriente da Augusto a Tiberio (Cappadocia, Armenia, Media Attropatene)* (Bari: Adriatica Editrice).

Papachatzes, N.D.

1974 Παυσανίου Ἑλλάδος Περιήγησις: Ἀττικά (Athens: Ekdotikê).

Parassoglou, G.M.

1978 *Imperial Estates in Egypt* (American Studies in Papyrology, 18; Amsterdam: A.M. Hakkert).

Parente, F.

1984–85 'Flavius Josephus' Account of the Anti-Roman Riots Preceding the 66–70 War, and its Relevance for the Reconstruction of Jewish Eschatology during the First Century A.D.', *JANES* 16–7: 183-205.

1994 'Onias III's Death and the Founding of the Temple of Leontopolis', in Parente and Sievers (eds.) 1994: 69-98.

Parente, F., and J. Sievers (eds.)

1994 *Josephus and the History of the Greco-Roman Period: Essays in Memory of Morton Smith* (SPB, 41; Leiden: Brill).

Parker, P.

1960 'John and John Mark', *JBL* 79: 97-110.

Parker, R.E.

1933 'The Reputation of Herod in Early English Literature', *Speculum* 8: 59-67.

Parker, S.T.

1986 *Romans and Saracens: A History of the Arabian Frontier* (ASOR Dissertation Series, 6; Winona Lake, IN: Eisenbrauns).

Parr, P.J.

1965 'The Beginnings of Hellenisation at Petra', in *VIIIe Congrès International d'Archéologie Classique 1963* (Paris: de Boccard): 527-33.

1968–69	'The Nabataeans and North-West Arabia', *BIA* 8–9: 250-53.
1970	'A Sequence of Pottery from Petra', in J.A. Sanders (ed.), *Essays in Honor of Nelson Glueck: Near Eastern Archaeology in the Twentieth Century* (Garden City, NY: Doubleday): 348-81.
1978	'Pottery, People and Politics', in R. Moorey and P. Parr (eds.), *Archaeology in the Levant: Essays for Kathleen Kenyon* (Warminster: Aris & Phillips): 203-209.

Patrich, J.
1982	'A Sadducean Halakha and the Jerusalem Aqueduct', in *JC* 2: 25-39.
1988	'Reconstructing the Magnificent Temple Herod Built', *BR* 4.5: 16-29.
1990	*The Formation of Nabatean Art: Prohibition of a Graven Image among the Nabateans* (Jerusalem: Magnes Press).
1994	'The Structure of the Second Temple: A New Reconstruction', in Geva (ed.) 1994: 260-71.

Paul, G.M.
1990	'Josephus the *Epitome de Caesaribus* and the Grain-Supply of Rome', *AHB* 4.4: 79-83.

Peckham, J.B.
1968	*The Development of the Late Phoenician Scripts* (Cambridge, MA: Harvard University Press).

Peng-Yoke, H.
1962	'Ancient and Mediaeval Observations of Comets and Novae in Chinese Sources', *Vistas in Astronomy* 5: 127-225.

Peters, F.E.
1977	'The Nabateans in the Hawran', *JAOS* 97: 263-77.
1978	'Romans and Bedouin in Southern Syria', *JNES* 37: 315-26.
1983	'City Planning in Greco-Roman Syria', *DaM* 1: 269-77.

Peters, J.P., and H. Thiersch
1905	*Painted Tombs in the Necropolis of Marissa (Marêshah)* (London: PEF).

Petersen, H.
1958	'Real and Alleged Literary Projects of Josephus', *AJP* 79: 259-74.

Pfeiffer, R.H.
1926	'Edomitic Wisdom', *ZAW* 44: 13-25.

Pflaum, H.G.
1960–61	*Les carrières procuratoriennes*, I (Paris: Librairie Orientaliste Paul Geuthner).

Phythian-Adams, W.J.
1921	'History of Askalon', *PEFQS*: 76-90.

Piattelli, D.
1990	'The Jericho Inscription Concerning Theodotos, Apeleutheros of the Empress Agrippina', in Kasher *et al.* (eds.) 1990: 75-83.

Pittakes, K.S.
1835	*L'ancienne athènes, ou la description des antiquités d'Athènes et de ses environs* (Athens: M.E. Antoniades).

Pixner, B.
1985	'Searching for the New Testament Site of Bethsaida', *BA* 48: 207-16.

Polotsky, H.J.
1962	'The Greek Papyri from the Cave of the Letters', *IEJ* 12: 258-62.

Pope, H.
1947   *Foreigners in Attic Inscriptions* (Philadelphia, PA: The Jewish Publica-
            tion Society Press).
Porten, B.
1968   *Archives from Elephantine: The Life of an Ancient Jewish Military
            Colony* (Berkeley, CA: University of California Press).
1981   'The Identity of King Adon', *BA* 44: 36-52.
Poulsen, V.H.
1960   *Claudische Prinzen: Studien zur Ikonographie des ersten Römischen
            Kaiserhauses* (Baden-Baden: B. Grimm).
Préaux, C.
1978   *Le monde hellénistique*, I–II (Paris: Presses Universitaires de France).
Premerstein, A. von
1932   'Das Datum des Prozesses des Isidoros in den sogenannten heid-
            nischen Märtyrerakten', *Hermes* 67: 174-96.
Prentice, W.K.
1908   *An American Archaeological Expedition to Syria 1899–1900.* III.
            Greek and Latin Inscriptions (New York: Century).
1922   *The Princeton University Archaeological Expeditions to Syria in
            1904–5 and 1909. III.B. Greek and Latin Inscriptions, Northern Syria*
            (Leiden: Brill).
Price, J.J.
1991   'The Enigma of Philip ben Jakimos', *Historia* 40: 77-94.
1992   *Jerusalem under Siege: The Collapse of the Jewish State 66–70 C.E.*
            (Jewish Studies, 3; Leiden: Brill).
Pritz, R.A.
1988   *Nazarene Jewish Christianity* (Leiden: Brill).
Puchstein, O., D. Krencker, B. Schulz, and H. Kohl
1902   'Zweiter Jahresbericht über die Ausgrabungen in Baalbek', *JDAI* 17:
            87-124.
Puech, E.
1983   'Inscriptions funéraires palestiniennes: Tombeau de Jason et ossu-
            aires', *RB* 90: 481-583.
Pummer, R.
1982   'Antisamaritanische Polemik in jüdischen Schriften aus der intertesta-
            mentarischen Zeit', *BZ* 26: 224-42.
Qedar, S.
1986–87   'Two Lead Weights of Herod Antipas and Agrippa II and the Early
            History of Tiberias', *INJ* 9: 29-35.
1989   'A Coin of Agrippa II Commemorating the Roman Victory over the
            Jews', *SM* 39: 33-36.
Quinn, J. D.
1961   'Alcaeus 48 (B16) and the Fall of Ascalon, 604 B.C.', *BASOR* 164:
            19-20.
Raban, A.
1989   *The Harbours of Caesarea. I. The Site and Excavations* (BAR Interna-
            tional Series, 491; Oxford: BAR).

Rabinowitz, I.
1956   'Aramaic Inscriptions of the Fifth Century B.C.E. from a North-Arab
            Shrine in Egypt', *JNES* 15: 1-9.
1959   'Another Aramaic Record of the North-Arabian Goddess Han-'Ilat',
            JNES 18: 154-55.
Rahmani, L.Y.
1971   'Silver Coins of the Fourth Century B.C. from Tel Gamma', *IEJ* 21:
            158-60.
Rainey, A.F.
1969   'The Satrapy "Beyond the River" ', *AJBA* 1: 51-78.
1980   'The Administrative Division of the Shephelah', *TA* 7: 194-202.
1982   'Wine from the Royal Vineyards', *BASOR* 245: 57-62.
1983   'The Biblical Shephelah of Judah', *BASOR* 251: 1-22.
Rajak, T.
1973   'Justus of Tiberias', *ClQ* 23: 345-68.
1983   *Josephus: The Historian and his Society* (London: Gerald Duckworth).
1987   'Josephus and Justus of Tiberias', in Feldman and Hata (eds.) 1987:
            81-94.
1990   'The Hasmoneans and the Uses of Hellenism', in Davies and White
            (eds.) 1990: 261-80.
1991   'Friends, Romans, Subjects: Agrippa II's Speech in Josephus' *Jewish
            War*', in L. Alexander (ed.), *Images of Empire* (JSOTSup, 122; Shef-
            field: Sheffield Academic Press): 122-34.
1994   'The Jews under the Hasmonean Rule', in *CAH* 9 (2nd edn): 274-309.
Ramage, E.S.
1987   *The Nature and Purpose of Augustus' Res Gestae* (Historia, Einzel-
            schriften, 54; Stuttgart: Franz Steiner).
Ramsay, W.M.
1893   *The Church in the Roman Empire before A.D. 170* (London: Putnam's
            Sons).
Rapaport *see* Rappaport.
Rappaport, U.
1969   'Les Iduméens en Egypte', *RP* 43: 73-82.
1970   'Gaza and Ascalon in the Persian and Hellenistic Periods in Relation to
            their Coins', *IEJ* 20: 75-80.
1981a   'The First Judean Coinage', *JJS* 32: 1-17.
1981b   'Ascalon and the Coinage of Judea', *PdP* 36: 353-66.
1981c   'Jewish–Pagan Relations and the Revolt against Rome in 66–70 C.E.',
            in *JC* 1: 81-95.
1983   'John of Gischala in Galilee', in *JC* 3: 46-57.
1994   'Where was Josephus Lying—in his *Vita* or in the *War*?', in Parente
            and Sievers (eds.) 1994: 279-89.
Rappaport, U., J. Pastor, and O. Rimon
1994   'Land, Society and Culture in Judaea', *Transeuphratène* 7: 73-82.
Rast, W.E.
1981   'An Ostracon', in N.L. Lapp (ed.), *The Third Campaign at Tell el-Fûl:
            The Excavations of 1964* (AASOR, 45; Cambridge, MA: ASOR): 113-
            15.

Bibliography 449

Rathbone, D.W.
1986 'The Dates of the Recognition in Egypt of the Emperors from Cara-
calla to Diocletianus', *ZPE* 62: 101-31.
Rawlinson, G.
1881 *The Religions of the Ancient World* (New Delhi: Award Publishing
House [repr. 1980]).
1889 *History of Phoenicia* (London: Longmans, Green and Co.).
Rees, W.
1951 'Archelaus, Son of Herod', *Scripture* 4: 348-55.
Reich, R.
1990 'The "Boundary of Gezer" Inscriptions Again', *IEJ* 40: 44-46.
1992 'Caiaphas Name Inscribed on Bone Boxes', *BARev* 18.5: 38-44, 76.
1994 'Ossuary Inscriptions of the Caiaphas Family from Jerusalem', in
Geva (ed.) 1994: 223-25.
Reifenberg, A.
1935 'Portrait Coins of the Herodian Kings', *NCir* 43: 169-76.
1950 *Ancient Hebrew Arts* (New York: Schocken Books).
1953 *Israel's History in Coins* (London: East and West Library).
Reinach, T.
1914 'Le mari de Salomé et les monnaies de Nicopolis d'Arménie', *REA*
16: 133-58.
Reinhold, M.
1933 *Marcus Agrippa* (Geneva and New York: W.F. Humphrey Press).
Reisner, G.A., C.S. Fisher, and A.G. Lyon
1924 *Harvard Excavations at Samaria 1908 to 1910*, I–II (Cambridge, MA:
Harvard University Press).
Rémy, B.
1976–77 '*Ornati* et *ornamenta quaestoria, praetoria* et *consularia* sous le Haut-
Empire romain', *REA* 78–9: 160-98.
Rey-Coquais, J.-P.
1973 'Inscriptions grecques d'Apamée', *AAS* 23: 39-84.
1977 'Inscriptions grecques et latines découvertes dans les fouilles de Tyr
(1963–1974): Inscriptions de la Nécropole', *BMB* 29 (whole volume).
1978 'Inscription grecque découverte a Ras ibn Hani: Stèle de mercenaires
lagides sur la cote syrienne', *Syria* 55: 313-25.
1989 'Apport d'inscriptions inédites de Syrie et de Phénicie aux listes
de divinités ou à la prosopographie de l'Egypte hellénistique ou
romaine', in L. Criscuolo and G. Geraci (eds.), *Egitto e Storia Antica
dell'Ellenismo età Araba: bilancio di un confronto* (Bologna: Clueb):
609-19.
Rhoads, D.M.
1976 *Israel in Revolution 6–74 C.E.* (Philadelphia, PA: Fortress Press).
Ribichini, S.
1988 'Beliefs and Religious Life', in S. Moscati (ed.), *The Phoenicians*
(Milan: Bompiani): 104-25.
Richardson, P.
1986 'Law and Piety in Herod's Architecture', *SR* 15: 347-60.

1877   'Inscriptions grecques provenant du recueil de Cyriaque d'Ancone',
              BCH 1: 286-94.
Ritmeyer, K., and L. Ritmeyer
1989   'Reconstructing Herod's Temple Mount in Jerusalem', *BARev* 15.6:
              23-42.
Ritmeyer, L.
1992.   'Locating the Original Temple Mount', *BARev* 18.2: 24-45, 64-65.
Rivkin, E.
1978   *A Hidden Revolution* (Nashville, TN: Abingdon Press).
Robert, L.
1925   'Inscription grecque de Sidon', *Syria* 6: 365-66.
1938   *Etudes Epigraphiques et Philologiques* (Paris: Champion).
Robinson, J.A.T.
1976   *Redating the New Testament* (London: SCM Press).
Robinson, S.E.
1985   '4 Baruch', in *OTP* 2: 413-25.
Roddaz, J.-M.
1984   *Marcus Agrippa* (Rome: Ecole Française).
Rogers, P.M.
1980   'Titus, Berenice and Mucianus', *Historia* 29: 86-95.
Rogers, R.S.
1953   'The Neronian Comets', *TAPA* 84: 237-49.
Roller, D.W.
1983   'The Problem of the Location of Straton's Tower', *BASOR* 252: 61-66.
1992   'Straton's Tower: Some Additional Thoughts', in R. Lindley Vann
              (ed.), *Caesarea Papers: Straton's Tower, Herod's Harbour, and Roman
              and Byzantine Caesarea* (JRASup, 5; Ann Arbor, MI: University of
              Michigan): 23-25.
Romer, F.E.
1978   'A Numismatic Date for the Departure of C. Caesar?', *TAPA* 108:
              187-202.
1979   'Gaius Caesar's Military Diplomacy in the East', *TAPA* 109: 199-214.
Ronen, I.
1988   'Formation of Jewish Nationalism among the Idumaeans', in Kasher
              1988: 214-39.
Roos, A.G.
1941   'Die Quirinius-Inschrift', *Mnemosyne* 9: 306-18.
Rose, D.G., and L.E. Toombs
1976   'Tell el-Ḥesi, 1973 and 1975', *PEQ* 108: 41-54.
Rosenbloom, J.R.
1978   *Conversion to Judaism: From the Biblical Period to the Present*
              (Cincinnati, OH: Hebrew Union College Press).
Rosenfeld, B.-Z.
1988   'The "Boundary of Gezer" Inscriptions and the History of Gezer at
              the End of the Second Temple Period', *IEJ* 38: 235-45.
Rostovtzeff, M.
1941   *The Social and Economic History of the Hellenistic World*, I–III
              (Oxford: Clarendon Press).

| 1957 | *The Social and Economic History of the Roman Empire* (rev. P.M. Fraser; Oxford: Oxford University Press, 2nd edn). |

Roth, C.
1962   'The Year-Reckoning of the Coins of the First Revolt', *NC* 2: 91-100.

Roth, M.T.
1987   'Age at Marriage and the Household: A Study of Neo-Babylonian and Neo-Assyrian Forms', *CSSH* 29: 715-47.

Rothenberg, B., and J. Glass
1983   'The Midianite Pottery', in J.F.A. Sawyer and D.J.A. Clines (eds.), *Midian, Moab and Edom* (JSOTSup, 24; Sheffield: Sheffield Academic Press): 65-124.

Roussel, P.
1933   'Epitaphe de Gaza commémorant deux officiers de la garrison ptolémaïque', *Aegyptus* 13: 145-51.
1987   *Délos Colonie Athénienne* (repr.; Paris: de Boccard).

Rowe, A.
1930   *The Topography and History of Beth-Shan*, I (Philadelphia, PA: Pennsylvania Museum University Press).

Rowley, H.H.
1940   'The Herodians in the Gospels', *JTS* 41: 14-27.

Roxan, M.M.
1991   'Greek and Latin Documents from Masada', *CR* 41: 458-59.

Safrai, Z.
1994   *The Economy of Roman Palestine* (London: Routledge).

Saller, R.P.
1987   'Men's Age at Marriage and its Consequences in the Roman Family', *CP* 82: 21-34.

Sandars, N.K.
1985   *The Sea Peoples: Warriors of the Ancient Mediterranean* (London: Thames & Hudson, 2nd edn).

Sanders, E.P.
1985   *Jesus and Judaism* (London: SCM Press).
1992   *Judaism: Practice and Belief 63 BCE–66 CE* (London: SCM Press).
1993   *The Historical Figure of Jesus* (London: Allen Lane, Penguin Press).

Sandison, A.T.
1967   'The Last Illness of Herod the Great, King of Judaea', *MH* 11.4: 381-88.

Sartre, M.
1981   'Le territoire de Canatha', *Syria* 58: 343- 57.

Saulcy, F. de
1869–70 'Note sur quelques monnaies d'Ascalon, frappées pendant le règne d'Hérode, puis par Salomé sa soeur, et par Archelaüs', *AN* 3.2: 253-58.
1874   *Numismatique de la Terre Sainte* (Paris: J. Rothschild).

Saulnier, C.
1984   'Hérode Antipas et Jean le Baptiste: Quelques remarques sur les confusions chronologiques de Flavius Josèphe', *RB* 91: 362-76.

Saumagne, C.
1966   'Saint Paul et Félix, procurateur de Judée', in R. Chevallier (ed.),
             Mélanges d'Archéologie et d'Histoire offerts à André Piganiol, III
             (Paris: S.E.V. P.E.N.): 1373-86.

Schalit, A.
1933   'Josephus und Justus', *Klio* 26: 67-95.
1954   'ΚΟΙΛΗ ΣΥΡΙΑ from the Mid-Fourth Century to the Beginning of the
             Third Century B.C.', *SH* 1: 64-77.
1962   'Die frühchristliche Überlieferung über die Herkunft der Familie des
             Herodes', *ASTI* 1: 109-60.
1967-68   'Die "Herodianischen" Patriarchen und der "Davidische" Herodes',
             ASTI 6: 114-23.
1969   *König Herodes: Der Mann und sein Werk* (Berlin: de Gruyter).

Scharlemann, M.H.
1968   *Stephen: A Singular Saint* (AnBib, 34; Rome: Pontifical Biblical
             Institute).

Schenk, W.
1983   'Gefangenschaft und Tod des Täufers: Erwägungen zur Chronologie
             und ihren Konsequenzen', *NTS* 29: 453-83.

Schiffman, L.H.
1987   'The Conversion of the Royal House of Adiabene in Josephus and
             Rabbinic Sources', in Feldman and Hata (eds.) 1987: 293-312.

Schillinger-Häfele, U.
1986   *Consules, Augusti, Caesares: Datierung von römischen Inschriften und
             Münzen* (Stuttgart: Limesmuseums Aalen).

Schmitt, G.
1982   'Zum Königreich Chalcis', *ZDPV* 98: 110-24.

Schmitt-Korte, K.
1990   'Nabataean Coinage—Part II: New Coin Types and Variants', *NC* 150:
             105-33.

Schmitt-Korte, K., and M.J. Price
1994   'Nabataean Coinage—Part III: The Nabataean Monetary System', *NC*
             154: 67-131.

Schottroff, W.
1982   'Die Ituräer', *ZDPV* 98: 125-52.

Schove, D.J.
1984   *Chronology of Eclipses and Comets AD 1–1000* (Suffolk: The Boydell
             Press).

Schumacher, G.
1886   *Across the Jordan* (London: PEF).

Schürer, E.
1890   *A History of the Jewish People in the Time of Jesus Christ*, I
             (Edinburgh: T. & T. Clark).

Schwabe, M., and B. Lifshitz
1974   *Beth She'arim II: The Greek Inscriptions* (New Brunswick, NJ: Rutgers
             University Press).

Schwartz, D.R.
1982   'KATA TOYTON TON KAIPON: Josephus' Source on Agrippa II',
            JQR 72: 241-68.
1983   'Josephus and Nicolaus on the Pharisees', *JSJ* 14: 157-71.
1983–84   'Josephus on the Jewish Constitutions and Community', *SCI* 7: 30-52.
1990   *Agrippa I: The Last King of Judaea* (TSAJ, 23; Tübingen: Mohr).
1992   *Studies in the Jewish Background of Christianity* (WUNT, 60; Tübin-
            gen: Mohr).
1994   'Josephus on Hyrcanus II', in Parente and Sievers (eds.) 1994: 210-
            32.
Schwartz, J.
1962   'Note complémentaire', *IEJ* 12: 135-36.
1990   'Once More on the "Boundary of Gezer" Inscriptions and the His-
            tory of Gezer and Lydda at the End of the Second Temple Period',
            IEJ 40: 47-57.
Schwartz, S.
1986   'The Composition and Publication of Josephus's "Bellum Iudaicum"
            Book 7', *HTR* 79: 373-86.
1990   *Josephus and Judaean Politics* (Columbia Studies in the Classical
            Tradition 18; Leiden: Brill).
1991   'Israel and the Nations Roundabout: 1 Maccabees and the Hasmonean
            Expansion', *JJS* 42: 16-38.
1993   'John Hyrcanus I's Destruction of the Gerizim Temple and Judaean–
            Samaritan Relations', *JH* 7: 9-25.
1994   'On the Autonomy of Judaea in the Fourth and Third Centuries
            B.C.E.', *JJS* 45: 157-68.
Sear, D.R.
1982   *Greek Imperial Coins and their Values: The Local Coinages of the
            Roman Empire* (London: Seaby).
Seeligmann, I.L.
1948   *The LXX Version of Isaiah: A Discussion of its Problems* (Leiden:
            Brill).
Segal, A.
1978   *The Hippodamic and the Planned City* (Beer-sheva: Bun-Gurion Uni-
            versity).
1989   'Theatres in Ancient Palestine during the Roman-Byzantine Period',
            SCI 8–9: 145-65.
Segal, P.
1989   'The Penalty of the Warning Inscription from the Temple of
            Jerusalem', *IEJ* 39: 79-84.
Sellers, O.R.
1933   *The Citadel of Beth-Zur* (Philadelphia, PA: Westminster Press).
Sellwood, D.
1980   *An Introduction to the Coinage of Parthia* (London: Spink, 2nd edn).
Sevenster, J.N.
1968   *Do You Know Greek?: How Much Greek could the First Jewish Christ-
            ians have Known?* (NovTSup, 19; Leiden: Brill).

Seyrig, H.
1955   'Remarques sur les monnaies des Artaxiades', *RN* 17: 111-22.
1965   'Un Officier d'Agrippa II', *Syria* 42: 31-34.
1968   'Seleucus I and the Foundation of Hellenistic Syria', in W.A. Ward (ed.), *The Role of the Phoenicians in the Interaction of Mediterranean Civilization* (Beirut: The American University): 53-63.
1970   'L'inscription du tétrarque Lysanias à Baalbek', in A. Kuschke and E. Kutsch (eds.), *Archäologie und Altes Testament: Festschrift für Kurt Galling* (Tübingen: Mohr): 251-54.
1971   'Le monneyage de Hiérapolis de Syria à l'époque d'Alexandre', *RN* 13: 11-21.
1985   *Scripta Varia, Mélanges d'archaéologie et d'histoire* (Bibliotèque archéologique et historique, 125; Paris: Librairie Orientaliste Paul Geuthner).

Shahîd, I.
1984   *Rome and the Arabs: A Prolegomenon to the Study of Byzantium and the Arabs* (Washington, DC: Dumbarton Oaks).

Shatzman, I.
1991   *The Armies of the Hasmonaeans and Herod* (TJAJ, 25; Tübingen: Mohr).
1994   'The Limits of Empire: Review Article', *IEJ* 44: 129-35.

Shaw, B.D.
1984   'Close-Kin Marriage in Roman Society?', *Man* 19: 432-44.
1987   'The Age of Roman Girls at Marriage: Some Reconsiderations', *JRS* 77: 30-46.

Sherk, R.K.
1980   'Roman Galatia: The Governors from 25 B.C. to A.D. 114', in *ANRW* 2.7.2: 954-1052.
1984   *Rome and the Greek East to the Death of Augustus* (Translated Documents of Greece and Rome, 4; Cambridge: Cambridge University Press).

Sherwin-White, S.M.
1976   'A Note on Three Coan Inscriptions', *ZPE* 21: 183-88.
1978   *Ancient Cos* (Hypomnemata, 51; Göttingen: Vandenhoeck & Ruprecht).

Sherwin-White, S.M., and A. Kuhrt
1993   *From Samarkand to Sardis: A New Approach to the Seleucid Empire* (London: Gerald Duckworth).

Short A.R.
1953   *The Bible and Modern Medicine* (London: Paternoster Press).

Shutt, R.J.H.
1985   'Letter of Aristeas', in *OTP* 2: 7-34.

Sievers, J.
1989   'The Role of Women in the Hasmonaean Dynasty', in Feldman and Hata (eds.) 1989: 132-46.
1990   *The Hasmoneans and their Supporters: From Mattathias to the Death of John Hyrcanus I* (Atlanta, GA: Scholars Press).

Simons, J.
1952   *Jerusalem in the Old Testament, Researches and Theories* (Leiden: Brill).
Sivan, R., and G. Solar
1994   'Excavations in the Jerusalem Citadel, 1980–1988', in Geva (ed.) 1994: 168-76.
Skaist, A.
1978   'A Note on the Bilingual Ostracon from Khirbet el-Kôm', *IEJ* 28: 106-108.
Small, D.B.
1987   'Late Hellenistic Baths in Palestine', *BASOR* 266: 59-74.
Smallwood, E.M.
1956   'Domitian's Attitude toward the Jews and Judaism', *CP* 51: 1-13.
1957   'The Chronology of Gaius' Attempt to Desecrate the Temple', *Latomus* 16: 3-17.
1962   'High Priests and Politics in Roman Palestine', *JTS* 13: 14-34.
1967a   'Gabinius' Organisation of Palestine', *JJS* 18: 89-92.
1967b   *Documents Illustrating the Principates of Gaius, Claudius and Nero* (Cambridge: Cambridge University Press).
1970   *Philonis Alexandrini Legatio ad Gaium* (Leiden: Brill).
1976   *The Jews under Roman Rule* (Leiden: Brill).
Smith, G.A.
1935   *The Historical Geography of the Holy Land* (London: Hodder & Stoughton, 26th edn).
Smith, J.Z.
1980   'Fences and Neighbors: Some Contours of Early Judaism', in W.S. Green (ed.), *Approaches to Ancient Judaism*, II (Chico, CA: Scholars Press): 1- 25.
Smith, M.
1971   *Palestinian Parties and Politics that Shaped the Old Testament* (New York: Columbia University Press).
1978   'Rome and Maccabean Conversions: Notes on 1 Macc. 8', in E. Bammel *et al.* (eds.), *Donum Gentilicium* (Festschrift D. Daube; Oxford: Clarendon Press): 1-7.
Smith, R.H.
1990   'The Southern Levant in the Hellenistic Period', *Levant* 22: 123-30.
Snyder, W.F.
1940   'Public Anniversaries in the Roman Empire', *YCS* 7: 223-317.
Soards, M.L.
1985   'Tradition, Composition, and Theology in Luke's Account of Jesus Before Herod Antipas', *Bib* 66: 344-63.
Soggin, J.A.
1984   *A History of Israel* (London: SCM Press).
1989   *Introduction to the Old Testament* (London: SCM Press, 3rd edn).
Solin, H., and M. Kajava (eds.)
1990   *Roman Eastern Policy and Other Studies in Roman History* (Commentationes Humanarum Litterarum, 91; Helsinki: Societas Scientiarum Fennica).

Sordi, M.
1983   *The Christians and the Roman Empire* (ET A. Bedini; London and Sydney: Croom Helm).

Spaer, A.
1977   'Some More "Yehud" Coins', *IEJ* 27: 200-203.
1984   'Ascalon: From Royal Mint to Autonomy', in Houghton *et al.* (eds.) 1984: 229-39.
1986–87   'Jaddua the High Priest?', *INJ* 9: 1-3.

Speidel, M.P.
1982–83   'The Roman Army in Judaea under the Procurators', *AS* 13–4: 233-40.

Sperber, D.
1974   *Roman Palestine, 200–400: Money and Prices* (Ramat-Gan: Bar-Ilan University).
1986   *Nautica Talmudica* (Ramat-Gan: Bar-Ilan University).

Speyer, W.
1967   'Der Tod der Salome', *JAC* 10: 176-80.

Spijkerman, A.
1972   'The Coins of Eleutheropolis Judaeae', *LA* 22: 369-84.

Stager, L.E.
1976   'Farming in the Judaean Desert during the Iron Age', *BASOR* 221: 145-58.
1991a   'When Canaanites and Philistines Ruled Ashkelon', *BARev* 17.2: 24-37, 40-43.
1991b   'Why Were Hundreds of Dogs Buried at Ashkelon?', *BARev* 17.3: 26-42.
1991c   'Eroticism and Infanticide at Ashkelon', *BARev* 17.4: 34-53, 72.
1991d   *Ashkelon Discovered* (Washington, DC: Biblical Archaeology Society).
1993   'Ashkelon', in *NEAEHL*: I, 103-12.
1996   'The Fury of Babylon: Ashkelon and the Archaeology of Destruction', *BARev* 22.1: 56-69, 76-77.

Stap, A.
1859   'Sur les deux prétendus Hérode-Philippe a propos d'une généalogie des Hérodes', *RG* 8: 580-92.

Starcky, J.
1960   'Pétra et la Nabatène' in *DBSup,* 7: 886-1017.
1971–72   'Arca du Liban', *CO* 10: 103-13.
1985   'Les inscriptions Nabatéennes et l'histoire de la Syrie Méridionale et du nord de la Jordanie', in J.M. Dentzer (ed.), *Hauran* 1.1 (Paris: Librairie Orientaliste Paul Geuthner): 167-81.

Stark, K.B.
1852   *Gaza und die philistäische Küste* (Jena: F. Mauke).

Stein (see also Kushnir-Stein), A.
1981   'Some Notes on the Chronology of the Coins of Agrippa I', *INJ* 5: 22-26.
1984–85   'The Undated Coins of Agrippa II under Nero', *INJ* 8: 9-11.
1992   'Gaius Julius, an Agoranomos from Tiberias', *ZPE* 93: 144-48.

Stern, E.
1981   'The Province of Yehud: The Vision and the Reality', in *JC* 1: 9-21.

1982   *Material Culture of the Land of the Bible in the Persian Period 538–332 B.C.* (Warminster: Aris & Phillips).

1984   'The Persian Empire and the Political and Social History of Palestine in the Persian Period', in *CHJ* 1: 70-87.

1988   'The Walls of Dor', *IEJ* 38: 6-14.

1989   'The Beginning of the Greek Settlement in Palestine in the Light of the Excavations at Tel Dor', in S. Gitin and W.G. Dever (eds.), *Recent Excavations in Israel: Studies in Iron Age Archaeology* (AASOR, 49; Winona Lake, IN: Eisenbrauns): 107-24.

1993   'Dor', in *NEAEHL*: I, 357-68.

1994   'A Phoenician-Cypriote Votive Scapula from Tel Dor: A Maritime Scene', *IEJ* 44: 1-12.

Stern, M.

1960   'A. Schalit's Herod', *JJS* 11: 49-58.

1971   'Ananias ben Nedebeus', *EncJud* 2: 293.

1974a   'Chronology', in CRINT 1.1: 62-77.

1974b   'The Reign of Herod and the Herodian Dynasty', in CRINT 1.1: 216-307.

1975a   'The Reign of Herod', in *WHJP* 7: 71-123.

1975b   'The Reign of Agrippa II', in *WHJP* 7: 176-78.

1976   'Aspects of Jewish Society: The Priesthood and Other Classes', in CRINT 1.2: 561-630.

1981   'Judaea and her Neighbors in the Days of Alexander Jannaeus', in *JC* 1: 22-46.

1982   'Social and Political Realignments in Herodian Judaea', in *JC* 2: 40-62.

1986   'Review of T. Rajak, *Josephus*', *JRS* 76: 324-26.

1987   'Josephus and the Roman Empire as Reflected in "The Jewish War"', in Feldman and Hata (eds.) 1987: 71-80.

Stieglitz, R.R.

1993   'Straton's Tower: The Name, the History, and the Archaeological Data', in Biran and Aviram (eds.) 1993: 646-51.

Strange, J.F., and T.R.W. Longstaff

1984   'Sepphoris (Sippori) 1983', *IEJ* 34: 51-52.

Strugnell, J.

1959   'The Nabataean Goddess al-Kutba' and her Sanctuaries', *BASOR* 159: 29-36.

1985   'A Note on Alexander Polyhistor', in *OTP* 2: 777-79.

Sukenik, E.L.

1942   'The Temple of the Kore', in J.W. Crowfoot *et al.*, *Samaria-Sebaste*. I. *The Buildings at Samaria* (London: PEF): 62-67.

Sullivan, R.D.

1973   'Diadochic Coinage in Commagene after Tigranes the Great', *NC* 13: 18-39.

1978a   'The Dynasty of Emesa', in *ANRW* 2.8: 198-219.

1978b   'The Dynasty of Judaea in the First Century', in *ANRW* 2.8: 296-354.

1978c   'The Dynasty of Commagene', in *ANRW* 2.8: 732-98.

1978d   'Papyri Reflecting the Eastern Dynastic Network', in *ANRW* 2.8: 908-39.
1979   'King Marcus Antonius Polemo', *NC* 139: 6-20.
1980   'The Dynasty of Cappadocia', in *ANRW* 2.7: 1125-68.
1990   *Near Eastern Royalty and Rome, 100–30 BC* (Toronto: Toronto University Press).

Sumner, G.V.
1967   'Germanicus and Drusus Caesar', *Latomus* 26: 413-35.

Svoronos, I.N.
1904   *Τὰ Νομίσματα τοῦ Κράτους τῶν Πτολεμαίων*, II (Athens: P.D. Sakellarios).

Syme, R.
1953   'Review of A. Degrassi, *I Fasti Consolari*', *JRS* 43: 148-61.
1956   'Some Pisones in Tacitus', *JRS* 46: 17-21.
1958   *Tacitus*, I–II (Oxford: Clarendon Press).
1968   'People in Pliny', *JRS* 58: 135-51.
1973   'The Titulus Tiburtinus', in *Akten des VI. Internationalen Kongresses für griechische und lateinische Epigraphik* (Vestigia, 17; Munich: Beck): 585-601.
1981   'Governors Dying in Syria', *ZPE* 41: 125-44.
1983   'Tigranocerta: A Problem Misconceived', in S. Mitchell (ed.), *Armies and Frontiers in Roman and Byzantine Anatolia* (British Institute of Archaeology at Ankara, Monographs, 5; BAR International Series, 156; Oxford: BAR): 61-70.
1995   *Anatolica: Studies in Strabo* (ed. A. Birley; Oxford: Clarendon Press).

Syon, D.
1992   'Gamla—Portrait of a Rebellion', *BARev* 18.1: 20-37, 72.

Sznycer, M.
1979   'Deux noms de phéniciens d'Ascalon à Démétrias (Thessalie)', *Sem* 29 (1979): 45-52.
1980   'La partie phénicienne de l'inscription bilingue greco-phénicienne de Cos', *AD* 35: 17-30 [publ. 1987].

Tadmor, H.
1966   'Philistia under Assyrian Rule', *BA* 29: 86-102.
1994   'Judah', in *CAH* 6 (2nd edn): 261-96.

Talbert, R.J.A.
1984   *The Senate of Imperial Rome* (Princeton, NJ: Princeton University Press).

Tarn, W.W., and M.P. Charlesworth
1934   'The Triumvirs', in *CAH* 10: 31-65.

Taylor, J.E.
1993   *Christians and the Holy Places: The Myth of Jewish-Christian Origins* (Oxford: Clarendon Press).

Taylor, J.S.M.
1992   'The Ethnarch of King Aretas at Damascus: A Note on 2 Cor. 11,32-33', *RB* 99: 719-28.

Taylor, V.
1966   *The Gospel according to St Mark* (Grand Rapids, MI: Baker Book House, 2nd edn [repr. 1981]).

Tcherikover, V.A.
1937   'Palestine under the Ptolemies (A Contribution to the Study of the Zenon Papyri)', *Mizraim* 4–5: 9-90.
1959   *Hellenistic Civilization and the Jews* (ET S. Applebaum; Philadelphia, PA: The Jewish Publication Society of America).
1964   'Was Jerusalem a "Polis"?', *IEJ* 14: 61-78.

Teixidor, J.
1977   *The Pagan God: Popular Religion in the Greco-Roman Near East* (Princeton, NJ: Princeton University Press, 1977).

Thackeray, H. St. J.
1929   *Josephus the Man and the Historian* (New York: Jewish Institute of Religion).

Thalmann, J.-P.
1990   'Tell 'Arqa, de la conquête assyrienne à l'époque perse', *Transeuphratène* 2: 51-57.

Thee, F.C.R.
1984   *Julius Africanus and the Early Christian View of Magic* (Hermeneutische Untersuchungen zur Theologie, 19; Tübingen: Mohr).

Thoma, C.
1994   'John Hyrcanus I as Seen by Josephus and Other Early Jewish Sources', in Parente and Sievers (eds.) 1994: 127-40.

Thomasson, B.E.
1984   *Laterculi Praesidum I* (Gothenburg: Radins).

Thompson (see also Crawford), D.J.
1984   'The Idumaeans of Memphis and the Ptolemaic "Politeumata"', in *Atti del XVII Congresso Internazionale di Papirologia*, III (Napoli: Centro Internazionale per lo Studio dei Papiri Ercolanesi): 1069-75.
1988   *Memphis under the Ptolemies* (Princeton, NJ: University Press).

Thompson, W.E.
1967   'The Marriage of First Cousins in Athenian Society', *Phoenix* 21: 273-82.
1972   'Attic Kinship Terminology', *JHS* 91: 110-13.

Tod, M.N.
1933   'A Greek Epigram from Gaza', *Aegyptus* 13: 152-58.

Toher, M.
1987   'The Terminal Date of Nicolaus' Universal History', *AHB* 1.6: 135-38.

Torrey, C.C.
1898   'The Edomites in Southern Judah', *JBL* 17: 16-20.

Toynbee, J.M.C.
1978   *Roman Historical Portraits* (London: Thames and Hudson).

Trell, B.L.
1982–83   'Phoenician Greek Imperial Coins', *INJ* 6–7: 128-37.

Tsafrir, Y.
	1982	'The Desert Fortresses of Judaea in the Second Temple Period', in *JC*
		2: 120-45.
Tscherikower *see* Tcherikover.
Tufnell, O.
	1977	'Lachish', in *EAEHL*: III, 735-46.
Turner, E.G.
	1954	'Tiberius Iulius Alexander', *JRS* 44: 54-64.
Tushingham, A.D.
	1972	'A Hellenistic Inscription from Samaria-Sebaste', *PEQ* 104: 59-63.
	1986	*Excavations in Jerusalem, 1961–1967*, I (Toronto: Royal Ontario
		Museum).
Tzaferis, V., and M. Peleg
	1988–89	'Banias 1988—Vaulted Building', *ESI* 7–8: 10-11 [publ. 1990].
Tzaferis, V., and R. Avner
	1989–90	'Banias 1989', *ESI* 9: 3-4 [publ. 1991].
Tzaferis, V., N. Feig, A. Onn, and E. Shukron
	1994	'Excavations at the Third Wall, North of the Jerusalem Old City', in
		Geva (ed.) 1994: 287-92.
Ulrich, E.
	1984	'The Greek Manuscripts of the Pentateuch from Qumran, including
		Newly-Identified Fragments of Deuteronomy (4Q LXXDeut)', in A.
		Pietersma and C. Cox (eds.), *De Septuaginta* (Festschrift J.W. Wevers;
		Ontario: Benben): 71-82.
Unnik, W.C. van
	1962	*Tarsus or Jerusalem: The City of Paul's Youth* (ET G. Ogg; London:
		SPCK).
Urbach, E.E.
	1959	'The Rabbinical Laws of Idolatry in the Second and Third Centuries
		in the Light of Archaeological and Historical Facts', *IEJ* 9: 149-65,
		229-45.
	1966	*Class-Status and Leadership in the World of the Palestinian Sages*
		(Jerusalem: Israel Academy of Sciences and Humanities; *PIASH* 2.4
		[1968]).
	1977	'Jewish Doctrines and Practices in Halakhic and Aggadic Literature',
		in S.W. Baron and G.S. Wise (eds.), *Violence and Defence in the
		Jewish Experience* (Philadelphia, PA: The Jewish Publication Society
		of America): 87-112.
Urman, D.
	1995	'Public Structures and Jewish Communities in the Golan Heights', in
		D. Urman and P.V.M. Flesher (eds.), *Ancient Synagogues: Historical
		Analysis and Archaeological Discovery*, II (SPB, 47; Leiden: Brill):
		373-617.
Ussishkin, D.
	1977	'The Destruction of Lachish by Sennacherib and the Dating of the
		Royal Judaean Storage Jars', *TA* 4: 28-60.
	1993	'Lachish', in *NEAEHL*: III, 897-911.

Vaggi, G.
1937   'Siria e Siri nie documenti dell'Egitto greco-romano', *Aegyptus* 17: 29-51.

Valency, M.J.
1940   *The Tragedies of Herod and Mariamne* (New York: Columbia University Press).

Vanderhooft, D.S.
1995   'The Edomite Dialect and Script: A Review of the Evidence', in Vikander Edelman (ed.) 1995: 137-57.

Vardaman, J.
1974   *'Corpus Inscriptionum Herodian[ar]um I'* (unpublished dissertation, Baylor University, Waco, TX).
1975   'Herodium: A Brief Assessment of Recent Suggestions', *IEJ* 25: 45-46.

Vardaman, J., and E.M. Yamauchi (eds.)
1989   *Chronos, Kairos, Christos: Nativity and Chronological Studies Presented to Jack Finegan* (Winona Lake, IN: Eisenbrauns).

Vaux, R. de
1965   *Ancient Israel: Its Life and Institutions* (ET J. McHugh; London: Darton, Longman & Todd, 2nd edn).
1973   *Archaeology and the Dead Sea Scrolls* (Eng. rev. edn; London: The British Academy).

Vikander Edelman, D. (ed.)
1995   *You Shall Not Abhor an Edomite for he is Your Brother: Edom and Seir in History and Tradition* (SBL and ASOR, Archaeological and Biblical Studies, 3; Atlanta, GA: Scholars Press).

Vincent, L.H.
1923   'IV. Les fouilles américaines de Beisan', *RB* 32: 430-41.

Vincent, L.H., and Stève, M.A.
1954   *Jérusalem de l'Ancien Testament*, I (Paris: Librairie Lecoffre, Gabalda).

Visconti, E.Q.
1811   *Iconographie grecque*, III (Paris: Imprimerie de P. Didot l'Ainé).

Visconti, P.E.
1880   *Catalogo del Museo Torlonia di Sculture Antiche* (Rome: Tipografia Tiberina).

Votschinina, A. (ed.)
1974   *Musée de l'Ermitage, le portrait romain: Album et catalogue illustré de toute la collection* (Leningrad: Editions d'Art Aurore [in Russian and French]).

Wacholder, B.Z.
1962   *Nicolaus of Damascus* (Berkeley, CA: California University Press).
1973   'The Calendar of Sabbatical Cycles during the Second Temple and the Early Rabbinic Period', *HUCA* 44: 153-96.
1983   'The Calendar of Sabbath Years during the Second Temple Era: A Response', *HUCA* 54: 123-33.
1989   'Josephus and Nicolaus of Damascus', in Feldman and Hata (eds.) 1989: 147-72.

Walbank, F.W.
1972   'Nationality as a Factor in Roman History', *HSCP* 76: 145-68.
Waldbaum, J.C.
1994   'Early Greek Contacts with the Southern Levant, ca. 1000–600 B.C.: The Eastern Perspective', *BASOR* 293: 53-66.
Warmington, B.H.
1969   *Nero: Reality and Legend* (London: Chatto & Windus).
Wasserstein, A.
1995   'Non-Hellenized Jews in the Semi-Hellenized East', *SCI* 14: 111-37.
Waterman, L.
1937   *Preliminary Report of the University of Michigan Excavations at Sepphoris, Palestine, in 1931* (Ann Arbor, MI: Michigan University Press).
Watzinger, C.
1935   *Denkmäler Palästinas*, II (Leipzig: J.C. Hinrichs).
Webster, G.
1985   *The Roman Imperial Army* (London: A. & C. Black, 3rd edn).
Weidner, E.F.
1939   'Jojachin, König von Juda, in babylonischen Keilschrifttexten', in *Mélanges Syriens offerts à M. René Dussaud* (Paris: Librairie Orientaliste Paul Geuthner): 923-35.
Weinberg, S.S.
1969   *Post-Exilic Palestine: An Archaeological Report* (Jerusalem: Israel Academy of Sciences and Humanities; *PIASH* 4.5 [1971]).
Weiss, Z.
1993   'Sepphoris', in *NEAEHL*: IV, 1324-28.
Welles, C.B.
1934   *Royal Correspondence in the Hellenistic Period* (New Haven, CT: Yale University Press).
1938   'The Inscriptions', in C.H. Kraeling (ed.), *Gerasa: City of the Decapolis* (New Haven, CT: ASOR): 355-494, 575-616 (indices), pls XCV-CXXXVIII.
Wenning, R.
1981   'Griechische Importe in Palästina aus Zeit vor Alexander d. Gr. Vorbericht über ein Forschungsproject', *Boreas* 4: 29-46.
1987   *Die Nabatäer—Denkmäler und Geschichte* (Novum Testamentum et Orbis Antiquus, 3; Göttingen: Vandenhoeck & Ruprecht).
1991   'Nachrichten über Griechen in Palästina in der Eisenzeit', in J.M. Fossey (ed.), *Proceedings of the First International Congress on the Hellenic Diaspora from Antiquity to Modern Times. I. From Antiquity to 1453* (Amsterdam: Gieben): 207-19.
1994   'Eine neuerstellte Liste der nabatäischen Dynastie', *Boreas* 16: 25-38.
White, L.M.
1987   'The Delos Synagogue Revisited: Recent Fieldwork in the Graeco-Roman Diaspora', *HTR* 80.2: 133-60.
Whittaker, C.R.
1974   'The Western Phoenicians: Colonisation and Assimilation', *PCPS* 20: 58-79.

Widengren, G.
1977   'The Persian Period', in J.H. Hayes and J.M. Miller (eds.), *Israelite and Judaean History* (London: SCM Press): 489-538.
Wiesenberg, E.
1956   'Related Prohibitions: Swine Breeding and the Study of Greek', *HUCA* 27: 213-33.
Wightman, G.J.
1985   'Megiddo VIA-III: Associated Structures and Chronology', *Levant* 17: 117-29.
1993   *The Walls of Jerusalem* (Mediterranean Archaeology Supplement, 4; Sydney: Meditarch).
Wilhelm, A.
1894   'Kietis: Zu Tacitus und Josephus', *AEM* 17: 1-6.
Wilkinson, J.
1974   'Ancient Jerusalem: Its Water Supply and Population', *PEQ* 106: 33-51.
Will, E.
1983   'Un vieux problème de la topographie de la Beqâ antique: Chalkis du Liban', *ZDPV* 99: 141-46.
Williamson, H.G.M.
1987   *Ezra and Nehemiah* (Old Testament Guides, 13; Sheffield: Sheffield Academic Press).
1988   'The Governors of Judah under the Persians', *TynBul* 39: 59-82.
Wilson, N.G.
1967   'The Libraries of the Byzantine World', *GRBS* 8: 53-80.
Winnett, F.V., and W.L. Reed
1970   *Ancient Records from North Arabia* (Toronto: Toronto University Press).
Wintermute, O.S.
1985   'Jubilees', in *OTP* 2: 35-142.
Wiseman, D.J. (ed.)
1973   *Peoples of Old Testament Times* (Oxford: Oxford University Press).
Wolters, P.
1888   'Der Grabstein des Antipatros von Askalon', *MDAI*(A) 13: 310-16.
Wooley, C.L.
1953   *A Forgotten Kingdom* (Harmondsworth: Penguin Books).
Wright, G.E.
1959   'Samaria', *BA* 22: 67-78.
Wünsch, R.
1902   'The Limestone Inscriptions of Tell Sandahannah', in Bliss and Macalister 1902: 158-87.
Yadin, Y.
1962   'Expedition D—The Cave of the Letters', *IEJ* 12: 227-57.
1966   *Masada: Herod's Fortress and the Zealot's Last Stand* (London: Weidenfeld & Nicolson).
1971   *Bar-Kokhba: The Rediscovery of the Legendary Hero of the Last Jewish Revolt against Imperial Rome* (London: Weidenfeld & Nicolson).
1974   'Four Epigraphical Queries', *IEJ* 24: 30-36.

1985   *The Temple Scroll* (London: Weidenfeld & Nicolson).
Yadin, Y. (ed.)
1976   *Jerusalem Revealed: Archaeology in the Holy City 1968–1974* (Jerusalem: IES).
Yadin, Y., and J. Naveh
1989   'The Aramaic and Hebrew Ostraca and Jar Inscriptions from Masada', in Aviram *et al.* (eds.) 1989a: 1-68.
Yeomans, D.K., and T. Kiang
1981   'The Long-Term Motion of Comet Halley', *MNRAS* 197: 633-46.
Zayadine, F.
1981   'Recent Excavations and Restorations of the Department of Antiquities (1979–80)', *ADAJ* 25: 341-55.
Zeitlin, S.
1919–20   'Megillat Taanit as a Source for Jewish Chronology and History in the Hellenistic and Roman Periods', *JQR* 10: 49-80 (Chs 4-6), 237-90 (Chs 7-12).
1950–51   'A Chronological Error on a Stamp of Israel', *JQR* 41: 243-44.
1963   'Herod: A Malevolent Maniac', *JQR* 54: 1-27.
1965–66   'Did Agrippa Write a Letter to Gaius Caligula?', *JQR* 56: 22-31.

INDEXES

INDEX OF REFERENCES

Note: Given the nature of this book, the index of primary sources can by no means claim to be complete. It is basically a large sample. The section on documentary evidence is particularly selective.

OLD TESTAMENT AND APOCRYPHA

PSEUDEPIGRAPHA

NEW TESTAMENT

5.2	296	25.12	385	*2 Apoc. James*	
10.22	368	25.13-27	322	4	386
12.12	238	25.13	382	61–62	386
19.25	270	25.21	385		
		25.23	98, 382	*Chronicle of Jerahmeel*	
Acts		25.25	385	37.1-14	38
4.6	222, 383	26.1-32	322		
4.25-27	196	27.1	334	*Gos. Pet.*	
5.17	383	27.9-12	386	4–5	195
6–7	284	28.30	392		
6.1	142			*Gos. Phil.*	
6.9	124	*Romans*		*Cod. II,*	
9	332	9.10-13	38	59.7-10	270
9.36	161	16.10-11	270, 313		
12	301			*Gos. Thom.*	
12.3-5	378	*Galatians*		*Cod. II*	
12.17	301	1.39	301	43.25-34	270
12.20-21	303	2.1-9	301		
12.21-23	380			*Hist. of Joseph the Carp.*	
12.23	303	*Philippians*		32	161
13.1	270	4.22	313		
15.1-35	301			*Josippon*	
15.13	301	*1 Thessalonians*		10.71	90
15.22-41	283	1.1	283	29.9-11	90
16.37-38	283			59.2-3	90
19.25	270	*Revelation*			
21.37	106	11.1-13	301		
21.38	385				
22.3	106	New Testament Apocrypha			
22.28	106	and Nag Hammadi			
23.1-5	282	Writings			
23.16-19	106	*1 Apoc. James*			
23.35	222	*Cod. V*			
24.1	282	40.25	270		
24.10	319				

RABBINIC AND POST-RABBINIC

Mishnah		*Ḥul.*		*Kil.*	
Ab.		12.1	120	6.4	56
5.21	144	139b	120	*Par.*	
				3.5	220
'Abod. Zar.		*Ket.*			
3.4	118	3.7	144	*Roš Haš.*	
		5.8	56	2.4	320
Bikk.		10.5	144		
3.4	102			*Šab.*	
				24.3	120

JOSEPHUS

CLASSICAL AND POST-CLASSICAL AUTHORS

DOCUMENTARY SOURCES

INSCRIPTIONS, PAPYRI, OSTRACA, COINS, ETC.

Naveh, J. 37, 40-43, 45-48, 56, 57, 68, 77, 79, 102, 144, 218, 324, 395
Negbi, O. 63, 84
Negev, A. 42, 45, 65, 230, 231, 268
Netzer, E. 99, 113, 122, 125, 126, 190, 227
Neusner, J. 102, 124, 170, 171, 218, 250, 259
Newell, E.T. 260
Nicolaou, I. 161
Nicols, J. 274
Niemeyer, H.G. 46
Niese, B. 180, 336
Nikiprowetzky, V. 325
Noldius, C. 24
Noth, M. 40

Oakeshott, M.F. 39
Obbink, D. 81
Oded, B. 224
Oden, R.A. 118
Ofer, A. 67
Offord, J. 239
Oppenheimer, A. 186, 250
Oren, E.D. 40, 62, 66, 76, 79, 83, 96, 121, 136, 162, 180, 214
Orentzel, R.E. 329
Østergård, U. 28
Otto, W. 25, 104, 125, 126, 156, 182, 209, 221, 223, 224, 369

Page, D.L. 137
Palmer, E.H. 127
Paltiel, E. 190, 335
Pani, M. 228, 253, 258, 260
Papachtzes, N.D. 119
Parassoglou, G.M. 248
Parente, F. 54, 325
Parker, P. 301
Parker, R.E. 23
Parker, S.T. 97
Parr, P.J. 39, 40, 42, 63, 64
Pastor, J. 57
Patrich, J. 118, 126, 295
Paul, G.M. 326
Peckham, J.B. 46
Peng-Yoke, H. 389
Peters, F.E. 63

Peters, J.P. 62, 70, 76, 79, 82, 121, 136, 180, 188, 235, 269, 335
Petersen, H. 199, 321
Pfeiffer, R.H. 38
Pflaum, H.G. 192
Phillips, S. 24, 121, 133, 369
Phythian-Adams, W.J. 104, 116, 121, 133
Piatelli, D. 320
Pittakes, K.S. 137, 307
Pixner, B. 238
Pleket, H.W. 126
Polotsky, H.J. 293
Pope, H. 63
Porten, B. 45, 50
Poulsen, V.H. 138
Prèaux, C. 124
Prentice, W.K. 290, 314, 335
Price, J.J. 96, 202, 336, 375, 390, 394
Pritz, R.A. 332
Puchstein, O. 272, 328
Puech, E. 77
Pummer, R. 63

Qedar, S. 47, 50, 77, 96, 128, 130, 131, 233, 338
Quinn, J.D. 47

Raban, A. 370
Rabinowitz, I. 44
Rahmani, L.Y. 50
Rainey, A.F. 39, 44, 45, 57, 60, 68
Rajak, T. 81, 87, 104, 109, 203, 235, 326, 330, 383, 393, 396, 397
Ramage, E.S. 259
Ramsay, W.M. 258
Rapaport, see Rappaport
Rappaport, U. 50, 53, 57, 62, 67, 68, 82, 83, 89, 116, 121, 131, 136, 180, 204, 214, 325, 369, 394
Rast, W.E. 77
Rathbone, D.W. 287
Rawlinson, G. 117, 303
Reed, W.L. 44
Rees, W. 229
Reich, R. 186, 221
Reifenberg, A. 136, 312
Reimann, O. 256

INDEX OF ANCIENT NAMES AND PLACES

Latin names are listed under the *gentilicium*, except of those people known by familiar forms, such as the Emperors. Names of members of the Herodian dynasty may be used in conjunction with the prosopography found in Appendix 1.
Numbers in square brackets indicate implied references. This is not a full index.